Other books coauthored by Mike Samuels, with Hal Z. Bennett:
The Well Body Book
Spirit Guides: Access to Inner Worlds
Be Well
Well Body, Well Earth

By Mike and Nancy Samuels:
Seeing With the Mind's Eye: The History, Techniques and Uses of Visualization
The Well Pregnancy Book
The Well Child Book
The Well Child Coloring Book
The Well Adult

By Mike Samuels:
Healing With the Mind's Eye

Mike Samuels, M.D., and Nancy Samuels

The well baby book

REVISED AND EXPANDED FOR THE 1990s

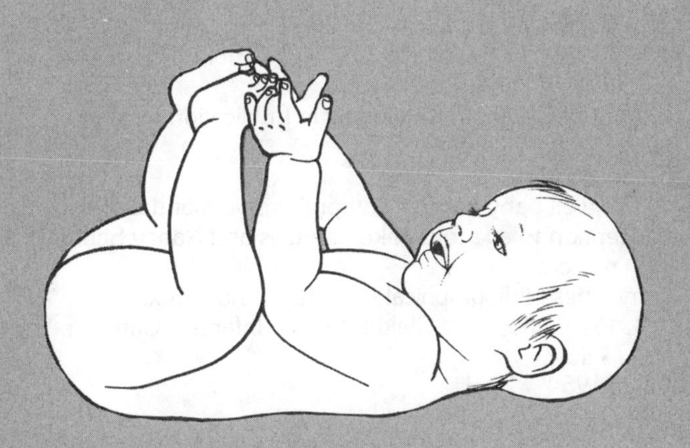

ILLUSTRATED BY WENDY FROST

SUMMIT BOOKS
NEW YORK LONDON TORONTO SYDNEY TOKYO SINGAPORE

Summit Books

Rockefeller Center
1230 Avenue of the Americas
New York, New York 10020

First Summit Books Edition 1979

SUMMIT BOOKS and colophon are trademarks
of Simon & Schuster

Manufactured in the United States of America

10 9 8 7 6 5 4 3 2 1
10 9 8 7 6 5 4 (pbk)

Library of Congress Cataloging in Publication Data

Samuels, Mike
The well baby book: a comprehensive manual of baby care, from
conception to age four/Mike Samuels and Nancy Samuels; illustrated by Wendy Frost.
p. cm.
Includes bibliographical references and index.
1. Pregnancy. 2. Childbirth. 3. Infants—Care. I. Samuels, Nancy.
II. Title.
G525.W54 1991
649'.1—dc20 90-26702
CIP

ISBN 0-671-73413-X
ISBN 0-671-73412-1 (pbk)

To our sons: Rudy and Lewis

Acknowledgments

We want to thank all the people who made special contributions to this book—Florence, Hope, Laurie, and Greg for baby-sitting; Dr. Fred Miller for medical advice and suggestions; Dr. Marshall Klaus and Dr. Brad Berman for medical advice on the second edition; Dr. I. Samuels for photographs; Jim Silberman for encouraging us to write a baby book; Chris Schillig for her thoughtful editing and general positivity on the first edition; and Dominick Anfuso for his care in revising the book.

Contents

Section III
Treating illness: medical information and self-help

List of Charts

Chapter 6 The Newborn: Birth Through the First Few Months

Chapter 7 The First Year: From Newborn to Toddler

Section I

A new view of baby health

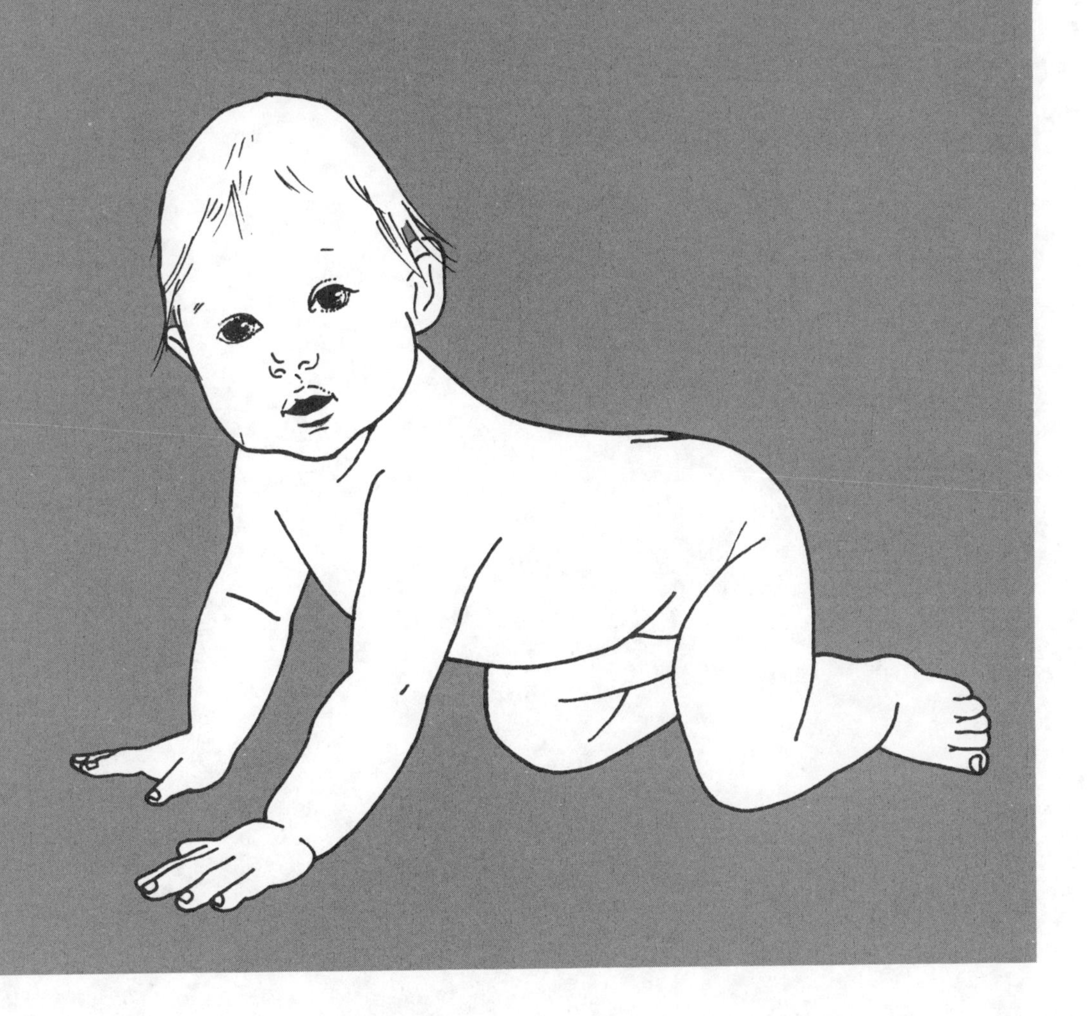

Chapter 1

About the well baby book

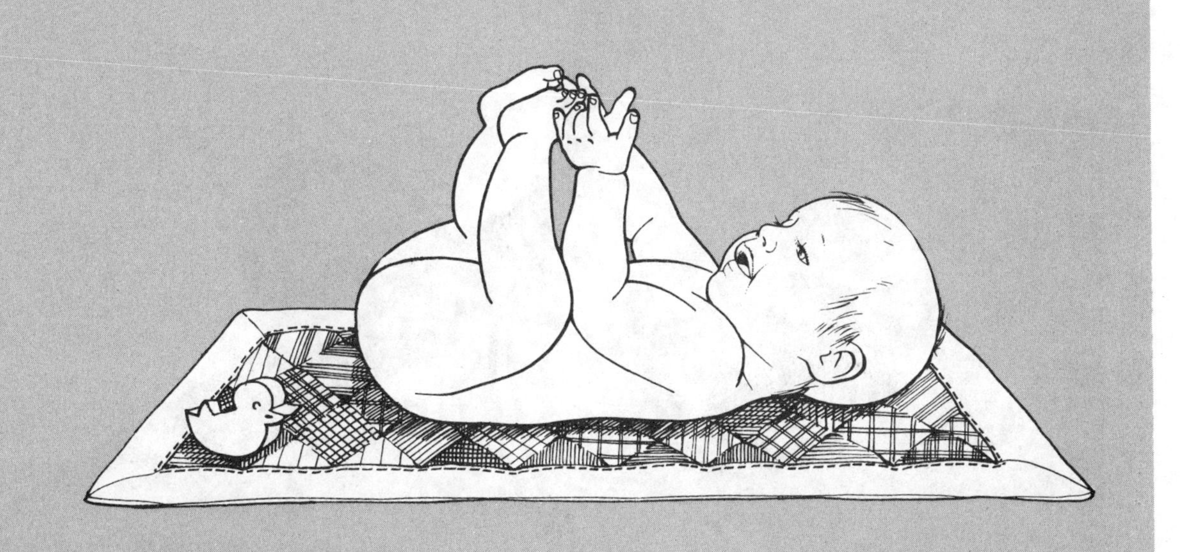

The Well Baby Book was written out of our love for babies. We began it shortly after our second baby was conceived, wrote about infancy in the months after his birth, and finished the book as he learned to stand and play with his four-year-old brother. Much of the manuscript was written with the baby in one of our laps. In a real sense our children helped us write this book. Their presence made its concerns real and gave us an involvement that could not have existed without our intimate contact with young babies.

Babies have tremendous gifts to give parents—a fresh, innocent vision, an almost total connection with the here and now, and a capacity for finding joy and involvement in whatever they encounter. Viewed from this perspective, they become wordless teachers of wisdom. A baby's look or action can instantly banish a parent's worries and stimulate warm feelings of joy and love. When parents can see a baby as endlessly fascinating, their lives become richer and more enjoyable. But if they only see a baby as trouble-

Three cheers for babies! This book was written out of our love for babies—our own and others.

some, problematic, or sickly, they miss the joy of parenting and become anxious and frustrated.

Our goal in writing this book was to help create happy, healthy babies. Health must be thought of as the well-being of the whole child, including physical, mental, social, and spiritual harmony. The first four years are crucial to the child's lifelong sense of well-being. The kinds of habits children acquire and the skills they learn in these years shape their bodies and influence the kinds of diseases to which they may become susceptible. Parents are the key to children's health and growth because they are the babies' models and they shape the overall nature of the babies' environment. This environment is inseparable from the parents' own growth and fulfillment. When parents feel the greatest possible pleasure, they relate to babies with the greatest possible interest and enjoyment.

Much of the manuscript was written with the baby in one of our laps.

In this book we give no dogmatic solutions or advice about child-rearing; rather we try to give parents a broad, new understanding of growth and development as well as health and disease, to help them find their own solutions to the problems of raising children. Inevitably there are times when parents, either through ignorance or lack of ideas, have trouble dealing with a situation or do not encourage habits that will contribute to the health of their baby. And there are many times when a baby is ill or hurt that parents worry unnecessarily. We want to minimize such times and give parents a way of successfully handling such situations.

In the second section of *The Well Baby Book* we provide information on babies' natural growth and development, on common, age-related concerns, and on how a parent can use the techniques of relaxation and imagery to promote a happier, healthier family. In the last twenty-five years there has been a veritable explosion of information about infants and their capabilities. Knowledge about the normal unfolding of infant development will relieve many of a parent's worries, and knowledge of ways that other people have handled new or difficult situations will give parents ideas on how to cope with those situations themselves. To enjoy life with a baby, parents have to create their own family style. We have included a great deal of information on and exercises for relaxation and imagery to help parents evolve their own positive way of relating to the baby. Relaxation involves consciously relaxing the muscles of the body and clearing the mind; imagery is "seeing with the mind's eye," and it involves consciously using mental imagery. We have found that these skills are useful for relieving worry and tension, for getting in touch with intuitive feelings, for communicating with the young baby, and for bringing about change. Relaxation and imagery allow parents to see which solutions advised by experts or other parents seem right to them, or to form entirely new solutions by tapping their own creative abilities. When parents make decisions in harmony with their feelings, they create an environment that is positive and healthy for the baby. This is true preventive medicine. It is the preventive medicine of the future—creating health and controlling disease through the relation of body, mind, and environment.

The third section of the book contains a wealth of information on the common accidents and illnesses of early childhood, as well as information on drugs, immunizations, and how to use the doctor. The book describes symptoms, gives home remedies when they are applicable, tells what the doctor does and why, and most important, it explains what is happening. It does what the doctor should do, but often can't. All too often the busy pediatrician doesn't have the time to answer questions or educate parents, and too often parents are afraid to voice their own questions and concerns. Answering questions is basic medical education. It follows a course similar to our other books, including *The Well Pregnancy Book* and *The Well Adult,* taking the mystery out of medicine and making available information that up to now has only been the province of medical personnel.

The more parents understand about childhood illness, the more they can do to deal with it and prevent it. This book contains a great deal of

Directly before and after the birth of our second baby we stopped work, then returned to the manuscript to write the chapters on "Birth" and "The Newborn."

information about the *common* illnesses of infancy. In fact, it contains as much information about common conditions as many medical textbooks. But unlike medical textbooks or lay medical encyclopedias, the book deals only with the illnesses a baby is likely to get, not with uncommon conditions. When the rarest disease is presented next to the most common, and described in a similar format with the same medical terms, parents are likely to become confused and frightened. Few parents can tell what their child actually has from among the vivid descriptions, and they come away with frightening images of rare complications and highly uncommon conditions. Not interspersing rare diseases with common conditions, not dwelling on bizarre complications, and simply concentrating on the diseases that a pediatrician usually sees make this book reassuring and truly relevant.

In fact, this is probably the most unfrightening and useful book written on baby medicine. We try to concentrate on what a parent can do to promote health, and we include a section on prevention in the description of each illness. We hope to encourage parents to treat illness in the earliest stages, to make them realize that they can exert a powerful influence over their baby's health. When a baby is ill or hurt, parents often fear the worst. But most common health problems actually get better by themselves or are easily treated. Many can be prevented or eliminated by knowledge of good health habits.

Understanding helps to replace fear with respect for the body's healing powers. If a parent has faith in the baby's healing abilities, the baby senses this and is strengthened by it. Researchers are just beginning to find out how important mental attitude and outlook are to health. They are discovering that relaxation and imagery can directly alter the body's physiology to promote healing. We show how parents can use these skills to become calm when their baby is ill or hurt and to transmit healing energy to their baby. We also show parents how to use games to teach older babies how to relax and use healing imagery by themselves. The greatest benefits of these skills can be realized if they are experienced and learned at the youngest possible age. Infants learn these skills unconsciously and benefit from them even before birth. Our work and experience have shown us more and more clearly what profound, lifelong resources relaxation and imagery can be in healing disease, as well as in promoting health.

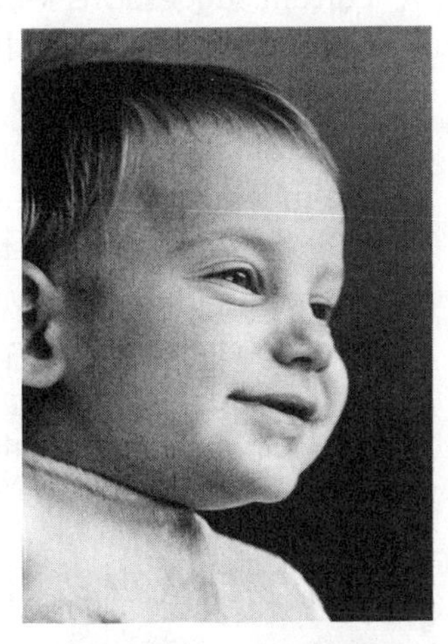

Our goal in writing this book was to help create happy, healthy babies and make parenting a joyful, positive experience.

This book is unique among baby books, both in the kinds of information it contains and in its outlook on health and disease. We want parents to take pleasure in the health and presence of their babies. To that end we've assembled much fascinating and enlightening knowledge about child development, relaxation and imagery, and baby medicine. The information that we found increased the beauty of all babies in our eyes and made us happier, higher, and more excited. We hope that in reading this book parents will share our feelings and look at their own baby with increasing feelings of love and joy. In that way parents will greatly enhance the positivity of their life with the baby and create an environment for health.

It was with great pleasure that we undertook the second edition of *The Well Baby Book.* We were delighted with the success of the first edition and the warmth with which it was received. Many readers have told us how reassuring and positive the book was. It has been our goal to keep that aspect of the book unchanged.

A unique aspect of *The Well Baby Book* is its emphasis on the whole baby and the whole parent. Holistic medicine, including relaxation and imagery, sees the mind and the body as one. Over the years mind-body health has grown and flourished, and physicians have seen how support, reassurance, and love can help foster good health. Changing attitudes will help young parents cope with the inevitable stresses of raising young children. The first section of this book presents new information on mind/baby health as it relates to the well-being of young babies.

In the ten years since *The Well Baby Book* was originally published, dramatic changes have occurred in our culture and in pediatrics. The young mother of today is more likely to be working full time, and her baby is more likely to be in daycare from an early age. More parents of young children are divorced or live alone. Likewise, parents have more concerns relating to child care, television viewing, and behavioral problems. The second section of the book, dealing with child development and practical concerns, reflects these social changes. In the field of behavioral pediatrics researchers have completed many studies on temperament, crying, toilet training, sibling rivalry, and self-feeding. To meet parents' growing interest in these concerns, we have included new information on these subjects.

Finally, many changes have taken place in the diagnosis and treatment of common childhood illnesses. We have revised almost all of the illness discussions, including information on causes, self-help, medical treatments, laboratory tests, and drugs, plus the latest immunization schedules, current suggestions for CPR, and descriptions of some rare infant conditions, such as Sudden Infant Death Syndrome and AIDS.

In the intervening years professionals and lay people have become increasingly aware of how important love, reassurance, and support are to the mental and physical health of the young child. For this reason we are even more committed to the underlying philosophy of *The Well Baby Book* and to helping with the wonderful but often difficult task of raising babies. The more that parents know about common occurrences in child illness and development, the better they can deal with parenting, and the happier and healthier their children will be.

Chapter 2

A short history of babies

The way in which a society views its babies is a reflection of the way in which that society views the universe. This view is greatly influenced, however, by the patterns of infant health and illness found in that society. Nonliterate societies saw themselves as intimately bound to the past and future through ancestors and spirits. They viewed babies as a link in a chain, as visitors from the world of the spirits who temporarily took their place in the world of physical reality. Parents accepted children—both their conception and their death—as a phenomenon over which they had little control. Childbirth and day-to-day child-rearing practices in such societies were largely natural; that is, they were not dictated by individual authorities. The way mothers gave birth and cared for their children stemmed from instinct, convenience, and age-old cultural patterns. A woman was com-

Child-rearing patterns in nonliterate cultures were not dictated by individual authorities but stemmed from age-old practices. Ia Orana Maria, *by Paul Gaugin, The Metropolitan Museum of Art, bequest of Samuel A. Lewisohn, 1951.*

monly attended during childbirth by other experienced women—usually family members or midwives—and sometimes by her husband. Babies were delivered naturally—without anesthetic—and with a minimum of intervention. In general, no birth control was practiced, so infants were naturally spaced at two- to three-year intervals due to the mother's continuous nursing. A very high percentage—between one-quarter and one-half—of these babies died before the age of four, largely from bacterial infections. Such staggering infant mortality inevitably conditioned the society's view of babies. Parents wanted and loved their babies but realized that many would not survive beyond infancy.

With the growth of population and the formation of city cultures, the baby's role became more complex and even less secure. Infant mortality due to disease remained high and was significantly increased by the widespread practice of infanticide. During the Middle Ages the killing of infants—especially females—was not infrequent, especially among the poor. During economic hard times, children were often sold into slavery or abandoned and left to die.

Keeping watch over a gravely ill child used to be an all-too-common event. As late as 1700 more than half of all babies died before reaching the age of five. Flemish engraving by Franz van din Wyngaardt, Les Veillenses, *The Metropolitan Museum of Art, Harris Brisbane Dick Fund, 1925.*

As late as the mid-1700s in Europe, three-quarters of all infants died before reaching five years of age. While abandonment and infanticide were still practiced, most of the children died of infectious diseases such as smallpox, diphtheria, plague, and gastroenteritis, diseases which killed many adults as well. Perhaps the single largest cause of infant deaths was diarrhea caused by poor sanitation. Due to a lack of sewage disposal and running water, disease-causing bacteria were to be found everywhere in the environment. Infants would take in bacteria at the breast, on food, even off their own hands. Then they would contract gastroenteritis, an intestinal infection, which would result in severe diarrhea. Since there was no effective treatment, infants would lose most of their small amount of body fluid, become dehydrated, and die in a matter of days. So little was understood about sanitation and spread of illness that parents felt powerless to prevent the death of a baby. Infant mortality was highest in poor, overcrowded sections of the cities, but was little better in wealthy or rural areas.

Several other factors also contributed to the survival problems of infants at this time. One was the use of sucking horns and cans, the forerunners of modern-day bottles. The need for cleanliness of feeding apparatus was not understood, and the milk itself often became contaminated due to the lack of effective storage means. Also many infants were fed by paid wet nurses who frequently practiced extremely poor breastfeeding hygiene and sometimes took very poor care of the infants in their charge.

During the 1800s, the staggeringly high infant mortality rates dropped significantly. The drop was partly due to the development of a vaccine for smallpox, but largely it was due to the introduction of new standards of hygiene made popular by Lister's concept of germs and antisepsis. Cleanliness was the doctor's primary weapon against gastrointestinal and respiratory infections—the scourges of the nineteenth century. The revolution

In the 1700s and 1800s many women hired wet nurses to suckle their babies. The poor hygiene often practiced by wet nurses was thought to contribute to fatal bacterial infections among their charges. Diane De Poitiers *(1370), by Francois Clouet, National Gallery of Art, Washington, Samuel H. Kress Collection.*

in hygiene coincided with a new concern for the health and safety of children. Infant welfare movements successfully fought for the passage of laws regulating the employment of women around the time of childbirth and for the registration and examination of people who engaged in child care.

One of the pioneers of the infant welfare movement, M. Morel de Villiers, the mayor of a tiny French town from 1880 to 1890, instituted procedures which cut the town's infant mortality rate from thirty per hundred to zero. All pregnancies were registered by law beginning at the seventh month, and all births had to be recorded. Every mother who remained in bed for six days following delivery was given an allotment of twenty cents. A law was passed making it compulsory to sterilize all cow's milk that was to be fed to infants. It also became mandatory that all infants be seen and weighed every fortnight on a communal scale to check on their health. Any illness in an infant had to be reported within twenty-four hours and sick infants were given free medical care. Any wet nurse who did not comply with these public health procedures would lose her qualification certificate. Finally, a bonus of fifty cents was given to any woman who could produce a one-year-old baby in good health. By the turn of the century all the western European countries and the United States had passed infant welfare legislation which encouraged infant follow-up as well as improved sanitation. Such preventive medical procedures were the forerunners of modern well-baby care.

London bills of mortality for children below the age of five

Years	*Deaths per 100 children*
1750	75
1770	65
1790	50
1830	35
1880	15
1900	15

Improved hygiene had had such a pronounced effect, radically lowering the incidence of infectious diseases, that attention now turned to eliminating other serious contagious disease. Immunization research brought vaccines for diphtheria, whooping cough, and more recently polio. The discovery of sulfonamides and antibiotics in the 1930s and 1940s has reduced or eliminated the serious complications of pneumonia, severe ear infections, bone infections, tuberculosis, and rheumatic fever. By 1964 the infant mortality rate had dropped to less than three per hundred in the United States and less than two per hundred in England. Of these, most are due to serious congenital malformations, birth trauma, and complications of prematurity —very few of them are now due to infectious disease. Not only has the death rate continued to go down, but equally important, the incidence of serious and crippling illnesses in children has dropped tremendously in industrialized countries.

Sanitation, immunization, and antibiotics have led to a dramatic change in illness patterns in young children. Coupled with new methods of birth control and a declining birth rate, this has profoundly changed the way in which babies are viewed. Until rather recently, the birth of a baby has not been completely a matter of choice. Particularly in earlier times the birth of a child has imposed real hardship on parents who, in turn, have found it difficult to care for their children. It is probably this kind of cycle that led to the practice of infanticide and abandonment. Even those children who were wanted often had a very uncertain future due to illness and disease. Both of these factors must have tended to make the child's position with the parents less central. Large families were the rule, lowering even more the amount of direct, individual attention children might receive from their hardworking parents.

Children who did survive were expected to begin to assume adult tasks at a very early age—indeed, as soon as they were physically able. Boys were expected to do physical labor and girls were expected to take care of younger siblings and help with the work of the house. Thus childhood, as a defined time with roles, duties, and privileges unique to itself, did not exist much beyond infancy. In a very real sense, childhood might end by the age of five or six.

Starting in the seventeenth century, philosophers began to call attention

In the 17th century large families were the rule, even among the rich, due to lack of effective contraceptive methods and the desire to make up for high infant mortality rates. The Copley Family *(1650), by John Singleton Copley, National Gallery of Art, Washington, Andrew W. Mellon Fund.*

to the life condition of children and to suggest that changes should be made in the way children were treated. Such thinking eventually led to the creation in modern society of a separate role for children as opposed to the idea that children were merely little grown-ups or weak adults. Extra and special attention was given to children's education, and children came to be valued for what they were and would become, as well as for what work they could immediately do.

Religious leaders and philosophers like John Locke came to hold that children must be purposefully molded into moral, hardworking adults who would meet the needs of society. Children did not seem to behave in this manner naturally, and thus there arose, for the first time, the concept that children were naturally depraved and must be forcibly socialized in order to break their innate selfishness and lawlessness. The purpose of education was not so much to awaken children's minds, as their natural right, but to teach them discipline, self-control, and proper moral values, as their duty.

In the later half of the eighteenth century an opposing view of children was proclaimed by the French philosopher Jean-Jacques Rousseau, who spoke out for the rights of the child and the individual. He believed that society thwarts and restricts the natural development of the child. Rousseau held that the child has an intuitive sense of right and wrong and will inevitably develop into a socialized person if his natural curiosity is stimulated rather than restricted. According to Rousseau the child raised in this manner will be a superior person.

Since the seventeenth century, child-rearing methods have largely been dictated by one kind of expert or authority or another. Their methods have been shaped by their philosophical view of man and designed to nurture their ideal adult. The role of authority has changed from philosophers and religious leaders to doctors, educators, and psychologists who specialize in child development. Their specific instructions have varied widely. But all the experts can be thought of as fitting on a continuum somewhere between Locke and Rousseau, between "native depravity" and "innate nobility," between deliberate training by intervention and the stimulation of naturally unfolding abilities. One set of experts advocates authority, discipline, and scheduling, the other recommends permissiveness, openness, and internal motivation. Viewed subjectively, the Lockean model has been considered cruel and confining, while the Rousseauean model has been considered liberating and kind. On the other hand, Rousseauean methods have been charged with creating confusion, delinquency, alienation, disorientation, and lack of useful skills, whereas Lockean methods have been believed to foster order, security, productiveness, and a sense of belonging.

In the early nineteenth century, the dominant view of child-rearing continued to hold that the playful child was on the road to hell. Around 1840, however, a new philosophy began to emerge which held that the mother should nurture her child so as not to injure its sensibilities and potential. By the time of the Civil War, a public controversy had developed over child-rearing, one side reflecting the theory that children were potentially bad or evil unless molded, the other side reflecting the idea that children were sacred beings who ought to be helped to grow and develop. Despite this ideological struggle, childhood was still not viewed as a separate developmental phase from adulthood in terms of social, economic, or physiological conditions. The field of social science had yet to arise; the disciplines of psychology and sociology did not exist. Thus there had been no research on child development to support either theory of child-rearing. Moreover, children had no voice or rights, and were in the control of their parents or employers.

In 1871, American Jacob Abbott wrote a famous treatise called *Gentle Measures in the Management and Training of the Young.* Its theme was that any parental training should take into account the child's physiological and mental level of development. Abbott urged that parents be tolerant in their child-rearing practices and avoid stooping to anger or violence. At about this time, universities began to undertake the first systematic study of child development. However, the popular literature on child-rearing was still a debate between the proponents of discipline and the proponents of love. The idea of stimulating development in various ways was unheard of.

As the twentieth century began, there was new and profound interest in how young children developed. Arnold Gesell, at Yale University, was the first person to study a number of children over a period of years, using scientific methods. During the same period, Sigmund Freud first made public his theory on infantile sexuality. Freud's views focused attention on the idea that the adult personality was shaped by the child's experiences. As the twentieth century continued, more and more credence was given to the importance of the systematic study of childhood in terms of child-rearing practices. Nevertheless, until very recently, there were few studies that pointedly backed up the judgments of childhood authorities.

During the first half of the twentieth century, the advice on child development that was cited as factual rarely was. Hallmarks of emotionally based advice were the way authorities dealt with the child's natural urges in relation to thumb-sucking, masturbation, and toilet training. The 1914 edition of *Infant Care,* published by the United States Children's Bureau, observed that infant masturbation was an injurious practice that should be eliminated through mechanical restraints, if necessary, by tying the baby's hands and feet to the sides of the crib. By 1921, the Bureau simply recommended pinning the infant's sleeves to the sheets. By 1930, the Bureau had determined that masturbating represented a temporary phase that the baby would naturally pass through. Likewise, child-rearing practices dealing with thumb-sucking and toilet training underwent similar evolution from extreme intervention to a more progressive attitude. From 1914 to 1921, mothers were advised to tie up their baby's hands to prevent the infant from thumb-sucking, a "disgusting" habit that deformed the baby's mouth and caused it to drool. At the same time, mothers were warned not to use a pacifier. The most rigorous of toilet training advice did not emerge until 1921 when mothers were advised to begin such training at one month, with the goal of having the child completely toilet trained by the end of one year. Later advice was more moderate.

It is important that parents realize that pediatricians and child experts give advice of two kinds. Some is based on scientific studies, but much of it is based on personal experience, opinion, and philosophy. However, many parents have turned over child-rearing decisions to the experts, in the belief that the experts had not only more knowledge, but better knowledge, knowledge of the TRUTH. Initially the experts' power was based on the authority of religion; now it is based on the authority of science. In reality, child-rearing methods even today are based more on philosophy and beliefs than on facts. Proposed methods are shaped by the expert's own upbringing and experiences. Studies can be found to support or justify almost any child-rearing dictum. A piece of advice will be promulgated by experts, become popular, exist briefly as a fad, only to be supplanted by an opposite or different piece of advice based on an equal number of studies or promulgated by an equally persuasive authority.

In recent years, many studies have provided valuable information for parents. Increasingly, studies are based on knowledge of neuromaturational landmarks and on the experience of large numbers of infants. One striking point underscored by research over the last decade is the tremendous variability in babies' temperaments. Wide individual differences exist in activity levels, adaptability, and ability to self-soothe. Variability in temperament calls for variability in child care. Parents must compassionately evaluate both their baby and themselves as they evolve ways to deal with daily situations. For example, frequent night waking is now known to be more common among infants with low sensory thresholds. Thus, rather than becoming upset and blaming themselves, parents of babies who are known to be sensitive may be better off to lessen stimuli and provide a calm situation. The new behavioral studies attempt to provide guidelines that are in harmony with the baby's development. An example of such information is the fact that infants do not develop a reflex for swallowing solid foods until three or four months. Thus it is not useful to feed young babies solids since they will spit most of the food out. There are many areas, however, in which research has still not been able to provide definitive behavioral guidelines for parents of newborns.

An important issue currently facing many new parents is the timing of when a mother should go back to work. Studies on day care for children under a year are interpreted differently by different experts. Some view the data as showing that early daycare has disadvantages; others see it as positive (see p. 191). At this point, parents cannot make a decision based purely on rational guidelines. The issue is so complex and so individual that families need to concentrate on finding the best solution for themselves.

Piaget's theory on learning in infancy and early childhood

Object permanence

Birth–2 yrs.	Babies differentiate themselves from objects and gradually become aware of the effects of actions.
Birth–1 mo.	Images cease to exist when out of sight.
1–4 mos.	Begin to sense objects still exist when out of sight.
4–8 mos.	Can recognize some objects from their parts; can follow objects that are thrown or dropped.
9–12 mos.	Can locate object after it is hidden out of sight.
12–18 mos.	Can find object after watching it be tucked away in several different locations.
18–24 mos.	Can figure out from clues where an object is located, without actually seeing it be hidden.

Causality

Birth–1 mo.	Baby acts reflexively.
1–4 mos.	Primary circular reactions: learns to recreate satisfying sensations (e.g., thumb sucking) by itself.
4–8 mos.	Secondary circular effects: learns to recreate accidentally caused effects (e.g., shaking the crib to make a mobile move).
12–18 mos.	Tertiary circular effects: deliberately varies behaviors (experiments) to create new effects.
18–24 mos.	Can understand indirect causality (e.g., winding up a toy will make it move).

Play

4–8 mos.	Approaches all objects with same behavior (e.g., suck on it, bang on it, drop it).
9–12 mos.	Carefully inspects new objects; can play peek-a-boo with hidden object.
12–18 mos.	Understands the functions of specific toys (pushes car, holds telephone receiver to ear). Pretends to do activities with body (e.g., pretends to drink from toy cup).
18–24 mos.	Engages in symbolic play with toys (e.g., "feeds" a doll).

Erikson's theory on the tasks of early childhood

Age	*Task*	*Favorable outcome*
0–1 yr.	trust versus mistrust	trust optimism
1–2 yrs.	autonomy versus doubt	self-control feelings of adequacy
3–5 yrs.	initiative versus guilt	purpose and direction ability to initiate activities

The increasingly rapid alteration of child-rearing methods can be looked upon as a historical rhythm, a true union of opposites in which one, by its very existence, creates and maintains the other. As a culture changes, the needs of its people at any moment change, thereby requiring and shaping different child-rearing methods. If parents understand their relationship to the rhythm, they can relax in the knowledge that there is no one right method to choose. Rather, parents are in the exhilarating position of being able to place themselves at a point on the continuum that feels right to them and their child. Parent and child are no longer slavishly forced to repeat the past but together can create child-rearing methods responsive to their changing needs. Finally, parents and babies become the experts.

Chapter 3

The new medicine for babies

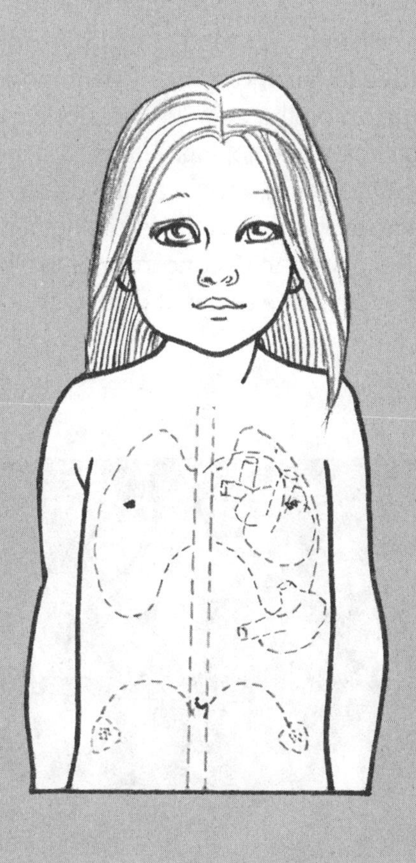

Illness in young children raises an age-old fear in parents. When a baby becomes ill, parents frequently worry unnecessarily about whether the situation is serious, and images of death or danger cross their minds. Such images have a valid basis in history. Until quite recently infant mortality rates were very, very high. One hundred years ago almost one out of every five infants died before the age of five and that represented a phenomenal advance in infant survival over the previous century. Since that time medicine for babies has progressed from largely trying to keep babies alive, to treating large numbers of babies who were seriously ill, to mostly treating well babies and babies with common minor illnesses. Thus, the age-old fear of an apparently healthy baby dying is no longer based in reality. Now the death of a baby from illness is a rare occurrence. Even serious illness in young babies is unusual.

Along with the elimination of most serious infectious diseases of childhood has come the proliferation of huge, technical, research-oriented medical centers. This is the atmosphere in which most pediatricians have been trained. Thus the pediatrician's orientation and skills are directed toward those diseases of childhood which are still life-threatening. The incidence of most of these diseases is low, and many of them are even rare. Ironically, once pediatricians are in practice, they spend more than 80 percent of their time seeing well babies for routine infant care and babies who are only mildly ill.

Up till now the mood of medicine for babies has remained tinged with fear due to historically high infant mortality rates and, more recently, concentration on the rarer life-threatening diseases. However, a new medicine for babies is developing. It relates to the large majority of babies whom the pediatrician sees—well and almost-well babies. The new medicine relates to increasing the overall *well-being* of all children to optimal levels. New medicine for babies concerns not just babies, but *their environment and their interactions with it.* It deals with educating parents about the healthiest

Parents have always worried when children become ill, but today serious illnesses are rare and this almost-instinctual worry is no longer grounded in fact. The Good Mother, *by Jean Honoré Fragonard, M. H. de Young Memorial Museum, gift of Mrs. Herbert Fleishhacker.*

environment for babies, about the infant's physical needs (nutrition, sleep, exercise, cleanliness), and about the emotional and social needs of the baby for love, stimulation, and communication. The new medicine involves allaying unsubstantiated fears and reassuring parents about the baby's strengths and their own. It tries to demystify medicine and teach parents basic information about how the body functions in health and illness, including solid information about childhood illnesses that will enable parents to handle many minor problems at home and to understand and not fear those problems that require a doctor. The new medicine also uses relaxation and imagery to alter the body's physiology so that it actually prevents illness and heals disease.

This new medicine is evolving from a marriage of two new fields: self-help medicine and holistic medicine. Self-help medicine focuses on ways parents can actively participate in the health of their children and themselves. It emphasizes early diagnosis and practical, effective home care for common illnesses which will prevent many diseases from becoming serious. Often increased knowledge and awareness of health can actually help parents prevent their children from getting sick at all. Holistic medicine focuses on making people aware of the root cause of illness. It deals with people's view of themselves and illness and the way in which this view affects their *whole* lives, including rest, exercise, sleep, nutrition, body movement, and mind states. This knowledge is also important in healing disease and staying healthy.

Up to now the main focus of infant health has been on external organisms that can cause illness. This focus is shifting to the infant's own body. Medical researchers are now interested in not only what diseases infants get, but in which infants get those diseases and why. Why some people get certain diseases—as infants or later in life—is a recent question for modern medicine. Up to now this question has been left to philosophers and religious scholars. Only a small number of the people who are exposed to a bacterium or virus *actually* become ill. One of the most dramatic examples of this fact concerns meningitis, a serious infection of the lining of the spinal cord. The bacteria that cause meningitis are quite common and actually are widely distributed. Studies have shown that at some time in their lives, 100 percent of the population have meningitis bacteria living in their bodies. Yet only an extremely low percentage of the population ever gets meningitis, 1 person per 100,000.

Another interesting observation that doctors have made is that a relatively low number of people in any population have most of the illnesses. Everyone can cite some people who are always healthy and other people who are always sick. Research has been done on just this point—those who are always ill versus those who are never ill. One study dealt with individuals who contracted common upper respiratory illnesses (infectious diseases). In general each group was distinguished by several characteristic factors. The people who were often ill or got sick tended to be "dissatisfied, discontented, unhappy, resentful." They saw themselves as "loaded with outside responsibilities, worries, and frustrations." Indeed, as a group, they were exposed to many more serious life stresses.

Perhaps one of the most remarkable studies involved giving people nose drops that were supposed to contain infectious cold virus. In fact, the nose drops contained no virus. A high percentage of the people in the group who had frequent colds actually developed a cold after being given the nose drops. Very few people became ill in the group that rarely had colds. The study shows how strongly people's bodies are affected by what they believe.

The basic theory of new medicine is that whatever a person does—on the social and emotional as well as the physical plane—affects that person's body. Each person's body has aspects about it that are genetically determined. These genetic factors and predispositions are then acted upon by the whole environmental spectrum from the time of conception onward. The basic interaction between body and environment takes place through nerve and hormone mechanisms. A person reacts to outside stimulation with pleasure or anxiety. Any reaction triggers the nervous system, which in turn stimulates the pituitary and the adrenal glands to secrete hormones, which in turn cause physiological changes throughout the entire body. The most common body-wide changes are the fight-or-flight response to fear or anxiety, and the relaxation response to pleasure. The fight-or-flight response causes increased heart rate, dilation of bronchi, decrease in bowel tone and constriction of blood vessels in the bowel, increase in sphincter tone, increased release of glucose by the liver, increase in body metabolism, and dilation of blood vessels in the muscles. The relaxation response is basically the physiological opposite of the fight-or-flight response. It causes a decrease in heart rate, constriction of the bronchi, an increase in bowel tone and blood flow, and lower metabolism.

In the last decade, researchers have learned a great deal about how stress affects a baby's health. Stress is now defined in a much broader way. Whereas it used to refer simply to events that made people anxious or upset, or changed their routines, stress is now regarded as an individual's feeling or perception that he or she can't cope with a situation. The person doesn't see himself being able to meet a goal. Emphasis has shifted from external to internal, from events to perceptions. When people continually feel that they cannot achieve their goals in situations, they develop a sense of helplessness which lowers the immune system.

Researchers currently think that certain attitudes aid people in dealing with situations that are stress-producing. Primary among these attitudes is a sense of *self-efficacy*. If people believe they can cope with a situation, they do not tend to perceive it as stressful. Research has shown that people who have confidence in their ability to deal with a situation actually have lower levels of stress hormones in their blood than people who feel they cannot cope. Social psychologist Suzanne Kobasa studied the personality characteristics of people who seemed resistant to the harmful effects of stress. She referred to the group of traits they shared as *hardi-*

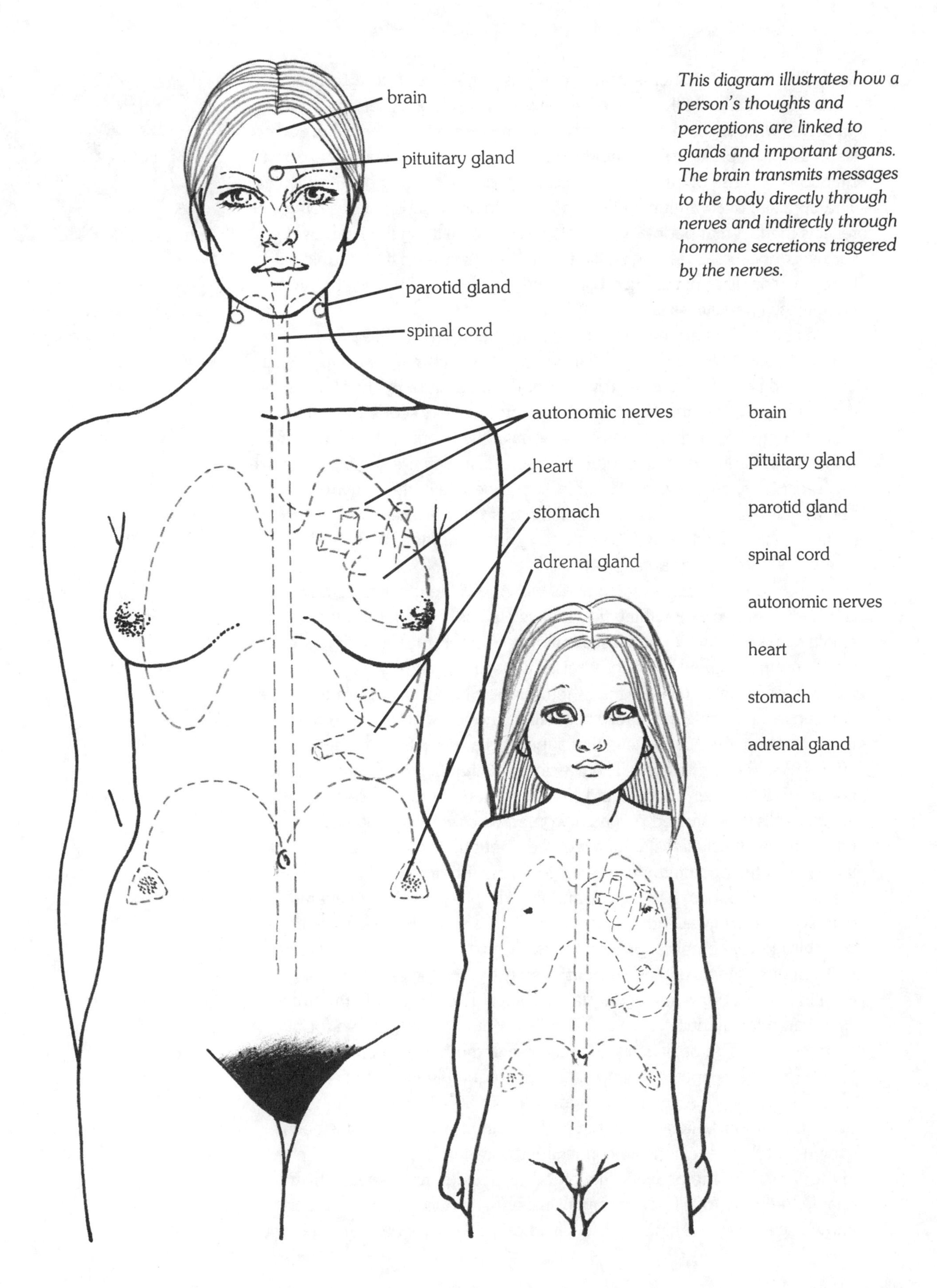

This diagram illustrates how a person's thoughts and perceptions are linked to glands and important organs. The brain transmits messages to the body directly through nerves and indirectly through hormone secretions triggered by the nerves.

ness. The three main elements that comprised hardiness were control, commitment, and challenge. *Control* involves people's belief that they can influence what is going on around them. The opposite of control is powerlessness, or helplessness. *Commitment* involves a sense of curiosity about situations, a sense of involvement and purpose concerning one's activities. The opposite of commitment is alienation. Finally, a sense of *challenge* reflects the fact that people view the world as something they can deal with, as opposed to viewing it as a threat. Kobasa found that people with hardy personalities experienced one-tenth the illness of those who did not have these characteristics.

Social support that makes expectant mothers feel loved, nourished, and satisfied has been shown to lower complications in pregnancy.

The concept of hardiness is important for babies as well as parents. For a mother and father, a sense of hardiness helps in coping with the realities of parenting and facilitates a growing bond with their baby. For babies, a developing sense of their own autonomy and ability to cope is key to optimum growth, both in terms of personality development and in terms of health. If babies learn to soothe themselves, if they are stimulated to see the effects they can have on the objects and people in their environment, and are allowed to participate in making their own choices in regard to matters such as feeding and toilet training, they are more likely to develop a sense of hardiness at an early age.

Another area of new research deals with the value of support. *Support* is broadly defined as anything that makes a person feel good, function effectively, and have an optimistic outlook. Support makes people feel loved, nourished, and satisfied. It raises their self-esteem and makes them feel part of something larger than themselves. Support can stem from relationships with people, from religious beliefs, hobbies, community affiliations. Researchers now believe that support is a resource in resisting the effects of stressful situations. The classic study that first demonstrated the relationship between support and stress was done by psychologist Katherine Nuckolls. She studied pregnant women who were dealing with stressful situations. Nuckolls asked the women about their marriage, their family, and their community in order to assess the degree of personal support each of them had. She found that despite the stressful events going on in their lives, those women who had strong support experienced one-third fewer complications in pregnancy and delivery.

Another striking study on support dealt with the illness patterns of children in a foundling home and a state nursery. The children in the home were cared for by nurses, the children in the nursery were cared for by their mothers. The babies raised by their own mothers gained weight better, were less susceptible to illness, and consequently had a lower mortality rate. Researchers now understand much more about how stress, hardiness, and support interact with the body's immune system. It has been shown that there are intricate connections between the brain and the immune system, the body's white blood cells and lymph nodes which enable the body to kill foreign organisms and produce antibodies. This knowledge has given birth to a new field called *psychoneuroimmunology.*

Scientists have discovered that there are nerves leading to the organs where immune cells are produced—the thymus, lymph nodes, spleen, and bone marrow. Researchers have even found that there are autonomic nerve endings in the immune tissues of the tonsils, appendix, and the Peyer's patches of the intestines. Finally, the white blood cells of the immune system also respond to chemical messengers from the central nervous system. White blood cells have receptors on their surfaces that bind to hormones, neurotransmitters, and neuropeptides. Neuropeptides, such as *endorphins,* are found in the brain and are associated with pain sensation and the processing of emotions. The endorphins are self-produced pain relievers that are released during relaxed states. They have been shown to increase pain tolerance during childbirth. Thus the relaxed state can result in enhanced immune function and stress in decreased immune function. Increasingly, research has shown that the brain interacts with the immune system.

There have been numerous studies on how stress affects the rates of infectious disease in children. The most well-known study was done by pediatric researcher Roger Mayer. He studied the incidence of strep throat in a group of children who were basically healthy and noted that one-fourth of the strep throats occurred shortly after a family crisis. He also found that children with strep throat were four times as likely to have experienced stressful episodes prior to becoming ill. Another study done by Dr. Klaus Roghmann dealt with the effects of stress on all types of illness in a group of children. Roghmann found that the probability of illness on a stressful day was double the normal rate for both mothers and children. The day after a stressful episode, the probability tripled. Studies have also shown that the duration of upper respiratory illnesses is prolonged in children who are under a great deal of stress.

Fascinating new research studies point to the fact that early experience profoundly affects the health of a child in terms of the immune system's ability to fight infection. One of the initial studies in this area dealt with immune differences between a group of rats that had been handled extensively from birth versus a group that had not. The group that had been handled had a better immune response, that is, they produced more antibodies in reaction to a foreign substance. The results of this study provoked further research on the effects of early behavioral interaction. Another study showed that when young monkeys were separated from their peer group, their immune function was impaired. An even more dramatic study with young monkeys showed that when mothers and babies were temporarily separated for two weeks, immune function decreased during the period of separation, but returned to normal when the mothers and babies were reunited. Finally a study with mice showed that litters who were removed from their mothers for four hours a day and were weaned at 15 days as opposed to 21 days had a depressed immune response.

Although it is difficult to generalize from these studies, they point to the fact that mother-baby interactions may profoundly affect infants' susceptibility to infection. Many of the topics covered in this book relate to the social interactions a baby experiences, including prenatal stress reduction, newborn-infant bonding, attachment, and daycare. The more positive these interactions, the better it will likely be for the baby's health.

All people—including babies in the uterus—react accordingly to whatever is *perceived* as pleasure or anxiety. The fight-or-flight response produced by the nervous system is the body's general response to what is mentally identified as stress. Each individual has his or her own pattern of stress identification which begins to develop even while in the uterus. This system is probably partly genetic, but mostly it is learned. Thus what one person perceives as stress, another may not. Prolonged stress, due to any cause, produces physical and mental illnesses of all kinds. It does so by lowering the individual's resistance to disease in general—including all infectious agents—and by creating muscle tension which affects the blood flow and environment of any specific organ, making it more susceptible to disease. Constant, unrelieved tension requires energy to keep muscles contracted (even slightly) and results in the buildup of toxic waste products around muscle cells.

Medical science has long known that perception of stress affects health and disease. One study found that a group of people who were frequently ill had stressful experiences similar to those of a rarely ill group, but the frequently ill group tended to view the stressful experiences as "*emotional* and *interpersonal problems*," while the healthier group felt they were "*interesting* and *satisfying experiences*." Similarly, studies have shown that streptococcal and viral respiratory illnesses were four times as frequent after stressful family episodes and that streptococci were found most often in children insecure in their parental relationships.

Another study focused on the differences between well children and children who had a variety of illnesses for which they were hospitalized. The study found that the families of the ill children were "more disorganized" and the children were exposed to a greater number of threatening and disruptive changes, such as serious illness or death in the family, departure of a close friend, displacement of the child outside the home. The researchers noted that the illnesses generally developed during a period of great flux in the children's life. The researchers also noticed that the families were less cohesive, the ill children related "more poorly" with their parents, and the mothers functioned "less adequately in their mothering roles." The researchers believe that illness is caused by many variables, including biological, psychological, and sociological factors. Each of these variables is affected by stress, adjustment mechanisms, and by the extent to which stressful situations are resolved.

Parents teach babies to handle stress by learning to handle stress themselves. Babies learn patterns of coping intuitively; they observe how parents perceive and deal with stress and then they imitate the parents. Parents attune children to stress in two ways—first, they provide children with their

Parenting the child "without"

New understanding of the child "within" has led adults into programs in which they learn to re-parent themselves. This chart adapts adult re-parenting messages to nurture and reduce the stress on a young child.

Age	*Messages for healthy growth*	*Appropriate nurturing*
0–6 mos.	I will meet your physical needs	Feed, deal with crying
	I'm glad you were born	Talk
	I like to hold you	Hold, fondle
6–18 mos.	I will give you attention and love without conditions	Unconditional love and positive feedback
	I will let you explore and make messes, but keep you safe	Protect from harm
18–36 mos.	I am not afraid to set limits for you	Begin disciplining with consequences
	I'm not afraid of your growing up	Help child solve problems using cause and effect
	I will not let you control me	Establish limits
	I will help you know your own feelings	Verbalize feelings
3–6 yrs.	I will teach you to have your own power	Encourage problem solving
	I will teach you appropriate behavior	Allow expression of fear
	I like your feelings	Point out what will make people like you

most visible *model* for dealing with stress, and second, parents provide a particular *environment,* which sets up many of the stressful conditions their children will encounter.

Whenever parents react to stress in their own life, they demonstrate to their children ways of reacting to stress. Parents can deal with stress as a challenge or as a problem, they can react to stress with excitement or depression. They may resolve it successfully and then relax, or they may remain under chronic stress.

Of course, no parents can, or should, eliminate stress entirely. And no parents can always deal with stress completely to their satisfaction. But it's important that parents realize that the way they handle it can truly be a form of preventive medicine. Thus if parents foster an environment in which their child can learn to recognize and deal with stress of all kinds, they will raise a child who is most likely to be healthy from infancy to adulthood.

The purpose of this book is to help create healthy babies by giving parents skills in both self-help and holistic medicine. The next section of the book contains much information about normal growth and development in the early years of childhood. And there is information on routine child care which can help parents meet the baby's basic needs in a healthy way. This section also deals with parents' feelings and the special requirements of living with a young child. It shows how parents can use relaxation and imagery to relieve stress, get in touch with their feelings, and evolve effective solutions. Taken together, all this information helps parents create an environment that is optimally stimulating and satisfying for themselves and their baby. At a very real level this part of the book functions as a holistic tool, helping parents to lower and deal with stress. The last section of the book educates parents about the most common accidents and illnesses of childhood. The orientation is toward early diagnosis, home treatment, and future prevention. This information helps parents to participate actively in the health care of their child. In so doing parents can become the practitioners of the new medicine for babies.

Creating health: child development, practical concerns, and holistic skills

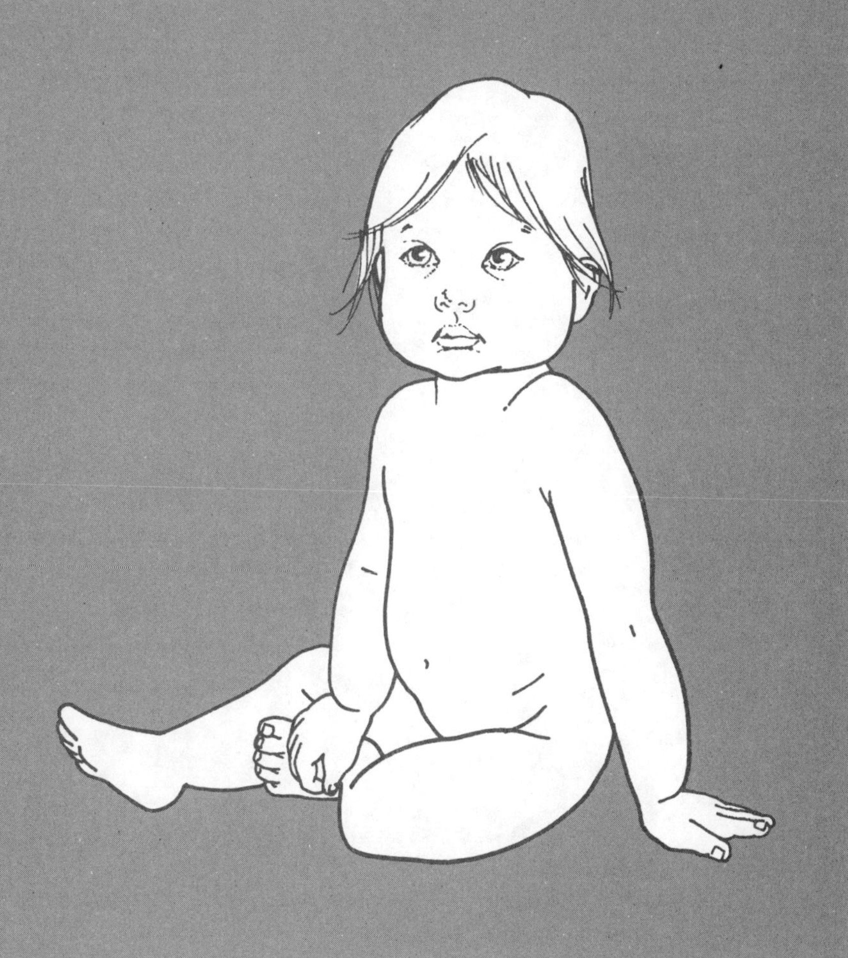

Chapter 4

The baby before birth

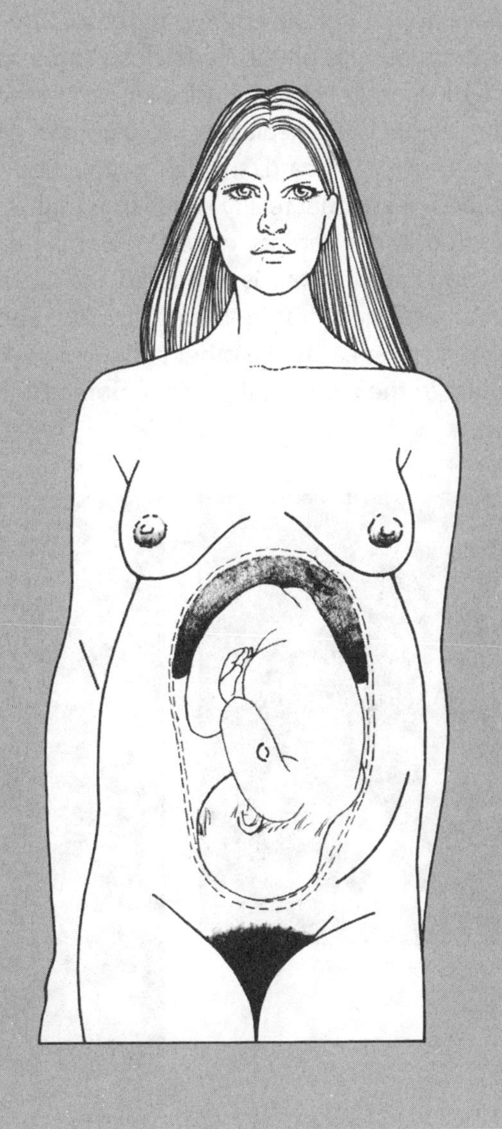

Birth as an event

For centuries the Chinese have dated a baby's age from the time of conception. Under this system most of the baby's first year of life is spent within the mother, developing. This time of development, although profoundly altered by birth, nevertheless is simply part of the overall developmental continuum. Seen in this context, birth becomes *an event* in the life of the child, not the start of the child's life. In Western society, the baby's age is dated from the time of birth. And correspondingly, Westerners tend to think of birth not as a landmark, but as the beginning of the baby's life. Birth *is* the start of some new physiological and psychological functionings, but *in actuality, the newborn baby has been alive and aware for some months.*

Historically, reluctance to recognize the unborn baby as a living person probably stems from a real fear of losing the baby during pregnancy, birth, or shortly after. Ignorance about the time of conception and about early development of the embryo probably also played a role. Even though an unborn baby is physically as close to the mother (and even the father), as *all-present,* as he or she will ever be, yet the baby remains, for nine months, largely out of immediate sensory contact with the parents. That is, the baby can't be seen, heard, smelled, or touched directly. Just as the baby's experience of external reality is buffered and altered by the uterine condition, so, too, is the parents' experience of the baby.

Spiritually as well as physically, the unborn baby is often viewed as being in an especially fragile, transitory state. The baby in utero seems to have one foot on earth, the other in heaven—one in the material world, the other in the realm of the spirits. Some African tribes continue to regard the

In many cultures babies are viewed as fragile creatures who are not spiritually safe until the proper religious ritual has been performed. Left: The Circumcision *(1656), detail, by Rembrandt van Ryn, National Gallery of Art, Washington, Widener Collection.* Right: The Presentation in the Temple *(1389), detail, by Hans Memling, National Gallery of Art, Washington, Samuel H. Kress Collection.*

The moment when a woman learns she is pregnant is an emotional time. Even a woman who has long wanted a baby has mingled feelings of joy, awe, and fear. Left: The Annunciation, *(1334), detail, by Giovanni di Paolo, National Gallery of Art, Washington, Samuel H. Kress Collection.* Above: The Annunciation, *Master of the Retable of the Reyes Católicas. M. H. de Young Museum, gift of the Samuel H. Kress Foundation.*

newborn baby as a spirit visitor for seven days after birth. At this time it is assumed that the baby's spirit will remain on earth and the baby is ceremonially named. Only then is the baby recognized as a living person. Similarly, many Christians believe the newborn baby is not safely in God's hands until the baby has been baptized and consecrated to the Lord. It is at baptism that the baby is officially given a name and recognized before God.

Much of the ancient fear and ignorance about the unborn baby are dissipating as we learn more about the time between conception and birth. Increasing knowledge is increasing the awe and respect we have for the unborn baby and is causing us to regard the unborn baby as a real person long before birth, a person who is in many ways as affected by the *external* environment as a baby outside the uterus. And knowledge is indicating important ways in which parents can affect the health and future development of their baby before it is born.

More and more, research is showing that virtually everything done by the parents—especially by the mother—affects the unborn baby. The baby reacts to the mother's emotional state both directly and indirectly. The baby's health at birth and afterward is dependent on the expectant mother's own health, on her nutrition, and on the drugs she has used during pregnancy and delivery. Moreover, studies show that the unborn baby can respond to external stimuli such as sound and light and can *learn* long before birth. All of this information is causing a radical change in the way expectant parents are relating to the unborn baby. Expectant parents are no longer viewing the time of pregnancy as a totally passive period of waiting; they are viewing it as the initial phase in actively assuming parental roles and adapting to a new member of the family.

Growth before birth

All parents wonder how the baby actually develops in the uterus and are excited when they begin to learn about it. A mental image of development helps expectant parents to relate and become emotionally close to the coming baby. And more knowledge of intrauterine development enables a woman to understand what is unfolding within her body and helps both parents to create a good environment for the baby's growth.

Conception (fertilization)

Growth and development inside the uterus is an astonishing, extraordinary, nine-month process that begins with the merging of sperm and egg in the top of the *fallopian tube,* which connects the ovary to the uterus. Half the baby's chromosomes come from the sperm, half from the egg. They join and make one special cell, which divides a number of times and forms a ball of several dozen cells during the first four days of merging. During this time the fertilized egg, or ovum, travels down the fallopian tube and enters the uterus.

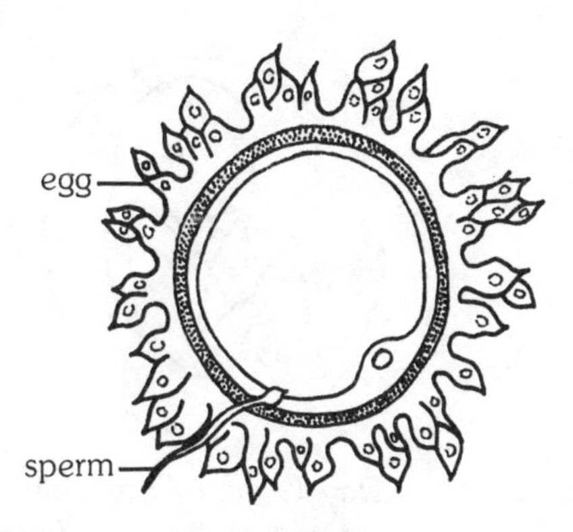

Day 1: Conception takes place when a sperm cell penetrates the egg.

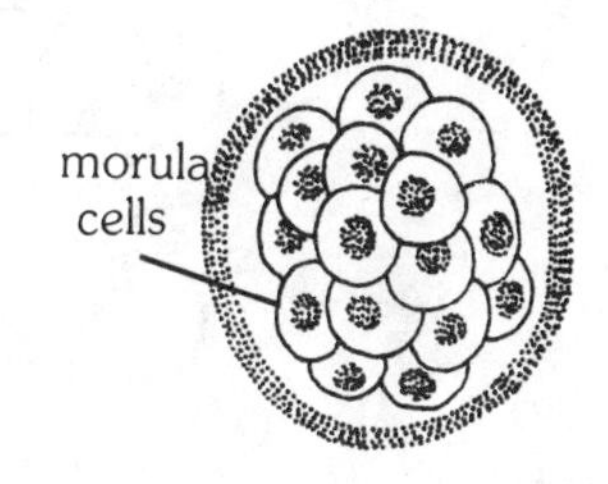

Days 1 through 4: The fertilized cell divides several times and forms a solid ball.

Ovum (0–2 weeks)

Upon reaching the uterus around the fifth day, the cells of the ovum begin to divide rapidly and form a *hollow* ball. Initially this ball floats freely in the uterus. Meanwhile, a major change is taking place as the cells, for the first time, become specialized into inner and outer layers. The inner cluster of cells will actually become the embryo, or baby, while the outer layer will eventually form the placenta, or specialized tissues that link the baby's blood supply with that of the mother. Around the seventh day, the outer layer develops little projections called *villi,* which burrow into the wall of the uterus, which in turn has been developing specialized blood spaces to surround the villi and thereby nourish and remove wastes from the baby. The process of *implantation* is the result of a complicated chemical/physical interaction between the mother's body and the developing embryo.

Embryo (2–8 weeks)

Once the ovum is implanted, the inner and outer layers themselves begin to undergo specialized changes. The outer layer evolves into the fetal mem-

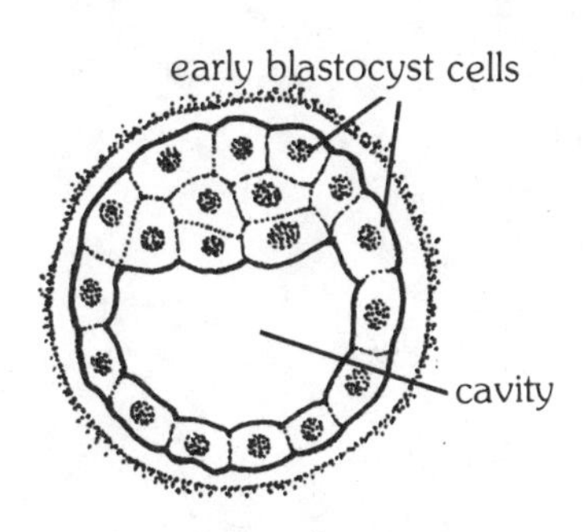

Day 5: A hollow ball is formed after further rapid cell division.

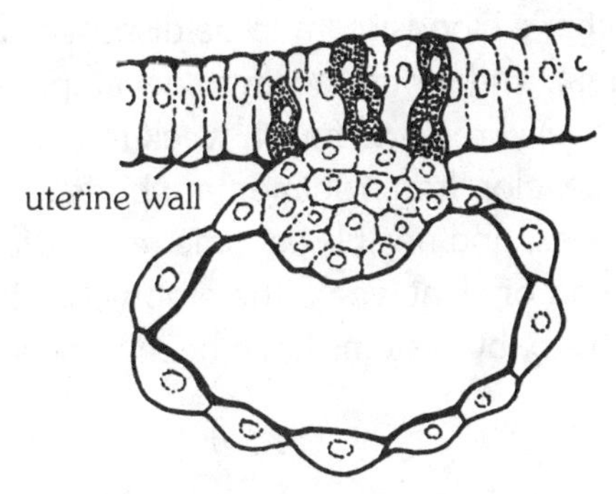

Day 7: Implantation takes place when the hollow ball burrows into the wall of the uterus.

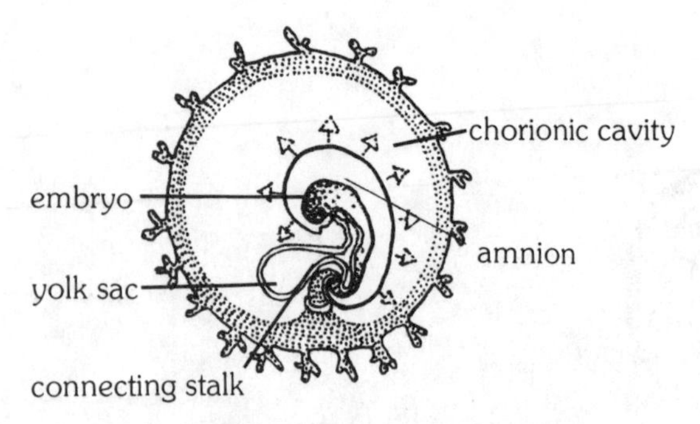

Day 7 on: The dividing cells begin to specialize into an inner layer, which will form the baby, and an outer layer, which will form the yolk sac and later the umbilical cord.

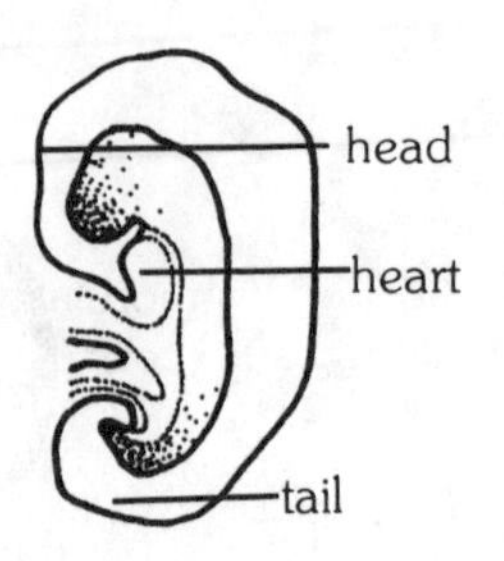

Day 14 on: The inner layer itself begins to specialize and forms a head, tail, and primitive heart.

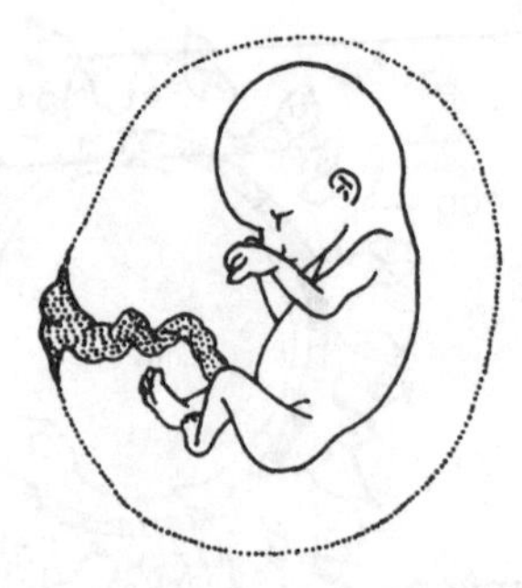

Day 49 on: All the body systems are basically formed and the embryo is almost recognizable as a baby.

branes, the *amnion* and *chorion,* which initially form the yolk sac and later the umbilical cord which links the embryo to the mother via the placenta. Meanwhile, the inner layer of the ovum is evolving into three distinct layers of tissue: outer (ectoderm), middle (mesoderm), and inner (endoderm). From the ectoderm will develop the baby's skin, hair, nails, parts of teeth, glands, sensory cells, and nervous system. From the mesoderm will develop the baby's inner skin layer, muscles, bones, circulatory system, and excretory system. And out of the endoderm will develop the baby's gastrointestinal tract, inner organs, and some glands.

In the third week the embryo begins to change from a ball to a pear shape. Thereafter it develops a head and tail, a neural groove along the back, and a primitive heart which actually pulsates and circulates the embryo's blood.

By the fourth week the amnion and chorion have formed a primitive stalk through which the embryo's blood travels, adjacent to the mother's blood but separated by a membrane. Across this membrane, oxygen, nutrients, antibodies, and hormones pass to the embryo, and waste products pass back to the mother's bloodstream to be disposed of. During the fourth week the head, brain, and mouth begin to develop, as well as the gastrointestinal tract and liver. From the fourth week to the eighth or ninth week, the arms and legs develop from rudimentary buds to recognizable form. Likewise the eyes, ears, and nostrils become recognizable, and the sex organs form. By the end of eight weeks the embryo is almost recognizable as human and all of its baby systems have been basically formed.

Fetus (8 weeks–delivery)

During the third month finger- and toenails form, as well as bones and individual facial characteristics. At eight weeks the nostrils close with skinlike plugs and by two weeks later the eyelids fuse shut.

For the first time the fetus spontaneously moves its arms and legs—a by-product of both muscular and nervous development. These movements are so minute and the fetus is so small that the mother does not notice them. Studies show that at this stage the fetus out of the uterus actually moves in response to touch. At eight weeks the fetus also begins to show recognizable brain-wave activity.

4th month (12–16 weeks)

During the fourth month the placenta finalizes its form. The fetus's movements become even more pronounced and for the first time the mother becomes aware of them. A fetal water cycle evolves—the fetus swallows and excretes the amniotic fluid, the sea-water-like liquid in which it floats. By the time the baby is born, it is swallowing as much as two cups of fluid a day. By sixteen weeks, early fecal matter, called *meconium,* is already collecting in the baby's intestinal tract. The mother, meanwhile, is absorbing the amniotic fluid and producing new fluid at a constant rate.

5th month (16–20 weeks)

By the fifth month the fetus is basically formed and most of its organ systems are functioning, yet it could not survive apart from the mother. The last half of pregnancy is largely taken up with growth and the fine development of organ systems.

During this month the baby becomes capable of its first sucking responses and can grip with its hands. The eyelids are still fused, but blinking movements begin. The bones of the ear, including those of the middle ear which make sound conduction possible, ossify, or harden.

6th month (20–24 weeks)

During the sixth month, the baby's skin, nails, and hair take on adult form. The baby also starts to develop fat and vernix, the oily substance which protects the baby from the amniotic fluid and covers the baby's skin at birth. At this point the nostrils reopen and the baby begins to make muscular breathing motions. The brain-wave patterns by now are usually similar to those seen after birth. The waves are believed to originate from the more highly evolved part of the brain, the *thinking* brain. They reflect beginning activity in the fetus's hearing and visual systems.

7th month

By the seventh month the eyes are completely formed and can perceive light. The eyelids now reopen. The taste buds of the tongue are functional.

If born at twenty-eight weeks the fetus has a good chance of surviving. Even though an average baby will remain in the uterus another twelve

Size of the baby before birth

4 weeks:
1/5 inch long
8 weeks:
1 inch long
12 weeks:
3 inches long,
3/4 ounce
16 weeks:
3 1/2 inches long
20 weeks:
10 inches long,
8–9 ounces
24 weeks:
14 inches long,
2 pounds 8 ounces
28 weeks:
16 inches long,
4–5 pounds
32 weeks:
18 inches long,
5–5 1/2 pounds
9th month:
20 inches long,
6–9 pounds

weeks, the fetus at twenty-eight weeks can actually see, hear, smell, taste, and perceive touch.

Between twenty-eight weeks and birth the baby's muscle tone increases, as well as its sucking and swallowing skills. The baby develops definite periods of alertness or awakeness. The nervous system undergoes further development. A fatty sheath called myelin is laid down around the nerve fibers. This sheath speeds up and makes easier the transmission of nervous impulses. The sheathing process is not completed until after birth. In fact, many physiological/maturational processes are not complete until after birth or, in some cases, until adulthood.

Stimulation before birth

The schedule of fetal development shows that birth is not altogether the beginning or the end it was once thought to be. The growing baby can sometimes survive in the outside world up to four months before the average time of birth. In fact, most of the fetal systems are basically developed and functioning halfway through pregnancy. Research shows that all the baby's senses are functioning by seven months and that the baby in the uterus is "thinking" and "perceiving" in a way similar to what it will do in the days after birth. This is not so surprising in light of what we now know about babies who are born prematurely. Premature babies have slightly less muscle tone, less developed reflexes, and different sleep patterns than full-term babies. But they are certainly capable of responding to light, sound, and touch. Thus it is important that, as fetal development progresses, the baby in the uterus be considered a sensing, functioning person who responds to stimulation from the environment. For expectant parents this may mean a radical change in the way they view their coming child. The baby is truly present at everything they do, but in an altered way.

Developmental researchers now believe that the stimulation a baby gets in the uterus is actually essential to the baby's differentiation and development. The pregnant woman automatically provides a great deal of the baby's stimulation before birth. Her movements, heartbeat, and breathing all affect the developing fetus. The baby's sense of touch is stimulated by the mother's movements, and the mother's heartbeat and breathing provide a constant sound stimulus. The fetus does much to stimulate itself as well. The baby's own motor responses, as well as the maternal environment, stimulate its developing muscles and nerves. One study has shown that normal development of the palate, the roof of the mouth, is dependent on the fetus's actually moving its mouth (mouth opening reflex) while in the uterus.

Studies done on chick and duck embryos show that to a remarkable extent the embryo elicits responses from itself which are crucial to its later development and to its postnatal life. When the duck's limbs are long enough to reach the head, their touching causes the beak to move. Animal research shows that the fetus moves from its earliest stages. The primitive heartbeat (seen in the human embryo at three weeks) causes movements of the trunk and head. Movements such as these are not idle motions. For example, the duck embryo makes swimming motions with its feet as soon as the webs between the toes develop. Like other embryos, the human fetus moves constantly and stimulates itself by touch.

A slightly different but quite fascinating aspect of fetal self-stimulation concerns rapid eye movement (REM) sleep. This is the stage of sleep associated with dreaming or the experience of images in adults. REM sleep is now believed to supply intense stimulation to the central nervous system. An adult spends an average of 15 to 20 percent of sleep (approximately one hour) in REM, but a newborn spends 50 percent of its time (approximately eight hours) in REM. Before the thirtieth week in the uterus, probably *all* of the fetus's sleep is REM.

The baby's sleep patterns in the uterus

Interestingly enough, REM sleep in the fetus goes along with high levels of hormones which stimulate growth and intellectual development. Therefore, some scientists deduce that in the uterus and shortly after birth the baby is involved in a kind of self-stimulation of the nervous system which may actually aid in brain growth and differentiation.

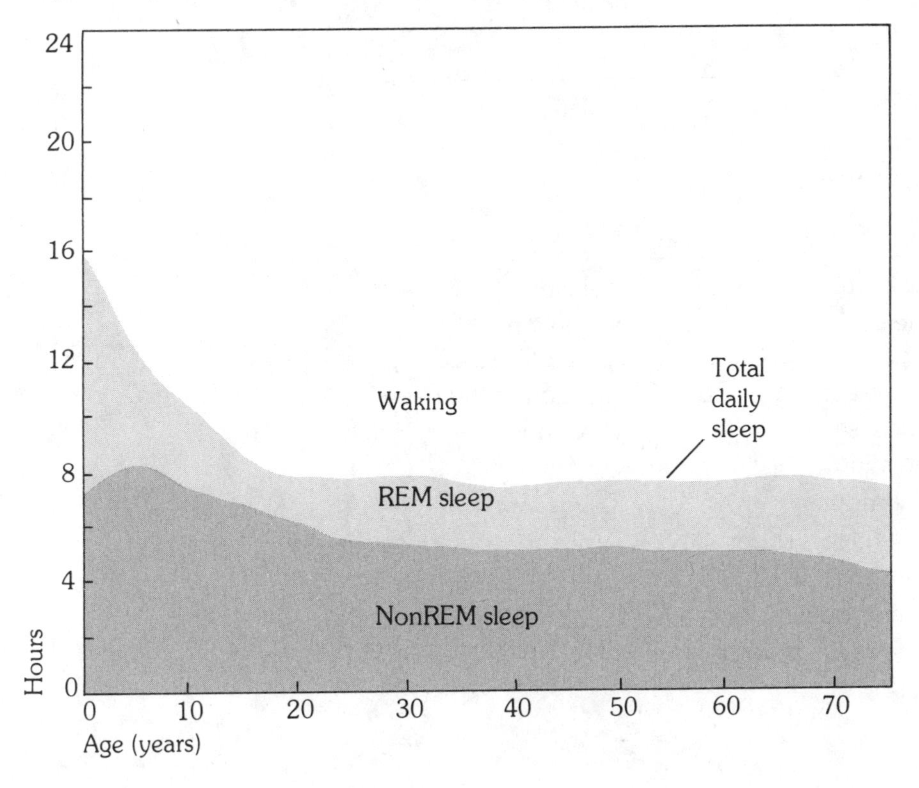

The newborn spends a great deal of time sleeping, much of it in REM sleep.

In addition to self-stimulation and maternal stimulation, the baby reacts to the external environment. Women have always observed that the fetus reacts to any sudden loud sound with violent kicking or moving. Scientists can add that the baby's heart rate increases at the same time. Many mothers have also noticed that the fetus moves in response to music, or noises like the washing machine and vacuum cleaner.

Scientists now know that the fetus responds to everything in its world from every early on. Animal studies have shown that prenatal nutrition, exposure to drugs, chemicals, and hormones, as well as physical and mental stress, can all affect the newborn baby. These effects on the baby are

How parents can stimulate the baby before birth

By 28 weeks of development, all of the senses of the unborn baby are functional.

Mother's activity	*Effect on the baby*
Movements, including dancing, yoga, walking, swimming, and resting Sex, massage Sunbathing, showering	Stimulation of touch perception and balance
Speech and singing, especially the mother's Music and gentle repetitive or rhythmic sounds	Stimulation of hearing
Exposing the mother's belly to direct light, especially the sun	Stimulation of visual perception
Conscious relaxation, meditation, and deep-breathing exercises Interesting and stimulating experiences for the mother, especially ones that have a short period of excitement, followed by a release of tension and by rest Balance and harmony in the mother's daily life	Stimulation of the baby's whole body

wide-ranging, including altered body rhythms, activity levels, emotionality, and learning patterns. All of the causal factors are interrelated, and they can join to affect the fetus in large and small ways. No parent can completely control the environment of the developing baby. In fact, scientists know little about how some things affect the unborn baby. At the present time, much is known about what stimuli can be harmful; much less is known about what stimuli can help the baby. Nevertheless, there are things the parent can do to affect the fetal environment beneficially. It is up to each couple to create their own positive environment for their baby—based not only on scientific knowledge, but on their own intuition of what is right. Everything the parents do to stimulate themselves stimulates the baby.

The unborn baby's nutrition

A pregnant woman's physical state directly affects the fetal environment, and in turn is dependent on her nutrition, rest, relaxation, exercise, and the external environment. The more favorable these factors are for a mother, the better the health of her baby will be.

Obviously, the state of a mother's health does not begin with pregnancy, but is the result of earlier incidents and lifelong patterns. Research has shown that an inadequate diet throughout her childhood increases the likelihood of a woman later giving birth to a premature infant, because an inadequate diet not only undermines her general health, but teaches her poor food habits which are likely to persist through pregnancy. Thus the past as well as the present influences the baby's health.

Whatever the mother's past health, much can be done during pregnancy to ensure her well-being and the baby's. An adequate diet throughout pregnancy is a basic necessity for both. The fetus derives *all* of its nutrition from the mother—at first, indirectly from the yolk sac, and later, directly from the mother's bloodstream via the placenta and the umbilical cord. The baby is literally formed from the nutritional elements consumed by the mother. Not only does the baby "feed" entirely from the mother, the baby *may* get preferential treatment. For instance, if a mother's diet is low in iron, the baby will receive most of the iron the mother ingests, thereby depleting the mother's iron reserves. The result can be an anemic mother, perhaps even an anemic baby.

Scientists have done a number of studies on the effects of diet on the fetus. Malnutrition among pregnant women can be a cause of low-birth-weight infants who are more likely to have a variety of medical problems. Animal studies show that the babies of malnourished animals had fewer brain cells, smaller internal organs, and fewer placental cells.

Nutritionists and doctors agree that optimum nutrition (see pages 42–43) for the pregnant mother results in a reduction of newborn illness and

Special diet for morning sickness

Symptoms such as nausea and vomiting are usually mild and disappear by themselves early in pregnancy.

Small, frequent meals consisting mostly of sandwiches or cereals are most easily tolerated.

Liquids should be taken in small amounts between meals.

Milk is easily digested and provides high protein and calcium.

Increased nutritional demands of pregnancy

Nutrient	*Prepregnant need*	*Pregnant need*	*How the nutrient is used*	*Which foods supply the nutrient*	*Recommended daily amounts**
Protein	46 g	75–100 g	Rapid growth of the baby, the amniotic fluid, the placenta, the mother's uterus, breasts, and blood volume	Dairy products:	
				Milk	1 qt
				Cheese	2 oz or ½ cup
				Eggs	2
				Yogurt	½ cup
			Storage reserves for labor, delivery, and lactation	Meat, fish, and fowl	2 servings (6–8 oz)
				Grains, legumes, nuts, bread, cereal, dried beans, rice, pasta	1 to 2 servings by choice
Calories	2100	2400	Increased energy metabolism and energy needs	All foods, particularly carbohyrates and fats	Supplied by the recommended amounts of all the foods
			Conserve protein		
Minerals					
Calcium	800 mg	1200 mg	Formation of baby's bones and teeth, and increased maternal needs	Milk, cheese, grains, egg yolks	As above
				Leafy vegetables	1 serving
Phosphorus	800 mg	1200 mg	Formation of baby's bones and teeth, and increased maternal needs	Milk, cheese, lean meats	As above
Iron	18 mg	18 mg, plus 30–60 mg supplement	Mother's increased blood volume, and baby's liver storage	Liver or organ meats	1 to 2 servings per week
				Other meat, eggs, grains, leafy vegetables, nuts, dried fruits	As above
Iodine	100 micrograms	125 micrograms	Increased maternal metabolism and production of thyroid hormone	Iodized salt	Daily in cooking
				Seafood	1 to 2 servings per week

Magnesium	300 mg	450 mg	Enzymes in energy production and muscle action	Nuts, soybeans, cocoa, seafood, dried peas and beans	Occasional servings
Vitamins					
A	4000 IUs	5000 IUs	Cell, tooth, and bone gowth of the baby	Butter, cream, fortified margarine	2 tbs
				Leafy vegetables, liver, egg yolk	As above
D	0	400 IUs	Absorption of calcium and phosphorus for teeth and bones	Fortified milk, fortified margarine	As above
E	12 IUs	15 IUs	Growth and maintenance of red blood cells	Vegetable oils, leafy vegetables, cereals, meat, eggs, milk	Supplied by recommended amounts above
C	45 mg	60 mg	Growth, formation of connective tissue and blood vessels, aid in iron absorption	Citrus fruits, strawberries, melons, papayas	1 to 2 servings
				Broccoli, green peppers, tomatoes, chili peppers, potatoes	Occasional servings
Folic acid	400 micrograms	800 micrograms, plus 200–400 supplement	Increased maternal metabolism	Liver, green vegetables, lentils, nuts	1 serving
			Prevention of a rare form of anemia		
			Formation of red blood cells and cell nuclei		
B complex	Different for each B vitamin	Slightly higher	Increased energy metabolism	Meat, beans, milk, cheese	As above

*The recommended daily amounts or their equivalents, *taken together*, supply the average needs of a pregnant woman.

death. To have an optimum diet during pregnancy, an expectant mother must meet the *increased* nutritional demands of her body.

In the United States today it has been found that a surprising number of pregnant women have inadequate diets. By no means is all inadequate nutrition due to lack of money. It is often due to a combination of poor diet habits and the extensive exposure to junk foods.

It is quite important that a pregnant woman not just eat "enough," but that she analyze her diet throughout pregnancy and make sure that it is adequate in all the basic nutritional categories. A good diet for mother and baby has been shown to be especially important during "vulnerable periods" of fetal development: 15–20 weeks after conception and 25–40 weeks after conception.

Preparations for nursing

During pregnancy, hormones cause changes in the woman's breasts which prepare her for nursing. The tubules, or little passages, in the breasts increase in number and size and form the tissue structures which actually produce the milk. There are several things that an expectant mother can do to assist her body in preparing for nursing.

A good enriched diet for the mother.

Adequate stores of fat obtained during pregnancy will supply 200–300 calories a day for the first three months after the baby is born. This represents ⅓ of the energy in the milk.

Nipple conditioning may help to prevent nipple soreness during the early days of nursing:

1. Frequently expose the breasts to air and sunlight throughout pregnancy.
2. Don't wear a bra, or open the flaps on a nursing bra to allow the nipples to rub on clothing and become desensitized.
3. Pull on nipples and roll them between thumb and forefinger daily during the last three months of pregnancy. This exercise is especially important for women with fair or sensitive skin and for those who have flat or inverted nipples.

Find out basic information about breast-feeding from the doctor, other mothers, the La Leche League International, and books (see charts, pages 122–25).

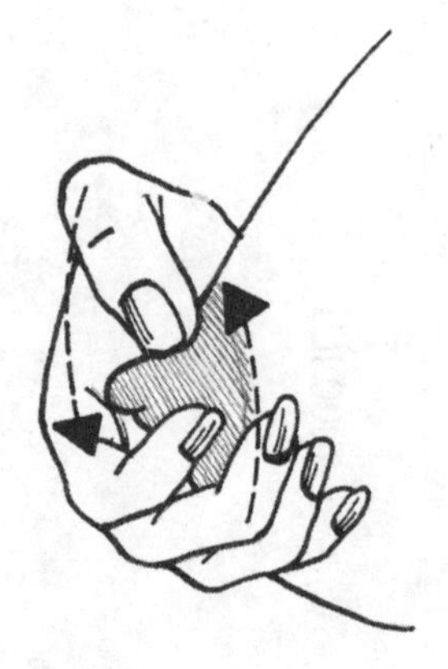

Nipple-toughening exercises may be an important aid in preventing nipple tenderness in the early days of nursing.

Pregnancy is a good time for women to become more aware of their normal diet patterns as well as the recommended prenatal nutritional requirements. During pregnancy many women experience cravings for specific foods or are repulsed by certain others. Often these feelings turn out to be medically sound. For example, many pregnant women have an increased desire for milk which parallels the baby's need for protein and calcium. Some pregnant women lose their regular appetite for such things as alcohol or pasta, which are high in carbohydrates and low in most other nutrients.

The question of healthy weight gain during pregnancy has been debated for decades by obstetricians and researchers. For years obstetricians tended to advise women to hold their weight gain to twenty pounds since obesity is correlated with greater complications in pregnancy and delivery. More recently it has been found that pregnancy is no time to restrict weight radically and certainly not a time to diet by withholding calories or salt. Healthy women produce healthy babies over a wide range of weight gains—from a few pounds to as many as sixty. What's important is that the mothers get the right amounts of the right foods. The average weight gain during pregnancy is now twenty-five to thirty pounds. Two to four pounds are usually gained during the first three months, and thereafter about a pound a week. These are just average figures and women should not be encouraged to try to hold to them.

Guide for pregnant women who are vegetarians

Eat a wide variety of foods to meet increased protein, vitamin, and mineral needs.

Combine grains, legumes, nuts, and seeds to obtain whole protein.

Use iodized salt or supplement iodine.

If no milk is used, supplement calcium and vitamins B_{12} and D.

How weight gain is distributed in pregnancy

	Weight (Averages)
The baby	7.5 pounds
The placenta	1.0
The amniotic fluid	2.0
Increase in the uterus's weight	2.5
Increase in the breasts' weight	3.0
Increase in the mother's blood	4.0
Increase in the mother's fat stores needed for energy	4.0-8.0
Total	**24–28 pounds**

How drugs, smoking, and alcohol affect the baby before birth

In addition to the foods a mother eats, the chemicals she is exposed to can affect the fetus. At this point it is believed that everything taken by mouth or injected into the pregnant woman reaches the fetus. The thalidomide tragedy of the early sixties showed that even medical drugs considered "safe" for the expectant mother could be severely harmful to the unborn baby at certain times during pregnancy.

Sometimes drugs can harm the fetus but not the mother. This is because the fetus is developing and evolving new structures; the mother is not. Also, what is the right dose for a person the size of the mother represents a massive dose for a tiny baby. Finally, drugs are not completely digested or metabolized by the baby because the fetal liver is not fully developed until some time after birth. Therefore drugs can affect the baby differently from the mother.

The safest course is for the expectant mother to take no drugs—prescription or nonprescription—throughout pregnancy. And the most significant thing an expectant mother can do in order to avoid taking drugs is to keep herself healthy. In addition to getting good nutrition and rest, she can take reasonable measures to avoid exposing herself unnecessarily to infectious agents and to conditions that predispose toward infections. Avoiding illness is not always possible. And the pregnant woman should know that there are drugs that have been used safely in pregnancy.

There is no question that smoking during pregnancy affects the developing baby. Cigarette smoke contains an astounding 68,000 chemicals, many of which are harmful. While an expectant mother is smoking a cigarette and for 15 minutes thereafter, the blood vessels in the placenta clamp down, reducing blood flow to the baby. In addition, chemicals such as cyanide and nicotine cross the placenta and cause profound physiological changes in the baby, such as an increase in heart rate and a constriction of blood vessels. Additionally, the baby experiences a high concentration of carbon monoxide, which further reduces the baby's oxygen supply. As a result, babies born to mothers who smoke have lower than average birth weights, a condition which is associated with an increase in all types of complications. This effect is dose related, but is seen to take place even when a woman smokes under ten cigarettes a day. Women who smoke are also more likely to give birth prematurely or even have a spontaneous abortion early in pregnancy. Finally, maternal smoking during pregnancy is thought to negatively affect the baby's health, including neurological and intellectual maturation. At birth, these babies are less responsive to sound and are less readily soothed by sounds. During childhood, those babies whose mothers smoked during pregnancy have higher rates of hospitalization and higher frequency of skin and respiratory diseases.

Although this is a distressing picture, there is good news. Within days of a mother's quitting smoking, the baby's oxygen increases by 8 percent. Moreover, when mothers are able to quit during the last trimester, the risk of perinatal death is no longer greater than for nonsmokers.

Drugs that can have an adverse effect on the baby during pregnancy

aminopterin
diethylstilbestrol
iodides and propylthiouracil
phenytoin
tetracyclines
thalidomide
valproic acid
warfarin
cigarette smoking
alcohol
Dilantin
lithium
streptomycin
barbiturates
diazepam (Valium)
amphetamines
heroin
morphine
cocaine
marijuana
LSD
methotrexate
podophyllin
oral contraceptives
retinoids
aspirin
Flagyl
sulfonamides
caffeine

In the past twenty years, there have been a growing number of studies on the effects of maternal alcohol consumption. Alcohol as a drug, or chemical, causes birth defects and increased chances of spontaneous abortion early in pregnancy. In 1973 researchers identified a group of malformations seen in the babies of mothers who drank heavily during pregnancy. This group of abnormalities, referred to as *fetal alcohol syndrome,* includes mental retardation and congenital malformations of the head, face, skeleton, and heart.

The syndrome was identified among babies whose mothers were heavy drinkers or drank in binges, but more recently it has been observed in babies whose mothers drank 1–2 ounces of alcohol a day, which is equivalent to an 8-ounce glass of wine, two beers, or two mixed drinks. In addition to fetal alcohol syndrome, moderate maternal drinking is also associated with low birth weight and neurological difficulties among offspring.

A number of other substances can also have adverse effects on the developing baby. These range from substances as common as caffeine and aspirin to less commonly used ones such as barbiturates or illegal drugs. In very high doses, caffeine has been linked to fetal death. In low doses, it acts as a stimulant on the baby. Marijuana affects the baby's hormonal balance and is associated with increased prematurity, low birth weight, and fetal distress. All the addictive drugs—cocaine, heroin, Demerol, and morphine—have very serious effects on the developing fetus, and newborns of addicted mothers are born addicted.

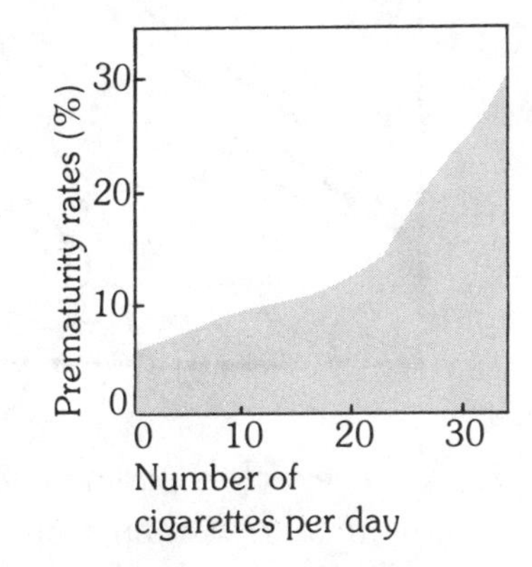

The more cigarettes women smoke per day, the greater is the probability of their babies being born prematurely.

Effects of maternal smoking on the developing baby

- increased carbon monoxide
- decreased oxygen
- increased heart rate
- increased stress hormones
- increased incidence of serious illness and death
- increased likelihood of low birth weight

Rest and sleep

One of the major things an expectant mother can do to contribute to the baby's and her own overall good health is to see that she gets adequate rest throughout pregnancy. This is an area in which most expectant mothers receive the strongest signals from their body, and they would do well to heed these signals. Many women find that they may be more easily fatigued when they are pregnant and that it takes longer for them to regain their energy. The energy requirements of pregnancy are undoubtedly greater than usual. Not only is the mother's body responsible for the synthesis of a whole other being, but her body is altering its own structures, carrying much more weight, generally doing more work, and feeling the effects of unusual hormonal changes. All of which predisposes her to greater physical and emotional fatigue.

The pregnant woman can't necessarily count on her body to react to exertion or stress in a familiar way. Things that formerly were not tiring may now be. What one hour's work and a half hour's rest might have accomplished before pregnancy may require two hours' work and an hour's rest during pregnancy. When a woman has specific tasks or goals she wishes to accomplish, she is wise to begin early and allot more time than usual.

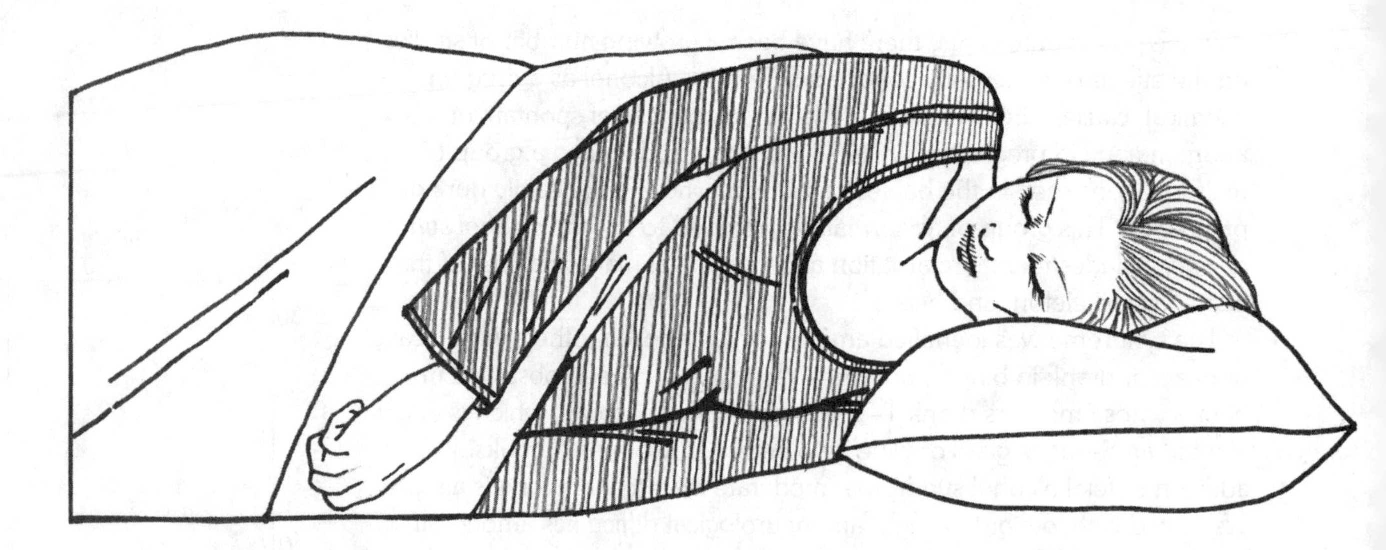

Adequate rest is important to the developing baby and to the expectant mother. At times during pregnancy almost all women find themselves in need of extra sleep.

The factors pertinent to both exertion and rest can vary widely from woman to woman, from month to month and week to week during pregnancy, and from one pregnancy to another for the same woman. The point is, it is important for a pregnant woman to pay continuous attention to her body's signals. In any questionable situation, she is wise to err in the direction of getting too much rest rather than too little.

The more quickly a person becomes aware of fatigue and begins to rest, the more quickly the body will get rid of the metabolic waste products that cause fatigue and will mobilize new energy reserves. Deliberate, deep relaxation in which muscular tension is systematically released relieves physical or emotional stress and maximizes the body's ability to recuperate (see page 60).

Understanding work, fatigue, and rest cycles is especially important to the workingwoman and to the woman who already has children. Both of these women may find they have to alter their established routines in order to feel well rested during pregnancy. The exact changes that may be necessary are impossible to anticipate accurately. And fixed preconceptions of how much energy she should have will simply keep a woman from being aware of and flexible about her body's needs.

Tied in with the pregnant woman's rest and exercise are her sleep patterns. Sleep requirements and patterns frequently alter with the onset of pregnancy and throughout the months that follow. Again, the expectant mother must pay attention to her body's signals. She may find she needs more or less sleep at different times. She may find she needs to go to bed earlier, sleep later, or take naps.

Sleep patterns provide a dramatic example of the relationship between maternal behavior and the life and environment of the fetus. The subtle advantages of getting adequate sleep during pregnancy are beginning to be demonstrated in research studies.

When the mother sleeps she has rapid eye movement (REM) sleep in cycles throughout the night. REM sleep is associated with high levels of growth hormones. These hormones cross the placenta and reach the baby. They are believed to stimulate brain growth in the baby. Conversely, maternal fatigue results in stress hormones reaching the baby. In high levels these hormones can harm the fetus. It would seem that when a pregnant woman is in tune with her sleep needs and is well rested, she is providing the optimum environment for the growth and development of the well baby.

How the mother's emotions affect the baby before birth

People connected with the care and development of very young children—parents and professionals alike—are coming to realize how important it is for the health and happiness of the baby and the parents if both mother and father are prepared for and positive toward parenting. The feelings and attitudes of both the mother and the father are major factors in the baby's health and well-being. This relationship between parental attitudes and infant health begins at conception, because the baby in the uterus directly shares the mother's emotions at a physiological level. Much about the physiological mechanisms for this is now well known. The mother's emotions result from her thoughts and perceptions. Thoughts and perceptions activate a part of the mother's nervous system called the autonomic nervous system, and a part of the brain called the hypothalamus. In turn the nervous system and the hypothalamus affect the tension of the muscles and the output of certain glands. If a thought or perception is stressful, the mother's pituitary gland secretes a hormone called ACTH which causes her adrenal gland to release other hormones—cortisone and adrenalinelike substances. All of these substances actually bathe the early embryo and later cross the placental barrier and enter the bloodstream of the unborn baby.

Just as stressful perceptions result in increased autonomic nervous activity, so nonstressful or pleasurable perceptions result in a group of beneficial physiological changes that have been termed the *relaxation response.* Relaxed pleasure states in the expectant mother result in an optimal uterine environment for the baby. Deliberately concentrating on positive thoughts and mental pictures (imagery), including ones concerning the baby, significantly increases the physiological changes which lead to the relaxed state. (See programmed imagery later in this chapter.)

There are undoubtedly other effects on the unborn baby caused by the mother's psychological state. Certainly the baby must be affected by the mother's level of muscular tension, her heart rate, respiratory rate, metabolic rate, electrical fields, and her body's acid-base balance. All of these factors are demonstrably affected by the mother's emotional state. As scientific research continues into parapsychology, it is possible that correla-

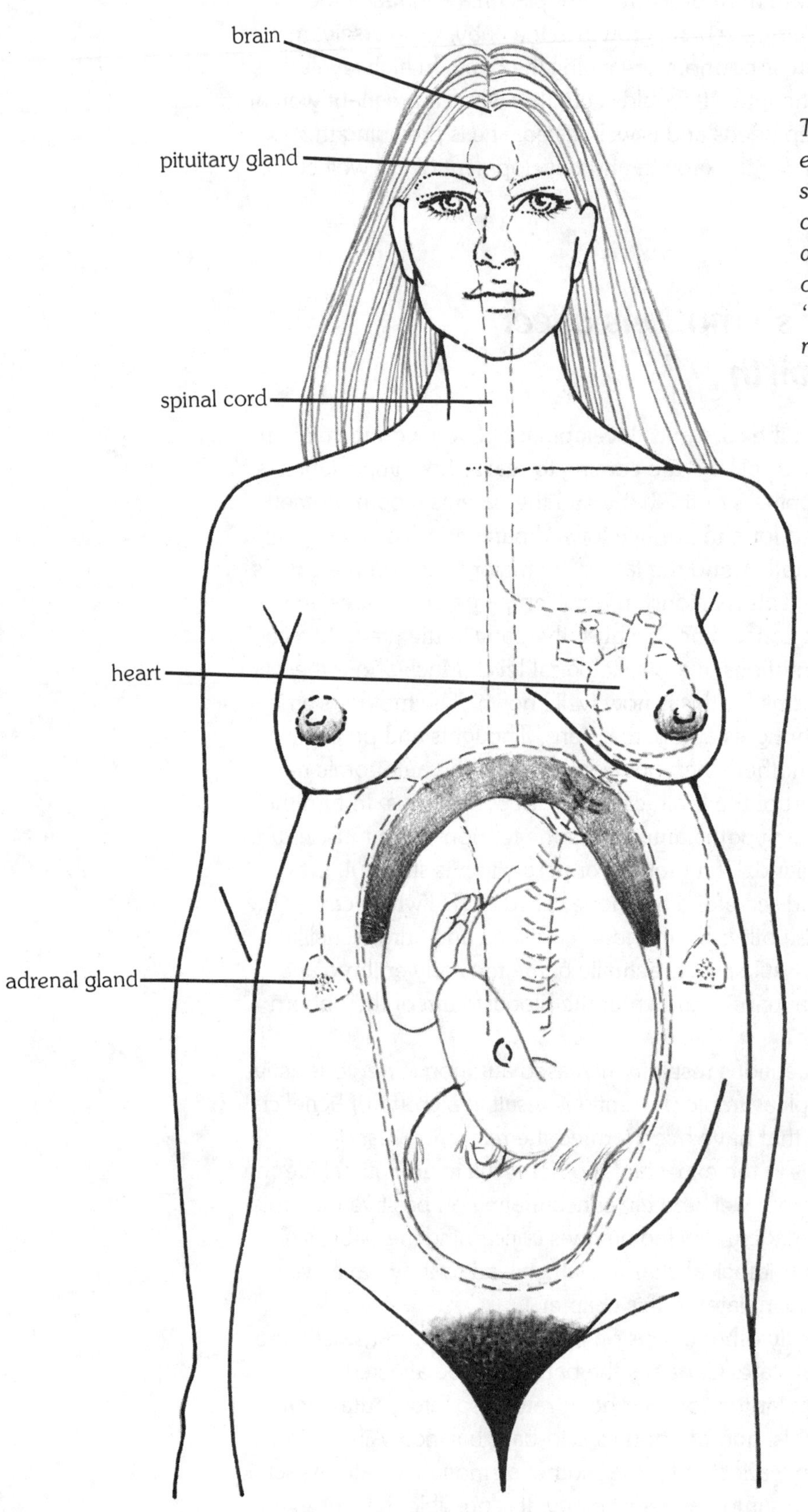

The mother's thoughts and emotions alter her hormonal secretions, which in turn cross the placental barrier and affect the baby. This is one way in which the baby is "tuned" to the mother's responses during pregnancy.

tions will be found between maternal and fetal brain-wave patterns (telepathic communication) and between maternal and fetal electromagnetic energy levels (auras).

Years ago researchers discovered that when the mother experienced emotional stress, fetal movements increased several hundred percent and continued for several hours after even a brief period of stress. If the stress continued for weeks, so did the increased fetal activity. Researchers also found that mothers who experienced a high degree of stress during their pregnancy had babies with lower birth weights. It was further demonstrated that mothers who underwent severe emotional stress during pregnancy often had infants who were irritable, hyperactive, and colicky. Other researchers found that such infants tended to be restless and cried a lot. Studies have also shown that anxiety decreases a pregnant woman's ability to absorb nourishment. A mother can fail to retain up to twice as much nitrogen, phosphorus, and calcium as the baby needs.

A mother's attitude toward being pregnant has even been shown to affect the baby. One study found that mothers who said they disliked being pregnant had a higher percentage of upset babies. Another study showed a correlation between colicky babies and mothers who, during their pregnancy, expressed doubts about their ability to care for the baby. It would seem that the expectations a pregnant woman has about her forthcoming baby are largely borne out. That is, mothers who had the most positive images before birth had the closest, most satisfying relationships with their babies after birth.

Studies with laboratory animals have shown an even broader relationship between the life of the mother and the health and behavior of the infant. Children of mothers who were exposed during pregnancy to severe stress—noise, shock, overcrowding, or hormone injections—showed permanent behavioral changes regardless of whether they were raised by their own mothers or by foster mothers who had not been stressed. The infants showed increased bowel activity, fear of new situations, and decreased learning ability. Even more remarkably, animals whose mothers, when they were infants, had been handled by scientists were heavier and more confident in new situations than control animals whose mothers had not been handled. Similar results were found among the grandchildren of the handled animals.

All of these studies point to the fact that it is likely that a mother's feelings, experiences, and perceptions during pregnancy profoundly affect the health and behavior of her baby. Most assuredly, the levels of stress hormones in the mother's bloodstream directly affect the unborn infant. Thus everything a prospective mother can do to *make herself happier and more content, to reduce and deal appropriately with stress,* will have a beneficial effect on the subsequent health and happiness of her baby.

One of the most important factors that affects a pregnant woman, and therefore the fetus, is the relationship she has with the baby's father. Pregnancy invariably brings with it many changes in the mother's feelings toward the father and vice versa. It is a strong negative influence on a pregnancy if the relationship is stressful. Poor marital adjustment and the absence of the father have been found to be associated with maternal emotional stress and, subsequently, colicky babies. Anything that the mother *perceives* as stressful stimulates the autonomic nervous system, the hypothalamus, and the adrenals, producing lasting effects on the unborn baby. Thus the more positive the mother's relationship with the father, the better the baby's fetal environment will be. In this way the father's role in pregnancy goes far beyond contributing half the baby's genetic constituents. His actions and attitudes have a direct effect on the mother and the fetal environment. The primary role of the father throughout the pregnancy is to be supportive—both emotionally and physically—toward the expectant mother. It is important that the father, like the mother, deal with his own feelings and intuitions so as to lower his own stress and tension. At times during pregnancy the mother's state may be so emotional that she will have difficulty in seeing beyond a problem to a solution. At such times the father's reassurance and supportiveness can be invaluable to the mother.

The primary role of the father throughout the pregnancy is to be supportive—both emotionally and physically—toward the expectant mother. Two Bears, Eskimo. The Metropolitan Museum of Art, Harris Brisbane Dick Fund and Houghton Foundation, Inc., gift.

Prenatal care and medical concerns

Good prenatal care is true preventive medicine and is essential for optimizing the health of mother and baby. In the Netherlands, where prenatal care is emphasized, it is thought to be responsible for a very low infant mortality rate. Most women routinely go through their prenatal visits to the doctor or midwife without problems, but regular visits can help to detect any problems, and early treatment of high blood pressure, gestational diabetes, small-for-date babies, or twins or breech presentations increases the chances of making sure the baby will be healthy.

In addition to spotting problems in the early stages, prenatal care has emotional and educational aspects which are the primary considerations for the great majority of women who have healthy, uncomplicated pregnancies. The mother's routine appointments allow her to become familiar with the person or persons who will assist her in delivering the baby. During her prenatal visits, the mother can establish a relationship with the doctor or midwife based on trust and understanding, and the doctor or midwife likewise has a chance to get to know the mother. At each stage of her pregnancy, the mother has a chance to talk about the medical, emotional, and practical things that concern her. Finally, she becomes accustomed to dealing intimately with her body in the presence of medical people. Often this takes some time, particularly for women who have not been pregnant before and are not used to going to doctors.

In the United States prenatal care typically involves a mere 6 to 12 hours total. The mother-to-be sees the doctor or midwife once a month until the time she is 32 weeks pregnant, again at 34 and 36 weeks, and then weekly until the baby is born. The first visit is usually a long one in which the doctor or midwife does a complete history and physical. Also during this appointment, the mother (and often the father) have a chance to interview the practitioner and find out how he or she handles a normal labor and delivery. Subsequent visits involve a briefer evaluation, some routine lab tests, and a question-and-answer period.

During prenatal care, routine laboratory work is done on the mother. A blood sample is drawn from her arm for several tests: a *hemoglobin test* makes certain she is not anemic, a *VDRL* rules out *syphilis,* and a *rubella antibody titer* determines if she has immunity to German measles. This sample is also used to establish her blood type and whether she is Rh positive or negative. In the event that the mother is Rh negative, she is often given a *RhoGam* shot at 28 weeks to prevent the formation of antibodies against the baby's blood type (which used to be the cause of "blue babies"). A urine sample is taken to do a routine *glucose test* to make sure the mother is not developing *gestational diabetes,* a *protein test* to make sure she is not developing proteinuria, and a culture to make sure she does not have a kidney or bladder infection.

Babies with neural tube defects (as well as other rare congenital malformations) show higher than normal levels of a chemical called *alpha-fetoprotein (AFP).* This substance crosses the placenta and can be detected in the mother's blood at about 16–18 weeks of gestation, but the maternal test can show many false positives.

Diagnostic tests used during pregnancy

Over the last twenty years medical technology has made incredible progress in its ability to test for serious problems while the infant is still in utero. The result has been an entire new field called *perinatology.* It combines the fields of obstetrics and pediatrics in dealing with the growing baby before birth.

A number of perinatal tests and procedures have become so common that they need to be included in a book such as this. However, not all tests will be used on every mother. In general, there are specific criteria for each of the tests, although doctors differ in how broadly they apply the criteria. One doctor may use a particular test almost routinely, while another doctor will use it only under certain circumstances. Often a doctor will talk with parents and make the decision to use a test in consultation with them.

Despite the frequency with which some of the tests are used, the conditions the tests screen for are generally uncommon or rare. The point is not that the incidence of these problems has risen during recent years, but that doctors can now screen for conditions that once couldn't be diagnosed before birth. As a result, doctors tend to use the tests fairly widely. For mothers, the technical nature of these procedures, combined with their unknown outcome, may cause much concern. The more expectant parents know about the tests and the low incidence of problems, the more reassured they are likely to be.

Amniocentesis

Amniocentesis is the most important test that can be done before birth to diagnose serious, non-treatable hereditary diseases and congenital malformations in the fetus. In this procedure, 25–35 cc. of amniotic fluid are withdrawn from the uterus during pregnancy. From the sample, fetal cells can be grown in a tissue culture. The chromosomes in the cells can be checked and various biochemical *assays* or tests can be done if indicated.

In addition to transmissible diseases, amniocentesis also identifies fetuses with *Down's syndrome* (formerly called *Mongolism*). The risk of Down's has long been known to increase with maternal age. So with the growing number of mothers over 35, the test has become increasingly popular with both parents and obstetricians. Its use has grown exponentially. Of all amniocentesis tests today, 80 to 90 percent are done for *advanced maternal age.* As maternal age rises, there is an increase in the number of Down's syndrome babies, as well as babies with other rarer chromosomal abnormalities that also result in congenital malformations.

Down's syndrome or *trisomy 21* is a genetic disorder in which the affected individual has 47 chromosomes rather than the normal 46. The Down's syndrome person has an extra number 21 chromosome. In addition, there is a whole group of physical characteristics that distinguish the syndrome, including short stature and a special facial structure with an *epicanthal fold* at the outer corner of the eyelid. But the most constant feature of Down's syndrome is mental retardation. IQ's vary from 20 to 80, though most range from 45 to 55, which is considered moderate retardation.

Doctors do not know why Down's syndrome is more prevalent among older women, although some researchers speculate that the mother's eggs, which have remained in the middle of a cell division since before her birth, do not always divide perfectly as they age. Other researchers think that trisomy 21 may be caused by maternal thyroid abnormalities or exposure to radiation or viruses.

The overall incidence of Down's syndrome in the United States is one in 800 live births. The risk increases as the mother's age goes up: at 25, the mother's risk is one in 1,205; at 30 it is one in 885; at 35 it is one in 365; at 40 it is one in 109; at 45 it is one in 32; and at 49 it is one in 12. When amniocentesis first came into general use, research geneticists recommended it for every mother over age 40. Now the age has arbitrarily been lowered to 35. No significant change occurs at age 35, but doctors feel that the procedure is safe enough to justify its use even in this younger age group.

Three major studies have shown that amniocentesis is a remarkably safe procedure for both mother and baby. From 1971 to 1973, The National Institute of Child Health and Human Development (NICHD) ran an extensive study of amniocentesis to assess the risk of injuring the fetus or causing maternal infection or hemorrhage. There was no increase in fetal loss rate, perinatal problems, birth weight, neonatal complications, or birth defects in the amniocentesis group. There also were no differences among the babies in growth, development, or behavior at one year.

Ultrasound

Ultrasound or *pulse-echo sonography* is a procedure in which high-frequency sound waves—vibrations that can pass through air, liquids, or solids—are used to build up a visual image of the baby in the uterus. Ultrasound, like all sound waves, bounces back when it encounters material of a different density. This is the way a ship's *sonar* works, as well as the way bats navigate. When the wave bounces back it causes a quartz crystal to send out a tiny burst of electricity which is picked up and translated into a dot of light on a screen. By scanning the mother's abdomen and building up a series of dots, a picture of the baby emerges.

Ultrasound sonograms have three important advantages over previous diagnostic techniques. First, they are non-invasive; that is, they gather information without directly entering the uterus. Second, their imaging does not involve X-ray radiation which is known to be dangerous to the fetus. Third, ultrasound is a fast, easy procedure which causes the mother no discomfort.

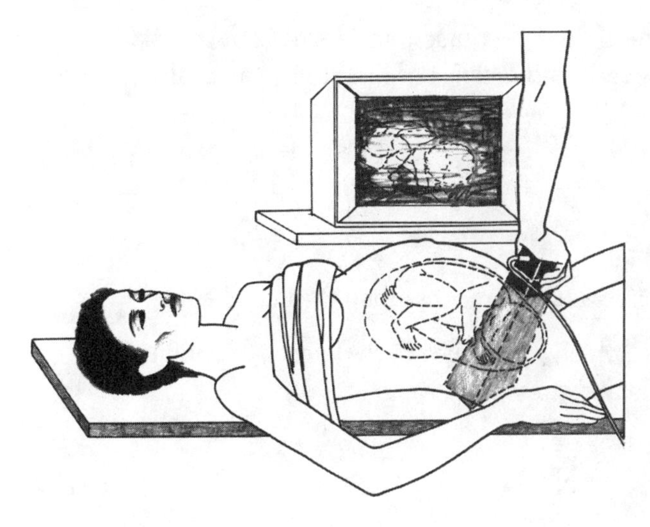

Ultrasound is a technique in which high-frequency sound waves are used to build up a visual image of the baby. It is a commonly used diagnostic procedure because it is non-invasive and doesn't involve radiation.

Common concerns of pregnant women

Regular exercise helps expectant mothers develop physical stamina and makes them feel better.

Nutrition

Get a balanced diet to meet increased nutritional needs, paying particular attention to getting extra protein and calories.

Gain an average of 25–30 pounds: approximately 10 pounds by 20 weeks, and another 15 pounds in the remaining 20 weeks.

Take iron, folic acid, and vitamin C supplements in the second and third trimesters.

Eat a high-fiber diet with lots of fruits and vegetables to avoid common problems with constipation and hemorrhoids.

Exercise

Do pelvic and abdominal exercises throughout pregnancy.

Avoid straight sit-ups, weight lifting, or other exercise that involves holding the breath because they elevate intra-abdominal pressure.

Do aerobic exercises at a conversational pace.

Precede exercise with a slow warm-up and follow with a slow stretch-out.

Work to maintain good posture: keep pelvis and shoulders back, chin up.

Lift from a squatting position to prevent back strain.

Sex

There is no medical reason to limit sexual intercourse or orgasm at any time during pregnancy *unless* there is a specific threat of abortion or premature labor.

Vary positions to accommodate the woman's changing size and shape.

Use techniques other than intercourse to achieve sexual satisfaction, based on the needs and feelings of the mother and father.

Chemicals and drugs

Stop smoking.

Stop drinking.

Limit caffeine in coffee and soda to less than 2–4 cups a day.

Do not use cocaine (which may cause birth defects) or marijuana (which may cause fetal distress).

Continued

Do not take any prescription or over-the-counter medication without consulting your obstetrician.

Do not expose yourself to solvents or other dangerous chemicals at home or in the workplace.

Stress

Pregnancy and birth are natural phenomena but they require change and adaptation.

Use relaxation techniques to deal with stress.

Pamper yourself with daily activities that are enjoyable.

Share concerns with relatives and friends in frequent, intimate conversations.

Attend a prenatal group for support as well as for information.

Set aside quiet times with the father to discuss hopes, concerns, points of conflict, and plans for the pregnancy, birth, and newborn period.

Rapidly seek reassurance for questions and worries.

Immunizations

Do not be vaccinated for rubella or mumps during pregnancy.

Avoid flu or polio shots unless there is a serious epidemic.

Avoid a tetanus-diphtheria shot unless the mother has never been vaccinated or has not been vaccinated within ten years.

The following vaccines are acceptable if necessary to meet travel requirements: typhoid, yellow fever, cholera, and Hepatitis A.

Rabies immunization is acceptable if necessary.

Personal hygiene and bathing

Brush and floss teeth regularly to prevent cavities and gum disease.

Avoid putting soap or drying agents on the nipples or areola in preparation for nursing; creams or lanolin are all right.

There is no medical reason to limit tub bathing or swimming because water does not enter the vagina except under pressure (but be careful of slipping in the tub).

Do not douche without instructions from the obstetrician.

To prevent toxoplasmosis, wash hands after handling red meat and use gloves to handle kitty litter.

Continued

Clothing

Wear loose, comfortable clothing; avoid clothes or stockings that are tight and may restrict circulation.

Choose clothing that can adjust as size and shape change; maternity clothes are generally not needed until the fourth or fifth month, although they may be more comfortable.

A well-fitted maternity or nursing bra provides support and relieves or prevents breast discomfort, upper backache, and breast sagging; nursing bras open to allow the nipples to rub freely in preparation for nursing.

Breast size generally does not change after the fourth month of pregnancy.

Wear low-heeled comfortable shoes which help to maintain good posture, prevent backache and leg cramps, and avoid falls due to changes in balance.

A maternity girdle will provide abdominal support and help to prevent backaches if a woman has loose abdominal muscles, is obese, or has had a number of previous pregnancies.

Support hose or leotards will help women with leg swelling, varicose veins, or leg cramps.

Cotton underpants lessen the chances of rashes or vaginitis.

Employment

There is no medical reason for a woman not to work during pregnancy, provided she remains healthy.

Women should avoid sitting or standing in one position for long intervals; women in sedentary jobs should walk at frequent intervals.

It is recommended that a woman rest during lunch and during morning and afternoon breaks.

It is important that a woman's work not cause her to strain physically or become too fatigued.

Women should feel free to stop work or cut back if they become chronically fatigued or feel themselves under constant emotional stress.

A woman's work should not expose her to dangerous chemicals or physical hazards such as radiation or high levels of microwaves.

Continued

Travel
Provided a woman is healthy, there is no medical reason to restrict travel, including airplane travel.

The mother should wear seat belts in cars, placing the lap strap below her abdomen and the shoulder strap above it.

A woman should be sure to move about every several hours when traveling to promote circulation and prevent leg swelling or an inflamed, blocked vein.

Avoid fatigue, stress, and big alterations in rest and diet; particularly avoid *missing meals* in the last half of pregnancy to prevent *ketosis*, a condition that can cause premature labor.

If traveling in the last months, a woman should have alternative delivery plans; women traveling to remote areas should realize that they may find themselves removed from conventional maternity care.

When to call the obstetrician
Doctors tell expectant mothers to contact them day or night if there are any of the following symptoms, which may indicate problems needing immediate attention. Although these symptoms don't always mean there is something wrong, it is important to discuss them with the doctor both for your own reassurance and to guarantee that if there is a problem it can be treated before it progresses.

visual problems: blurred vision, double vision, or spots in front of your eyes

swelling of face or fingers

severe headache

muscle irritability

convulsions

abdominal pain

persistent vomiting after the first trimester

blood or fluid from the vagina

chills or fever

burning on urination

unusual change in the baby's movements, especially a long absence of movement

Relaxation and imagery in pregnancy

Relaxation

In recent years relaxation has played an increasingly important role in childbirth and medicine. Almost all natural childbirth systems use relaxation to make the mother as physically and mentally comfortable as possible during labor and delivery. Tensed muscles and fear are responsible for most of the discomfort in childbirth. Relaxation relieves muscle tension, anxiety, and mental tension. When muscles relax, circulation functions better to bring in nutrients and remove toxic waste products, thereby altering the body's physiological state. In a relaxed physiological state, a person actually perceives things differently; that is, a person perceives situations as being less stressful and anxiety-producing. Resolving stress has beneficial effects for the unborn baby as well as the expectant mother.

One of the most detailed systems for teaching people to relax was worked out by the muscle physiologist Edmund Jacobson. Complete instructions are given in several of his books, including *How to Relax and Have Your Baby*. Briefly, Jacobson begins by teaching a person to be aware of how tension and relaxation feel. Surprisingly, most people are not aware of what tension and relaxation feel like. Jacobson directs people to contract their muscles, one at a time, then "let go" and experience the sensation of complete relaxation in the same muscle or group of muscles. For example, lie in a comfortable position with your hands resting at your sides. Raise one hand slightly by bending it at the wrist and you will feel muscles in the top of your forearm contract and tense. If you let your hand go limp, these muscles will relax and your hand will drop. With practice you will become aware of the subtle difference in feeling between a contracted muscle and a relaxed one. If you're not sure of the tension, lightly rest the fingers of your other hand on top of your forearm and feel the muscle contract when you raise your hand. Jacobson directs people to work on all areas of the body, one by one, contracting muscles and then deeply relaxing them. Most people find they are least aware of small amounts of tension in the muscles around the eyes, jaw, and pelvis. Presently not many people teach Jacobson's *progressive relaxation* because it's a lengthy system.

The most popular current technique for teaching relaxation is *autosuggestion,* which can generally be taught in a short time. Usually the teacher recites the directions slowly as the people do the exercise. After people know the exercise, they can give the instructions to themselves mentally. In using this book people can have someone read them the exercise slowly, can tape-record the exercise and play it back, or can simply read the exercise over several times until they can mentally give themselves the instructions. The basic idea is what's important, so the exercise needn't be memorized word for word. People who are unfamiliar with this kind of

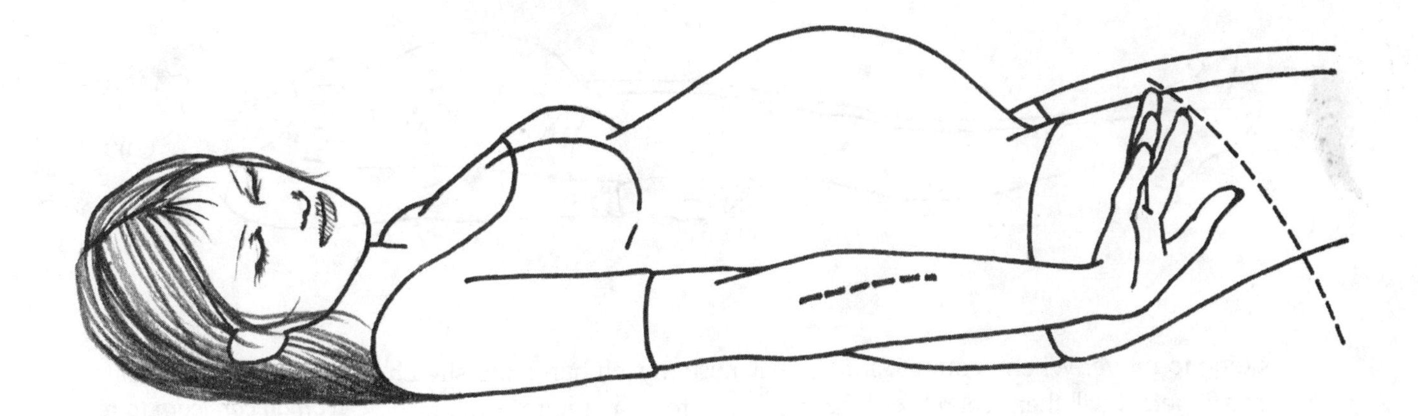

By raising a hand slightly a person can feel muscle contraction or tension in the forearm. Learning what tension and relaxation feel like can help a woman to relax during labor.

exercise may find that they feel a little awkward at first and wonder if anything is happening. But doctors can measure actual muscle relaxation and other physical changes even if the people themselves don't notice anything. Each time people do the exercise, they will become more aware of the subtle feelings of deepening relaxation.

Here is an example of a relaxation exercise that uses autosuggestion: Find a tranquil place where you won't be disturbed. Lie down with your legs uncrossed and your arms at your sides. Close your eyes, inhale slowly and deeply. Pause a moment. Then exhale slowly and completely. Allow your abdomen to rise and fall as you breathe. Do this several times. You now feel calm, comfortable, and more relaxed. As you relax, your breathing will become slow and even. Mentally say to yourself, "My feet are relaxing. They are becoming more and more relaxed. My feet feel heavy." Rest for a moment. Repeat the same suggestions for your ankles. Rest again. In the same way, relax your lower legs, then your thighs, pausing to feel the sensations of relaxation in your muscles. Relax your pelvis. Rest. Relax your abdomen. Rest. Relax the muscles of your back. Rest. Relax your chest. Rest. Relax your fingers. Relax your hands. Rest. Relax your forearms, your upper arms, your shoulders. Rest. Relax your neck. Rest. Relax your jaw, allowing it to drop. Relax your tongue. Relax your cheeks. Relax your eyes. Rest. Relax your forehead and the top of your head. Now just rest and allow your whole body to relax.

You are now in a calm, relaxed state of being. You can *deepen* this state by counting backward. Breathe in; as you exhale slowly, say to yourself, "Ten. I am feeling very relaxed . . ." Inhale again, and as you exhale, repeat mentally, "Nine. I am feeling more relaxed . . ." Breathe. "Eight. I am feeling even more relaxed . . ." Seven. "Deeper and more relaxed . . ." Six. "Even more . . ." Five (pause). Four (pause). Three (pause). Two (pause). One (pause). Zero (pause).

You are now at a deeper and more relaxed level of awareness, a level at which your body feels healthy, your mind feels peaceful and open. (It is a level at which you can experience images in your mind more clearly and vividly than ever before.) You can stay in this relaxed state as long as you like. To return to your ordinary consciousness, mentally say, "I am now

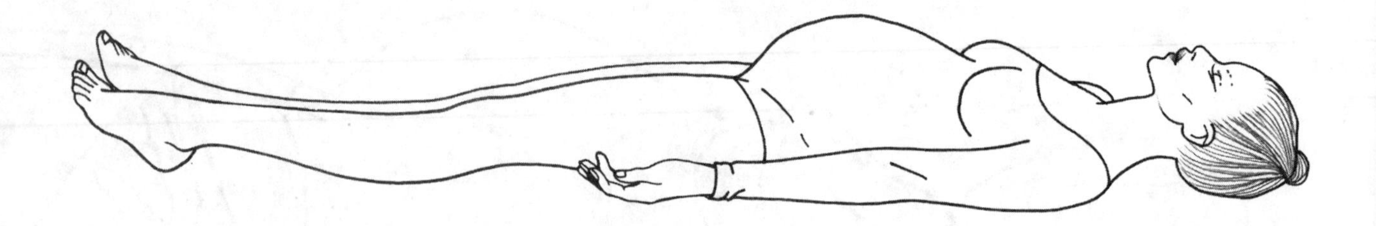

going to move. When I count to three, I will raise my left hand and stretch my fingers. I will then feel relaxed, happy, and strong, ready to continue my everyday activities."

The more profoundly a woman can learn to relax her whole body at will, the more comfortable she can make herself during labor.

Each time people relax, by any method, they find it easier and they relax more deeply. People experience the sensation of relaxation as tingling, radiating, or pulsing. They feel warmth or coolness, heaviness or a floating sensation. When people have practiced a method of relaxation several times, they may be able to relax deeply just by breathing in and out and allowing themselves to let go.

Imagery

Most men and women don't assume they will simply get married and begin having children. Our culture no longer uniformly supports such expectations. This change in expectations is due to improved methods of contraception, to the real problems of overpopulation, and finally to related changes such as the great increase in the number of working married women and the increase in the number of couples who are living together but are not married.

Having a baby is perhaps the ultimate act of faith. It clearly involves taking on a number of responsibilities for an almost totally dependent creature. In this culture, many new parents have little practical knowledge about the responsibilities of infant care. No matter how much time expectant parents spend preparing for and learning about the coming baby, the baby represents a long plunge into the unknown. There is no greater change that adults normally undergo within a relatively short time than the birth of a baby. Often the change is especially great with first babies and with so-called change-of-life babies. Virtually all expectant parents—consciously or unconsciously—anticipate the dramatic quality of this forthcoming change and have questions within themselves about it.

Expectant parents must question, evaluate, and create their own role as parents. Today people approach parenthood as an act of choice, a choice many of their contemporaries have not made, and inevitably their feelings toward the experience must be mixed. More than ever, expectant parents probably have both pleasurable and anxious imagery about what parent-

When to use relaxation during pregnancy

Use the exercise just described to relax your body, which will in turn relax the uterine muscles and the baby.

Relax your body and mind in order to relieve worries.

Relax your body and mind when you are upset, angry, or unhappy.

Relax your body when you are fatigued.

Relax your body and mind before going to sleep.

Relax your body and mind at particular stress points during the day.

Relax your body when you feel sick or physically uncomfortable.

Relax a part of your body to anesthetize this part.

Relax your body completely at the first sign of any illness, to help prevent or heal disease.

hood will bring. The more people can become aware of their own positive and negative images toward parenting, the more they can prepare themselves for it. This means exploring images, elaborating the pleasurable ones, and seeking out the roots or *causes* of the fearful ones. It further means figuring out how to (re)structure life-styles so as to maximize those aspects of parenting that the mother and father *are looking forward to* and resolve or minimize those things that they are not looking forward to.

Ideally, people deal with their major fears about parenthood before they even conceive a child, or certainly before the baby is born. In actuality, people never deal with all their ambivalences beforehand, but they can work toward that goal, which will tremendously heighten the pleasurable aspects of parenting. The first step is for people to get in touch with their dominant images of pleasure and fear, and to follow these fantasies.

Relaxing and concentrating on mental images is now an important technique in medicine. This process is called *imagery*. Through *imagery* people can get in touch with inner feelings, envision goals or the future, and make changes in their lives to harmonize with their feelings and accomplish their goals. Actually people visualize all the time without even realizing it. They picture things in their mind's eye, see events from the past, envision plans for the day, picture the solutions to problems they are working on in art, science, and everyday life. Although most people visualize constantly, they don't make conscious use of this skill.

Potentially, imagery is one of the most useful tools people have to improve their lives. With practice, imagery becomes even more powerful.

Age-old imagery techniques in religion and medicine are being discovered anew and adapted to many fields. Meditation helps people relax and clear their minds, imagery allows them to use this clear mental space to learn more about themselves and improve their lives.

We've divided imagery techniques into two basic categories, receptive and programmed. *Receptive imagery* involves clearing the mind and then letting images arise spontaneously. It is used to get access to inner feelings and ideas. It is one of the basic techniques used in all forms of psychiatry, and it can be used to get in touch with feelings about parenthood. *Programmed imagery* involves choosing and holding images, rather than just letting them arise. Concentrating on particular images has specific effects on people's mental and physical states and on their lives. Thus programmed imagery is useful in achieving goals and making changes.

We will give instructions for both programmed and receptive imagery. The instructions are simple and easy to follow and a person's ability to perform them will improve with repetition. Before doing the exercises, people should be familiar with the relaxation exercise we just described on pages 60–61. In fact, we suggest that people do the entire relaxation exercise as a preface to both imagery exercises. As people become accomplished at relaxation, they will find that the abdominal breathing that begins this exercise will be enough.

Receptive imagery for expectant parents—getting in touch with feelings

Find a quiet space where you will be undisturbed, a place where you feel at ease. Make yourself comfortable. Let your eyes close. Breathe in and out deeply, allowing your abdomen to rise and fall. As your breathing becomes slow and even, you will feel relaxed. Imagine the relaxation in your whole body deepening by stages. You are now in a state in which your mind is clear and tranquil. You can visualize vividly and easily. Your mind is open and receptive. Imagine your mind is like a screen and you can see images relating to your feelings about pregnancy and being a parent. For example, imagine the kind of delivery you would like. You can look at these images as long as you wish. Some images will make you feel good, some images will make you feel uncomfortable. Simply note the images; do not dwell on the emotions. Each time you visualize in this way, the images will be clearer and flow more easily. To return to your ordinary state, count slowly from one to three, and gently move some part of your body. Allow yourself to return slowly, and open your eyes when you feel ready to do so. You will now feel rested, calm, and ready to evaluate and interpret the images that have come into your mind.

Using receptive imagery before the baby is born

There are a number of questions that generally come to mind when a woman finds she is expecting a baby. Receptive imagery can help her find the answers within herself. To do this she should follow the receptive imagery exercise, looking for images relating to the questions that concern her. The expectant father can also use this technique to explore concerns he has about the coming baby.

Subjects to think about	*Examples of specific questions and concerns*	*Typical positive or negative images that may come to mind*
Nutrition	What foods does my body crave?	Milk, leafy green salads, lean meats, and seafood
	What foods don't interest me now?	Alcohol, pasta, hot chili
Exercise	What kind of exercise appeals to me now?	Walking, swimming
Sleep	Am I getting enough sleep? Do I need naps?	Feeling sleepy in the afternoon
Sex of the baby	What sex will the baby be?	Image of a girl; image of a boy
Kind of delivery	What kind of delivery would be ideal for me?	A natural delivery with no drugs; a delivery that uses some kind of anesthesia so I don't feel the contractions
Method of feeding the baby	What method of feeding the baby makes me feel the happiest?	Nursing the baby; feeding the baby with a bottle only; nursing and occasionally using formula to give the mother time off
Preparations for the baby	What things do I feel are important to do before the baby is born?	Get a dresser? Buy a special cradle? Set up a whole room? Buy new clothes? Borrow well-loved baby articles from friends?

Feelings aroused by the prospect of parenthood

Pleasurable	*Fearful*
Parenting instinct; oceanic feelings of wanting a baby, stimulated by daydreams or sight of a positive parent-child experience	Fear of being tied down to responsibility; fear of being an inadequate parent or disliking the task
Pride in conceiving a child—female, fertility; male, potency	Fear of not being able to conceive
Earthy feeling of fullness, verdancy; harmony with natural rhythms	
Feelings about pregnancy itself	
Female feeling of being healthy, big, slow-moving, relaxed	Female fear of being "fat," ungainly, physically uncomfortable
Male feeling that woman looks soft, happy, glowing	Male fear of wife looking big and unappealing
	Fear of woman being sick
	Dislike of having to give up activities and habits, change life-style
Increased interest in sex; lack of concern over birth control	Decreased interest in sex; fear of somehow hurting the baby through lovemaking
	Fear of miscarrying
	Women's fear father will suddenly leave
Feelings about childbirth	
Excitement and joy at new life, at witnessing a profound, primeval event	Fear of participating in such a personal, physical event
Female pride in doing well	Female fear of pain, of not being able to deliver the baby without anesthetics

Continued

Pregnancy can be a warm, languorous, slow-moving, happy time.

Pleasurable	Fearful
Feelings about childbirth (continued)	
Male pride at helping mother, being needed	Male fear of not knowing what to do or not wanting to be there, of not loving the mother during labor
Feeling proud of and loving the baby	
Knowing instinctively how to care for baby	
Feeling that family is made richer by the birth of the baby	
Being happy at the baby's strength, health, physical perfection, sex	Fear of a difficult birth, of problems for the mother or the baby
	Fear of the baby not being healthy, well formed
	Disappointment over the baby's sex
	Fear of not loving the baby right away, of thinking the baby is ugly
Feelings about caring for an infant	
Touching baby, picking up, cuddling	Fear of picking up the baby; won't do it right; baby will cry
Rocking baby, watching baby sleep	Baby is fragile, can easily be hurt
Breast-feeding baby	Disgust at having to change dirty, smelly diapers
Taking baby to beach, hiking, picnicking with family and friends	Resent not being able to do things because of the baby; baby crying
Happy at thought of staying home, taking care of baby	Resent woman not working, bringing in extra money
	Resent being stuck at home

Continued

Pleasurable	*Fearful*
Feelings about caring for an infant (continued)	
	Fear of not having enough money to raise a child and having to give up own pleasures
	Fear of being left alone with baby, having to support the baby alone
	Feeling jealous of all the attention the baby gets, requires
Image of a healthy, strong baby	Fear of illness in the baby
	Fear of not being a good parent

Programmed imagery

Choosing and then holding specific images in mind is called *programmed imagery*. When a person deliberately concentrates on a relaxed, peaceful image, a number of physiological changes take place. Muscles relax, heart rate and blood pressure decrease, oxygen consumption of cells decreases, and respiratory rate decreases. Basically an opposite set of physiological changes takes place when a person concentrates on a frightening or stressful image.

A pregnant woman can use programmed imagery to reduce tension and physical discomforts. If she has had an upsetting day or her back is aching, she will be helped by focusing on an image that is relaxing to her. If an expectant mother occasionally worries about how she will feel in labor, she will be helped by deliberately picturing herself experiencing contractions in a calm, relaxed manner.

Here is an exercise in programmed imagery. Until people can relax easily and deeply they should follow the instructions for relaxation (pages 61–62) as a preface to this exercise: Find a quiet place where you will be undisturbed, a place where you feel at ease. Make yourself comfortable. Let your eyes close. Breathe in and out deeply, allowing your abdomen to rise and fall. As your breathing becomes slow and even, you will feel relaxed. Imagine the relaxation in your whole body deepening by stages. You are now in a state in which your mind is clear and tranquil. You can visualize vividly and easily. Imagine your mind is like a screen and you can see any image you choose. The image may be something you have seen, something you have imagined, something you would like to happen. Scan the image with your mind's eye and notice small details. The more closely you look at the image, the clearer and more vivid the details will become. When you visualize a scene, imagine you are really there. *Look* at your surroundings, *listen* to the noises, *smell* the air, *feel* the breeze. Be there. Enjoy all the sensations of the positive images you are holding. Experience your imagery as long as you wish. To return to your ordinary state, count slowly from one to three, and gently move some part of your body. Allow yourself to return slowly, and open your eyes when you feel ready to do so. You will now feel rested and calm. You will be able to return to the positive image you held more and more readily each time you do this imagery exercise.

Using programmed imagery before the baby is born

Image	*In order*	*For example, imagine*
Yourself in enjoyable scenes with a young baby	To maximize your positive expectations about becoming a parent	A family picnic in a meadow, taking a walk with the baby, showing the baby to relatives and friends
Yourself having fun taking care of a young baby	To strengthen your confidence about being a parent	Playing with the baby during its bath, feeding the baby, tickling the baby as you change its diaper
Yourself being pregnant and feeling radiant and healthy	To increase feelings of well-being and create good health during pregnancy	Walking exuberantly down a street in maternity clothes, feeling good when you wake up in the morning, happily eating all kinds of good foods
Yourself doing well during labor and delivery	To build up your confidence and relieve inevitable anxiety about labor and delivery	Being relaxed and focused during labor, joyful during delivery, calm and rested after delivery
A strong, healthy baby	To feel glad about the baby and relieve inevitable momentary concerns about the baby's health	A radiant, beautiful baby
Positive energy flowing into you and your unborn baby	To make yourself and the baby strong	Yourself and the baby bathed in warm sunlight

People invariably end such an exercise with a sense of well-being and energy. More than likely the unborn baby shares these sensations with its mother and benefits from them. Many people find that the images which they "program" in advance eventually do come about.

Nesting

There are many physical alterations that will increase the expectant parents' enjoyment of the pregnancy and help prepare for the baby. If ever there is a time for parents to concentrate on making their life easier and more pleasurable, it is during the months before birth. This is a time when women, especially, may become aware of intuitive feelings. Historically these feelings have been noted as cravings or urges, frequently having to do with food, rest, lovemaking, and material preparations for the baby.

Almost always the coming of a baby necessitates a number of changes in a woman's life. Change—even positive change—can in itself be stressful. Awareness of this helps the expectant mother make plans that will best coincide with her intuitive feelings. The coming of a baby means a woman must rearrange her time at the most basic level. If she's working at a job outside her home, she has to plan how much time she will take off and what arrangements she will make when she returns to work. Most women find it best to arrange in advance for people who can come in after the baby is born to help with cooking, housework, and laundry. The mother and father also have to set up their living space so as to make room for a new family member with specialized needs. For some parents this may mean considering a move. The most important thing about all of these decisions is that they make the mother—and the father—happy.

Strong feelings about preparing a physical space for the baby represent the so-called nesting instinct. Most women experience such feelings sometime in the latter part of the pregnancy. They may want to get a bed, a bureau, or a changing table for the baby. And they will want to be sure they have diapers and a basic supply of baby clothes. The amount of clothing and bedding that newborn babies require can vary widely depending on several factors. Babies need less clothing and use fewer diapers in warm weather. In the winter, babies need heavier outfits and blankets. Sometimes very young babies spit up after a feeding, which requires an extra change of clothes. If a newborn infant uses cloth diapers and doesn't wear rubber pants, the baby will need to be on rubber pads (puddle pads) and absorbent mats to soak up wetness. A baby without rubber pants will probably also soak its undershirt, nightgown, and blanket. If a baby is in rubber pants or disposable diapers, it will need less clothing and there will be less washing. However, newborn babies have fairly sensitive skin and may tend to get a rash from rubber pants or disposables which have *nonporous cover-*

ings. Finally, the number of outfits needed depends on how often washing will be done. The following chart is based on washing every other day and will give a range from minimal to generous. A complete newborn layette is fairly extensive and can be expensive. Baby clothes can be picked up at garage sales, rummage sales, or thrift shops. Many mothers have much of the newborn "gear" passed on to them from other mothers. Newborns rarely wear out their clothing—first, they grow quickly, and second, they need a number of outfits because they are changed so often. Often a woman will feel a great sense of relief and relaxation when she has gotten together all the articles she feels she needs for the coming baby. Practically speaking, such arrangements must be made sometime and they are better done before the baby comes; afterward the new mother will need to spend time caring for and adjusting to the baby. Many women feel an increased need for rest in the weeks immediately before (as well as immediately after) the baby's birth. Setting up for the baby's physical needs is often the last thing women feel they must accomplish before the birth, and finishing it signals an invaluable time for rest and looking forward to childbirth.

Following up nesting instincts is a good example of working out intuitive feelings. The results are both practical and psychological. Mothers receive many such intuitive messages during pregnancy, and the more they can tune in to these messages, the happier they will be and the better will be the fetal environment. Receptive imagery is an excellent way for parents to identify and explore these intuitive feelings.

Layette for the first 6–8 weeks

Clothing

2–3 dozen diapers (cloth)
2–3 pair diaper pins or clips (for cloth diapers)
3–6 pair rubber pants and/or
2–6 boxes of newborn disposable diapers
6–12 newborn undershirts
6–12 short-sleeved tops and/or long kimonos for warm weather
6–12 long drawstring nightgowns and/or newborn jump suits for cool weather and nights
2–6 warm buntings or sleep suits for daytime outings and nighttime sleeping in cold weather
1–2 sun hats (warm weather)
1–2 warm hats (cold weather)
2–3 pair washable booties
1–2 very small sweaters, preferably washable

Continued

Bedding
6–12 receiving blankets
6–12 sets of rubber pads and soaker mats to change baby on and protect laps and sheets
3–6 crib sheets
2–3 baby towels, extra soft, absorbent, possibly with a hood
3–6 baby washcloths—for frequent change and laundering
2–4 medium-weight, washable blankets

Supplies
Mild soap for bathing the baby
Mild soap for washing the baby's clothes
Fabric softener for the baby's diapers, clothes
Diaper bucket
Rectal thermometer
Baby oil, powder, or lotion (optional)
Orthodontic pacifier
Small, somewhat stiff hairbrush
Formula (for bottle-fed babies)
6–8 bottles for water, juice, formula

Equipment
Cradle, carriage, or crib for the baby to sleep in
Dresser or shelves to store the baby's clothes
Padded *secure* changing table or surface
Small, square plastic basin or baby bathtub
Infant chest carrier
Infant car safety seat
Portable bed or carry basket
Tote bag for baby diapers, clothes, etc.

Communication between the parents and the unborn baby—thought, touch, and emotion

Communicating with an unborn baby seems a strange idea at first. This is probably because most people assume the baby isn't really "there" until it's born. Until recently even doctors and researchers believed that the baby was an insensate bundle of reflexes at birth and for weeks afterward. Now researchers are realizing the baby is a functioning, feeling person long before it is born.

Common concerns before birth

Whether or not to breast-feed

Whether or not to have a boy circumcised

Whether to use cloth diapers or disposables

Arranging the baby's sleeping and changing areas, and buying necessary clothing and supplies

Making birth arrangements for the mother, for siblings

Deciding when the mother will stop work and return to work

Deciding what type of daycare arrangement will be best for the family and making arrangements for it

Parents are in communication with the unborn baby whether they are aware of it or not. By activity or the lack of it, the baby communicates to the parents much about its personality and its reactions to specific events. Startled kicking in response to sudden noises is familiar to most pregnant mothers. Babies in the uterus have characteristic levels and times of activity which give parents some idea of their personality even before they are born. Studies have shown that unborn babies who are active are also more active at six and twelve months after birth. Another long-term study has shown that unborn babies whose heart rate ranged widely with excitement showed similar cardiac variation at twenty years of age. Further, it was found that as children these individuals tended to be more imaginative and emotional.

Not only does the unborn baby communicate with the parents, the parents communicate with the unborn baby. As the mother perceives and reacts to things in her environment, her heart rate, respiration, hormonal levels, and muscle tension give the baby an impression of what she perceives. Studies have shown that newborns already have learned appropriate responses to such signals from the mother's body. When babies in a nursery are allowed to hear a tape recording of a mother's normal heartbeat, they become quiet, breathe evenly, eat well, and gain weight. When the recording of the heartbeat is speeded up above normal, the same babies become restless and cry. In other words, babies in the uterus come to recognize when the mother is anxious or frightened and they in turn become anxious. Thus throughout pregnancy there is constant physiological communication between the baby, the mother, and the environment (as perceived and filtered by the mother).

Most expectant parents tend to talk about the coming baby as if he or she were a person who is not yet there. Parents consciously think and talk about the unborn baby, and unconsciously (physiologically) communicate with the baby. Why not consciously talk *to* the baby? Just as parents croon to and talk to a newborn infant, they can similarly communicate with the unborn baby. The unborn baby cannot respond with words, but then neither does the newborn. What the newborn, and even the unborn baby, *can* do is respond to the attention and the feelings behind the parents' words. Talking directly to and about the unborn baby as if he or she were already present has advantages for both the baby and the family. The baby comes early to occupy an emotional and mental space as well as a physical space in the family's life. Talking to the baby causes everyone to relate to the baby as a real person. This eases the transition between before and after birth—between the baby's being in the uterus and being physically present. And it tends to make the whole family more aware of the baby and do things that are good for the baby.

One thing that enhances the quality of this verbal communication with the unborn baby is giving the unborn baby a name. Such a name is not usually intended to be the baby's real or final name, because it is unusual for the baby's sex to be known before birth. If parents choose an ungendered nickname, they are less likely to become set about getting a boy or a girl. Once parents have a way of referring to the baby without resorting to the ambivalent "he" or "she" or a nonspecific "baby," they will find they spend more and more time talking about and relating to the baby. This talk is not at all silly—it helps to prepare the parents for the reality of the newborn baby. Many expectant parents who communicate in this way with the coming baby are not surprised by the way the newborn acts and reacts. Often they feel they are already well acquainted with the baby.

Such communication can be especially important to fathers and older siblings because it expands their role with the baby during the pregnancy and gives them a much greater personal sense of rapport with the coming baby. The family can then relate to the expectant mother as two distinct people—Mother and Baby, rather than as Pregnant Mother or Big Mommy. The father will feel he already has a child he can talk to and do things for when he helps the mother cook, take care of the home, or set up a room for the baby. Likewise, older children will feel they already have a brother or sister they can talk to and do things for by helping the mother.

The unborn baby has still another means of communication—that of touch. From around the sixteenth week the mother begins to feel the baby moving. Expectant mothers often notice that the baby reacts with seemingly pleasurable movements when they engage in certain activities or do specific things. Some mothers feel the baby loves the warmth of sunbathing, the gentle pressure of swimming or taking a bath, the rhythms of lovemaking.

Soon mother, father, and children can put their hands on the mother's belly to feel the baby kicking, turning, and moving. In turn they can "hug the baby, rub the baby, play with" the baby. Some mothers routinely massage their bellies in a slow, gentle way. Even though all such touching is indirect, there is no question that the baby is capable of reacting to this stimulation in the uterus.

Tribal cultures have often believed that the shamans or medicine men could actually identify the spirits of unborn babies and talk to them. Cultures that believe in reincarnation have a religious model that supports and explains such intuitive communication. In such cultures babies are thought to be old spirits returning to the earthly plane for another life. The spirit of the baby, as distinguished from its body, is considered to be quite developed and therefore approachable through a kind of telepathy such as might take place between two people a distance apart. The last section of the ancient *Tibetan Book of the Dead* is a lengthy set of instructions for dying people on how to control the factors that will determine what womb they next enter, and therefore how their evolution will proceed. Famous yogins frequently tell of their memories of previous lifetimes.

In the West there is not the same kind of widespread cultural belief that up to now has encouraged attempts at intuitive or psychic communication with unborn babies. But with the growing interest in parapsychology and the scientific results coming from respected researchers, many parents will tend to put more faith in their intuitive thoughts and spend more time trying to communicate with the baby at this level. Since it is known that faith and motivation positively affect parapsychological phenomena, it is likely that future parents will have increasingly good results at such communication.

In tribal cultures, people believed that the shamans or medicine men could identify the spirits of unborn babies and talk to them. Spirit Babies, *by Wendy Frost, 1984. Pastel/graphite on lithograph, 18" x 24". Collection, Mike and Nancy Samuels.*

Mothers, fathers, friends, and even siblings often have strong feelings about the coming baby which are later borne out. *Receptive imagery* provides a technique for tuning in on these feelings about the unborn baby. Through receptive imagery a parent may catch a glimpse of the unborn baby and come to know the baby's personality. Even answers to direct questions about the baby may come in the form of visual images or thoughts.

Find a quiet place where you will be undisturbed, a place where you feel at ease. Make yourself comfortable. Let your eyes close. Breathe in and out deeply, allowing your abdomen to rise and fall. As your breathing becomes slow and even, you will feel relaxed. Imagine the relaxation in your whole body deepening by stages. You are now in a state in which your mind is clear and tranquil. You can visualize vividly and easily. Your mind is open and receptive. Imagine your mind is like a screen and you can see images appear and disappear. Turn your mind to the baby that is coming. The images that appear will contain information about the baby. If you have a specific question, mentally ask it. Watch the images that flow and pay attention to succeeding thoughts. Continue this communication as long as you wish. Each time you visualize in this way, the images and thoughts will be clearer and flow more easily. To return to your ordinary state, count slowly from one to three, and gently move some part of your body. Allow yourself to return slowly, and open your eyes when you feel ready to do so.

The working mother and planning ahead

Pregnancy is a time of great change and adaptation. This is especially true when the mother as well as the father works. In addition to dealing with the demands of work, the expectant mother has to deal with shifting needs for nutrition, stress, and exercise, and the physical changes her body is undergoing. Moreover, the working mother must decide on birth arrangements and shop for necessary supplies and clothing for herself and the baby. Finally the mother needs to plan for the time when she will stop working, when she'll resume work, and the day-care arrangements she'll need if she intends to return to work within the first few months. All of these things require a fair amount of time and energy, and the expectant mother is most likely to complete these tasks happily if she begins early and gets a feeling for what other women have done.

The specifics of a woman's *maternity leave* are affected by family economics, the policy of her employer, and her own needs and feelings. Currently the United States is the only industrialized country other than South Africa without a national maternity-leave policy that guarantees an official, paid time off. However, the 1978 Pregnancy Discrimination Act requires that companies with more than 15 employees treat pregnancy as they would any other temporary health disability. Women workers may not be fired, denied a job or promotion, or forced to leave the company or use vacation benefits because of pregnancy. The specific details of hospitalization, pay, and time off vary with the company and with its insurance policy. Eighteen states have their own laws regarding parental leave, and 95% of the largest firms in the country have some sort of official pregnancy leave. Of those, 40% pay full salary during maternity leave. In fact, about 40% of large companies currently offer 1–4 weeks of unpaid leave to new fathers. The overall picture in the United States is considerably less optimistic than that. One study showed that over half of all women got no paid maternity leave whatsoever, and that of those who did, the average time off was ten weeks, although a few companies grant as much as six months leave. Most fathers take only a few days off, using vacation or sick days.

For many parents, there is much more flexibility than a simple leave. A number of companies allow changing work schedules, flexible work time, part-time work, job sharing, and even working from home. Flexibility includes cutting back days or hours, and working early or late. Often husband and wife dovetail their hours to that one goes to work early while the other stays with the baby, reversing the situation as called for.

In terms of mother and baby health, there is generally no reason for the mother to stop working until her due date nears. The exceptions to this are hazardous working conditions (chemical or physical) and medical problems that require the mother to rest. In some cases mothers want to stop work earlier because of fatigue or because they want to have plenty of time to prepare for the baby, either physically or emotionally.

Likewise there are no routine medical concerns that dictate when a mother should return to work. It may be anywhere from several weeks to several months or years after the baby is born. The amount of time taken off after the birth really depends on a combination of economic concerns, the mother's wishes, the employer's needs, and the kind of day care the mother can arrange.

It is important to point out that expectant mothers, first-time mothers in particular, often cannot predict in advance how they'll feel about returning to work and leaving the baby for long periods. Sometimes mothers who thought they would miss work, find they do not; and mothers who thought they would not mind leaving their newborn, find that they do. On the other hand, some mothers find they are happier if they return to work fairly quickly, either because they like the socialization or the challenge of their work. Ideally, expectant parents should endeavor to figure out which arrangement will best suit them and their baby (see page 67).

Once parents feel fairly clear about their own desires, they can then begin to make whatever arrangements are necessary, both in terms of work and child care, leaving a certain amount of flexibility built in, if possible, to accommodate for changes. Many of the expectant mothers who read this book will find that they have more choice than they realize about maternity leave and scheduling, especially if they begin to explore the possibilities early. Once again, the key to serving the baby's needs best is flexibility. The needs of a newborn are quite different from those of a three-, six-, or twelve-month-old. Indeed, the great majority of new parents change their child-care arrangements at least once in the first six months.

If the mother plans to return to work within the first several months after her baby is born, it is imperative that she make child-care plans before the birth. Finding the right child-care arrangement takes a certain amount of time and reflection—the parents need to decide what type of arrangement they are seeking, and then they have to find the right person or place to fill that need. For first-time parents, it may be difficult to conceive of the complexity of their requirements, as well as the degree to which they will be dissatisfied if they do not like the person or place they hire.

Things to be considered are the parents' work schedules, their intuitive feelings about the baby and the caretaker's role, and the cost. There is no ideal, recommended length of time for a mother to be at home. The benefits of day care versus the disadvantages are a subject of debate. There is most concern about child care for babies under a year. We'll discuss specific needs and benefits for the baby in the chapters dealing with specific ages.

Considerations for the pregnant woman who works

How much time would you like to take off before and after the baby is born? How much time can you arrange for? Talk to other mothers of newborns about their solutions.

Early in your pregnancy, talk to your employer and negotiate an official time off, including maternity leave and/or sick leave, paid or unpaid; set flexible dates if possible. Plan to finish any major projects ahead of time, and help to train the person who will take over your work. If possible, arrange for a light schedule and/or part-time work at home after the birth. Keep in touch by phone.

Learn what child care involves from friends and classes.

Set up a schedule with your spouse so your individual responsibilities will be clear.

Make a decision about what type of child care will be best for you and your baby, visit the people, and make arrangements a month or more before you plan to go back to work so there is time for a trial period to work out any problems. If you plan to return to work within the first month or two, you will have much more time for these concerns before the baby arrives.

Get support from other working mothers and choose an obstetrician and pediatrician who are positive toward working mothers.

The cost of day care varies, ranging from free, such as help from a mother or mother-in-law, to expensive, as in full-time live-in help. In general, child care is not inexpensive. Child care provided by a relative or by the parents working staggered hours is the least expensive. Family care—that is, being taken care of by a family in their home—is mid-range in cost. Full-time caretakers or group care are usually the most expensive. Most children under three today are cared for by their own parents on staggered shifts, by relatives, or by paid caretakers in their homes or the baby's. Generally parents use a combination of care, with child care centers used more as the baby grows older. There are some financial subsidies for child care, especially group care, that are provided by state and federal programs. They are mostly available to low- and middle-income parents, especially single parents. Finally, there is tax credit for child care. It is not very common, but some companies, mostly large ones, do provide daycare for the children of employees. Unless a mother's salary is fairly high, the cost of day care can almost be prohibitive, especially if more than one child is in day care outside the home.

Chapter 5

Birth

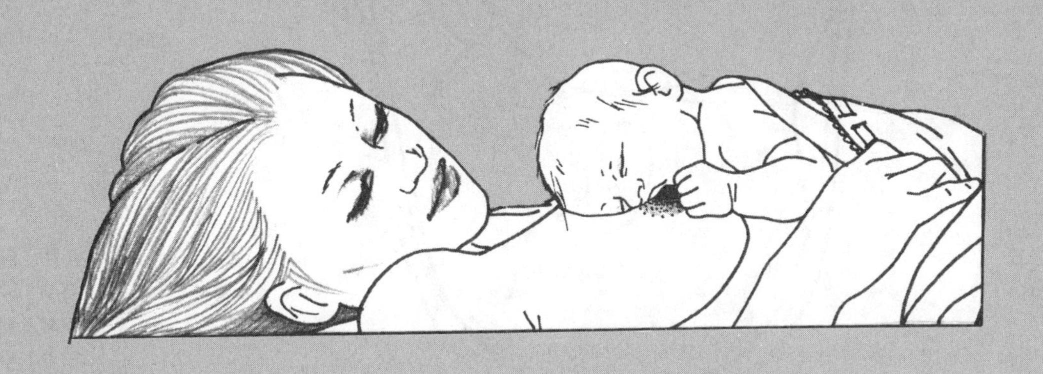

The baby's view of the birth sequence

The hours of labor and delivery are only a very small portion of prenatal life. Yet they are the climax toward which the baby and mother have been working for many months. This climax is so significant that in many ways labor and delivery stand apart from the rest of pregnancy. Many events take place during labor and delivery that are completely different from the rest of prenatal life.

Until the thirty-second week or so, the developing baby is wonderfully housed within the mother. The baby floats freely in a warm, liquid environment. There is ample room for the baby to move about, and the baby takes full advantage of this, making rolls, turns, and twists that the mother can feel. But around the thirty-second week, things start to become crowded.

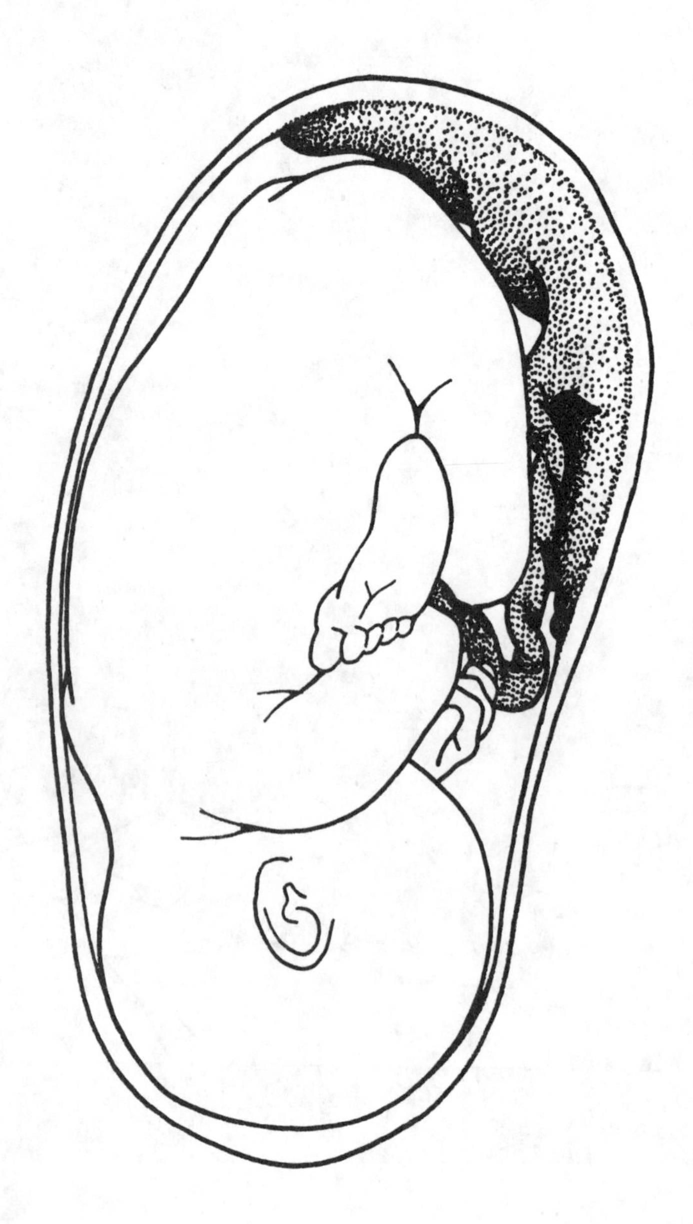

By the eighth month the baby's size is such that it now fills the uterus. Conveniently, the baby assumes an upside-down position in the pear-shaped uterus.

The growing baby now just about fills the uterus and is surrounded by relatively less amniotic fluid. As the baby's body starts to touch the walls of the uterus, the baby tends to be positioned by the shape of the uterus, which is much like an upside-down pear. The baby, who by this time is much longer than the uterus, curls up and assumes a pearlike shape also. The baby's back curves, the head tucks down toward the chest, and the knees are drawn up to the belly. In this position the baby is widest around its backside and flexed legs. Both baby and mother gradually come to be most comfortable if the baby's bottom goes to the large area at the top of the uterus and the baby's head goes to the smaller area at the bottom of the uterus. As the baby continues to grow, it tends to make fewer and fewer rolls and flips, and spends more and more time in this upside-down position. During the last few weeks of pregnancy, the baby does little moving other than kicking or punching with its feet and arms.

The upside-down position is ideal for making the descent through the birth canal at the time of delivery. For reasons that are still not fully understood, biochemical changes take place in the *baby* which cause labor to begin. The baby's body releases a hormone that crosses the placenta. In response to this hormone the mother's body releases another hormone called oxytocin. Meanwhile, the placenta stops manufacturing progesterone, the hormone that maintains pregnancy. This allows the oxytocin to stimulate uterine contractions.

The uterus contracts rhythmically and frequently, exerting pressure on the cervix. This pressure causes the cervix to change in shape from a narrow tube into a wide funnel through which the baby can squeeze. In addition to passing through the cervix, the baby, and most important, the baby's head, must pass through the mother's pelvic opening. The bones of the pelvis form a flattened oval which is wider from front to back than from side to side. The baby's head is large enough so that it can only pass through this oval ring at certain angles. In order to get through the birth canal—that is, in order to descend from the pelvic bones to the vagina—the baby actually must make several bends and turns.

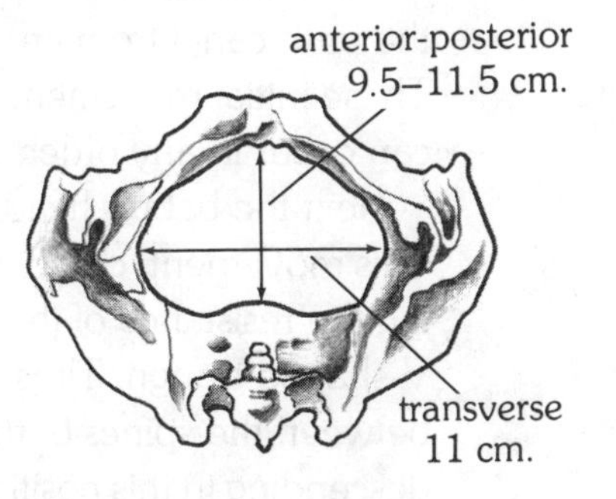

The pelvis is shaped like a flattened oval, narrower from side to side, and the baby's head bends and turns in order to pass through the pelvis during delivery.

The factors that cause the baby to descend are pressure of the amniotic fluid and the top of the uterus on the baby's backside, coupled with the baby's extending and straightening its body. The relatively small opening of the pelvic bones and the tight fit of the bottom of the uterus and the cervix exert strong pressures and actually cause the bony plates of the baby's skull to come together and change in shape. The soft spots of the skull and the ability of the plates to shift and overlap function in a marvelously adaptive way to reduce the pressure on both the mother and the baby in the transition stage of labor. The strength of this pressure is not to be minimized—the baby's head can actually remain molded or shaped for days after birth.

Once the top of the baby's head has passed the spines, or protuberances, on the mother's pelvic bones, it is said to be *engaged.* With most first babies, the head is engaged before labor even begins; with most subse-

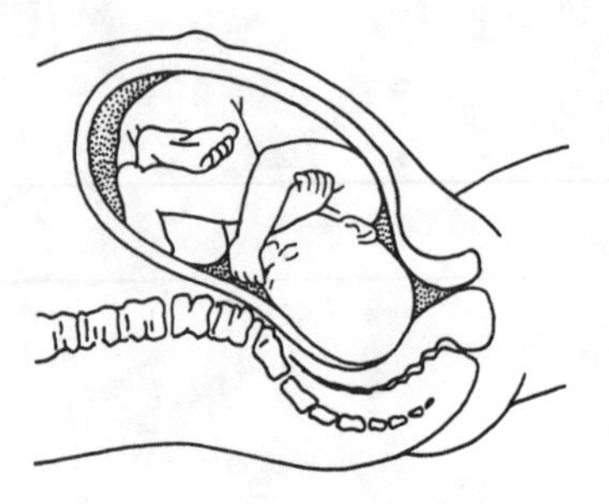

*As the baby's head passes the pelvic spines (*descent and engagement*), its chin tucks down toward its chest (*flexion*).*

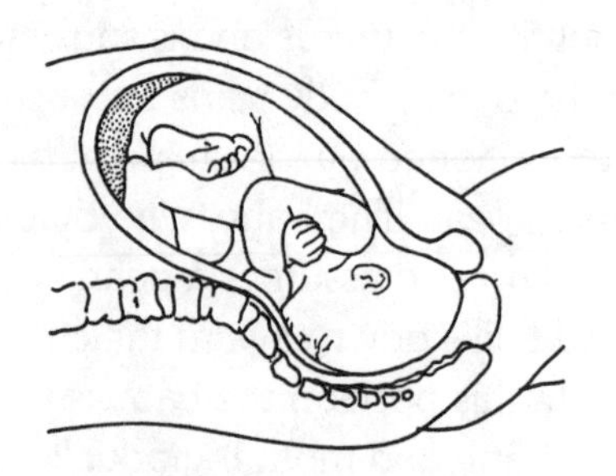

*The baby's head turns to face the mother's spine (*rotation*). This presents the narrowest part of the head to the narrowest part of the pelvis.*

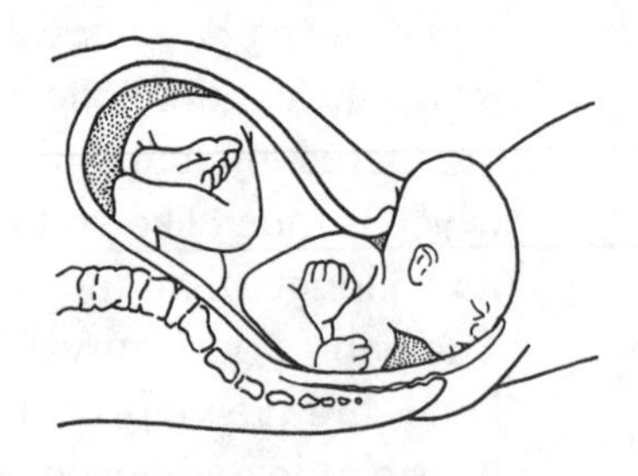

*The baby's head now bends backward in order to emerge from the vagina, which is slightly above it (*extension*).*

quent babies, the head is not engaged until labor is well under way. As the baby descends, the resistance of the cervix and surrounding tissues causes the baby to make the first of its several bends and turns. The baby bends its head forward tightly so that its chin touches its chest. This movement, called *flexion,* changes the effective diameter width of the baby's head relative to the birth canal from an average of 11.5 centimeters to 9.5 centimeters. These initial movements—engagement, beginning descent, and flexion—can occur in any order.

Next the baby's head rotates or turns so that it faces the mother's spine. This movement, called *internal rotation,* is caused by the baby's head meeting the resistance of the muscles along the mother's spine, which are like a V-shaped trough. Thus the narrowest part of the baby's head passes between the spines of the pelvic bones. The baby's head continues descending in this position until it first reaches the external lips of the vagina. Then the baby's head bends sharply backward, lifting its chin away from its chest. Since the baby is facing the mother's back, this motion allows the baby's head to come up and out of the mother's vagina, which is now behind the back of the baby's head. This bending movement is called *extension.* As the baby's head continues to bend backward, the lips of the vagina open and stretch. When the stretching of the vagina around the baby's head is at its maximum point, the baby is said to be "crowning." With further bending the baby's head actually emerges. Since the baby is still facing the mother's spine, the back of the head emerges first, then the top, then the forehead, nose, mouth, and finally the chin. Once the chin is free and the whole head is out, the baby's head falls forward (down) toward the mother's anus, then turns sideways when the baby turns its shoulders. The baby tends to turn naturally as its shoulders meet the resistance of the mother's spinal muscles. The shoulders slide into the V-shaped muscle trough at the back of the birth canal. Positioned this way, the baby's narrowest chest dimensions, front to back (rather than shoulder to shoulder),

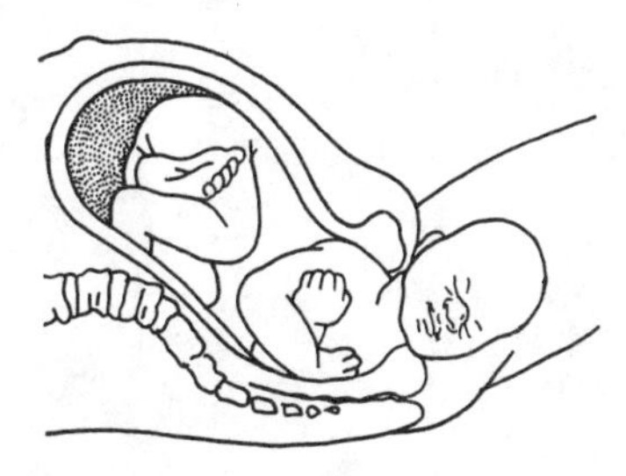

The baby's torso turns sideways in the birth canal so that its shoulders and chest can come through the widest dimension of the pelvis (external rotation).

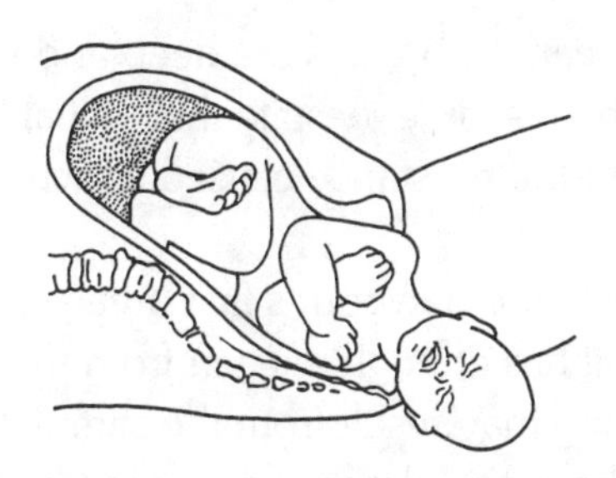

The baby bends down as the top shoulder is delivered and up as the bottom shoulder is delivered.

pass through the narrow opening between the spines of the pelvis. These movements are called *restitution* (when the head again turns sideways) and *external rotation* of the shoulders. After external rotation, the baby continues to move down the birth canal. The top shoulder emerges first from the vagina, followed by the bottom shoulder. The delivery of the baby is completed as the baby's hips slide down the trough at the back—once again presenting the narrowest part, front to back, to the area between the pelvic spines.

These intricate movements of the baby's are linked with the mother's contractions and her natural, overwhelming instinct to bear down. In a sense, the steps described above are simply parts of one long, flowing motion as the baby passes through the birth canal. The mother realizes the ultimate nature of this motion when she first senses that now the baby can only go forward, must continue descending and cannot return. At this point there is a sense of exhilaration to the mother's labors, as she and the baby perform their final joint steps in the dance of birth.

How the baby changes at the time of birth

At the time of birth, the newborn's lungs are filled with fluid. It is uncertain whether this fluid is fluid from the uterus that the baby has inhaled or plasma that has been secreted by the lungs themselves. Much of the fluid is forced out by pressure on the baby's chest as it passes through the birth canal. As soon as the pressure from the birth canal is released, the baby's chest expands elastically, drawing in air. Generally after this initial "elastic recoil," the baby begins to breathe by itself, using the muscles of the chest and diaphragm. The newborn's earliest breaths are deep and strong enough to inflate the lungs for the first time, despite their initial resistance to inflation (like a new balloon) and the resistance caused by whatever fluid remains in the lungs.

It is not yet known what triggers the newborn's first breaths, since moments after birth the baby still has enough oxygen from the placenta. Researchers believe that breathing may result from the stimulation caused by the cold, light, and noise of the external world, as well as by the decreasing level of oxygen in the infant's blood. The miraculous thing is that within several minutes after birth the newborn's lungs are expanding and contracting rhythmically, drawing air in and out, bringing oxygen to red blood cells and removing carbon dioxide.

As the baby passes through the birth canal, events take place that prepare the baby to adapt to life outside the uterus. The baby changes its circulation and its way of getting oxygen. These awesome changes, coupled with the expulsion of fluid from the lungs and the automatic recoil following the release of pressure from the birth canal, make it possible for the baby to get oxygen into its blood by itself, without the mother, as it breathes in and out for the first time.

From about eight weeks, the baby has had a well-developed fetal circulation. The baby's own blood picked up oxygen from the mother, across the placental barrier. This oxygen-rich blood reached the fetus through the umbilical cord. The blood went first to the heart, then to the rest of the baby's body. Some of the blood from the baby's body returned directly to the heart, some returned via the placenta where it was oxygenated. The baby in the uterus has a valve, or hole, called the *foramen ovale,* between the upper two chambers of the heart, and a special blood vessel called the *ductus arteriosus* by which most of the blood bypasses the fetus's nonfunctional lungs. The foramen ovale and the ductus arteriosus make it possible for both sides of the fetal heart to pump throughout the body the oxygen-rich blood from the placenta. In addition to these two unique structures, the fetus also has another special blood vessel called the *ductus venosus.* The ductus venosus allows much of the blood from the placenta to bypass the baby's liver and go straight to the heart.

Within moments after birth, two major changes occur in the baby's circulatory system. The first is breathing. Regular breathing causes blood to flow into the lungs in large amounts. There the blood receives oxygen directly from outside air for the first time. This blood then returns from the baby's lungs to the heart. The pressure of the returning blood causes the valve, the foramen ovale, to close between the upper-left and upper-right chambers of the heart. In the next several days the flap, or valve, adheres to the heart muscle and seals off permanently, aided by the baby's clotting mechanisms. The ductus arteriosus, the blood vessel bypassing the lungs, contracts by itself soon after breathing starts. Eventually it degenerates and simply becomes a fibrous ligament. The closure of the ductus arteriosus ensures that all blood that comes from the newly sealed-off right side of the heart will go directly to the lungs to get oxygen.

The second major circulatory change at birth is the closing off of the umbilical cord. For a few minutes after birth the umbilical cord continues to pulsate as blood returns from the placenta to the baby's body. But within a short time the umbilical cord shrinks by itself, even if it is not cut or tied. This happens in response to high levels of oxygen in the baby's blood from the first breaths, and from stress hormones in the baby's blood. The process is aided by handling of the cord and by the lower temperature outside the uterus. This constriction of the umbilical cord results in the closure of the ductus venosus, the blood vessel bypassing the liver. These circulatory changes complete the infant's immediate shift from fetal to newborn circulation.

In addition, more long-term changes are taking place in the chemical makeup of the baby's blood. One of the most important constituents of blood is hemoglobin, the molecule in the red blood cells that picks up oxygen and carries it to all the cells in the body. The fetus has a special type of hemoglobin (Hb-F) which picks up oxygen more easily than adult hemoglobin (Hb-A). Some researchers believe this may help to ensure an adequate supply of oxygen for the fetus during the critical early stages of development. At thirty-four to thirty-six weeks, the fetus has over 90 percent fetal hemoglobin (Hb-F). Over the next few weeks fetal hemoglobin declines in proportion to adult hemoglobin. By birth fetal hemoglobin has dropped to 75 percent. After birth the percentage continues to drop—to 10 percent by four months after birth, and to only 1 percent by six months after birth.

The baby's dual perception of birth

Throughout labor and delivery the baby continues to experience directly the biological processes of the mother's body through the placental exchange. Basically this means that, as throughout the rest of pregnancy, the baby is receiving oxygen, hormones, nutrients, and any drugs the mother is being given. The baby is aware of and affected by the mother's nervous state through her hormonal responses. Thus the mother's work, excitement, and any tension, discomfort, or anxiety that she experiences are transmitted to the baby. As always, the baby is also aware of the mother's state through changes in her breathing, heartbeat, and blood pressure, as well as changes in her body position, muscle tension, and voice. The baby's sense perceptions must change radically during labor and delivery, as the bag of waters breaks, and as movement down the birth canal progresses. Still the baby experiences labor and delivery through a dual perceptive system, as it has experienced all of prenatal life. Not only does the baby react to sensations, it is aware of the mother reacting to sensations. Birth is the climax and the end of this direct, continuous duality, which has existed since conception. From the point of view of the baby, then, birth is the beginning of separation and, in a sense, the beginning of true individuality.

But because the baby is still operating under a dual perceptive system, its experience of labor and delivery must be similar to the mother's. If the mother experiences birth as an intense, joyful event, the baby probably does likewise. If the mother experiences birth with anxiety, fear, and pain, the baby does too.

The mother's view of the birth sequence

Every pregnant woman wants to have the most comfortable labor and delivery possible. She wants this for herself, but such a birth experience positively affects the baby's health and well-being too. A relaxed, unafraid woman actually has a shorter labor, less complications surrounding the whole birth experience, and less need for depressant drugs and anesthesia. The shorter and less complicated labor and delivery are, the easier it is for the baby and the less likely are the chances of any fetal distress or lack of oxygen. Almost all women can deliver a baby completely naturally—that is, without any drugs or special medical procedures.

In the last hundred years there have been kaleidoscopic changes in Western obstetrical practices. Doctors, in their attempts to lower both maternal and newborn complications and mortality, have gradually increased the amount of medical intervention in the birth process. Specifically, doctors have increased the use of drugs, monitors, and surgical techniques. Most important, in their efforts to eliminate the relatively small percentage of serious obstetrical problems and tragedies, doctors have made birth into more of a medical situation than a natural event. In so doing, they have put birth in the control of medical specialists rather than the parents.

Today the average pregnant woman in this country has to deal with a number of alternatives that are peculiarly in conflict and can be tension-producing. In order to view birth as nonfrightening and to experience birth as a joyful event, each woman has to look at her own feelings and choose from among today's obstetrical alternatives the one that makes her feel most comfortable.

Moreover, women still have to deal with the folklore that describes childbirth as inherently and unavoidably unpleasant, dangerous, and painful. This vision springs from frightening accounts told by mothers, aunts, friends, and even men. The vision has been reinforced by the media and by the medicalization of obstetrics. Many obstetrical practices grow out of the idea that in childbirth there is always a potential emergency looming.

Most people who were born in the 1940s, 1950s, and 1960s were delivered in highly medical-technical situations. Their mothers were placed in unfamiliar surroundings, bereft of family and friends, given little information, and no say in what happened. Generally, women were drugged throughout labor and delivery, making it difficult for them to participate in, help, or enjoy the birth of their own child. Even in the 1970s and 1980s, this was still the case for women who had difficult vaginal births or unexpected cesareans. The vision of birth that these children derived from stories of their own birth may have a negative cast, either overtly or more subtly.

Since the 1970s many people, including medical people and parents, have begun to question why birth has come to be treated as a rare disease. And they have begun to wonder what effect this has on both mother and baby. Such questioning has resulted in a growing natural childbirth movement started by such European doctors as Grantly Dick-Read and Fernand Lamaze. In addition, women have become involved in a movement to reclaim their own bodies and destinies. The effectiveness of their demands for change as obstetrical "consumers" helped to encourage and spread new modes of childbirth: Most recently, concerned attention and demands for change have come to focus on the experience of the newborn in childbirth, as well as on the experience of the mother.

The main birth goals for the mother to seek are as much physical and mental ease as possible, as joyful an experience as possible, and the opportunity to establish a strong bond with her baby in the hours immediately after birth (see *Bonding*). The choice of the individual doctor, clinic, or midwife determines many of the alternatives in the birth situation. In most cases the health professional will have made many of these choices and have a fairly systematic way of working. Women should not be afraid to visit several doctors or clinics and ask them to describe in detail their standard birth procedure and the degree to which they will let the mother determine details of her delivery. Women can learn a great deal from friends who have already had children, from reading books on childbirth, and from visiting local hospitals or birth rooms. Every woman is unique and every birth is unique. The most important thing for a woman is to find the kind of childbirth situation that *makes her feel secure and confident.* It is helpful to the expectant woman (and the baby) if she has a positive imagery of the forthcoming experience and looks forward to it with interest and excitement, and without fear.

Choosing the doctor or midwife

The relationship that a pregnant mother and father have with their obstetrician or midwife is an important and intimate one. This person will assist the mother during labor and delivery, advise the parents of what is best for the baby, and affect the way the mother perceives the whole experience of pregnancy and birth. The mother's view of the birth process is an important factor in determining what happens to her and how she deals with her experience.

As much as a mother tries to visualize and choose what will happen to her during birth, she cannot fully control the process or its exact outcome. Birth is one of the great experiences in life, requiring the participants to give up specific expectations and views, and accept whatever unfolds. Thus the confidence that the mother and father have in the doctor or midwife becomes very important.

Childbirth requires a woman to let go and trust her body. To do this effectively, the mother must be in an environment in which she feels comfortable and has confidence in the people who are assisting her. The environment and the people who can best help a mother achieve these feelings will vary greatly from one woman to another. Every birth is unique, so it's not useful for expectant parents to organize a rigid plan of how they want the birth to take place. What's important is that each mother get in touch with her feelings about the kind of environment and people that will help her feel most at ease (see page 66).

Birth is a journey. As with any journey, one can plan the destination, but one cannot plan all of the events that will take place along the way, or even necessarily the exact route one will travel. Often the most meaningful and significant moments are the ones that are unexpected. And memories of the journey will have more to do with how one dealt with what happened than what actually happened.

Currently, there are two basic philosophies about childbirth. One of them wants to make the experience as natural as possible; the other advocates the general use of advanced technological procedures in the belief that this maximizes the baby's safety. A home delivery is the epitome of the first philosophy, whereas an electronically monitored delivery in a hospital is the epitome of the second. This dichotomy in obstetrical philosophies has resulted in a quandary for many pregnant women and for many care-givers.

Women today face more childbirth choices than ever before. In most parts of the country a mother may choose among delivery by a lay midwife, a nurse-midwife, a family practitioner, or an obstetrician. She can elect to give birth at home; in a "free-standing" birth center separate from a hospital; in an "alternative" birth room within a hospital; or in a traditional hospital delivery room. Within each of these settings, a mother has some choice among positions for childbirth, use of an episiotomy, and availability of drugs or monitoring.

An alternative birth room gives a mother the technical advantages of a hospital with some of the warmth of a home delivery.

Before interviewing doctors or midwives, a mother and father should develop a concept of the kind of birth they'd like to prepare for. Most expectant mothers have intuitive ideas which reveal their feelings about birth, their hopes and fears, and what will result in a joyful experience. But the ideas must be meshed with the realities of having a baby. To accomplish this a mother needs to talk to other mothers about their birth experiences, and begin to read about pregnancy and childbirth. After a mother has gained more specific information, it will be useful for her to do visualization exercises (imagery) to help her get in touch with a birth situation that is most comfortable. From all her talking, reading, and thinking can come a list of preferences that may be discussed when she interviews doctors and midwives.

The choice of a particular doctor or midwife is the most critical one in determining many of the alternatives in the birth situation. Each practitioner has his or her own set of beliefs and training, which condition or create the kind of medicine they practice. For example, a midwife may have been trained to walk a woman who is experiencing a slow first labor, whereas a doctor may have been trained to administer a drug to speed up contractions. The obstetrical style of the practitioner consists of his or her normal routines and responses to variations or complications in labor. While the expectant mother cannot determine everything that may happen during childbirth, she can choose the style and philosophy of the person who will deliver her baby.

A woman's choice of a doctor or midwife is generally made very early in pregnancy, or even before she discovers she is pregnant. An expectant mother's decision may be made on the basis of the medical insurance she has, by remaining with her regular gynecologist, through conversations with other mothers, by contacting professional organizations and support groups, or by obtaining a referral from another doctor she has seen. In order to make her choice on the basis of obstetrical philosophy, a mother must learn how the doctor or midwife handles specific situations—either by talking with other patients or, better still, by talking at length with the practitioner.

In speaking with a doctor or midwife, the mother and father should ask how the person handles both normal deliveries and cesareans, and they should express any specific concerns or requests they might have. While it will be impossible to find out exactly how a doctor or midwife will deal with every situation, the prospective parents will be able to get a feeling for the person's obstetrical style and personality, and whether or not their attitudes toward birth are similar. If there seems to be a serious disagreement over philosophy or an important issue, the parents should interview other doctors or midwives.

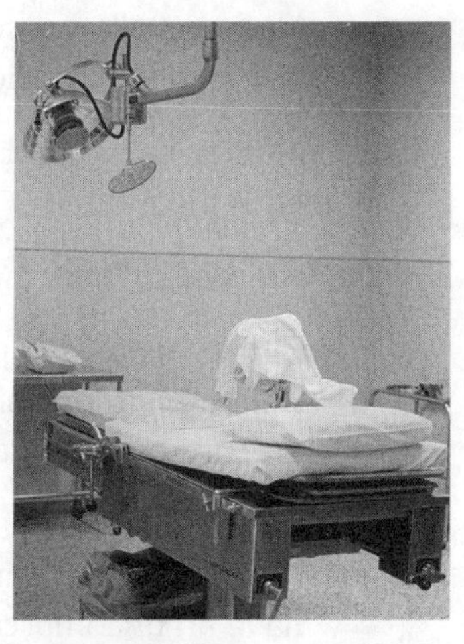

A hospital delivery provides access to the most up-to-date technology.

For many women, the process of selecting a doctor or midwife is neither quick nor easy. First, a mother should educate herself enough to decide what questions to ask, and then obtain the names of people whose philosophy and style are likely to match hers. Finally, if she is not sufficiently confident about the first person she sees, she may need to interview several others. This in itself can be time-consuming, costly, and even disconcerting.

The emphasis on choosing the right person to deliver the baby may seem unnecessary in the early part of pregnancy, but it's valuable to do in the first or second trimester because it enables the mother to build up a relationship with the doctor or midwife. Also, if differences become apparent and a woman is to make a switch, it is easier to do so early in the pregnancy. As pregnancy progresses, most women become attached to the practitioner they have been seeing and find it more difficult to make a break. Ultimately it is worth all the effort for the parents to find a doctor or midwife they trust and feel comfortable with.

For those women who are interested in natural childbirth, there are several well-known methods, such as Lamaze and Bradley, that are in wide use at this time (see page 90). Even these methods vary from course to course and doctor to doctor. An expectant mother can evaluate which method appeals to her most by reading basic books on the various methods, by speaking to the instructors and doctors, and by talking with women who have used the various methods.

Some women who decide to use natural childbirth may specifically decide to have the baby in a birth room or at home, instead of in a conventional hospital setting. If the choice is a home delivery or birth room, it will require selecting a doctor or midwife who will deliver in that particular setting.

Most doctors and midwives have their own obstetrical style. In an average delivery some doctors will virtually not intervene in the natural process, whereas others will routinely use a number of medical procedures. A doctor or midwife who delivers at home or in a birth room will generally be less likely to intervene. Home and birth-center deliveries now function to provide a relaxed, less medical atmosphere. Doctors and midwives who do *home* deliveries are still uncommon, but a growing number of doctors use birth centers or special birth rooms within their local hospitals.

Alternatives for childbirth

Non-interventionist obstetrics

Mother is allowed to move about freely in labor and delivery and pick her own positions.

Mother-baby bonding is emphasized and the baby is not separated from the mother.

No medicines or medical procedures are routinely used.

Birth is allowed to proceed in an instinctual, natural manner which is thought to optimize innate hormonal patterns that speed labor and produce natural opiates (endorphins) which make labor more comfortable, even ecstatic.

Not all mothers want or feel comfortable with this approach or have an uncomplicated labor or delivery.

Continued

Many doctors believe such an approach puts some babies at greater risk, although a number of studies indicate that it is as safe.

Truly non-interventionist obstetrics is most available in the United States in home deliveries or alternative birth centers, although a number of obstetricians who deliver in hospitals lean toward this philosophy.

Interventionist or technical obstetrics
Uses routine medical procedures such as monitoring in an attempt to optimize the health of all newborns.

Generally restricts mother's movements during labor and delivery.

Does not always emphasize mother's participation, choice, or sense of intimacy.

Definitely has a higher cesarean section rate.

Techniques are thought by non-interventionists to slow labor and sometimes actually cause labor and delivery complications.

Thought by proponents to be the safest system in terms of infant health statistics.

Currently most births in the United States lean toward the technical, although many obstetricians have personal philosophies which are relatively non-interventionist.

Natural childbirth
Mother participates fully in labor and delivery: works hard, feels all sensations, is often uncomfortable at certain points, but generally has profound feelings of joy and accomplishment.

Mother and baby have no side effects from drugs which may complicate bonding or early nursing.

Many methods are taught, including Lamaze, Bradley, Jacobson, Kitzinger, or individual systems. The trend is away from dogmatic systems (especially breathing techniques) and toward systems which allow the mother to follow her own body's signals.

Medicated childbirth
At present, anesthetics handled by skilled personnel have minimal side effects on the baby.

Barbiturates and Demerol given in low doses in early labor can help a mother who is very uncomfortable.

A continuous epidural (anesthesia injected around the spinal cord) stops all sensation below the waist, allows the mother to move her

Continued

legs and push, has minimal effects on the baby, and can be given during the entire later part of labor. It is generally considered the best anesthesia for the later part of labor, but may not be available in small hospitals without anesthesiologists.

A spinal (a single shot of anesthesia injected *into* the spinal canal) not only stops all sensation below the waist, it prevents the mother from pushing and means the baby must be delivered with forceps or a vacuum extractor. It is not given until late in labor.

Certain medications or some given in high doses depress the mother and baby. These include large amounts of Demerol or barbiturates, local nerve blocks like paracervicals, and general anesthesia.

Non-interventionists believe that some medications alter the natural process of labor and delivery and may slow labor.

Present at labor and delivery

Husband or father: familiar, loving, involved person who can be continuously present; may or may not be trained to coach mother in labor and won't be trained to deal with specific complications; occasionally may make mother more anxious during labor.

Nurse: training, interest in, and motivation for natural childbirth can vary widely; must follow hospital rules; not present continuously; goes off at end of shift regardless of mother's stage of labor; generally unknown to mother and not chosen by mother.

Labor coach or doula: assists mother continuously throughout labor and delivery; may be natural childbirth instructor, midwife, experienced friend, or, rarely, the doctor; varies in experience with dealing with labor complications; sometimes not allowed by hospital rules; considered by many to be one of the most important aspects of birth care; some birth experts feel the doula must be a woman.

Family members, friends, or siblings: may reassure mother by promoting a non-medical, intimate atmosphere, or may make mother more anxious (especially children); often not allowed because of hospital rules.

Others including residents, medical students, or hospital observers: may decrease personal or sexual atmosphere of birth; may make mother anxious and slow labor; essential in training future doctors, labor coaches, and midwives.

Continued

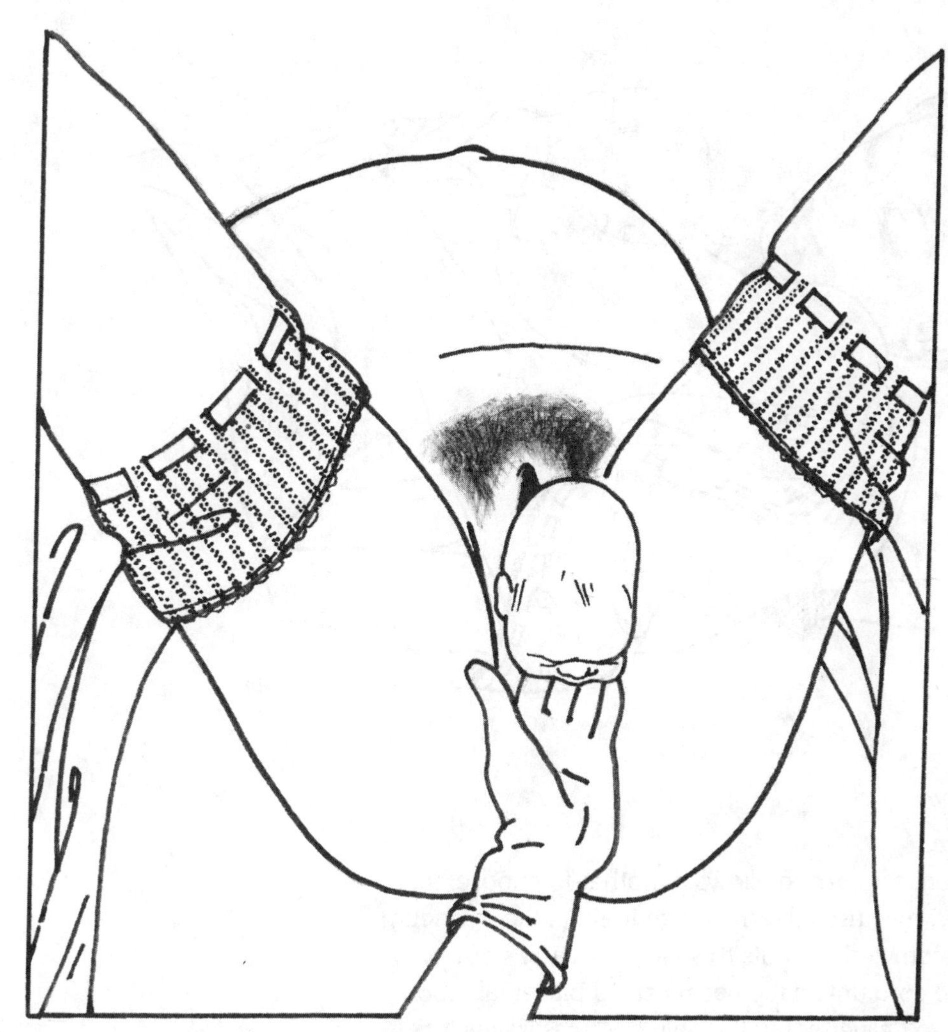

In the most dramatic moment of birth the baby's head crowns and begins to emerge from the vagina. This moment is especially exhilarating and moving for the mother if she is actually able to see the baby's slick, wet head coming out.

Labor procedures
The non-interventionist approach involves no routine shave or enema, allows the mother to wear her own clothes, does a minimum of internal exams to see how labor is progressing, monitors the fetal heartbeat intermittently, and encourages her to move about freely during labor and even drink juice or tea.

The interventionist approach may routinely use some medical procedures such as IV, continuous fetal monitoring, artificial rupture of the membranes, and drugs to stimulate labor or ease discomfort.

Continued

Delivery procedures

The non-interventionist approach allows a mother to choose her position for delivery; may use oil or massage to relax the perineum and avoid an episiotomy; dims lights to shield the baby's eyes; delays cutting of the cord until baby has received placental blood; allows the placenta to deliver naturally; only does cesareans for rare presentations or emergencies.

The interventionist approach uses a delivery table with stirrups, uses surgical lights; does routine episiotomies to prevent perineal tearing; may use forceps or a vacuum extractor to deliver the baby; uses drugs or manually extracts the placenta; routinely does cesareans for dystocia (failure of labor to progress), as well as for emergencies and breech and other presentations.

Procedures that affect bonding

Non-interventionists encourage bonding by placing the baby directly on the mother and allowing it to nurse and remain with the mother and father for at least an hour, often in private; by delaying weighing the baby and putting drops in its eyes, and in some cases by not routinely suctioning out the baby's nose and throat.

Interventionists may briefly take the baby to weigh, measure,

Continued

Bonding takes place when the baby is immediately placed on the mother's breast after birth and the two are allowed to look at and touch one another freely. The instantaneous and special bond thus formed continues for years and has special mental and physical benefits for baby and mother.

and examine it, suction out its nose and throat, give it vitamin K shots and eyedrops.

Some hospitals may routinely separate the newborn from its mother and place it in a nursery for variable amounts of time. This procedure does not allow bonding in the critical period of the first hour after birth.

Some hospitals have full rooming-in in which the baby remains with the mother continuously and she has primary responsibility for it. Bonding researchers feel this situation optimizes bonding, lessens the chances of postpartum depression, and eases the mother's transition to caring for the baby at home.

Hospitals and doctors vary in when they routinely send mother and baby home. Some mothers are uncomfortable with hospitals and do better at home; some mothers feel more comfortable and get more rest if they remain in the hospital for several days.

Site of delivery
Hospital delivery room—most readily available and most widely used by obstetricians; has emergency and surgical facilities available; hospital rules determine management of labor and delivery, who can be present at birth; very medical atmosphere—frightening

Continued

to some, reassuring to others; mother is moved from labor room to delivery room for final stage of labor.

Birth room—generally in or near hospital; emergency equipment available, surgical facilities near; warm, almost nonmedical atmosphere—often the medical equipment is hidden out of sight; mother doesn't have to move at last minute to another room to deliver baby; relaxed rules—for example, friends and children as well as husband can be present at birth; increasingly popular.

Home—relaxed, familiar atmosphere; mother is most in control here; anyone can be present, including children; not many obstetricians use; emergency equipment for infant resuscitation or maternal intravenous may or may not be available; midwife or doctor may or may not be experienced in newborn resuscitation; surgical equipment is only as near as hospital. Generally, health statistics for mother and baby excellent; considered by some to be optimum situation for mother-child bonding because of natural atmosphere and lack of separation of mother and baby. Said to foster the least jealousy and rivalry in other siblings because they are not separated from mother and share in baby's birth.

Babies, mothers, and cesarean sections

Indications for cesarean sections

Cesarean births are not considered dangerous for mother or baby. Doctors often choose to do cesarean sections in preference to difficult vaginal births because they believe it is safer and easier for both baby and mother.

Most cesarean sections are not planned ahead, but are decided on during labor, for a variety of medical reasons:

1. Labor does not progress normally because the baby cannot fit through the mother's pelvis—as shown by X rays taken during labor.
2. Baby appears to be in fetal distress—heart rate changes seriously, as detected by stethoscope or fetal heart monitor.
3. Labor does not progress normally because the baby is presenting in an unusual position—face first or chin, backside, feet (breech).

Continued

4. Labor does not progress normally because the uterus is not working properly—contractions aren't sufficient, cervix fails to dilate, baby's head fails to engage.

In other words, when labor is not going naturally, and it's the doctor's *judgment* that it won't, the doctor may choose a cesarean (1) because he believes it's absolutely necessary or (2) because it's safer and easier.

Some cesarean sections are planned ahead:

1. Repeat cesarean section. Some obstetricians routinely repeat sections for subsequent babies once a woman has had one because they believe the scar could be a weak point in the uterus during labor. Many obstetricians will deliver the subsequent babies vaginally provided labor is going well and there is no other reason for a section this time. Several recent studies have shown vaginal deliveries are safe in such cases.
2. The mother *obviously* has an inadequate pelvis (too small), which is unusual.
3. Serious medical problems exist in the mother, such as toxemia, diabetes, or placental abnormalities.

With repeat sections, special care is taken to make sure the baby is full-term because premature babies have higher incidences of hyaline membrane disease. The mother may be allowed to go into labor naturally or an amniotic tap can be done to determine the maturity of the baby.

Cesarean section rates

Presently the percentage of babies born by cesarean section varies widely from doctor to doctor, hospital to hospital, and country to country. They range from under 5 percent to over 30 percent.

Section rates are generally on the increase because of

1. Increased use of fetal heart monitors, whose data can sometimes be difficult to interpret, due to their newness.
2. Fear of complications from long labor, forceps deliveries, and fetal distress—and subsequent malpractice suits—versus the increased safety of cesarean sections and their widespread use and acceptance in the medical/legal communities.

Before choosing a doctor or hospital, an interested mother can find out their attitudes toward and their general rate of sections. Certain doctors and hospitals make an effort to deliver babies vagi-

Continued

nally, particularly those that are interested in natural childbirth and birth rooms.

Advice for parents and babies of cesarean sections.
In many cases the father can be present at the birth.

Cutting of the cord can be delayed until the blood flows out of the placenta.

The father if not the mother can request to hold the baby immediately after the delivery to "bond," provided the baby is breathing with no difficulty.

The baby is generally taken to the nursery, put in an incubator, and watched to make sure there are no problems (depending upon the reason for section), but the father may be able to stay with the baby and the mother will be able to see the baby soon.

Cesarean mothers can definitely breast-feed, but should realize the baby will be affected by the anesthesia and pain medication.

Relaxation and imagery can help ease discomfort around the mother's incisional site and promote healing.

Cesarean sections require a longer hospital stay because the mother is recovering from abdominal surgery. Some mothers find they are very tired and uncomfortable for a time, but most mothers recover with unexpected quickness.

Many mothers feel sad that they were unable to deliver vaginally, especially if they were studying natural childbirth, but feel better if they realize it was not their "fault," accept the doctor's judgment that it was better for them and the baby, and become involved in care of the baby rather than childbirth. For these mothers breast-feeding can be an especially rewarding experience.

Using relaxation and imagery for childbirth

Total body relaxation can contribute to both the comfort and the ease of labor and delivery. Relaxation helps to clear the mother's mind, relieves worries and anxieties and tension, and helps to relax the muscles around the uterus and vagina. Each of these adds to the mother's sensation of well-being and markedly lowers her sense of discomfort. The more at ease the mother is, the faster and simpler her labor is likely to be.

Remaining in a highly relaxed state is the goal of Jacobson's *progressive relaxation* method for natural childbirth. This and other methods of relaxation have enabled many women to deliver their babies without discomfort and without the use of any drugs. The more skilled a mother is at relaxation, the more skilled and confident she will be at using relaxation during labor and delivery.

In addition to relaxation, imagery is an effective technique in childbirth. Grantly Dick-Read, one of the original popularizers of natural childbirth, said that a woman's image of a physiological act determines whether she experiences pain or pleasure in the act. Dick-Read believed that fear of childbirth disturbs the nerve-muscle harmony of labor, resulting in tension which is interpreted by the mind as pain. Dick-Read believed that women are taught fear-producing images of childbirth by their culture. Thus he felt that a very important part of preparing for childbirth consists of educating an expectant mother to hold a positive image of childbirth. If a woman has an overall positive attitude, she will tend to be confident and relaxed. The more a woman knows about the natural changes taking place in her body during labor and delivery, the more she can attune her body to these changes and work with them.

In addition to a basic positive image of childbirth, there are specific images that can be useful at different points in labor and delivery. The specific images produce changes in perception and physiology which can relieve discomfort and help keep a woman in a continuous, overall state of relaxation.

Relaxation and imagery during labor and delivery

Relaxation is a key technique for labor and delivery and most natural childbirth systems make use of it. The more a woman practices deep body relaxation before labor begins, the more effectively she'll be able to use it during labor. Initially she should follow complete instructions for relaxation (see pages 60–62), and as she becomes familiar with the sensation of relaxing, she can simply follow the instructions and concentrate on remaining deeply relaxed for longer and longer periods. Labor and delivery vary greatly in length, but they most likely will last a number of hours. Thus it is good if a woman learns to stay relaxed and focused for an hour or more. When the muscles around the uterus are relaxed, the

Continued

woman is not fighting or struggling with the contractions and if she is *mentally* relaxed and tranquil as well, her perception of the experience is profoundly altered and she can work with her contractions. Images that a woman holds in mind while relaxed can greatly increase her ability to remain calm and tranquil. Like relaxation, imagery is a skill that improves and becomes easier with use and it is helpful if a woman practices it during pregnancy (see pages 62–64, 68–70 for complete instructions). Together, relaxation and imagery can make a woman more comfortable during labor and delivery and can help to make childbirth a tremendously rewarding and exhilarating experience.

Images for childbirth

I am calm and relaxed.
The baby feels my calmness and shares it.
The baby and I are rested and ready for the work we will do.
The baby is naturally doing just what it should.
My uterus is contracting by itself.
With each contraction my cervix is dilating a little more.
The contractions of my uterus are massaging the baby, hugging it.
My belly feels as if it is suspended in warm water, floating lightly. My abdomen feels almost as if it were separate from the rest of my body. I can watch the contractions come and go as if they were slow waves breaking on a shore.
My breathing is slow and even.
My legs, hands, and jaw are loose. My belly and bottom are loose.
The baby and I rest deeply in between one contraction and the next.
In a while the baby will be here. The baby and I are doing beautifully. The baby will be beautiful.
The baby is descending naturally. With each contraction the baby descends a little more.
The baby's head fits perfectly in my pelvis.
My hand against my back equalizes the pressure of the baby's head against my back.
Soon the baby will be here.
The baby and I are doing beautifully.
It feels good to push now. It is wonderful, exhilarating work.
The baby and I can still rest between contractions.
The baby is almost here.
My vagina stretches tight as the baby's head crowns, then emerges. I think of coolness, coolness.
I can see my baby's head.
Now the baby is here. The baby is beautiful.

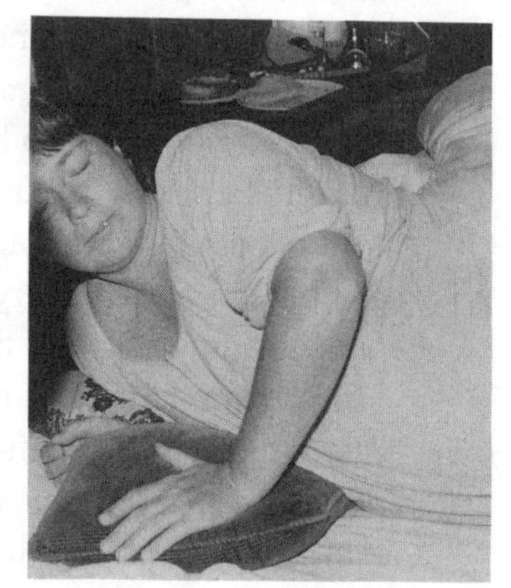

Relaxation and imagery can make a woman more comfortable during labor and delivery.

Philosophies about birth

Western society has tended to view birth as a traumatic experience for the baby as well as for the mother. The Bible has been translated as saying that women shall bear children in suffering—suffering which must then be shared by the infants. Many psychological doctrines view birth not just as trauma, but as the prototype of all future fear and anxiety. According to the doctrines put forth by Sigmund Freud, Otto Rank, and others, the birth process is considered to be physically painful for the baby. Uterine life, on the other hand, is thought to be ultimately blissful and secure, the total satisfaction of physical needs, complete union with the mother. Birth is seen as a painful interruption of this bliss, an irreversible break in the primal union, a sudden and terrifying shock for which the baby is not prepared. Moreover, birth becomes the initial abrupt thrust into the unknown and the beginning of the need for self-initiated activity—the birth of the ego. Suddenly the baby's most basic needs are no longer automatically taken care of; the baby has to cry in order to be fed. An "I" must be born who does things in order to satisfy basic needs, rather than having them satisfied without effort.

Eastern and occult thought view birth differently. But they likewise view birth as a sudden and shocking change from union to separateness. The Eastern doctrine of reincarnation holds that each individual or spirit is born many, many times. Every person is believed to have subconscious memories of these other lifetimes and may achieve conscious recollection of them. After death the spirit chooses a womb in which to take on a new physical body. At birth the spirit suddenly finds itself a mewling infant, unable to communicate or do things. This helpless condition is both shocking and frustrating. The soul goes from the perfection of the spiritual plane to the duality, coarseness, and problems of earthly existence—from spiritual lessons to learning the physical lessons of nursing, defecating, and moving. According to Eastern thought, almost everyone loses conscious memory of the spiritual plane as he or she makes this transition.

Recent research actually raises serious questions about the theories of uterine bliss, the idea that birth is painful and fear-provoking for the baby, and the idea that birth is the primal separation. The idea of uterine bliss is certainly subject to question since it is now known that the baby in the uterus physiologically "shares" or is affected by all the mother's emotions, including fear and anxiety. Thus it is unlikely that birth is the infant's first experience of terror, if indeed it has to be terrifying at all. Frederick Leboyer speaks poignantly of the infant's birth terror and shows pictures of newborns whose faces appear contorted with fear and rage. But he also shows that if the baby is brought into the world with gentleness, if the mother is able to participate joyfully in the birth, then the baby may enter the world so peacefully as to appear to be sleeping. Leboyer speaks of the terror and pain of the first breaths, yet everything has been preparing for just this event. Most babies breathe easily, naturally.

Rather than view birth as a shock for which the baby is not prepared, one can cite evidence for the fact that the baby is extraordinarily well prepared for both the physical and the mental aspects of birth and life outside the womb. At a physiological level the baby actually initiates labor and naturally executes the intricate series of turns by which it can most easily pass through the birth canal. Some researchers have even postulated that the pressure and squeezing the infant feels from contractions and in the birth canal help to provide necessary stimulation of the nervous system, which in turn will ensure the proper functioning of the baby's major organ systems, including respiratory and excretory, as is the case among animals.

During periods when the newborn is alert and awake, it eagerly takes in stimulation—seeing, hearing, and touching. From the first moments after birth the baby turns its attention to the mother's face and things around it. In fact, many babies seem to seek out stimulation and new experience. The newborn infant has an incredible array of reflexes and learning abilities which enable it to breathe, take oxygen into its own blood, and take nourishment for itself.

Birth then can be viewed not as trauma but as a perfectly coordinated series of movements, a dance, in which an innately prepared and relaxed mother and her baby move step by step from one phase of their lives to another. It is the essence of the flow of life that neither one can stop the dance, remaining fixed in space and time.

From the moment of conception the baby's destiny as a human being propels it onward. Truly the baby is meant to live its life outside, not inside, the womb. The womb is simply a temporary shelter for the baby until it is capable of making its way in the outside world. And it is quite possible that the love the baby first sees in its mother's eyes, seconds after its birth, is infinitely more pleasing than the warmth and darkness of the womb.

Western psychologists since Freud have speculated on the negative effects of the birth process. They have theorized that pain, anxiety, and the fear of death are the consequences of birth itself and that all of life is but an adjustment to separation from the mother. Failures in this adjustment are believed to lead both to mental and physical illnesses. When birth trauma is nonexistent or minimal, then the infant proceeds into life positively. Such an atraumatic birth may have beneficial effects on the baby's mental and physical health throughout its life. The baby may gain a sense of itself as being capable and a sense of basic trust that the world is benevolently continuing to meet its needs. And birth may become a model for successful coping with new and stressful situations, which is ultimately the underlying factor in the body's ability to prevent and heal illness.

And finally what of the theory that birth represents primal separation and the first profound experience of loneliness? How much of this is so, and need it be? Certainly the umbilical connection is over. But while in the uterus the baby "knows" the mother at a physiological, sensory level. If the newborn baby is put in immediate contact with the mother, then the baby continues its connection with the mother's heartbeat and respiration in an altered form. Likewise, the mother's voice, though altered in quality, will be familiar. All of these points form a bridge which links the baby's two worlds. Actually for the first few days and weeks the baby spends most of its time sleeping or feeding. Much of this time can be spent in close (skin-to-skin) contact with the mother, the known one. This contact both provides emotional security and supplies the baby's physical needs for warmth and nourishment.

Constant companionship during labor

One of the most important findings in recent years shows that *constant* attendance during labor has positive effects on the baby as well as the mother. Among 150 cultures studied by anthropologists, in all but one a family member or friend, usually a woman, remained with the mother continuously throughout labor and delivery. In their studies on bonding, pediatricians Marshall Klaus and John Kennell noticed that the presence of a supportive lay woman, whom they referred to as a *doula,* seemed to have a significant effect on the length of labor and complications of childbirth. Their early observations prompted them to undertake an extensive study in which half of all mothers were randomly assigned a doula early in labor. Indeed, among the mothers who were constantly attended by doulas, the average length of labor was 9 hours as compared to 19, the cesarean section rate was 12 percent versus 19 percent, and drugs and forceps were required only 7 percent of the time as opposed to 21 percent. Moreover, among the babies in the doula group, there was a lower incidence of fetal distress and difficulty breathing after birth. Immediately after birth, there were also differences in the way the mothers related to their babies: mothers in the doula group tended to stay awake longer and spent more time stroking and talking to their baby. The study showed that constant support during labor has far-reaching, positive benefits on both mother and baby.

Bonding between mother and baby

Bonding is a term that describes the process by which a mother establishes a special relationship with her baby. "Bonding" refers to the mother's ties to the baby, while "attachment" refers to the baby's tie to the parents, although the terms are often interchanged. Two fascinating groups of experiments add new dimensions to researchers' views of newborn learning and development. These studies show that the infant's behavior and learning patterns are tied to much more than the infant's purely physical needs. The infant's social, psychological, and intellectual development from birth is tied to its ability to release a chain of complex mothering activities.

One group of experiments centers around a phenomenon called *imprinting.* Some animals, for example, ducks, are known to follow the first moving object they encounter and to develop a special attachment to the object as if it were their mother. This attachment is strongest if it occurs within a certain number of hours from hatching, after which it diminishes as the duck actually becomes progressively more afraid of unknown moving objects.

Another group of studies concerns how infant monkeys relate to and are affected by objects meant to substitute for their mothers (*surrogates*). Monkey infants became emotionally attached to soft, fuzzy mother-substitutes even if their milk is supplied by a second surrogate mother made of bare wire. In moments of stress the infant monkeys selectively sought out the cloth mother and they were more inclined to explore new situations if the cloth mother were present.

There is now evidence that similar attachments are made by human babies and that such attachments are very important to the establishment of the most satisfactory or optimal mother-child relationship. Every animal species has specific maternal behaviors that are characteristic both before and after birth. These maternal behaviors involve prebirth nesting activities and the grooming and exploring of the new babies after birth. Like other animal species human mothers and babies seem to have a typical kind of behavior toward each other. This behavior is seen immediately after birth if the baby is not taken away from the mother. The mother and the baby participate in an intricate, interlocking dance of seeing, touching, and hearing. The mother holds and touches the baby. She strokes the baby's face, arms, and legs with her fingertips and within a few minutes rubs the baby's head and body with her hand. Throughout this exploratory touching, the mother faces the baby and looks into its eyes. Within a few minutes the mother naturally puts the baby to her breast to feed it.

Bonding between mother and child takes place naturally, based on inborn behaviors. Melanesian Mother and Child. *Wood; height: 36 1/8". The Metropolitan Museum of Art, The Michael C. Rockefeller Memorial Collection of Primitive Art.*

The baby likewise has its own behaviors that contribute to this special interaction and stimulate the mother's maternal behavior. From the beginning the baby looks at the mother and focuses on her face. When put to the breast, the baby repeatedly licks the area around the nipple. The mother characteristically speaks to the newborn in a special, high-pitched tone of voice. Studies have shown that the newborn can actually synchronize its movements to adult speech.

The complex interaction which takes place between mother and baby minutes after birth serves to unite them and prepare them for the special roles they will play for each other for months to come. The mother becomes *bonded* to the infant, and the infant becomes attached to the mother. The mother's bonding to the infant literally serves to ensure the infant's care and thereby its survival. The infant's attachment to the mother serves to ensure its own properly unfolding development. If allowed to, this bonding takes place naturally, based on innate behavior patterns of mother and baby that stimulate each other.

The bonding procedure in all species seems to be remarkably strong. But at the same time the mechanisms are delicate, time-dependent, and easily disturbed. Psychologists studying animal behavior have found out much about the effects of alterations in natural bonding. If a goat and her kid are not kept together during the first five minutes after delivery, the mother will refuse to care for the kid. This alienation can be reversed if mother and kid are forcibly put together in a small space within the first twelve hours. Then the bonding which normally would take place within a few minutes after birth *will* take place, but requires an average of ten days.

Studies on bonding have caused psychologists to suggest that there is a "maternal sensitive period," a time after delivery during which mothers form an attachment to their babies. While the attachment can take place later, the best time seems to be directly after birth. Human maternal bonding seems both more complex and more flexible than among other species. Human behavior, more than other animal behavior, is influenced by the higher centers of the brain. It is affected by the mother's expectations, imagery, and thoughts.

Two of the leading figures in the field of maternal bonding are pediatricians Marshall Klaus and John Kennell. As neonatologists they observed that premature infants were often returned to the hospital (after being sent home) due to *failure to thrive,* sometimes even because of child abuse. These observations, coupled with the knowledge that parents were deprived of physical contact with their infants in the neonatal nurseries, led Klaus and Kennell to study the effect of early maternal-infant contact on the bonding process. Klaus and Kennel found that mothers show distinct differences depending on when and how bonding takes place. Among two groups of mothers studied, one group was given routine hospital contact with their babies in the first three days, including simply a glimpse of the baby after delivery, brief contact at six hours, and thereafter for twenty-minute feedings every four hours. The second group of mothers (extended contact) were allowed to hold their naked babies for one hour within the first two hours after birth and then were allowed five extra hours of contact each day. One month after delivery the extended-contact mothers showed more eye-to-eye contact with their babies, more soothing behaviors, more fondling, and more reluctance to leave their babies. Another similar study showed that two months after delivery, mothers who had extended contact with their babies were more likely to be successfully breast-feeding. At one year the extended-contact mothers were observed to spend more time with their infants during a well-baby exam and, again, to show more soothing behavior. At two years these mothers exhibited greater verbal interaction with their infants and issued fewer commands. Interestingly enough, at three and a half years, the higher contact group of infants showed an average IQ fifteen points higher than the average of the control group. Moreover, a significant relationship was found between the infants' IQ and the amount of time their mothers had spent in eye-to-eye contact with them at one month.

Since Klaus and Kennell's early studies, there have been numerous

When does love begin?

Feelings of maternal love are not necessarily instantaneous. Mothers come to love their babies at different times.

During pregnancy	41%
At birth	24%
First week	27%
Later	8%

Adapted from Aidan MacFarlane.

studies that basically support and broaden their findings. However, there are still no studies that clearly demonstrate the amount of time mother and baby must be together in the first hours after birth. Klaus and Kennell emphasize that bonding is a complex social relationship between two people that is affected by many factors; it is not an instantaneous process like a bond established by epoxy glue. Each mother and baby are unique, and not every mother develops a close tie to her baby within the first few minutes or hours of contact after birth. British child psychiatrist D. W. Winnicott suggests that there is a period of *primary maternal preoccupation,* a period of heightened sensitivity that begins at the end of pregnancy and continues for several weeks after birth.

Bonding between father and baby

Fathers bond too—with absorption and preoccupation

Fathers tend to talk rapidly to baby

Father supports mother, enhances her self-esteem and assessment of mothering skills, protects her from outside concerns

Modern hospital procedure is based on total cleanliness, efficiency, and the capacity to deal with rare diseases and emergencies. While it has largely succeeded in these goals, its very success in these areas often interferes with the natural bonding process and causes the new mother to question her own intuitive knowledge of, and feelings for, her baby.

The effects of hospital procedure on the newborn infant must also be quite profound. Hospital newborn practices and nursery arrangements are already changing and will probably continue to undergo radical changes as more becomes known about bonding and as expectant parents make their feelings known. The more new parents understand about bonding, the more they can do to work within and around hospital procedures. Based on current knowledge, the most satisfactory bonding situation occurs when both the mother and baby are healthy and alert following delivery. This means that neither is drugged and the baby has suffered no oxygen deprivation in the birth process. The room is warm and dimly lit; the father is present; the mood of everyone in the room is relaxed and joyful. After being dried off and given a brief physical, the newborn is placed naked on the mother. The newborn is allowed to nurse immediately and remains with the mother. Nothing is done either to baby or mother that would diminish their sensual contact or spontaneous behavior with each other. This means delaying or eliminating the use of strong-smelling creams or soaps on the mother's skin, particularly around her breasts, and postponing the administration of silver nitrate eyedrops that are used to prevent a newborn eye disease.

Optimum medical conditions for the baby in the birth experience

For the large majority of mothers and newborns, meeting the conditions described below will create an optimal birth situation. If a

Continued

mother wants these conditions to be met, she can create a situation in which they are likely to be so. She does so by making choices that make her feel comfortable.

A calm, unafraid mother who is positively educated about what birth is, what her body is doing, and how to work with her body through relaxation and breathing.

A relaxed, supportive atmosphere for the mother throughout labor and delivery.

As little use of drugs as possible.

A dimly lit room, with no loud sounds.

After being dried off and having a brief physical, a healthy baby should be placed naked against the mother's breast and allowed to nurse or lick the mother's nipple. The baby's sucking reflex is strongest twenty to thirty minutes after birth.

A mother who is allowed and even encouraged to spend the first few hours quietly holding and communicating with the baby verbally, visually, and by touch.

Chapter 6

The newborn: birth through the first few months

Trust and positivity

The arrival of a new baby is one of life's most dramatic and exciting events. It is a landmark, a rite of passage, a means of reconnection with the natural order and with one's own past. Having a baby irrevocably ties a person to cycles of birth and death. There is a sense of affirmation, of positivity. A new baby engenders acceptance and forgiveness of the past, and renewed promise and hope for the future. Emotions run high for everyone closely connected with the baby. The immediacy, newness, and unpredictability of this time shatter rational forms and habits in a beautiful and positive way. This shattering is a gift that does not necessarily happen many times in a lifetime. Such abrupt, poignant change forces a person to break out of the confines of everyday life and experience a personal rebirth. Both the immediate and distant past are transformed and seen in a new light. There is an overwhelming feeling of wonder, correctness, and joy.

Almost inevitably situations of such shattering newness and change also bring with them moments of fear and doubt—fear of the unknown and doubts about one's ability to cope with it. One can even speculate that these feelings of fear and doubt were passed to us as infants by our own parents. Certainly in our society such feelings are almost universal in parents of first babies. These feelings prepare new parents for the task at hand and alert them to gaps in their own knowledge. Most fears in the first few weeks are easily resolved or prove to be groundless. Almost all parents have a humorous and touching story of some anxious moment they had with their first baby.

The newborn has an incredible radiance which evokes universal awe and love. The Nativity *(40), detail, by Petrus Christus, National Gallery of Art, Washington, Andrew W. Mellon Collection.*

To see a newborn is to be humbled, to forget our own egos, to realize how little we do to affect the mystery of creation. The Adoration of the Magi *(1085), by Fra Angelico and Fra Filippo Lippi, National Gallery of Art, Washington, Samuel H. Kress Collection.*

Experience has shown both parents and pediatricians that the most useful attitude to adopt in the first weeks is one of *trust and positivity.* The mother has instinctive knowledge of what to do for the baby, while the baby itself has powerful reflexes and drives guiding its behavior. A healthy baby is not delicate. In this sense appearances are deceptive. A healthy baby is actually quite resilient. Some experienced pediatricians go so far as to say that there is almost nothing a parent can do (unwittingly) to harm a young baby.

The newborn's appearance

The newborn baby is a magical, wondrous person who has an incredible impact on everyone. There is something awe-inspiring, even a little frightening, about these small, perfect creatures who are so like adults and yet so different. The sight of a newborn awakens thoughts about the mystery of creation and man's lack of control over it. To be exposed to a newborn is to be humbled, to be taken away from our egos, when we realize how little we've consciously done to create this person.

Studies have shown that the newborn's very shape and proportions—the largeness of the head in comparison to the body, the small mouth, chubby cheeks, and large forehead—all tend to draw people's interest and attention. Indeed, newborns are so different from adults and even from older children that the differences themselves deserve attention. Such a description of the special characteristics of the newborn is reassuring to most first parents, and it helps concerned parents realize that their baby is all right.

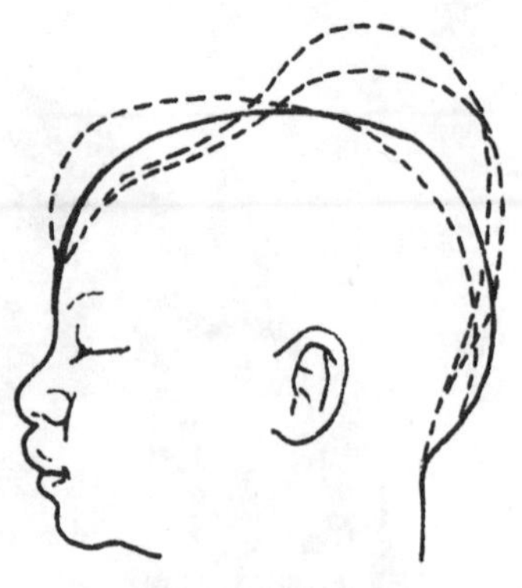

During the first few days after birth the newborn's head remains molded, *or shaped by the pressures of the birth canal. The drawing shows several common shapes caused by molding.*

Newborns have special body proportions. Evolution has taken a direction that favors the development of the human brain over the rest of the body structures, and favors the larger size of the more conscious part of the brain. The relatively large head and the smaller, less mature body make it necessary for the human infant to be nurtured by its mother for a longer period than most other animals.

The average newborn weighs around seven pounds and is twenty inches long. The shape of the newborn's head almost always remains molded for a week due to the pressures experienced in the birth canal. The infant's head is able to change in shape during birth because the bones of the skull are relatively soft and are still only connected by fibrous tissue. In two places the fibrous margins between the bones are actually open; these are called the fontanels, or "soft spots." In these areas, the bony plates of the skull are not yet fused. The larger, anterior, fontanel, in the midfront of the skull, is diamond-shaped and may measure up to 4 centimeters (2 inches) in width. The rear, or posterior, fontanel is barely the size of a fingertip and generally closes by four months. The fontanel area is soft and normally pulsates with the baby's heartbeat. When the baby is upright, the anterior fontanel may even be slightly depressed. Parents need not fear touching the soft spots. These areas fuse in normal growth by the time the baby is nine to eighteen months old. The soft spots have always attracted the attention of parents because they constitute one of the most striking differences between the newborn and the adult. The fontanels are more apparent if the newborn has little hair. Among the Hopi Indians the fontanels were regarded as the place where the baby's spirit entered its body.

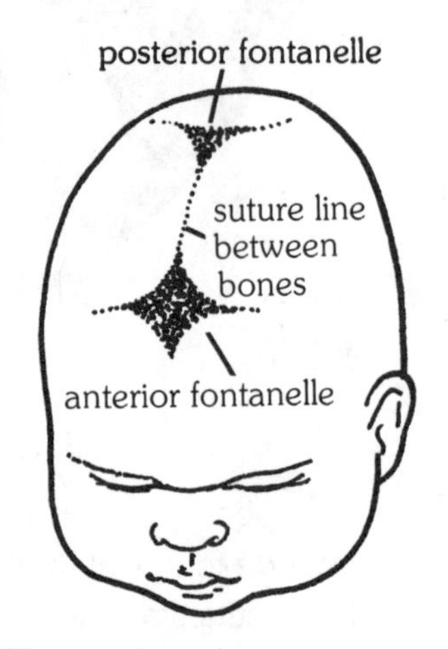

The newborn has two spots on the head, the fontanels, *where the skull plates have not yet grown together. Touching the soft spots will not hurt the baby.*

At birth the baby's skin is naturally covered with a yellow, somewhat greasy substance, the *vernix caseosa,* which is secreted by the fetus's skin glands. In the uterus, the vernix protects the fetus's skin from the effect of the long exposure to a liquid environment. If not deliberately washed off, the vernix comes off by itself in a few days. The newborn's body is also covered with fine, scarcely visible hair, called *lanugo,* which disappears during the first month. At birth the baby often has a full head of hair. This, too, is often shed in the first month and is not necessarily the color the baby's hair will be later. Some babies develop a full head of hair quite quickly; others have little hair for months.

Skin color at birth varies depending on the baby's racial background and state of activity. Newborns are slightly red at birth and remain so for a few hours. The newborn's skin flushes when the baby cries or becomes very active. During the first several days after birth it is not uncommon for the newborn's feet and hands to appear slightly bluish, as circulation at the end of the arms and legs is not yet well developed. This bluish tinge is most likely to be seen when the baby is cool (for instance, when the baby is being changed). The infant's hands and feet are normally several degrees cooler than the rest of the baby and this in itself does not mean the baby is cold. The newborn's skin may appear mottled, especially after a bath. This is normal and relates to the developing circulatory system.

In the first week after birth, many babies develop a yellowish tinge to their skin called *jaundice.* This coloration, which affects 60 percent of healthy full-term infants and 80 percent of preterm infants, is caused by an accumulation in the skin of a breakdown product of red blood cells called *bilirubin.* In older babies this breakdown product is removed by the liver and excreted in both urine and feces. But in a newborn, the liver is not fully functional. This is the cause of *physiologic jaundice,* a common condition which generally becomes noticeable about the second or third day, peaks between the second and fourth, and begins to disappear about the fifth to seventh day after birth. One out of two hundred babies develops another normal condition called *breastmilk jaundice,* which starts between the fourth and seventh day, peaks in the third week, and disappears by itself. In rare instances jaundice can be caused by a medical condition. For that reason, babies with jaundice are given a physical exam and a blood test for bilirubin. If bilirubin levels are very high in physiologic jaundice, the baby will be hospitalized and given phototherapy (full-spectrum light) in the nursery. This treatment increases the breakdown of bilirubin, which is toxic in high levels.

Newborns commonly have a variety of "spots" on their skin, most of which are not seen in adults or older children. There may be tiny, whitish bumps, called *milia,* on the nose. These are caused by plugging of the skin pores and they spontaneously disappear within a few weeks. Some newborns have birthmarks which are permanent or which disappear or fade as the baby grows up. There may be bluish-black areas, called *mongolian spots,* over the baby's back, buttocks, and genital area. These spots, which normally disappear in a year or so, are seen in 90 percent of dark-skinned babies. Another kind of birthmark, called a *café-au-lait spot,* is a light brown oval less than an inch in diameter which can be found anywhere on the body. It persists throughout life. What are commonly referred to as birthmarks are small, permanent, brown to blue dots. All the birthmarks in this first group are caused by excesses of skin pigment.

Another group of birthmarks is caused by overgrowth of blood vessels; the most common variety of these marks is called a *salmon patch.* They are light red areas most frequently seen on the back of the neck ("stork bites" or "angry spots"), eyelids, and in the middle of the arm. Some may persist, but most disappear in a matter of months or years. Small, red, rubbery lumps, called *strawberry birthmarks,* can appear anywhere on the body in the first month after birth. They also disappear in childhood.

Normal newborn skin conditions

- Milia—white dots on face in about 50% of newborns
- Acne—pimples on face, from 3 weeks to 6 months
- Mongolian spots—black-blue spots on back, buttocks, genital area in about 90% of Black, Indian, and Asian babies
- Café-au-lait—light brown patches in 10–20% of babies
- Salmon patch—light red area on neck or eyelids in 50% of all babies; eyelid patches fade, neck patches may fade
- Strawberry birthmarks—red lumps; may appear at around 3 weeks of age, disappear as child grows

The newborn's skin is rather delicate and is much more susceptible to normal rashes than an adult's. Up to half of all newborns between one and four days old develop from two to one hundred half-inch red spots which likewise disappear by themselves in a couple of days (*erythema toxicum neonatorum*). Not infrequently the baby's skin peels around crease marks—particularly in the wrists, feet, and armpits. During the first month after birth many infants temporarily develop pimples that look like acne on the forehead, cheeks, and chin (baby acne).

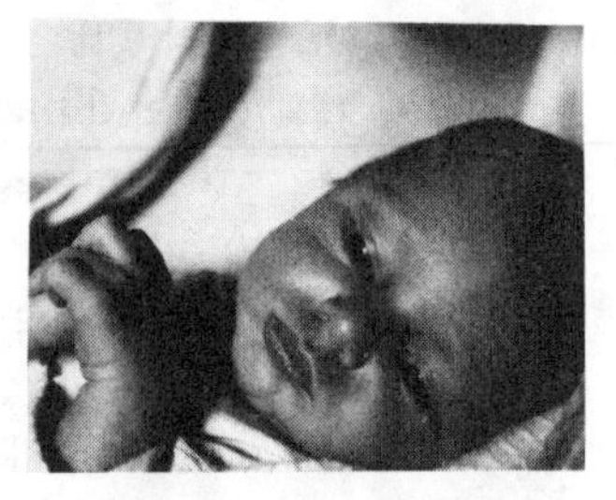

Studies have shown that the newborn's high forehead, round face, and wide-set eyes evoke nurturing feelings in adults.

As we've mentioned, the face of the newborn has characteristics that are particularly attractive to the parent—the high forehead and the roundness of the face. The eyes of all babies are grayish-blue at birth, which is not necessarily an indication of what color they will be. Puffiness of the eyelids is not uncommon with newborns and spontaneously disappears in a day or two. Excess tearing, redness, swelling, and even a watery or pussy discharge may follow administration of silver nitrate drops.

The newborn's nose is characteristically flat and wide and gives no hint yet as to what its adult shape will be. The nose as well as the mouth is commonly filled with amniotic fluid at birth. As soon as this fluid has been cleared or sucked out, the baby breathes through its nose at a rate almost double that of an adult—thirty to forty breaths per minute. The baby's nostrils can often be seen to flare with increased breathing effort.

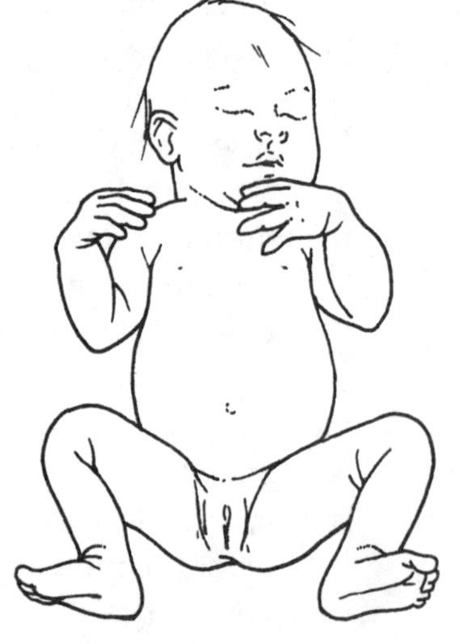

The newborn's belly appears remarkably large, especially after a big feeding, and it moves in and out as the baby breathes.

The baby's mouth is well defined and highly mobile. In the first few days the baby may develop blisterlike areas (sucking blisters) on the lips. These are not unusual and disappear by themselves. The baby's tongue is proportionately shorter than that of an adult. Parents sometimes worry the baby is "tongue-tied," since the frenulum, the connective membrane under the tongue, appears to attach so far forward. Actually, this is normal; the tongue grows rapidly and soon moves freely.

Because of the way the baby's belly bulges, its torso is quite unlike that of the adult. The baby breathes abdominally—that is, the belly rises and falls with each breath—whereas adults often breathe high in their chest. The lower ribs, which are still soft after birth, may be observed to draw in on inhalation—especially if the baby is crying. Like a puppy's or a kitten's, the baby's stomach may stick out visibly after a normal feeding. This is because, compared to an adult, the baby ingests enormous volumes of food relative to its weight and body size.

The baby's umbilical cord begins to dry and turn leathery immediately after it is cut and tied. This is due to the fact that the slight length of cord still attached to the baby is no longer getting any blood through the arteries, which have contracted. Actually the remnant of the cord dries up and falls off with the help of bacteria that digest the dead skin cells. The bacteria produce the somewhat rotten odor that may be noticed right before the stump falls off. This process takes place in five to ten days and should not be sped up by the parents. A slight bulge around the umbilical cord (umbilical hernia) may develop in the first month. It is not uncommon and is not dangerous. It generally disappears by the end of the first year.

The newborn's genitalia (the boy's scrotum, the girls clitoris and labia minora) are proportionately large and often are swollen at birth. In an uncircumcised boy the foreskin normally adheres to the penis and should not be forcibly retracted. The foreskin naturally separates and becomes retractable as the child grows older (generally by around three years). Many doctors no longer believe there are medical reasons for routine circumcision.

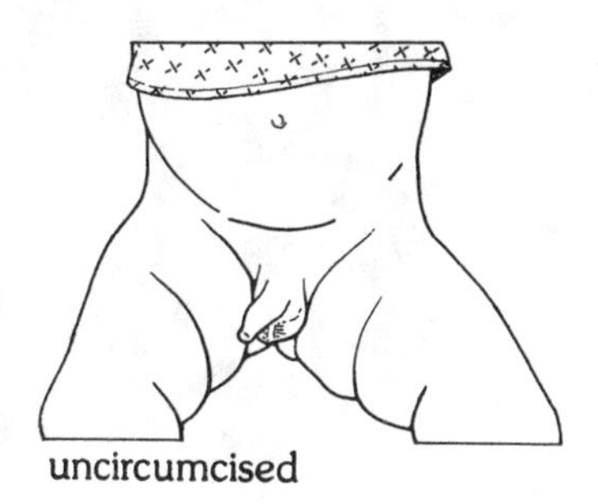
uncircumcised

Newborn girls often have a vaginal discharge in the days after birth. It appears as white mucus and may be tinged with blood. The discharge generally reaches its maximum by three to five days and ends by three weeks. Breast engorgement may develop during the same period in both girls and boys. Babies may actually secrete milk (colostrum) from their nipples. In older times this was called witch's milk. Both of these discharges or secretions are caused by maternal hormones which crossed the placenta before birth.

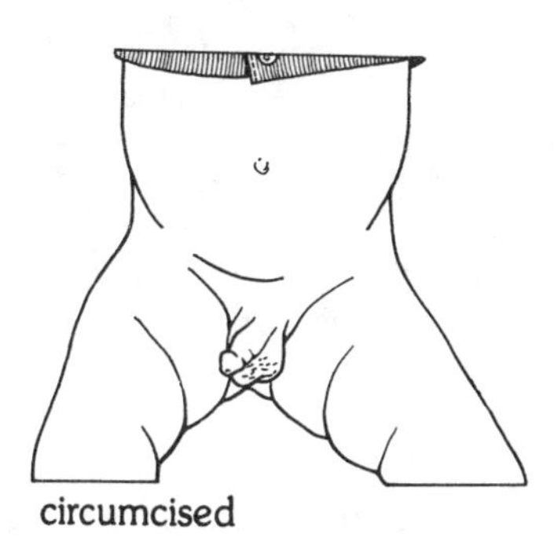
circumcised

The newborn will generally pass its first stools within twenty-four hours after birth. These first stools, called *meconium,* are black and tarlike. They are formed of amniotic fluid and cells that the baby has ingested during the final weeks in the uterus. Most babies will pass several stools containing meconium before their digestive tract is clear. Over the next several days the baby will pass *transitional* stools, which are loose, greenish-brown, and may contain milk curds. By the time the baby is about a week old, the stools will attain their regular color and consistency.

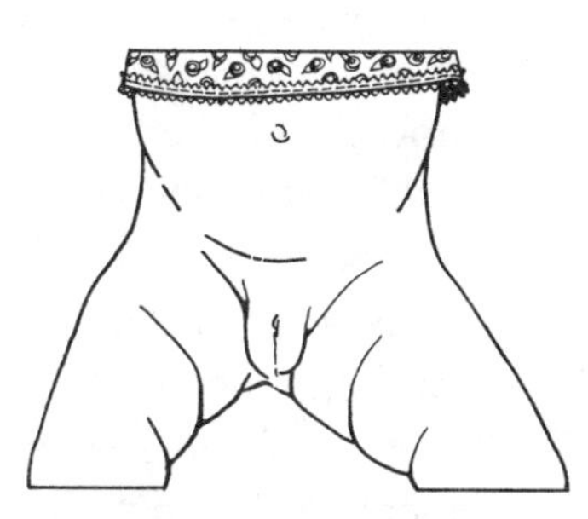
Newborn genitalia appear large and swollen.

Breast-fed babies typically have yellow to green, odorless, soft, pastelike stools, but these can vary widely in color, consistency, and frequency. Nursing babies can have anywhere from several stools a day to one or two a week. Breast milk is naturally laxative and babies who nurse rarely are constipated, even if they appear to strain when passing a stool. The baby is not constipated unless the stool is dry and hard. The stools of bottle-fed babies tend to be darker in color and have a stronger odor. Generally, bottle-fed babies have less frequent stools and they are more prone to constipation than breast-fed babies.

The newborn's states of attention

From birth every baby begins to develop its own unique rhythms as it alternates between sleep, drowsiness, alert inactivity, waking activity, and crying. Researchers refer to these types of activity as the baby's *states.* Parents who observe closely soon become experts on their own baby's states. The classic study on infant states simply involved a researcher observing four infants in a nursery for sixteen hours a day. This researcher, Peter Wolff, described newborn activity as consisting of the following conditions and spontaneous behaviors: In *deep sleep* the infant has a smooth, even breathing rhythm and closed eyelids with no eye movements. During

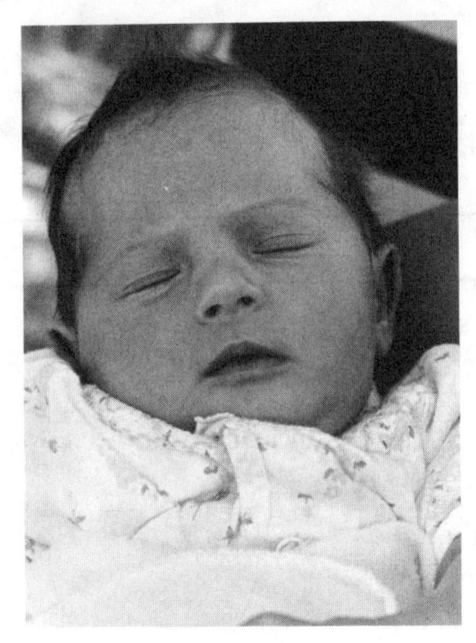

The newborn spends much of its time asleep.

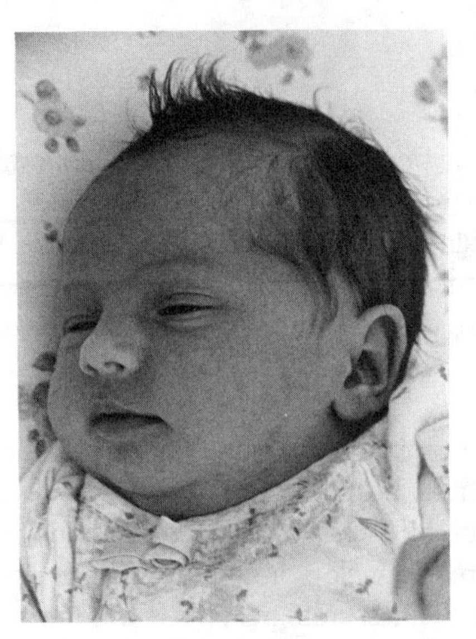

In the drowsy state, the newborn's eyes are half open and appear not to be focused.

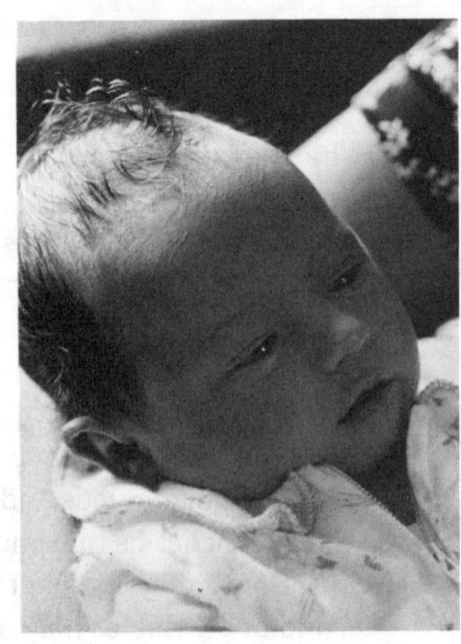

In the quiet alert state, the baby looks around quietly and intently, taking in information about the outside world.

deep sleep the baby's muscle tone is quite flaccid. In fact, the baby's muscles are so relaxed that when an arm is lifted and then let go, it will simply drop. Almost every new parent has been surprised, even frightened, by how deeply newborns can sleep. During deep sleep babies may frequently exhibit startle reactions (see *Newborn Reflexes*). In *active sleep* the baby alternates between rapid and slow breathing, makes random movements of its limbs, trunk, and face. The baby may smile, frown, lick its lips, writhe, or gently stir. During active sleep, rapid eye movements (REM) may be observed beneath the baby's closed lids. *Drowsiness* is the intermediate state between waking and sleeping. The baby intermittently opens and closes its eyelids. The eyes themselves may appear glassy and unfocused and may roll upward under the baby's sleep-heavy lids.

In the *quiet alert state* the baby's eyes are open, bright, and focused. The baby is inactive in that it does not smile, grimace, or make many movements. What the baby does do is try to follow specific sounds and sights by moving its eyes and head.

In the *active alert state* the baby is physically active and its skin may even flush with exertion. The limbs, trunk, face, and head are in motion and the eyes are open. The final state Wolff describes is *crying,* in which the baby makes noises and vigorous movements. The baby may shed tears and its skin may flush during vigorous crying. Wolff observed that crying and gross activities such as kicking and hand sucking were most frequent before meals, and he theorized that the baby's activity level goes up as need and tension mount.

Since this study was done in 1959 researchers have generally agreed with and elaborated on Wolff's work. Brain-wave EEG research has shown that the newborn's rapid eye movement state is linked to adult

Common concerns at birth

Breast-fed babies eat on demand, which may be as often as hourly or as long as 4–5 hours when the baby is sleeping (breast-feeding mothers need to add 500 calories and 2 quarts of water to their diet). Bottle-fed babies generally take about 2–3 ounces every 3–4 hours. Babies usually need to be burped, and spitting up is common. *Transitional stools* that are loose and greenish-brown are normal in the first days after birth. The baby does not always cry because of

Continued

dreaming, but differs from adult REM sleep in several ways. Newborns spend a much greater number of hours (about eight) and a much greater proportion of their total sleep in REM. Also, newborns have distinct REM *waking* states when they are sucking or drowsy, as well as REM sleep states. Adults do not exhibit these REM waking states except during meditation.

Spontaneous smiling by newborns occurs only during REM states. Researchers have also observed that the quiet alert state frequently occurs when a crying newborn is picked up and soothed, and they speculate that this state is the best one for infant learning in the sense of dealing with or observing outside stimuli.

Every baby and every parent is different

While all babies are naturally endowed with fantastic capabilities, each baby is unique in the way it responds to the world. From birth each baby is an individual. And each mother is unique. Thus every mother-child interaction will be a special one—broadly like others, but distinct in many respects.

Researchers have found a number of areas in which newborns show great variation. As all parents know, babies vary in the amount of time they spend sleeping, crying, or being quietly alert. From birth, babies vary in muscular activity, some babies being very active, while others are very still. Babies even vary in the amount of movement they make while asleep. Babies also differ in their sensitivity to stimuli, their general irritability, and their response to frustration. One study has revealed that babies even vary in terms of how hard they suck for nourishment. In general, babies who respond vigorously to one stimulus respond vigorously to others. Not surprisingly, babies (like adults) also vary in their physiological responses to stress, showing wide differences in autonomic nervous system function, as indicated by heart rate, breathing rate, and skin temperature. There is no doubt, however, that each newborn has its own special personality. In fact, many parents feel they recognize their newborn. That is, they notice similarities in prebirth activity and postbirth behavior. Newborn behavior is more than a matter of general needs and reflexes, and it is not capricious in that a very active newborn is unlikely suddenly to become a very passive baby.

In 1977, based on many years of study, child development researchers Stella Chess and Alexander Thomas published a study about individual differences among babies. They observed that newborns and young infants exhibited different characteristics in their spontaneous and reactive behavior. These behavioral characteristics were labeled as *temperament,* and were thought to be inborn. Chess and Thomas described three normal variants in temperament: the easy child, the difficult child, and the slow-to-warm-up child. The *easy child* was regular, adaptable, had a posi-

hunger. Sometimes the baby is happy to suck on its fingers or a pacifier, or be rocked.

Newborns have variable sleep patterns and don't settle down for several months. They may sleep as little as 2–3 hours at a time, or as much as 5–6.

Sneezing and hiccups are common in newborns.

The umbilical cord comes off in about a week. Call the doctor if it is bloody or red.

Breast engorgement and breast secretion normally occur in some babies; girls may have a bloody vaginal discharge. Both are a result of maternal hormones that cross the placenta before birth.

Jaundice (a yellow cast to the skin) is common and usually not serious, but should be seen by the doctor.

Infants should always be in safety seats when in cars.

Newborns are resilient, strong, and will usually remain healthy.

tive approach to new stimuli, and was predominantly positive in mood. These children were found to quickly develop regular sleep and feeding schedules, adapt easily to school, and have a high frustration tolerance. By comparison, the *difficult child* was biologically irregular, withdrew from new stimuli, had difficulty adapting to change, and frequently had negative moods. These children had irregular sleep and feeding schedules, did not adapt easily to school, frequently had loud crying spells, and were easily frustrated. The *slow-to-warm-up child* was not particularly irregular, had negative but mild responses to new situations, and over time gradually showed quiet, positive responses. It is important that parents realize that all of these temperaments are normal variations in behavior. They do not necessarily reflect the quality of parenting or attention that the baby experiences. In general, child-rearing advice and practices are most effective if they are geared to the temperament of the individual baby. Thus parents should not rush a slow-to-warm-up child into new situations, nor punish a difficult child for becoming frustrated or not quickly adapting to changes.

The most important point shown by the studies about individual differences is that parents should expect their newborns to be unique individuals. We do not expect all adults to be the same, or to be simply passive or active, so parents will enrich their relationship with their baby if they approach the baby as a person first, and only then as active or passive.

The parent-newborn relationship can be one of real interpersonal exploration, of real give-and-take. Viewing the baby in this way means the parent is most likely to observe newborn behavior patterns in a meaningful way and to use these observations to stimulate the baby in directions of positive growth.

The parent is an equal partner in the relationship with the baby. That is, the behavior of the mother and father is as much a matter of their own personalities as it is a matter of reacting to the baby's personality. If parents observe their own behavior, they will find that they have characteristic ways of reacting to certain situations, just as the baby does. Some parents respond immediately to a baby's cries, some respond only after the baby has cried for a bit. There are some babies who are easily comforted and some who are harder to soothe. Ideally the parent assesses his or her own style of relating, as well as the baby's style, and then figures out the most harmonious way to meet both their needs.

It is important to reiterate how different individual babies are and to realize how great their capability is for adapting to differing parent styles. Innately, unconsciously, what the baby wants is for the parent to be happy, because only then does the baby—who is both dependent on the parent and intuitively sensitive to the parent's moods—feel secure and happy. Many parents want so strongly to be "good" parents that they constantly worry if they are being negligent or selfish and are always ready to blame themselves. This worrying does not positively alter or deal with a situation. Indeed, unhappy parents eventually will even begin to resent the baby for making them feel bad about themselves. What is needed is an open, flexi-

Common concerns at the one-month visit

Sleeping: few babies sleep through the night yet, but most are beginning to sleep for longer periods at night.

Babies will continue to cry for a variety of reasons, but most parents will now be able to differentiate the cries, and will be able to soothe the baby appropriately.

Feedings should be longer but spaced further apart as the baby eats more at one time. Bottle-fed babies should get 3–4 ounces per feeding. Spitting up is still common.

Babies should never be left unattended on dressing tables or dining tables.

To prevent rash, expose diaper area to air for a few minutes several times a day.

When babies begin early vocalizations—cooing, gurgling, and laughing—the parents should reinforce them.

ble, experimental approach to problem situations. In time, such an approach will yield a creative, individual solution.

Newborn nutrition: mother and baby and breast-feeding

The Crowned Madonna Nursing Her Child *(1400), by Taddeo di Bartolo, M. H. de Young Memorial Museum, gift of the Samuel H. Kress Foundation.*

One of the newborn's chief activities is feeding. Nursing is a natural, lovely, time-consuming act. Remarkably, the newborn is ready right after birth to tackle this whole new way of getting nourishment. Just as it instinctively switches from relying on its mother for oxygen to breathing by itself, so the newborn readily switches from the passive nourishment of the umbilical cord to the more active nourishment of the nipple.

Babies who are born naturally and immediately put to the breast, first lick and soon suck at the nipple. The newborn is equipped with a number of reflexes that make nursing easy and natural. The first is *rooting,* a reflex that helps the baby locate the nipple and get the nipple in its mouth. If the baby feels a touch stimulus at either side of its mouth, the baby will turn its head toward that stimulus; if the baby feels the stimulation at the center of its lips, it will open its mouth and take in the nipple or the object that has caused the stimulation. At this point the *sucking reflex* takes over and the baby

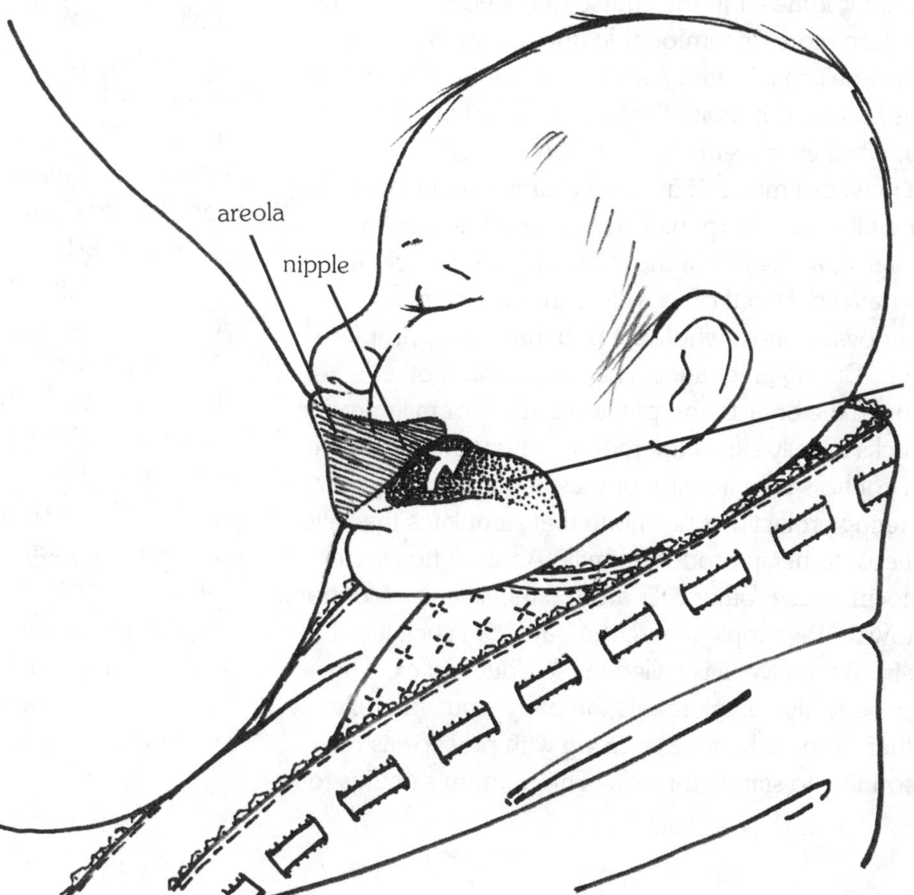

When the baby becomes proficient at nursing it takes most of the areola into its mouth, pressing the nipple upward with its tongue. In this position the baby uses its gums to squeeze milk from the glands behind the areola.

instinctively begins to suck at the nipple with powerful and exquisitely synchronized movements of the lips, tongue, gums, and jaws. The baby's lips slide over most of the areola, the darkened portion of the breast, fixing the baby's mouth and minimizing the swallowing of air. The baby then partially closes its mouth so that its gums press on the milk ducts under the areola, squeezing milk toward the nipple and into the baby's mouth. At the same time the baby presses its tongue upward, squeezing the nipple against the roof of its mouth. Drawing the nipple farther into its mouth with its jaws and cheeks, the baby exerts firm suction on the nipple, which brings out the milk. Meanwhile the baby—with the mother's cooperation—manages to align its head so that it is able to breathe freely through its nose while it is sucking. All these movements quickly become remarkably coordinated. Nursing-like movements actually start while the baby is in the uterus, are functional at birth, and are perfected with practice.

Studies show that the sucking reflex is strongest about twenty to thirty minutes after birth. If the baby is not put to the breast then, its sucking reflex diminishes and does not return until the end of the baby's second day.

When the baby's mouth fills with milk, the *swallowing reflex* is engaged. The baby instinctively knows not to breathe in while swallowing, although some early mistakes may be made which will result in episodes of coughing. The baby is protected from getting milk in its lungs by a well-developed *gagging reflex.* When milk goes down the windpipe rather than the esophagus, the baby automatically coughs in an effort to expel the milk.

Normally, babies swallow some air in the course of a feeding and later burp it up. Some babies are more uncomfortable due to swallowed air and may need more help in expelling it. Patting or rubbing the baby's back or chest usually helps. This may be done with the baby lying flat on its stomach or being held vertically, whichever seems to work better.

Not infrequently the newborn may spit up a small amount of milk during or after the feeding, or while being burped. This happens because the sphincter, or muscular valve, at the top of the stomach does not yet fully close, allowing food to travel back out of as well as into the stomach.

Just as the baby is endowed with a whole set of behaviors to promote nursing, so is the mother. During pregnancy, changes in the mother's hormonal levels have changed the breasts and prepared them for milk production. The baby's first sucks initially signal the mother's hypothalamus, the part of the brain which controls the pituitary, or master gland. The pituitary gland responds by secreting prolactin, a hormone that stimulates the cells in the breast, called *alveoli,* to begin producing milk. Another hormone from the pituitary, oxytocin, causes other cells around the alveoli to contract and squeeze the milk toward the nipple where the baby can suck it out. This squeezing of milk from the alveoli is called the *letdown reflex.* The mother's letdown reflex perfectly complements the baby's nursing reflexes. The baby and the mother become better at nursing with practice as her body gets used to responding to stimuli for milk. The primary stimulus for

Advantages of breast-feeding

Breast milk is the natural food for babies, supplying all necessary nutrients for the first months of life.

Breast milk is sterile and does not have to be bottled or heated.

Breast milk is associated with fewer feeding problems due to allergy or intolerance: less diarrhea, spitting up, colic, or eczema.

Breast milk is high in maternal antibodies against bacteria and viruses, protecting the baby against polio, mumps, influenza, and encephalitis.

Breast milk promotes growth of healthy lactobacillus in the baby's digestive tract and inhibits growth of *E. coli.*

Nursing has psychological advantages for both mother and baby, and has been shown to affect mothering and attachment.

Nursing gives the baby prolonged early tactile, visual, and interpersonal contact.

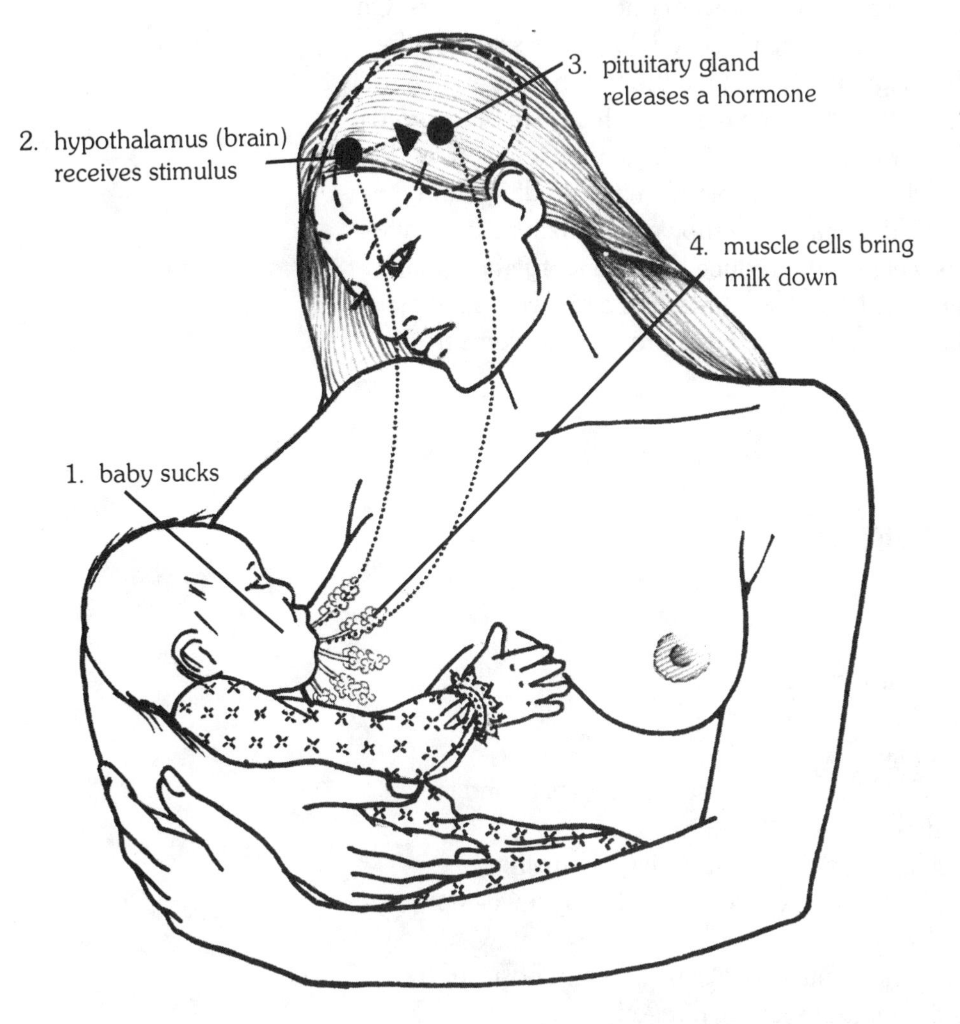
3. pituitary gland releases a hormone
2. hypothalamus (brain) receives stimulus
4. muscle cells bring milk down
1. baby sucks

The mother's breasts release milk, not in response to simple suction, but due to a complex reflex. In order for the letdown reflex to occur, the mother needs to be relaxed and perceive an appropriate stimulus. Thus the new mother may sometimes drip milk when the baby isn't nursing or may be unable to let down as soon as the baby starts to nurse.

milk production is the baby's sucking. The more frequently and longer the baby sucks, the more milk production is built up. Conversely, the shorter the time and less often the baby nurses, the less milk will be produced. Thus the more the mother nurses in the first days after birth, the more quickly her milk supply is built up.

Emotions and the mother's psychological state have a tremendous effect on the letdown reflex because they control the messages the hypothalamus sends to the pituitary gland. The letdown reflex is easily upset by anxiety and fear, as well as by confusion, distraction, and fatigue. This is especially true in the early days of nursing when the mother's reflex is not fully conditioned. The letdown reflex is promoted by rest, relaxation, and most important by confidence, and may be signaled by a tingling or burning sensation in the breasts, a sudden feeling of fullness in the breasts, and by milk dripping from one or both breasts. The mother may also experience uterine cramps because oxytocin stimulates the uterus as well as the alveoli to contract. Hearing the baby cry or even thinking about the baby may cause the letdown reflex to work, occasionally making milk squirt from the mother's breasts. If the baby is not going to nurse, the mother can stop the flow by pressing firmly on her breasts with the palm of her hand.

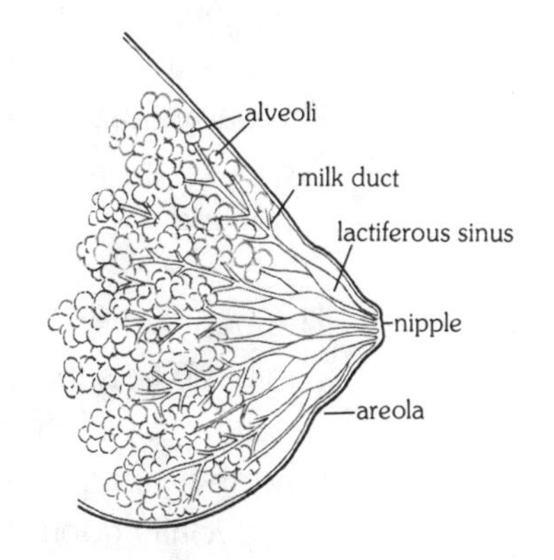
alveoli
milk duct
lactiferous sinus
nipple
areola

Milk is produced in alveoli of the breast, passes down the ducts, and collects in the sinuses behind the areola, the darkened portion of the nipple. Muscles around the ducts help to bring the milk to the nipple.

Letting the baby feed on demand ensures the baby is getting enough milk. There are wide variations in the baby's nursing demands, and it's not uncommon for newborns to want to nurse every one and a half hours. On an average, the newborn on a self-demand schedule nurses six times the first day, seven the second, eight the third, nine the fourth day, eight and a half the fifth day, eight the sixth, and seven the seventh day. In other words, the frequency tends to increase for the first few days, then level off, and eventually drop down. Studies now favor total demand feeding during the first week. The demand schedule has been shown to benefit milk production, maximize the baby's weight gain, reduce breast engorgement, and may reduce nipple tenderness. Night feedings in the early weeks are especially important to build up the milk supply and prevent problems from engorgement.

Information on nursing

Basic facts

Almost all women can nurse successfully.

Colostrum is secreted the first 1–4 days.

Milk comes in 3d–6th day.

Breast engorgement is likely when the first milk comes in and is possible in the first few weeks.

Sore nipples are most likely on the 4th–5th day of nursing.

Nursing is a learned skill. It can take mother and baby a week or more to become fairly skillful.

Worries and tenseness impair nursing. Relaxation and positive imagery stimulate the mother's *letdown reflex.*

The more the baby nurses, the more the mother's milk supply builds up.

The baby nurses more frequently and for longer periods during growth spurts; the milk supply increases in 1–3 days of heavy nursing.

The baby grasps most of areola in its mouth when nursing.

The baby gets most milk in the first 5–10 minutes of nursing.

A newborn with 5–6 wet diapers a day is getting enough milk.

A mother needs lots of fluids to produce milk. Milk and water are especially good for mother. Mother needs high-protein, high-calcium diet (see table pages 42–43). Note: brewer's yeast supplies large amounts of protein and B vitamins which are needed to fight fatigue and stress, which lower milk production.

Birth control pills reduce milk supply substantially, and some types actually alter the protein and fat composition of the milk.

Continued

How often and how long?

No single answer. Solutions range from feed on demand for as long as the baby nurses to feed on a timed schedule for a varying amount of time per side.

Mothers who have fair or sensitive skin and who have not done *nipple toughening exercises* during pregnancy should be careful of sore nipples from prolonged nursing in the baby's first days.

Initially try 7–10 minutes on the first side, a little longer on the other side. Time may be limited at first to prevent sore nipples in sensitive mothers. Gradually increase the time on each side until you and the baby are comfortable (10–15 minutes a side). At first baby will want to nurse every 2–3 hours, occasionally hourly, and occasionally with one longer stretch. Frequent nursing in the first days probably helps bring in the milk more quickly.

Positions for nursing

Mother sitting, mother lying down (see illustration).

Pillows are used to prop up mother and baby.

Continued

There are several common positions for nursing. Sometimes a baby will seem to prefer one or another. The new mother may find her nipples are less tender if she varies her position from feeding to feeding. Her breasts are less likely to become engorged if she alternates breasts at each feeding.

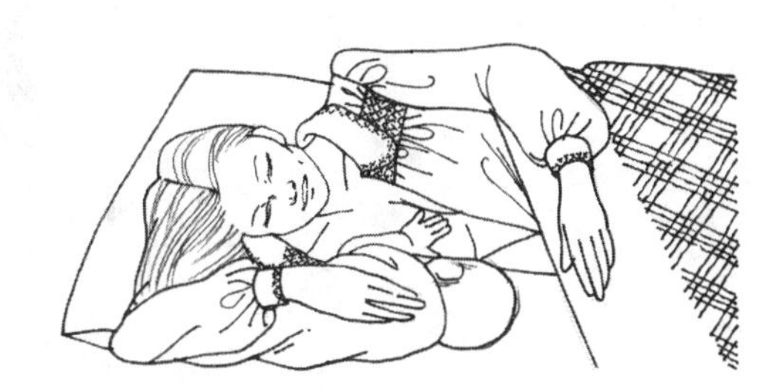

Babies don't like to have their nose covered or their head turned forcibly while nursing.

Mother can use her thumb and forefinger to squeeze areola and keep baby's nose free while nursing.

Problems getting the baby on the nipple in the early days

Both baby and mother can become frustrated if the baby has trouble getting on at the beginning of nursing. The mother should seek out a comfortable position and a quiet place to nurse and she should try to relax so her letdown reflex will work. Holding the nipple securely between two fingers, she should touch the baby at the corner of the mouth to stimulate its rooting reflex.

Newborns do not like something *stuck* in their mouths and may even try to spit out the nipple. Keep the baby's nose away from the breast by holding the nipple between two fingers.

Don't put the baby on when it is very excited. Put the baby on when it is just waking up or has been rested or soothed. This

Continued

Any initial problems with nursing usually pass within a few weeks. A sense of humor about it all helps keep things in good perspective until nursing becomes easy and relaxed. Rest on the Flight into Egypt *(1509), by Lucas Cranach the Elder, The Metropolitan Museum of Art, gift of Felix M. Warburg and his family, 1941.*

also prevents the baby from "jawing," or playing with the nipple and causing sore nipples.

Bundle the baby if its hands get in the way.
Try different positions for nursing.
Try the other breast.
Hand-express some milk if nipples are engorged.

Encourage the baby to take most of the areola in its mouth.
Get the baby sucking vigorously on an orthodontically shaped pacifier first, then gently remove the pacifier and put the baby on the nipple.

Tips for relieving engorgement in the early days of nursing

Use nursing bra for support.
Nurse frequently enough at both breasts to prevent engorgement (limit the amount the baby nurses on the first side, so the baby doesn't fall asleep and not nurse the second side).
Manually express or pump milk if necessary.

Tips for sore nipples during early nursing days

Give baby a pacifier between nursings.
Apply lanolin and mild creams to protect nipples.
Don't let baby chew on nipples.
Allow nipples to dry after nursing.
Sunbathe nipples.
Apply dry heat to nipples—a heater or even a light bulb will do.
Limit nursing to short times and try not to nurse more frequently than every couple of hours.
Avoid engorgement by not going long stretches between nursings or nursing on only one side at a feeding.
Change baby's nursing position to alter pressure on sore areas of nipple.

Sore nipples generally are most tender about 4–5 days after delivery if the baby feeds on demand; they will be tender later if the baby is kept to a schedule.

The baby does not physiologically "need" to eat for a day or so after birth. It is adequately provided with body water and does not yet really need nutrition (sugar, protein). The baby's food stores balance the fact that the mother's milk does not "come in" in any quantity for one to three days. This does not mean that the baby gets nothing from the early nursing or that it will be frustrated by such sucking.

The initial nursing time helps to develop the very important early bonding between mother and newborn. In turn, this bonding paves the way for a close mother-infant relationship. The early nursing also gives the baby a chance to perfect its nursing skills and stimulates an early and abundant supply of milk in the baby's mother. Finally, this early nursing supplies the baby with a substance called *colostrum,* which is present in the mother's breasts even before birth. Colostrum is a thick, yellowish, milky substance. It is higher in protein, vitamin A, and minerals than later breast milk, and lower in carbohydrates and fats. Colostrum is even easier to digest because of the lower fat content, and it has a mildly laxative effect which helps the baby clear its digestive tract of *meconium,* the early, greenish-black stools that have accumulated while in the uterus. The colostrum also contains antibodies which are thought to act directly in the bowel to help prevent infections in the newborn. In essence, colostrum seems to be the ideal starter food. It is secreted by the mother for one to four days and slowly changes to *transitional milk.* Transitional milk is secreted for the next two to three weeks, by which time it assumes the characteristics of mature breast milk. Just as colostrum is the ideal starter food, so mature breast milk is the ideal nourishment for the growing infant.

Hints for vegetarian nursers

Make sure you get extra calories and extra protein— extra milk is the usual source.

If milk is not used, combine grains to get complete protein.

Get extra calcium from large amounts of green leafy vegetables.

Composition of milk

	Human (average)	*Cow's (average)*	*Enfamil**	*Similac**	*Soyalac†*
Calories/oz	20	20	20	20	20
Protein (g/100 mg)	1.1	3.3	1.5	1.7	2.0
Carbohydrate (g/100 mg)	6.8	4.8	7.0	1.6	6.0
Fat (g/100 oz)	4.5	3.5	3.7	3.4	4.0
Minerals (g/100 mg)	0.2	0.7	0.35	0.38	0.28
Sodium (Na)	6.5	2.5	10.9	11.2	12.6
Potassium (K)	14	35	17.9	18.2	21.7
Calcium (Ca)	16.5	62	32	33	21
Chloride	12	29	11.3	15.1	
Phosphorus (P)	4.5	5.3	32	30	17

Milks also differ in vitamins, particle size, and curds.

*Artificial milks made from cow's milk. †Artificial milk made from soy protein.

Studies have shown that all (nonhuman) animals do best when they are fed milk from their own species. Breast milk has real differences from other milks. It may sound ridiculous to mention this, but humans are so adaptive and inventive that they have almost created a problem where nature has provided a solution. A study of the differences in carbohydrate, protein, fat, mineral, and vitamin content of specific animal milks leads to the common-sense conclusion that every species produces a milk tailored to the needs of its young. Myths as to the superiority of one or another animal milk over human milk stem from the relatively few instances in which a mother was unable to nurse because of being severely undernourished or ill. This is rarely the case today. The only medical reason for the baby not to breast-feed is if the mother has active tuberculosis, typhoid fever, or malaria.

There are a number of demonstrated advantages to breast-feeding. Breast-fed babies have fewer problems with food and feedings. It is not uncommon for babies to have allergic reactions to or difficulty in digesting cow's milk and prepared formulas. This accounts for the number of specialty formulas, such as soy milk, that are on the market. Studies show that infants fed cow's milk have seven times as great an incidence of eczema and a higher incidence of respiratory illnesses during the second six months of life. Studies have also shown that breast-fed babies are not as likely to become obese in later life. Obesity in the first six months is caused by the growth and multiplication of fat cells that is associated in later life with a tendency toward obesity and heart disease, strokes and high blood pressure.

Breast-fed babies actually have an entirely different normal group of bacteria living in their digestive tract, as well as a different acid-base balance in their digestive tract. Breast-fed babies' intestinal bacteria are mainly lactobacillis, similar to those found in yogurt and given to people with digestive problems. The bacteria in babies fed cow's milk are predominantly of the coliform family, of which certain *E. coli* varieties can cause serious infection and diarrhea in newborns. Like colostrum, breast milk contains antibodies against bacteria and viruses. These antibodies slow or stop the growth of disease-causing organisms, including influenza, encephalitis, polio, mumps, and *E. coli.* These antibodies have definitely been shown to protect infants while they are nursing, but do not provide protection after the baby is weaned.

Breast-feeding provides important psychological benefits for the newborn. It ensures that the newborn has prolonged physical contact with the mother, whom the baby has come to "know" while in the uterus. The baby recognizes the mother's heartbeat and other rhythms of her nervous system, as well as her voice, warmth, touch, and smell. This continuity would certainly seem to benefit the newborn's developing sense of security and trust in the outer world. Studies have shown that newborns actually have different patterns of sucking and breathing when they are sucking from the breast rather than from a bottle. Mothers who breast-fed their babies tended to touch, smile at, and rock their babies more often. Nursing moth-

Drugs and breast-feeding

Probably safe
acetaminophen (e.g., Tylenol)
amoxicillin
aspirin
digoxin
Dilantin
indomethacin
prednisone
propylthiouracil
theophylline

Probably safe, but may make the baby sleepy
codeine
methadone

Probably unsafe
alcohol
atropine
birth control pills
bromides
estrogen
Flagyl
narcotics
reserpine

Absolutely contraindicated
chloramphenicol
diethylstilbestrol
gold salts
immunosuppressants
iodides
meprobamate
tetracycline
thiouracil

ers tended to talk to the babies in gaps between sucking, and touch the babies while they were sucking. Bottle-feeding mothers tended to touch and talk to their infants randomly during feedings. In this study bottle-feedings were generally ended by the mother, whereas breast-feedings were ended equally by mother and newborn. Thus it would seem that the synchronized "dance" between mother and newborn that starts at birth and is later continued and added to during early feedings is altered by whether the baby is fed from the bottle or the breast.

Recommended daily allowances for nursing mothers

Good nutrition begins before birth—it begins with the mother and her food habits. If the mother enjoys a good diet throughout pregnancy, her baby will be well nourished at birth. And her baby will receive the best food possible in the early months if it is breast-fed. In order to give her baby the best start, it is important that the nursing mother maintains a diet that is adequate for herself as well as the baby. The nursing mother needs a third more calories and almost twice as much protein as a woman who is not nursing. She actually needs more protein and more calories than she did in the last three months of pregnancy.

Nutrient	*Nonpregnant need*	*Pregnant need*	*Nursing need*	*Food sources*
Protein	46 g	75–100 g	66–70 g	Milk, cheese, eggs, meat, grains, legumes, nuts
Calories	2100	2400	2600	Carbohydrates, fats (200–300 calories per day during the first three months after birth come from the mother's stored fat)
Minerals				
Calcium	800 mg	1200 mg	1200 mg	Milk, cheese, grains, leafy vegetables, egg yolks
Phosphorus	800 mg	1200 mg	1200 mg	Milk, cheese, lean meats
Iron	18 mg	18 mg + 30–60 mg supplement	18 mg	Liver, other meats, eggs, grains, leafy vegetables, nuts, dried fruits
Iodine	100 micrograms	125	150	Iodized salt, seafood

Continued

Nutrient	Nonpregnant need	Pregnant need	Nursing need	Food sources
Minerals (*Continued*)				
Magnesium	300 mg	450 mg	450 mg	Nuts, soybeans, cocoa, seafood, whole grains, dried peas
Vitamins				
A	4000 IU	5000 IU	6000 IU	Butter, cream, fortified margarine, green and yellow vegetables
D	0	400 IU	400 IU	Fortified milk, fortified margarine (and sunshine)
E	12 IU	15 IU	15 IU	Vegetable oils, leafy vegetables, cereal, meat, eggs, milk
C	45 mg	60 mg	80 mg	Citrus fruits, berries, melon, tomatoes, green vegetables, potatoes
Folic acid	400 micrograms	800	600	Liver, green vegetables
B complex:				
Niacin	13 mg	15 mg	18 mg	Meat, peanuts, beans, peas
Riboflavin	1.2 mg	1.5 mg	1.9 mg	Milk, liver, grains
Thiamin	1.0 mg	1.3 mg	1.4 mg	Meat, grains
B_6	2 mg	2.5 mg	2.5 mg	Grains, liver, meat
B_{12}	3 micrograms	4	4	Milk, eggs, meat, cheese

During the first four months of life, breast milk provides all the necessary nutrients that the growing baby needs. Often dentists and pediatricians recommend supplementary fluoride be given. Some pediatricians also recommend supplementary vitamin A, vitamin C, and iron. The C content of breast milk varies with maternal intake. The baby generally has adequate supplies of iron for at least the first four months. These supplies are stored up during the later months of pregnancy, and it is actually questionable whether iron from supplemental sources is absorbed by newborns.

Bottle-feeding

Although most pediatricians and pediatric organizations strongly recommend breast-feeding, particularly in the first weeks and months, there are mothers who choose to bottle-feed, either entirely or as a supplement. The reasons for this are many and varied: some women bottle-feed because of their work schedule, others because they fear that they will have problems, that nursing will adversely affect their breasts, or that nursing will limit their time. Many mothers breast-feed at first, but plan to wean the baby entirely after a few months. It is important to point out that experts encourage mothers to breast-feed initially, even if they only plan to do so for a short time.

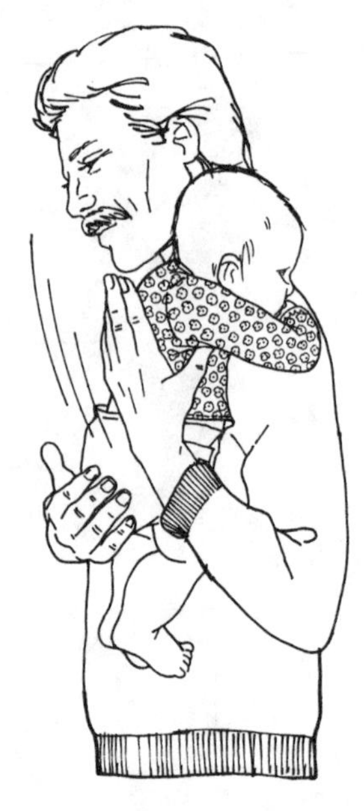

New babies often swallow air as they nurse and need help to burp or they can become uncomfortable. The classic method is to put the baby high up on one's shoulder and gently rub or pat the baby's back until it burps.

At this point, nutritional studies of bottle-fed and breast-fed babies show little difference because the commercial formulas are engineered to be similar to breast milk. Common formulas are made of nonfat cow's milk, demineralized whey, lactose, and soy and coconut oils. Basically, the scheduling and environment for bottle-feeding should be as much like breast-feeding as possible. The mother or care-giver should be relaxed, unhurried, and comfortable. The baby should be hungry and held in a comfortable position similar to nursing, that is, close to the mother and in eye contact with her. The bottle should not be propped up since that deprives the baby of sensual, interpersonal contact, and the baby is more likely to choke. Moreover, babies whose bottles are routinely propped up have a higher rate of ear infections.

Commercial formulas only require dilution with water, and refrigeration after opening. Bottles and nipples should be washed in hot, soapy water; they do not require sterilization. The new bottles have anatomically shaped nipples and collapsible plastic liners which lessen the amount of air the baby swallows. Pediatricians recommend heating the bottle to body temperature, although the baby is not harmed by drinking cooler milk. Before feeding, the temperature of the milk should always be tested on the skin on the inside of the wrist.

Pediatricians recommend feeding bottle-fed babies on demand, just as breast-fed babies are. This generally comes out to 6–9 feedings per day when the baby is a week old. The baby will be hungry every 2–4 hours, depending on the baby's stomach-emptying time. In general, bottle-fed babies feed less often than breast-fed babies, but are more likely to spit up a small amount at the end of a feeding. Feedings take from five minutes to a half hour. Each bottle should contain more than the average amount the baby drinks, but the baby should never be forced to finish the bottle. Full-term newborns consume about 1 ounce per feeding during the first few days. This increases to 2–4 ounces by 7–10 days. The feeding size goes up about 1–2 ounces per month, so that by five months the baby takes 6–8 ounces per feeding, eventually leveling off at 7–9 ounces. The number of feedings per day, which is 6–9 initially, drops to an average of 4–5 at two to five months, and 3–4 thereafter.

Cares and concerns of the first weeks

Especially for first-time parents there are many questions that arise in the first days after birth about practical matters of baby care. These questions usually take the form of "Am I doing this right?" "Should the baby be doing this now?" and "Is it normal for the baby to do this?" These questions arise because most first-time parents in our culture have actually had little or no practical experience in dealing with newborns. When new parents can't easily find answers to questions or solutions to problems, they may become confused and anxious. They want to do what's best for their baby, only they aren't sure what that is, or they can't decide which of two solutions seems better, or no solution seems to work.

Minor concerns and feelings of confusion and guilt can be magnified by several factors. First, in the days after birth the mother's body undergoes great hormonal changes which influence her mood and make her more emotional than usual. Second, both parents (and baby) are experiencing the stress of a radical change in living patterns. Finally, both parents are generally operating with much less sleep than usual, which also affects their moods. This lack of sleep follows the tremendous physical exertion and the emotional excitement of labor and delivery. What sleep the parents do get is periodically interrupted by demands of the newborn infant.

How new parents can avoid fatigue

Most new parents experience considerable fatigue in the first few weeks, due to extra work, extra company, stress, and lack of sleep. In general the more often the baby wakes at night, the more tired the parents are. Here are helpful suggestions to make things easier:

Take naps during the day *as soon* as the baby goes to sleep.

Go to sleep very early at night. It's only necessary for a few nights and it really helps.

Reduce or eliminate visitors—especially ones who are stressful—limit their stay, set the time and length of the stay in advance.

Make a conscious effort to rest; stay in bed; undertake nothing extra; simplify all household routines, especially meals, cleanup, and baby laundry.

Be alert to early signs of fatigue.

Get help from friends and relatives, especially for household tasks.

Adjust nutrition for increased stress—institute a nursing diet—try taking brewer's yeast (mother *and* father).

Make use of relaxation exercises, meditation, and imagery.

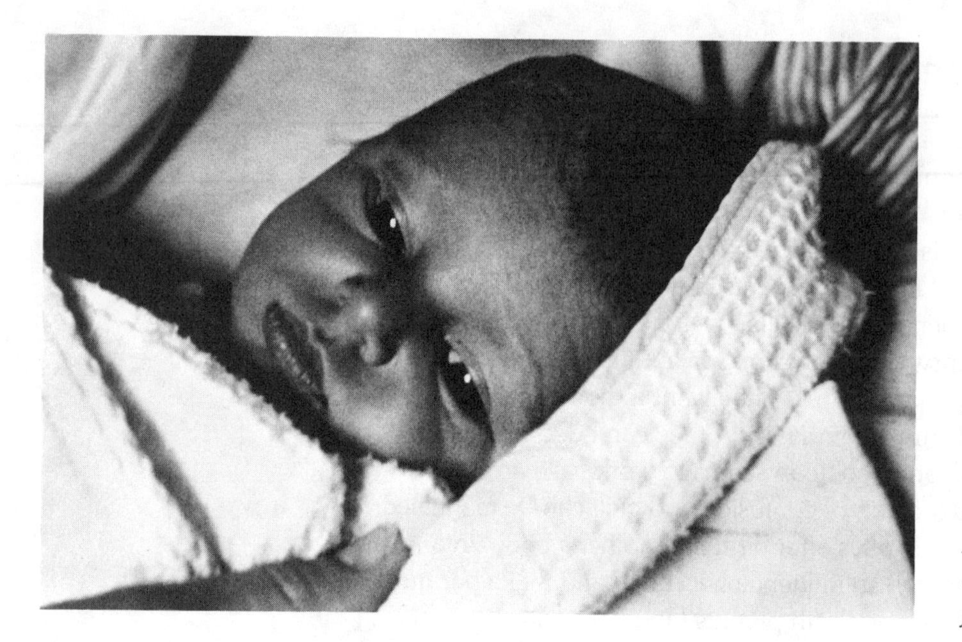

No matter how perfect or beautiful the newborn is, it always represents a radical change in the parents' life. Inevitably there are moments of anxiety and concern in the first few days.

Using relaxation after the baby is born

The first days after birth are generally joyful and exciting, but they can also be stressful and tiring. Relaxation and imagery are excellent tools for relieving tensions and making this the special time the parents have looked forward to. Relaxation is particularly helpful to the mother who is undergoing hormonal changes and adjusting to the new demands of nursing. Complete instructions for relaxation are given on pages 60–62 and for imagery, pages 62–70.

Mothers: Relax your whole body to relieve fatigue.

Mothers: Relax your whole body before nursing, to allow your letdown reflex to work—this is one of the most important uses of relaxation in this book.

Mothers: Relax your whole body, and specifically the pelvic area, to relieve postdelivery discomfort from the episiotomy and/or vaginal stretching.

Mothers and fathers: Relax your whole body to relieve worries and anxieties about the baby, and about being a parent.

Mothers and fathers: Relax your whole body when the baby is upset—it will help relax the baby as well.

Mothers and fathers: Relax your whole body to induce sleep.

Using imagery after the baby is born

Visualize	*In order to*	*For example, visualize*
A strong, healthy baby	Feel good about the baby and relieve inevitable moments of concern	Your baby, radiant, beautiful
Positive energy flowing into yourself and the baby	Make yourself and the baby strong	Yourself and the baby bathed in warm sunlight
Yourself in happy moments with your young baby	Maximize positive feelings about parenting and relieve moments of tension and doubt	Your most enjoyable times with your baby—nursing, falling asleep together, walking your baby
Yourself deftly taking care of your baby	Strengthen your confidence as a parent—especially in moments of confusion or frustration	Yourself expertly diapering and bathing your baby
Good nursing	Relax and help stimulate milk production and the letdown reflex	The milk coming down from the outer areas of the breast to the nipple; imagine your baby nursing hungrily
The baby being calm and quiet	Help soothe the baby when it is crying or overtired	The baby lying quietly, surrounded by peaceful energy

The whole situation results in a special state of consciousness which is unique to new parents. Characteristically they alternately experience moments of great elation and great depression. One moment they feel great pride and a sense of universal connectedness. The next moment they feel overwhelmed at the thought of the enormous responsibilities that lie ahead and wonder if they should ever have had a baby at all.

In this emotional state of mind, all parents at times tend to become greatly concerned about what are essentially minor physical points. The first reassuring fact for parents to remember when questions arise about the baby—as they inevitably do—is that the baby is basically healthy; otherwise the doctor who examined the baby after birth would have spoken to the parents. *The chances are extremely remote that any infant will suddenly become seriously ill or manifest a hidden abnormality in the days after birth.* This is a litany anxious parents can repeat to themselves until they can discuss anything that they are really concerned about with their doctor.

Whatever the baby is doing is most likely natural for that particular baby. And it's unlikely that whatever concerned parents do in response will hurt the babies, because babies are innately hardy. New mothers and fathers *naturally* have strong parental instincts which, when coupled with common sense, yield a reasonable solution to almost any problem. And new parents need to realize that a solution isn't necessarily wrong if it doesn't agree with baby books or relatives. In fact, researchers are finding that parents' intuitive solutions are often best. *Book solutions, which are generally theoretical, often change with the times.*

Taking care of the newborn

The newborn baby has approximately the same body temperature as an adult, but is unable to maintain its body temperature against cold external temperatures as well as an adult. Researchers speculate that this is because the newborn has a very thin layer of fat. In effect, the newborn baby is not "well insulated." A baby actually loses heat to the surrounding air four times as fast as an adult. In order to maintain its normal body temperature, the newborn needs an environment higher in temperature and narrower in range. Studies have shown that when babies are just born they need an external temperature between 88° and 92° F (31° and 34° C). For the *first two weeks* after birth, *naked* infants need a room temperature of at least 80° F. A receiving blanket wrapped around the baby raises the temperature around the baby by about ten degrees. For the first several weeks babies should be kept bundled, or parents should see that the baby's room is kept quite warm. Particular care should be taken when the baby is bathed, because the baby will tend to cool off even more quickly than normal due to the evaporation of water from its skin. The bathroom should be warmed with a heater and the newborn should be dried, wrapped, and warmed up reasonably quickly after its bath (see Newborn Bathing).

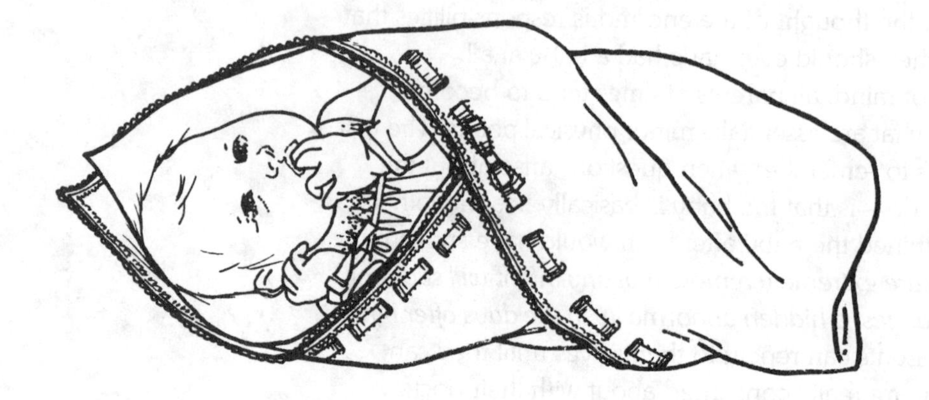

Newborns lose heat easily and need to be bundled up except in very warm temperatures.

Parents shouldn't be anxious about the baby's temperature, but they should be aware of the fact that newborns do lose heat much more quickly than an adult. Parents should not necessarily be upset if an infant's hands and feet feel cold. The infant's hands and feet are normally cooler than the rest of the body due to the infant's immature circulation. In fact, the hands and feet may even appear bluish for the first several weeks. To see if the infant is really getting cold, the parent should feel the infant's body, not its hands or feet.

There's no reason not to take the newborn outdoors for brief outings if the weather is warm or if the infant is well bundled. But parents should be aware that a strong wind effectively lowers the temperature. Actually, most parents instinctively tend to keep a newborn indoors and keep it well wrapped.

There is no need to bathe a baby for the first several days, or even very often after that. The baby's waxy vernix covering protects the skin for days if not washed off, and the vernix eventually comes off by itself. It's good to wash off the diaper area with warm water and a little mild soap after the baby has a bowel movement.

Newborn bathing

The bathing room should be warm.
The bath water should be approximately at body temperature.

All necessary supplies for the bath, and for later dressing, should be within easy reach. The newborn should never be left alone in the bath or on the changing table.

A wet, soapy baby is very slippery—and requires both hands of the parent. A baby can be soaped up while lying on the changing table, then rinsed off in a small amount of water (sponge bath). There are several inserts available to keep a baby from slipping in a bathtub. A baby can be bathed in the sink, in a small rectangular plastic tub that fits in the sink (the baby is less like to slip), in commercial baby bathtubs, in a bathinette, or in the regular tub with an adult.

Babies naturally fear lack of support.

Some babies don't like being on their back or their stomach. Other babies actually like being submerged and splashed.

Baths can be fun if the baby is bathed in a way that it likes.

Continued

When wet, newborns are very slippery, and they can easily become cold. Except for the diaper area, babies do not need bathing any more often than adults.

Most babies don't like to have their hair washed. Avoid shampoo in their eyes by giving them a sponge-bath shampoo while they are lying down on the changing table or in the tub. Moisten hair with a wet cloth; lather slightly. Scrub with a soft hairbrush to remove any flakes on the scalp *(cradle cap),* and rinse with a washcloth or cup. Don't be afraid of the soft spot.

Pat baby dry with a towel; don't scrub with the towel—especially around the diaper area. Baby towels are especially absorbent; some conveniently come with a hood.

Babies don't really need bath oil, lotion, powder, or creams unless they have a rash. But many babies love a gentle message with oil (avoid the oil if the baby has acnelike pimples).

Diapering

Disposable diapers—ecologically disastrous, but convenient; quite expensive, easy to put on, sometimes cause a rash in newborns. May leak around the legs, but generally soil less of the baby's other clothing; especially good for trips.

Cloth diapers—available in woven cotton, terry cloth, or flannel, prefolded or not, in different thicknesses; available from diaper services; must be washed fairly frequently; can be used with or without wool diaper covers or rubber pants; can be "custom-folded" to fit the baby (see illustration). May come with Velcro fastenings.

Diaper routine—change baby when wet or soiled. How often depends on the baby, the thickness of the diapers, whether or not the baby is changed at night. A newborn uses six to ten diapers a day. Double cloth diapers or nighttime disposables can go through the night.

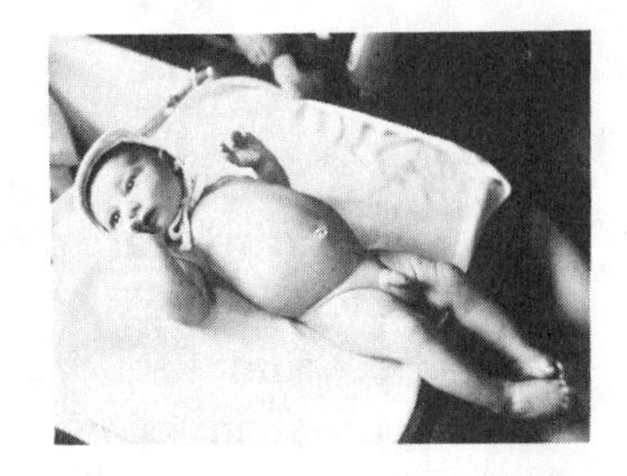

Diapering can be a play time for the newborn, who spends much of its time asleep. It is a chance for the baby to move its body and look about.

diaper folding for newborn

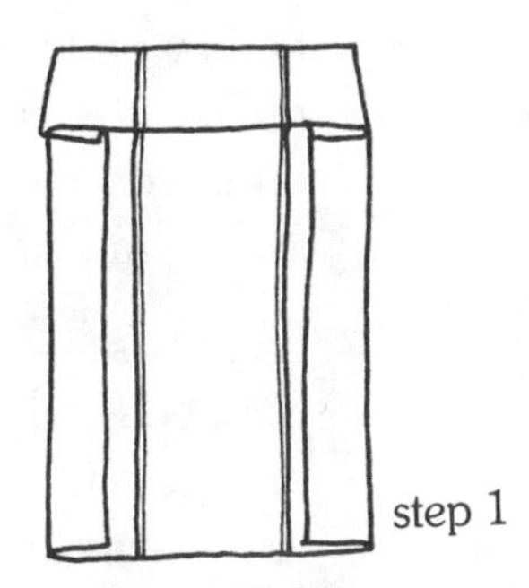

step 1

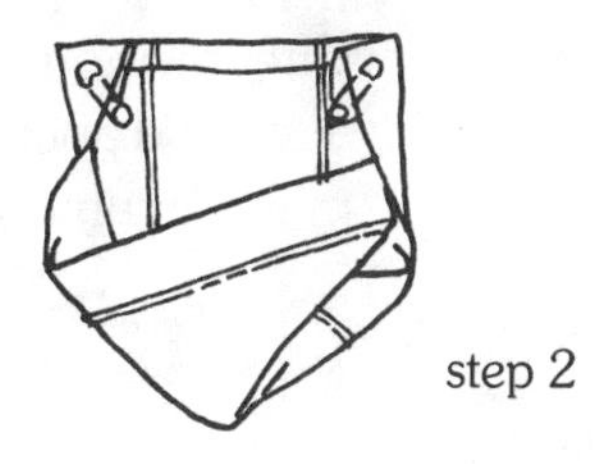

step 2

diaper folding for older baby

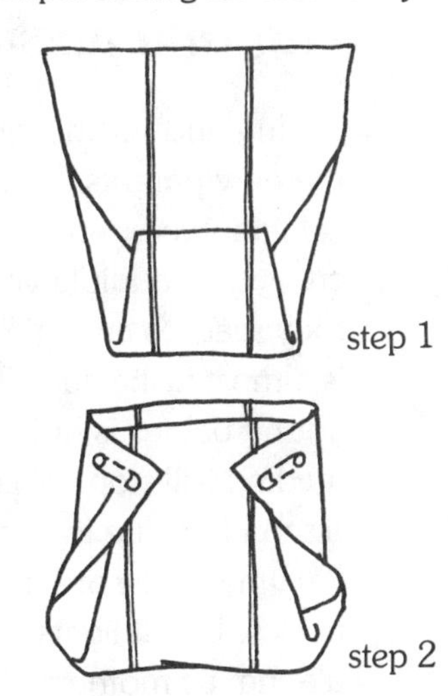

step 1

step 2

Cloth diapers can be folded in several ways to provide a "custom fit."

At this point, diapering poses an ethical dilemma for parents who are concerned about the environment, but who like the convenience of disposable diapers. Prior to toilet training, the average baby uses 8,000–10,000 diapers, a quantity representing ten to twenty trees per child. Disposable diapers now constitute 2 percent of the solid waste in landfills around the country. Disposables are made from a combination of wood pulp products and plastic, and estimates are that it will take up to five hundred years for them to decompose. Moreover, their disposal is introducing untreated fecal bacteria and viruses into groundwater and streams near landfills. It is not known how long the new so-called biodegradable diapers will take to decompose, but they still contribute to waste disposal problems and expense, and water pollution.

The alternatives to disposable diapers are washing diapers at home or using a diaper service. Cloth diapers are cheaper than disposables in the long run and cause fewer rashes. A 1988 consumer study showed that plastic diapers averaged 35 cents per diaper, whereas the average diaper service charged 7–11 cents per diaper, and home-washing cost 3 cents per diaper (after the initial investment). On a monthly basis this averaged $84 for disposables, $26 for diaper service, and $9.50 for home-washing.

Cloth diapers need a covering to prevent them from leaking and to minimize the baby's clothing changes. Plastic pants do prevent leaking, but they trap moisture and heat next to the baby's skin, and make diaper rashes more likely. Currently, many mothers use heavy wool diaper covers (e.g., *Biobottoms*) with cloth diapers. These covers have Velcro fastenings that eliminate the need for pins.

Everyday care

Cord care—falls off by itself due to bacterial action. Thus it naturally smells bad. The cord clamp should be removed by the second or third day. Cord stump should be kept clean and dry to prevent infection. Diaper should be kept below cord so as not to wet or rub. A small discharge can be cleaned with cotton and a little alcohol. Infections are uncommon. They are indicated by red, hot, swollen skin around the navel. Drops of blood, a scab, raw spots, or a smelly odor are all normal.

Fingernails—grow quickly and can cut the baby or scratch the mother during nursing. Parents can bite off nails gently or cut with blunt-ended scissors. Scissors are often hard to use because the baby won't hold still—scissors may be best used when the baby is drowsy. Many nightgowns and shirts for newborns have little flaps on the ends of the sleeves that can be flipped to prevent the baby from scratching itself while asleep.

Ears, nose—ear wax or nasal mucus, if excessive, can be gently removed with a cotton swab. Occasionally a small rubber bulb syringe is used to suction out the baby's nose if it is very congested and seems uncomfortable, or can't nurse.

Circumcision care—Vaseline should be applied to the incision line at each diaper change until healed. A few drops of blood are normal. Circumcisions rarely become infected.

Crying and fussiness—soothing the baby

Crying and soothing patterns are of great importance to the newborn and the new parents. To parents, crying is much more than a mere psychological variable or an observable state. Only a psychologist could describe crying as "audible vocalizations." Parents cannot simply observe crying; they react to crying. The need to soothe a fretful infant and stop the crying is almost instinctual. The most common reason for crying among very young babies is hunger. When hunger is the cause of crying, nothing but feeding will stop the crying for very long. Other causes of crying are physical discomfort due to heat, cold, gas, or uncomfortable clothes. And babies will cry when they are frightened or startled by such things as sudden loud noises, bright lights, cold hands, or cold water. Researchers are now speculating, as mothers and fathers long have, that newborns also cry out of need for affection or stimulation and in response to frustration.

All babies cry. It is their most potent means of attracting attention. Hearing their baby cry can be one of the most distressing things that new parents

Causes of crying

- Hunger, need to suck
- Pain—gas, indigestion, colic
- Discomfort—diaper rash, straining to defecate, too cold or too hot
- Wet diapers
- Fear—sudden movement, loud noises, precarious (unsupported) position
- Uncomfortable position
- Overstimulation
- Lack of body contact —need to be held and touched
- Boredom—lack of stimulation or attention
- Tension—from self or others
- Fatigue
- And, of course, the unknown

have to deal with. If the parents know why a baby cries, they can meet the need, but problems arise when new parents don't know why the baby cries and then wonder if it is wise to constantly soothe the baby. Sometimes new parents do not realize when the baby simply needs to be fed, burped, or changed; or they don't provide enough stimulation for a bored baby; or they overstimulate a tired or difficult baby.

Crying does not necessarily mean the baby is unhappy. Initially it is a means of attracting attention. Some researchers even believe crying is necessary to release tension. Most primitive cultures try to keep the baby from crying by very frequent nursing (as much as twelve times in three hours).

Recent studies by developmental psychologists and pediatricians have shown what "normal" crying is. In a study of eighty middle-class newborns, T. Berry Brazelton found that the *average* time spent crying was 2 hours a day at two weeks, increasing to a peak of 3 hours a day at six weeks, and dropping down to 1 hour a day by twelve weeks. All babies tended to cry most in the early evening, a particularly stressful time in many households. Other researchers have noted that parents vary greatly in how upset they become over "normal" crying.

Babies vary tremendously in temperament, in their ability to be soothed, and in what soothes them. Two personality types seem to engage in the most crying: the *difficult baby* and *the baby with a low sensory threshold.* In the case of a baby with a low sensory threshold, crying is often a matter of the baby being overwhelmed by too much sensory input.

Colic is a poorly defined condition in which an otherwise healthy baby cries excessively. Some pediatricians classify as colicky those babies who cry paroxysmally more than 3 hours a day, three days a week. Often these babies draw up their knees and have obvious gas, causing parents to report that the babies have abdominal discomfort. But no studies indicate any abdominal problem or that these babies are fundamentally different from other babies.

Happily, pediatricians have found that specific changes in care-giving will usually reduce excessive crying. New studies have shown that babies cry 25 percent less if they are carried next to an adult's body at least two hours a day or are suckled more often. If parents do both these things, the baby should experience a significant reduction in crying. Other experts suggest soothing the baby with a pacifier or a heating pad, and providing less stimulation in terms of external stimuli (light, noise, commotion), less frequent picking up and putting down of the baby, or repeated attempts to feed the baby. By changing their soothing routines and by being alert to what seems most effective with *their* baby, parents can expect to see a noticeable decrease in the baby's crying within 2–3 days.

Some babies seem to have a need to suck that goes beyond their need for nourishment. Pacifiers are one way to meet this need. Such babies may happily suck on a pacifier for long periods of time, and this activity seems to soothe them. Things that might ordinarily disturb the baby only result in

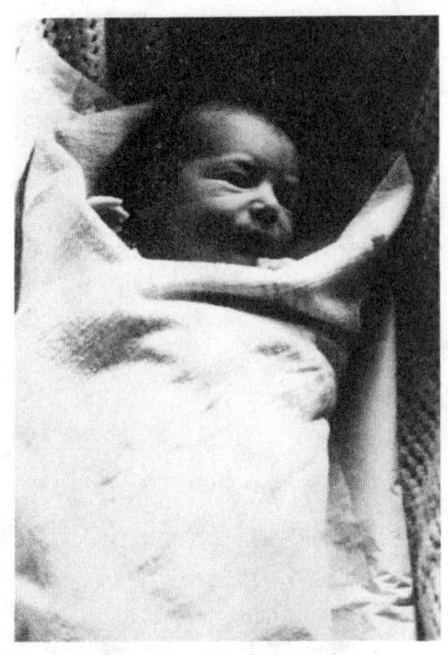

A baby can be soothed by many things—rocking, feeding, attention, or even being bundled up.

Soothing techniques

- Feed the baby
- Burp the baby
- Change diaper
- Pick up on shoulder —hold
- Rock the baby
- Walk the baby
- Pat baby while it lies on stomach
- Talk to baby
- Put baby where it can see action
- Distract baby— engage baby's attention visually with a moving object or with the sound of a music box (see page 147)
- Give the baby a pacifier
- Use heating pad or hot water bottle
- Play quiet, serene music

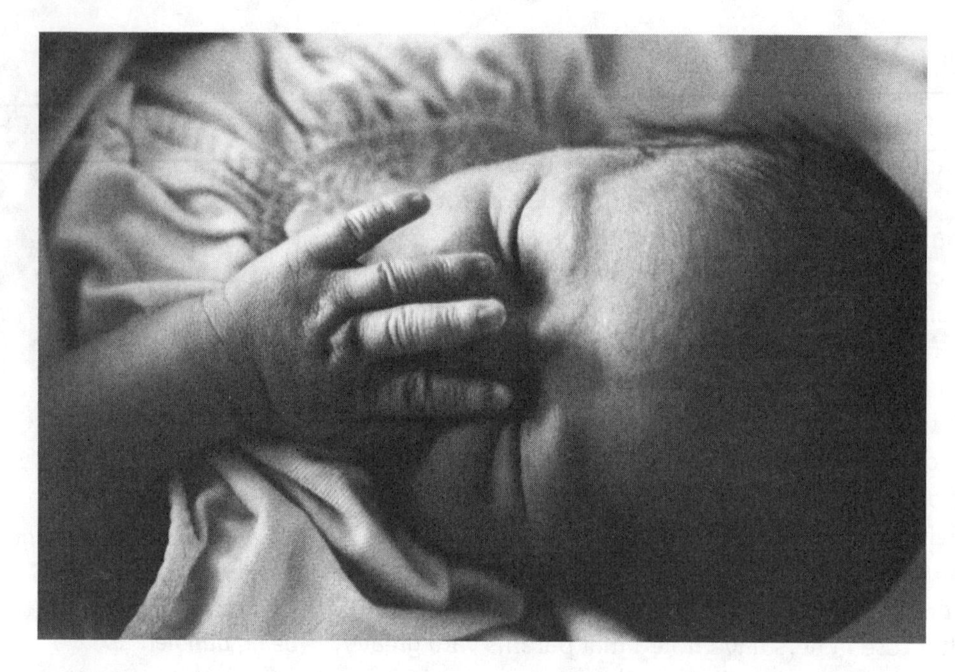

Newborns have strong sucking needs and often will happily suck for hours on their fingers, pacifiers, or toys.

more vigorous sucking on the pacifier. Some people feel that pacifiers cause dependence on objects and that babies who use pacifiers eventually learn to comfort themselves with the pacifier. It is true that very young babies can "lose" their pacifier, whereas they cannot "lose" their fingers. Babies generally lose interest in pacifiers between six months and a year if they are not encouraged to keep using them. To put it more accurately, the babies become equally interested in a wide variety of other objects when they begin to increase their manipulative skills. Care should always be taken not to give the baby the pacifier instead of food when the baby is actually hungry. Dentists recommend orthodontically shaped pacifiers to prevent causing later problems with alignment of the child's bite, but sucking on their thumb or a pacifier will not have adverse effects before the age of four, by which time most children have naturally given up this sucking.

Self-consoling behavior is a major developmental task of infancy. For a newborn, deliberately sucking on its fingers or a pacifier is truly the beginning of autonomy. These activities are a means by which the baby can make itself happy. Once babies master "non-nutritive sucking," they are less likely to cry.

Newborn capabilities

In the past ten years behavioral scientists have learned things that have literally changed their whole way of looking at the baby in the first few months of life. These new insights deal with the newborn's abilities and with the relationship between the instinctual behavior of the mother and the newborn. All of this information has important implications for the baby's health during infancy and later life. Basically, the studies show that the infant is incredibly capable, far more capable than was previously thought. It is now known that from birth the newborn can see, hear, smell, respond to touch, and learn—and can do these things remarkably well. Moreover, each infant is truly unique in its activity levels and responses. From the first, the infant forms a powerful social relationship with the mother and plays an active role in interacting with its environment. Likewise the mother, seeing and touching the baby right after birth, forms a profound bond with the infant which evokes maternal behavior.

As far back as the late 1930s researchers were beginning to learn about the responsiveness of the baby in the uterus. But most psychologists of that time held the view that the capabilities of the *newborn* were largely undeveloped and that the *newborn's behavior was entirely reflexive.* Even now there are major textbooks in child development that state that the newborn behaves as if it had no higher brain centers, that is, like a primitive reflexive animal. It is still taught in some medical schools that newborns cannot see in a meaningful way.

During the last decade we have learned that, to the contrary, infants only hours old have acute pattern vision. At a distance of ten inches, infants can resolve or focus on eighth-inch stripes. Infants fix their gaze on specific targets and deliberately choose to look at patterns rather than solid colors, and look at facelike patterns rather than others. Immediately after birth infants are truly capable of "seeing" a face at close range. This visual ability immediately fosters interaction with the mother, which in turn gives her pleasure and stimulates her maternal feelings.

The newborn's hearing abilities are also remarkably sharp. The newborn can tell the difference between two sounds which are only one note apart. They can even distinguish between sounds of different length, volume, and rhythm. Furthermore, as every parent knows, different kinds of sounds have different effects on the newborn. Rhythmic sounds of low pitch, such as the sound of a normal heartbeat, tend to soothe a baby. Sharp, high-pitched sounds tend to frighten babies and cause them to stop moving. It is probable that the newborn's reactions to sound are conditioned by months of hearing the mother's heartbeat and even her voice. One study has shown that in a nursery in which the sound of a normal heartbeat was continuously played, the newborns cried less, breathed more deeply, and gained more weight than another group who did not hear the heartbeat. We also know that newborns generally are more responsive to women's voices than to men's.

Newborns can also distinguish between different odors and tastes. Infants turn their heads and increase their activity levels in the presence of strong odors. By eight days of age they show a stronger tendency to turn toward the odor of their own mother rather than toward the odor of another person.

The newborn is capable of and actually learns, from the time of birth, and an increasing number of people even believe that babies learn while in the uterus (see Chapter 4, "The Baby Before Birth"). The baby's reactions

A partial list of the newborn's reflexes

Name	*To elicit*	*Baby's movements*	*Possible use to baby*
Moro, or startle	Suddenly change position, dropping baby's head backward, or make a loud noise next to baby	Throws out arms and legs, then pulls them back convulsively	Attempt to grab mother for protection, comfort
Root	Touch cheek or area around mouth	Turns head toward stimulus	Nursing aid
Suck	Touch mucous membranes inside of mouth	Sucks on object	Nursing aid
Grasp	Touch palm of hand or sole of foot	Closes hand or curls foot	To hold mother while feeding, being carried
Babinski	Stroke outside of sole of foot	Large toe curls up	Unknown
Hand to mouth	Stroke cheek *or* palm	Turns head toward stroke, bends arms up, and brings hand to mouth; mouth opens and sucks	Feeding aid; may help to clear baby's air passage
—	Bright light in eyes	Closes eyes	Protects eyes
Blink	Clap hands	Eyes close	Protects eyes
—	Cover mouth	Turns head away and flails arms	Prevents smothering
—	Stroke leg	Other leg crosses and pushes object away	Protection
Withdrawal	Give baby a painful stimulus	Baby withdraws	Protects baby
—	Place baby on belly	Holds head up, then turns	Prevents smothering
T N R (tonic neck reflex)	Turn baby's head to side	Whole body arches away, arm and leg move to "fencing" position	Helps in birth
Step	Stand baby	Baby walks	Practice walking movements

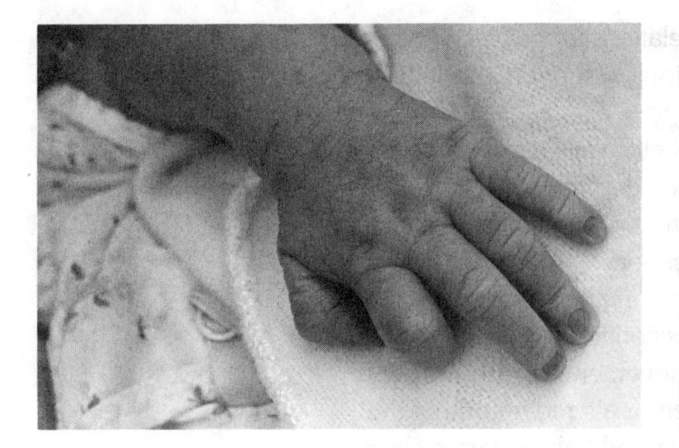

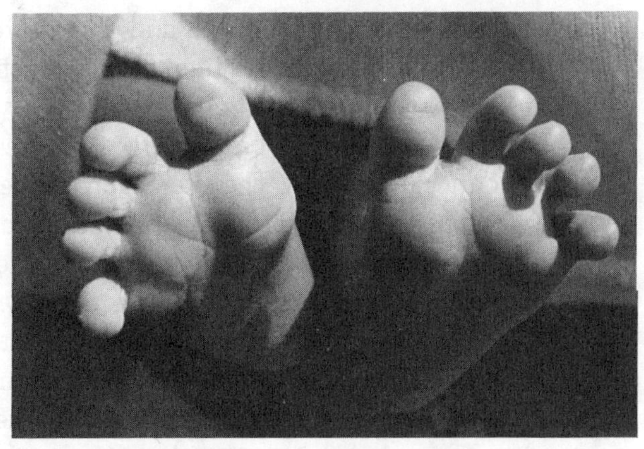

The newborn's hands and feet are always a source of amazement because they are so perfectly and minutely formed.

at birth to sound and other stimuli are not random. And the newborn learns by habituation, which is regarded as the simplest form of learning. That is, the baby eventually reacts to a repeated sight or sound with lessened interest. Thus we know that infants can store an event in memory and recognize when a change is made.

Infants even learn to adjust their sucking patterns to the supply of milk from a machine. The more milk at hand, the harder they will suck; whereas when the supply of milk is stopped, the infants stop their sucking. When the flow of milk from the valve is associated with the ringing of a bell, infants quickly learn to suck in response to the signal. Psychologists call this *Pavlovian conditioning.* Also, infants learn to turn their heads differently to right or left if milk is only presented to one side. Further, if right and left sides are paired to different sounds, infants learn to associate the proper side with each signal. This clearly goes well beyond reflexive behavior. What is even more striking is that the infants studied relaxed and smiled when they succeeded in turning their heads in the right direction. Babies who actually were too full to drink any more were still seen to turn their heads in the correct direction and smile! The younger the baby, the more trials it took to learn any new situation. Infants who failed to find the milk eventually started to show signs of distress—both by facial expression and by higher pulse and breathing rates. Some very distressed young infants responded to the frustrating situation by becoming completely motionless. Mothers who have carefully watched their babies in frustrating situations agree with these findings.

The mother-baby dance

At birth the baby has remarkable sensing and learning abilities, well-developed reflexes that foster survival, and inborn behaviors that assist the bonding interaction with the mother. All of these natural capacities instantly set up an intense social, emotional, and physical relationship between mother and baby. This relationship automatically functions to support and fulfill the deepest needs of both mother and baby.

From the first, mother-baby interaction takes place in a cyclic, synchronized, dancelike pattern. The interaction has been described by Dr. T. Berry Brazelton as consisting of several phases. *Initiation,* the first phase, consists of one of the partners engaging the other's attention. This first phase is immediately followed by *mutual orientation, greeting behavior,* or *play dialogue.* In these phases there is mutual interaction in the form of face-to-face smiles, noises, talk, and rhythmic circular movements. In the last phase, *disengagement,* the interchange is finally broken or altered by one of the parties. These early interactions between mother and baby occur in short cycles several times a minute. Brazelton speculates that the periods of interaction are brief because the baby would be overwhelmed by more continuous stimulation at this point. If the mother fails to respond for a time, the baby becomes concerned and repeatedly attempts to engage the mother again in their dialogue. If the baby cannot regain the mother's attention, it eventually withdraws and becomes motionless.

These cyclic patterns of interaction between mother and baby probably start in the uterus and are influenced by both physiological factors and sensations that the fetus experiences. For its whole uterine life the baby has been exposed to the mother's nervous patterns, and for months the baby has been stimulated by the sound of the mother's heartbeat and voice.

This highly complex, spontaneous relationship naturally sets itself up in the first few weeks after birth, without the conscious design of mother or baby. *Mother and baby will naturally develop their relationship* if not directed by well-meaning experts (be they relatives or physicians) and if given warm support. The process demonstrates why trust and positivity are the most useful guides for new parents.

Stimulation of the newborn

From the moment of birth the newborn is awesomely capable of interacting with its environment. The baby possesses remarkable inborn powers for getting stimulation and satisfaction from other people. The baby's parents, and particularly its mother, instinctively complement the baby's actions and answer its needs. Everything that happens to and around the newborn in the first few days and weeks provides the baby with stimulation, with material for its earliest learnings in the external world. In the first few days most parents instinctively tend to shield the baby from too much stimulation and from stimulation that is too strong. Such action is based in part on the parents' own feelings as well as on the baby's reactions themselves. Frequently in the days after birth the parents, and especially the mother, feel a need for rest, for a quiet time to adjust to the momentous physical and psychological changes of the last few days. For both the baby and the parents, birth represents a shock, a great change. A shattering of habits and expectations inevitably built up during the months of pregnancy now takes place. Such a shock is a gift—for only thus can parents and baby let go of old patterns and be ready to meet the new ways that will be necessary, that remain to be worked out. Unknown situations need to be met without fixed expectations, but with positivity and flexibility. This allows for the unparalleled learning that both parents and baby undertake in the first few weeks.

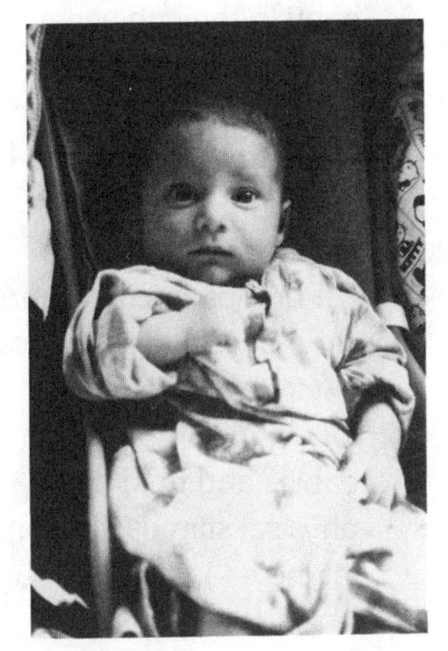

Newborns are remarkably capable and have a voracious appetite for new stimulation. Infant seats allow babies to spend more time in a vertical position, observing the world around them.

Although stripped bare of many habitual ways of acting, neither baby nor parent is left unprepared for this transition into a new life. The very lack of known ways allows instinct and deep emotion to guide behavior. These instincts and emotions, when allowed to function most naturally, produce a situation in which baby and parent fulfill each other's needs. It is the nature of instinct that both baby and parent basically act as they do spontaneously and without conscious effort. Cultural learnings and the parents' own upbringing definitely influence their behavior, but in addition, parents have a body of age-old knowledge and intuition that also guides them. By simply letting go and doing what feels right, parents naturally balance cultural and instinctual knowledge. The resulting interaction appears deceptively simple to an observer. In fact, psychologists are just now beginning to recognize the richness and the complexity of this early parent-child relationship. Psychiatrists have long speculated on the incredible importance of this relationship, but have largely confined themselves to speculation rather than to concrete observation and practical advice. The synchronous after-birth dance in which mother and infant engage each other's attention is one example of such deceptively simple interaction. Another such relationship concerns infants' body movements, which are synchronized to the speech of adults who are talking to them. Babies may appear to be making excited but random motions, but slow-motion analysis of sound movies shows that even one-day-old infants are actually moving parts of their bodies in a precise, shared rhythm with adult speech patterns. Thus we can conclude that newborns participate in the speech structure of their culture through millions of tiny gestures long before they talk. Mirroring the linguistic forms of adults, babies are building into their bodies the rhythms and nuances of language months before they learn to speak themselves.

Contrary to what researchers said for years, newborn babies are not only capable of taking in a wide variety of stimulation, they actually seek it out. The people, objects, and events that make up the household provide basic early stimulation for the newborn. These things can be an endless source of fascination for the baby, *if* the baby is allowed and encouraged to interact with them. All too often parents do not realize what social creatures young babies are and how much stimulation they crave. Sometimes parents simply concentrate on the infant's physical needs for nourishment, warmth, and cleanliness, without realizing the infant's needs for sensing social activity, and demonstrations of love. If a baby has to spend most of its time in a crib or carriage, it is environmentally as well as emotionally deprived. The baby in the crib generally hears and sees very little, is separated from outside social activities, and has no means of feeling the reassuring presence of its mother other than her voice. It is important to remember that during its life in the uterus the baby has been exposed to constant movement and touching, as well as to a constant sense of the mother via her heartbeat, respiration, and voice.

Perhaps the most important stimulation for the newborn is touch. In the early days after birth, touching of all kinds provides a link to the crowded environment of the last days in the uterus. Among animals, lack of early touching can be life-threatening. Human mothers naturally touch their babies and hold them against their skin. The babies' need for this kind of physical stimulation continues to be of great important throughout infancy—indeed, throughout life.

Stimulation of touch and movement

Nursing the baby
Giving the baby its hand or a pacifier
Holding the baby—especially against the skin—in a variety of positions (baby carriers allow parents to work while holding the baby)
Changing the baby's diapers
Bathing the baby
Rubbing or stroking the baby (massage)
Rocking the baby—in arms or in a cradle or carriage
Walking the baby
Taking the baby out in a car or carriage
Doing exercises with the baby—stretching the limbs, holding the baby in such a way that it can try to hold up its head, etc.
Touching the baby with different kinds of textures, materials
Allowing the older infant to experience different temperatures, wind, sunlight, etc.

Gentle exercise is good for the newborn. The baby's arms and legs can be bent in and then extended, alternately. Also, to encourage head control, the baby can be held upright while its head is slightly cradled. Such "exercises" promote muscle development and growth.

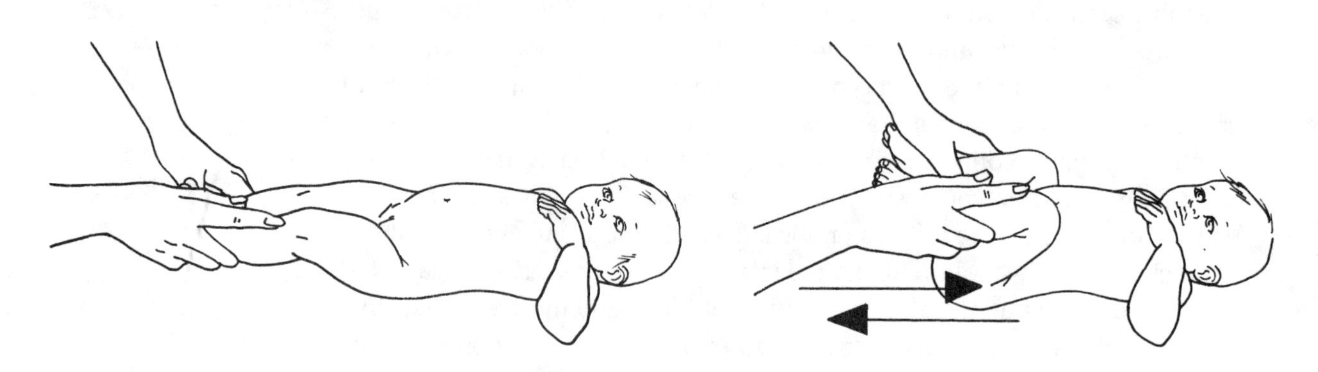

Like touching, noise or sound sensation is not entirely new to the newborn. During the last months in the uterus the baby's hearing has been functional and the baby has heard the mother's breathing, heartbeat, digestive sounds, and voice, as well as isolated loud sounds from the external environment. In the early days after birth the mother's voice, heartbeat, and breathing provide familiar sounds that link the baby to its earlier life in the uterus. Slow, gentle, rhythmic sounds tend to be soothing and may even lull the baby to sleep. Faster, louder rhythms and sounds tend to stimulate the baby. Sudden loud noises put a newborn on alert and frequently cause a full-body startle and sometimes crying. All babies love being talked to and sung to. Adults and children naturally seem to talk to babies in soft, high-pitched tones. It is no accident that baby talk, lullabies, and music boxes have been used for centuries to interest and soothe babies.

Forms of sound stimulation

Voices—especially the mother's (hearing conversation, as well as being talked to directly, stimulates language development)

Music boxes

Soft rhythmic sounds like the mother's heartbeat, clocks, the characteristic squeaks of a rocker or cradle

Rattles

Music

(Music mobiles, rattles, and faces in direct conversation all stimulate both the auditory and the visual sense systems.)

During the last months in the uterus the baby is already visually capable and may even see strong outside lights. Indeed, at birth newborns are capable of acute vision, but shut their eyes in very bright light. The newborn is most interested in complex objects—particularly human faces. Newborns prefer patterns to solid colors, and moving objects to still ones. In the first few weeks the baby's focus is limited to about 7½ inches (19 centimeters) away. Objects farther away or much closer are simply out of focus. Often when objects are brought much closer, the immature muscles of the eye cause the eyes to cross and stick or cause one eye to drift to one side. The newborn's large eyes and compelling gaze naturally cause most parents to stimulate the baby's vision.

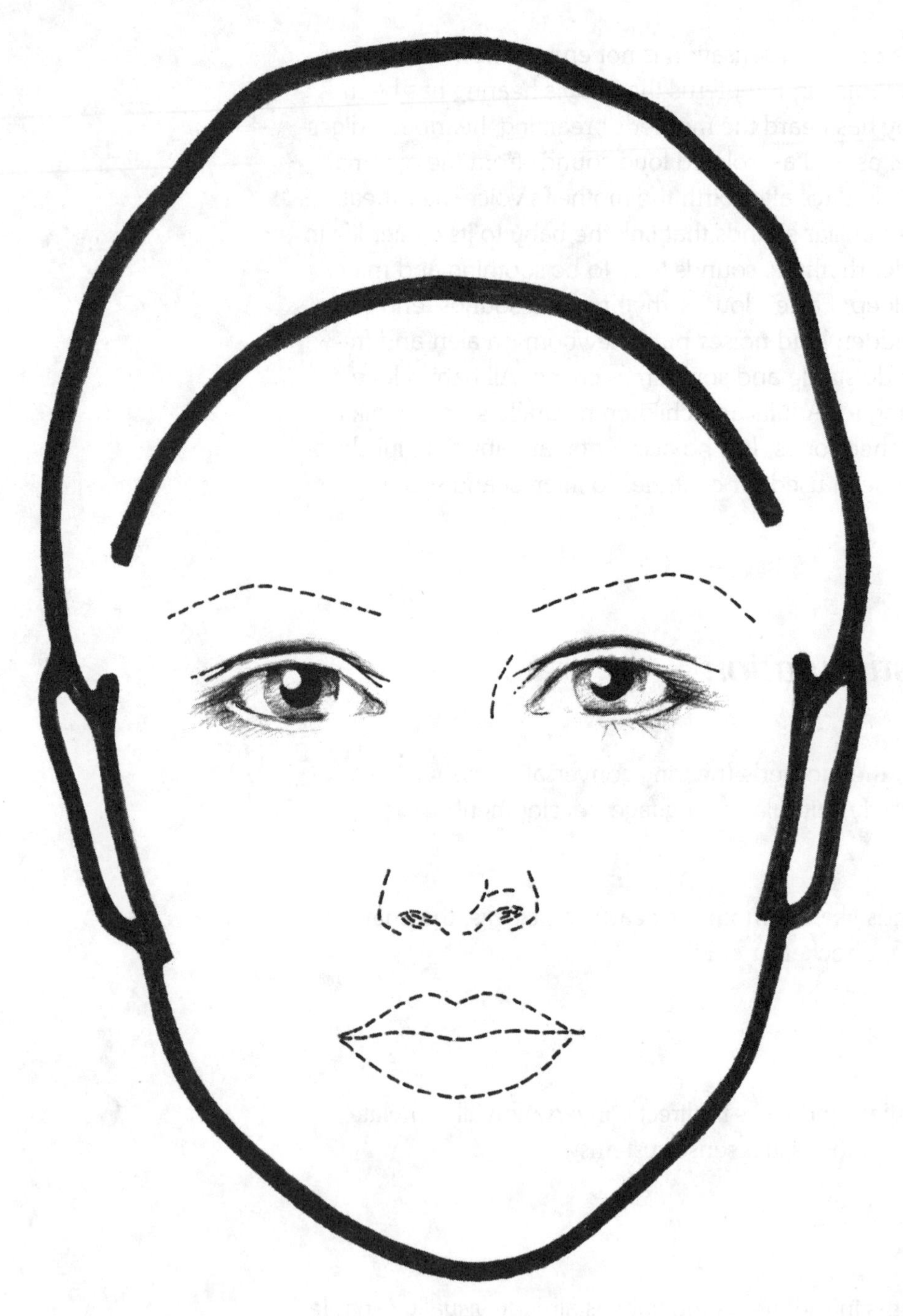

Newborns naturally look at round shapes with clear edges, such as faces, nipples, or targets. Gazing at a target is interesting for the newborn and stimulates visual development.

In general, newborns respond to stimuli that they like and withdraw from stimuli that don't interest them or which overwhelm them. Attention and inattention are the newborn's way of guiding the parents to what it wants and needs to grow and learn. Sensory stimulation can actually cause growth. For example, when a baby sees something, nerve cells grow and circuits are formed in the optic area of the brain; the muscles of the eye are exercised and produce more muscle fibers. Visual stimulation and exercise develop muscular coordination and greater perception and discrimination.

Kinds of visual stimulation

Targets and bull's-eye shapes (the mother's nipple and areola are a natural target).

People's faces in eye-to-eye contact—especially the mother's face while nursing.

Toys—especially with faces, human or animal that have large, staring eyes. (If such an object is placed within reach, the baby will soon be stimulated to try to touch or hit it.)

Moving objects—toys that wind up and move, mobiles, wiggling fingers.

Vertical and semivertical positions (for example, infant seats) encourage the baby to look about alertly.

Patterns—on pillows in the crib, in the shirts of people who hold the baby.

A variety of interesting objects in the crib and carriage—a single different object can be placed 3 to 4 inches from the baby whenever it is put down.

Generally red seems to be the color babies are most interested in.

Soft lights are very compelling—especially the boundary between a light and a dark background—even out of focus. (The light should never be too strong, as the baby will stare directly at it for long periods.)

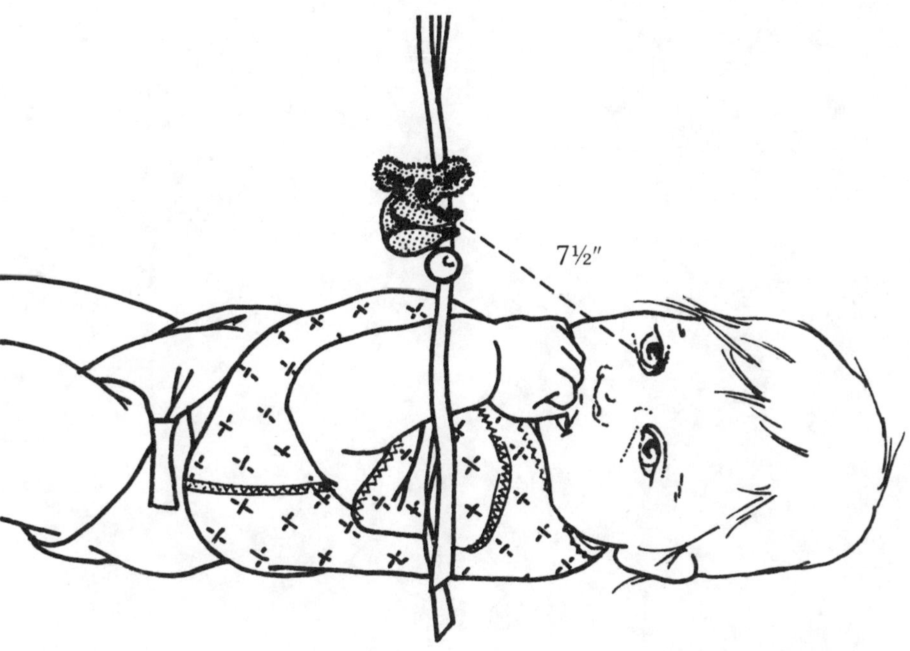

The newborn focuses best at a distance of 7½ inches. The baby will visually explore objects, such as doll faces, that are placed nearby in the crib.

What may appear to adults as random, purposeless, or uncoordinated activity is actually critical practice in developing adult sensory-mental skills. In a real way this kind of activity is the baby's work. The newborn phase of this work involves the baby's getting used to its body in relation to the external environment. From the beginning the baby's whole home environment plays a profound role in the way and rate at which the baby develops—physically, mentally, and socially.

Chapter 7

The first year: from newborn to toddler

Old patterns, new patterns

By the time the baby is two to three months old, the shocking newness of its presence has largely disappeared. By this time the parents know a great deal about their baby. Most situations that arise are familiar, and the parents have routines for dealing with them. These routines relieve much of the uncertainty and tension of the newborn period.

The poignancy of the early weeks, the intense alterations of mood, and the shattering of old habits are supplanted by a calmer period in which both parents and the baby can enjoy the comfort of familiar ways. The baby has made the initial adjustments to its body, has learned to deal with basic functions, and generally seems calmer and more relaxed. By this time the baby is good at feeding—the mother's letdown reflex works well and the

By the time the baby is three or four months old, the family is really beginning to feel itself a unit. The Fisherman's Family, *by Carl Anthony Tollefson, oil on canvas, 12" x 11". Collection, The Whitney Museum of American Art.*

Common concerns at four to six months

Thumb-sucking is normal and not harmful at this age and may be self-consoling.

Most parents start solid food in this period, beginning with cereal, then adding fruits and vegetables. The doctor may recommend supplementary iron, fluoride, and vitamins.

Separation anxiety is normal toward the end of this period.

By now, most babies sleep for at least one long stretch during the night.

Safety-proofing the house becomes essential as the baby begins to crawl.

Babies may be uncomfortable as teeth begin to erupt. Refrigerated pacifiers and teething biscuits may be helpful. Parents should begin to clean the baby's teeth at night with a wet cloth.

The baby gets the gift of the parents' whole lives. Textile hanging, Indian Notable, Wife and Child, *detail (c. 1615–1640), the Metropolitan Museum of Art, gift of Mrs. Albert Blum, 1920.*

baby takes the nipple or bottle readily. The baby's sleep patterns are becoming more predictable and the household has adjusted somewhat to the baby's cyclical waking and sleeping. The mother's body has readjusted to a nonpregnant state and she probably has all her customary energy back. If there are older brothers and sisters, they have, by now, begun to accept the continued physical presence of the new baby.

With renewed energy the whole household begins to take up many of its former pursuits, incorporating or making arrangements for the new baby. The baby, in turn, now becomes more of a participating member of the family. With a first baby, parents undergo a joint metamorphosis, from independent adults to a family with the responsibilities and interests of one nonadult member. At this point the work of the parents involves creating a life-style which continues to allow for the fulfillment and growth of each parent, and which also meets the physical and emotional needs of the baby.

The happier and more fulfilled the parents are in their own lives, the better a model they will provide and the more energy and enthusiasm they will bring to meeting the baby's needs. In addition to giving the baby the gift of life, the parents give the baby the gift of their own lives. The baby spends its time enmeshed in and absorbing all aspects of the parents' lives without any conscious effort on their part. The baby experiences the way the parents react to the world, sensing when they are happy or unhappy, energized or tired, relaxed or anxious. The baby experiences the basic rhythms of the household and the physical environment of the parents—the sights and sounds of the home and the neighborhood. The baby also observes and absorbs the way in which the parents deal with new experiences and stressful events. The baby learns how the parents handle such situations—when they become alert or tense and how they finally relax.

Of course, the baby takes in the parents' whole lives in a nonjudgmental manner. To some extent the baby is the recipient of responses, objects, and life-styles that have passed from one generation to another as parents act and react in ways taught to them by *their* parents. All parents have aspects of their lives that please them and aspects that do not—both are assimilated by the baby. Thus the parents' happiness is not only important to themselves, it is the root of the baby's happiness. Rather than sacrifice themselves for their baby, parents need to *fulfill* themselves for their baby.

As the baby passes out of the newborn stage and its needs and abilities change, the parents are confronted with continuing choices. As the baby's needs change, so do the parents' responsibilities. Parents will also find their own needs and interests changing—in expected and unexpected ways. A mother who had expected to resume work quite quickly may find she still wants to focus primarily on taking care of the baby. On the other hand, a woman who intended only to take care of the baby may find herself drawn to outside activities not concerned with her infant. A father may find that, with the lower tension of the postnewborn period, he tends to spend more time taking care of the baby and playing with it. The important thing is that both parents find a balance between their own needs and those of the baby.

Common concerns at nine to twelve months

Babies can begin eating table foods and feeding themselves finger foods (a messy but important step). Babies should not be allowed to eat tiny, hard, round foods like peanuts or carrot sticks. Parents can start to introduce potentially allergic foods such as orange juice, cow's milk, and eggs.

Babies can begin drinking from a cup. They can manage a cup with a spout by themselves.

Safety devices at stairs, doors, and windows become essential as the baby becomes increasingly mobile. Tables need to be cleared of tablecloths and objects that the baby can pull down. The baby has to be protected from heaters, fireplaces, plugs, and food on the stove.

Landmarks of development

All babies learn basic motor skills more or less in the same sequence, but all babies do not master these skills at similar ages. In fact, babies vary *widely* in the age at which they achieve certain physical landmarks—so widely that it is difficult even to make a chart of averages that accurately reflects what any real infant will do. A real baby always does some things earlier and some things later than an average chart shows, because age of accomplishment varies with both environment and genetics. Child-rearing practices can accelerate landmarks in all babies, but nonetheless, some babies will still naturally achieve a particular landmark earlier than others.

Babies do not always learn at a constant rate. They often learn in spurts and jumps that are sometimes quite dramatic. A baby who has never rolled over can literally be rolling over quite deliberately and skillfully within a week.

Parents often attach great significance to the age at which their child achieves a certain landmark. They feel proud if the baby is "early" or worry if the baby is "late." Neither feeling is particularly justified. All normal babies reach the landmarks at some point. Early achievement is not necessarily an indication of greater intelligence or coordination, nor does late achievement always indicate retardation or disease. Often a baby who is slow in one area, for example, large movements, is concentrating on another area, such as developing its visual ability. Sometimes slowness in a particular area simply indicates lack of stimulation in that area.

Big muscle control and movement

There are three general guidelines that characterize infant growth and development. The first rule is that *control of movement proceeds from the head downward;* second, *motor control of the limbs develops down the limbs,* for example, arms before wrists and wrists before fingers; third, *movements progress from general to specific,* from diving at an object to reaching for the object with one hand.

Motor development actually begins in the uterus, as early as parts of the body are being differentiated and formed. The first flutters that an expectant mother feels around the sixteenth to eighteenth week are actually graceful, flowing movements of the baby's limbs and body. But even before this, as early as nine weeks, a fetus is making swimming movements. All the movements that babies make in the uterus contribute to their muscular capabilities at the time of birth. Indeed, the amount of motor control babies have at birth is quite remarkable. When placed on their stomach, newborns can turn their head from side to side, and thus prevent themselves from being suffocated. By about one month babies can lift their heads slightly off the surface on which they're lying. By this time also, babies' movements and posture have become more relaxed than at birth, when they were somewhat stiff and jerky.

During the next several months babies continue to perfect their head control. First, babies begin to lift their head higher and higher while lying on their stomach. Somewhere around three months, babies are able to raise their chest as well as their head by putting their arms out in front and pushing. Soon the baby will be able to hold its head fully upright and turn it from side to side.

During this same period the baby will also be gaining control of its head when propped in a sitting position or held upright. At first the baby's head simply flops from side to side and needs support. As the baby gains control over the large muscles in the neck, it will be able to hold its head steady in an upright position for longer and longer periods of time. By about three months the baby will be able to steady its head when propped in a sitting position. At first the baby's head will bob forward and back, then remain steady and tilted slightly forward, and finally remain steady and perfectly upright.

For the first several months the baby's head will fall backward if the baby is lifted up or pulled to a sitting position by the arms. This is usually the last type of head control to be fully mastered and is probably the hardest. As the baby perfects other head movements, the "head lag" when being

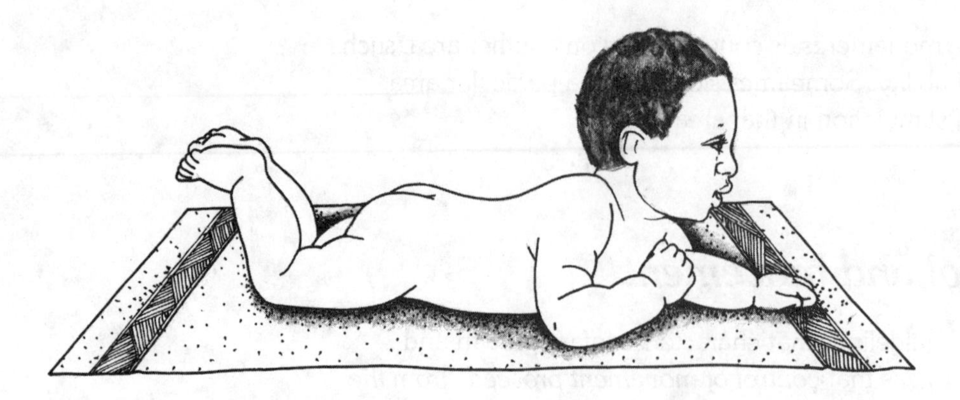
The first important motor landmark of the newborn is learning to steady and lift its head.

pulled upright will gradually diminish. At this stage some babies love being pulled to a sitting position and will laugh delightedly as many times as this "game" is repeated.

Head control is no small achievement for a baby. Compared to an adult, the baby's head is four times bigger in proportion to the body. For adults it would be like trying to move about with a large, heavy object on top of their head. Head control greatly expands the young baby's world, which is largely visual because the baby lacks mobility. With increasing head control, a baby can take in more and more visual information. Greater head control also means a baby can be more selective about what it looks at.

Head control also has another advantage for the babies. It actually helps a baby learn to roll over from stomach to back. Babies first manage to roll over from front to back by using the head as a kind of pendulum. Once babies can lift their head up quite high, they can tilt their head to one side and use the weight to pull their whole body over. Often the baby rolls over initially by accident. The baby may be quite surprised, even a little frightened, when it happens for the first time.

Crawling is a highly variable motor landmark. Some babies crawl early, others hardly crawl at all.

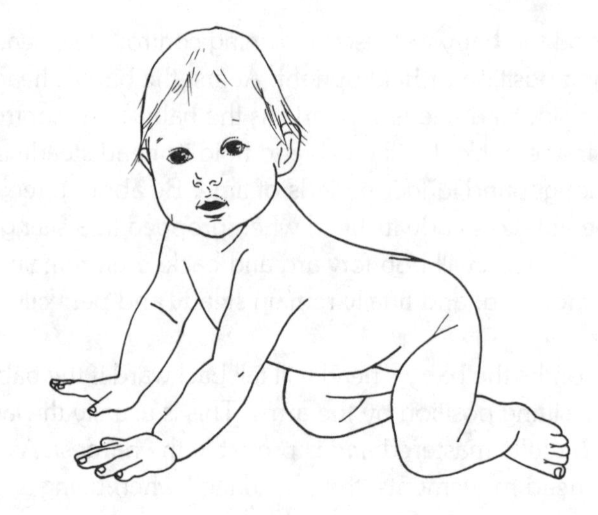

Rolling over from back to front generally follows rolling over from front to back. It is probably more difficult, and it only happens by accident when the baby is on a sloping surface. Rolling over represents a giant advance in mobility for the baby, but adds an extra burden to the parents' responsibilities. The parents must now be especially careful to see that the infant does not roll off any high surface such as a bed or changing table.

Sitting is an important landmark that makes playing alone much easier for the baby.

During this time period the baby learns to sit without support, which is another big advance. It enables the baby to use both hands to play with objects and to observe the world for longer periods with less exertion. The sitting baby is more like other family members now as it confidently sits, looks around, and absorbs all.

Next comes crawling. Babies vary greatly in their achievement age and style of crawling. In fact, crawling is not usually listed as a developmental landmark just because the variability is so great. Some babies crawl a lot, some never. Sometimes a baby who has worked out a very effective means of crawling will walk later than a noncrawler who has no other means of locomotion.

The last gross motor skill to develop during this stage is walking. Walking actually begins with the baby's ability to stand and bear weight on its legs, which starts when the baby can be supported in a standing position. In the early months babies are only able to bear part of their weight and only for brief periods. By around six months most babies are able to bear their own weight fully while they are standing, if someone steadies them. Often babies will flex their knees momentarily, then return to a standing position. Once babies have really mastered standing, they soon learn to pull themselves up and stand alone by holding on to furniture. Most babies enjoy the sense of power they feel at being able to stand and often become tremendously excited, bouncing up and down and squealing as they hold on. As they gain confidence in their balance, they will begin to let go of their support and stand momentarily without help of any kind. Some babies will then learn to stoop and recover; others will simply grab back onto their support.

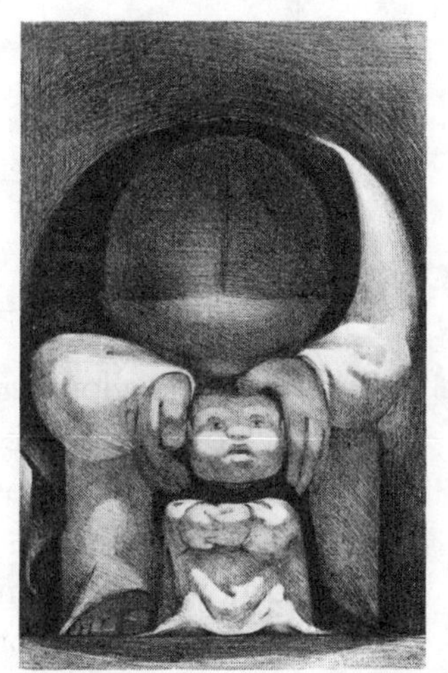

The parent hovers over the baby—alternately worrying and giving encouragement as the baby is about to take its first steps. First Steps, *by Jean Charlot. Lithograph, The Metropolitan Museum of Art, Harris Brisbane Dick Fund, 1940.*

The next development is for the baby to begin walking with help—either by moving from one piece of furniture to another or by holding on to an adult's hands. Babies sometimes begin to walk with support as soon as they learn to stand with support, but most babies spend a long time just viewing the world from the vantage point of their new upright position.

Somewhere between ten and sixteen months most babies learn to walk well with no support at all. There is great variation in how long each baby spends in the various prewalking stages and in the exact sequence of stages a particular baby undertakes. Some babies even approach walking from a high crawling position. That is, they begin to stand by pushing themselves up from a crawl. This method provides no support for their hands and inevitably seems to involve a number of falls. Walking represents a great step forward for a baby, both literally and figuratively, because it makes a baby truly mobile for the first time in its life and gives the baby its first real sense of independence.

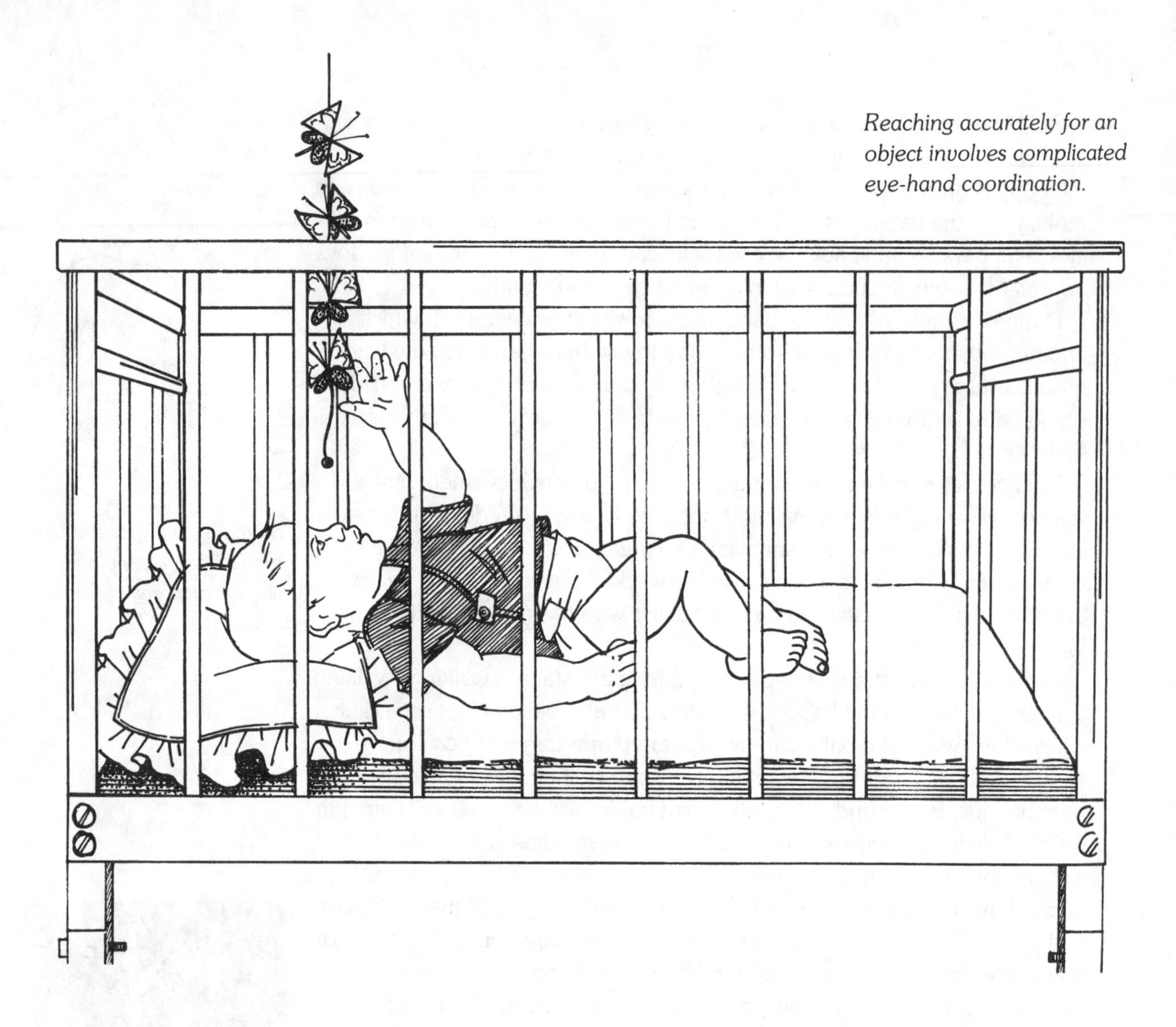

Reaching accurately for an object involves complicated eye-hand coordination.

Fine muscle control and movement

Fine motor development largely refers to eye-hand coordination. The significance of eye-hand coordination cannot be overemphasized. It is one of the human species' most distinctive characteristics and it is linked to the complex developments of the human brain.

Fine motor development begins in the first days after birth and progresses alongside the gross motor landmarks, but not necessarily in conjunction with them. The newborn learns to fix its eyes or stare, and subsequently learns to follow moving objects with its eyes. In the first several months the baby learns to follow an object a short distance to the left or right, and finally learns to follow an object across its whole field of vision from one side to the other. At the same time the baby learns to move its head as it follows objects with its eyes.

Babies are actually born with a well-developed grasp reflex; if you stroke their palms, they will automatically curl their fingers tightly around the stroking object. Gradually the baby learns to grasp objects deliberately as well. While the baby is perfecting its voluntary grasp, it is also figuring out how to reach out. The baby is not only learning to control the muscles of the arm and hand and explore by touch, it is learning to coordinate arm-hand movements with the visual images it sees. At about three months all this work culminates in the baby's ability to see an object, reach out, grasp the object, and hold it for a minute. Having mastered grasping, the baby then learns to pull an object to it so that it can proceed to find out more about the object with its mouth. Often babies are able to grab an object and get it to their mouth much earlier than three months. Generally they do so with a series of movements consisting of swipes and grabs.

By around the middle of the first year babies' fine motor development is such that they can see a tiny object such as a raisin and rake it in with their fingers. Around this time babies also begin to oppose thumb and palm, thereby greatly improving their ability to grab large objects. This is the beginning of the true grasp that is characteristic of humans and other primates. The infant later adds two other hand skills to its developing repertoire. It learns to reach out with both hands and grab two objects simultaneously, and it learns to pass an object from one hand to the other.

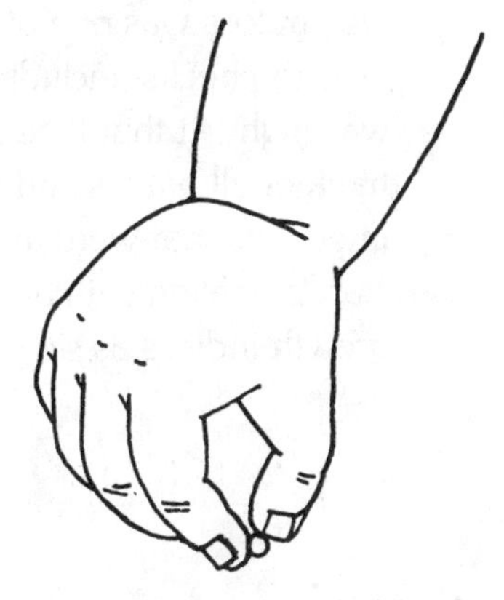

Opposing thumb to forefinger in pincer fashion enables the baby to pick up small objects and represents the beginning of true fine-motor development.

Between about six and nine months the baby begins to poke at objects with its forefinger and to oppose thumb and forefinger in a pincerlike movement. The latter movement is the forerunner of the ability to grasp tiny objects and it is the beginning of truly fine motor coordination. At first the baby will need to rest the side of its hand on a flat surface as it pinches the tiny object, but in a few months the baby will be able to reach out neatly and pluck up small things.

Growth patterns

Infant growth charts indicate the relationship of a mythical average infant to all the infants in a culture. Such charts represent a true average—some children are bigger, some are smaller. The average figures for all babies for each month in the first year go to make up a growth curve. The most commonly used growth charts plot weight, height, and head circumference, and show curves for small, medium, and large babies.

Charts represent averages—every baby is unique! Every baby will approximately follow the pattern, but probably not exactly. Real babies grow in spurts; therefore sometimes a baby may be above the average curve, at other times below it. In truth, every baby will have its own individual curve, which is dependent on a number of factors: the actual number of weeks the baby is at birth (gestational age), the size of the baby at birth, the baby's body type, and the baby's genetic background (both the size of the parents and the way in which they grew). The baby's diet, exercise, activity level, and health also affect the curve. With all of these factors at work, no two children grow exactly alike. Not even two siblings will grow exactly alike, although they may grow along *similar* curves. And one growth pattern is not necessarily "healthier" than another.

In general, parents are more concerned about growth increments, especially about weight gain, than the pediatrician is. Parents often view weight gain as an indication of their parenting ability and a measure of the child's total wellness. The cultural philosophy on babies seems to be "bigger is better." No doubt this is left over from a time when it was not uncommon for babies to become severely ill in infancy due to diseases now rare, and weight loss was one of the earliest indications that a baby was ill. Periodic growth checks, including weighing, were instituted when infant mortality was high. At that time checking growth became society's way of keeping track of all babies and finding those who were sick due to spoiled milk or infections that were the result of unsanitary conditions. Today the pediatrician is dealing with an entirely different situation, and views the baby's growth indices as simply one factor in assessing the baby's overall health.

Rough rules of growth

Doctors have worked out many rules of thumb in order to have some simple way of describing growth that will cover most babies. These "formulas" apply to *all* babies even less than the growth curves. They are included here mostly because they are fun, not because they are a true indication of health or normal growth.

"At birth the average infant weighs 3333 grams—or 7 pounds 5 ounces."

"The baby loses 10 percent of its birth weight in the first few days and regains it by about ten days."

"The baby gains about 1 ounce a day during its first few months."

"From three months to a year, the weight of the baby in pounds is equal to its age in months plus eleven."

"The baby doubles its birth weight between four and six months of age, triples its weight at the end of a year, and quadruples it at the end of two years."

"The average baby is 20 inches at birth and grows 10 inches the first year, 5 inches the second year."

Babies gain a relatively large amount of weight per month for the first six months. The rate of gain slows down between six and twelve months, then slows down even more after twelve months. If babies continued to gain weight at their initial rate, they would weigh over five hundred pounds by the age of twenty!

All babies are fairly close in weight and length at birth. The range between light and heavy, short and tall, increases continuously throughout the first twelve months. Thus the average growth curves are roughly similar at the start, but diverge more and more.

First year nutrition: starting solid foods

Frequently it is the pediatrician who determines the infant's diet, going so far as to specify exactly what the infant "should" be eating, especially in the early months. All pediatricians have a feeding schedule, but they often differ widely in what foods they recommend and when they suggest introducing them. These schedules are mostly a matter of experience and personal preference rather than scientific research. In fact, there is no one "right" feeding schedule that has been *proved* best for babies.

Since the early part of this century doctors have tended to introduce solid foods earlier and earlier and in almost all cases babies have prospered. But the practice of very early feeding of solids is open to question because studies of stool samples show that most of the food passes through undigested. The young baby is not able to break down the complex molecules in many fats, carbohydrates, and protein. Milk is certainly nutritionally superior to the cereal, vegetables, and fruits which may be introduced in the first few months, and it is more easily digested.

If a very young baby is fed a great deal of solid food, it can even interfere with the baby's milk consumption. Most very young babies probably spit out a lot of the solids they are fed. Babies don't develop the ability to swallow voluntarily until about three months, which makes it difficult, if not impossible, to feed them solids until then.

When should solid foods be started? Medically there is no *one* age at which solid foods should be introduced. Milk provides adequate nutrition for the first half year. For most babies the introduction of solid foods is largely a matter of individual choice—the baby's and the mother's. Many experienced mothers feel that babies indicate in some way when they are ready for something more than milk. A baby may begin to appear still hungry at the end of its regular feeding, or may begin to show great interest in the food that the family eats. A mother may want to introduce solid foods for social or stimulatory reasons. Solid food is a whole new kind of activity for the baby, it makes the baby more a part of the family, and, at the same time, represents a real step toward eventual independence. Often fathers and older siblings are happy at last to be able to "feed" the baby themselves.

Introducing solid foods is a gradual process. Starting to feed solids, especially to a very young baby, can be a time-consuming task. Some babies balk at solid food or simply push it back out, still on their tongue. A young baby has to learn what to do with the lump on its tongue. At first the baby may simply be interested in tasting food, not swallowing it. Once a baby has learned to swallow, it may show interest in food for a while and then become bored. In any case, there's no reason to fight over solids because the baby is getting most of its nutrition from its milk and will continue to do so for at least several more months. With a change in foods or another growth spurt, the baby's interest in solid food will return.

The order and timing of introducing various solids is largely a matter of personal preference—both the pediatrician's and the mother's. The most widely used schedules begin with a single grain cereal, usually rice. Other cereals may be introduced next, or the baby may simply go on to plain vegetables and/or fruits, of which mashed banana and applesauce are the most popular. In general, meat purees are the last category of solid food to be introduced.

Traditionally, solid foods have been introduced one at a time, about a week or more apart. The only medical reason for this is that if the baby is sensitive or allergic to a particular food, the mother and doctor will more readily know which one it is. Many pediatricians believe that a *young* baby's digestive system is less able to handle certain foods and that the baby is

Foods that are commonly withheld from infants because they may result in allergy

Some doctors feel strongly about potentially allergenic foods, others do not. Especially if parents have a family history of allergy, they are probably wise to delay the introduction of these foods.

Food	Age
Oranges and other citrus fruits and juices	6–9 mo
Regular homogenized or skim cow's milk	9–12 mo
Wheat (in quantity)	6–9 mo
Eggs—yolks	9 mo
Eggs—whites	12 mo
Chocolate	12 mo
Fish	12 mo

First solid foods

The baby's swallowing mechanism is not fully developed until around three months.
Begin solids when the baby stares at food, reaches out, or seems hungry after feeding.
Usually starting time of baby's interest—4–6 months.
Begin with the blandest foods; gradually introduce the spicier foods.
Begin with highly pureed foods; gradually introduce chunkier foods.
Here is the most widely used progression:

First		
Cereal	Rice, barley	Easy to fix, feed, digest; filling, not high in protein, may have added iron
Second		
Fruits	Pureed bananas, prunes, apricots, apples, peaches	Flavorful, most babies like, contain vitamins, somewhat laxative
Third		
Vegetables	Green beans, peas, carrots, potatoes	High in vitamins, flavorful
Fourth		
Meats	Chicken, beef, liver	High in protein (high in natural iron—liver)

Start with small amounts—let the baby taste.
Often the baby pushes some food back out, especially at first.
Don't force the baby to eat when it's not hungry.
Don't force the baby to eat foods it doesn't like.
Food should not be steaming hot or ice-cold. Precooked meats and vegetables do not necessarily have to be heated.
Use a small spoon; long-handled, rubber-coated ones are nice.
Let the baby have its own spoon to hold when it begins to grab for the feeding spoon.
Make sure the baby sits up to eat. A baby on its back is more likely to inhale food and choke.
Make sure the baby is *securely* fastened in its high chair or infant seat. *Don't leave a baby on a table in an infant seat,* belt or no belt. Babies have been known to flip infant seats off tables.

Food requirements recommended by the National Academy of Sciences

	0–2 mo	*2–6 mo*	*6 mo–1 yr*	*1–2 yr*	*2–3 yr*	*3–4 yr*	*Sources*
Calories	480	770	400	1100	1650	1400	
Protein	8.8	14	17	25	25	30	Milk, eggs, meat, cheese, beans, peanut butter
Vitamins							
A (IU)	1500	1500	1500	2500	2500	2500	Liver, greens, carrots, cantaloupe, apricots, squash
B_1 (mg)	0.5	0.5	0.5	0.7	0.7	0.7	Soy, liver, asparagus, greens
B_6 (mg)	0.4	0.4	0.4	0.7	0.7	0.7	
B_{12} (mg)	2	2	2	3	3	3	
Niacin (mg)	8	8	8	9	9	9	
Riboflavin (mg)	0.6	0.6	0.6	0.8	0.8	0.8	
Folacin (mg)	0.1	0.1	0.1	0.2	0.2	0.2	
C (mg)	35	35	35	40	40	40	Oranges, citrus, cabbage, greens, strawberries
D (IU)	400	400	400	400	400	400	Milk, cheese
E (IU)	5	5	5	10	10	10	Enriched cereal, beans, greens, liver, meat, eggs, prunes
Calcium (g)	0.6	0.6	0.6	0.8	0.8	0.8	Milk, cheese, egg yolks
Iron (mg)	10	10	10	10	10	10	Liver, dried legumes, fortified cereals

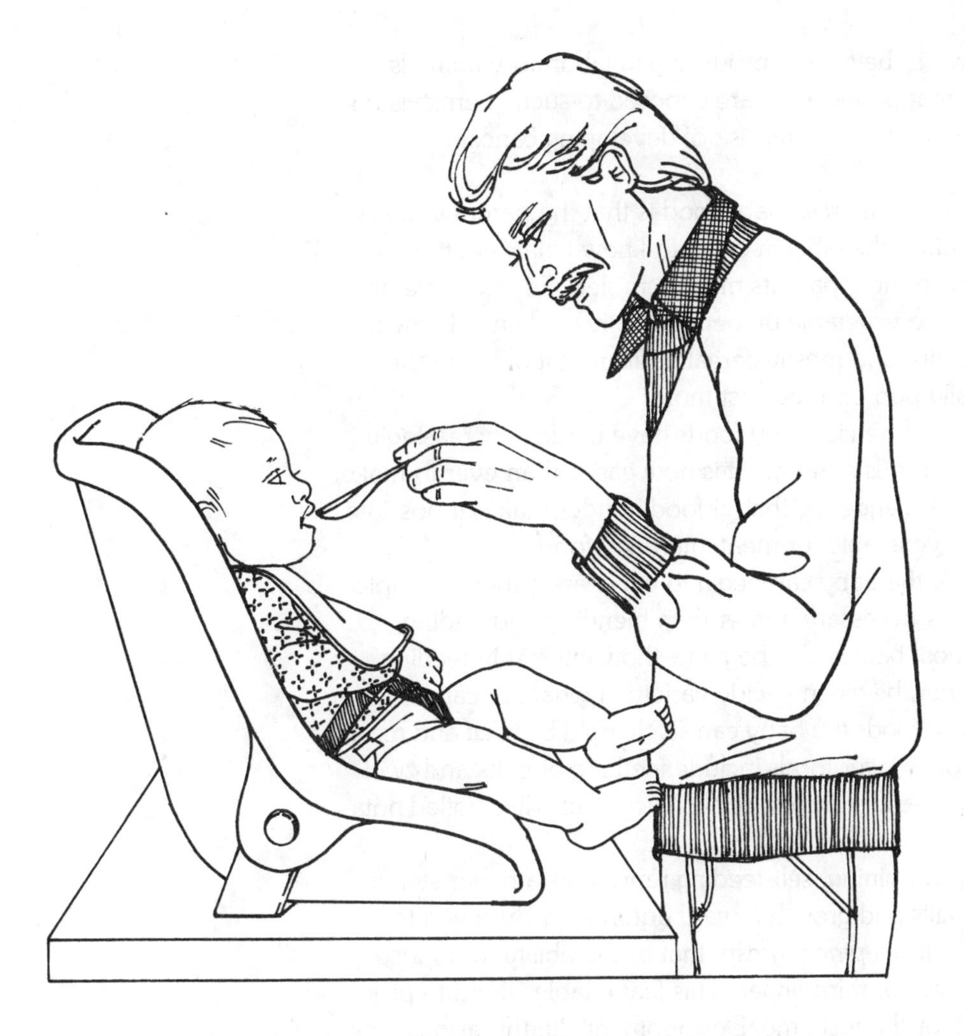

The age at which babies show interest in solid foods is highly variable.

therefore potentially more likely to react to such foods if they are introduced early. These pediatricians feel that if foods that are commonly allergenic are withheld till six months or a year, the baby's immune system is less likely to respond to them and allergy to such foods will be prevented for the baby's whole life. Not all doctors believe in this theory, and the incidence of food allergies is sufficiently low so that some pediatricians do not delay the introduction of any particular foods. But the number of problematic foods is small enough that many parents (especially those with family histories of allergy) decide to delay some or all of these foods.

At first the baby's solid food needs to be rather completely pureed to prevent the baby from choking. Some babies tend to be fussy eaters and may spit out even small lumps. An incredible array of pureed foods is now commercially available. Unfortunately, some commercial foods contain unnecessary salt, sugar, starch, food colorings, MSG, and/or preservatives. Many people believe that the additives are not only unnecessary, but may actually be harmful. It has been found that certain hyperactive three- and four-year-olds show dramatic improvement when put on an additive-free diet. Some researchers have also expressed serious concern about routinely feeding young infants additives (like Red Dye #2) which, in large doses, have been shown to be cancer-producing in laboratory animals. These researchers feel that people who are exposed to such chemicals for their whole lifetime may have a greater risk of developing cancer as adults.

Another problem with commercial baby food is that the parent virtually has to read the fine print on the label in order to know what is in the food other than additives. Even then, parents may be misled. For example, the mixed meals like meat and vegetable dinner generally contain little meat (which means little protein) and mostly cereal or filler. Not only are the mixed meals nutritionally poorer, they cost more.

These drawbacks to commercial baby foods have made it increasingly popular to prepare baby foods at home. It is now easier than ever to make homemade baby food. A blender or (baby) food grinder makes it possible to turn almost any fruit, vegetable, or meat into baby food.

After six months or so, the baby can begin to eat coarser foods. Simple mashing may be all that's necessary, rather than blending and adding water. By six months most babies also begin to show interest in feeding themselves. They can then be given a wide variety of what are called "finger foods." These are foods the baby can safely hold by itself and mash with its gums and tongue. Finger foods include teething biscuits and zwieback, French bread crusts, and stringless cooked vegetables like boiled potatoes or carrots.

Like weaning and toilet training, self-feeding represents a major step in the baby's mastery of skills and growth toward autonomy. By seven to nine months babies develop a *pincer grasp,* that is, the ability to oppose their thumb to their second or third finger. This feat enables them to pick up small pieces of food for the first time. Developmentally, this also corresponds to a period of maximum appetite and weight gain, and the ability to sit up in a high chair and swallow chunks of food without gagging. Thus babies are physiologically motivated to master self-feeding at this point. By fourteen months their appetite has dropped off considerably as their rate of growth slows, and it's more of a struggle to get them to eat.

Many pediatricians will recommend that parents encourage the baby to be basically self-feeding and off strained foods by ten to twelve months. The baby is given soft, small chunks of food that are easily picked up and chewed, such as Cheerios, macaroni, and small cubes of chicken. Initially, foods should be chopped to the size of fruit cocktail, and should be served one at a time, rather than all at once. If the baby gags at first, it may be best to go back to strained foods for a few days. Initially, babies will eat only with their fingers, which admittedly is messy, but by the age of two, they can begin to use a spoon. When the baby finally does achieve self-feeding, it's a great convenience to the parents because the baby can eat at the table with the family, and can generally eat the same foods as the rest of the family. Despite the food that falls to the floor and the cleanup it necessitates, when a baby begins self-feeding it can be a time of fun for all the family.

Care must be taken in the choice and feeding of all finger foods, especially when they are first introduced. Parents should always watch an infant who is eating any finger food. Fruits like apple, pear, and peach should have the skin removed. And babies should never be given small hard foods like raisins or nuts, or foods that readily break into little pieces like some crackers. Babies can easily choke on foods like this. Even little pieces of teething biscuit can cause a small baby to choke or spit up (see *Choking* in the *Emergency Medicine* chapter). Sometimes babies aren't actually that hungry, they just want something good to taste that they can gnaw on. In this case, the baby can be given a long piece of celery or carrot (scraped to bring out the flavor).

By one year most babies are being fed the same foods as the rest of the family, only mashed or finely cut up. Hard raw foods, unpeeled fruit or vegetables, large chunks of meat, nuts and seeds are *not* suitable, unless the baby has enough teeth and skill to chew them.

The second main food concern during the first year is what liquids to feed the baby and when. The baby gets its most substantial nutrition from milk, whether it's from the mother or a commercially prepared formula. As a rule there is no medical reason to introduce liquids other than milk for the first four to eight months. In fact, any other liquid given in quantity is likely to decrease the amount of milk the baby is drinking. On the other hand,

There is often a special aura of peace and security about the nursing mother and baby. Madonna and Child, *detail, by Adriaen Isenbrant. Courtesy of The Art Institute of Chicago.*

occasionally feeding a baby diluted apple juice can help to free a long period of time for the nursing mother, while giving the father, siblings, or grandparents an expanded role in the baby's care. Supplemental juice or water can also be beneficial in extremely hot weather or when the baby has a cold.

There is increasing evidence that breast milk is medically the most advantageous liquid for babies. And research is pointing toward breast-feeding for a longer rather than a shorter time. Briefly (to review the discussion in "The Newborn" chapter), infants being fed breast milk during the first year show fewer episodes of diarrhea or gastrointestinal infection. This is due to breast milk's content of antibodies and to the fact that breast milk encourages the growth of lactobacilli (as opposed to *E. coli*) in the infant's digestive system. Breast-fed babies also have a substantially lower incidence of respiratory tract infections, middle ear infections, herpes virus infections, and candida or monilia of the mouth (thrush). Also, bottle-fed babies show a higher incidence of asthma and eczema, as well as allergy to cow's milk products. And babies fed on cow's milk have a much greater tendency to become obese, which is now thought to be associated with obesity in adulthood and with the development of heart disease, high blood pressure, and diabetes. Some researchers believe that a minimal allergic reaction to cow's milk may later cause a buildup of cholesterol in a person's arteries.

Studies show that regular cow's milk (as opposed to breast milk, evaporated milk, and commercial formulas) is less well absorbed by an infant's digestive tract. Some commercially prepared formulas more closely match the chemical composition of breast milk. In addition, commercial formulas are less likely to cause allergies than homemade cow's milk formulas. The complex protein structure of cow's milk is partially broken down in commercial processing.

The trend now is to encourage mothers to breast-feed initially, to breast-feed longer (seven months to one and a half years), to delay the introduction of solid foods, and to delay feeding the baby straight cow's milk until after one year.

General facts about baby food and how to make it

Commercial

All kinds of baby foods are readily available canned and precooked.

They have a long storage life before being opened.

Continued

Most contain many additives, fillers, etc.—labels must be read carefully, even those of so-called "natural baby foods"—but some pure, natural baby foods are available.

Mixed dinners contain mostly fillers and/or vegetables—not meat.

Commercial foods must be stocked or purchased independently of the parents' meals, but require no preparation. Heating is optional.

Adult foods

Some commercial adult foods are fine "as is" for babies: for example, plain applesauce, cream of rice cereal.

Homemade baby foods

Either hand-mashed, blended, or ground. A few things can be mashed by hand; most have to be cooked first: bananas, ripe peas, potatoes (sweet and regular), squash, egg yolks.

Virtually all meats, vegetables, and fruits can be blended, either raw or cooked. Special baby blender jars are available; large amounts can be made at one time and refrigerated or frozen in ice cube trays for individual servings. Electric blenders provide fresh baby food, but are expensive, noisy to operate (frighten babies), and time-consuming to clean. Most foods need water or some other liquid added to get a good consistency.

Many foods can be ground in a hand baby food grinder. Hard foods and some uncooked foods may be hard to grind. Hard grinders enable parents to feed baby small portions of almost anything they eat. They are portable, inexpensive, convenient, nonfrightening (no noise). Grinders enable parents to know exactly what they are feeding the baby—fresh, pure foods. Ground foods generally require some water, milk, or juice to moisten them—especially when the baby is very young. They don't necessitate special shopping, but may require planning around what the baby can eat. They are available at baby stores, health food stores, and some of the larger department stores.

Starter foods

Cereal and grains

Infant precooked dehydrated cereals like rice, barley, oats, wheat—no cooking necessary; just add water and stir. Very convenient, nonrich, can be mixed with fruits to enhance taste.

Continued

Adult hot cereals—some adult hot cereals, like cream of rice, contain no additives, need only brief cooking, and do not need to be ground up. Others like oatmeal, rice, bulgur wheat, and pasta, including farina, must be cooked and ground up.
Adult dry cereals—for example, Grape-Nuts or Cheerios—can be ground with water or milk in a grinder or blender.

Fruits
Apples, bananas, peaches, pears, apricots.
Regular canned or fresh fruit can be ground or cooked and mashed (for example, applesauce, baked apples).
Dried fruits can be soaked or cooked, then ground—for example, prunes, apricots. They are especially useful in winter months.

Vegetables
Carrots, green beans, peas, potatoes, winter squash, broccoli, spinach.
Fresh or frozen: cook, then mash or grind. Canned: simply mash or grind. Can be mixed with meat.

Meats
Chicken, beef (steak or hamburger), liver, pork, lamb, and turkey.
Cook, then grind. Can be part of the adult's meal or boiled separately (with vegetables for a complete meal). Leftovers are handy and can be ground fresh each day.

Dairy products and miscellaneous
Yogurt (an excellent instant baby meal—very good for lunch or emergencies, and also when traveling).
Cottage cheese—mash or grind.
Puddings, custard, gelatin desserts, ice cream. No extra preparation necessary; all contain protein.

Drinks
Water.
Milk—preferably breast milk; canned, evaporated, or formula up to about 1 year, then regular cow's milk.
Fruit juices—apple, prune, apricot.

Finger foods

Initiate self-feeding; offer finger foods at 7–9 months.
Baby must be sitting up, watched for choking initially.
Good for snacks, present a challenge to the baby, and keep baby occupied.
May ease teething discomfort (chilled things even cool the gums).

Continued

Foods to eat	***Foods to chew on***
Zwieback	Thick chunks of carrot
Infant teething biscuits	Thick pieces of celery
Stale bagels, French bread crusts	
	Foods to avoid
Fruit cocktail	Nuts
Hard crackers	Corn
Scrambled eggs	Popcorn
French toast	Hard apple
Bits of cheese, dry cereal, rice	
Banana	
Chopped spaghetti or macaroni	
Boiled chicken	

Breast-feeding for the working mother

The pleasures and advantages of breast-feeding cause many mothers to wish to continue even when they return to work. Often mothers do not have to start working again for two or three months. Even if the mother expects to wean at that point, the baby will receive significant nutritional, immunological, and psychological benefits from breast-feeding (see page 120) which make it worthwhile for the mother to nurse even for this length of time. There is much that the new mother can do to ease the transition of going back to work while continuing to nurse. In a few cases, mothers who work part-time are able to arrange their work schedule so that they can nurse the baby before they leave, on a break, and again when they return. In most cases, however, the baby will have to be fed from a bottle while the mother is away. If so, the mother should begin feeding the baby from a bottle that has a breast-shaped nipple well in advance of the mother's returning to work, but no earlier than six weeks of age since it's hard for the baby to learn both nursing and bottle-feeding skills in the early weeks.

A battery-powered breast pump is a convenient way for a mother to express and store milk when she is working.

At least initially, in order to keep up their milk supply and to stockpile milk in the freezer for several weeks before work, the mother should learn to pump or manually express milk.

When the mother finally does return to work, the specifics of her schedule and that of the baby will depend upon the hours she's away, and how much breast milk she intends to supply for the baby. The older the baby gets, the longer it naturally tends to go between feedings. By three months, the average baby can go about four hours between feedings.

Likewise the mother is able to go that long without becoming engorged or uncomfortable, as she would have in the early weeks. The most complicated situation arises when the mother wishes to supply all of the baby's milk herself, and she works long hours. In that case, the mother will need to be able to express milk in a private room during her breaks, be able to store the milk in a refrigerator, and have a thermos for transporting it home. In some cases it may be best to maintain the same schedule on the weekends.

If the mother cannot or doesn't want to express milk at work, she can still continue to nurse at home. The mother's milk production is flexible enough to allow her to omit some feedings, especially after 10–12 weeks. Earlier than that, she may need to spill some milk just to keep herself comfortable and to keep up her milk supply. Meanwhile, the baby can be given formula during the mother's work hours.

Weaning

Weaning is a very important matter that affects the mother as well as the baby (especially if the baby is nursing). From the baby's point of view weaning may mean either giving up the breast or giving up the bottle; thus the baby can actually be weaned twice, from breast to bottle and from bottle to cup.

Medical evidence leans toward later weaning, but there is no one medically "right" time. It *is* advisable that the *nursing* mother slowly wean her baby, dropping one feeding at a time or just gradually nursing less and less often. This allows the mother's hormonal system to return to its prepregnant state slowly. To stop nursing all at once can be a shock to the mother's system and may involve some breast discomfort as well as mood depression. Emotionally and physically weaning is very important to the baby as well. Physically, weaning means the baby is giving up a major source for getting nourishment. The more rapidly a baby is weaned, the more important it is that the parents make sure the baby is getting adequate amounts of milk from the new source—be it cup or bottle. Emotionally, the baby is giving up something nourishing and pleasing, a source of love and comfort since the day of birth. At the same time the baby is gaining new independence and separation from the mother.

Drinking from a cup is a skill that takes time for babies to learn. Most aren't capable of holding a cup by themselves and drinking from it until the second half of the first year.

Different babies wean in different ways. Some babies literally wean themselves, others wean in response to their mother's wishes. Some babies wean rather willingly, others—depending somewhat on their age—may need a bottle, especially before going to sleep.

Most often, when and how the baby weans is initiated by the mother and adjusted according to how the baby responds. Going to a cup involves learning a whole new set of skills, particularly if the baby is encouraged to hold the cup by itself. Like all new learning, it takes time and depends greatly on how much positive reinforcement is given. Babies generally aren't ready to wean to a cup earlier than seven to nine months, physically or emotionally. At around nine months some babies naturally seem to have a lag in their interest in breast-feeding. This lag goes along with the baby's growing mobility and greater sense of itself. Many mothers take advantage of this natural lag to wean, but mothers do wean considerably earlier, for example, at about three months. Other mothers and babies happily nurse through the second and even the third years. What is important here is what pleases both mother and baby. Certainly after a year, if the mother feels constrained by the nursing regimen, there is no reason not to drop several feedings, or gradually wean completely. There is no demonstrated medical advantage to nursing past nine months to a year, and prolonged

Weaning suggestions

Babies vary widely as to when and how quickly they drop feedings, whether they go to the cup or the bottle.

When you decide to wean, try to take advantage of possible natural lags in interest: 4–5 months, 7 months, 9–12 months.

Avoid sudden weaning, particularly when the mother is resuming work at the same time.

Don't be surprised if both mother and baby are somewhat depressed and sad at weaning.

If weaning is very gradual, there will probably be some lapses.

Institute cup or bottle milk feedings to compensate for dropped feedings.

Begin to use cup or bottle well ahead of weaning, to ensure good nutrition and a smooth transition.

If possible, drop one feeding at a time, rather than several.

If breasts become full, a minute or two of nursing on each side will relieve but not really stimulate milk production.

Below 7–8 months, wean to a bottle; over 7–8 months, wean to either a bottle or a cup.

Try to spend the same kind of quiet, close times with the baby, even though the baby is nursing less.

The age of weaning is highly variable in our culture. In the second half of the first year, the baby can still enjoy the physical and social benefits of breast-feeding.

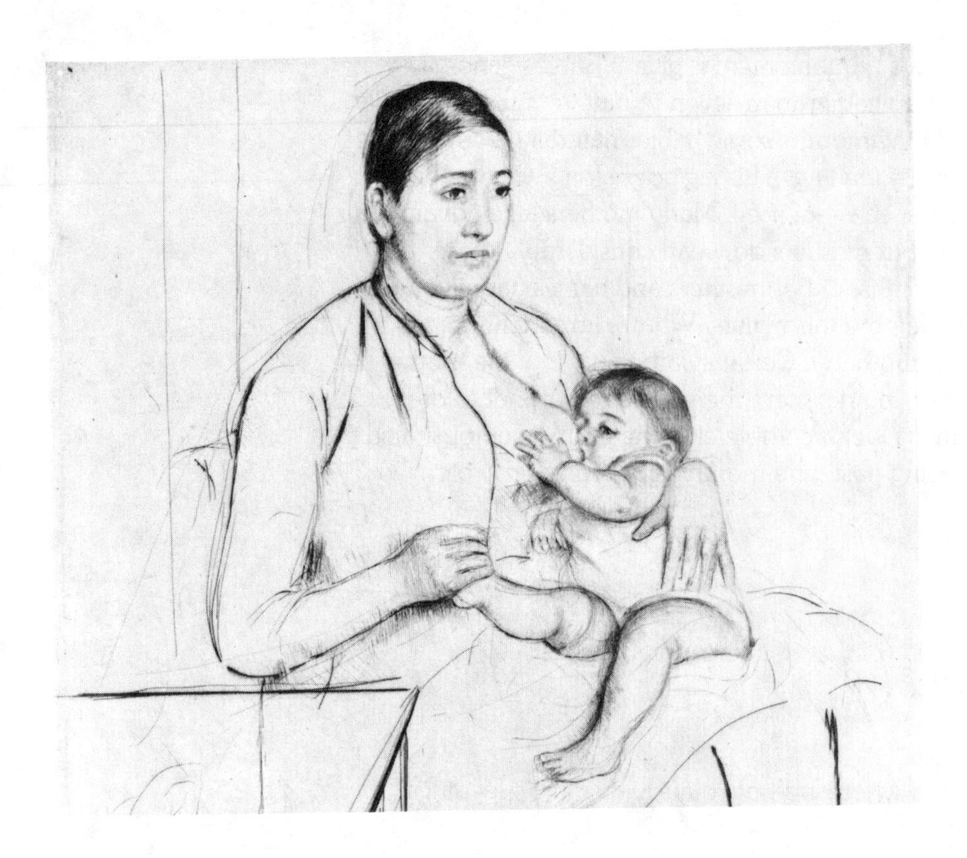

Gradual weaning allows the baby to master a new skill without too much pressure. Nursing, *detail, by Mary Cassatt. Courtesy of The Art Institute of Chicago.*

nursing may not really help the baby if the mother finds herself nursing reluctantly. The mother's need for independence is a real factor here and varies widely from mother and baby to mother and baby. It's also important for mothers to recognize their own expectations as to when a baby should be weaned. Rather than hold to a culturally approved schedule, women should be encouraged to follow their own feelings (and the baby's reactions) as to when and how to wean.

Like self-feeding and toilet training, weaning from the breast represents a maturational landmark that has emotional as well as physical implications. Weaning involves mastery of new physical skills and gives the child greater independence from the mother. Ideally, weaning becomes an occasion for growth rather than conflict. Gradual weaning—dropping one feeding at a time—allows the baby to master a new skill without too much pressure, and allows mother and baby to adjust to the new pattern. If initiated too early, the baby may miss the emotional closeness of nursing or being held and given a bottle, and may find it difficult to make the transition.

At about one year, the baby can go directly from nursing or bottle-feeding to a cup. If the baby is weaned from the breast before nine months, he or she will have to go to a bottle. If nursing goes on for eighteen months, child or mother may become more reluctant to give it up. Generally, the nighttime feeding is the last one to be dropped with nursing or bottle-feeding. Bottle weaning is similar to breast weaning. As a baby goes from bottle to cup, parents can gradually decrease the amount of milk in the bottle by an ounce at a time.

Mothers who return to work in the first year may face special problems around weaning. Many pediatricians feel that even part-time nursing is preferable to complete weaning in the first year because the baby still receives the nutritional, immunological, and emotional benefits of nursing. In the first few months after birth, new mothers will probably need to use a breast pump when they are at work, but after several months they may find they are able to nurse nights and weekends without having to express milk during the day, and the baby can simply be given formula while they are at work.

Sleep patterns and sleeping through the night

Babies spend a great deal of time sleeping, especially in the first weeks after birth. Gradually they begin to sleep fewer hours overall and fewer times during the day. Babies' sleep needs vary depending on the activities of the previous day. A baby will often sleep more than usual after a hectic day, an upset, or an injury, and a baby may also sleep more for a couple of days if it is in a growth spurt or if it is sick.

These generalizations notwithstanding, every baby has its own sleep needs and sleep patterns. Some babies routinely sleep for long periods, others do not. Some babies sleep through the night starting very early and spend most of the day awake. Others nap frequently during the day and wake during the night, taking a longer time to adopt an adult pattern.

Recent research has revealed much about the variability of normal infant sleep patterns. Sleep patterns reflect babies' temperaments, how mature their nervous systems are, and the way in which they have been conditioned by their environment. Most babies have a natural awake period between five in the afternoon and nine at night. About 70 percent of babies sleep from midnight to five in the morning by three months of age; by six months 83 percent do, and by a year, 90 percent do. Between nine and twelve months, 25–50 percent of babies will resume waking at night because of dreams or nightmares. Often this behavior persists until age two. Babies with a low sensory threshold and babies who are breast-fed are more likely to wake at night.

By six weeks many babies have one long stretch of sleep—about six hours—which, if parents are lucky, falls roughly between midnight and six in the morning. Between six weeks and three months, sleep is generally tied to feeding schedules. Thus a baby wakes up when it is becoming hungry.

When a very young baby wakes, it may spend some time alert but not hungry. The longer the baby has been asleep and/or the less it had to eat at last feeding, the sooner the baby will be hungry after waking. The baby may also spend a varying amount of time alert and awake after a feeding.

As the baby grows, its sleep patterns become less reflexive and more amenable to scheduling. Without even realizing it, the parents modify the baby's innate sleeping habits by the habits of their household. The more attention and stimulation the baby gets during the day, the more likely the baby is to stay awake, and perhaps the more likely the baby is to sleep at night. The more quickly parents attend to slight cries and movement in sleep, the more the baby will become accustomed to short sleeps and frequent rousings.

By the time the baby approaches six months, its feeding and sleeping cycles have become less and less tied to each other. The baby begins to have long awake periods during the day, punctuated still by one, two, or even three naps. The more regular the household pattern, the more regular the baby's sleep patterns are likely to be. As the baby sleeps less and less during the day, many parents become increasingly concerned about having the baby sleep through the night (if it has not already begun to do so).

Most pediatricians say not to expect a baby to regularly sleep through the night (eight hours or more) until it weighs 10 or 11 pounds. Some babies do, but most still need a night feeding. Babies vary tremendously in their need for night feedings. Those who are large, quiet, bottle-fed, or who are awake most of the day are most likely to sleep through the night sooner. Babies who are light, active, breast-fed, or who sleep a lot during the day are more likely to want night feedings. Breast milk is more easily and quickly digested than cow's milk, meaning a breast-fed baby may get hungry again quicker. Also, breast-fed babies may not get as much milk in a single feeding until their mother's milk supply has built up. This buildup can take a while.

Parents sometimes condition their baby to night feedings without even realizing it, and there are a number of things parents can do to try to get a baby to sleep through the night (see chart). In spite of all efforts, some babies may continue to wake up during the night even past the first year. Many mothers report that out of desperation or sheer tiredness they have allowed their (older) baby to cry itself back to sleep. Several nights in a row of this admittedly disturbing routine will usually alter the baby's pattern of waking.

Somewhere between nine months and a year, new considerations enter into night waking. By now there is no question of the baby being unable to go for eight or more hours without food. Waking is more a question of habitual action and perhaps a question of developing separation anxiety. The baby may want the comfort, the sociability of nighttime feeding. Some people feel that babies of this age are also beginning to experience nightmares for the first time, or they may be cutting teeth. Such factors can make this period a difficult time to get a baby to sleep through the night. It may be easier if efforts are made to alter the baby's nighttime waking before (or after) the baby reaches nine months.

Many parents notice that their baby goes through periods of sleeping through the night, only to begin waking again. A renewal of nighttime waking may merely be the result of a hard day. Or it may be the result of nightmares, teething, or a change in the baby's routine. If the parents want the baby to return to sleeping through the night, efforts should be made before the baby becomes reaccustomed to waking in the middle of the night.

Suggestions for parents when they want the baby to sleep through the night

Stimulate baby during day; keep baby awake.

Give baby a large feeding just before parents go to sleep:
- Delay the last (or second to last) feeding through rocking, pacifying, talking, or stimulating.
- If necessary, gently wake the baby by picking up, talking, changing diapers, then feed.
- Encourage the baby to nurse at both breasts.

Do not immediately attend to drowsy, fussy cries in the middle of the night. See if the baby can get back to sleep by itself; otherwise the baby becomes conditioned to waking between sleep cycles and needing some attention before going back to sleep.

At night put the baby in its own bed, in its own room, or a very quiet place.

If the baby cries enough to need to be picked up, don't feed, but first try to rock the baby back to sleep.

Don't play with or talk to the baby a lot during night feedings, no matter how awake and cute. Save conversation and stimulation for daytime.

Don't bring the baby into the parents' bed and let it sleep there till morning; it is more likely to be disturbed.

Try feeding the baby cereal in the evening; it may help the baby to sleep through changes in its sleep cycles.

Sleep physiology

As the baby grows older its sleep patterns change. In addition to requiring less total sleep (from an average of sixteen hours at birth to about thirteen hours by a year), the percentage of time spent in rapid eye movement sleep (REM) decreases. The amount of non-REM, or deep, sleep remains rather constant at around eight hours, while REM sleep—active, dreaming sleep—decreases from about eight hours to about four hours. In addition to dreaming, REM sleep is characterized by intense neurological activity, higher levels of growth hormones, and brain growth. During REM sleep there is great variability in heart rate, breathing rate, and body movement. The stimulus

By the time the baby is three or four months old its sleep patterns are becoming more defined.

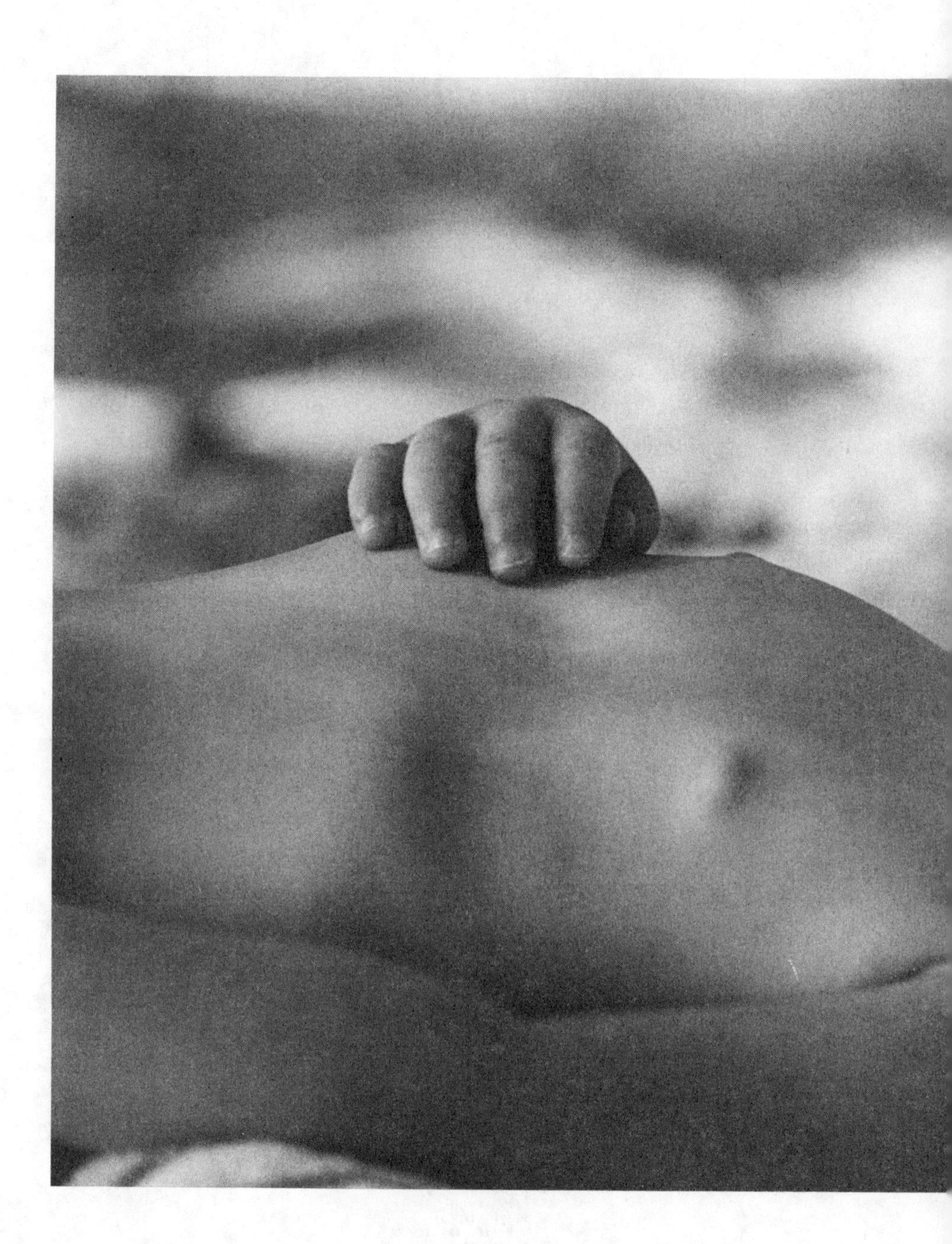

for this activity is thought to originate in the lower brain, the *pons*. The cerebrum, the higher brain, is unable to differentiate between stimulation from the pons and stimulation from external experiences. (This may be likened to an adult's experience of thinking a dream is real while dreaming.) As the baby spends more time awake, it receives more external and less internal stimulation.

Much of the REM activity in young infants is difficult to distinguish from half-awake behavior. The young baby actually has rapid eye movements and brain-wave patterns characteristic of REM sleep when it is involved in drowsy sucking and crying. "Half-awake" REM patterns disappear by

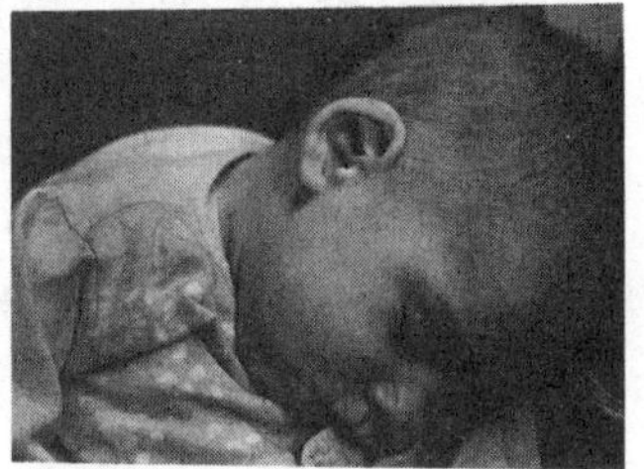

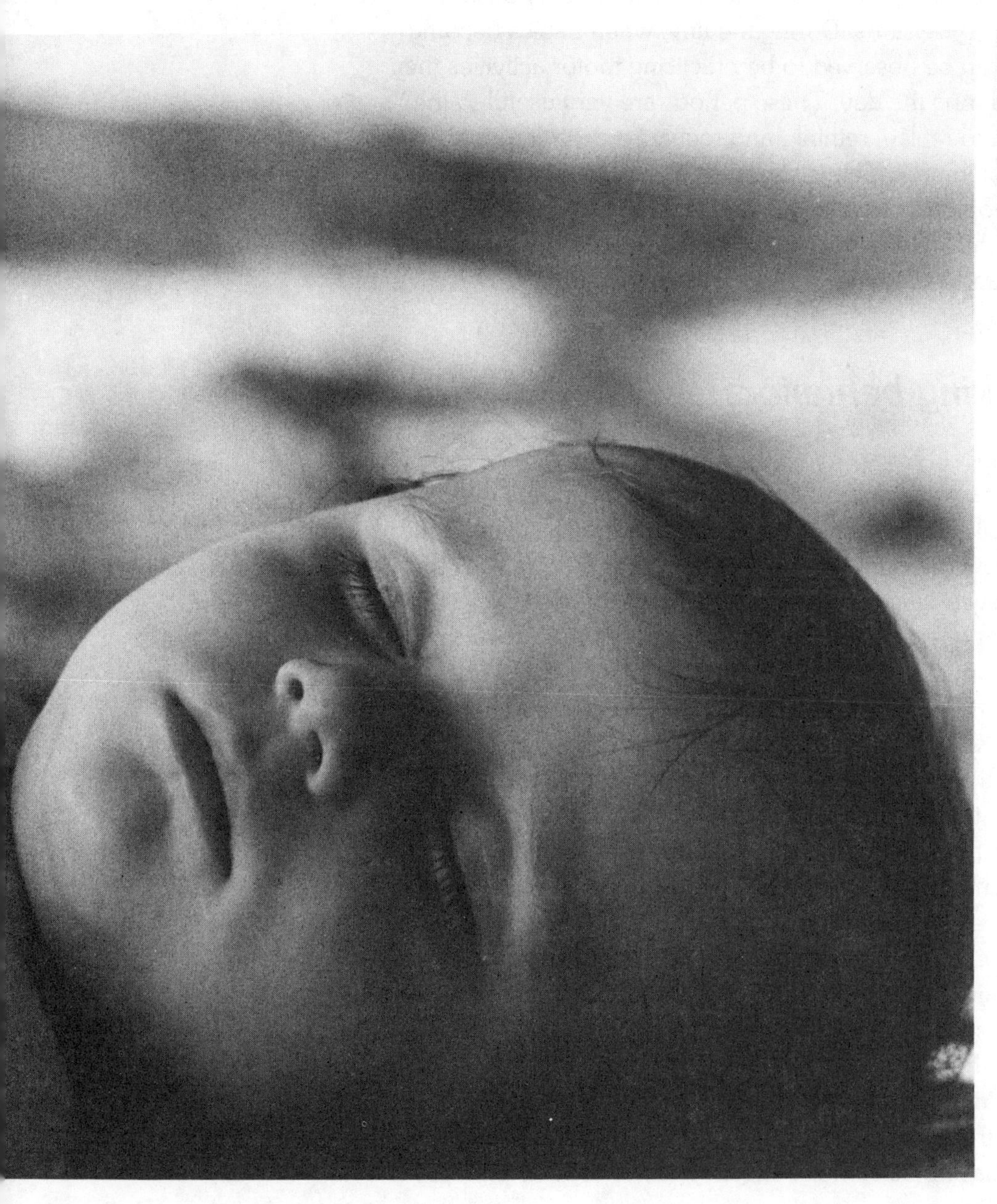

about three months. Also the brain-wave pattern of the infant in REM sleep stabilizes and attains a more adult character.

Other behavioral changes are also observed in infants around three months. Certain fussy behavior decreases and the infant more actively starts and ends contact with its environment. So three months appears to be a maturation step with changes in sleep as well as awake activity. The changes seem to be related to each other. For example, infants decrease the amount of waking and sleeping REM stimulation as they learn to get stimulation from the outside world.

From three months onward babies' sleep has most of the characteristics of adult sleep; running in cycles of three to four hours, each cycle has REM and non-REM phases. Between cycles infants may rouse to a semialert state where they may suck, cry, rock, and move. Then they go back to sleep as the next sleep cycle starts. During the time when babies become semialert, they often can be observed to be practicing motor activities they have tried to master during the day. These periods are very useful to the infants, allowing them to replay, rethink, and reenact activity important to their growth and development. This is similar to an adult's waking at night and thinking about problems of the day and visualizing different solutions. Probably infants also think about their "problems" (reaching out, sitting, etc.), visualize them, and experience the possible solutions.

Sucking and rocking behaviors

During the first year, most babies develop some type of sucking or rocking behavior. Sucking behaviors are most common when babies are quiet, restless, or about to fall asleep. Babies may characteristically suck on their thumb, fingers, toes, or lip. Some rhythmically kick their feet, or rock their head or body; a few even repeatedly bang their head. Interestingly, sonogram studies show that babies engage in sucking behaviors in utero. In fact, it is not uncommon for babies to be born with sucking blisters on their lips or hands. Hand-sucking is seen in all newborns within the first few hours of life, the average time being just under an hour. These findings seem to indicate that sucking movements are instinctual and are related to development of the nervous system. T. Berry Brazelton speculates that sucking is self-consoling behavior that babies engage in because it is pleasurable and under their control.

Thumb-sucking generally starts in the early months and peaks at around 18–24 months. In the United States 50 percent of all babies develop a thumb-sucking habit. Some babies suck on the corner of a favorite blanket; others tug their earlobe or twist their hair as they suck. If these habits persist in the older child, they are often associated with times of stress. Most babies naturally give up thumb-sucking by themselves somewhere between three and four years of age. Up to about the age of four, thumb-sucking has no deleterious effects. It is not considered a psychological problem and does not have adverse effects on tooth alignment. After the age of four, however, persistent thumb-sucking requires dental consultation because it can cause problems with the alignment of the front teeth.

Rhythmic behaviors, including body rocking, head rolling, and kicking, are common in infancy and early childhood. Kicking generally begins around three months of age and occurs in almost all babies during moments of excitement, either due to happiness or unhappiness. Often babies will flex and extend their hands and arms in the same rhythm as their legs. Body rocking generally begins around six months of age, and can occasionally be violent enough to break a crib. Depending upon how the behavior is defined, such rocking occurs in 20 percent to 90 percent of all children. Some babies sit up and rock their whole body; others rest on their elbows and knees, and rock back and forth. Such rocking is most likely to occur when babies are listening to music, are falling asleep, and/or are by themselves. Head rolling only occurs in about 10 percent of all babies, and generally begins around one year of age. Head rolling takes place when the baby is lying on its back, and involves turning the head from side to side. If persistent enough, the motion can rub the hair off an area on the back of the head. Generally body rocking and head rolling are transient behaviors that disappear by the time the child is two. The most dramatic repetitive behavior that babies engage in is banging their head against the sides of their crib. Such head banging takes place in 5–15 percent of normal children, and begins around a year. Over half of all babies who bang their heads have previously engaged in body rocking or head rolling. Often babies will also suck on a favorite blanket or suck their thumb at the same time. Even though head banging may look and sound as if the baby is hurting itself, it is rarely dangerous and babies often appear happy while they are engaged in it. Although head banging takes place in some autistic children, it is not a cause for alarm in children whose behavior is otherwise normal. Head banging generally disappears by age three or four.

Sexual development in infancy and early childhood

Most people believe that the sexual organs do not function until puberty, but in fact, the ovaries and testes begin to form in utero at about seven weeks, and have already undergone enormous changes by birth. The production of male hormones is responsible for the development of the male genitourinary systems. The external genitalia begin to form in both sexes at around the twelfth week of gestation. Sonogram studies have shown that boys even have spontaneous erections in utero. Likewise, newborn males have been observed to have erections as early as two days after birth. As every parent of a boy knows, such erections are often related to fullness of the bladder and take place just before or after urination. Erections are also associated with general arousal, including stretching, crying, and thumb-sucking. Often erections take place during sleep. When they occur during REM sleep (see page 39), they are accompanied by smiling, and tonguing or mouthing behaviors.

Sigmund Freud postulated a major theory of infant sexuality. He believed that sexual impulses in infancy are similar to those in adults, in that they both involve excitation and satisfaction. Freud believed that in the infant this arousal stemmed from instinctual desires, similar to sucking, and was pleasurable. Freud theorized that sexual behavior begins in an immature form in the newborn, and continues throughout the life cycle.

Studies have shown that stimulation of the genitals leads to erections in boys and to smiling and cooing in older infants of both sexes. Masturbation, that is, rubbing of the genitals, is common in both boys and girls in the early years, and is universal by the age of five. Around the turn of the century and for some years thereafter, doctors and parents considered such behavior bad or harmful, and tried to stop it. Presently, pediatricians consider such behavior normal and harmless. Some sexual researchers believe masturbation in young children is simply a pleasant tactile experience, while many psychologists and psychiatrists consider it to be a crucial landmark in sexual development. In any event, most child experts believe that parents should not reprimand or frighten a child about such behavior. Likewise, some degree of interpersonal sex play is common by the age of five, and does not appear to have negative effects.

First year capabilities and needs for learning

During the first year the baby learns the basic skills of controlling its body, understanding stimuli, and relating to the world. Perhaps at no other time in its life will the baby learn so much so quickly. Learning begins with the infant's capabilities at birth and continues as the infant has new experiences and reaches new maturational landmarks. New capabilities arise continuously and in spurts, singly and in groups. During the first year the baby masters an incredible array of motor skills—more or less in a sequence—culminating in grasping and walking. The baby also learns to recognize, order, and make meaning out of what it perceives. And the baby learns to react to experience—to feel enjoyment, trust, fear, and frustration.

Babies actively seek stimulation and experience. They seem to have a powerful innate drive to learn and to be competent. Babies achieve the greatest learning when helped by their parents in a stimulus-rich environment. They enter the world as relatively helpless creatures, unable to meet their own needs and with limited ability to communicate these needs. The more efficiently and readily parents are able to meet their babies' needs, the happier the babies will be and the more quickly they will learn. The better parents understand their baby's developing capabilities, the more they can help and the more interest and enjoyment they will find in the baby's development. Having some idea of the general timing and sequence of their baby's capabilities allows parents to participate in and stimulate learning rather than waiting for it to occur.

When babies stare at objects around them they are actually learning to organize their experience. By observing similarities and slight differences, babies form basic concepts.

What the baby sees

Understanding what newborns can see provides explanations for why they behave as they do and suggests ways parents can work with babies.

Initially the newborn is visually most interested in edges or boundaries and tends to single out one edge to fix on for a time. Probably this is why babies in the first month often stare at the parents' hairline rather than at their eyes. Young babies also like to look at lights and window margins. At around two months babies begin to shift from staring at the border of an object to scanning the entire object and staring at features within the borders. At the same time the baby will begin to seek out the parents' eyes and stare at them.

Both the baby's ability to focus over distance and its ability to see sharply improve steadily. By the time the baby is three months old, its eyesight is virtually equal to an adult's. Researchers now believe that babies have a tremendous visual appetite and that their attention is generally directed for the longest times toward visual stimuli that vary slightly from things they are already familiar with. Faces are one of the earliest visual concepts the baby comes to understand. When a baby can recognize the basic shape of a face, it will begin to look preferentially at drawings of faces in which the features have been slightly moved or changed.

Infants become interested in a scene or object they see either because of meaning, movement, or shape. Once they have learned to recognize the object or scene, they quickly become bored with it. But a scene that is totally different will interest infants less than a scene that is slightly changed in size, shape, pattern, etc. The fact that infants prefer slight changes in scenes means that their interest is not random. Possibly the infant is comparing a new or changed scene with a memory of a familiar scene. In order to identify similar features, babies must use the techniques of comparison. In this way babies eventually learn to organize their visual perceptions into concepts. That is, babies begin to class similar perceptions together and make generalizations as to what constitutes a face, a smile, etc.

In the early months parents can provide their baby with significant visual and intellectual stimulation simply by presenting the baby with an array of frequently changing, slightly different objects or scenes. Everyday life does this automatically if parents realize and expose babies to a variety of scenes.

The onset of babies' interest in moderate differences between visual stimuli is two to three months. This new visual interest is paralleled by landmarks of growth in the infant's brain, including the appearance of alpha waves and a leveling off of the growth of nerve cells.

Older babies continue to enjoy changing visual stimuli. Without changing stimulation they may quickly become fussy or sleepy. Researchers found that ten-month-old infants presented with complex visual-motor tasks developed longer attention spans and picked up greater visual detail than children who had not been given such tasks. Parents reported that babies in the study who did the tasks also responded more smoothly to a variety of situations in the home.

We now believe that infants have inborn abilities to perceive depth. This means that from a very young age the infant perceives the world as three-dimensional.

It used to be said that infants were completely at the mercy of their perceptions, that their world was total confusion. Now it appears that infants actually are able to concentrate selectively on one aspect of a situation, while shutting out other aspects of it. This is similar to an adult's ability to read a book and not hear a conversation that is going on in the next room.

Broadening social skills and language

Between one and two months the infant begins to smile responsively as well as smile reflexively in REM sleep. It is most likely to happen in response

Grandmothers often play marvelous, age-old games that are both social and educational.

to cooing baby talk or the mother's smiling face. By this time the infant will make real eye-to-eye contact with a person and participate in a prolonged social interchange. By two months the infant is beginning to produce new sounds ("sh," "coo," "oo"), as well as making familiar throaty noises and gurgles. Increasingly, the baby makes noise to initiate social contact. Such sounds eventually replace crying as a means of getting attention. By about three or four months the baby has begun to squeal and laugh and show definite discrimination about things in its environment. The baby not only recognizes its parents, it recognizes and may show a strong preference for specific objects. The baby shows pleasure in enjoyable situations and may cry if a social interchange is cut off.

Somewhere around a half year the baby begins making repetitive sounds—first vowels, then consonants. This is often referred to as babbling. By about nine or ten months these babblings have come to sound like baa-baa, ma-ma, and da-da. By this time the baby will begin to imitate speech sounds and gestures such as waving. The baby will engage in social activities such as clapping hands, playing peekaboo, and feeding itself crackers. By about its first birthday the baby will begin to use its first words.

Attachment, separation anxiety, and safe-base exploration

In the nuclear family (mother, father, and their children only) the baby forms a strong attachment to the person who principally takes care of it, usually the mother. This attachment is shown by the liveliness of the baby's response to the mother and by the baby's anxiety or emotional withdrawal at any significant separation from the mother. Babies as young as ten days show disruption of their accustomed feeding and sleeping patterns when they are separated from their mother. This is not surprising when one considers that the baby has been attuned to the mother's patterns for nine months in the uterus and has also participated in strong initial bonding directly after birth, as well as in the early days of life.

The mother's lap is a timeless symbol of comfort and safety. Egyptian sculpture, Isis and Horus, *The Metropolitan Museum of Art, Rogers Fund, 1945.*

Human babies show distress, mourning, and disruption of development when they are separated from their mothers. The degree to which any one baby is *affected* is influenced by the baby's age, by the length of separation, by the intensity of the relationship that has been formed with the mother, and by the quality of the relationship set up with the substitute caretaker.

As the baby matures and gets to know its mother better, the attachment to her grows. During the first three or four months the baby seeks stimulation from the mother and learns to pick out her face and voice. In these first few months the baby is literally in touch with the mother's body much of the time. The infant learns that the mother is the greatest and most depend-

By the end of the first year, babies show great attachment to their mothers. This attachment is demonstrated by loving gestures as well as by staying physically close to the mother. Left: Le Baisir, *detail, Mary Cassatt. Drypoint and aquatint in color. The Metropolitan Museum of Art, Gift of Paul J. Sachs, 1916. Right:* Enfant Nu, *Mary Cassatt. Drypoint and aquatint in color. The Metropolitan Museum of Art, Gift of Paul J. Sachs, 1916.*

able source of stimulation and response. As the attachment deepens, the infant increasingly has long periods of eye-to-eye contact with the mother, alerts to her voice, and learns to smile in response to her face. In the next three or four months the baby learns to differentiate the mother (and other close people) from strangers. By this time the baby follows the mother around with its eyes. In the last half of the first year the baby's attachment to the mother begins to affect its behavior toward the world around it. The mother seems to provide a "safe base" from which the baby feels secure enough to explore its surroundings. The security of the mother is especially important in new or stressful situations. The older baby (twelve months) may cling to the mother or protest when it is to be separated from her. Even before a baby shows separation anxiety, it may show shyness or fear around strangers.

Thus in the second half of the first year, a special pattern develops. In this period the baby begins to become mobile and likewise begins to take the initiative in interactions. The baby has by this time formed a definite concept of "mother," of other familiar people, and even of familiar places, and shows positive attachment to these "concepts." The baby is beginning to discriminate among people and among objects, and is starting to see itself as separate from other objects and people, can visualize them when they are not present, and thus is capable of missing them when they are absent.

Although the baby is beginning to understand itself as separate from other people, it is still dependent on them to supply both its physical and emotional needs. The baby uses familiar persons and situations as bases from which to explore the unfamiliar and often feels anxiety when no familiar base is present.

Infant anxiety toward the unknown manifests itself in three phenomena: stranger anxiety, separation anxiety, and safe-base exploration. Typically, young children in all cultures exhibit these phenomena, though at somewhat varying ages in different cultures. At around six to eight months, most American babies stop being responsive to strangers and begin to view them guardedly, even with alarm. Some babies stop smiling at strangers and even cry when they are approached by unfamiliar people. These reactions generally peak a few months after they begin and then gradually subside. *Stranger anxiety* is usually less if the baby is in the mother's lap or if the baby is in a very familiar setting. If the baby has been exposed to strangers throughout its life, it is less likely to develop strong stranger anxiety.

By the end of the first year most babies are becoming noticeably shy around strangers. This is a natural phenomenon that occurs to some degree among children in all cultures.

Separation anxiety generally begins in American babies around the age of ten months and does not begin to disappear until somewhere around twenty-four months. When an infant is placed in an unfamiliar setting or is with unfamiliar people, it will generally cry and not move about unless there is something familiar as well. A baby will also cry when its mother starts to leave, and as the baby gets older it may even attempt to follow the mother. Like stranger anxiety, separation anxiety is greatly decreased or even eliminated if the baby is frequently left with other familiar people, is familiar with the place where it's left, or if the child has become accustomed to the mother's leaving.

The third anxiety phenomenon is *safe-base exploration.* As a baby becomes mobile it starts to explore and investigate the world at its own initiative. If the mother is present when an infant begins to explore, it will vocalize, move about, and may even go into adjoining strange areas out of sight of the mother, returning occasionally to check on her presence. In so doing, the baby begins physically and mentally to separate itself from its mother and her surroundings. Psychologist Erik Erikson has said that the ability to let the mother out of sight is the baby's first social achievement. Indeed, the ability to "let go" of the mother is the basis of the child's learning and development in the next several years. This behavior is a sign of the baby's ego development. It shows that the baby has "internalized" the mother—that is, the mother has, as Erikson says, become an "inner certainty as well as an outer predictability." This process of internalizing the mother is based on the infant's past experience, from which the baby comes to have a sense of trust in the fact that the mother will (always) come back. This basic trust is built up each time the mother leaves the baby and then returns to warmly attend to the baby. These leavetakings are initially rather brief and can gradually become longer and longer as the baby's trust and memory grow.

A well-known child development researcher, Mary Ainsworth, speculates that the dynamics of mother-infant interaction which develop in the infant's first nine months determine the baby's ability to use the mother later as a safe base and resolve the stress of separation and new situations. *Ideally*, Ainsworth says, the infant shows a smooth balance between exploration and seeking out the mother. In such a situation the infant knows at all times where the mother is; occasionally seeks physical, visual, or verbal contact with the mother; and after separation or in a strange situation directly seeks physical nearness and contact with the mother until it feels soothed. Mothers of such infants were found to be generally responsive to the baby's needs, readily available and accepting, but not interfering. Ainsworth noted that if a mother generally rejects an infant, the infant will not seek to be near the mother. If a mother interferes *or* pays no attention to a baby, the infant will show distress when the mother leaves, but will be ambivalent toward the mother when she returns (avoidance-attachment). The whole interaction between the infant and its familiars (most notably, mother, father, home) in the first year is the model for how the infant will react to unfamiliar or stressful situations in the future.

Advice for the working mother

One of the most significant changes to affect the family in the last several decades is the rise in the number of working mothers who have very young children. By 1987, 52 percent of mothers with children under the age of one were working. These women must not only deal with the normal concerns of mothering a young child—nutrition, growth, behavior, etc.—they must also deal with the demands of work, commuting, and schedule juggling as well. While they admittedly find it somewhat hectic and fatiguing, many women manage all these roles, and even find it very fulfilling. To do all this happily, mothers need to have a positive attitude, great flexibility, a good sense of organization, the ability to set priorities and make decisions as to what one can and can't do, and the ability to get outside help when it's needed.

In the chapter on pregnancy, we discussed planning for maternity leave and thinking about arrangements for the baby when the mother returned to work. During pregnancy these concerns have a theoretical, slightly unreal quality. At the least, the problem of returning to work seems a long way off, especially for a first-time mother. Now with mother, father, and baby somewhat settled into their new roles, the topic of returning to work comes up in earnest, although the solutions vary tremendously with each family. Returning to work is very different depending on whether the baby is two months old or ten months. Moreover, there are great differences depending upon whether the mother works full- or part-time, whether she has a flexible schedule, whether she can work at home, and whether or not she has a job that is very demanding and/or requires a long commute.

Other factors that influence the mother's return to work are the baby's temperament and feeding/sleeping habits, whether or not there are older children to take care of, and the degree to which the father is able to help the mother with all of this. Mothers may find they want or need more time off after the second baby than the first, and/or they may find that daycare for two is so expensive it makes work less economically valuable.

Critical to the ease of the mother's return to work is the kind of daycare she arranges and how comfortable she feels in leaving the baby. There are two main aspects to daycare. The first is the amount of care the parents need, which is determined by the way their schedules work out. The second is the type of daycare the parents choose and can afford.

There are several basic ways that two working parents balance family and career. At one extreme, both husband and wife work full-time, and the children are cared for by others. At the other extreme, both parents work, full- or part-time, dovetailing their schedules so that someone is always home. A third alternative is that both parents work full- or part-time, and child care is used to cover the time that neither parent can be home. In another arrangement, one or both parents work at home, with or without daycare for part of the time. Finally there is the traditional, but increasingly less common, model—one parent works full-time while the other parent remains at home until the baby reaches a certain age. Obviously, these different types of work schedules result in different daycare arrangements. Moreover, there are often shifts in the parents' needs, especially in the first year. Many mothers take as much time off as possible after the baby is born, then shift to working at home, then to going in part-time, and finally to returning to their full complement of hours.

Most children under the age of two or three months are taken care of at home—either the parents' home or the caretaker's home. A smaller number are taken care of in a daycare center. In home care, there are several basic options. First, by working at home or dovetailing their schedules, the mother and father manage to take care of the baby at home. Second, the baby is cared for at home for some number of hours a day by a relative or friend. The advantage here is that the caretaker is loving and dedicated, and is personally involved in the baby's development. Furthermore, this type of arrangement often costs little or nothing. Although not uncommon, this is not the typical arrangement, especially if the mother works full-time.

In the third instance, the baby is cared for at the home of a caretaker who also looks after other children (her own or others') of varying ages. This is the most common type of early daycare arrangement. The advantages of this type of arrangement are that the baby has a constant relationship with a few people, the location is usually nearby, and the parent can readily develop a close relationship with the caretaker. The greatest disadvantages are that the quality of such caretaking varies widely, and there may be a number of other children who also require the caretaker's attention. Only one out of ten family-care workers is licensed. However, the

Infant daycare alternatives

Full parental care based on staggered parental schedules

Advantages

- baby is not separated from parents:
  - maximizes attachment
  - parent gets to know baby
  - baby exposed only to parent's values and child-rearing practices
- baby stays in familiar surroundings
- minimum exposure to outside bacteria and viruses
- inexpensive

Disadvantages

- parental fatigue
- parents may have to work inconvenient hours
- parents can spend less time with each other
- staggered hours
- not possible with certain careers

Continued

licensing does not guarantee that the care is good. Licensing only certifies safety standards in the home at the time of inspection. Thus it is extremely important that the parents evaluate both the caretaker and the home—in person and on a regular basis (see chart).

A fourth option is that the baby is taken care of at home by a live-in or non-live-in person who may or may not do housework. The big advantage of this arrangement is that the baby has one-to-one care in a familiar environment. In addition, this arrangement is the least work for the parents, if they can afford it. There is no travel time and no shifting of baby equipment; and the caretaker may do varying amounts of housework and evening and weekend care as part of the job. The disadvantages are that a live-in arrangement affects the parents' privacy and may not be long-lasting. Live-in care-givers include mother's helpers, foreign-born workers, professional nannies, and au pairs. These care-givers can be hard to find, expensive, and often contract for a minimum period of time. They are located through word of mouth, newspaper advertisements (yours or theirs), or agencies. Agencies are the most expensive, but in general they do a good job of screening applicants and they guarantee satisfaction. If the parents make the arrangements themselves, they usually interview potential care-givers on the phone, then conduct a personal interview that includes interacting with the baby, and finally, check the person's references carefully. Throughout the process, the parents need to think about whether they can imagine the person in their home taking care of their baby while they are at work.

Finally, the least common option is that babies under a year may be taken care of in daycare centers that have special arrangements for very young children. A good infant center will have trained personnel and a low ratio of caretakers to babies. The advantages of such centers are they are not as expensive as private care and generally have subsidies for low-income mothers; they are stable; and they offer long hours for parents who need them. Many parents, mothers in particular, have times when they feel guilty or unhappy about leaving a young infant in daycare. It's important to deal with these feelings even if they cannot be completely resolved. The situation can always be made better. First, the parents will feel better if they make sure that they spend focused time with the baby when they're at home. Dishes and laundry can wait. Second, the parents may feel better if they are able to cut back the number of hours the baby spends in daycare by making further changes in their own schedules. It's important to realize that most parents have no option other than to have the mother work. Nevertheless, all mothers need some time on their own. From this point of view, a mother can't and shouldn't expect to be with her infant all the time. Time out, whether it's working or attending to other concerns, can help to "recharge" the mother. An unhappy, overworked mother is unlikely to do her best as a parent. This is really part of the larger issue that no parent is perfect. Many new parents find they have impossibly high standards for themselves as parents. No one can be a

Care by a relative

Advantages

- care-giver loves baby, is emotionally involved
- care-giver will be long-term figure in baby's life
- increases family ties
- inexpensive or free
- setting is familiar

Disadvantages

- may cause family conflicts over hours, scheduling arrangements, child-rearing practices
- older relatives may have physical limitations

Continued

Care by a grandmother is loving and dedicated. Photo by Dr. I. Samuels.

super parent—this becomes even more apparent as children get older. It's enough for a parent to do a loving and conscientious job.

Even in the best of daycare situations, problems can arise. Parents will feel better and their baby will benefit from efforts to deal with these problems. This is a situation in which it is better for parents to be somewhat overprotective and to be quick to speak out about their concerns, because the baby cannot speak for itself. There is much that parents can do to ensure that daycare arrangements function optimally. Beyond seeing that the daycare situation meets basic standards in a variety of areas, parents need to try to develop a good rapport with their baby's caretaker, and make sure that they allocate sufficient time for this purpose. In doing this, they'll not only get to know the care-giver on a personal level, they will find out how their baby is doing when they're at work.

Even within these categories, there are tremendous differences depending upon how many hours the babies spend in care, and how many other children are cared for at the same time.

In the end, the most important thing is that the baby seems happy and well cared for, and that the parents feel at ease with the arrangement they've worked out and with their own lives. Infant daycare is not always an ideal solution for the family, but, with thoughtful planning and loving care, it can be a positive experience.

Family care with a non-relative outside the home

Advantages

- baby is in a home setting, looked after by a single person who optimally gets to know the baby well
- may be near work or home
- usually flexible on hours
- moderate in price
- allows siblings to be with baby
- exposes baby to other children
- easy to find

Disadvantages

- quality of care varies, ranging from excellent to poor
- care-giver may have to look after several other children (including her own)
- care-giver may have a different philosophy on child-rearing
- atmosphere may not be stimulating
- baby is out of own home
- baby has to be dropped off
- baby is exposed to germs from other children

Continued

Concerns about infant daycare

Currently one of the greatest controversies in child development involves the long-term effects of daycare on children under a year. The question is, is daycare detrimental to the baby, and if so, how? This is an emotional, exceedingly complex social issue that touches on all aspects of life—psychological, social, political, and economic. Almost everyone approaches the issue with preconceived ideas, prejudices, and personal involvement.

Parents who need two incomes, companies that cannot afford long maternity leaves, and many feminists who see child-rearing as a potential loss of freedom hope that studies will support the view that early child care is either beneficial or not harmful. Many other people, including parents, pediatricians, and psychologists, are concerned that early daycare may have adverse effects. The interpretation of the results of the research on daycare in the first year is controversial, but the weight of evidence at this time seems to indicate that there is some reason for concern. This finding does not apply to daycare for older children, however. In fact, there is some evidence that daycare for children over two years may be beneficial.

Concern over infant daycare stems from the fact that it has long been known that early infancy is a special time for mother and baby in terms of getting to know each other, becoming attuned to each other's rhythms, and forming attachments. In psychological terms, a main task of the baby during early infancy is believed to be the formation of a secure attachment to a primary care-giver. When such an attachment develops, the infant feels that he or she has a safe base from which to explore the world and interact with others (see page 185). Attachment is paradoxically the beginning of independence and self-esteem. Research shows that young babies can form multiple attachments, but it is generally believed that one primary care-giver whom a young baby learns to love and trust is ideal. This concept stems from research in orphanages which showed that infants did not develop normally if they did not have a primary caretaker (see page 24). Based on these old studies, researchers recently undertook detailed studies on babies who had been cared for by someone other than their mother for twenty or more hours per week during the first year. These babies' attachment to their mother was measured using a standard test called the *Strange Situation,* which has succesfully predicted how attached a baby is to its mother. In the test, the mother leaves the baby with a stranger who attempts to be comforting. When the mother returns, if the baby greets the mother and appears comforted by the mother's presence, the attachment is said to be *secure.* If the baby avoids or resists contact with the mother, the attachment is considered *insecure.*

The most disturbing research on infant daycare comes from studies by Jay Belsky, a child researcher at Pennsylvania State University. Belsky found that babies under a year who were in non-maternal care more than twenty hours per week were more likely to be classified as insecurely attached to their mother and father than children who did not have as much non-maternal care. A number of studies by other researchers have also demonstrated that these babies showed increased avoidance and insecurity in the Strange Situation, backing up Belsky's work. However, several other studies have failed to demonstrate any association and insecure attachment. In all the studies, there was a great variation within the groups. Even in Belsky's studies, more than half the daycare infants did establish a secure attachment with their mother.

More recent research growing out of the work on the Strange Situation has dealt with the effect of maternal stress, maternal attitude, and the gender of the baby. Belsky found that the babies who become insecure were more likely to be male, and to be fussy and difficult, and the mothers were more likely to be less satisfied.

In addition to attachment and secure behavior, other research has been undertaken. Several studies have shown that there is no difference in intelligence or language development between babies in non-maternal care and a control group. However, there have been studies that indicate that daycare babies have improved social relationships with both children and adults. Still other studies have found negative behaviors such as increased aggression, decreased cooperation, greater frustration, and more social withdrawal among daycare infants. Although these behaviors were not in a pathological range, they were similar to babies who had been rated as insecure. These results, combined with that of security-attachment studies,

Live-in or non-live-in care at home

Advantages

- baby is in own home
- parent may be at home, but doing work
- siblings will be present
- hours may be more flexible
- care-giver may do other work in house
- early exposure to a second language if care-giver is non-English speaking

Disadvantages

- expensive
- may be hard to find
- may affect family privacy if care-giver lives in
- care-givers may have different philosophies of child-care which may lead to conflict with the parent
- care-giver may not be a stable figure for the baby, may leave suddenly
- care-giver turnover is common
- care-giver may not stimulate English language skills if she is not English speaking

Continued

have led Belsky to characterize non-maternal care in the first year as a risk factor. He observes that the data raises concern about "non-parental care as we know it in the first year of life." Belsky also states that although infants who are cared for by their mother can have such problems as well, mothers tend to be more responsive to signals of insecurity and are more likely to meet a baby's needs.

All child development experts do not share Belsky's view of this material, however. Alison Clarke-Stewart of the University of California agrees with Belsky's research but questions the long-term results of the data. She questions whether an insecure assessment in the Strange Situation is the same for babies of working and non-working mothers, and even whether the test was meaningful. She notes that the object of the test is to create a stressful situation in which the baby seeks its mother's reassurance, and she points out that a baby who has been in daycare is accustomed to being left with strangers and may not even need comforting when the mother returns. She also says that one can interpret Belsky's data in two different ways. One is that a young baby has a 39 percent increased risk of insecure attachment if the mother works. Another way of looking at the results is that the probability that an infant will be securely attached is only 10 percent less than normal if the mother works. Clarke-Stewart questions the studies that show that daycare babies are more aggressive and cites other studies which show advanced social development. Her conclusion is that the daycare children are not insecure and socially maladjusted, but think for themselves and want their own way. She also cites studies showing that infant daycare babies did better on intelligence tests at 18–36 months, although non-daycare babies caught up quickly. A Swedish study of first-year daycare showed very positive results. These children were later found to score well on cognitive tests and receive positive ratings from teachers in social and academic attributes. However, there are several major differences between Swedish and American infant daycare. First, all mothers are given 6–7 months off with 90 percent of pay, and most take it. Thus daycare generally does not begin in the early months. Second, daycare is consistently of high quality whether it be home care or a daycare center. Care is free, and workers are trained and licensed. Infants in high-quality university research centers in the United States have also basically shown positive results.

These two diverse interpretations of the material show how complex the question of non-maternal care in the first year really is. Neither parents, pediatricians, nor researchers have a definitive answer to the problem. In fact, as of 1988, well-known child development experts showed a wide range of opinions that go beyond the conclusions of Belsky and Clarke-Stewart. At one extreme, Burton White, author of *The First Three Years of Life,* has stated that he believes daycare should be avoided through the third year. Selma Fraiberg, author of *Every Child's Birthright,* tends to agree with White. Mary Ainsworth, who developed the Strange Situation and pioneered in the field of attachment, feels that mother-child attach-

Child-care center

Advantages

- care-givers are often trained
- center is generally a stable situation
- environment can be stimulating in terms of learning and relating to other children, adults
- cost may be subsidized

Disadvantages

- few centers deal with very young children
- care is institutional rather than home-like; child generally has less one-to-one care
- care is generally expensive
- baby is exposed to a large pool of germs
- baby must be dropped off
- turnover is high among care-givers

ment may be compromised by early daycare. Dr. T. Berry Brazelton, well-known pediatrician and author, urges parents to stay home whenever possible. We believe that ideally the baby should be taken care of by the mother and father for the first three to six months, and then only be in part-time care until about a year. We also recognize that in our culture this may not be possible for all parents and babies until there is a guaranteed, paid maternity leave for all mothers. At the opposite end of the spectrum, researchers B. Caldwell, Jerome Kagan of Harvard, and S. Scarr who wrote *Mother Care/Other Care,* believe that the effects of good daycare are benign.

Good daycare may not be as easy to obtain as many people assume. UCLA psychologist Carollee Howes has found that among a group of 18–24-month-old children cared for in their own homes or that of a family, most had already experienced two to three changes in a non-maternal care-giver, and some as many as six. In infant centers, the turnover is even greater. Approximately half the workers leave each year, presumably due in part to the low pay scale.

In 1985 Yale University set up a panel to make recommendations about infant daycare concerns. Despite the wide range of views expressed by panel members, all agreed on the necessity of a policy of paid infant-care leave for mothers for a minimum of six months. They also agreed that all families should have access to good-quality, affordable infant care thereafter. As of 1980, the Federal Interagency Day Care Regulations proposed a set of guidelines for minimal standards: one adult for every three children in infant daycare, and one adult for every four toddlers. They also proposed that child care workers have training. Only three states meet these standards.

If there is any consensus about infant daycare, it seems to lean toward maximizing mother-baby contact, especially in the first few months. Researchers seem to agree that early daycare may affect child development—with the magnitude and risk/benefits being determined by the infant's whole environment and the quality of daycare. Thus each parent must determine how much time to spend with the baby in the first year. Those mothers who must or who choose to work in the early months should attempt to spend as much time as possible outside of work with the baby, and should make every effort to ensure that the baby's daycare is of good quality.

Characteristics to look for in a care-giver

Care-giver seems to love babies and be at ease with them.

Care-giver has a warm, stable, positive temperament and seems to get along with parents and siblings.

Care-giver appears neat and clean, seems dependable.

Care-giver can meet parents' needs in terms of hours, can do housework, drive, shop, and take baby out.

Care-giver has a similar child care philosophy and style, especially in regard to discipline and values.

Care-giver has the ability to stimulate the baby.

Stimulation in the first year

Many studies have been done on the effects of stimulating the infant in the first year. Basically, all studies point to the fact that stimulation tends to both accelerate mental and physical development and diminish boredom and withdrawal. The older infant, like the newborn, seeks stimulation and seems to thrive on it. In studies of laboratory animals stimulation has been shown to produce an increase in brain weight, the number of brain cells, and in activity of enzymes involved in sending nerve impulses. These physical changes are permanent. More researchers theorize that the behavioral changes observed among infants as a result of stimulus enrichment affect adult behavior as well as the baby's present actions.

Beginning as early as two months babies show differences in behavior based on environmental stimulation. Studies reveal that institutionalized babies with generally impoverished environments show "more avid [but] less selective" attention toward visual patterns, while babies from private homes more quickly become bored with the patterns. Infants raised in normal homes are used to looking at diverse visual stimuli and are more skillful at dealing with them. Older infants raised in institutions show severe effects from lack of stimulation. These infants are basically apathetic, make few demands on the environment, and few attempts at social interchange. They appear depressed and often cry listlessly. The greater the deprivation infants suffer and the longer they endure it, the more severe are the results and the harder the results are to reverse. But in an enriched environment with varied, appropriate stimulation, deprived infants can recover their curiosity, liveliness, and sociability.

In a rich, full relationship between mother and baby, the mother naturally stimulates the baby through her attention and encouragement. Mother and Child, *by Pablo Picasso. Courtesy of the Art Institute of Chicago.*

Parents vary widely in the amount of stimulation they give to young children at different stages. It is rather typical for infants to spend large amounts of time unattended, in a crib, for the first several months. As the infants grow older and begin to spend more time awake, they become both more engaging and more responsive, and their parents generally spend more time talking, holding, and playing with them.

Just as deprivation produces negative effects, enrichment produces positive effects. The more babies are introduced to stimuli on a par with their developmental capacities of the moment, the faster and more ably the babies will develop. At the most basic level, the more mothers and other people look at, touch, hold, and talk to babies, the more the babies will explore, vocalize, manipulate, and learn. Real direct attention develops in babies the confident expectancy that their actions will affect the environment and produce results. This attitude is important not just to specific behaviors, but to all learning. The sense of competence thus instilled goes beyond intellectual learning to social and emotional adaptation patterns. Positive patterning increases babies' ability to deal with frustration and stress. Early stimulation may actually arouse the body's stress system (the "adrenocorticosteroid mechanism"), and this experience may produce better ability to handle later stress experiences. Animals that have been stimulated or stressed in infancy withstand adult stress better and are less timid at exploring new situations.

A famous child development study by Mary Ainsworth showed that infants in Uganda were quite advanced in motor and language development during the first year. Ugandan infants sat, crawled, stood, and walked much earlier than average American babies. The infants also knew their own name, and used two or three words earlier. From her studies Ainsworth concluded that the accelerated development was due to infant caring methods. Typically, the Ugandan infant has a very close relationship with its mother in the first year of life. This relationship includes beast-feeding on demand and a great deal of physical contact. The babies are either carried upright on the mother's back or sit face outward in her lap. Thus the baby is constantly exposed to and stimulated by the mother's experiences. Ugandan babies are also given special training to teach them to sit without support. This training is preparatory to a naming ceremony, held at about three months. The infants spend approximately fifteen minutes a day sitting in a shallow hole with their back further supported by a cloth bound around the waist. Once the baby can sit and crawl, it is allowed complete freedom to move about. Ainsworth found that upper-class Ugandan infants who were raised in a more Western manner showed the same schedule of motor development as European babies. The upper-class Ugandan infants were kept in cribs, breast-fed on schedule, and not carried about nearly as often.

How to stimulate your baby's big muscle control

Providing a rich environment for the baby helps to stimulate its growth and development optimally and can be a source of interest and fun for both the baby and the parents. Such stimulation teaches the baby to relate to the world with interest and positivity and may accelerate the baby's development. By learning to use its body skillfully, the baby gains a sense of competence and self-direction.

Head control

Hold infant upright (supporting its head initially), first while stationary, then while walking or dancing.

Carry infant about in a carrier or pack as soon as head control is sufficiently well developed.

Put infant on its stomach—encourage infant's natural tendency to lift head by presenting interesting sights and sounds (for example, the mother's face or voice) where the baby will have to look up at them.

Gently pull the baby to sitting position.

Rolling over—front to back, back to front

Encourage baby to hold its head up while on its stomach.

Let baby spend time on its stomach on a soft, safe, roomy surface (for example, bed, playpen, rug).

Put the baby on a slight tilt or depress the surface (for example, bed) with your hand to encourage rolling over by gravity.

Continued

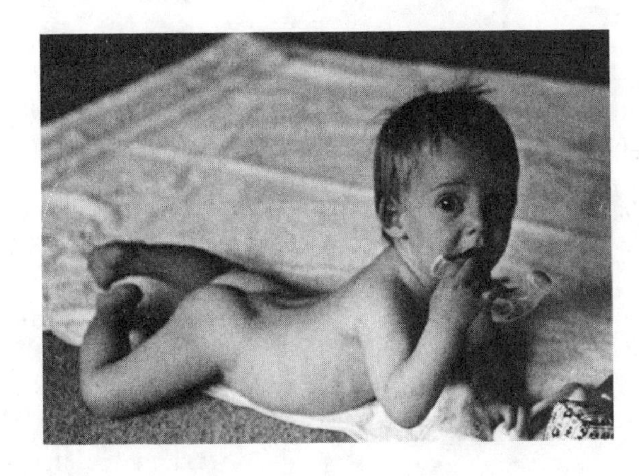

Putting the baby on its stomach encourages raising the head, rolling over, and finally crawling.

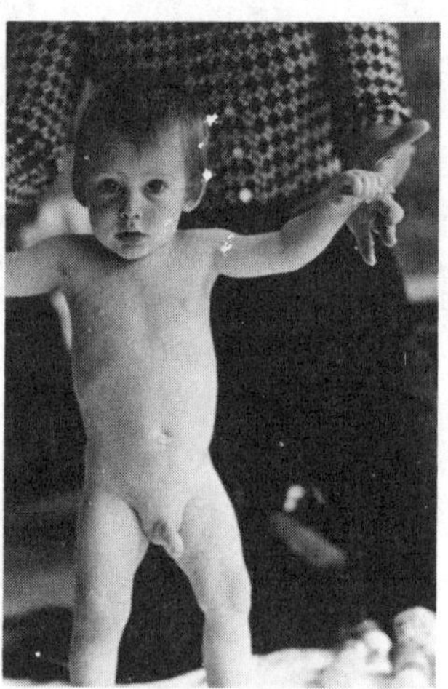

Holding the baby upright stimulates the big muscles and develops the balance needed for standing and walking.

Gently roll the baby over.

Put something interesting above or next to the baby's head.

Sitting up
Support baby in sitting position with hands.

Prop baby in a soft, safe place.

Continued

Set baby on floor with legs open and hands in front on floor.

Pull baby gently to a sitting position.

Creeping, crawling
Put baby on stomach in safe place with sufficient room to move about.

Put an interesting object in front of the baby, but just out of reach, or call to baby.

Hold hands behind baby's feet so baby can push off—repeat as baby moves forward.

Standing/walking
Hold baby upright; let baby bear weight on feet; "walk" baby while supporting its weight.

Put baby in hanging jumper, mobile walker.

Stand baby against sturdy, graspable furniture—for example, chair, playpen, low table.

Encourage baby to take steps holding on to hands for balance, not support.

How to stimulate your baby's fine muscle control

Eye control—following and focusing

Hold baby upright (stimulates visual alertness).

Place visually interesting objects (including people) close enough for baby to focus on (approximately 7–10 inches for the very young infant) and gradually back away (by 3–4 months the baby is ready to focus over long distances).

Place baby where it can see contours (especially ones with great dark and light contrast) and faces and facelike patterns.

Provide baby with a variety of interesting things to look at; frequently change the objects and the baby's position.

Continued

When the baby is turned away from the mother it is exposed to outside stimulation.

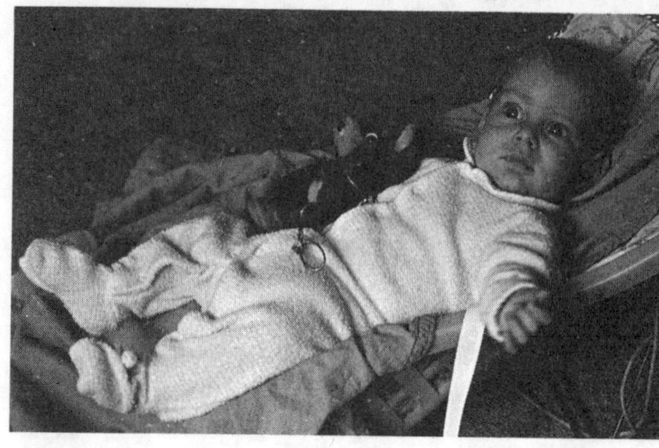

Placing the baby in an upright position where it can see things stimulates eye control.

Slowly move interesting objects across baby's visual field or point them out.

Place baby where it can see moving objects like mobiles, wind chimes, or windup toys at close range.

Eye-hand coordination

Put objects in baby's hand to stimulate grasp, then gently pull.

Place baby where its arms can touch objects or where its hands can hit at objects or reach and pick up interesting, easily graspable objects such as small soft blocks, animals.

Continued

Handing small objects to the baby stimulates beginning eye-hand control.

Hand objects to the baby; have baby hand them back: small soft blocks and rubber animals, rattles, tiny toys, finger foods.

Encourage baby to put safe objects in its mouth—fingers, finger foods, or toys.

General body stimulation

Bathe the baby—in water and sunlight.

Massage the baby, with or without oil. Stroke the baby's body from the center outward in a slow, even rhythm; delicately pat and knead the muscles and spine; gently extend the arms and legs.

Hold baby upright (stimulates visual alertness).

Rock baby.

Dance with baby.

Spin baby about gently.

Exercises for the baby

Flexibility

Gently move the baby's limbs, flexing and extending all the joints.

Put the baby in yoga positions—many are natural and merely need to be stimulated by putting the baby in a position that usually leads to one of the asanas (yoga positions):

Lying on stomach, arms outstretched, head raised (cobra)
Lying on stomach, with arms, legs, and head raised (open bow)
Cross the baby's arms
Bring leg to opposite shoulder, shoulder to opposite leg—very gently

Strength

Back and neck
"Baby airplane"—hold baby firmly about the middle and raise smoothly over head (baby needs a fair amount of head control to learn this).

Legs
"Baby bicycle"—lay baby on back, hold both the baby's ankles, and alternately push and pull the baby's legs. (Earlier) variation: push and pull legs simultaneously.

Arms
"Baby boxer"—lay baby on back, hold baby's wrists, and alternately push and pull baby's arms. (Earlier) variation: push and pull arms simultaneously.

Grasp

Put fingers in baby's hand(s) and gently pull.

Neck, back, arms, stomach

"Baby sit-ups"—lay baby on its back, grasp baby's wrists, and gently pull baby up to a sitting position (requires some head control to begin with).

Legs

"Baby knee bends"—hold baby securely in a standing position, lower baby as its knees bend, and steady baby as it pushes to a standing position again.

Continued

Swimming and sunbathing are stimulating to the baby's whole body.

"Baby jumps"—hold baby securely in a standing position, lower baby as its knees bend, and spring baby into the air as it naturally pushes upward. (*Note:* bouncing chairs and hanging jumpers allow the older baby to do these exercises without help.)

General body

Swimming—many swim teachers have special courses for infants.

Spiritual stimulation for the baby

"Discipline"

Gently and patiently repeat the action you want the baby to do.

Continued

Specific exercises can help to strengthen the baby's developing muscles and promote healthy growth.

The spiritual bond between mother and baby deepens as the baby grows. The baby comes to realize that the mother is the source of its sustenance, and the mother in turn begins to have a sense of the baby's unfolding personality. Top left: Raphael, The Alba Madonna *(24), National Gallery of Art, Washington, Andrew W. Mellon Collection. Top right: Giovanni Bellini,* Madonna and Child, *The Metropolitan Museum of Art, The Jules S. Bache Collection, 1949. Bottom left: Domenico Veneziano,* Madonna and Child *(332), National Gallery of Art, Washington, Samuel H. Kress Collection. Bottom right: Gentile de Fabriano,* Madonna and Child *(366), National Gallery of Art, Washington, Samuel H. Kress Collection.*

"Balance" or rhythm

If the baby is very excited, bring it back to an active but nonexcited state by clapping, shaking a rattle, or by rocking or patting the infant in the baby's own rhythm, then gradually slowing to a more balanced pace.

Continued

A baby can even be brought into balance by the sound of another person's breathing at close range. This can also help to calm the anxious or excited parent.

Massage done in a slow, relaxed manner helps to calm an overexcited baby.

"Concentration"

Give the child an interesting, beautiful thing—a toy, a fruit, a flower; whatever attracts the child's attention most—and let the child play with it without interruption.

"Friendliness," generosity

Smile and speak warmly to the baby.

Smile and speak warmly to others.

Repeatedly give something to a child in a loving manner and gently ask the child to give it back.

"Relaxation"

Slow down the baby's rhythm if necessary (see *Balance*).

Put the baby in calm, quiet surroundings.

Expose the baby to calm, quiet people.

Put the baby in a comfortable position.

Produce in your own mind the thought of rest and peace.

Imagine your peaceful thoughts are flowing to the baby.

Pass your hand over the baby and imagine relaxation is flowing into the baby.

Look into the baby's eyes and think of the baby going to sleep.

Harmony with nature

Nature is regular; therefore do everything concerning the child with regularity.

Showing the baby the beauty of nature in calm, quiet surroundings stimulates the baby's sense of awe and wonder.

Social stimulation for the baby

Infant needs

Love—a warm, accepting, available, cooperative person; a stable, dependable relationship that involves physical, visual, and verbal contact.

Self-worth—value the child for itself.

Role models—people who embody the kind of social being it is hoped the child will become.

Continued

Protection—physical care and safety.

Security—emotional care that provides a safe base from which to explore the world. This is the start of basic trust.

Positivity—a parent who approaches situations with optimism.

Exposure to other significant adults. This extends basic trust.

Exposure to strangers—provides a model for how to relate to them.

Separations from parent that are brief, nontraumatic, and enjoyable—lead to self-confidence and independence.

Reinforcement of baby's social behaviors (for example, smiling, babbling)—leads to sense of self as effective.

Exposure to and participation in a variety of social situations—leads to confidence and ease of handling.

Language stimulation—help your baby to vocalize and understand words

Talk frequently to the baby in a slow, distinct voice. Use normal words and sentences. Emphasize basic sounds.

Expose the baby to the richest language environment possible, adult conversations.

Repeat back sounds the baby makes.

Pause after saying something to the baby to allow the baby time to respond vocally (and with gestures).

Show delight when the baby responds to or initiates sounds.

Respond to the baby's cries differentially—that is, learn the baby's language, as well as exposing the baby to yours.

Concentrate on a few simple important words when the baby appears about ready to actually talk (for example, ma-ma, da-da, hot).

Hold the baby and talk face to face.

Continued

Show the baby pictures or objects when introducing a new word.

Talk beyond the baby's ability to vocalize because the baby understands more than it can say.

Expose the baby to a variety of objects and experiences with new words.

Read to the baby.

Repeat and expand the older child's remarks.

Give the child experiences to talk about and talk about the child's experiences.

Encourage attentive listening; in turn listen attentively to the child.

Sensory stimulation

Provide the baby with a rich variety of experiences. Help the baby to focus its attention and follow up its natural interest in objects and experiences that are basically similar, but differ a little. For example, if the baby is interested in a cup, give it cups of different sizes and shapes to explore and play with. Such exploration will help the baby become aware of both differences and similarities and will help it learn what the object can do; for example, a cup holds something to drink. This is the beginning of concept formation and learning how to make generalizations.

Sense	*Varieties of experience*	*Stimulating objects or situations*
Visual	Different colors and tones, sizes, shapes, forms	Infant seats, backpacks
Auditory	Music, speech, singing scales; take note of frequency, pitch, volume, duration, rhythm	Radio, records, music boxes, toy instruments, and toys that make noise such as rattles or bells

Continued

Sense	Varieties of experience	Stimulating objects or situations
Tactile	Textures, temperatures, consistencies (wet/dry/sticky)	Toys, household objects, food, etc.; bathing, water, sun
Kinesthetic	Sizes	Graduated cups, balls of different sizes
Olfactory	Odors	Foods, flowers, perfume, etc.
Gustatory	Tastes	Sweet, sour, and salty foods

"Baby tours"—present the baby with a series of stimuli one after another. A tour can be designed simply to show a variety of stimuli, such as a bed, a chair, a door, or can concentrate on stimuli that are similar, like several rattles.

Imagery for the baby up to a year

Receptive imagery provides parents with a means to get in touch with the baby's feelings and to have a sense of just what kind of parenting the baby needs at any time—the stimulation, the limits, the encouragement that the baby needs now to fulfill its developing potentials best. In an open, relaxed state, parents will receive images and feelings about the baby that can be their guide. For example, a parent may look at a cranky, crying infant and suddenly realize that the baby is terribly frustrated by its lack of mobility or bored by a situation that is no longer stimulating. Or a parent may watch a baby playing with a rattle and suddenly realize that shaking is no longer a challenge, that the baby is ready to have a toy that disassembles and goes back together. In a sense, visualizing a baby's feelings is a form of telepathy or psychic reading. This kind of insight is similar to communication with the unborn baby that was discussed in the prenatal chapter. Research has shown that telepathic communications take place most often between parents and children. This sort of insight frequently happens spontaneously, but using receptive imagery, parents can make such insight happen deliberately. Parents will feel that they *know* what the baby is thinking.

Here is a receptive imagery exercise for parents. Make yourself comfortable. Breathe in and out deeply, allowing your abdomen to rise and fall. Deeply relax your whole body in stages. You are now in a state in which your mind is open and receptive. You can visualize vividly and easily. You are connected to your baby and your baby is connected to you. Time and space are different at this level—their possibilities are not limited. Visualize your baby . . . imagine how your baby feels—picture what your baby needs . . . picture how you can help the baby. Stay in this state as long as you wish.

Parents can do this exercise either when they are alone or when they are actively caring for the baby. They can even do it briefly, almost unconsciously, in the midst of an activity. Receptive imagery can help parents be closer to their baby. Parents can get a feeling for when the baby is getting tired, hungry, or bored; for why the baby is frustrated or crying; for the kinds of food the baby wants to eat; for the tasks or toys the baby needs to stimulate its physical or mental development.

Using relaxation and imagery up to one year

Take advantage of the baby's naps to relax yourself deeply.

Take several deep breaths and relax if you are frightened, frustrated, or angered by the baby; if you ever feel like hitting the baby; if the baby cries continually, falls, throws food on the floor, etc.

Take a few minutes to relax in the hectic time before dinner, after the baby goes to bed, in the midst of a busy day, before nursing.

The baby's naptime has always been a time for mothers to relax and do quiet work. La Marquise de Pastoret, *detail, by Jacques Louis David. Courtesy of the Art Institute of Chicago.*

Here is a brief relaxation and imagery exercise for parents. Close your eyes. Take several deep breaths, allowing your abdomen to rise and fall. As your breathing becomes slow and even, you will feel relaxed. Imagine that your body is light, almost weightless. Picture yourself floating in air, surrounded by a field of warm light. Hold this image until you feel quite rested and calm. When you feel ready, count to three and open your eyes.

This feeling of calmness and relaxation can continue for several hours and will relax your baby too. Even a few minutes of relaxation can totally change a person's day. Relaxation can break an expanding bubble of tension and increase a person's energy, accomplishment, and enjoyment.

Using imagery for getting in touch with feelings and picturing positive situations in the first year

Parents make many decisions that affect both their lives and the baby's in the first year of the baby's life. Often they make these decisions based on cultural patterns or on other people's suggestions, without really getting in touch with their own feelings. It's important for people to realize whether or not they are in harmony with what they do and what happens to them. Life with a young baby can be especially confusing at times because many things a parent does for the baby are unfamiliar or are done so quickly as to preclude much thought.

If parents let images of situations come to mind and then become aware of the feelings the situations arouse, the parents can see whether or not a particular alternative is in harmony with their feelings.

Should the baby be allowed to cry when it is put down to sleep?

When will the baby begin to eat solid foods?

When will the baby be weaned?

When will the baby sleep through the night?

When will the baby begin to stay with other people?

Will the mother return to work, and when?

How much time will the father plan on taking care of the baby?

Once a decision is made, a parent can hold that particular image in mind (programmed imagery) to increase good feelings around the situation. For example—

Picture the baby doing well with a sitter.

Continued

Picture the baby eating solid foods and enjoying it.

Picture the baby sleeping peacefully through the night.

Picture the mother enjoying her return to work.

Chapter 8

The older baby

The older baby is more and more a person in its own right, reaching out with its own personality, needs, and desires. The Stocking, *detail, by Mary Cassatt. Drypoint. The Metropolitan Museum of Art, bequest of Mrs. H. O. Havemeyer, 1929. The H. O. Havemeyer Collection.*

By the time the baby reaches a year, its needs and impact have become greater than ever. The baby has become very much a part of the *family* in a different sense than in the earlier months. By a year, the baby's presence is no longer a novelty. The cute, custodial stage has passed as the baby acquires new skills and ranges more widely into the parents' house, time, and lives. Parents begin to look at the baby with a new sense of permanence and wonder. The baby is more and more a person in its own right, with its own personality characteristics, needs, and interests.

Big muscle development

Walking is one of the great developmental landmarks of infancy. That sounds like walking is an all-or-none phenomenon that is achieved overnight, and in one sense, it is. A baby who has shown only minimal interest in walking and who has taken only a few hesitant steps may one day begin walking with determination and never go back to crawling again. Yet the way that baby walked initially bears no resemblance to the way the baby walks a week, a month, or a half-year later.

When the baby first begins to walk, its feet are widely spaced so it can keep its balance.

At first the baby walks with a widespread stance, feet rolled in, toes pointing out. As the days and weeks go by, the baby's halting gait becomes smoother, and as the baby's confidence in its balance grows, the stance narrows. Meanwhile the baby's arches are growing stronger and the baby starts to walk more on the flat part of its feet. Gradually the toes start to turn in as well and the baby begins to walk in a straighter line.

With further improvements in balance the baby becomes able to stoop and recover, as well as walk. The baby's hands, once used as steadying devices, now are free to pick up objects and carry them. The baby is able to engage in new kinds of play as it has less need to concentrate on the act of walking itself.

Walking actually becomes habitual, even nonchalant, somewhere in the first half of the second year. And straight walking gives way to new variations. The baby learns to walk backward, generally quite easily. Around eighteen months the baby learns to walk *up*stairs, one step at a time, holding on to someone's hand for support. Walking downstairs in this manner does not come for another few months. About this time the baby first learns to run in a characteristically stiff and jerky manner. The baby becomes considerably more adept at both stair climbing and running toward the end of the second year. By this time the baby can climb up and down stairs by itself, usually starting each stair with the same foot. The baby can also run quite fast and smoothly without falling.

Between the ages of two and four most children learn a wide variety of gross motor skills. These skills develop as the child's capacities mature. But they also are tied to stimulation and experience. Thus there may be more than a year or two's range in the normal development of a particular skill. Generally boys seem to achieve most of the gross motor landmarks earlier than girls. Probably this is mostly due to practice and shows the great importance at this point of exposure and encouragement.

Almost all the newly acquired gross motor skills of the two-to-four period are "playground skills." At first the child repeatedly practices the movement in an unskilled way. Then as the child becomes proficient at the movement,

The safest way for young babies to get down stairs is to back down.

Big motor landmarks—1 to 4 years

Doctors and child development researchers commonly consider certain activities to be landmarks of the second to fourth years. These landmarks are simply abilities that are *somewhat* age-related and are also easy and fast to observe or test for.

At 2 years
Balances on one foot for 1 second

Jumps in place

Pedals tricycle

Can jump with both feet together

At 3 years
Balances on one foot for 5–10 seconds

Hops on one foot

Catches and bounces ball occasionally

Can walk putting heel to toe

A child needs encouragement and safe equipment to learn motor skills such as climbing and swinging.

How to help your child with big motor stimulation

Expose the child to large outdoor areas that are safe and contain objects or equipment that naturally stimulate big motor activities—for example, jungle gyms, swings, slides, ladders, ropes, platforms, balance beams, seesaws, balls, and bicycles.

Encourage the child to choose activities that it is weak in as well as ones it excels at.

Expose the child to indoor toys and activities that stimulate big motor development, such as push-pull toys, rocking horses, hanging bars, hobbyhorses, and balance toys.

Provide the child with props that stimulate big motor kinds of dramatic play—for example, Batman capes, playhouses.

Teach the child games and activities that require big motor action such as tag, hide and seek, Simon sez, and dancing.

Large outdoor areas naturally encourage the child to run and jump.

Common concerns during the second year

The baby's appetite generally decreases in the second year.

As self-feeding begins, babies frequently spill and make a mess.

Weaning to a cup is common in this period.

Most babies continue to nap in the afternoon, often for long periods.

Toilet-training readiness and interest begin to appear. Parents should introduce the potty chair when they wish to start training.

Parents should begin to set limits, using verbal praise and reprimands, and physically removing the child from situations when necessary. Eventually, the concept of time-out can be introduced.

Parents can stimulate children by reading aloud, playing games, and engaging in physical activities with them.

Many parents now arrange group daycare or social play.

Parents need to take appropriate safety measures with tub and pool use, with cabinets that contain poisons or sharp objects, and with objects that can cause choking or suffocation (e.g., plastic bags, chewing gum).

Parents should limit the baby's television viewing and monitor what programs are watched.

Thumb-sucking, masturbation, pacifiers, and security blankets are all normal at this age.

Nightmares and separation fears are common at this age, and the child should be reassured and given help to resolve them.

it begins to incorporate the new skill smoothly into the course of play—sandwiching the skill in between two or three other motor activities or building up a stunt, a fantasy, or a game around the new skill. Many of the two-to-four-year-old skills involve the use of materials and, in fact, are inseparable from them—skills such as throwing, kicking, catching, pedaling, steering, and climbing. Even those skills that do not require materials become intimately bound up with the course of play. Indeed, a great proportion of the child's time and learning at this age is spent in large motor play.

Artists through the ages have recognized the beauty and pleasing proportions of the older baby's body. Left: Eros Sleeping, *Greek sculpture, 250–150 B.C. The Metropolitan Museum of Art, Rogers Fund, 1943. Right:* Reclining Boy, *by Andrea del Verrocchio, M. H. de Young Memorial Museum.*

Fine muscle development

Fine motor development between one and four years involves continued development of the small muscles of the hand in conjunction with vision. Unlike big motor activities, fine motor development demands a relatively still body. Yet much of the one-to-four period is characterized by running, walking, climbing—in short, by big-motor activities. Indeed, these big activities are so characteristic and so recently acquired that relatively little mention of fine motor activities is usually made in descriptions of the toddler and the preschool child. But very important fine motor skills are usually being achieved in this same period of time, in between the running, jumping, and pedaling that are so common. In fact, some of the big motor skills, such as climbing, throwing, and steering, overlap and reinforce the use of the hand in conjunction with visual perception.

Fine motor development breaks down into two basic categories. The first involves using the hands to reach out for, grasp, and move an object. The second category, which grows out of the first, involves grasping a tool and using *it* to accomplish a goal.

By the end of the first year the baby has made real progress in its ability to grasp objects. Not only can the baby grasp with its whole hand, it has learned the basic refinements of grasping—opposing thumb to palm and thumb to forefinger. Thumb-to-palm opposition enables the baby to grasp larger objects firmly. The pincerlike grasp of thumb-to-forefinger enables the baby to pick up small objects in a precise fashion. During the second year the baby learns to use the pincerlike grasp to "do something." For example, a baby not only picks up an object such as a raisin, it drops the raisin into a bottle. About this time the baby also learns to pile small blocks on top of one another to make a stack. As the baby gets older it is able to make a taller and taller stack without having the blocks topple. This feat demonstrates the baby's increasing muscular precision and eye-hand coordination. The baby is learning to set goals and consciously direct the movements of arm and hand. This skill is no small achievement. It involves the perfection of nerve and muscle circuits that produce a complicated motion, requiring a number of muscles coordinated smoothly and dexterously. The eyes have to tell the brain where the hand is in relation to the object, and the brain in turn has to constantly send corrective signals to the muscles.

The second category of fine motor development involves sustained grasping and the use of one of a variety of tools: crayon, pencil, paintbrush, hammer, saw, screwdriver, scissors, fork, spoon, knife, etc. The forerunners of all such movements probably are shaking rattles and putting things in the

The ability to make a stack of blocks represents real development of visual skills and fine muscle control.

mouth, actions that involve some precision in moving an object. Once a child has learned to grasp a tool in a usable manner, it can then do something to *another* object to achieve a particular result. For example, once a baby has learned to hold a pencil or crayon, it can make marks on a paper. With practice the child's grasp and movements become more and more adept, and the marks that are made become more and more precise. Early in the second year the baby spontaneously begins to scribble if given a crayon or pencil. By midyear the child can draw lines as opposed to simply making marks. By about the end of the second year the child can draw a crude circle. As the child approaches four, it can, with practice, draw and copy increasingly complicated (geometric) figures.

Tool use stimulates the growing baby's fine muscle control and its sense of cause and effect.

Using a spoon requires expertise in eye-hand coordination and grasp. It also encourages the baby's sense of competence and independence.

As a child's grasp develops, so does its interest in feeding itself. Even before a year a baby may start to grasp a cup and drink by itself. This action represents a refinement of the inborn hand-to-mouth reflex coupled with grasping. Later the baby starts to use a spoon to stir and to bring food to its mouth. The stabbing motion of the fork is a more adroit movement and follows stirring motions. Dexterity with a spoon or fork does not come till around sixteen months.

Children between one and four spend much of their time in action-oriented activities involving materials. That is, their gross and fine motor play frequently involves doing something to an object. Small objects involve the hands and eyes in small movements. Developing fine motor skills has two important consequences. First, such skills have great usefulness in

During the second year the child's rate of growth slows, and they become taller rather than heavier.

everyday life as the child learns to feed and dress itself, as well as amuse itself with many of the small toys that require fine manipulation of the hands. Second, fine motor skills of the one-to-four period are tied to intellectual development. Manual dexterity and the use of tools are linked to understanding concepts and solving problems.

How to help your child with fine motor stimulation

Expose the child to toys that fit together, stack, etc.: blocks, puzzles, pouring containers.

Provide the child with children's hand tools including hammers, saws, scissors, etc.

Encourage the child to use pens, pencils, paintbrushes, and paper in free play as well as in activities that require reproducing or tracing.

Teach the child games that require fine motor coordination: action songs, finger play games, card games, sorting games.

Growth patterns

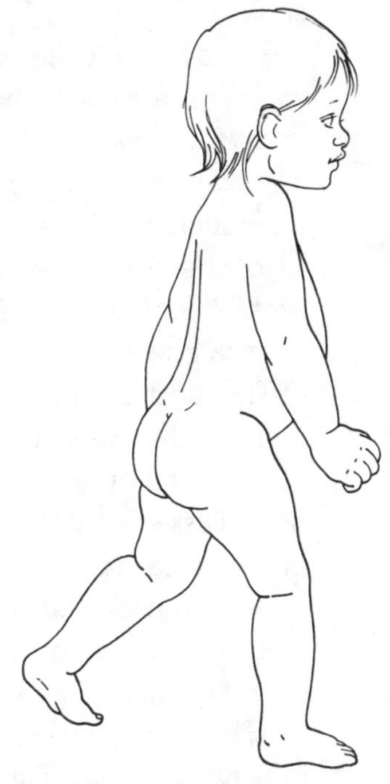

Two-year-olds develop a characteristic swayback and potbelly, which they will lose toward the fourth year.

During the second year the baby's physical growth slows down. The baby grows taller as opposed to fatter, gaining more in height than in weight. The baby actually loses much of its layer of subcutaneous fat and thus its chubby, babyish look. The baby also begins to develop the swayback and protuberant abdomen that are characteristic of the second and third year. The accompanying chart contains figures for height and weight gain that are averages. They obviously do not apply to all children individually, but indicate general growth patterns.

In the second year the average child gains 5 inches (12.7 centimeters) and a mere 5 pounds (2.5 kilograms). The child's birthweight is approximately quadrupled by the end of the second year. The circumference of the baby's head increases by 2 centimeters—less than an inch. But by the end of the second year the baby's brain has reached four-fifths of its adult size.

During the third and fourth years weight and height gains are fairly constant. The child gains about 4 to 5 pounds (2 kilograms) each year and will continue to do so through the ninth year. The child grows 3 to 4 inches (8½ centimeters) in the third year, and from then on 2 to 3 inches (6 centimeters) per year until puberty. During the fourth year the child thins down and loses its swayback and potbelly, attaining more graceful proportions.

Growth formulas

From 1 to 6 years
Weight in pounds = (age in years × 5) + 17

From 2 to 14 years
Height in inches = (age in years × 2½) + 30

Nutrition

By about one year of age most babies are eating table foods along with their parents. In addition they may have one or more snacks in between. The chances are great the baby has been or is being weaned from the breast and is drinking from a cup, a bottle, or both. Most one-year-olds are quite proficient with finger foods, but generally are still not very adept with spoon or fork. Coupled with their newfound independence, this may lead them to prefer foods that can be cut in small pieces and eaten by hand. Parents can foster self-feeding at this period and save themselves a great deal of trouble by limiting the number of messy, spoon-fed foods they serve.

The average one-year-old has six to eight teeth—all front teeth or incisors. This means the baby can now bite and tear, but still has to use its gums for chewing. When the molars come in during the course of the second year, the baby will be able to start chewing on larger pieces of food and tough, hard ones. Until the child has molars and is used to the mechanics of chewing and swallowing, foods that can be choked on should be prohibited. Nuts, seeds, and potato chips are especially dangerous because they can be inhaled.

The most common food concern that parents have in the years between one and three is whether their child is eating enough. They wonder how the small amount of food the child eats allows it to grow and have the boundless energy characteristic of this age. The answer to this question lies in several facts. First, between one and three years the child's growth rate slows tremendously. This means the child needs smaller quantities of food relative to its weight. Second, the average adult in this country tends to overeat, whereas most two-year-olds have not yet been conditioned to do so. Third, unlike most adults, young children often have substantial snacks in between meals. Thus they don't need to eat as much food at any one meal.

Another food concern of parents in these years is that a child sometimes has periods when it is disinterested in food in general or when it refuses specific kinds of foods. Eating is tied to growth, and probably most of the child's growth occurs in spurts. These spurts correspond to periods when the child is eating readily and frequently, while disinterest corresponds to the periods in between growth spurts. A fascinating study done in the 1930s actually showed that when children were free to select their own foods, they not only ate enough, they selected a balanced diet. *However,* they did not necessarily eat a balanced meal at each sitting. The amount the children ate varied, with some foods being eaten in excess and others being refused. But over a period of days and weeks the children selected a nutritionally adequate diet. At each meal the children were given a dozen different foods to choose from, including raw and cooked vegetables, eggs, cereal, milk, etc. The children often ate a bizarre meal, consuming as many as ten eggs at once or eating strange combinations of foods. They generally paid no attention to adult tastes or habits and sometimes began their meal with dessert.

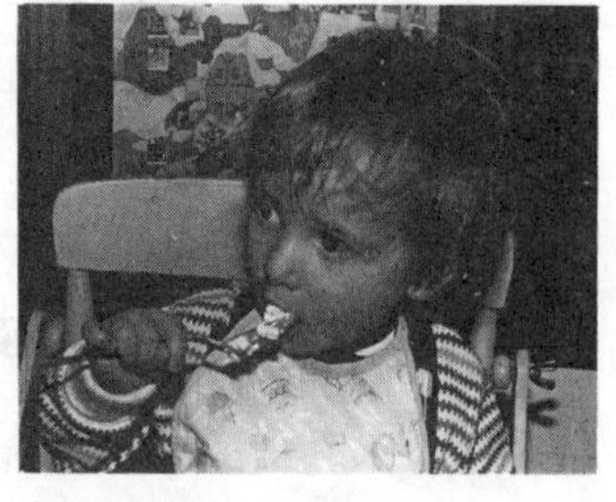

By one year, the baby is beginning to feed itself. Parents need to have patience because the baby often feeds itself slowly, sloppily, and in smaller amounts than they expect.

One of the children in the study who was known to have rickets (severe vitamin D deficiency) ate large quantities of cod-liver oil, which is rich in vitamin D. At the point the child stopped eating cod liver oil, X rays demonstrated that the rickets had been cured. It has long been known that laboratory animals deficient in calcium, magnesium, B vitamins, or specific amino acids will voluntarily select a diet rich in the particular elements they need. This is an example of the "wisdom of the body," that is, of the body's natural tendency to meet its own needs and keep itself healthy.

The demand feeding study shows that children are capable of choosing a sound diet if they are provided with a variety of nutritionally rich foods, but obviously every child cannot be given a dozen choices at every meal. However, children's ability to choose foods can be respected and they can be offered a variety of nutritionally sound foods. This is the age when children begin to acquire important lifelong food habits. What people—children or adults—eat not only provides for growth and sustenance, it determines to a large extent their overall health, their resistance to diseases, and their ability to heal.

Young children should be encouraged to eat good foods, in a slow, relaxed manner, when they are hungry. "Feeding problems" of children are rarely due to illness or allergy. They usually are the result of a conflict between the children's natural inclinations and the parents' wishes. Parents may be expecting a child to eat too much, to eat something the child doesn't like, to eat too fast, or to eat when they are not hungry. Children also react to various kinds of stress at mealtime—arguments, confusion, too much activity, impossible standards for table manners, even food problems of other family members.

In addition to eating because of hunger, the toddler begins to eat by habit. The child learns these habits from the family, by their example. Parents who are concerned about their child's nutrition do well to look at their own food patterns. Consistent overeating, eating rapidly or under stress, or simply eating too much junk food or sweets are all habits that a child quickly learns and imitates. Likewise, eating reasonable portions, eating in a calm, slow manner, and eating foods high in protein and vitamins are habits a child learns by example.

Sleep

By one year most babies have dropped down from an *average* of sixteen hours of sleep a day at birth to an average of thirteen and a half. This figure declines only slightly in the next three years. By four years of age the average amount of sleep per day is twelve hours. These figures include time spent napping. An older child who still naps every day is likely to get up early or stay up late.

There is, of course, wide variation around these averages. Some children regularly require as little as ten hours of sleep by the age of four, while others still require as much as fourteen. Individual children themselves often vary in the amount they sleep. As in eating, there may be wide fluctuation in the amount children sleep each day. But their sleep needs are generally rather stable over a period of weeks.

Most children probably sleep more when they are in the middle of a growth spurt. Heavy physical activity, intense emotional excitement, and physical accidents or illness may also tend to increase the child's need for sleep. Children who are coming down with a cold may take an unexpected nap or nap for an unusually long time. Younger children will sometimes fall asleep directly after a period of intense stimulation such as a frightening accident or a temper tantrum.

While children tend to balance their body's needs with the amount they sleep over the long run, they can often be insensitive to fatigue on a given day. Many elements in the environment can stimulate a child to stay awake even when tired. Noise, excitement, or any kind of special event can be distracting and keep a child awake. Rather than fall asleep, the overstimulated child may forcibly keep itself awake. From considerably under a year a child is physiologically capable of keeping itself awake. In time parents can become aware of a child's early signs of fatigue. Unusual fussiness, crankiness, irritability, "bad behavior," or temper tantrums are often a sign of fatigue. Excessive quietness, lethargy, lack of appetite, or outright drowsiness can also be signs of too little sleep.

If tired behavior occurs in the morning, it is a sign the child did not have enough sleep the previous night. If tired behavior occurs in the late afternoon, it is a sign that the child has had a tiring day and needs to get to bed early. Chronic fatigue not only increases the likelihood of behavior problems, it lowers resistance to disease.

A child's sleep patterns are greatly affected by the habits of the household. Some children regularly take naps until the age of four. This is probably due in part to sleep need, but it is also due to the parents' encouraging such a routine. Under different circumstances these same children could go to bed early and not nap at all. Parents can do a lot to encourage infant

A quiet, close moment before bed helps the child to slow down and prepare for sleep. La Bonne et l'Enfant, *detail, by Mary Cassatt. Print, drypoint. The Metropolitan Museum of Art, Gift of Paul J. Sachs, 1916.*

Sleep hints

Be aware of signs of fatigue in a baby—whining, crying, mumbling, falling, poor coordination.

Two-year-olds generally don't like to go to sleep and will often become overtired if allowed to stay up.

A baby or older child who is really overtired can have trouble falling asleep.

Nighttime rituals help—quiet periods, bedtime stories, bedtime animals and/or blankets.

Make bedtime a set time that is generally not dependent on sleepiness or behavior (parents may tend to let children stay up longer if they are clearly not tired or if they are behaving unusually well). This helps to avoid nightly scenes, because bedtime is a habit, not a decision.

Structure bedtime and naps around the family routine, and around the realistic sleep needs of the individual child.

Don't make bedtime too abrupt or too soon after mealtime or heavy play.

Children drop naps by eliminating them some days or by falling asleep later and later in the afternoon, not by taking shorter and shorter naps in any orderly way.

Toddlers often wake in the night because of toilet training, vivid dreams, or teething discomforts.

Sleep is the body's way of renewing its energy, and it can be important in preventing and healing disease.

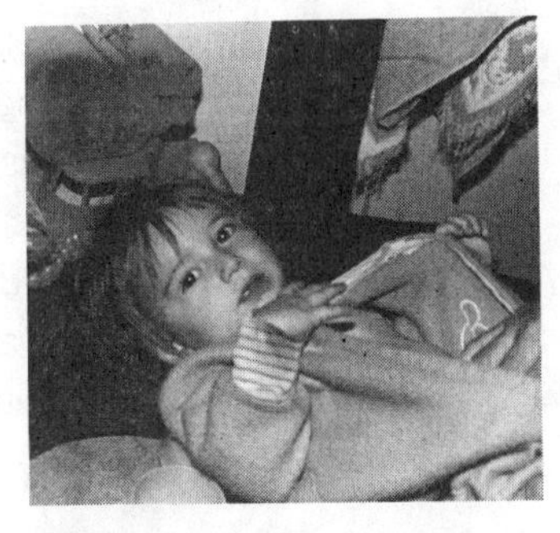

The older baby hardly ever wants to go to sleep and will become overtired if allowed to stay awake too long.

sleeping patterns that are in harmony with their household and that meet the children's needs at the same time.

Just as children will become used to different sleep times, they also will tend to become conditioned to any presleep routine that is regularly followed. Indeed most children seem to like and even need such ritual. In general these routines are not to be quickly changed. If a routine is suddenly altered, a child may object strenuously or find it difficult to fall asleep. It is no accident that almost every child and parent evolves a complex bedtime ritual. Most children seem to need help in bridging the time between the fast-paced rhythm of the day and the slow, deep rhythms of sleep. Loving assurances, peace, and quiet all seem particularly appropriate to the end of the day. Traditionally, bedtime has been the time for talking over the day, hearing stories, and saying prayers. Bedtime is often a close, poignant, spiritual time. Much of the closeness of this time is lost if the child is very tired, if the parents are very tired, if bedtime is rushed, or if bedtime has become a nightly battle between the parents and child.

Many of the sleep problems of these years arise from conflict between the child's sleeping patterns and the parents' schedule. In addition to problems about napping and going to sleep, problems may arise about sleeping through the night. Waking to nurse is replaced in the older group by other reasons for waking in the middle of the night. Sometimes children who have been regularly sleeping through the night will begin to wake again.

Physiologically, a child normally experiences several periods of very light sleep during the night. The older baby, like an adult, experiences four to six sleep cycles per night. Each cycle lasts sixty to ninety minutes and consists of deep sleep followed by REM (rapid eye movement) dreaming. In between cycles are the periods of very light sleep. The child is most likely to wake, partially or totally, in these light sleep periods. The child may toss around, whine, cry, even talk, and then go back to sleep.

Some children habitually wake between cycles, usually at about the same time each night. This is more likely to happen if the parents respond immediately to the child's noises. Children who are cutting molar teeth may wake crying a number of times during the night. Also, children are more likely to wake when they are just learning to keep dry at night. The child may wake after wetting the bed or in time to go to the bathroom, or the child may wake more frequently during this period of toilet training, just *because* it is deliberately trying to wake up when it needs to go to the bathroom.

Throughout these years children also wake in response to dreams, partic-

Many babies enjoy a warm, relaxing bath before bedtime. The Bath, *detail, by Mary Cassatt, National Gallery of Art, Washington, Chester Dale Collection.*

Quiet bedtime rituals help ease the baby's transition from activity to sleep.

ularly nightmares. Parents may first observe this situation when young babies wake suddenly from active, rapid eye movement sleep and appear to be frightened. Older children will tell parents that they have been wakened by a frightening dream. All children seem to experience nightmares. Studies show that a large number of four-year-olds (30 to 50 percent) awake frequently from nightmares, but a significant number of younger babies do also.

Toilet controls

Control over bladder and bowel is based on both intentional training and the development of the nervous system. To the extent that control is based on physical maturity, it is a developmental landmark much like sitting or walking. To the extent that it is based on learning and cultural patterns, control is an act of socialization. Like walking and talking, toilet controls frequently get mixed up with parental feelings of achievement, pride, and annoyance. There is no doubt that parents have less work once a child has achieved this control. Therefore it makes sense for parents actively to encourage control when a child is developmentally ready.

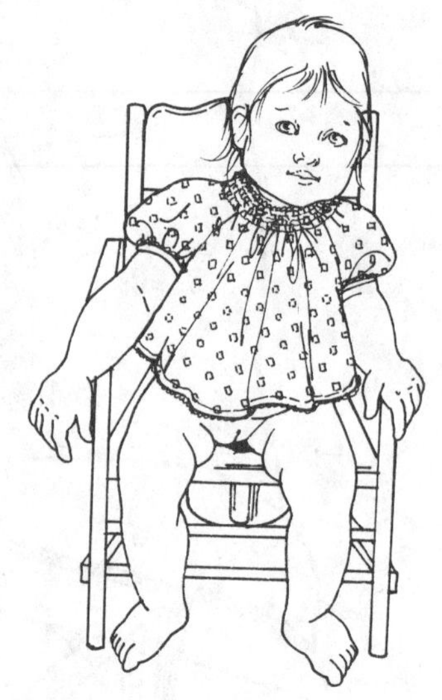

Potty training is a matter of the baby's maturational readiness and the parents' encouragement and help.

Toilet training also represents a major developmental step in terms of the child's growing sense of autonomy, as it relates to both mastery over his or her own body and independence from parental control. This type of developmental skill cannot be accomplished forcibly. Problems arise if parents expect mastery before the child is physically capable of it, or before the child becomes motivated to achieve such control. It is very important that toilet training not become a negative experience because the child is not yet capable of it, and likewise that it not become a battle of wills because of the child's growing sense of being a separate individual who needs to make decisions for him or herself. Like weaning and self-feeding, toilet training can be a positive growth experience if children are encouraged to master these new skills at the appropriate time and are praised for their efforts.

Voluntary control of the sphincters first becomes possible between the ages of 12–18 months. Before this time, "potty training" simply means training parents to anticipate the child's needs or observe the child's earliest signs of need. This process certainly saves soiled diapers and communicates the parents' values to the child, but it does not mean the child has actually achieved voluntary control. Bladder control is demonstrated when the child doesn't urinate for 2–3 hours at a time, and has dry diapers.

Voluntary control over elimination or urination can actually begin only when a child is able to distinguish the sensations that precede having a bowel movement or urinating. The child first begins to be aware of these sensations when it realizes it has wet or soiled its diapers. Then it gradually becomes aware of the process as it is happening. The child may develop such awareness spontaneously or the parent may need to point out what's happening and the results. In either case, parents' matter-of-fact recognition and their interest will act as reinforcement to the child's awareness. At the same time the parent can begin to make the child aware of the desirability of going to the bathroom in a potty or toilet.

With encouragement the child will reach a point where it can inform the parent when it is about to go. At first the child may be able to warn the parent, but may not be able to hold back the natural functions for very long. With practice the child will be able to anticipate its needs earlier and delay going for longer and longer periods of time.

Sensory development is the first stage in control. This means that the child must be able to perceive, recognize, and understand a specific set of nervous impulses from its own body, then it can develop motor control, which involves learning to consciously direct the muscles of the sphincters to contract. Both kinds of body learning take place gradually, and in both

Toilet habits—hints and aids

The baby has natural periods of body awareness—about 12–18 months for bowel control, about 1–2½ years for bladder control.

Point out wet or soiled diapers to the baby, and have adults and older children provide a model by showing the baby that they use the toilet.

When children wear few clothes, or are without diapers, they become aware of their physiological functions more readily—thus summer may be a better time to toilet train than winter.

Reinforce good performances and simply note mishaps. All children have lapses, especially in periods of tension or stress. Mastery generally takes several months.

Potty chairs are easier for the child to use and are less frightening for very young children than training seats that fit on the toilet.

Nighttime bladder control follows daytime control by anywhere from several months to a year.

Limit fluids before bed when a child is first staying dry at night. Keep the room warm and have the child use the toilet right before going to bed.

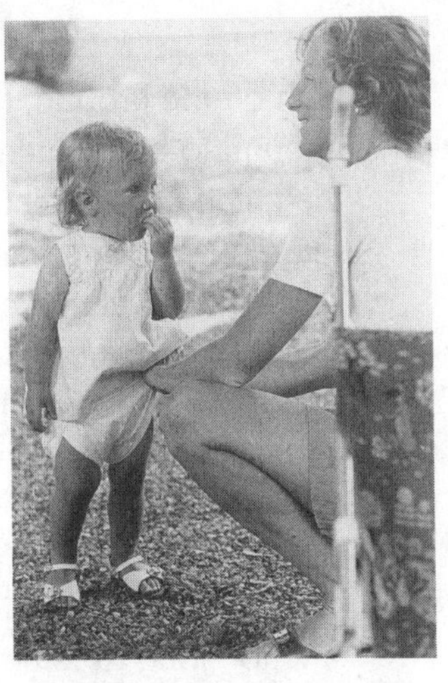

The first step toward toilet control is awareness of being wet or soiled. Parents can encourage this kind of awareness by pointing it out to the baby.

stages the child can easily be distracted or confused by other stimuli—from his or her own body or from outside. Thus, initially, lapses in toilet training, or "accidents," are the rule rather than the exception. Moreover, children vary tremendously in the age at which they gain voluntary control due to differences in development, reinforcement, and the personality and interest of the child. A number of physical and emotional factors can also affect the timing of control. Stress, the amount of liquids the child has consumed, the temperature of the house, can all have an effect on lapses or accidents. Some parents begin toilet training efforts shortly after the baby's first birthday, but many do nothing until the child is almost two.

Even after a child has achieved a degree of control, he or she will generally need help with the mechanics of urinating and eliminating—especially at night or in unfamiliar places. Locating and getting to a toilet or potty, removing clothes that are in the way, seating oneself, wiping oneself, and reclothing oneself all present formidable obstacles to the young child and may require adult help for some time after voluntary control has been established. It is very important to sustained control that the parent assist the child in these mechanics and make them as easy as possible.

Most pediatricians recommend that a potty chair be used initially for toilet training. Many children are intimidated by toilets because they're high off the ground, the seats are too large for them, and flushing is noisy enough to be frightening. Children sometimes have fantasies of falling into the toilet, being sucked into the toilet when it flushes, or of being bitten by sea monsters or snakes in the toilet bowl. Occasionally children confuse having a bowel movement with having a baby, and fear flushing the baby away. Such concerns are not as outlandish as they sound, and some adults can even recall similar fears and concerns. The advantages of a potty chair are that children can seat themselves, they can't fall in, and their feet can touch the floor which helps some children to push during a bowel movement. Once toilet training is actively begun, children must be kept in training pants during the day. Diapers are too cumbersome and take too long to remove—for the adult as well as the child. The use of training pants gives children a greater sense of control over the process, as

Concerns of the third and fourth years

Children should now be eating table foods and feeding themselves. Junk food should be limited, especially at snack time.

Most children continue to nap in the afternoon, a few for long periods.

Children's independent behavior should be encouraged. Children can begin to dress themselves, and pick their own activities.

Parents should continue to set appropriate limits and consistently apply time-outs when necessary.

Children should be encouraged to talk and take part in family discussions.

Children need companionship and intellectual stimulation at this age; most start preschool. At home they can be read to, given puzzles, shown how things work, and engaged in conversations.

Children need to be taught safety rules in regard to climbing, riding bikes, crossing the street, and going near water. Children can give up their car seat and use regular safety belts when they reach 40 pounds.

About 85 percent of children are toilet trained in the daytime by three years of age; 70 percent are night trained.

Parents should brush the child's teeth with a soft brush, and the child should see the dentist for the first time.

does letting them dump out the potty, and eventually letting them wipe themselves.

The child's control over bowel movements precedes control over urination by as much as a year and a half. Bowel movements are less frequent and tend to be more regular. Young children seem much more cognizant of the feelings that precede a bowel movement. Defecating tends to involve an active pushing process; urinating tends to occur more spontaneously. Daytime bladder control comes next and may precede nighttime control by twelve months or more. The age on daytime control can be from little more than a year to over three years.

Nighttime control over urination is hardest for the child and is the last to develop. The child literally has to make the entire process of awareness and restraint unconscious, programming a part of its mind to control bladder (and bowel) restraint automatically during the night.

Social development

In the second year the child's life is transformed by its newfound mobility and increased ability to communicate. Mobility frees the child from its mother and permits real interaction with the object world. This interaction with the object world is enhanced by the child's increasing fine motor control which allows the child to explore objects in new ways. The baby demands the mother's full attention less and less, and spends increasingly long periods playing alone but near the mother. The baby loves the mother no less, but objects hold new challenge and fascination.

The older baby loves to explore the world quite independently.

The baby is so full of this new world of objects that it wants to share new discoveries with the mother and find answers to questions raised in its explorations. So the baby tries to communicate all this—first through gestures and then through its growing vocabulary and understanding of grammar and conceptual schema. Not only does the baby communicate about objects, it is better able to communicate its physical wants and needs. The baby is becoming more discriminating about its body and can begin to let the parents know of hunger and the need to defecate.

During the second year the baby begins to take more responsibility for itself. It shows interest in and is now physically able to participate in a number of daily routines. The baby gets better and better at drinking from a cup and using a fork and spoon. Sometime during the second year it begins to take a real interest in the procedure of dressing—raising its arms to have shirts removed, pulling down elasticized pants, and lying down to have its diapers changed. To a parent who has been struggling to dress an increasingly heavy baby, this new interest comes as a joyful gift. The baby also shows interest in helping with many simple, visible tasks involved in running the household, and willingly carries objects, scrubs, sweeps, or holds dustpans. At this point the baby spends much of its time actively imitating the actions of the parents.

The toddler can work and communicate best with adults, especially the parents. If put in a room with another toddler, the first baby is likely to take minimal notice of the second. Instead the baby will play with whatever interesting objects are at hand. Two toddlers will generally play *alongside* each other, not *with* each other. This is referred to as *parallel play*. Their awareness of each other is often shown only by playing with a toy the other has just had or by vying for the toy the other child presently has. As the second year progresses the child will have more and more interaction with another child, both physically and verbally.

With increased mobility and more active exploration, the child can for the first time put itself into situations where it isn't wanted or ones that are dangerous. These situations require the parents to set limits on the child's behavior and exercise discipline for the first time. This discipline may accompany initial pressure on the child to control its bladder and bowel. Thus it is during the second or third year that the child generally meets head-on with the first real expectations and limits on its behavior.

The child's growing sense of autonomy from within meets growing cultural controls from without. For many parents and children this can be a difficult time that overrides numerous pleasures of this age. The child's sense of frustration may express itself as obstinacy, negativity, aggression, or even as temper tantrums. "The terrible twos" sums up parents' feelings about the problems of this age.

Temper tantrums are common in the second year. Unpleasant as they may be, they reflect the child's natural drive toward autonomy and mastery of new skills. By recognizing these needs, parents can often avoid flare-ups before they even arise. For example, toddlers often throw tantrums when they are frustrated by a new task. Helping children accomplish some part of the task or a similar skill, and praising them for it, can resolve the situation positively. Just before children master a major developmental task such as walking or talking, they may feel a general sense of frustration that colors all their interactions. Occasionally, young children have tantrums because they are afraid of something, and are either unable or unwilling to verbalize it. In such situations the parents' intuition and insight can work to prevent problems. Tantrums very commonly arise when parents set limits on the child's emerging independence. This type of outburst can sometimes be avoided if the child is made aware of what he

The older baby loves to imitate and loves to help with household tasks.

or she *can* do, as opposed to cannot do. If, despite reasonable measures, the child throws a tantrum anyway, some form of "time-out" should be used that temporarily removes the child from the immediate situation. Very young children can be picked up and held, older children can be sent to their room for only as long as it takes them to regain control of themselves. Active, intensely responsive children tend to have the most emotional outbursts. Parents need to realize that such tantrums are due in part, not to perverse feelings or "meanness," but to the child's temperament and style of reacting. Most important, parents should avoid battles with the child over weaning, self-feeding, and toilet training. If parents work to meet the child's needs for independence, and set known consistent limits, they will decrease the incidence of tantrums.

One of the major developmental tasks for preschool children is learning the limits of behavior expected of them, and developing the self-control to adhere to those limits. This is quite a challenge for both parent and child, because children's growing mastery of skills and developing sense of autonomy require that they constantly be testing the limits that are put upon them. However, all parents need to discipline their children. Discipline need not be punitive; in fact, it is more effective if it reinforces good behavior. The goal is not merely submissive or automaton-like behavior on the part of the child, but growing self-control and self-esteem, and increasing ability to handle the world by themselves.

Behavior modification techniques are very effective in dealing with difficult discipline problems. The basic principles of behavior modification are (1) all behavior is learned, and shaped by its consequences; (2) positive consequences make it more likely the behavior will be repeated, and conversely, negative consequences make it more likely behavior will not be repeated. The three components of any behavior modification system are rules, rewards, and negative reinforcers. The rules are the limits that the parents, care-giver, or preschool sets. Rules of the highest priority are based on a concern for ensuring the safety of the child, and preventing harm to others. Another priority is caring for property and preventing its destruction. Finally, limits involve honoring the rights of others. Limit-setting should not become a battle of wills in which one person—be it parent or child—becomes the winner, and the other person becomes the loser. Again, the goal is for children to learn to control their actions and emotions so that they can accomplish self-appointed tasks and learn to receive positive feedback from the people around them.

Rewards that will encourage a particular behavior include attention, praise, and immediate gratification which is generally supplied in the form of stickers, treats, or gifts. In the long run, attention and praise are the most important, but there are definitely difficult situations in which parents may find it useful to resort to more tangible forms of reward. Useful types of negative reinforcement include ignoring a behavior, issuing verbal disapproval, enforcing a "time-out," and taking away privileges. Physical punishment should be avoided. Children with discipline problems are

Time-out

A time-out is a very effective discipline.

Child is placed in "isolation" in a crib, playpen, chair, or room.

The time-out should include a short period after crying stops.

Child remains "out" only until it regains control and agrees to cooperate.

The older child becomes increasingly social and engages in play with other children—at first simply playing alongside and later playing elaborate shared games.

often aggressive to begin with, and physical punishment tends to make this worse.

Studies have shown that the most effective negative reinforcer in terms of a serious infraction is the "time-out." It is important that parents keep in mind that too much punishment or too severe a punishment can become abusive. Not only can children be abused physically, their spirits can be damaged by verbal abuse, excessive restriction of privileges, or lack of attention. If few rules have been imposed on a child, there is often a difficult period when parents initially begin to set limits. It is essential that positive reinforcements far outweigh the negative each day, and that parents spend some time in pleasurable activities with their child each day. Unless children basically feel loved, no type of discipline will be successful. Conversely, when children feel loved, they are more likely to respond positively to limit-setting because their parents' approval is so important to them.

During the third and fourth years the child becomes more and more social in its orientation. It begins to show interest in its peers as well as its parents, and parallel play gives way to *shared play*. This process is facilitated by the child's growing mastery of motor and language skills, which enlarge the possibilities for play, and make possible more elaborate games. The child increasingly involves itself in fantasy, imagination, and role-playing, assuming the role of the parent, or pretending to be a wild animal or well-known hero.

Characteristics of good child care

Caretakers are warm, attentive, enjoy children, and make the children feel secure and at home.

Caretakers are skilled enough to meet the children's physical needs.

Caretakers provide a rich environment, with interesting indoor activities and good playground space and/or equipment.

Caretakers stimulate the children intellectually, encourage their growing independence and self-reliance, reward their mastery of new skills, and help the children solve problems, overcome fears and weaknesses, and relate to the world in a positive way.

During these years of increasing socialization and autonomy, the child becomes more and more able to function by itself both in the home and outside. It learns to dress by itself, go to the bathroom by itself, play by itself, and may begin to attend a nursery school or daycare center. Often the child swings wildly from being independent and self-assured to clinging and dependent. These swings in behavior are sometimes mirrored in bladder control and waking at night. In these years the child also begins to show interest in sexual identification and plays differentially with boys and girls. The child becomes interested in where babies come from and in its genital organs.

Daycare

By the time the baby has reached a year, the parents have begun to make plans around the baby and pursue interests that involve the baby. This results in the first development of a true family style, which is a highly individual matter. Family style involves how much time the parents spend with the baby, what they do when they are with the baby, and the quality of that time. There are virtually as many styles as there are families. The satisfaction that each parent and child takes in their family style depends upon how fulfilled each one is by the time they spend apart as well as by the time they spend together.

The years from one to four involve growing *independence* on the part of both the baby and the parents. Along with the child's growing independence go longer and longer periods of physical separation from the parents.

During these periods of separation the child still requires physical care, and the quality of that care has profound effects on the child—and, indirectly, on the parents.

Throughout these years the child needs adults who are interested, loving, stimulating, and, most important, who function as a safe base for exploration. It is important that other adults who take care of the child, as well as the parents, have these qualities. The more time the child spends apart from the parents, the more important it is that other adults provide both a safe base and stimulation.

The child has an intense need to explore the physical world through manipulation of objects and words, as well as through fantasy play. This earliest exploration is basically accomplished alone, or with an adult. Somewhere between one and three the child begins to need other children to explore and play with, first in parallel play, later in cooperative efforts.

Just as the child has an urge to explore and to do things apart from the parents, so the parents have needs to know themselves apart from their child. The intense caretaking of earliest months does not go on forever and cannot provide a basis for a permanent life-style. Just as the child's life and the family life must grow and change, so must the individual lives of the parents. The more fulfilled parents of young children are, the more fulfilled they will be in later years, and the happier and more stimulating the environment they will provide for their growing child.

Child-care arrangements for the older baby

Baby-sitter
Grandparents or other relative
Close friend and/or other mother
Teenager
Paid, traded, or free—usually for short periods
Day or night
Usually temporary
At home or at sitter's

Nanny or professional sitter
Usually permanent
Full-time or part-time
Live-in or not
At home or at sitter's

Continued

Many mothers form cooperative play groups or exchange babysitting to provide their children with care and also give them a chance to socialize. Such arrangements also give the parents some free time.

Cooperative play group

Organized, exchanged group baby-sitting
Usually 3–6 children
Each parent has children at home one day a week (children are at other homes 2–4 days)
Usually half-days, mornings or afternoons
Commonly for children 18 months–4 years
Free, but requires some parent initiative, organization, and time
Care is as good or bad as the individual parent's efforts

Nursery school—daycare situation

Private, church, cooperative, or federally funded
Range from birth through kindergarten age; generally start at 2 years 9 months if the baby is toilet trained
Include an extremely wide variety in styles, techniques, atmosphere, teacher training, cost, and required parent involvement
Time ranges from 3 to 10 hours per day, 2 to 5 days per week, just during regular school year or 52 weeks per year
Curriculum ranges from (1) simply supervised free play, (2) skilled teaching on what's happening at the moment, within a scheduled routine, (3) highly structured activities, including number and reading readiness tasks, to (4) Montessori programs, in general highly structured activities and specially designed equipment emphasizing sensory understanding and quiet, ordered, self-directed work

Close relatives bring a special love to child care.

Things to consider in choosing a child-care arrangement

Different parents have different educational goals, and children have different educational skills and needs depending on their age, experience, and background. Here is a list of general considerations to use in evaluating a preschool situation or daycare center:

Does the classroom feel good?
Do the children seem happy and involved?
Are the children doing interesting work?
Are the teachers warm, attentive, and relaxed with the children?
Are the teachers working with the children or talking to other adults, doing paperwork, etc.?
Can the teachers discuss their goals for the class? What is the program?
Is there sufficient stimulation in most areas for the children?
- Motor—big and fine motor equipment and games
- Intellectual—problem solving, logical reasoning
- Preschool skills—reading readiness
- Fantasy—opportunities and space for dramatic play
- Creativity—unstructured work, raw materials

Continued

Social skills—forming strong, constructive relationships with other children and adults
Group work and skills—learning to be with other children and work in a group
General information—how do things work? grow? etc.
Is there a reasonable amount of sturdy, age-appropriate equipment readily accessible to all the children and arranged so as to be inviting?
Can the parents afford the program?
Does the program provide enough time for the parents? for the child? (a minimum of 2 half-days a week is necessary for a child to develop a sense of school continuity).

Language acquisition

The most recent theories on language acquisition, like those on motor development, postulate that as the child matures physically it reaches a "readiness" of development. That is, language development unfolds in

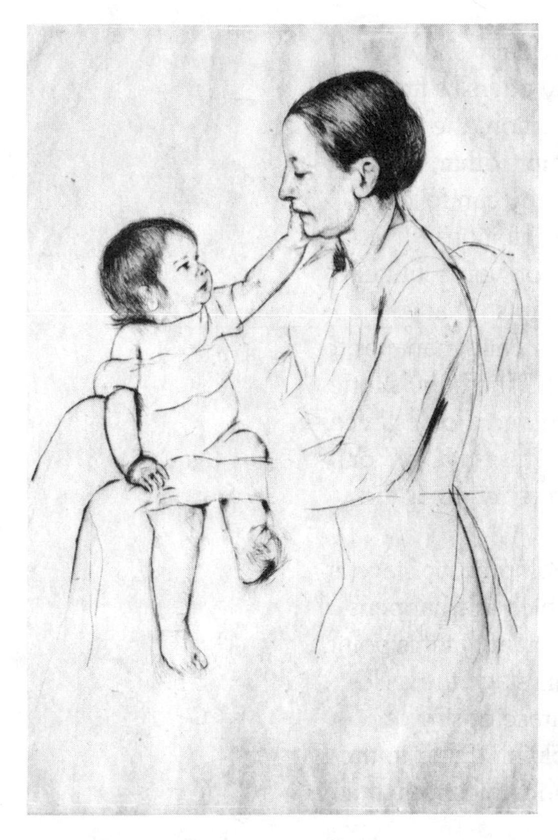

The baby learns to speak by hearing adults talk and by having objects named. La Caresse *(1891), detail, by Mary Cassatt. Drypoint. The Metropolitan Museum of Art, gift of Arthur Sachs, 1916.*

relation to physical growth and development. Language skills are based on brain maturation, which is related to both chronological age and the attainment of motor landmarks. In this case brain maturation is judged in terms of brain weight, the density of nerve cells in the cerebrum, and the presence and amounts in the brain of certain chemical substances.

Formerly, it was believed that language development was purely the result of exposure to, and selective reinforcement of, sounds from the environment. Thus if a baby said something like "ma-ma," everyone smiled and said wonderful. Or, alternately, the parents would *tell* the baby to say "ma-ma," and praise any effort in this direction. But such theories really fail to account adequately for the fact that in a period of *only* thirty months (roughly between the ages of eighteen months and four years), the child goes from saying single words to a large vocabulary and mastery of basic sentence structure and grammar. The old theories also failed to account for the fact that children frequently understand and use words or sentences in ways that are not imitative, in ways they have never heard. Often children will even invent their own words for things or combine parts of words in novel ways.

The present language development theories combine the idea of appropriate stimulation and reinforcement. Some researchers even postulate that the brain is naturally structured to interpret language and understand grammar and syntax. They look upon language as a natural human function, somewhat like walking, which develops as the child grows, and is aided by stimulation. Just as there is a sequence in which walking unfolds, so there is a general sequence in which language unfolds.

Language begins with babbling. At around a year, the baby shows definite signs of understanding particular words and actually utters its first real words. During the whole period of early language acquisition, the baby understands and responds to language that is more complex than it is able to vocalize. For example, by about fifteen months the baby can follow simple commands and a few months later can follow prohibitions.

During the second year the baby adds to the number of words it utters and begins to use single words to express complex concepts. That is, the baby uses single words to stand for whole sentences. The child manages to do this largely through adultlike intonation and inflection. The baby's tone may express declaration, exclamation, question, or command. For instance, a baby may say "hot" so as to mean "That is hot" or "This is HOT!" or "Is this hot?" or "Don't touch—HOT!" This period is referred to as the *holophrastic stage* of language development.

Somewhere toward the end of the second year the holophrastic stage is succeeded by the *telegraphic stage*. The exact age at which this happens, as well as the exact number of words in the child's vocabulary at this point, is highly variable, highly individualistic. In the telegraphic stage the child begins to put two or three words together to make a phrase or simple sentence. Like telegrams, these messages are remarkably brief and to the point. Omitting conjunctions, prepositions, pronouns, and adjectives, they

How to encourage language development

Talk to the child about what it sees and does.

Use a variety of words, and increasingly use long, complete, and complex sentences.

Try to understand the child's earliest attempts to say words.

Give information in verbal as well as physical form.

Answer and ask questions.

Repeat and expand what the child says.

Orient the child to new words by pointing out objects and later by explaining what a word means in terms of things the child already knows.

Read to the child frequently—daily if possible.

Teach the child nursery rhymes and songs.

manage still to convey a wealth of information. Interestingly enough, these abbreviated sentences are generally constructed in a proper grammatical fashion with subject and verb in the right order.

Between the ages of two and three the child's vocabulary grows from about fifty words to over a thousand. Somewhere around the middle of the third year, the child enters a golden period of language acquisition. The child seems to learn new words every day. Moreover, it strings together new words and forms increasingly complex sentences. At this point the child's speech flowers with prepositions, articles, conjunctions, and complicated forms of the verb "to be." Although the child still makes many

Reading to the child encourages language development.

By sharing experiences and getting explanations, the child takes on adult views of reality. Feeding the Ducks, *by Mary Cassatt. Color etching. Sight: 11 11/16" x 15 3/4". The Metropolitan Museum of Art, bequest of Mrs. H. O. Havemeyer, 1929. The H. O. Havemeyer Collection.*

grammatical slips, some quite funny and some quite endearing, the basic structure of grammar is there.

Learning

During the second year the child's play begins to shift in emphasis. Up to now play had been focused on manipulating and exploring objects as they exist. In the final step of this stage the child becomes able to visualize or imagine actions or situations that have not occurred. In other words, the child can picture new possibilities in its mind without resorting to trial and error. The Swiss expert on child development, Jean Piaget, calls this *internal experimentation* or *inner exploration.* The process involves manipulation of symbolic images. It is about this time also that the child begins to grasp the permanence of objects. That is, the child now comprehends that if a pillow is put in front of a teddy bear, the teddy bear is still there. *Object permanence,* like internal experimentation, involves the use of images or symbolic representations. The child can now deal with objects and situations that it cannot immediately perceive with its senses as real. It is also about this time that the child first begins to use and understand a number of words. Words, like images, are symbolic representations and can likewise be manipulated in new, inventive ways. Piaget calls the stage from approximately one and a half to seven the *preoperational stage.* In this stage the child can use images and words to represent objects and actions formerly grasped only by directly perceiving the sensory stimuli themselves.

Between one and four, children continue to explore the world around them actively and add to their stores of information. Their ability to name objects and events greatly increases their ability to organize their own experience, develop concepts, and communicate an idea to others. Language acquisition also enables the child to pose questions. And questioning enables the child to explore new possibilities, to find out about problems of their own posing, and to get at the huge stores of information that reside in adults. As the child matures, its verbal and visualization skills enable the child to discriminate and identify different forms, colors, and sizes. Likewise the child begins to understand the basic concepts of time, space, number, and quantity. From one to four the child is discovering and being specifically programmed to look at the world in the same way that adults do. This includes a linear view of time, a view of space and objects as being both real and separate from the child, and a view of quantity that involves discrete individual units.

Good toys encourage the child to manipulate and develop concepts about the physical world.

The child also begins to consolidate discrete elements in its personality as well as learn the personality of its family and culture, taking in the values, motives, beliefs, goals, and rules of its family and culture. This process takes place largely by identification and imitation. The child learns to associate basic emotions—pleasure, pain, fear, frustration, and anger—with certain kinds of situations, and it learns aggression, altruism, ambition, sex roles, self-reliance, obedience, and responsibility from the example of significant adults and from reinforcement or disapproval of the child's own behavior. In the broadest sense, the child learns how to behave in society. It learns what the culture perceives as right and wrong and eventually internalizes this information in the form of a conscience. According to Freudian psychoanalysts the superego starts to develop at the beginning of this period with the earliest prohibitions (no-no) and takes final shape at the end of this period after the child has accepted that its sexual yearnings for the parent of the opposite sex can never be fulfilled (resolution of the oedipal situation).

Allowing the child to explore the world with its physical senses provides it with important basic information.

Tours of places like aquariums and zoos expand the child's world.

Providing intellectual stimulation

Exposure to basic forms and their names through manipulative toys and finding-and-matching games.

Exposure to colors and color names by pointing them out and through matching games.

Exposure to size and quantity through graded toys (stacking cups, blocks, etc.) and comparison games.

Exposure to number concepts—counting a variety of real objects using natural counting situations; counting games such as lotto, dominoes.

Exposure to spatial orientation—finger games and big motor games that involve back, front, near, far, up, down, left, right.

Exposure to time and time-based concepts—relating regular events (bedtime, schooldays, seasons) to their times; relating past and future to more and more distant events.

Encourage a lengthening attention span through interesting activities, limited to one at a time in a quiet, uncluttered space. Activities may be free-form or may have realistic goals that the parent has demonstrated to the child, self-initiated or suggested by the parents.

Encourage understanding of cause and effect by demonstrations, explanations, and questions about simple physical events.

Continued

Strollers make it easy for parents and children to spend time in museums, zoos, and aquariums.

Encourage free exploration of the world around:
- Safe objects and educational toys that the child can take apart and reassemble
- Tours of the home, neighborhood, zoo, ocean, etc.
- Adult explanations of names, labels, books

Encourage visualization and fantasy:
- Play role games
- Provide props and costumes
- Talk about fantasies, dreams
- Play guessing games about animals, people, places, objects (I have four legs and say meow—who am I?) in which clues are given to build up a picture
- Give the child frequent opportunities to play with other children, as well as alone

Encourage the child to generalize through skillful questions and the comparison of like features. Encourage observation of similarities and differences.

Imagination

Personality development, socialization, and learning all take place in response to experience and imagination. One of the hallmarks of the child's life in this period is the richness and vividness of its imagination. Imagination becomes equal to and combines with physical sensation and manipulation as a means of learning about the world. The child can turn a block into a truck and become the truck's driver, then transform the truck into a ship and become its captain. As the child grows older its ability to envision different roles and situations increases, and it learns to share these visualizations actively with other children and adults. This results in intricate and beautiful dramatic play in which several children interact in imaginary roles using a variety of materials around them as their costumes and props. The same characters and tableaux may be sustained for a long period of time or the children may leap about from situation to situation and from character to character. While the children are playing, their imaginary world takes on a reality of its own, gaining their whole attention without in any way deluding them about the objective world. Useful details of the real world are abstracted and highlighted, while irrelevant details are simply dismissed until they can be made useful.

The young child is a master visualizer. Visualization is the ability to see with the mind's eye, and make those inner images take on reality. It is the tool of the child's work and play, allowing the child to break through the restrictions of the physical world and transcend its own size, motor skills, and immaturity.

One of the most striking examples of fantasy play is the *imaginary playmate.* Sometimes children around the age of two or three talk to and play with an imaginary companion known only to themselves. This companion is a person, an animal, or an object that the child generally has never seen. The child experiences the companion as a particularly vivid figure whose characteristics may remain stable over a number of years. The child interacts with the companion or companions as if it or they had an independent reality of their own. Usually when asked if it can see the companion or if the companion is "real," the child will quite readily say yes. Generally the child can name the companion, describe it, and talk about it at length, but can give little or no explanation for the companion's continued presence. Eventually the imaginary companion disappears as readily and mysteriously as it first appeared.

Older children play vivid imaginary games, taking on special roles in relation to their toys.

Sometimes imaginary companions may function as helpers or teachers in the child's life, giving advice, instruction, and reinforcement. Similar phenomena are frequently encountered among the children of nonliterate tribes. It is interesting to note that in such cases the companions often persist into adult life and are considered by the tribe to be valuable helpers. In Jungian psychotherapy, adult patients seek to discover and work with figures similar to imaginary companions. Some psychic readers report that they receive their information from such figures.

Psychic skills

Young children often "see" and point out to their parents objects or persons that the parents can't see. Such images may be imaginary or "real." The existence of real psychic phenomena has been demonstrated in parapsychological experiments over the last thirty years. *Clairvoyance* (knowledge of an event a person can't see or hear), *precognition* (knowledge of the future), and *mental telepathy* (transmission or reading of thoughts) are examples of psychic phenomena. Some psychologists believe that psychic ability first begins in the preschool years and naturally goes along with the development of the child's mind. Psychologists have found that some fantasy images described by young children actually were taking place elsewhere or took place later. Many parents have experienced telepathic situations with their children in which either the child suddenly vocalizes what the parent has been thinking or in which the parent anticipates a statement or action of the child. Unfortunately, little work has been done on the extent to which parents and children share thoughts. Such closeness probably begins when the child is an infant or is in the uterus, and is, of course, of a nonverbal nature. An example of this is when a nursing mother wakes just before her baby cries to be fed. Until recently our culture has tended to suppress and discount events of this nature. As a result parents have not reinforced such experiences in their children or themselves. Like any landmark, psychic ability is likely to disappear if ignored and strengthened if encouraged.

Dreams

Another type of fantasy imagery experienced by children is dreams. Like adult dreams, children's consist of a succession of images from known and unknown sources. Often the images are tied together in seemingly illogical ways and do not follow any rational sequence. Children awaken and cry, particularly if their dreams are vivid and frightening. Parents tend to emphasize nightmares in connection with children's dreams, probably because

In many cultures, children's dreams are accorded great significance. Here a child who later founded a Buddhist sect dreams of conversing with ancient Buddhist masters. Chigi Daishi as a Child, *detail, unknown artist. Courtesy of The Art Institute of Chicago.*

children so often do awaken from a frightening dream and need to be comforted. In reality, the percentage of nightmares the child experiences is quite low.

Studies of brain-wave activity during sleep show that the young child, like the adult, experiences an average of four to six dreaming periods a night. With encouragement the older child (two to four) can recall many dream images and talk about them. It is interesting to note that in some non-Western cultures, most notably among the Senoi of the Pacific, children are encouraged to talk about their dreams each morning. Dreams play a large part in their lives and are accorded great respect.

One-to-four-year-olds are more likely than older children to be awakened by their dreams, or to moan or cry out. Their dreams seem to be particularly vivid. Children sometimes have difficulty distinguishing between a dream and waking reality, and they may look for characters seen in the dream after they wake up. Or they may ask if something that happened in a dream is really true.

The subjects of nightmares in the one-to-four age group are similar to waking fears. Almost half the children's dreams are about strange and fearful animals. Such dreams are much less frequent among school-age children. Other common subjects of one-to-four-year-old dreams are personal difficulties, problems of friends and pets, darkness, and being harmed.

Daytime fears

In addition to nighttime fears, all children of this age group experience daytime fears. These fears seem to be inborn as well as based on experience. The innate nature of some of these fears suggests that such responses may have had survival value. These earliest basic fears are of sudden loud

Almost all older babies develop daytime fears that are generally outgrown in time. Repose, *by Mary Cassatt. Courtesy of The Art Institute of Chicago.*

noises, lack of support (falling over an edge), and impending collision. Some researchers believe that all newborn primates are innately fearful of new situations. By six to nine months the baby shows visible fear of strangers, and subsequently shows fear when the mother leaves. A child of this age shows much less fear of novel situations when the mother is present. As the child's images and symbol systems develop, its fears become associated with imaginary images as well as with real situations. By three to four the child is most likely to be afraid of imaginary creatures, darkness, being alone, animals, threats of danger, or abrupt, sharp warnings.

Children often develop fears as a result of physically or emotionally frightening experiences. For example, a child who has a severe fall on the stairs may become afraid to go up and down stairs by itself. Fears based on experience sometimes spread to associated, but noncausal, features of the frightening situation. A child who falls down the stairs at night may become afraid of the dark as well as afraid of the stairs. In such cases the child links the pain or fear of the primary situation with other perceptions or even thoughts that were experienced at the same time. When this happens a child's fears may appear to others as illogical or without cause. Often it is difficult to determine the cause of such "associated" fears—especially if the child is not yet very verbal.

Children also become afraid of things that they know other people fear. This is particularly true if the frightened person is a parent, an authoritative figure, or a friend. Fear can be highly contagious in this age group. If a boy

When the child develops a fear, parents can help by giving reassurance and encouraging the child to talk about it.

watches a friend get hurt on a bicycle, he may become fearful of bike riding himself. If the friend merely gets a scrape, but a teacher or the friend's mother becomes visibly upset, the boy may likewise become fearful.

Child development researchers and psychologists have found that the way adults respond to children's fears may help the children to overcome them. Talking about the child's fears, respecting the child's feelings, and helping the child deal with the feared situation can help the child to overcome its fears. Ignoring fears, punishing or ridiculing the child, and forcing a child into a confrontation have little success in helping a child deal with its fears and may even do harm.

Positive ways of dealing with childhood fears

Accept the child's feelings, its difficulty in dealing with the fear.

Explain the fearful situation in detail.

If possible, discuss the actual source of the fear (it may take some time for the child or the parent to find the cause).

Set an example of fearlessness and/or expose the child to other children dealing successfully with the feared situation—but do not make fun of the child.

Desensitize the child to the fear by bringing the child to the situation in steps.

Continued

Suggest—verbally and by action—things the child can do (or think about) in the situation which will strengthen the child's confidence and give the child a measure of control over the situation (for example, a child who is afraid of loud noises can be told to cover its ears until the noise stops).

Give the child a positive, reassuring environment around the feared situation (for example, you can give a child who is afraid of the dark a night-light, a "security" blanket, company till the child falls asleep, and/or the knowledge that if the child wakes it can call out to the parent).

Birth of a sibling

One of the most important life changes for any child is the birth of a sibling, but it is especially important for the firstborn, who has been an only child up to that point. With the birth of another child, older sibs must radically adjust their understanding of their relationship to their parents. The firstborn goes from being the sole focus of the parents' attention to sharing its time and energy with the all too time-consuming infant. No matter how often the parents say they will love the older child just as much, the child may find this hard to believe. If there are several sibs, the youngest of them may feel the most displaced since its role as "baby of the family" has now been taken over.

Many factors affect the way the older sib perceives the new baby. Age difference is a primary consideration. Generally, in terms of adjustment, the arrival of a new baby is most difficult for sibs between two and five years of age. Children of this age find it hard to understand the changes in the emotional climate of the household and the new demands on the mother's time. Children older than five have a more rational grasp of the situation and more of a life of their own; children under two are less aware of what's happening. Girls generally have an easier time adjusting to the birth of a sibling, possibly because they often take on the female mothering role.

Older siblings are affected by the baby long before the birth, even before the mother becomes pregnant if there is much talk about the decision. There are also major changes for older siblings during the pregnancy, no matter how much the parents try to minimize the differences. Certainly the parents shift some of their attention to the arrival of another baby, and the mother experiences radical physical and hormonal changes throughout the pregnancy. The mother's moods often fluctuate, her physical needs for sleep change, and she may tire more easily. Young children notice and may be disturbed by the mother's change in shape, and the fact that she is less likely to carry them and hold them on her lap. Another potential problem area concerns heightened expectations of older sibs. Once the mother becomes pregnant, parents often attempt to speed up weaning, toilet training, and sleeping through the night. In some instances older children have to share their room with the baby, and changes are made in the room even before the baby arrives.

Older siblings have to readjust their relationship with their parents after a younger brother or sister is born.

Once the baby arrives, older sibs experience a significant decrease in attention because the mother and father are not only fascinated with the new baby, there is much for them to do in terms of caretaking. If older siblings feel stressed by the arrival of the new baby, or "abandoned" because of the mother's hospital stay, they are likely to be more irritable, cry more, regress in their behavior (for example, have toileting accidents), and exhibit self-consoling behaviors such as thumb-sucking. Older children may demonstrate anger, either through tantrums or negative remarks about the baby. Although it is rare for older siblings to actually attempt to hurt the baby, it should be made clear that they can express their feelings verbally or emotionally, but not physically.

There are many things parents can do to make the birth of a sibling easier for an older child. Sibs should be told what's happening well before the birth, though the exact timing depends on the age of the siblings. Children's questions, anatomical and otherwise, should be answered in a brief, positive, and factual manner. Every question does not need a lecture. Reading books on birth and, if possible, watching an animal give birth, will help the child understand what's happening. Older sibs should be involved in planning for the coming baby, and made to feel a part of the new family group. They should be made to feel that it is "their" baby as well. Parents should also mention realistically, and with humor, the demands and stresses the new baby will put on *all* members of the family, and the help the mother will need in taking care of the baby.

Throughout the pregnancy, the parents should make a specific effort to spend clear, focused time with the siblings, and to get the children involved in projects and activities of their own that will continue after the baby is born. If possible, any major life changes for sibs, such as weaning, toilet training, or entering a new school should be scheduled to take place well before the birth. Thus, any problems with the change will not tend to be associated with the baby. The arrival of a new baby requires tremendous adaptation by itself.

The arrangements for sibs during the birth should also be clear and coordinated well in advance, especially since the father will most likely be with the mother. If possible, the children should be involved in the planning. Overnight plans should be made, as well as daytime arrangements. Children should be told where the mother will give birth, and approximately how long she will be away from home.

How sibling order affects children

Firstborn and only children tend to be higher achievers, more conforming, less popular with peers, and more anxious.

Parents tend to spend more time with firstborns, talk to them more, and put more pressure on them.

Later-borns tend to be more popular, and more affectionate and aggressive with peers.

Middle children tend to be socially active and independent.

Youngest children tend to be gregarious, less susceptible to social pressure, and less responsible.

Small families tend to produce less tension and resentment. Children in small families tend to be higher achievers and have a better self-concept.

Large families tend to be more family-centered and more authoritarian, and the father tends to be more involved. Children in large families have to deal with more rules and more chores.

Sibling spacing: firstborns tend to be higher achievers if there is an interval of 3–4 years before another child is born. If sibs are born close together, they are more likely to be treated alike, at the level of the younger child.

In terms of achievement and intellectual stimulation, youngerborns and closely spaced sibs benefit from increased attention and encouragement, and from being recognized as individuals.

Effects of television viewing on the preschooler

Television is one of the major, if not *the* major, agent of socialization for our children. The effects of television viewing have been extensively researched, yet most parents know nothing about the results of these studies. As of 1980, the average preschooler watched twenty-nine hours of television per week—between three and four hours a day. By the time the average child reached high school, he or she had spent more time watching TV than in any other single waking activity. Again, this is not something most parents are aware of or think about very often.

Extensive television viewing has preponderantly negative effects on a broad range of developmental parameters. Not only does TV have negative psychological effects, it prevents children from engaging in other activities that would have positive effects. The most widely studied effect has to do with violence. Television viewing produces increased aggressive behavior and increased acceptance of violence. These studies are so convincing that as early as 1972 the Surgeon General of the United States issued the warning, "A causal relationship has been shown between violence viewing and aggression. TV violence is harmful to the viewer." Since that time, the violence portrayed in television shows has been unrealistically blunted to give the appearance that violent acts produce neither pain nor visible injury; people often survive unbelievable assaults, and those who die do so offscreen. This surreal type of violence is thought to produce further desensitization.

The second major effect of extensive TV viewing is the blending of fantasy and reality. This is especially significant for young children who have not yet learned to distinguish fantasy from reality. Adults are able to realize that what is portrayed on TV generally has nothing to do with the reality of life, either their own or what they see around them. Young children who have not even reached the age of reason are totally unable to make such distinctions. Many segments of the population, including minorities, old people, women, children, and even men are not portrayed as they really are, either in terms of their activities or their reactions. Television is a land of fast cars, speedboats, flashy women, and detectives. Beyond this, children see an estimated 20,000 commercials a year, which likewise present an abbreviated or unreal life-style. All 20,000 of these messages are expertly produced pieces designed to convince people that happiness and fulfillment result from the consumption of material objects, which in reality are often dangerous or unhealthy. Studies of seven-year-olds have shown that the more they watch TV, the more thay believe the distorted reality they see on it.

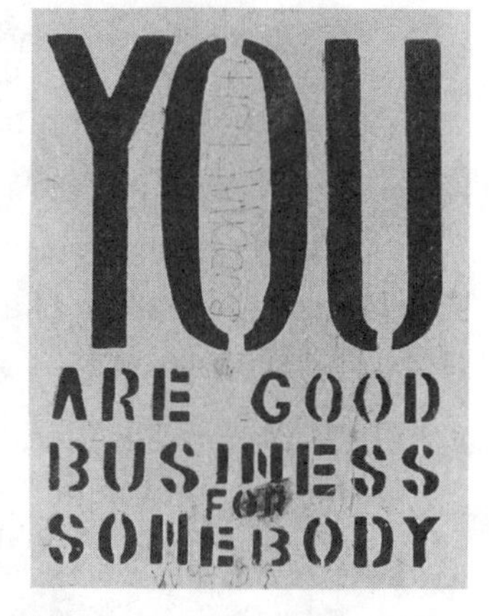

The average child watches 20,000 commercials a year on television.

For young children television is a significant source of information—much of it misinformation—about sex and sexual roles. Most often TV tends to trivialize sex or make it a tool with which to manipulate people. Sex is rarely portrayed as part of a meaningful relationship. TV is not a source of biologically correct facts, rather it emphasizes the more unusual sexual practices such as prostitution and brief sexual encounters.

Dr. T. Berry Brazelton has written about the fact that television encourages a passive stance toward the world. Television images are so compelling that, while nursing, a young baby will often look at a TV screen in preference to its mother's face. Later, as young children become able to interpret the action, they become overwhelmed by the implications and shut down emotionally because they do not know how to deal with the information they see. Many social scientists are concerned that the passivity induced by TV viewing prevents children from participating fully with friends, hobbies, school, and family.

The effects of television on cognitive skills are very complicated, but studies suggest that television viewing has a negative impact on learning as well as motivation. The rapid shift of images on TV tends to reduce children's attention spans. In the early years, even *Sesame Street* was criticized for the speed at which it presented information. Some researchers even believe that the lack of eye movement necessitated by television viewing may contribute to reading problems in preschoolers. On the positive side, there is no question that young children have a greater store of information than before the advent of TV.

What should parents do to reduce the negative effects of TV on young children? Researchers and educators suggest there is much that can be done. First, parents can limit the amount of time that children watch TV. Unfortunately, a study of first graders found that only 70 percent of their parents do this. A number of researchers believe that based on the results of studies, preschool children should not be allowed to watch any television. Because of both social pressures and the convenience of using TV as a baby-sitter, few parents are willing to restrict TV totally. Generally, parents either limit the number of hours that the TV can be watched per day, or they only allow the children to watch certain shows or watch at certain times. Some families limit TV viewing to Saturday morning, others to several hours a day. Restricting children to specific programs has the added effect of screening what the children watch, and making sure that what they watch is educational. It has been shown that programs such as *Sesame Street* and *Mr. Roger's Neighborhood* increase children's understanding of positive kinds of behavior, and increase their recognition of letters and numbers. Watching programs along with children and talking about what is being shown will help to counter many of the negative effects of TV. Parents can increase children's understanding and perspective by commenting both negatively and positively on what is portrayed, and by explaining the purpose of commercials. Finally, parents can encourage alternatives to TV viewing. Reading aloud to children, playing board games or engaging in physical activities with them, and simply holding family discussions are valuable alternatives to TV. Moreover, children thrive on the direct, one-to-one attention such activities involve.

Young children and divorce

By the 1980s, for the first time, divorce had become common in the United States among the parents of young children, creating huge changes in life-style and requiring great adaptation on the part of both parents and children. Psychologist Judith Wallerstein points out that research into the effects of divorce has lagged behind the social changes of the last few decades, but studies do give some indications of what to expect. By the mid-1980s, 30–40 percent of all children experienced divorce. Among children whose parents split up, 90 percent remain with the mother, although joint custody is an increasing trend. Of divorced mothers and fathers, over 75 percent remarry.

For children, the crucial event in the divorce process is the period immediately after one of the parents leaves home. Prior to this event, there is a period of disruption or decreased family function when one or both of the parents are unable to carry on their parenting roles and responsibilities as effectively as before. Because the divorce is usually sought by one parent, and only reluctantly agreed to by the other parent, there is often a great deal of anger and depression in the household before separation occurs, and often afterward as well. The parents are absorbed with their own problems and generally they are less available, either physically or emotionally. In the immediate period after separation, children are often left in new child-care settings for long periods of time. Wallerstein comments that "the separation and its aftermath are remembered by many children as the most stressful period of their lives." The breakup produces a period of shock and "mourning" for the family that has been lost. Often, children are unaware that a breakup is impending, presumably because the parents have gone out of their way to hide their problems. Ironically, for the children the "suddenness" of the separation makes the situation especially hard to deal with. Most children do not remember either parent as being sensitive to their needs during this critical time. While this is not surprising, considering the turmoil, emotional and otherwise, that the parents are going through, it is most unfortunate for the children. Likewise, there is generally little emotional support for the children apart from their parents—either from relatives, school, church, pediatrician, or friends. Frequently, parents fail to seek support that might be available for either themselves or the children.

The immediate way in which children respond to their parents' separation is greatly influenced by the child's age. Preschoolers commonly show regression in those skills most recently acquired. For example, a child who has just mastered toilet training may again have accidents. Children may also return to self-consoling behaviors such as thumb-sucking, using a security blanket, or masturbating. Although young children may not understand or be aware of all the problems surrounding their parents' separation, they often feel neglected, and they may experience fears of abandonment or starvation. As a result, children may have difficulty going to sleep and may become more upset than usual about routine separations such as preschool drop-offs. Frequently, young children become more irritable and demanding with their parents, and more aggressive with siblings and peers.

Fortunately there is much that parents can do to make the process of separation less threatening for young children. Interestingly, the preschooler is easier to comfort and reassure than the older child. Verbal assurances that everything will be all right, focused periods of attention, and an effort to maintain stable routines will help the younger child deal with the situation. As a result, symptomatic behavior will often disappear, sometimes within a matter of days or weeks. It is important that the parents make an effort to maintain good communication with the child, giving

Helping a preschooler cope with divorce

Explain the purpose of the separation.

Emphasize that your child is not to blame.

Reassure your child that he/she will be taken care of, giving specific information as to forthcoming housing and daycare changes.

Strive to maintain predictable routines.

Give your child extra attention at separation times (bedtime, drop-offs, etc.), specifically noting pick-up arrangements.

Work to minimize friction with your former spouse.

Seek to ensure that your child maintains a relationship with the other parent.

Seek outside support for yourself and your child. Consider professional help if you or your child is having great difficulty with the situation.

clear, simple explanations for what has happened. Young children can best understand separation in terms of an end to the fighting and unhappiness. It is crucial that young children understand they did not cause the divorce, cannot prevent it, and do not have to choose between the parents. It is also important to tell children what is likely to occur in the future, emphasizing what will happen in terms of the child's daily routines, and what will happen to the other parent.

In regard to long-term effects, certain factors are more likely to produce well-adjusted, happy children. The key issue is for the children to maintain a good relationship with each of the parents, in whatever arrangement allows both mother and father to parent responsibly. Children make the best adjustment to the separation if they believe that it has relieved tension in the household and can or will enhance the quality of their life. Children are most likely to have this sense if their parents have been able to successfully resolve the divorce in their own minds. If the parents still feel anger and recriminations years after the initial separation, it makes it harder for the children to accept the divorce. If the parents are each able to establish a new, secure environment, the children's lives and attitudes will reflect it. In this case the children have a sense that the new living arrangements are truly better, which puts the difficulties of the initial separation into perspective.

Remarriage is a big factor in the new household that each parent establishes. On the average, the mother remarries within two to three years. Generally, she enters the new marriage with more realistic expectations and greater flexibility. The children's relationship with the stepparent and new siblings takes time and effort. Children below the age of eight usually form new relationships fairly quickly and adapt to the new situation fairly happily. Often remarriage enhances the lives of these children, who benefit from the increased happiness of their parents.

Economic effects on children

The baby's health and development are profoundly influenced by its environment, including both economic factors and social institutions. Both poverty and affluence have their own characteristic, wide-ranging effects. By far the most severe effects are caused by poverty.

As of 1980 in the United States, 17 percent of all children under eighteen were living below the poverty level, many of them in households headed by a single parent. By the year 2000, 40 percent of children under sixteen will spend some part of their childhood in a single-parent family. Children in poor families are more likely to become ill, to have a wide range of developmental difficulties, to miss school, to have high lead levels in the blood, to have hearing difficulties as a result of ear infections, to live in unsafe housing, and to die of all causes at any age. These statistics point up how important it is that low income parents get support. Pregnant women need adequate prenatal care, including good nutritional information. Likewise, it is important that mothers get comprehensive medical care for their children, especially during the early years when there are profound changes in growth and development. Unfortunately, this can be difficult for many low-income parents because of the present medical funding in the United States. Early daycare can provide a support network for parents with low incomes, as well as developmental and behavioral expertise.

Single-parent families have special problems in relation to children's health and well-being. The income of a single mother is one-third that of a married couple. As a group, single mothers have been found to be as attentive and involved in their mothering as women who are married. Two of the major problems that single mothers face are isolation and overload. The time they spend in work and child care diminishes the amount of time they have to maintain outside relationships. Overload is the result of the fact that they are solely responsible for the economic, psychological, and physical well-being of themselves and their children. Having to readjust to a lower standard of living is a siginificant cause of depression, anger, and feelings of helplessness among single parents and recently divorced parents. For a single parent, support of some kind is crucial—whether it be from relatives, friends, or a support group. Despite all these problems, single parents often do well because they are relieved to be out of a bad relationship, and they may enjoy their new personal freedom and time alone if the other parent has the children part of the time. For children of divorced parents, contact with the non-custodial parent is the most important type of support they can receive.

Affluence also has positive and negative effects on the growth and well-being of children. Parents with high incomes are able to provide many advantages for their children in terms of financial stability, education, medical care, nutrition, possessions, travel, and exposure to social and cultural resources. However, surprisingly, studies have shown that affluence can also have negative effects on development. Parents who are aware of such potential difficulties can work to minimize them. The major problem caused by affluence is the weakening of the parent-child relationship and family ties. Many high-income parents lead busy lives and have long absences from home. Because these parents are able to hire substitute caretakers who provide good physical care, they may not realize how much of their parenting responsibilities are being left to the caretaker. It is important that affluent parents spend time with their children and see that they are given nurturance, love, and support, as well as limits and goals. Only if the parents spend significant periods of time with their children will they be able to transmit their own values, concerns, and traditions. Several problems can arise with substitute caretakers (see page 191). Frequent turnover can be confusing and may ultimately lessen the child's ability to form strong attachments. Also, some caretakers are largely custodial and provide little intellectual stimulation, while others tend to indulge the children and have low expectations of them socially and emotionally. Another problem faced by affluent children is the fact that their parents may put significant pressure on them to succeed at all endeavors starting at an early age. They may expect their child to achieve developmental landmarks

Helping single parents cope

Seek support from family and friends.

Get together regularly with other single parents.

Join baby-sitting co-ops and carpools.

Cooperate with other parents in children's activities.

Get outside household help if possible, even occasionally.

Join single parent self-help groups such as Parents Without Partners, or church or school groups.

Make use of schools and community agencies in terms of family activities and afterschool care.

Regularly schedule time for yourself to do activities you enjoy.

Be realistic in expectations of yourself and your children.

Plan ahead—for both outside activities and time to recharge.

such as toilet training very early, or to be intellectually bright enough to get into the most competitive preschools. It's important that successful parents love their children for who they are, accepting the growth and progress the children can make on their own initiative. Like all youngsters, affluent children need their basic needs satisfied, including receiving ready praise for their daily accomplishments. At the same time, affluent toddlers also need to be given appropriate responsibilities and not have every whim gratified instantly. In those terms, children's basic needs and developmental tasks are the same, regardless of whether their parents are low-income or high-income, and whether or not both parents work.

Teaching the older baby to use relaxation and imagery

Young children are naturally relaxed most of the time, and they are superb visualizers, for they believe in images because they have not yet put adult limitations on the nature of reality. For this reason, young children tend to be highly suggestible.

Although children intuitively understand what relaxation and imagery are, they cannot deal with the concepts verbally. The concepts can best be communicated by example and activity. The parent is really teaching the child to be aware of its natural skills and to begin to consciously control those skills. When words are used, parents should refer to familiar, concrete things that children can picture and feel.

Here are some imagination games to play with children to help them relax. Tell the child you have a pretend game to play. Have the child lie on its back, on a soft mat or a bed, with legs uncrossed and arms at its sides. Tell your child to pretend, picture, or imagine that

Its body is as heavy as metal
Its body feels heavy like a giant rock
Its body is as light as a cloud
Its body feels like whipped cream
Its body is floating like a balloon
Its body feels like wet spaghetti
Its body feels like a wet mop (washcloth, sponge)
Its body feels like a rubber person
Its body feels like a bowl of Jell-O
It's a snowman
Its body feels as cool as an ice cube
It's lying in a cool pool of water
It's lying in the sand on a warm day at the beach
Its body feels as warm as a roll from the oven, a towel from the dryer, hot water from the faucet

It's sleepy
Its eyes are heavy and closing

Try several of these images. Ask the child to give others. See which images are the most effective for your child. To check for deep relaxation, and to demonstrate it for the child, pick up the child's arm and let it drop. When the child is deeply relaxed, its arm will drop limply.

Imagining how the body feels is only one type of pretend game. Children also enjoy and should be encouraged to take on other characteristics, because pretend games not only help to teach a child to feel specific characteristics, they teach it how to control feelings deliberately. When children know how to turn feelings on or off consciously, they can relax at will when they are hurt or upset, feel courage when they are frightened, become happy when they are bored or sad.

Here are some imagination games to play with children to teach them certain useful feelings. Tell the child that you have a pretend game to play. Say to the child that certain animals and people are good at certain things, and that when the child pretends to be one of these animals or people, the child will become like them. The good feelings the animals have will make the child feel happy.

Children naturally make everyday objects into props for fantasy games.

Using relaxation for parents of an older baby

Life with an older baby becomes increasingly interesting but can become more hectic and may be complicated by the addition of another baby. Parents will find that it is still helpful to use relaxation themselves, as well as to teach it to their older baby. Complete instructions for learning to relax are given on pages 60–62. With practice, parents will find they can become very relaxed simply by taking several deep breaths or by imagining feelings of relaxation flowing into their body.

Relax briefly and take several deep breaths whenever you are frightened, frustrated, exhausted, or angered by the baby—for example, if the baby is hurt, breaks something, refuses to cooperate, makes a mess, becomes overexcited, or won't listen.

Still, take advantage of time when the baby is napping or playing happily to relax yourself deeply.

Take a few minutes to relax in the hectic time before dinner, after the baby goes to bed, in the midst of a busy day, or when the baby becomes overtired.

Tell your child to pretend, picture, imagine it is

A lion—the brave king of the jungle
A deer—a fast runner of the forest
An elephant—who's strong enough to pick up whole trees with its trunk

Pretend games can be used at specific times to help the parents and the child, as well as to have fun. Relaxation and visualization images can be used when a child is tired, overexcited, sick or hurt, frightened, unhappy, frustrated, or bored.

Using receptive imagery for parents of an older baby

Receptive imagery gives parents a means of getting in touch with their own feelings about the older baby and with the baby's feelings about the world. In this way imagery can add to the parents' relationship with the baby and help the parents make their decisions empathetic about it. If parents relax and imagine how the baby feels and picture what the baby needs, they can see things with the baby's eyes. If parents let images of situations—present and future—come to mind and they become aware of the feelings those images arouse, then the parents will realize which alternatives are in harmony with their own life. Complete instructions for imagery are given on pages 62–67.

Consider these images from your own point of view . . . and from the baby's point of view:

When should the baby be toilet trained?

How much sleep does the baby need? When should the baby go to bed?

When should the baby give up its nap?

When should the baby give up its bottle?

When should the baby begin to go to a sitter's, a play group, nursery school, or daycare center? How often and how long?

When (and if) the mother should return to work—part-time? fulltime?

What foods does the baby need?

What activities are enjoyable for the baby? for the parent?

Treating illness: medical information and self-help

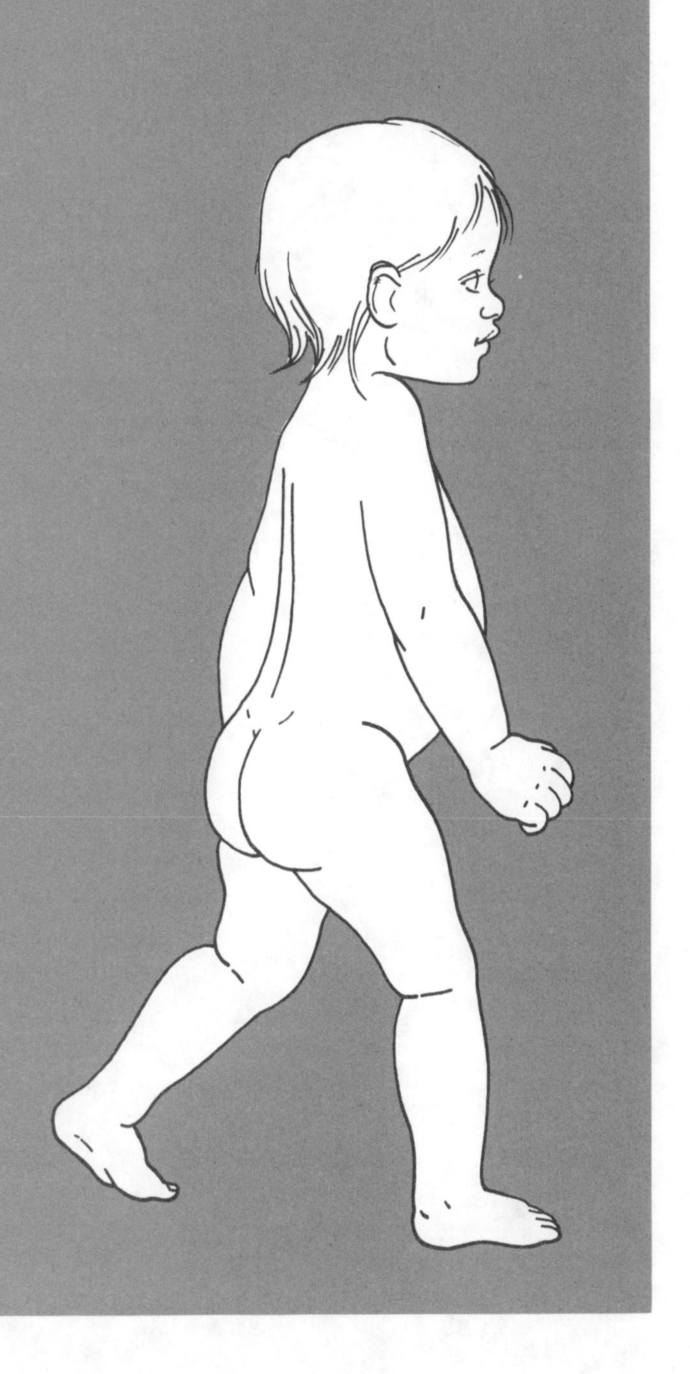

Chapter 9

Diagnosis and treatment of common medical problems

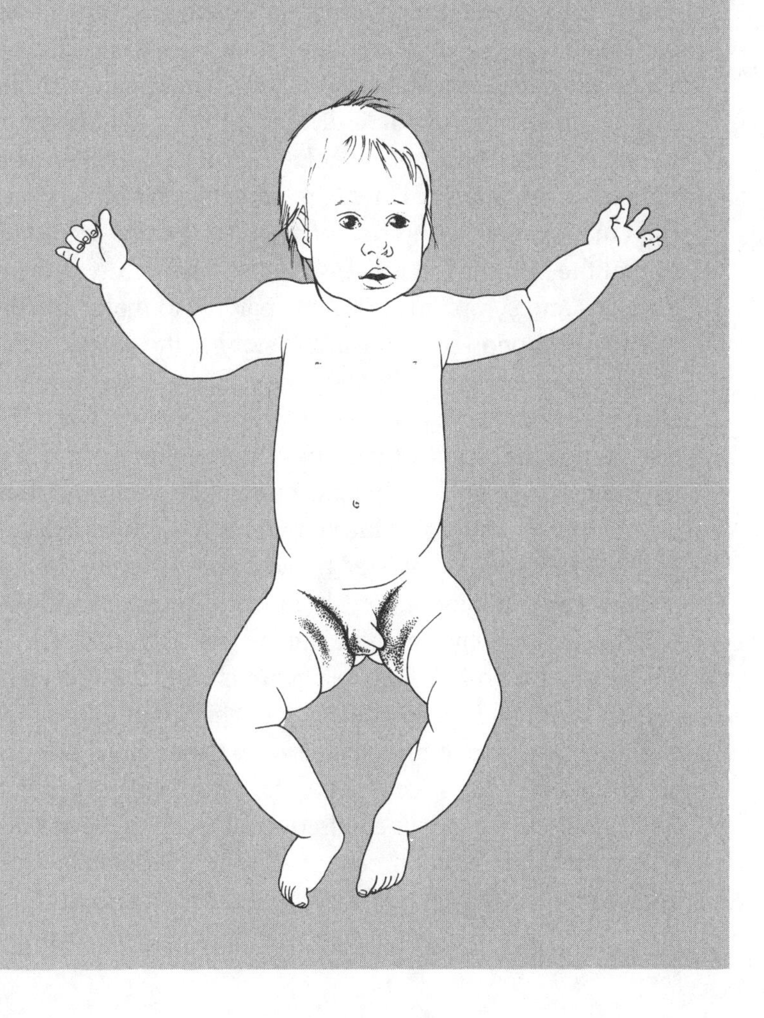

How the chapter is arranged

This part of the book is designed to help parents deal with a child's illnesses. It contains a great deal of relevant and comprehensive information about the most common illnesses of early childhood. Unlike a medical encyclopedia, it does not intersperse very rare diseases with very common ones. This helps to make the section useful and not frightening. The information in this section is quite complete. Each discussion of an illness contains practically all the information of a medical textbook. But it is presented in a way that parents can understand and use. The material was written so as to relieve parents of unnecessary worry and enable them to cope effectively with minor illnesses.

The goal of this section is to educate parents about illness and help them participate more effectively in their child's health care.

The section on medical conditions is especially arranged for usefulness and rapid access. The diseases are grouped by organ systems. For example, diseases of the ear are together and are grouped with other diseases of the head. Likewise, all diseases of the skin are together. The organ systems are arranged as follows: skin, head, chest, abdomen, and finally infectious diseases of the whole body. Grouping diseases by organ system can help parents find out what (if anything) is wrong with their child. For example, if a child's eyes are tearing, the parent can rapidly skim the eye diseases.

Each disease discussion is divided into five major sections: *Signs and symptoms, Description, Self-help, The doctor,* and *Prevention. Signs and symptoms* lists signs of illness the parents can see, as well as symptoms the child may complain of. The signs and symptoms are listed in outline form so that the information is accessible at a glance. In many cases, skimming the signs and symptoms will allow parents to make an early diagnosis.

The *Description* section tells the story of the illness, explains what's going on. There is a discussion of what causes the illness and what physiological changes are occurring in the child's body. Other things that are discussed are the normal course of the illness, things that make the illness more likely to occur, and possible problems or complications and their likelihood. The goal of this section is to educate parents so they have a clear understanding of the illness and are relieved of unnecessary worry. Lay people often have poor or garbled information about many illnesses, and this is a cause of needless worry which may be transmitted to the child.

The section on *Self-help* tells parents what they can readily do at home to help their child speed healing and feel better. Often the Self-help section is all that's needed to treat the disease. Especially if diagnosis and treatment are started early, this section may save the family a trip or call to the doctor. Early self-help treatment can frequently keep an illness mild. A doctor who is genuinely interested in patient education essentially will tell patients the information contained in the *Self-help* section and the *Description.* Self-help medicine is a new field which is getting great attention from public health and many consumer groups. Its goal is to help people participate effectively in their family's medical care.

The section on *The doctor* tells when to go to the doctor and describes how the doctor diagnoses and treats an illness. It explains what the doctor does and why, giving parents insight into how the doctor thinks about illness. It shows what steps the doctor takes to diagnose an illness and eliminate other possible causes for the symptoms. This section takes the mystery and apprehension out of a visit to the doctor. To some extent it also gives parents a criterion for evaluating their medical care against the typical treatment described in the book.

The *Prevention* section describes self-help techniques the parents can use to prevent the illness from occurring, spreading, or recurring. This section describes the way in which the illness spreads and thus how it can be avoided. We hope parents will make this the most used section of the book. In addition to giving specific things to do, this section promotes an attitude of health awareness. It tells parents how to tune in on their children's bodies and their environments in order to align the two for maximum health. When this awareness becomes second nature, it creates a life-style in which illness is less likely to occur or become severe.

Finally, there are several things this chapter is *not* designed to do. It is not designed to replace the doctor completely. In fact, it makes clear when the doctor's special skills and reassurance are necessary. And this chapter does not deal with rare or complicated conditions that generally need continuous medical treatment. The diseases that are dealt with are the truly common ones, the ones that take up the great majority of parents' and doctors' time and concern.

The skin

Diaper rash (primary irritant contact dermatitis)

Description

Diaper rash is extremely common; probably every baby has it some time in infancy. Some babies seem more prone to diaper rash because of inherently sensitive skin. Generally it is fair-skinned children who tend to be more sensitive.

Diaper rash is one of a number of *primary irritant contact dermatitises*. That is, it is an inflammation of the skin due to direct exposure to an irritating agent. The redness and swelling are the result of increased blood flow and greater amounts of moisture in the skin cells. The fatty junctions between cells are replaced by water, the cells are stretched apart, and the normal protective barrier of the skin is broken. The body deals with this situation by bringing in increased amounts of white blood cells to prevent or fight infection.

The inflammation is caused by a combination of factors: irritating chemicals, moist heat, and mechanical abrasion. The irritating chemicals are the urea in the urine itself, intestinal enzymes which are present in feces, and ammonia, which is produced in the diaper when urea is broken down by bacteria. Leftover detergent or chemicals in cloth diapers can also act as irritating agents. Moist heat is produced by the baby's urine and sweat in conjunction with body heat. The heat and humidity are sealed in by rubber pants or the plastic outer layer of disposable diapers. They prevent evaporation, which is both cooling and drying. Mechanical abrasion produced by too vigorous scrubbing with a washcloth or towel or stiff, scratchy diapers can add to the problem when the skin is already irritated.

More severe rashes (three or more days) may become raw and oozing in spots, may develop pimples and whiteheads, and may become secondarily infected with yeast (*Monilia*). A yeast infection is caused by a fungus called *Candida albicans* which is normally found in low numbers around the genital area and mouth. Secondary yeast infections are most common around folds of skin where moisture is trapped. They appear as bright red patches that are sharply demarcated (satellite lesions).

Signs and symptoms

Redness in the diaper area

Slight swelling of the reddened areas

"Thickening" of the skin, with shiny areas and deepened skin lines

Possibly raw and oozing areas with pimples

Possibly sharply demarcated red patches

Self-help

There is no one correct procedure for treating diaper rash. Treatment involves eliminating the causal factors, and varies depending on the severity of the rash. Parents have to alter their diapering routines until they find what works best for the baby—and for them. The goal of all changes is to minimize exposure to irritating substances, eliminate bacteria from the diapers, and keep the affected areas dry.

The doctor

Parents should call on the doctor when the rash becomes raw, bright red, or infected—or if the baby is very uncomfortable. The doctor will determine whether the rash is infected with bacteria and/or yeast and, if so, may prescribe an antibiotic ointment to lower the number of bacteria, or nystatin to lower the number of yeast. The doctor may also prescribe a corticosteroid cream to reduce the swelling and redness, and give the skin a chance to heal. Antibiotics, nystatin, and particularly corticosteroids are strong medicines and generally they are not needed or recommended, especially for long-term use. Most rashes respond to early and consistent treatment at home.

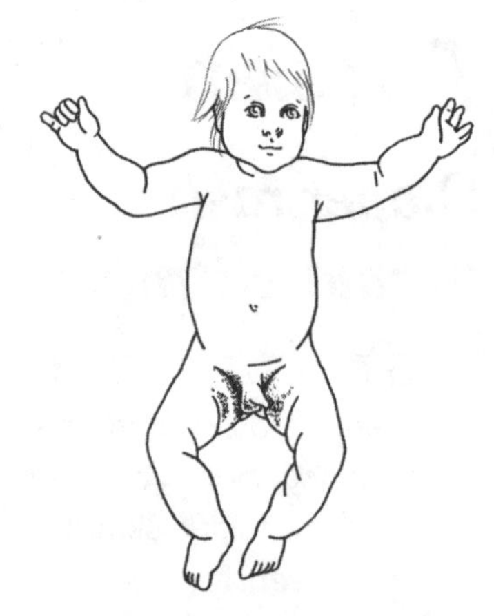

Diaper rash occurs around the genital area and in the skin folds of the legs. If diaper rash is attended to promptly, it is not likely to require medical attention.

Prevention

The best prevention for diaper rash is to follow a good cleanliness routine for the baby: reasonably frequent changes, washing with mild soap, exposure to sun and fresh air. Early treatment will avoid most serious rashes and decrease the duration of a rash. Parents who are familiar with their baby's typical skin reactions can become aware of situations that are likely to lead to a rash and take care to avoid them.

Suggestions for treating diaper rash

Changes can be instituted one by one depending on how severe or persistent the rash is. In general, the earlier a rash is treated, the more quickly it will respond.

Change diapers more frequently than normal or put baby in double diapers.

Gently rinse or wash the diaper area with lukewarm water and mild soap, especially after a bowel movement.

Continued

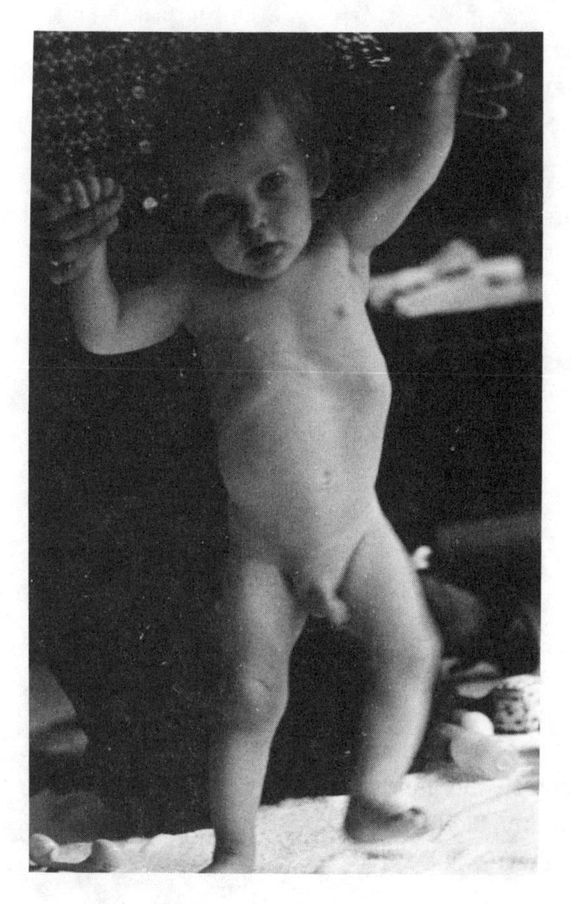

Exposing the baby's bottom to air and sunlight specifically helps cure diaper rash.

Dry the diaper area thoroughly after washing, using a blotting action, never rubbing.

Expose the diaper area to air, heat lamps (at a safe distance), or sunlight. The sun's ultraviolet rays actually kill bacteria, as well as dry the skin.

Apply a drying agent like talcum powder or cornstarch. (*Note:* Talcum powder is abrasive to the lungs and should not be inhaled; cornstarch in the presence of moisture can be a medium for the growth of yeast, that is, *Candida,* or *Monilia.*)

Apply a nonprescription cream or ointment such as A and D, Diaparene, or a thin coat of zinc oxide. These basically form a barrier to protect the skin from irritating agents and may also be healing or antibacterial. (*Note:* The baby's skin must be completely clean and dry or the cream simply traps moisture and bacteria against the skin and aggravates the problem.)

Let the baby go without diapers whenever possible.

Eliminate or decrease the use of rupper pants or plastic-coated disposable diapers, particularly at night or whenever the baby will not be changed for a long time.

Change diaper liners or the brand of disposable diapers, temporarily. Switch from cloth diapers to disposable or vice versa. Disposable diapers can be scratchy and trap moisture; cloth diapers can harbor ammonia and bacteria. (See below.)

Wash cloth diapers in milk soap, dry them outdoors, in sunlight—the ultraviolet rays kill bacteria. (Otherwise boil or wash diapers in an antibacterial preparation.)

Prickly heat

Description

Babies generally develop a prickly heat rash when they are overdressed and the weather is hot and humid. The rash starts in small areas and then spreads. Prickly heat is most common on the back of the neck, the ears, and the chest. It is caused by blockage of the ducts in tiny sweat glands. If only the tip of the duct is blocked (*miliaria crystallina*), a tiny, clear pimple is visible. If more than the tip is blocked (*milaria rubra*), there will be

Signs and symptoms

Groups of very tiny, liquid-filled pimples on the upper trunk redness around the base of the pimple. Prickly heat occurs most often in young babies and rarely seems to bother them. The rash generally is not long lasting (see *Milia* in Chapter 6, "The Newborn").

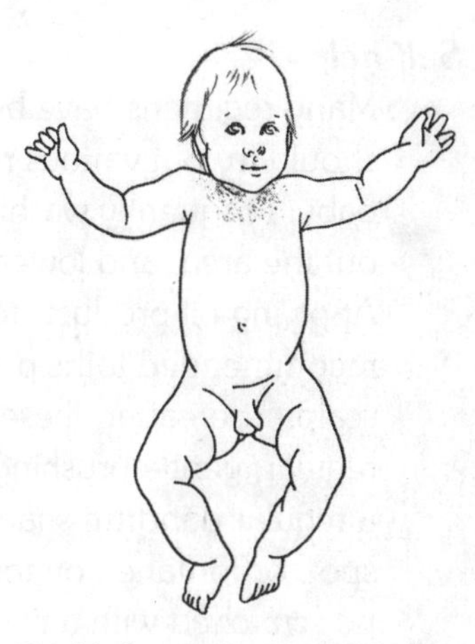

Prickly heat occurs most often on the neck, upper back, and chest.

Self-help

A baby with prickly heat should be kept cool and dressed in loose, lightweight, "breathable" clothes. Cornstarch or talcum powder (powder is abrasive to the lungs and should not be inhaled) can be sprinkled on affected areas. A bath with baking soda and water (1 teaspoon bicarbonate of soda to 1 cup of water) is cooling and soothing.

The doctor

The doctor can be called on to diagnose the rash if it persists.

Prevention

On hot days babies should be kept in cool clothes and in the shade to minimize the incidence of prickly heat. Frequent cool baths are good if a baby perspires a lot.

Cradle cap and "baby acne" (seborrheic dermatitis)

Description

Seborrheic dermatitis is a very common skin condition in young babies. Cradle cap and baby acne are thought to be related to hormones transferred from, or stimulated by, the mother's body in the last weeks of pregnancy. This hormonal stimulation causes the overproduction of a waxy, oily substance called *sebum.*

Plugging of the sebaceous glands by the excess wax leads to inflammation and the formation of pimples. These pimples most commonly occur on the face, but they may also be seen on the scalp and the skin in the genital area. Such pimples, or acne, come and go during the first three or four months, but eventually they go away completely by themselves. Often the pimply condition reaches a peak around three to four weeks after birth.

Cradle cap produces flaky, crusty, orange-colored patches around the eyebrows and on the scalp. This condition may persist for months and will not clear completely unless the scales are removed.

Seborrheic dermatitis is rarely of any medical consequence to the baby, but severe cases, especially of facial acne, are not pretty. This may distress parents and affect the way they relate to the baby, and that is of consequence. Parents should not feel silly about their concern, but they should realize that the condition is truly only skin-deep and will pass in time.

Signs and symptoms

Red swollen areas with pimples, primarily on the face

Dry flaky areas, especially around the eyebrows

Dry, flaky, crusty patches on the scalp

Self-help

Many regimens have been used to relieve seborrheic dermatitis. Parents should try out various routines and see which works best for them and their baby. Frequently washing pimply areas with a mild soap removes oils, dries out the area, and lowers the chances of secondary infection of the pimples. Applying oil products tends to make pimples worse, but it is sometimes recommended to help soften crusts of cradle cap around the eyebrows and scalp. Thereafter, these crusts can be removed and kept to a minimum with regular, gentle brushing with a somewhat stiff brush, and/or washing with a regular dandruff shampoo. Parents should not be afraid to brush the soft spot, or fontanel, on top of the baby's head. The crusts may even need to be scratched with a fingernail. This procedure should be done carefully because it is more likely to result in inflammation or rawness, and it is more uncomfortable for the baby. Gentle brushing can be somewhat like a massage and babies seem to enjoy the stimulation. Parents may even find that brushing serves to satisfy their own needs to "preen" the baby.

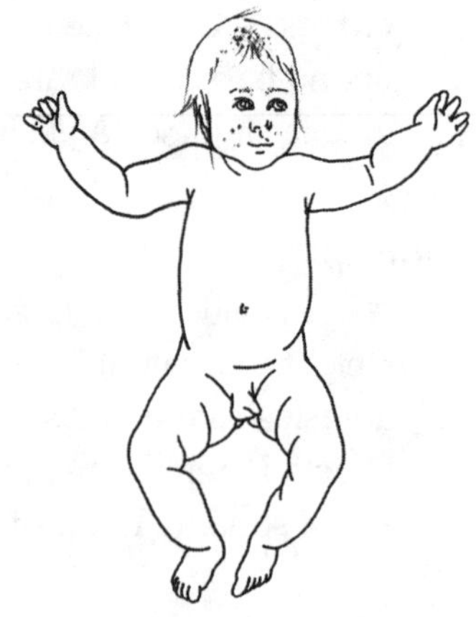

Cradle cap consists of crusty areas around the scalp and eyebrows. Baby acne occurs most often on the face.

The doctor

Generally the doctor reassures parents that the condition will clear and that it is not a hazard to the baby. In persistent or severe cases the doctor may prescribe steroid antibiotic creams for pimples or selenium (dandruff) shampoo for scalp encrusting.

Impetigo

Description

Impetigo is a skin infection generally caused by streptococcus or staphlyococcus bacteria. Both staph and strep bacteria are commonly found in the environment. Thirty to 40 percent of healthy people normally have staphylococci living in their nasal secretions. Healthy newborns normally have staph around their umbilical cord and genital area as well.

Infections result when staph or strep overgrow. This overgrowth is probably a result of lowered resistance and a break in the skin. Children are particularly susceptible to impetigo infections. They tend to have more skin abrasions, get dirtier, and if left to themselves, wash less than adults. The incidence of impetigo relates somewhat to the overall cleanliness of a child's environment.

Impetigo commonly appears on the face, arms, legs, and diaper areas, but can spread to other areas. An infection often starts with one pimple and then develops into clusters which open when they pop or are scratched. Eventually a raw area develops with characteristic honey-brown crusts made from elements of plasma and spent white blood cells.

Signs and symptoms

Red areas with pimples and characteristic honey-brown crusts

Blisters, itching

Children scratch infected areas to relieve the itching and often pick up bacteria under their fingernails. The bacterial spread readily—from one site to another and from one child to another. Around the nostrils is one of the most common sites of impetigo because young children frequently pick their noses.

If impetigo in a newborn is not treated, it can spread over large areas of the body, enter the bloodstream, and become a serious condition. This is because newborns have had limited exposure to bacterial infections and therefore their resistance is not great. Any newborn suspected of having impetigo should be seen by a doctor. In older children an infection, if untreated, will spread more slowly, but it may cause a fever. Even in mild cases the infection can sometimes be quite persistent, but usually it responds to assertive local treatment over a period of five to seven days.

Impetigo is a bacterial skin infection occuring most often on the face (nostrils, lips), limbs, and diaper area.

Self-help

Impetigo is best treated by cleanliness. The infected areas should be scrubbed vigorously with soap and water until the crusts or scabs come off. Then an antibacterial cream like Neosporin or Bacitracin should be applied. This regimen should be followed three times a day until the infection has cleared up. The parents should wash their hands frequently as well.

In addition to scrubbing infected areas, it is important to have children follow a stepped-up routine for general cleanliness. Children should be washed more frequently and carefully—paying special attention to the hands and the area around the nostrils. Fingernails should be trimmed back to lessen the chances of collecting bacteria underneath. And antibacterial cream can be applied to the nails and nostrils to minimize spread. Cream around the nostrils is sticky and seems to keep children from picking their noses. If infected areas can be covered with clothing, it tends to cut down on scratching and subsequent spread. The child's clothes and linens should be changed frequently and washed in hot water.

The doctor

The doctor should be seen if the child is a newborn, if the child runs a fever, if large areas are infected, or if the infection is persistent. In severe cases the doctor will prescribe a course of antibiotics (injectable or oral) in addition to the local treatment described above.

Prevention

Impetigo is a soap-and-water disease. General cleanliness tends to prevent infection, and it becomes of major importance in environments where impetigo is common. Special attention should be given to personal washing and to cleaning kitchen, bathroom, and toys. Children should use their own towel and washcloth, and their sheets should be changed frequently.

Staph and strep bacteria are generally present in the environment and

Washing with soap and water generally helps to prevent impetigo and is especially important if a child has a playmate with impetigo.

some people can carry and spread bacteria without being ill, but most transmission probably occurs from a person with a visible, oozing infection.

Newborns should be kept away from children with impetigo. Older children who are in contact with a child who has impetigo should wash their hands and face more frequently and pay more attention to keeping normal cuts and abrasions clean. If one member of a family has impetigo, that person should promptly begin assertive treatment to prevent other family members from becoming infected. A child who has a number of open sores or is running a fever should minimize contact with other children for one to two days or until the infection is under control.

Fungal infections including ringworm

Signs and symptoms

Scaly red, raised patches about an inch in diameter, ring-shaped and often with a clear center

Local itching

Patches on the scalp appear as thick, broken-off hairs with red scaling skin below

Description

Ringworm is an infection of the superficial layer of the skin or scalp. It is not caused by a worm, but by a highly specialized variety of fungi that live only in the skin. Fungi are actually a family of plants that lack chlorophyll (mushrooms are a form of fungi). Ringworm is generally transmitted from person to person, but occasionally it may be transmitted from a dog or cat. It is fairly contagious and should be treated, otherwise it can spread and form new patches. The itching associated with ringworm can be quite uncomfortable.

Self-help

Ringworm of the skin is easily treated with a topical cream called Tinactin (Tolnaftate), which is available without prescription. The cream is applied

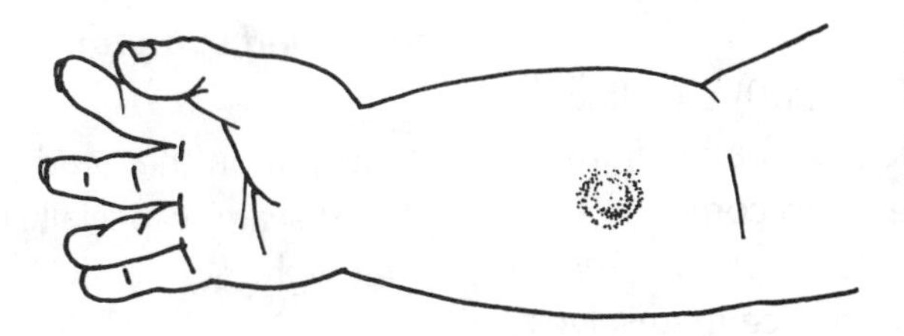

Ringworm is a fungal infection of the skin which appears as a red ring with an open center.

two to three times a day in small amounts. The infection should be visibly better in about seven days. Treatment should be continued for a week after all visible signs of ringworm are gone. The topical cream does not enter the hair in sufficient amounts to cure ringworm of the scalp, which requires a prescription drug that is taken by mouth.

The doctor

A doctor diagnoses ringworm of the scalp with the aid of special ultraviolet light. Under this light the fungus glows greenish-white. The spores of the fungus can actually be seen under the microscope if a small scraping of the fungus is put in a solution of potassium hydroxide.

Ringworm of the scalp is treated with an oral prescription drug called griseofulvin, a drug which has caused liver cancer in mice. The course of treatment lasts six weeks. The hair should be shampooed frequently to remove loose hairs and fungal spores. In severe cases it may be necessary to cut the hair and wear a cap to prevent infecting others.

Ringworm of the skin is also diagnosed by a microscopic examination of a skin scraping in potassium hydroxide solution. Ringworm of the skin responds readily to the nonprescription cream Tinactin.

Prevention

The best prevention is to avoid contact with known cases and to treat promptly cases that arise—whether in people or animals. Infected children should bathe frequently, use their own brush and comb and clothes, and these should be washed frequently in hot soapy water.

Head lice

Description

Head lice (*pediculus humanus capitis*) are tiny insects that live and breed in human hair and spread rapidly from one person to another. They are different from animal lice. Head lice are commonly found in crowded cities and, increasingly, in affluent suburban communities. Occasionally they become epidemic in a particular nursery or elementary school. The eggs hatch in a week and are mature enough to reproduce in two more weeks. If separated from their human hosts, the lice will die in less than a day.

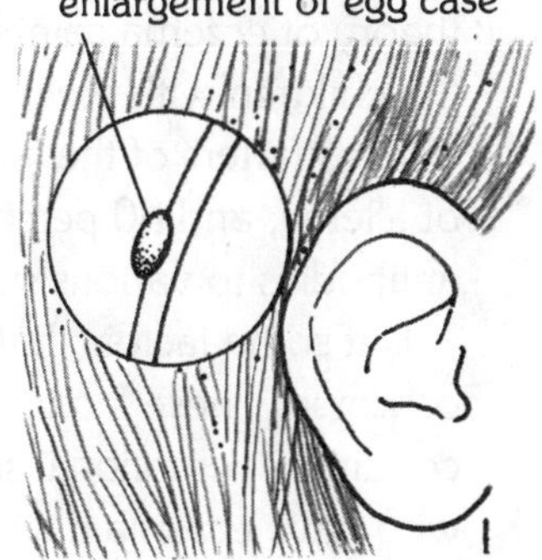

Head lice can be detected by finding shiny white egg cases at the base of hair shafts. The lice themselves are too small to see.

Self-help

Several nonprescription pyrethrum liquids (e.g., *RID, A-200*) are effective in eliminating head lice when left on for ten minutes. After bathing, the dead nits (eggs) and lice can be removed with a fine-tooth comb.

Clothes and bed linens should be washed in hot water to prevent reinfection. Ten minutes in 120°F water will kill the nits and the lice themselves.

The doctor

The doctor diagnoses head lice by looking closely at the hair with a magnifying glass and finding the egg cases. The most effective treatment for head lice is a prescription insecticide called Kwell Shampoo. Some doctors prefer not to use this drug because it can be toxic to the nervous system, and it has been shown to cause cancer in animals.

Prevention

General cleanliness, prompt treatment of known cases, and avoiding contact with new or untreated cases lowers the chances of getting head lice. Thorough cleaning of linens, clothes, and household surfaces is important in preventing new cases and reinfection.

Signs and symptoms

Itching on the head and scalp, especially at night

Tiny white egg cases (like grains of rice) that are attached to single hairs

Dot-size brown or black lice on the hair or clothes

Red pimples near the base of the hair shafts, neck, or ears

Eczema (atopic dermatitis)

Description

Eczema is an inflammation of the skin. It usually appears in young children around 1–4 months old. Often it eventually disappears by itself when the child is about 3–5 years old. The actual cause of eczema is unknown although doctors have thought for years that it is an allergic reaction. It has been shown that the appearance of the rash correlates with the introduction of such foods as cow's milk, eggs, wheat, or oranges. The allergy theory of eczema gained support from the fact that more than a third of the children with eczema have or develop asthma or hay fever. Moreover, three-quarters of the families of children who have eczema have a history of allergy, and 80 percent of children with eczema have high levels of antibodies to various substances.

But some factors that are unrelated to food allergies make eczema better or worse. These factors include sweating, skin temperature, and weather conditions, emotional stress, colds and infections, and clothing. Children who have eczema have very sensitive skin in general and their condition is irritated by many factors that do not produce a rash in most children.

Eczema can occur as an acute condition that clears up or it can develop into a chronic condition that gets better and worse sporadically. Eczema can involve one small patch or it can involve a larger area of the child's

Signs and symptoms

Redness, crusting, and dry, thickened oval patches of skin usually on the back of the knee, inner surface of the elbow or the hands, cheeks, scalp, and trunk

Itching of affected areas

body, and it can become secondarily infected with staph or strep bacteria. Severe or chronic eczema can cause intense, uncomfortable itching, and it can be unsightly. Such eczema may be frustrating, but it is treatable, and treatment does make a difference.

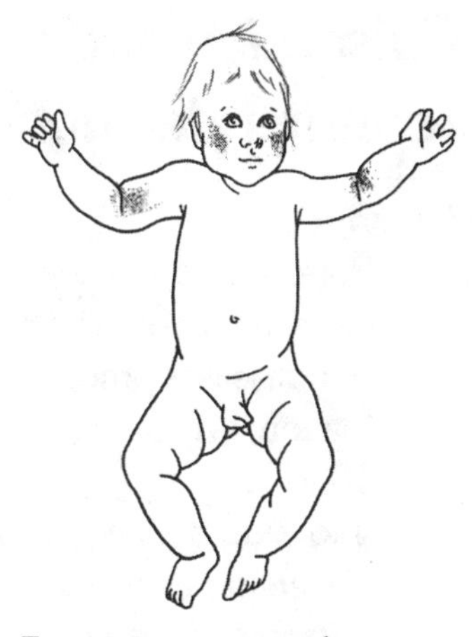

Eczema is a crusty skin inflammation usually found on the inside of the elbows, behind the knees, or on the hands, face, or trunk.

Self-help

Treatment of eczema basically involves adding moisture to the skin and protecting the affected areas from irritating substances. Frequent washing and strong soaps are actually drying. Moisturizing is accomplished by *short* baths or showers and pat drying, followed by the application of lubricating oils or ointments. These oils and ointments can be based on lanolin or on an oil emulsion. Alpha-keri, Eucerin, and Nutraderm are common non-prescription lubricants. Humid weather also tends to make eczema better.

A child with eczema should be dressed in comfortable, nonirritating clothes, such as cotton. Wool, in particular, can be mechanically irritating. (See *Asthma.*) Strong soaps and shampoos should be avoided. Mild soaps such as Dove and Ivory are preferable. Keep fingernails short and cover hands with socks if necessary to prevent scratching.

Some parents find their child is helped by removing from the diet foods that were *introduced* only 2 to 4 days before the rash appeared. Real improvement may not take place for several weeks on a restricted diet. This can be confusing to parents because eczema can become better or worse over the course of a few days without any dietary manipulation. If several foods are suspected, the parents can experiment by removing the foods from the child's diet one by one. Alternatively, the parents can remove all commonly allergenic foods (unprocessed cow's milk, wheat, eggs, oranges) and add them back one by one over a period of weeks. Isolating food agents can be tedious and frustrating, but worthwhile.

The doctor

Doctors diagnose eczema with a history and a simple visual examination. They may examine a scraping of the affected area to rule out a fungal infection (see *Ringworm*). The doctor may prescribe an antihistamine (e.g., Benadryl) to relieve itching, and/or a mild corticosteroid cream, that will help reduce the inflammation and swelling. Most often corticosteroids will take a week or more to show progress. If the rash is secondarily infected, the doctor may prescribe an antibiotic.

Prevention

There is no known regimen that absolutely prevents eczema. In general parents should be careful about the skin irritants and even the allergenic foods that a child comes in contact with, particularly if the child has sensitive skin or if there is a family history of eczema or allergies. Breast-feeding and delayed introduction of allergenic food are strongly recommended for these children.

Poison ivy and poison oak (contact dermatitis)

Description

Poison ivy and poison oak are inflammations of the skin that appear suddenly after contact with one of these plants. They are the most common skin diseases among children between the ages of 2 and 20. The inflammation is an allergic reaction to a chemical in the plant's oils, and it appears 18 to 72 hours after exposure. The height of the eruption generally occurs 4 to 7 days after exposure. The inflammation often appears as a line of blisters on exposed areas of the body where the child brushed a leaf. The irritating oils can get on the hands and under the nails and then be spread to other areas. The liquid that comes out of the blisters is simply plasma and does not cause the rash to spread. The blisters and the surrounding areas generally are intensely itchy.

Poison ivy and poison oak can be gotten in any season of the year from contact with the plants' leaves or even from the stems. Children are most likely to get the rash in the spring when the plants contain the most oil. At this time of the year the shiny, red-green leaves cover large areas of the woods. Pets sometimes bring home the allergenic oils on their fur, but usually a child gets poison ivy or poison oak after a walk in the woods. The smoke from burning the leaves can also cause poison oak.

Signs and symptoms

Intense itching

Redness and swelling of the skin

Red pimples

Blisters filled with clear liquid which oozes out and forms dry crusts

Self-help

The nails and hands should be scrubbed carefully with a nailbrush and soap to wash off the oil and prevent spreading. A nonprescription lotion such as calamine can be applied to itchy areas. The child should be kept cool; heat and sweating generally make the itching worse. A cool bath with baking soda or *Aveeno* added helps to relieve the itching. And the child should wear loose clothes. The itching tends to be forgotten if the rash is covered by clothing. Cooling by evaporation probably gives the most relief from itching. This is the principle of calamine lotion, and it can also be achieved simply by wetting the skin with cool water.

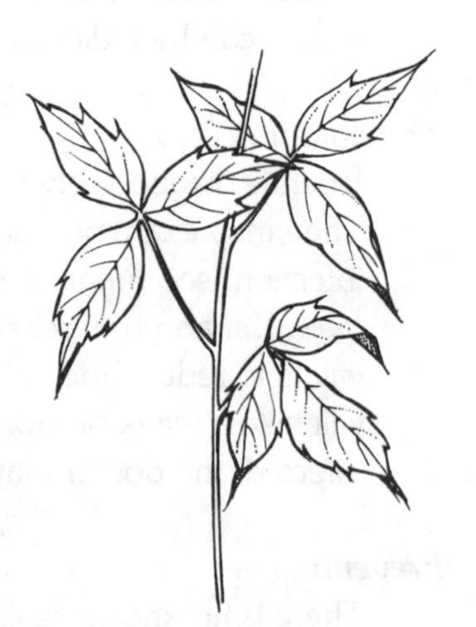

Poison oak and ivy are common plants in rural areas. Both have three shiny, reddish-green leaves that come off a single stem.

The doctor

In severe cases when the child is very uncomfortable or there is significant swelling around the eyes, nose, or genitals, the doctor may prescribe an oral steroid. The drug is given over a week's time, starting with a large dose and gradually tapering down. Response to steroids varies from rapid improvement to little or no progress. Some children show renewed symptoms when the drug is finished (rebound effect). Oral steroids have significant side effects and problems, so most doctors use them only in severe cases. Some prescribe topical steroid creams which are not as strong and do not have as many side effects.

Children are most likely to get poison ivy after playing in untended woods or fields.

Prevention

Teaching a child to identify and avoid the plant is the best prevention. Toddlers and younger children should be watched in areas where poison oak or poison ivy may be present. Plants near the house should be chopped out or possibly sprayed. If parents believe a child has touched the plant, they should wash the child immediately with soap and water, taking special care with the nails and hands. If thorough washing is done within a matter of hours, the rash may be prevented or minimized. Clothes that may have the oil on them should be removed carefully and washed in hot, soapy water to prevent further spreading.

The head

Eye infection (conjunctivitis or pinkeye)

Description

Conjunctivitis is an inflammation of the mucous membrane (conjunctiva) which surrounds the eye and lines the inside of the eyelid. It is the most common eye problem in young children, and it is usually caused by a viral or bacterial infection, but it can be caused by irritants such as smog, chemicals, smoke, or dust in the air. Children who have allergies sometimes develop a conjunctivitis during allergy attacks.

Bacterial conjunctivitis characteristically has a greenish yellow discharge that looks like pus or mucus. Viral conjunctivitis usually has a more watery-looking discharge. Viral or bacterial conjunctivitis often accompanies a common cold, but it can occur by itself. If the discharge is profuse and sticky enough, it can seal the child's eyelids or lashes together. This can be very frightening to young children, and painful if they try to open their eyes forcibly. The eyelids are most likely to be stuck together upon awakening in the morning or after a long nap.

The child's body generally cures an eye infection within two weeks, but medical treatment often shortens the healing to 2 or 3 days, particularly in cases of bacterial conjunctivitis.

Newborns are susceptible to conjunctivitis if their mother has chlamydia or gonorrhea at the time of the birth. The newborn's eyes can become infected with these organisms during passage through the birth canal. If untreated, gonorrheal conjunctivitis can cause blindness. In most states antibiotic or silver nitrate drops must, by law, be put in all newborns' eyes to eliminate the chance of conjunctivitis. Silver nitrate is not effective against chlamydia. Unless promptly washed out with water, the silver

Signs and symptoms

Mucusy, puslike, or clear discharge from the eyes

Redness and swelling around the edges of the eyelid

Itching, soreness, and/or a feeling that something's in the eye

Eyelids stuck together—especially upon awaking

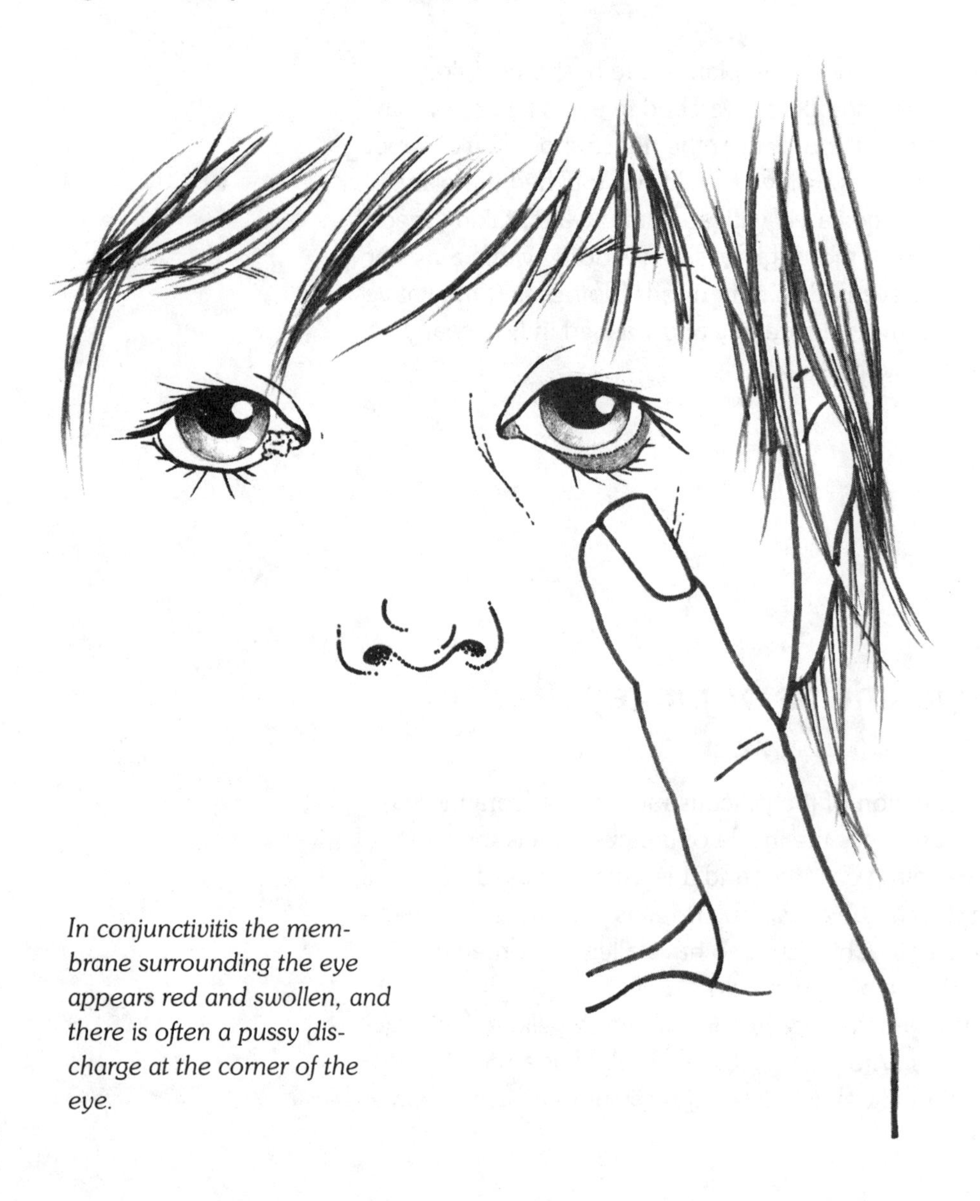

In conjunctivitis the membrane surrounding the eye appears red and swollen, and there is often a pussy discharge at the corner of the eye.

nitrate drops themselves often cause an irritative conjunctivitis in newborns one to two days after the drops are administered. Generally the irritative conjunctivitis clears up by itself in 2 to 3 days.

Self-help

To make the child more comfortable, the eyelids should be gently washed 3 or 4 times a day with warm water. Washing must be done if the eyelids are stuck together, and it may take a few minutes to dissolve the dried discharge. Often when the discharge is sticky, children tend to rub their eyes, which can cause further irritation and prolong the inflammation. Nonprescription eyedrops such as Murine or Visine—or even sterile water—may be soothing and they can be used to wash out irritants like dust (see below). In cases of conjunctivitis due to an irritating substance like smoke, smog, or airborne dirt, children should be protected from further exposure to the irritant as much as possible.

The doctor

The diagnosis of conjunctivitis is generally made on the basis of a visual exam, but occasionally doctors will want to take a culture. When a conjunctivitis is accompanied by large amounts of discharge, doctors will usually treat it with antibiotic drops or ointment. The antibiotic is given 3 or 4 times a day until a few days after the symptoms have cleared. This usually takes about a week.

Ointments are less uncomfortable, easier to administer, and need not be used as often because they last longer. But, unlike drops, ointments produce a film over the eye which interferes somewhat with normal vision. Some children find this objectionable. Drops are most easily administered if children lie down or sit with their head tilted back. Some doctors suggest putting a drop in the lower eyelids or corner of each eye while the eyelids are *closed.* When children open their eyes the drops should roll in.

It is not uncommon for children to dislike getting either drops or ointment. Drops sometimes sting, and ointment temporarily makes vision blurry. Since the medicine must be administered 3 or 4 times a day for several days, it is important that parents work out the best possible routine. Children who are frightened may be reassured if parents themselves try the drops first.

Prevention

Parents should avoid exposing a child to irritating substances, especially if the child has had an irritative conjunctivitis before. They should also avoid exposing a child to children who have runny eyes and other symptoms of a cold. Some types of infectious conjunctivitis are readily transferred from one child to another. If an infectious conjunctivitis is suspected, children should be encouraged to wash their hands more frequently and should be reminded not to rub their eyes.

Sty (hordeolum)

Description

A sty is actually a tiny abscess or walled-off infection in the hair follicle at the base of an eyelash. The infection is caused by staphylococcus bacteria. Sties usually last for several days, and can be quite uncomfortable. They often develop a white head, burst, and drain spontaneously. Sties tend to recur.

Self-help

A warm, moist washcloth should be placed over the sty 3 or 4 times a day. Such a hot compress helps increase blood flow to the area, bringing in extra white blood cells to engulf the bacteria. Warm compresses are most effective if they are left on for 15 minutes or more.

The doctor

Sometimes a doctor will prescribe an antibiotic eye ointment or drops in the beginning stages of the inflammation. (For administration of drops and ointment, see *The doctor* under *Eye infection—conjunctivitis.*)

Prevention

As with all staph infections, careful hygiene may help to prevent reinfection or passing on the disease. Children should wash frequently and use their own towels and washcloths.

Signs and symptoms

A small red swelling on the edge of the eyelid

Tenderness and pain in the sty and in the surrounding area

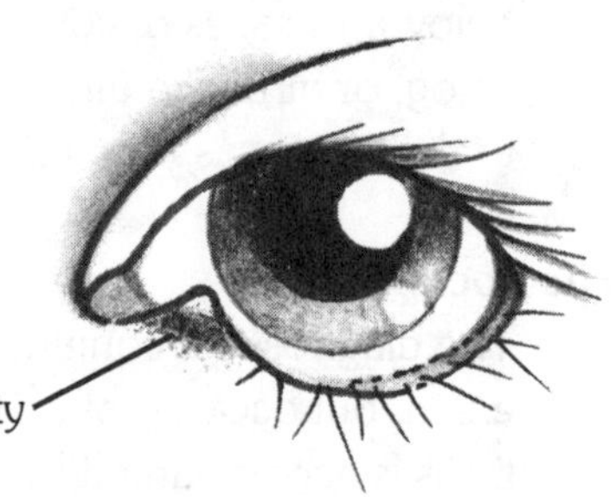

A sty is an infection of an eyelash follicle and appears as a small red swelling on the edge of the eyelid.

Blocked tear ducts

Description

In some newborns the duct or canal between the nose and the tear gland in the corner of the eye fails to open completely. The blockage keeps tears from draining normally into the nose. As the child grows older the duct usually opens by itself so that 80 percent are clear by eight months of age.

Self-help

Frequent, light massaging of the tear gland sometimes helps to open the duct. The parent should gently rub from the corner of the eye downward along the side of the nose. Massaging can be done twice a day for a few months. Crusts should be removed with warm water.

The doctor

If the condition does not clear spontaneously or with massage by the time the baby is eight months old, the doctor should be seen. Usually a pediatrician will suggest that the baby be seen by an ophthalmologist who will open the duct by inserting a small probe. This procedure is usually done in the hospital under a general anesthetic.

Signs and symptoms

Persistent tearing from the inner corner of the eye in newborns

Crusting and mild discharge around the eye

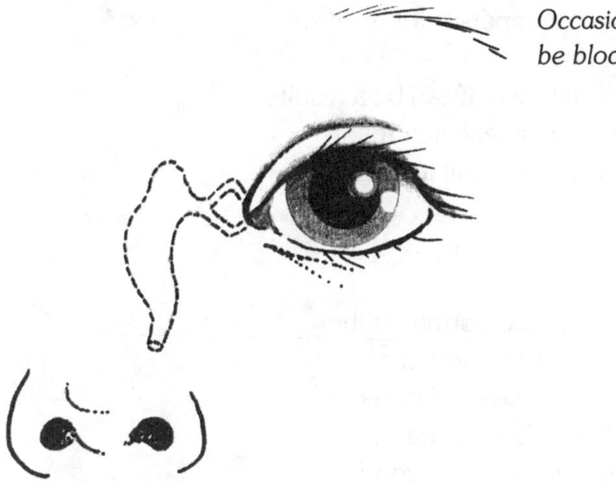

Occasionally a tear duct can be blocked in a newborn.

Occasionally a blocked tear duct becomes infected and develops a pussy discharge. If this happens a doctor should be seen promptly. The doctor will treat the infection with antibiotic drops.

Prevention

A blocked tear duct is a congenital condition and there is no known prevention.

Crossed eyes (strabismus), walleye, or wandering eye

Description

Strabismus is a condition in which the eyes are not properly aligned due to unequal strength and faulty balance in the muscles surrounding the eye. This improper alignment causes double vision. When children are seeing double, they may tilt their head to one side or close one eye in an effort to overcome it. Children with double vision often have difficulty walking and may become fussy and irritable. In time, children unconsciously learn to suppress the image sent by one eye (the nonaligned). Over a period of years the lack of "use" of this eye results in a decrease in central vision due to lack of stimulation. The eye actually loses its ability to see straight ahead.

Ophthalmologists say that less than 5 percent of all children have strabismus in some form. The onset of strabismus may be shortly after birth or in the third year of life. Almost all newborns up to the age of six months occasionally have one eye wander or cross. This is due to the fact that the infant's eye muscles are not yet well coordinated and the infant has poor focus at near and far range. In general, newborn eye wandering or crossing

Signs and symptoms

Abnormal position of one or both eyes that is not temporary

of eyes lasts only a few minutes, but occasionally it can persist for weeks. In that case the doctor should be seen.

The specific cause of permanent strabismus is unknown. It can be a result of uterine development, and occasionally it can be a genetic trait that is inherited. It can also be due to birth injury or to a severe viral infection of the nervous system.

Self-help

Occasional episodes of crossed eyes in young babies are normal. If the baby's attention is attracted to one side or the other with a toy, then the baby's eyes will usually "unlock." Often a newborn's eyes will cross more than once a day, leading a parent to suspect the baby's eyes are simply tired. In any case, if the baby's eyes cross briefly, it is probably good to temporarily avoid making the baby's eyes follow fast movements from far to near. The parent should also avoid holding objects too near the baby's eyes because this normally requires the eyes to turn toward each other in order to focus.

The doctor

A strabismus that lasts for several weeks or develops after the age of six months will not be outgrown and should be treated *early* by an ophthalmologist. In addition to visual inspection, there are two simple tests which can help the doctor confirm the diagnosis, particularly in cases where there is little displacement of the eyes. One test involves seeing whether light reflected in the child's eyes is at corresponding points in both eyes. A second test involves covering one eye and then the other while a child looks at an object. The eye that is being uncovered will move if the child has strabismus.

Diagnosed cases of strabismus are treated with special glasses that stimulate the weak eye to align, and by covering the good eye in order to develop good central vision in the weak eye. Treatment may take weeks, months, or years to relieve the strabismus. The earlier medical treatment is started, the better it works. In cases that do not respond to medical treatment, eye-muscle surgery may be advised. One of the problems in nonsurgical treatment of strabismus involves the child's adjustment to wearing patches and glasses.

Prevention

There are no known ways to prevent strabismus, but prompt treatment prevents permanent loss of vision in the affected eye.

Teething problems (dentitio difficilis)

Description

Teething refers to the discomfort a child feels as the teeth penetrate the gums. As the teeth emerge, the gums can become inflamed, swollen, and painful. The amount of discomfort varies greatly from one baby to another, from one tooth to another, even from day to day. The average baby is constantly experiencing tooth eruption from three months to over two years. A baby can show symptoms for as much as four months before a tooth comes through. Sucking, either at the bottle or the breast, increases the blood supply to the baby's gums and may temporarily increase swelling and discomfort. When a tooth finally erupts, the swelling subsides. The timing of eruption is highly variable. For example, the central incisors normally erupt anywhere from birth to over a year. Some families have a history of early or late eruption, which is almost never a matter of concern.

The eruption of the first baby molars at around a year generally causes a baby the most difficulty, including possible loss of appetite and waking at night. Parents notice the wakefulness because most often the baby has already been sleeping through the night. Old wives' tales would have parents believe that teething can cause fevers, colds, and diarrhea, but there is little evidence for this. On the other hand, it is possible that difficulty with tooth eruption may lower a child's resistance to illness and may be the cause of some unexplained fevers.

Signs and symptoms

- Irritability
- Drooling
- Rubbing gums, chewing on objects
- Fretful sleeping

Self-help

Somewhat paradoxically, the best treatment for sore gums involves letting the baby chew on smooth, firm, unbreakable objects. There are currently on the market a large number of teething rings and exercisers, including

Eruption chart

Tooth	"Average" age of eruption (months)	
	Lower	Upper
4 central incisors	6	7½
4 lateral incisors	7	9
4 eye teeth (cuspids or canines—pointed)	16	18
First molars (flat chewing teeth)	12	14
Second molars	20	24

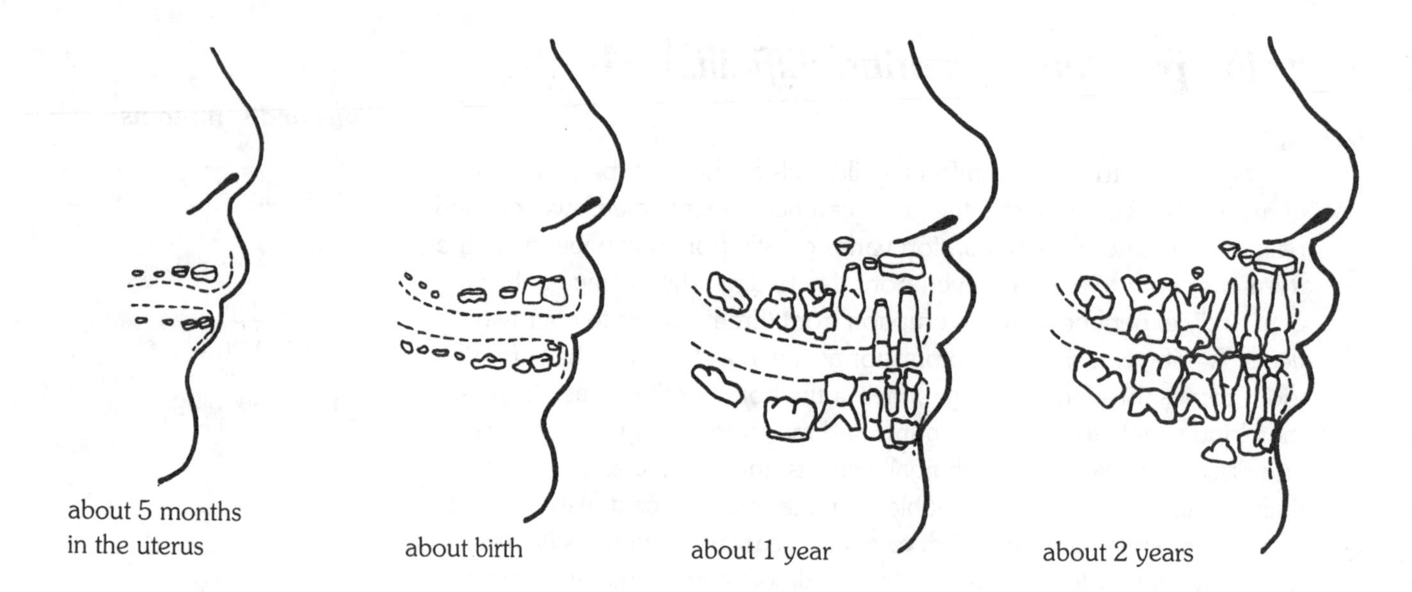

These diagrams show the average development of the baby's deciduous ("baby") and permanent teeth at various ages. The teeth are shown before they come through the gums and after they erupt. Permanent teeth are shown forming above and below the baby teeth.

water-filled ones that can be chilled to help numb the gums. Letting the baby suck on an ice cube wrapped in a handkerchief is an old device for numbing the gums. Some babies find relief simply by rubbing their gums with their fingers or in having someone else "massage" their gums. Older babies seem to enjoy chewing on zweiback, teething biscuits, or frozen foods like beans. Some parents find that the nonprescription gum-numbing medications and acetaminophen (e.g., Tylenol) are helpful.

When babies are very uncomfortable because of sore gums, they sometimes specifically avoid or lose interest in sucking. Strenuous sucking increases the blood supply to the already swollen, tender gums. If babies take milk or juice from a bottle, it may make it easier if the hole in the nipple is enlarged. Or babies may enjoy taking liquid from a cup. In either case, it is soothing to the gums if the liquid is slightly chilled.

The doctor

The doctor should be consulted if the baby develops a fever or other signs

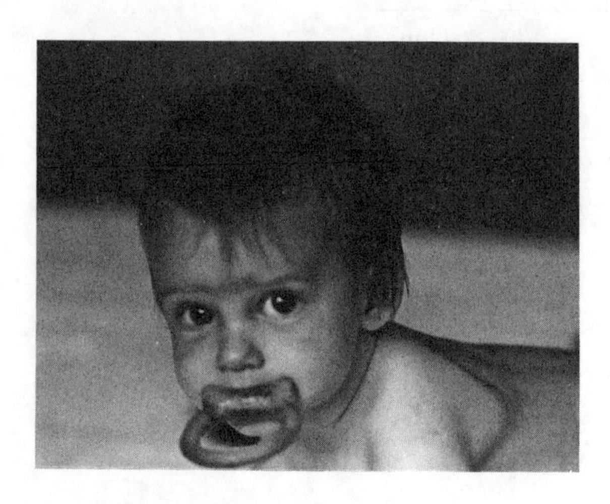

Children whose gums are sore from teething often enjoy chewing on hard rubber toys or water-filled toys that have been chilled in the refrigerator.

of illness. Dentists sometimes suggest cutting the gums, which used to be a more common practice, but this is not thought to be a good idea.

Prevention

Teething is not a disease; it is a normal physiological process. Some babies do seem to experience more discomfort with teething than others. There really is no way to prevent it, but things can be done to ease the baby's discomfort.

Cavities (dental caries)

Description

Cavities represent the destruction of tooth structures by acid-forming bacteria which are normally present in the mouth. These bacteria break down refined carbohydrates, particularly the form of sugar called sucrose. The end product is an acid which dissolves the calcium in the tooth enamel. Other kinds of bacteria normally present in the mouth form deposits called plaque on the teeth. This plaque tends to harbor the acid-forming bacteria and allows them to digest the tooth enamel more readily.

Dental caries have been a very common problem in young children, but recently fluoridated water, better hygiene, and less dietary sugar have decreased the incidence. Susceptibility to caries runs in families, as does resistance, but diet habits and oral hygiene definitely play a major role too. Carbohydrates and sugars that tend to stick to the teeth or that are kept in the mouth for prolonged periods provide acid-producing bacteria with a constant source of "food." The small particle size of some foods—especially highly refined ones—makes those foods easier for bacteria to work on. Moreover, foods with small particle size tend to adhere to the teeth more easily. The constant presence of food in the mouth—either due to frequent, sweet snacks or always sucking on a bottle of juice—is especially bad. A constant sugar bath on the teeth can result in a serious condition in which all of the child's teeth are severely affected with caries. It is particularly important that a child does not go to sleep with food on the teeth because saliva production declines then, and the teeth are not naturally rinsed.

Parents cannot tell whether their child is susceptible until after the teeth have erupted. If highly susceptible children are allowed to go to sleep with bottles in their mouth, they can develop severe cavities by one and a half or two years of age. To avoid this condition, called "milk bottle syndrome," dentists advise that parents do not allow babies to get accustomed to going to sleep with a bottle or that they only give the baby a bottle of water.

Signs and symptoms

Brown spots on teeth that do not brush or scrape off

Self-help

There is no home treatment once a cavity has developed. Assertive prevention before a cavity has developed is the best treatment.

The dentist

Early and regular visits to the dentist are necessary once all the child's teeth are in or by two and a half or three years of age. Babies generally have regular visits to the pediatrician but surprisingly they often do not go to a dentist early enough. Pediatricians do not routinely refer babies to dentists unless *severe* caries are seen. So it is the parents' responsibility to see that the baby gets early and regular dental care, including a routine examination and X rays.

In an initial visit the dentist will usually "count" the teeth, clean the teeth to remove plaque, probe the teeth for cavities, and possibly take X rays. The earlier the first visit, the less likely the child is to have cavities. Visits that simply involve observation and cleaning help the child become accustomed to the dentist, the office, the equipment, and the routine. This makes the child more at ease when cavities do have to be filled. If there are no cavities at the first visit, return visits are scheduled for six months or possibly four months later, depending on the condition of the child's teeth and the family history of susceptibility.

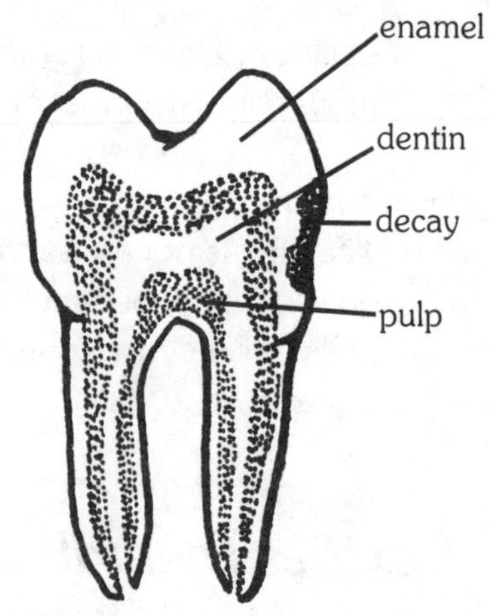

Cavities result when tooth enamel is dissolved by acid that is produced by bacteria feeding on sugar.

Many parents do not realize the importance of treating caries in "baby" teeth and the value of early treatment. Cavities in baby teeth can become deep enough to produce serious toothaches. In some cases if cavities are not treated early enough, the tooth may have to be extracted. This is particularly bad in the case of back teeth. Children normally have some of their baby teeth for as long as ten years.

If baby teeth have to be extracted prematurely, it may be years before the permanent teeth come in, and the permanent teeth are more likely to come in in the wrong position. This necessitates long, expensive orthodontic treatment.

Prevention

The more susceptible a child's teeth are, the more important prevention becomes. Since a parent can't be certain of how susceptible the child is, it is wisest to establish good preventive habits for every child. The four most important facets of prevention are (1) control of diet, (2) oral hygiene, (3) use of fluoride, and (4) dental checkups. Control of diet involves eliminating or minimizing the use of sugar and sweets, and avoiding frequent use of foods that cling to the teeth (for example, sticky candy and certain kinds of crackers). Oral hygiene involves cleaning the teeth to remove food particles and prevent plaque from building up.

Fluoride is an important aid in prevention of decay. Studies have shown that children who are born and raised in an area where the water has high fluoride content have 60 percent fewer caries than children raised in an area with low fluoride. For this reason many water districts across the country now routinely add fluoride. If the local water does not contain high amounts of fluoride, parents should consider giving their child fluoride tablets or drops. Some pediatricians prescribe fluoride in vitamin preparations beginning as early as one month. Such treatment is considered useful up to

Good teeth and diet

Avoid sweets—especially sticky candy and candy that stays in the mouth for a prolonged time (hard candy, suckers, and chewing gum).

Avoid high-sugar foods—sugared breakfast cereals, cakes, cookies, ice cream, dried fruit.

Avoid "sticky," highly processed foods whose ingredients are finely ground—many cereals, crackers, breads, and snack foods like caramelized crunch, cheese puffs, and chips.

Avoid sodas, juice "drinks," juices that have sugar added, and even juices that are naturally high in sugar.

Never allow infants to suck on bottles for hours, particularly if they contain sweet juices and especially before going to sleep.

Avoid frequent snacking because less saliva is produced between meals—saliva is acid-neutralizing.

Provide rough foods like apples, carrots, and celery which have a natural cleansing action on the teeth.

Encourage nonsweet foods for snacks—cheese, yogurt, fresh vegetables, and fruits.

Oral hygiene

"Clean" a baby's teeth with a wet washcloth before bedtime.

Parents should brush a child's teeth until the child has enough coordination to do it properly. Brush before bedtime, or more often if the child is susceptible.

Floss a child's teeth if cavities develop between the teeth.

Teach a child to rinse the teeth when brushing can't be done.

the age of six to eight, but it is most valuable in the first few years when active formation of the permanent teeth is still taking place. Thereafter fluoride can help to lower the number of cavities.

Finally, early and regular checkups are an important part of any prevention program. Prompt treatment will keep cavities from becoming large and will make the need for extractions unlikely.

Common cold (acute nasopharyngitis, inflammation of the nose and back of the throat, rhinitis)

Description

The common cold is an infection of the upper respiratory system—the nose and throat—caused by a virus or bacteria. There are at least a hundred different viruses and a number of different bacteria that cause cold symptoms. Most colds are probably caused by viruses. If the initial inflammation is severe enough or persistent enough, a child's resistance may be lowered and then bacteria may multiply in the already inflamed areas. More severe colds tend to be bacterial as well as viral in nature.

Colds in some form are by far the most common illness of infancy and early childhood. As all parents know, children vary greatly in their susceptibility to colds, which occur at any time of the year but are most common in fall and winter. Colds are generally most frequent in the first five years of life. Children in this age group may average as many as eight colds a year and each may last several days to several weeks.

Signs and symptoms

- Running nose
- Sneezing
- Fever
- Mild sore throat
- Cough
- Tiredness, muscle aches
- Crankiness
- Lack of appetite

How the body fights the cold. In an uncomplicated cold the child's body is quite capable of healing itself. This is as true for an infant as it is for an older child.

Some of the organisms (especially viruses) which cause the common cold have been found to live normally in the nose and throat. Thus some viruses may be present in a latent state all the time and only cause the symptoms of the common cold when they multiply. The body reacts to a particular kind of virus (or bacteria) by producing antibodies which specifically attach to these virus particles and render them harmless. This is the principle on which immunization is based. Once such antibodies have been produced, they prevent reinfection by that particular virus or keep a reinfection from becoming severe. There is no medicine that directly attacks viruses; antibiotics are only effective against bacteria, and thus are of use only if the viral infection becomes complicated by a bacterial infection.

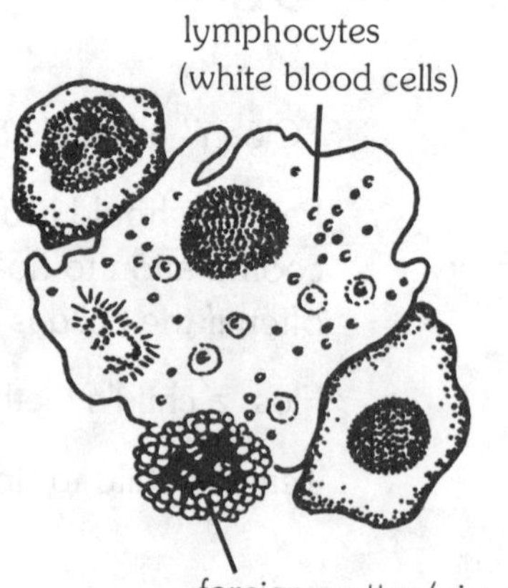

The body cures a cold by producing antibodies which engulf and kill the virus.

Cold symptoms and onset. A cold begins with local symptoms such as nasal congestion, a runny nose, or sneezing. A runny nose represents the body's attempt to rid itself of the virus. When an infection starts, the lining of the nose swells. Then white blood cells are brought into the area to produce antibodies and engulf the virus. Along with the white blood cells and virus, the top layer of cells lining the nasal passages sloughs off and is included in the mucus discharge. (After the cold is gone new cells grow and the top layer renews itself.) In order to clear out the dead virus, antibodies, and white blood cells, the body needs fluids. With high fluid levels the secretions of the nose and throat become thinner and less congested, making it easier for the body to expel the virus.

If the trachea, or windpipe, becomes infected, the child gets a cough. In an effort to fight the infection, the windpipe produces a mucus discharge or phlegm. The child naturally coughs in order to get rid of this discharge. If the child does not have sufficient fluids, the discharge can become sticky and difficult to cough up. A "tight" cough not only slows healing, it can hurt.

Another symptom of a cold is fever. Fever is a generalized body response as opposed to a specific response like a sore throat or runny nose. The cold's virus probably does not live as well at higher temperatures. After a period of just fever, lasting as long as 12 to 24 hours, the cold can disappear or localize in the nose or throat. Fevers in young children tend to be high because their temperature regulation mechanisms are not yet mature. In general there is nothing dangerous about fevers, even those as high as 104° F or 40° C. The reason that there is such concern about high fevers is that on rare occasions a rapidly rising high fever may lead to convulsions (see *Emergency Medicine* section). Parents often tend to overbundle a child with a fever, and a child's temperature cannot drop naturally if the child is wrapped up warmly. Bundling, like the fever itself, tends to increase the child's needs for fluids.

A cold is often signaled by a change in behavior: the child doesn't want to eat or is too tired to play. Rest is important since the body expends great energy to synthesize antibodies and white blood cells to fight the virus. Babies and young children often sleep for long periods during a cold, especially during the feverish stage. Children with a cold should not be expected to eat normally for two or three days. There is no danger in not eating much for this period of time.

Fahrenheit-Centigrade equivalents

F.	C.
96.8	36
97.6*	36.4*
98.6**	37.0**
99.6***	37.6***
100.4	38
102.2	39
104	40
105.8	41

*Normal armpit temperature
**Normal oral temperature
***Normal rectal temperature

Colds in infants under six months. Babies under six months generally have fewer colds than other young children, because infants probably have some immunity due to antibodies transmitted to them in the uterus and, if they are nursing, through breast milk. Infants—especially if they are first babies—also tend to have less contact with children who have colds.

A cold in a baby under a year appears different from a cold in an older child. The baby is more likely to run a fever, perhaps even a high fever, and it often appears irritable and restless. This change in behavior and personality may be one of the first symptoms to alert parents to the illness. Babies under a year may be very bothered by nasal congestion because they are naturally nose breathers. Moreover, congestion interferes with their ability to nurse or take fluids from a bottle. Colds in the young infant are also frequently accompanied by general achiness, vomiting, and mild diarrhea. (See *Gastroenteritis.*)

Colds in the one- to two-year-old. A cold in a one- or two-year-old is different from a cold in a baby. The colds often come on quite suddenly. The child can awake after a nap looking flushed and feeling hot to the touch. When the temperature is taken, it is often 101° F or 102° F, and may even be as high as 104° F (40° C). The child will probably feel a little listless and its eyes will generally appear glazed, but it may not seem to be very bothered by the high temperature. The child will talk and smile fairly normally, but in a softer, more vulnerable way. Generally localized symptoms like a runny nose or cough will appear the next day. The fever will begin to drop, but may persist for several days.

Colds in the three- to four-year-old. The older child of three to four generally reacts to a cold more like an adult in that he or she will experience local symptoms before the onset of the fever. Often the older child will be sufficiently verbal and aware enough to describe preliminary symptoms such as achiness or sore throat. As the child progresses, the child will begin to sneeze, have a running nose, and a low-grade fever. Within a day or so the fever will drop and the clear, runny nasal discharge will turn to thick green or yellow mucus as the body begins to rid itself of the virus. The child's nostrils may become inflamed and sore from the irritation of constant moisture and wiping. An uncomplicated cold such as this may persist for as long as seven to ten days.

Complications of a cold. A complicated cold begins in the same way as an uncomplicated cold but it does not start to get better in the same way. Other symptoms will appear and the child's fever may return or rise.

Any simple cold can develop complications ranging from the minor to the more serious. Most are due to the fact that the mucous membrane lining the nose and throat is continuous with that of the larynx (vocal cords), bronchial tubes and lungs, middle ear, and sinuses. Live viruses can spread to any of these areas. Or, due to the inflamed condition of the mucous membrane, bacteria that live in the area and are ordinarily not harmful can begin to multiply and cause trouble. Spread of these bacteria can cause ear infections, croup, tonsillitis, bronchitis, or pneumonia. (See specific conditions for more information.)

Self-help

Treatment of a cold is based on two principles: (1) helping the body heal itself and (2) making the child more comfortable by treating symptoms, if necessary. There are several things that assist the body in healing itself. Extra fluids are extremely important because they help to break up mucus congestion and flush out virus and bacteria. Children should be encouraged

Taking a child's temperature

Clean the thermometer with alcohol or warm, soapy water, and rinse. If necessary, shake the mercury thermometer down below normal. Do not check the temperature directly after a bath, or (orally) after a child has had hot or cold foods or liquids. Digital or rectal mercury (fat bulb) thermometers are recommended for use with young children; oral mercury (thin end) thermometers are much more breakable. Temperature strips are not currently recommended because they are less accurate.

Armpit
Place bulb end of thermometer (any type) under armpit and hold arm snugly against body. Wait 3–4 minutes.

Continued

to drink as much or more fluid than normal, whichever ones they like most, including water, juice, or even soda. Probably the most commonly recommended fluid is filtered apple juice. If the child's stomach is upset, frequent small amounts of soda may be most easily tolerated at first. Some doctors feel that milk (and milk products) are mucus-producing and should be avoided or reduced in the early, acute stages of a cold. The one exception to this rule is breast-feeding, which should not be discontinued.

Another way of giving added fluid to the child is running a vaporizer. Vaporizers are particularly useful when a child has a cough. The vaporizer will make the child feel better because the moist air specifically loosens bronchial secretions, and possibly nasal congestion. As these secretions become thinner, they can be coughed up more easily and with less discomfort. Moisture from fluids and a vaporizer helps cure a cough and prevent complications like bronchitis and croup. (See *Bronchitis* for further treatment of coughs.) A cool mist vaporizer is recommended because vaporizers that boil water present a significant hazard in terms of burns.

Rest is also important in treating a cold because the body needs a lot of energy to heal itself. Parents can encourage rest by keeping the household quiet and avoiding tiring activities such as guests or outings. Every effort should be made to keep the child from getting fatigued, especially older children who may want to play as usual. Parents should find quiet activities for the child to do when not sleeping. Keeping the child warm conserves energy, too. This means keeping the house at a reasonable temperature and adjusting the child's clothing and blankets to the temperature of the child and the house.

The second principle of treatment involves relieving symptoms when they are uncomfortable. In general if a child is not uncomfortable, there's no need to treat any of a cold's symptoms. Relieving symptoms is not the same thing as curing the cold or killing the virus. It probably doesn't even hasten the child's recovery, except insofar as feeling better lets the child's body heal itself faster.

A fever, particularly a high fever, can make a child uncomfortable. Children with a fever can be undressed in a room of normal temperature as long as they are not shivering. The child should be allowed to cool off naturally. In the case of a high fever a child may be made more comfortable by sponging with lukewarm water, which cools as it evaporates. Cold-water sponging causes the child to shiver, and *retain* heat. Acetaminophen (e.g., Tylenol) is valuable if a child is uncomfortable. Aspirin should not be given for flu symptoms because it has been found to be associated with an increased incidence of Reye's syndrome, a rare but potentially fatal condition (see page 408).

Children are often bothered by stuffy or runny noses. Very young babies may have difficulty clearing thick or profuse mucus from their nose. In this case the babies will have problems nursing or taking a bottle. A special rubber bulb syringe may be used very gently to suction out the mucus if

Oral
Place bulb under child's tongue and have child close lips around thermometer, but not bite it. Wait 2 minutes or more. Oral mercury thermometers should not be used with young children because of the danger of breaking off the tip.

Rectal
Lubricate rectal thermometer with petroleum jelly or lubricant. Gently insert thermometer just far enough to cover bulb. This should be done carefully. Hold in place 2–3 minutes. Armpit and oral temperatures are easier to take, and are less upsetting for older babies.

the baby is uncomfortable. Some doctors suggest putting babies on their stomach in order to promote mucus drainage. Older children can be taught to blow their noses gently, with caution against blowing hard because it can block the eustachian tubes leading to the middle ear.

The doctor

Questions about a fever or other cold symptoms are the basis for most unscheduled calls to the doctor. A cold is usually the first illness a child gets and parents are almost always worried the first time their child gets a serious one. Most pediatricians encourage parents to call if they are worried by specific symptoms or if the child has a fever of 101° F or above. The doctor will want to assess whether or not the child's cold is complicated. If not, the doctor will generally advise home treatment, possibly including baby acetaminophen (e.g., Tylenol), keeping the baby cool, lots of fluids, a cool mist vaporizer, and saltwater nose drops. The parent should call again if the child isn't better in a day or so, or seems to be getting worse.

If the doctor suspects there is any possibility of a complication which should be treated, he will have the parents bring the baby in for examination. To determine whether or not the cold is complicated, the doctor will generally ask a series of questions. He or she may want to know (1) what the baby's temperature is, (2) whether the baby seems to have labored breathing, wheezing, or a croupy cough (bronchitis or croup), (3) whether the baby is pulling on its ear and seems to be in pain (ear infection), (4) whether the baby has severe diarrhea or vomiting (dehydration—see page 315 for signs), and (5) whether the baby seems very listless, sleepy, or unnaturally unresponsive (possibly indicating a more severe illness).

If he sees the baby, the doctor will check its temperature and do a basic physical, including looking at the baby's eardrums, listening to the baby's lungs, looking at the baby's throat and nose, possibly taking a nasal or throat culture to rule out a strep infection. The doctor will check the baby for great irritability or lethargy (and a stiff neck in a child over two), signs that might indicate meningitis (rare).

Recipe for saltwater nose drops

½ tablespoon salt

½ tablespoon baking soda

1 quart water

Use with purchased medicine dropper.

Prevention

Cold viruses are communicable from 24 hours before the onset of a cold to 5 days afterward. The incubation period for developing a cold after being exposed to a virus is highly variable—from 12 hours to a week or more after exposure.

Recent research shows that cold viruses are basically spread by hand-to-hand contact. When people touch their nose with their hands or a tissue, the virus is transferred to the objects or people that they touch afterward. The virus stays alive on objects or skin for several hours. If other people touch the virus with their hands, and then touch their nose, the transfer is made. Thus handwashing and disinfecting household surfaces are the major means of preventing spread. Coughing and sneezing do not spread nasal secretions, they spread saliva, which contains relatively little

Cold treatment

Helping the body heal itself

Rest

Sleep, quiet the household, avoid stressful outings, avoid vigorous play, encourage quiet play, TV

Warmth

Enough clothes for comfort; uncover, undress for comfort with fever

For a fever sponge child with warm water (not alcohol or cold water)

Diet

Eat what they want; don't force food

Drink as much fluid as is reasonable; encourage water, juice, even soda, mild tea

Vaporizer

Use a cool-mist vaporizer if child coughs, or is susceptible to croup, or if house air is very dry due to heat

Symptom relief

Fever

Remove clothes, sponge bathe, acetaminophen (e.g., Tylenol)

Congested or runny nose

Use a baby syringe if the child *can't* nurse; teach the older child to blow its nose; give plenty of liquids; use saltwater nose drops

Cough

Teach older child to cough to bring up mucus

Diarrhea

Stop solid foods; give fluids; nurse, but stop cow's milk; add a bland diet as the child recovers

Sore throat

Warm milk, or weak tea with honey

Vomiting

Stop solid foods, give small amounts of fluid until vomiting stops virus. Since parents or caretakers help young children when they blow their nose, the adults as well as the children need to wash their hands. Cleaning up used tissues presents another opportunity for the virus to be spread. In the case of a daycare center, adults can inadvertently spread the virus to themselves and to the other children if they do not wash their hands after each encounter with the virus.

Viruses can cause small-scale epidemics in families, preschool groups, and communities. A particular virus may make the rounds of a group of people for a month or so and then be replaced by a different virus. The more contact a child has with other children, the more likely that child is to catch the viruses that cause colds. Young children who live in isolated areas or stay at home most of the time are least likely to get colds. Children who go to daycare or preschool, or who have brothers or sisters who do, are the most likely to get colds.

The question of just when to keep a child at home bothers every parent at some time or other. Isolation definitely reduces spread, but if carried to extremes it affects children's social interaction and development of immunity. On the other hand, no isolation and lack of hygiene can result in virtually continuous colds (for example, eight a year, each one lasting several weeks) for a child, a family, even a school or community. During the most active stages a child should probably be kept home for the child's own comfort as well as to minimize passing the cold to others. Certainly, a sick child should be kept away from very young babies and very old people.

The better a child's general state of health is, the less likely the child will be to get a cold or to have a cold develop complications. A child who gets adequate nutrition, sufficient rest and exercise, and is basically happy, is more like to be in good overall health. Many parents fail to realize the importance of the general factors in a child's life that affect its susceptibility as much or more than specific factors such as a virus or bacteria. All pediatricians find that colds are not evenly distributed among their patients. Some children rarely get sick, while others seem to be sick rather constantly. Some of a child's susceptibility is undoubtedly inherited, but much of it is environmental, and much can be done to affect a child's "environment" to lower susceptibility. An emphasis on good nutrition and healthy snacks, and on sufficient sleep and prevention of fatigue, are basic to minimizing colds. Being aware of early signs of illness and teaching the older child to be sensitive to body signals can often prevent colds and lesson their severity. In particular, parents should be aware of the child's day-to-day energy level and fine state of health and gear the child's activities accordingly. For example, if a child seems a little tired and out of sorts, the parent may be wise to avoid the kind of long shopping trip that is always known to be tiring. A child's illness sometimes can be a message to the parents to make changes in their life, because a cold is often the result of fatigue and tension, but it also represents the development of basic immunity and is often unavoidable (see page 292).

Strep throat

Signs and symptoms

Running nose

Sneezing

Fever

Loss of appetite

Vomiting (occasionally)

Sore throat

Swollen neck glands

Description

Strep throat is a bacterial infection of the throat caused by Group A beta-hemolytic streptococci. A child with a strep throat is usually sicker than a child who simply has a viral sore throat. Often the child has a sudden onset of a high fever, feels very tired, and may vomit. The glands in the child's neck often swell and are tender to the touch. The back of the child's throat generally appears bright red and may be covered with white pussy spots called plaques.

Occasionally the child gets a skin rash, which looks like sunburn, in the armpits, leg creases, and body. This skin rash generally appears about a day after the onset of the fever and lasts several days. The rash is caused by a toxin released by the strep bacteria. Strep throat accompanied by this rash is a condition called *scarlet fever.* Most children do not develop scarlet fever when they have strep throat because most varieties of strep produce little toxin or because the children have natural antibodies to the toxin.

A number of years ago researchers found that a strep throat or scarlet fever could be followed by heart disease or kidney disease. These complications are thought to result from an unusual allergic reaction to the strep bacteria. Rheumatic fever can cause damage to the valves of the heart; glomerulonephritis can cause damage to the kidneys. These complications occur only in a small percentage (0.5–3 percent) of *untreated* strep infections.

Doctors now routinely treat all strep infections with penicillin in order to avoid these complications. Penicillin readily kills large numbers of strep bacteria, preventing complications, and possibly even speeding the body's healing of the infection. Generally within three days of beginning treatment, children feel much better, and by a week they have completely recovered. Children can return to normal activities, including nursery school, as soon as they feel better—a minimum of one day after starting treatment.

Self-help

See treatment for the simple cold, especially fluids and rest. Acetaminophen in proper doses will help relieve severe pain in the child's throat and glands. Eating smooth cold foods like ice cream or gelatin or drinking warm fluids like mild tea with honey may also help to soothe the sore throat. The older child can also be given throat lozenges. Warm, wet towels may relieve the discomfort of swollen neck glands.

The doctor

At present doctors vary widely in their handling of severe sore throats. Roughly a tenth of all *severe* sore throats with fever are accompanied by growth of strep bacteria. A diagnosis of strep infection is easily made with a throat culture. A culture is made by touching a cotton swab to the back of the throat and touching the swab to a medium for bacteria growth. Within 24 hours the culture will show strep growth if the person has a strep infection. The new rapid antigen detection test gives results in minutes, but it is somewhat less accurate. Some doctors use antigen tests, others prefer to culture, but an antigen test or culture is the only sure way to distinguish strep from a virus. In the early 1950s doctors treated all severe sore throats with penicillin, but now they generally wait for positive test results before starting treatment with penicillin.

Doctors do not treat simple viral sore throats with antibiotics because antibiotics are not effective against viruses. Moreover, doctors avoid unnecessary use of antibiotics because of possible side effects, including allergic reactions. Strep is highly communicable, and doctors sometimes routinely test and treat family members of strep cases. It has been found that 40 percent of the siblings of strep cases show a positive culture.

Researchers have found that to prevent possible complications of strep throat antibiotics have to be given for 10 days. It is important that medication not be discontinued as soon as the child begins to feel better, since 10 full days of penicillin are necessary to prevent regrowth of the strep bacteria and a renewed possibility of complications.

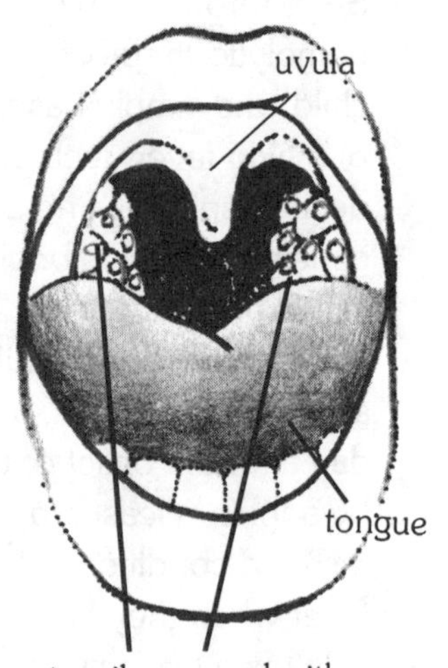

A strep throat appears bright red and there are often white dots of pus on the back of the throat and the tonsils.

Prevention

Strep bacteria are readily spread by touching, coughing, and sneezing. A child who develops strep throat does so rapidly after being exposed to the bacteria. The actual incubation period is 1 to 3 days. A child is contagious from the onset of symptoms until a day after penicillin is started, and for at least 10 days if, for any reason, penicillin is not started. A child should be kept away from other children from the time strep is first suspected until a day after treatment is begun. During this time it is important that parents pay special attention to routine cleanliness and minimize close contact between the child and others. Prompt treatment of sore throats helps to prevent further spread.

Tonsils and adenoids

Tonsils and adenoids are two pairs of lymph tissue located at the back of the throat. They help the body prevent illness by filtering out dead bacteria and virus, and they also assist in the manufacture of antibodies. They normally appear "enlarged" until a child is seven or eight, then gradually shrink in size.

For a number of years tonsils and adenoids were almost routinely removed by doctors. Tonsillectomy was something of a prepuberty rite. Even today, roughly a third of all American children have their tonsils removed. Enlarged tonsils were thought to be chronically infected and were considered to be the cause of recurrent colds, strep throats, fevers, allergies, even bad breath. In other words, they were blamed for almost everything.

Swollen tonsils are common in young children, but doctors no longer routinely advise their removal.

Research has shown that the removal of tonsils and adenoids does not result in a lower incidence of colds, sore throats, or strep throats. Good medical practice now calls for the removal of tonsils and adenoids only in specific cases such as obstruction of the nose or mouth, tonsillar abscesses, persistent nasal blockage, and mouth breathing.

If parents feel hesitant about a suggested tonsillectomy, they should feel free to ask for a detailed explanation of why the operation is necessary, and they should feel free to seek a second opinion. According to ear, nose, and throat experts, over 95 percent of all tonsillectomies done in the United States are unnecessary. Tonsillectomies can have emotional effects, as well as occasional medical complications.

Ear infection (acute otitis media)

Description

Acute otitis media is an infection of the middle ear which can be caused by a virus or bacteria. The middle ear is an enclosed area drained only by the eustachian tubes. These tubes connect the middle ear to the back of the throat (*see* diagram). Almost 75 percent of all children get ear infections.

Ear infections are the most common complication of a cold. They are often seen in young children who have a cold and fever and are irritable.

An ear infection develops when the mucous membrane lining the eustachian tubes swells and obstructs the drainage from the middle ear. Lymph tissue near the eustachian tubes can also swell and push against the tubes, causing a block. When the eustachian tube closes, extra fluid that is produced in response to the infection becomes trapped in the middle ear. The trapped fluid in the middle ear is an ideal medium for the growth of the virus and/or bacteria, and they multiply rapidly. The body brings more white blood cells and fluid into the area to fight the infection, and then dead virus or bacteria build up in addition to spent white blood cells and fluid.

This congestion and the swelling of the tissues exert pressure on the eardrum and on the sensitive nerve endings around the inner ear. The

Signs and symptoms

- Earache
- Fever (often)
- Pussy or bloody, drainage from ear
- Irritability
- Poor appetite
- Difficulty sleeping
- Tugging at ears
- Hearing loss
- Crying

pressure can be extremely painful. For many children an earache is the most severe, unrelenting pain they have ever experienced. The pain begins to subside when the pressure drops for any of three reasons: (1) the body begins to get ahead of the infection, fluid production drops, and the remaining fluid is absorbed by local cells, (2) the membranes of the eustachian tube shrink back to normal, causing the tube to open and allowing the middle ear to drain, and/or (3) the eardrum, which separates the middle ear from the external ear canal, spontaneously bursts and allows the fluid to drain out. Rupture of the eardrum commonly occurs in about a fifth of all ear infections. The rupture normally heals completely by itself within two weeks and need not be a cause for concern.

Ear infections are always treated with antibiotics to prevent complications. Before antibiotics, children sometimes had severe complications stemming from untreated bacterial ear infections, including hearing loss and infection of the mastoid bone behind the ear (*mastoiditis*). Antibiotic therapy has virtually eliminated both of these.

With treatment an ear infection heals in about one to two weeks. In almost all cases there are no long-term effects, although there is often slight hearing loss for up to three or four weeks after the infection.

Self-help

A child with an ear infection should be kept warm. A hot water bottle wrapped in a soft towel or a heating pad held against the ear often helps to ease the pain. Acetaminophen (e.g., Tylenol) can also be given to ease pain. Sometimes a vaporizer may help to loosen congestion. Analgesic

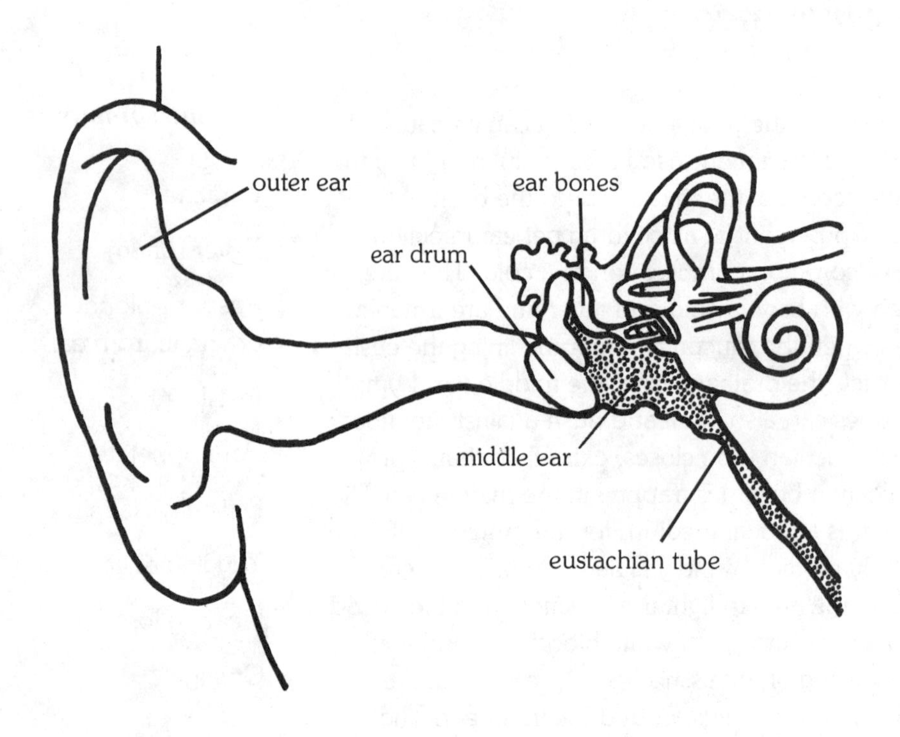

The middle ear is an enclosed area drained only by the eustachian tube, which enters the back of the throat.

eardrops and nose drops only rarely make the child feel more comfortable.

The doctor

The doctor diagnoses an ear infection by looking at the eardrum with an otoscope. If there is infection (either viral or bacterial), the drum will appear flaming red and sometimes swollen; a normal drum appears mirrorlike and silver-gray. Because of the commonness of ear infections, a doctor will examine the ears of all young children with a fever and cold symptoms.

Since the middle ear is inaccessible, there is no way the doctor can take a culture in order to distinguish between a viral or bacterial ear infection. Thus, due to the serious complications that can follow an untreated bacterial infection, doctors treat all ear infections with antibiotics. For the same reason, all children with significant ear pain and fever should be seen by a doctor. There are several strains of bacteria that cause ear infections. The doctor may treat the child with amoxicillin. Children who are allergic to penicillins are given erythromycin and sulfisoxazole, or trimethoprim. In any case the doctor will want to know if the child is *not* better within forty-eight hours, and will want to look at the child's ears again in ten to fourteen days to make sure treatment has been effective. If the drums still appear quite red on a follow-up exam, as occasionally happens, the doctor may switch to another antibiotic. Normally, a child feels much better within twelve hours of starting antibiotics and may even return to normal activities, including nursery school, within a day or two.

In addition to antibiotics some doctors also prescribe codeine for pain if necessary. Decongestants are still given by some doctors to relieve nasal congestion, but studies have not shown them to be effective. Decongestants often produce hyperactivity or sleepiness in children. For that reason some doctors tend not to prescribe them. Antibiotic eardrops are sometimes prescribed when the eardrum has perforated.

If the ear infection appears quite severe and the child is in excruciating pain, the doctor may suggest the child see a special ear, nose, and throat (ENT) doctor who will puncture the eardrum (*myringotomy*) to promote drainage and immediately lower the pressure and accompanying pain.

Prevention

Prompt and early treatment of a cold probably helps to prevent ear infections. Parents whose child frequently gets ear infections are wise to take special care. The child should be taught to blow its nose in a steady, gentle way so as not to force mucus up into the eustachian tubes. Some parents feel it helps to keep the child's ears covered in cold, windy weather, or when the child has mild cold symptoms. It can promote drainage if the child sleeps with its head slightly elevated. Very young babies, who are fed while lying down, may have a greater tendency to get ear infections.

Serous otitis media ("glue ear")

Description

Serous otitis media is a condition in which the middle ear becomes filled with fluid because the eustachian tube fails to drain adequately. When the eustachian tube becomes blocked, the tissues surrounding the middle ear absorb its air content, thereby creating a vacuum. To equalize the pressure created in the middle ear, the surrounding tissues then secrete fluid into the enclosed space. This fluid decreases the movement of the eardrum which in turn dampens the conduction of sound to the bones of the inner ear. This dampening effect gives the child the sensation of hearing under water. An older child will often complain about it. With a younger child the parents may first notice that the child seems less than normally reactive to sounds.

Often the cause of eustachian tube blockage is unknown. Doctors speculate that some children have narrow, twisted, or very short eustachian tubes. Allergies can cause chronic enlargement of lymph tissue or cause the eustachian tubes to be chronically inflamed. Untreated, poorly treated, or recurrent ear infections (acute otitis media) can also lead to fluid-filled ears. Two or three weeks after an ear infection, almost 40 percent of all children have some residual fluid behind the drum. The fluid disappears by itself in 95 percent of all cases within two to three months, but the child's ears should continue to be evaluated by the doctor during this time.

It is important to treat the condition to prevent the possibility of any permanent hearing loss and to prevent problems in the child's school and social life. Children with serous otitis media and hearing loss are sometimes thought by parents, teachers, and other children to be intentionally uncooperative, daydreamy, or dumb. Parents should inform teachers about children who have had serous otitis media with hearing loss and the children should routinely be seated near the teacher.

Signs and symptoms

Hearing loss

Minimal pain

A feeling of fullness in the ear

Self-help

Children with serous otitis media, and those who are prone to it, can sometimes be taught to clear their eustachian tubes by "popping their ears." The children should firmly hold their nose and, at the same time, close their lips and puff their cheeks out hard, then let go and swallow. An alternative is to have children blow into a balloon while holding their nose. Sometimes just repeated swallowing, pressing on the outer ear, or chewing gum will clear the eustachian tubes.

The doctor

The doctor diagnoses serous otitis media by examining the eardrum with an otoscope. The eardrum will appear pale, not normally shiny. Sometimes the doctor can see the shadow of fluid behind the drum or the drum will fail to move normally in response to a puff of air. The doctor may also do *tympanometry,* an electronic measure of movement of the eardrum, and/

or test the child's hearing since its temporary loss can be an indication of the presence of fluid in the middle ear.

In addition to suggesting home treatment the doctor may prescribe antibiotics for two to four weeks to deal with an unresponsive infection. In severe cases a pediatrician will refer the child to an ear, nose, and throat specialist who may make a small puncture in the eardrum (*myringotomy*) and insert a tiny plastic tube into this hole. This procedure may be done in the office or in the hospital. The tube is generally left in for about six months. The purpose of the tube is to break the vacuum in the middle ear and allow air to get in. The plastic tube acts as an alternate, external eustachian tube. Some doctors believe the tube insertion has good results, others have not found this to be the case. After the tube is removed, the eardrum heals by itself.

Prevention

Early and effective treatment of ear infections and of allergies may prevent episodes of serous otitis media. It may also help to teach a child how to keep the eustachian tubes open (see *Self-help*). This is especially important when a child is flying in a plane, going up in a rapid elevator, or when gaining altitude in a car. Observation by a doctor during episodes of glue-ear may prevent infections and permanent hearing loss.

Croup

Description

Croup is an inflammation of the trachea (windpipe), bronchi, and larynx (voice box) that is caused by the viruses that cause the common cold. In adults an inflammation of the larynx (*laryngitis*) causes hoarseness and loss of voice. In a child, the airway through the voice box is so narrow that laryngitis causes a characteristic barking cough and possibly difficulty breathing. It may also cause hoarseness.

Croup follows several days of a cold. Often the child has been mildly ill and coughing and may have run a slight fever. Typically croup comes on at night. The child suddenly wakes up with a harsh barking cough. The condition is not usually serious, and the coughing spells last only an hour or so. Sometimes the prolonged coughing may activate the gag reflex and the child may vomit. For unknown reasons, vomiting often promptly relieves the coughing attack. The next morning the cough generally becomes looser and more raspy. This may be the end of it or the barking cough may return, generally in less severe form, on subsequent nights. Occasionally the initial episode of croup may be quite severe, and the child may have real difficulty breathing which doesn't improve and requires prompt medical treatment (see *The doctor*).

Signs and symptoms

Barking cough

Difficulty breathing (if present, call doctor)

Hoarseness (possibly)

Fever (possibly)

Self-help

Very moist air usually is of great help to a child having a croup attack. Moist air relieves the swelling in the larynx and opens up the airway. The child will begin to breathe more easily almost immediately. Children often become upset by the fact that they cannot stop coughing. Parents should encourage the child to be calm (and be calm themselves) because this will help break the cycle of coughing. The child should be told to breathe slowly and evenly. Many children relax when they are told that moist air will stop the coughing and make the breathing easier. If there is any question of difficulty breathing, call the doctor.

Moist air can be generated quickly by running a cool mist vaporizer or humidifier in a small room, close to the child; by running a hot shower; or by running a sinkful of hot water and holding the child over it. If hot water is run in the sink, a towel or a piece of plastic can be used to create a makeshift tent over the child's head. Children should *never* be held near boiling water. The chance of accidents, and their severity when they occur, is just too great. Even hot water vaporizers are no longer recommended because the steam itself can scald a child who gets too close.

The vaporizer should be allowed to run all night, even after the child is again breathing easily. In general the moisture will keep the child from having another episode. But parents should sleep where they are readily able to hear if the child coughs again or calls out. Real croup is sufficiently frightening to the parents, as well as the child, that they will want to sleep near the child, particularly if it is very young. Even older children become

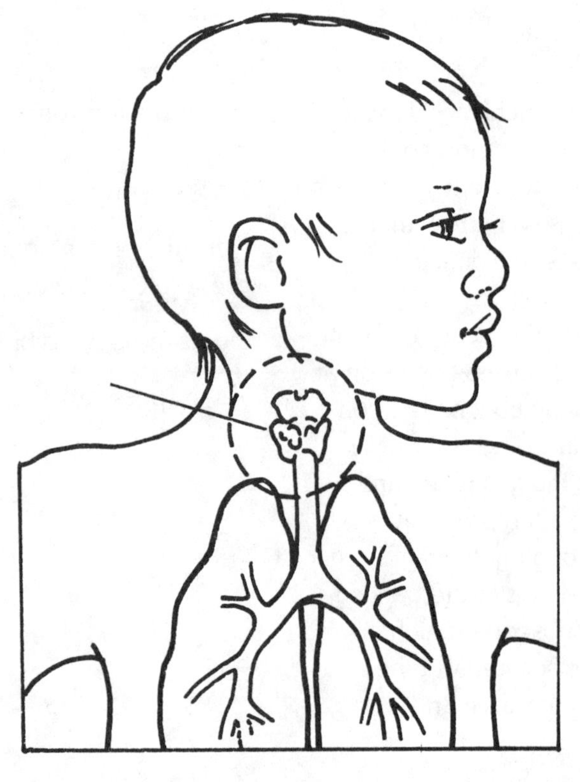

In croup the larynx becomes swollen, which causes a barking cough and difficulty in breathing.

quite frightened at the difficulty they had breathing and they may want company and reassurance even after the coughing has stopped.

The vaporizer should be run in the child's room for the next several nights, and even during the day to keep the moisture content of the air high. The child should be encouraged to drink large amounts of clear, room-temperature fluids (not cold fluids or milk or orange juice) in order to liquefy the mucus and reduce the swelling of the larynx. On succeeding nights parents should check on the child to make sure the cough is loose and rattly—not tight or barklike.

Symptoms of difficult breathing

Call the doctor immediately if the baby has difficulty breathing

Noisy, high-pitched inhalations

Increased chest retractions on inhalation

Arching neck to breathe

Rapid breathing rate

Poor color (pallor or blueness)

Increased anxiety and restlessness

Drooling and difficulty swallowing

The doctor

Croup has the potential of being a serious illness. The doctor should be called if the barklike coughing spell fails to respond to moist air within 45–60 minutes, if the child is also running a fever over 101° F, or if the child has *significant* difficulty breathing at any time. The doctor can even listen to the child's breathing over the telephone. It is a true medical emergency if the child is unable to get enough air. The doctor has several medications that promptly bring down swelling of the larynx in an emergency.

Prevention

Prompt treatment of a noisy cough is probably the best prevention for croup. Extra fluids and a vaporizer are especially important to help break up a tight cough. They are definitely indicated if the child has had previous episodes of croup (see *Bronchitis,* following).

The chest

Bronchitis

Description

Bronchitis is an infection of the trachea (windpipe) and the bronchial tubes leading to the lungs. The infection is usually caused by a virus and is generally a complication of a common cold. Bronchitis is most frequently seen in children under four. Some children, even whole families, seem more likely to have recurrent episodes of bronchitis, which can vary widely in severity from a mild cold with a loose cough to a cold with a fever and a severe cough.

At first the cough is dry, but after several days, mucus is produced in the bronchial tubes in response to the initial viral inflammation. Once mucus is produced the cough will become loose and noisy. Parents may hear squeaks, wheezes, or rattles with the child's breathing. These noises are caused by the movement of mucus in the bronchial tubes as the child breathes. An older child will cough the mucus up and spit it out; a young

Signs and symptoms

Coughing

Chest pain on coughing

Fever (sometimes)

Vomiting (sometimes)

child swallows the mucus and may occasionally gag on it and even vomit reflexively. Mucus that isn't liquefied and expelled can become a medium for bacterial infection and can drip down into the lungs. The faster the child can get the mucus out, the faster the condition will heal. Bronchial coughs normally get better by themselves within one or two weeks.

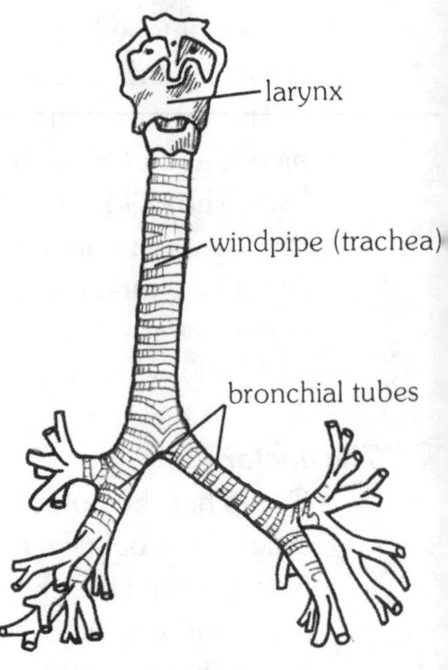

Bronchitis is an inflammation of the bronchi, the large tubes that go between the windpipe and the lungs.

Self-help

The child should be encouraged to cough to bring up the mucus and to spit it out. Repeated shallow coughing doesn't raise much mucus and is drying and irritating to the throat. The child should be encouraged to cough deliberately and deeply. Suppressant cough medicines should not be given, except at night if the child is being kept awake by shallow coughing spells. Antihistamines should not be given because they keep the child from coughing up mucus. Rubbing the chest with preparations like Vicks helps loosen and raise mucus and makes the child feel better. Children who seem fairly sick or have a fever should be kept indoors and quiet.

Moisture is most effective in helping to liquefy the mucus because it loosens the secretion so the child can cough it up. The child can get moisture by drinking fluids *in quantity* and by breathing air continuously moistened by a vaporizer. A very young baby should be encouraged to nurse frequently and may be given water or juice in addition. Bottle-fed babies should be given more water or juice and less milk than usual. Elevating the head of the bed and changing a child's position frequently also helps to promote mucus drainage.

The doctor

The doctor should be seen if the child has a fever over 101° F, has difficulty breathing, is wheezing on exhale (possible *bronchiolitis*), or appears to be quite ill. If the bronchitis is complicated by a bacterial infection, the doctor can prescribe antibiotics. He will also listen to the child's lungs to rule out pneumonia. If there is any question, the doctor may do a chest X ray.

Prevention

The best prevention is prompt treatment of a cold. Extra fluids and a vaporizer are most important if the child has a bad cough. Parents should be particularly attentive with children who have previously had bronchitis.

Pneumonia

Description

Pneumonia is an unusual complication of a cold. It is an infection of the lungs caused by a bacteria or virus. The tiny air sacs of the lungs, the alveoli, become inflamed and then fill with fluid. As the body fights the infection, white blood cells and dead bacteria or virus become mixed with the fluid, forming pus.

The alveoli are the places in the body where gas exchange takes place. Here oxygen from air that is inhaled into the lungs passes into the tiny blood vessels that surround the alveoli. At the same time carbon dioxide passes from the blood into the lungs to be released on the next exhale. As the alveoli become filled with pus, there is less area in the sacs for gas exchange. Consequently the child breathes in a forced and rapid way in order to get enough air.

Pneumonia is most common in the late winter and early spring. In children, pneumonia rarely develops by itself. A cold generally precedes pneumonia by several days. Instead of getting better the child suddenly becomes worse. The fever rises and the child begins to have difficulty breathing, taking rapid, shallow breaths and appearing to have trouble getting the air in and out. The child's nostrils may flare on inhaling and the center of the child's chest may sink in with each breath.

Children with pneumonia often have chest pain, particularly when they cough. In order to minimize their discomfort, children tend to take shallow breaths and lie on their side (typically with the inflamed lung down). Older children in particular tend to breathe mostly with the nonaffected lung. This lateral breathing may even be visible to the parent.

Pneumonia, that is bacterial pneumonia, used to be a dangerous disease, and still can be, but it responds promptly to antibiotic treatment. Viral pneumonia is generally less severe, with a lower fever (101° F as opposed

Signs and symptoms

- High fever
- Cough
- Difficulty breathing
- Rapid breathing
- Flared nostrils
- Chest retractions
- Poor color
- Intense anxiety
- Chest pain (possibly)

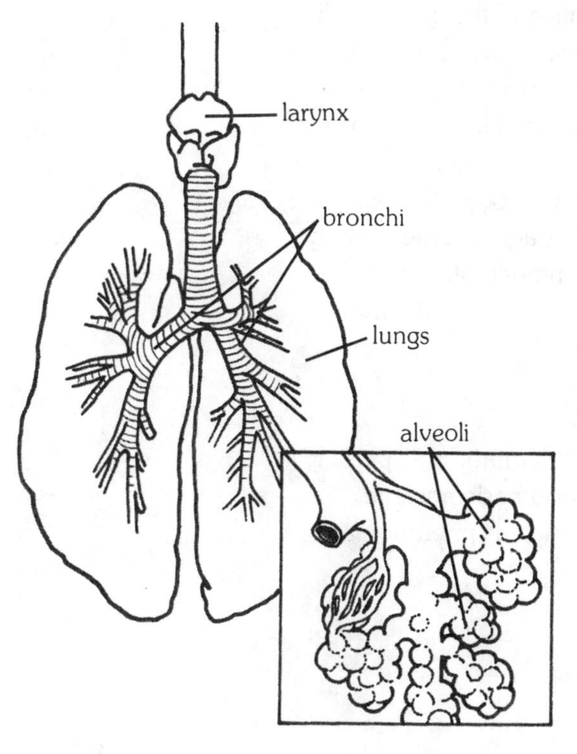

Pneumonia is an infection of the alveoli, the tiny air sacs of the lungs from which oxygen passes into the blood.

to 103° F to 105° F). Viral pneumonia doesn't respond to antibiotics, but generally gets better within a week to ten days, as does bacterial pneumonia that is treated with antibiotics.

Young babies under two years, and particularly under six months, are susceptible to a special type of pneumonia called *bronchiolitis.* This condition is caused by respiratory syncytial virus (RSV), the same one that causes most deep, serious coughs in babies. The bronchiolitis infection lasts about a week and is treated like other viral pneumonias.

Self-help

Any child with a fever and difficulty breathing should be seen by a doctor. Nonprescription treatment for pneumonia is the same as for bronchitis (see *Bronchitis*), but should always be under the direction of a doctor.

The doctor

The doctor should be called *at any time* about a child with a fever and difficulty breathing. Parents need not be alarmed, but should realize it is important that the child be seen promptly. The earlier pneumonia is treated, the less likely it will become severe.

The doctor diagnoses pneumonia (or rules it out) based on these factors: First, the doctor does a physical exam, including listening to the child's chest with a stethoscope. If the child has pneumonia, the doctor will hear decreased breath sounds and fine crackling noises called *rales* which are caused by the fluid in the alveoli. Second, the doctor almost always orders a sputum culture and white blood cell count. In bacterial pneumonia the number of white blood cells is abnormally high and the culture will reveal bacteria; in viral pneumonia the count may be normal and the culture will show no bacteria. Finally, the doctor will order a chest X ray. In bacterial pneumonias, the X ray shows a greater density in the affected areas of the lung. In viral pneumonias, there is often excess air trapped in the alveoli so the X ray appears less dense than normal.

If the diagnosis is pneumonia, the child may or may not be hospitalized depending on a number of factors, including the child's age and the severity of the illness. Bacterial pneumonia will be treated with antibiotics. In either case, the child will be given large quantities of fluid and kept in an environment of very humidified air.

Prevention

The best prevention is prompt treatment of early cold symptoms, especially coughs. Good general health, good nutrition, and good basic hygiene markedly reduce the likelihood of serious infections such as pneumonia.

The abdomen

Urinary tract infection (UTI)

Description

Urinary infections are caused by bacteria, usually *Escherichia coli. E. coli* is a normal inhabitant of the intestines, but not of the urinary tract. The urinary tract is normally sterile—free of all bacteria. Urinary infections usually involve only the bladder and the urethra, the tube leading from the bladder to the external opening. But infections sometimes go higher, involving the ureters, which are the tubes leading to the kidneys, and the kidneys themselves.

Urinary tract infections vary widely with regard to symptoms. They can even be present and show no symptoms other than a low-grade fever. For this reason doctors do a urine analysis on children with persistent low-grade fevers and no other symptoms.

When children under eighteen months have a urinary infection, they tend to show general symptoms such as tiredness, poor appetite, and even poor weight gain. In a more severe infection a child may vomit if the onset of the illness is rapid. Older children are likely to have local symptoms, such as frequent urination or burning pain on urination. Occasionally a child will have bloody urine, or abdominal or low back pain.

Urinary infections should be treated promptly with antibiotics to prevent damage to the kidneys which can occur in long-standing, untreated infections. Girls get UTIs much more often than boys, due to having a shorter, straighter urethra which makes infection by the bacteria easier.

Signs and symptoms

- Pain on urination
- Fever
- Abdominal pain
- Vomiting
- Frequent urination
- Back pain
- Bloody urine

Self-help

In addition to taking antibiotics prescribed by a doctor, the child should be encouraged to drink about twice as much fluid as usual.

The doctor

A urinary tract infection is diagnosed by doing an analysis and culture of a urine sample. With a young baby a special urine collecting bag may be taped to the child to catch a sample. This generally takes a short time and doesn't make the baby very uncomfortable. The results of the culture take a day, but blood cells and bacteria can be seen immediately under the microscope. The doctor will begin treatment on the basis of these findings. He will prescribe a 10- to 14-day course of a broad-spectrum antibiotic or a sulfa drug. The doctor will usually do a repeat culture 2 to 3 days after treatment begins, to make sure that the bacteria are gone and the urine is again sterile.

If a child has repeated urinary tract infections, the doctor may suggest doing an ultrasound exam or X ray of the urinary tract to see if there is an anatomical obstruction which is holding back urine and thereby setting up an ideal site for bacteria to grow.

Prevention

There is no specific prevention for urinary tract infections, but there are two suggestions which may be relevant to children who have had more than one infection. The children should be encouraged to urinate at normal intervals; some people believe that retaining urine for long periods may increase the possibilities of infection. And girls should be taught to wipe themselves carefully from front to back after a bowel movement, because *E. coli*, the most common cause of urinary infections, is a normal inhabitant of the lower intestinal tract.

Pinworms

Description

Pinworms is an intestinal infection caused by a tiny worm named *Enterobius vermicularis*. The adult worms live in the lower part of the large bowel, attached by their lips to the intestinal wall. The worms are very small, only 2 to 13 millimeters in length. At night the female worm detaches herself from the mucosa, crawls down the large bowel, and out the anus. Female worms deposit thousands of eggs in the skin folds around the anus, causing intense itching. The eggs are so small they are invisible to the naked eye.

Children reinfect themselves via fecal-oral transmission. The children scratch the anus to relieve the itching and thereby pick up the eggs on their fingers and under their nails. Afterward, when the children touch their mouth or pick up food, the eggs are transferred and later swallowed. The eggs travel to the small intestine and hatch there. The baby worms then travel to the large intestine, and attach to the wall. In less than a month they grow to adulthood and reproduce, starting the cycle all over again.

Pinworms are ubiquitous. An estimated 10 percent of the population of the United States probably has pinworms at any one time. Pinworms readily spread to others by touch and from eggs on clothing and bed linens.

Signs and symptoms

Anal itching, especially at night

Vaginal pain, or itching, in girls

No symptoms (sometimes)

Self-help

Pinworms are usually asymptomatic and do not need treatment unless the child is uncomfortable. The infection will go away as soon as the adult worms die, provided reinfection does not occur (see *Prevention*).

The doctor

The only really positive way to diagnose pinworms is to identify a sample of the eggs under a microscope. A sample is collected by touching a piece of sticky transparent tape to the child's anus. This should be done early in the morning before the eggs have dropped off or been removed by wiping after a bowel movement. The child should not be bathed before the sample is to be collected. Doctors often diagnose pinworms without the laboratory test simply on the basis of symptoms, because pinworms are the most common cause of nighttime anal and vaginal itching in children.

The doctor treats pinworms with one of several drugs: *mebendazole (Vermox), pyrantel pamoate (Antiminth),* or *pyrvinium pamoate (Povan)*. Because pinworms are so communicable, doctors generally treat all members of a family at the same time to prevent cycles of reinfection. Many doctors do not treat pinworms at all because they feel that pinworms are normal and go away by themselves. With proper hygiene a child will not become reinfected.

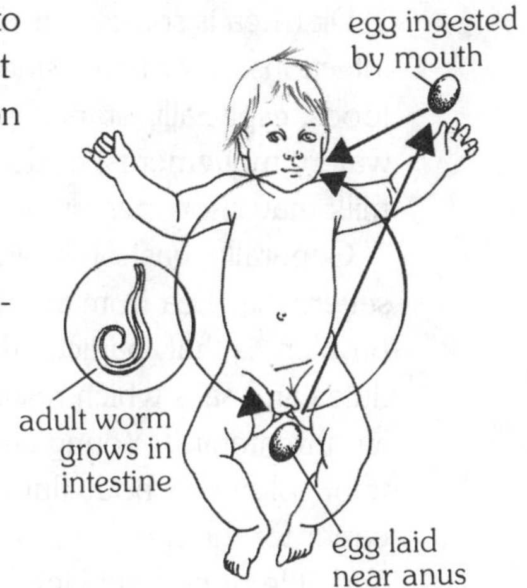

Pinworm eggs are ingested, then hatch and grow in the intestines. Adult pinworms lay their eggs in the skin around the anus, where children may pick up eggs on their fingertips and then ingest them.

Prevention

Cleanliness and good hygiene prevent reinfection and spread to others. Infected children should wear underpants while sleeping and their nails should be kept clean and short. The children should be told *not* to scratch their bare anus and to wash their hands after waking up, after bowel movements, and before eating. To kill loose eggs, the bedclothes and linens should be laundered daily in hot water. If reinfection is prevented, the adult pinworms will live out their life cycle and then die.

Gastroenteritis

Description

Gastroenteritis is a bacterial or viral infection of the digestive tract. It sometimes goes along with a respiratory infection (cold), but can occur by itself. The infection usually begins with a loss of appetite and a low fever. Nausea and stomachache are common, and the child may vomit. In addition to stomach symptoms, most children have some diarrhea, and among very young infants diarrhea may be the most prominent symptom. The diarrhea varies from simply loose to very watery stools; the number of stools may vary from one or two a day to ten or twelve. Real diarrhea involves an increase in the number of stools, as well as a change to a liquid consistency. Generally such a bowel movement is sudden, somewhat explosive, and may be accompanied by intestinal cramps.

In a young baby diarrhea generally appears as a yellow, brownish, or greenish stain on the diaper with flecks of mucus and undigested food. One or two watery stools or stools that are just a little looser than usual do not constitute diarrhea. Most often watery stools are a normal response to changes in diet.

Gastroenteritis generally goes away by itself within a couple of days. Most gastroenteritises are caused by a virus or by illness-causing strains of *Escherichia coli* bacteria. Occasionally other bacteria or rotavirus produce a more serious illness with much more severe symptoms, including sudden onset of a very high fever (104° F to 106° F).

Signs and symptoms

Nausea

Vomiting

Diarrhea

Stomachache

Loss of appetite

Fever

Other cold symptoms (possibly)

Diarrhea is sometimes due to causes other than gastrointestinal (GI) tract infections. It is often a side effect of antibiotics, for example ampicillin. New foods, especially orange juice and egg yolks, frequently cause one or two watery movements, as do spicy foods. Children who are allergic to cow's milk may show persistent mild diarrhea after its introduction.

Generally, gastronenteritis and diarrhea are not serious conditions, but *severe* diarrhea from any cause *can* become a medical emergency. The problem is that, particularly in infants, severe diarrhea can lead to a loss of fluids and salts which results in dehydration. And *extreme* dehydration is life-threatening. Young children, especially infants, have a relatively small total volume of body fluids as compared to adults. Therefore it is much easier for them to become dehydrated. With *many profuse watery stools* and little or no liquid intake, a young infant can actually become seriously dehydrated in less than a day. In severe cases an infant under a year can lose up to 10 percent of its weight in fluid—somewhere around a quart and a half. This may not seem like that much to an adult, but it represents a significant percentage of the infant's total body fluids.

In a baby, profuse diarrhea can cause dehydration much more quickly than in an adult because a baby normally excretes a much greater proportion of its fluid volume in urine and sweat each day than does an adult (25 percent versus 6 percent). Therefore, it is much more important that a baby drink a normal amount and not lose an excessive amount through vomiting or diarrhea.

The infant, like the adult, keeps its fluid volume balanced by taking in an amount equal to what it excretes. A child does not become dehydrated as long as it is taking in as much fluid as it is excreting. Thus the problem with diarrhea is not so much the watery stools, but making sure that the child takes in sufficient fluid and salts to balance what it is putting out. In any case of diarrhea, the child is excreting above normal amounts of fluid. A baby with mild diarrhea will need one or two extra feedings a day, or about one cup.

Historically, severe diarrheas—due to infection or contaminated milk or water—have been a major killer of young children. This is still true in many Third World countries and even on some Indian reservations in the United States. These are areas with a low standard of living—no plumbing, poor refrigeration, and poor hygiene. Better hygiene and better preparation and storage of formula and food all but eliminate toxic diarrheas in infancy. Better hygiene and sanitation have actually been responsible for the greatest decrease in infant mortality in history (see Chapter 2, "A Short History of Babies").

Nowadays most diarrhea in young children is not life-threatening and is, in fact, no more serious than a cold. Most gastroenteritises are healed by the body within two or three days and require little treatment other than additional fluids.

Self-help

A child with diarrhea needs more fluid than normal. Parents should encourage the child to drink extra liquids. Breast-fed babies should be allowed to nurse on demand. They can also be offered bottles of clear liquids such as dilute filtered apple juice; half-strength, liquid Jell-O; or a rehydration formula such as *Pedialyte* or *Lytren,* which contain salts and sugar, as well as fluid. Anti-diarrhea preparations are not recommended for infants. Discontinue formula, cow's milk, and solid foods until the diarrhea improves because they can be irritative to the inflamed GI tract. As the diarrhea improves, slowly begin to add mild foods—cereal, rice, bread, Jell-O. When the stools become normal, a normal diet can be resumed.

The doctor

The doctor should be called if the child appears to be really sick—that is, if it is running a fever over 101° F, if the child is having many watery stools or stools with mucus or blood in them, or if the child is vomiting and unable to hold down fluids.

If a child shows signs of dehydration, the doctor should certainly be called. With mild dehydration, children will simply be thirsty. In babies, this may be difficult to judge. As children become more dehydrated, they will show signs of having less fluid in their body: decreased urination, less tears, and dry mouth and lips. As dehydration becomes more severe, the symptoms become more obvious. The child appears listless and irritable, and the skin retracts more slowly than normal when pinched.

If the gastroenteritis is bacterial, as shown by a stool culture, the doctor will treat it with an appropriate antibiotic. Bacterial gastroenteritis is unusual. If the child shows signs of dehydration, is not keeping down fluids, and has profuse diarrhea, the doctor may hospitalize the child in order to replace fluids intravenously until the child can keep them down. Hospitalization for diarrhea is uncommon in the United States today.

Signs of dehydration

Thirstiness

Restlessness

Decreased tears

Dry mouth and lips

Decreased urination

Skin that retracts slowly when pinched

Prevention

Good nutrition and good overall health probably increase a child's resistance to infections of the GI tract. Mild gastroenteritises are best prevented by lowering the chance of spread. Direct contact with infected persons should be minimized and special care should be taken with routine hygiene. Transmission of gastroenteritis is fecal-oral—the stools contain the virus which is transferred to the child's or the parent's hands in diaper changing, handling, and wiping. The virus on the hands can then be transferred to the person's mouth, to food, and to others. So hand washing obviously becomes important when handling the baby, after going to the bathroom, and before eating or preparing food. In general, babies who are breast-fed show much lower incidence of gastroenteritis and diarrhea. If a child is on formula, the formula should be prepared and refrigerated carefully. And bottles and nipples should be washed thoroughly.

Prompt treatment of mild diarrhea with extra fluids and appropriate changes in diet (see *Self-help*) will prevent dehydration.

Constipation

Description

There are no fixed rules as to how often a baby *ought* to eliminate. Frequency varies widely with the particular child, the age of the child, and the child's diet. Thus if a baby fails to eliminate for several days, it is not *necessarily* constipated. The child is constipated only if the stools are hard and dry, and the baby has real difficulty passing them. A child is not constipated if it passes a stool of normal consistency.

Constipation most commonly results from diet or because stools remain too long in the lower bowel and excess water is absorbed. Everyone knows that certain foods tend to be constipating, whereas others are the opposite. High-protein foods, such as cow's milk, that are digested and absorbed tend to be constipating. Foods that have roughage that is not digested tend to promote elimination. Stools can remain in the lower bowel too long due to too little liquid intake, too little roughage, or due to poor bowel habits; for example, a child may avoid eliminating because of embarrassment, toilet training stress, or distraction.

Signs and symptoms

Very hard, dry, infrequent stools

Excessive straining to eliminate or inability to eliminate

Self-help

Almost all constipation can be treated by changes in diet or toileting rituals. A child who is or tends to be constipated should be encouraged to drink greater amounts of liquid and eat more foods with roughage. The child should also be encouraged to go to the bathroom as soon as it feels the urge to eliminate. Assertive home treatment almost always yields results within a day.

Preventing and curing constipation

Increase:

Liquids—water, fruit juices, especially prune juice
All fruits, especially prunes and raisins, cantaloupe
Bran
Whole grain products
Molasses and sweets
Salad, green vegetables
Salad oil, butter

Decrease:

Cow's milk
Cheese
Rice, pasta, bread
Highly processed breads and cereals
Chocolate

The doctor

Very unusually a child will actually be unable to pass a stool, even after dietary changes. In this case the doctor should be called. The doctor may suggest a stool-softening medicine, mineral oil, or a glycerin suppository. If constipation continues, the baby should be examined by the doctor. Stool softeners or enemas should not be routinely administered.

Prevention

Most constipation can be prevented by a good diet and reasonable toileting procedures. Parents need to pay attention to the child's stools, but not worry about them. If the child's stools begin to get hard, the diet should be changed. If the child routinely seems to be avoiding eliminating, parents should encourage the child to go more frequently, since the stools will be

The best approach to constipation is prevention. Certain foods help the baby to stay regular.

passed more easily. During toilet training everything should be made easy for the child. If the baby seems bothered by a regular toilet (seating arrangement, noise of flushing, etc.), try a potty chair. With an older child, make sure it can easily remove its clothing. Many preschoolers feel uncomfortable about eliminating away from home and they should be encouraged to go before leaving the house or when they return. Often nursery school children switch from going regularly in the morning to going in the afternoon when they have more time. Older children should be encouraged to pay attention to their body's messages and promptly heed the call. In this way a routine time may be established which will encourage regularity.

Allergy

Asthma

Description

Asthma is a disease that is characterized by episodes of wheezing and difficulty in breathing. In this condition the *trachea,* or windpipe, and the *bronchi,* the large airways leading to the lungs, are unusually responsive to a wide variety of stimuli. As a result, a significant portion of the airway narrows—a change which is reversible either spontaneously or with treatment. Asthma is relatively common in children. Approximately 5–10 percent of children show some signs of asthma, and of those children, 80–90 percent have their first symptoms before four or five years of age. Most of these children have mild asthma, but a few have severe attacks. In general, the prognosis is good; most asthmatic children are symptom-free by adulthood.

Asthma symptoms are produced by three physiological changes: contraction of the smooth muscles lining the airway, swelling of the mucous membrane lining the airway, and production of excess mucus. These changes cause obstruction and greater resistance in the airway, making breathing more difficult. In some children attacks are associated with allergies, in other children attacks are associated with other factors such as temperature, exercise, etc. In most children with asthma the airway is reactive to both allergic and non-allergic factors, although one factor may be more important than the other.

In allergic reactions, *allergens*—substances that people are allergic to such as dust, pollen, mold, and animal dander—stimulate cells in the lining of the airway to produce antibodies and release histamine. In non-allergic asthma attacks, other conditions stimulate nerve cells in the lining of the airway. These conditions include dust, smoke, air pollution, rapid changes in temperature, exercise, respiratory infections, or even emotional upsets. Both histamine/antibody production and nerve stimulation cause the airways to narrow, producing an asthma attack.

Asthma attacks are highly variable. They range from mild to severe, and can come on either slowly or suddenly. Usually they start with a cough that is initially tight, but later may bring up mucus. Next children may develop wheezing and prolonged expirations. If the attack progresses, the children may experience difficulty breathing.

Some children experience only the cough and shortness of breath and never develop the wheezing. In very young children, asthma attacks are not likely to be triggered by allergies. Frequently they follow a respiratory infection. The main symptoms are coughing and difficulty in breathing. Often infantile asthma is associated with repeated attacks of croup or bronchiolitis (see page 305). The older the child is when the first asthma attack occurs, the more likely it is to be allergy related. The severity and frequency of attacks are highly variable.

Signs and symptoms

- Coughing
- Difficulty breathing, rapid breathing, chest retractions
- Wheezing
- Sudden sharp attacks
- Shortness of breath
- Abdominal pain (possibly)
- Prolonged exhales
- Restlessness and apprehension during attacks
- Excessive secretions

Treatment

The general treatment for asthmatic children involves recognizing those factors which most commonly set off attacks and isolating the child from them. This process is referred to as environmental control and involves considerable experimentation with and manipulation of the child's surroundings. In addition to keeping the child away from specific substances known to produce attacks, it is commonly advised that children be kept away from *all* substances that are known allergens (see list following).

Fluids decrease the thickness of the mucous secretions and make breathing easier. It is important therefore to encourage asthmatic children to drink a lot of clear, room-temperature fluids, especially when a mild cough develops. A vaporizer is also helpful (see *Bronchitis*).

Training in relaxation techniques, imagery, and proper breathing have been shown to be effective in treating and preventing asthma attacks. When a person is afraid, breathing becomes more difficult. Thus a child who becomes frightened by an attack has an even harder time breathing and tends to have trouble relaxing. A cycle of tension and difficult breathing ensues. Also, if a child becomes anxious or frightened for any reason, the likelihood of an attack increases.

Relaxation tends to relieve the fear/tension cycle. When a person relaxes,

Environmental control of allergens

Household dust—do a major cleaning of the house, and especially the child's room, when the child is out of the house. Surfaces in the child's room should be mopped with soap and water. Household surfaces should be dusted daily with a wet cloth. Forced-air vents in the child's room should be closed and covered, and non-fan-driven radiant heat should be substituted. A high-efficiency particulate air cleaner (HEPA) or an electrostatic dust precipitator should be used.

Avoid flannel and wool rugs, sweaters, and blankets.

Avoid upholstered furniture and toys stuffed with plant or animal products.

Avoid animals, especially those with long hair.

Cover mattresses with a heavy plastic case.

Use synthetic blankets, foam rubber or Dacron pillows, and toys and furniture filled with synthetic stuffing.

Avoid allergic foods such as chocolate, nuts, eggs, and cow's milk.

Avoid pollen—keep windows closed during the height of the pollen season in spring. Eliminate flowering plants indoors.

Eliminate dust-catchers, piles of paper, Venetian blinds, and infrequently used items in child's closet.

Avoid damp, moldy areas or wash them with Zephiran chloride.

the bronchi and bronchioles open up, making breathing easier. Deep breathing increases the amount of air the child is getting, deepens the relaxation, and gives the child an activity to focus on. Imagery further deepens the relaxation, opens the air passages, and gives the child positive, physiologically effective images to concentrate on.

The doctor

A child with asthma should be under the supervision of a doctor. The doctor initially diagnoses asthma from a history of the child's breathing difficulties and from listening to the child's breath sounds during an attack. The doctor may order a chest X ray, pulmonary function studies to measure airway resistance, and possibly allergy tests. Treatment depends on the severity of the child's asthma.

A child with mild asthma is treated with drugs that affect smooth muscle tension and cause the airway to open up, such as *albuterol* (e.g., Proven-

Environmental control of non-allergens

Treat colds and respiratory infections promptly. Use a cool mist vaporizer and give extra fluids.

Limit exposure to sick people whenever possible. Increase hand washing when household members are sick.

Avoid factors known to trigger attacks, such as air pollution, paint fumes, strong cooking odors, all types of smoke, and cold drinks.

Avoid aspirin and sulfites.

Avoid rapid exposure to cold, and overexertion (especially in the cold). If necessary, moderate physical activity, but don't have the child avoid all activity.

Avoid unnecessary stress. Minimize frustrating situations, fighting, chaos, and exhaustion. Deal with anxiety-producing situations, including any preschool or daycare problems. Cope with stress in your own lives by relaxing and getting sufficient support (see page 60).

til, or Ventolin) or *metaproterenol* (e.g., Alupent). These drugs are either given in syrup form for very young children, or as an aerosol in a metered-dose inhaler. These drugs are only taken in response to the beginning of an attack in mild asthma conditions.

In moderate-to-severe asthma, the drugs are taken on a daily basis. In addition, the doctor may prescribe *cromolyn* as a preventative. This drug does not dilate the bronchi, so it will not stop an acute attack. Rather, it generally reduces airway reactivity. Children with more severe asthma may be given a steroid inhaler as well. Steroids reduce inflammation of the airway. The doctor may also recommend allergy desensitization shots.

A severe asthma attack is a MEDICAL EMERGENCY. The sooner the doctor is called, the better. Severe attacks sometimes require emergency room treatment or brief hospitalization. If necessary, the child will be given oxygen and strong bronchodilators, and will be watched closely.

Prevention

There is no specific, agreed-upon prevention for asthma. Since asthma is an allergy-related condition, it seems wise for parents to delay introduction of allergenic foods (see *Self-help*) for the first twelve months if there is a family history of asthma or allergy.

Parents who have a child with asthma can do a great deal to help the child lower the number of attacks and prevent attacks. This basically involves prompt treatment of colds, encouraging drinking of fluids, environmental control of allergens, and teaching the child relaxation and breathing techniques. Meeting a child's emotional and intellectual needs probably helps to lesson the likelihood of asthma attacks as well as many other diseases known to have a psychophysiological component.

Food allergies

Description

In addition to being allergic to external agents, babies can be allergic to the food they eat. As in other allergies, the child's body overreacts to a substance that most people don't react to at all—that is, the child's body produces antibodies that attempt to neutralize the offending substances. The most common foods to which babies are allergic are cow's milk, wheat, egg whites, fish, nuts, chocolate, pork, and melons. Many doctors believe that if introduction of these and other foods (see *First year nutrition*) is delayed, children are much less likely to become allergic because the immune system then does not become primed to these substances.

Symptoms of food allergy can vary widely. Mild symptoms, such as digestive upset and slight skin rash, can be vague and difficult to diagnose. Occasionally a child can have severe symptoms, such as swelling and redness of the skin (hives), difficulty breathing (asthma), or rarely, anaphylactic shock. True cow's milk allergy is very rare—its incidence is estimated at 0.5 percent. It begins within the first six weeks of life with vomiting and diarrhea that can be almost continuous.

Signs and symptoms

Diarrhea

Vomiting

Abdominal discomfort

Fatigue

Irritability

Headache

Rash

Eczema or asthma symptoms (see above)

Self-help

Parents who suspect a possible food allergy should stop feeding the baby the suspected food until they've had a chance to discuss the situation with the doctor. If the symptoms are more severe, the doctor should be called immediately.

The doctor

With mild suspected food allergies the doctor will try to determine if a baby is actually allergic by having the parents withhold the food for several weeks to see if the symptoms disappear. Then the doctor may have the parents reintroduce the food to see if symptoms return. If the food that's withdrawn has important nutritional value, such as milk, the doctor will suggest a substitute.

If the symptoms are severe, the offending food is usually obvious. If the doctor suspects true milk allergy, he may do laboratory tests to rule out other rare causes of vomiting and diarrhea in early infancy. If milk allergy is proven, the baby will be started on an antiallergenic formula such as soy milk. If a child has a proven allergy, many doctors will suggest that commonly allergic foods such as nuts, chocolate, egg whites, and fish be avoided.

Prevention

Studies have shown that breast-feeding lowers the incidence of allergies in early childhood (see *Breast-feeding* in Chapter 6, "The Newborn"). Delayed introduction of allergic foods is also recommended. At the same time parents should be careful not to jump to unproven conclusions about their child being allergic. This can lead to years of unnecessarily withholding nutritious foods and looking upon the child as sick.

Childhood diseases

Chicken pox (varicella)

Description

Chicken pox is a generalized viral infection which is highly contagious. Almost all people (80 to 90 percent) exposed to children pox get it, and almost everyone gets it in the childhood years. One case confers lifetime immunity. Children with chicken pox are infectious beginning 5 days before the rash appears and continuing for 6 days afterward. The virus is spread by direct contact and by airborne droplets from coughing and sneezing. The incubation period—that is, the time between exposure and appearance of the rash—varies from 11 to 21 days, usually 13 to 17.

One or two days before the appearance of the rash, children often develop a slight fever, a runny nose, and tiredness. But the rash can occur without any prior symptoms. It starts as red dots which are often seen near the hairline. The dots quickly turn into tiny, clear, fluid-filled pimples on a red base. Doctors describe them as dewdrops or teardrops. These teardrops break and scab over. New teardrops continue to form and break for a period of 3 to 4 days, appearing first on the trunk, then face, arms, and legs. The fever that accompanies chicken pox is usually highest at the point of greatest eruption. Typically, red dots, teardrops, and scabs can all be observed at the same time by the third or fourth day after the rash first develops. The crusts all fall off within 7 to 14 days and the skin generally heals without a blemish.

Chicken pox can range from a very mild infection with only a few pimples on the trunk to a more severe illness with literally hundreds of pimples and a high fever. The rash tends to be extremely itchy, and this often is the most uncomfortable symptom for the child.

Signs and symptoms

Rash

Itching

Fever

Running nose

Tiredness

Self-help

Treatment is aimed at relieving uncomfortable symptoms, particularly the itching, and at preventing a secondary bacterial infection of the rash (rare). The itching is relieved by cool baths; starch (1–2 cups per tubful) or baking soda (also 1–2 cups per tubful) may be added to the bathwater. Calamine lotion may also help.

To lower the chances of secondary infection, the child should be kept clean, the fingernails should be clipped, and hands should be washed frequently. Some doctors advise putting socks on the child's hands at night if the child is scratching vigorously. It is good to change the child's bedclothes and sheets daily while the rash is at its height. Acetaminophen (e.g., Tylenol) may be given for fever if the child is sufficiently uncomfortable. If itching is intense, the doctor may prescribe an antihistamine.

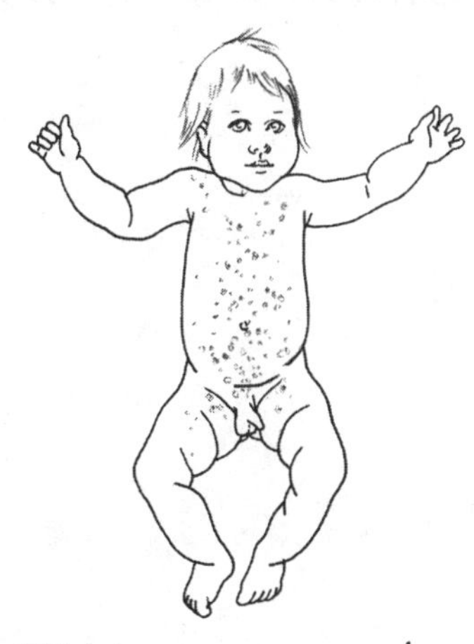

Chicken pox causes a rash which appears first on the trunk, then on the face and limbs. Pimples progress from red dots to crusts.

The doctor

The doctor is generally not necessary in diagnosing or treating chicken pox, but should be called if the child appears really ill or develops a secondary infection.

Prevention

A vaccine for the chicken pox is presently being developed and tested. Chicken pox is so mild and so communicable a disease that no attempt is made to prevent a child from getting it. Children are generally kept at home until the last new blister is scabbed over—partly for their comfort and partly to prevent huge epidemics.

Roseola infanta (exanthem subitum)

Description

Roseola is an illness caused by a virus, and its pattern is somewhat unique. A child initially gets a high fever (103° F to 105° F) for 3 to 4 days, with no other complaint. On the last day as the fever drops, a red rash appears, starting on the trunk and spreading to the arms. The rash disappears by itself in less than a day. The disease is self-limiting and not serious. Infrequently the onset of the disease can be accompanied by a febrile convulsion (see *Febrile convulsions*) caused by a sudden, rapid rise in the fever.

Roseola most often occurs in children between the ages of six months and three years. Once children have had roseola, they have lifetime immunity. It is unknown how contagious the disease is or how it's transmitted.

Signs and symptoms

High fever

Rash over the whole body

Self-help

Parents can give acetaminophen (e.g., Tylenol) in appropriate doses if a child is uncomfortable because of the fever. Lukewarm baths and extra fluids are also useful (see *Fever*). The rash is not uncomfortable and needs no treatment.

Childhood diseases (rashes)

Disease	*Rash*	*Infectious period*	*Incubation period*
Chicken pox	Red dots turn into fluid pimples on a red base, then scabs Rash starts on trunk, then spreads to arms and legs Rash progression takes 3–4 days	5 days before rash until 6 days after	11–21 days, maximum (13–17 days, usually)
Rubella (German measles)	Flushed, red, raised areas, fleeting Rash starts on face, then spreads to trunk and limbs Immunized children are not susceptible	7 days before until 4 days after	2–3 weeks, maximum (17 days, usually)
Measles	3-day cold before rash Pimples turn into large red areas around hairline, spread to face and body for 3 days Child looks ill Immunized children are not susceptible	4–5 days before until several days afterward	9–14 days
Virus infection	Widely variable and short Common cause of rashes in immunized children	Variable	Variable
Strep throat—Scarlet fever	Sore throat plus positive strep culture Red rough areas for 7 days Rash in skin folds	Variable	2–5 days

The doctor

A child with roseola generally does not need to see the doctor. The one exception is a child with a significant history of febrile convulsions. In this case a doctor may advise giving the child sedatives to decrease the chance of a febrile convulsion.

Prevention

There is no real prevention for roseola since little is known about the transmission. Not exposing other children to a known case probably helps to prevent spread.

Chapter 10

Emergency medicine

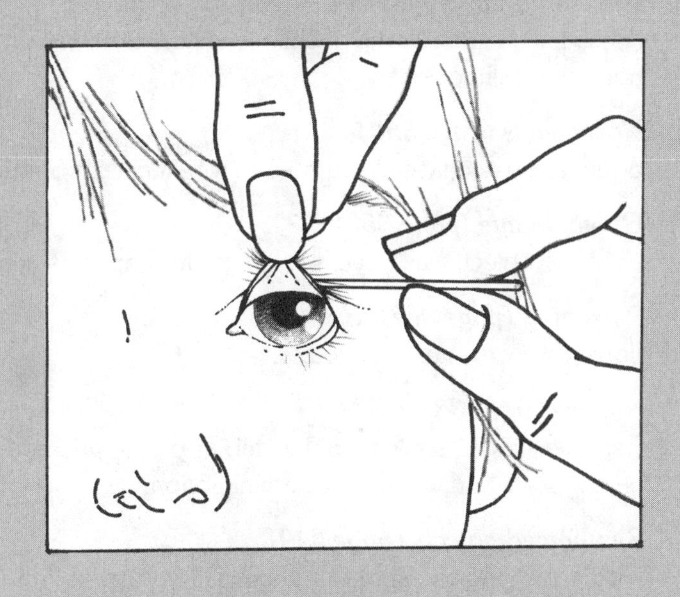

Emergency treatments

For further emergency instructions turn to pages listed below.

Bites (page 335)
Wash out; identify animal.

Bleeding (page 333)
Press on wound with gauze or cloth to stop heavy bleeding; wash out; evaluate for suture or bandage.

Blood under fingernail (page 354)
Heat paper clip to red hot and touch to nail.

Bumps, sprains, and broken bones (page 341)
Apply ice packs; immobilize a suspected fracture.

Burns (page 339)
Apply cold water or ice; if severe take to doctor.

Choking (page 359)
Baby under 12 months: put facedown, head lowest, then give four back blows. Next, with baby on back, push chest with two fingers four times. For child over one year: put child on back, put heel of hand between navel and rib cage; put second hand on top of first, and rapidly press inward and upward; repeat 6–10 times.

Convulsions, febrile (page 357)
Lower fever with cool soaks or lukewarm bath.

Electric shock/drowning (page 363)
If breathing or heart stops, do resuscitation until help arrives.

Head injuries (page 346)
Apply ice pack on bump; if child is unconscious or not behaving normally, call doctor.

Nosebleeds (page 350)
Squeeze nose between thumb and forefinger for 5 minutes.

Object in eye (page 352)
Look for object; wash eye; see doctor if symptoms persist.

Poisoning (page 367)
Force milk or water; call doctor.

Stings (page 338)
Remove stinger; soak in cool water, apply ice packs, a paste of baking soda and water, or calamine lotion.

Swallowed objects (page 349)
If object is long and sharp or large, call doctor.

This chapter deals with the most common accidents of early childhood—from the most minor cuts and scrapes to the most serious conditions. Children under four frequently have *minor* accidents, so frequently that minor accidents can be considered a normal part of growing up. All parents should understand and know how to treat these minor accidents so that they and their children will feel more comfortable. Minor accidents are more an everyday concern than a medical problem.

The goal of this section is to educate parents so that they can deal with accidents effectively and without unnecessary alarm. Most people are terrified of the specter of an accident occurring and wouldn't know what to do if one did occur. Learning the most medically effective way to respond to an accident will help to relieve much of this terror. A parent's confidence is directly transferred to a hurt child, at a nonverbal as well as a verbal level. Thus the way a parent acts when there is an accident determines to a large extent the way the child will act. Hysterical parents not only don't cope with the accident, they generally terrify their child. Calm parents not only are in a position to deal with the accident, they can reassure and relax the hurt child, which will lower the child's fear, pain, discomfort, and bleeding.

Most childhood accidents are not serious and they rarely are true emergencies in the sense that it is important to act or get help immediately. In almost all accidents parents have enough time to comfort and calm down the child and themselves, before they even evaluate the extent of the injury. Calming down is the first step in treating most cuts, scrapes, stings, bites, burns, bumps, falls, etc. The parent should hold, rock, and talk to a frightened child before instituting treatment. A parent can say, "I am here. . . . You are going to be all right. . . . You'll be all better soon. . . . Your body is healing the hurt right now. . . . It's getting better and better." Children are very susceptible to suggestion after the shock of an accident, and they are calmable. Not only can children's moods respond to positive suggestion, their bodies can actually respond at a physiological level. When children relax, their breathing slows, their pulse slows, and their blood flow changes. Experienced doctors who use hypnosis have even shown that bleeding can be markedly reduced or stopped in response to verbal commands like, "Your body knows how to stop the bleeding. . . . Your body will stop the bleeding now. . . ." Demonstrations like this show how important the parents' words and actions can be after an accident.

There are two accident situations in which prompt action is imperative: (1) when a child has stopped breathing due to choking, drowning, or electroshock, and (2) when a child is bleeding severely due to a large cut or puncture wound. If breathing has stopped, resuscitation should begin within minutes. If a child is bleeding *severely,* firm pressure should be applied directly. These situations are very unusual. All parents should read the sections concerning such accidents so that they will know beforehand what to do if such an emergency ever arises. In these situations there isn't time to look up medical treatment, and in other situations such as severe burns, poisonings, and head injury, some basic knowledge beforehand can be very useful.

Emergency preparedness

Learn or at least read about child CPR (see page 363).

Keep emergency numbers available next to phone:

Paramedics/Fire/ Police 911 or ______

Pediatrician ______

Poison control center ______

Hospital emergency room ______

Parents' work numbers ______
______

Responsible friend or relative ______

Also, list names of any serious illnesses or drugs prescribed.

Awareness is the key to accident prevention

Accidents are the most common cause of death in the age group from one to fourteen. Yet most serious accidents can be prevented. On a direct level, safety consciousness is the most concrete preventive medicine parents can do for their child. Accident prevention has two major facets: one is working with the child, the other is working with the child's environment.

It is a young child's job to explore the world; it's a parent's job to make sure the world is reasonably safe. The job of making a child's environment safe will change as the child grows and develops new physical and mental skills. Under each emergency discussion in this section there are specific safety suggestions, including suggestions relevant for different ages.

No house and no environment can be made completely riskless, nor should it be. This is the area where the parent works with the child. Initially the parent works with the child by knowing about the individual child's current motor skills and interests and about which skills will shortly be unfolding. Later the parent works with the child by educating the child about dangerous situations and how to handle them.

Babies are highly individualistic. Some are very active and highly mobile from birth, and these are most likely to have accidents such as falls at a young age. Some children simply seem to be accident-prone, which may be confined to a specific age, or it may be a general condition. Accident-prone children do not create accident situations by themselves. Their house and their relationship with their parents play a large part. Parents of children who are accident-prone or who are in a highly exploratory stage bear a special burden and have a special responsibility to observe their children and anticipate problem situations.

All children are more likely to have an accident at certain times. Children who are sick, tired, or cranky are more likely to have an accident, and the chances of an accident are more than double when the parent is also sick, tired, or cranky. Frequently this correlates with a particular time of day or a particular situation. For example, shortly before dinner is a time when parents are busy and both they and their child tend to be tired.

Children are also more likely to have an accident when they are wildly excited, trying to impress, or trying to keep up with older children. Finally, children are more likely to have accidents when they are distracted, unhappy, jealous, or worried. At times children may consciously or unconsciously use an accident to gain attention and sympathy. This possibility should not be overlooked when children suddenly start to have a number of accidents.

And all children have their particular accidents to which they are prone. Some children fall, some children pinch their fingers, some children get burned, some children ingest poisons. In fact, a study done on poisonings shows that 25 percent of all children who ingest poisons will have a second episode of ingestion within a year. The more parents understand their

Basic accident prevention

Use infant seats and seat belts at all times.

Use helmets and special bike seats for young children riding on bicycles.

Never leave young children unsupervised near streets or swimming pools, or in the bathtub. Pools and streams must be fenced off.

Put baby gates at top and bottom of stairs when babies are young.

Poison-proof the house: put all medicines and cleaning products out of reach. Lock lower cabinets.

Cover low electrical outlets.

Remove poisonous plants.

Prevent choking: keep small objects away from baby, and do not feed baby small hard chunks of food.

children's own tendencies, the more effectively parents can safety-proof their child's environment and work to educate their child.

Each accident discussion is separated into four sections: *Description, Self-help, The doctor,* and *Prevention. Emergency instructions for the parent are contained in the Self-help section.* This chapter is not designed to qualify a parent in first aid. In particular, it does not have detailed instructions for splinting, bandaging, suturing, or setting broken bones. Its goal is to deal with the common conditions parents are most likely to encounter and to instruct them in what to do until the doctor can be reached.

Cuts, scrapes, and puncture wounds

Description

Any scrape, cut, or puncture wound represents a break in the body's protective outer layers. Generally scrapes are the most minor of the group, but may be the most painful. By themselves, they rarely require a doctor's

Emergency advice for the parent and child

Breathe in and out deeply, allowing your abdomen to rise and fall. Deeply relax your whole body. Feel strong and capable—know that you will do your best. Feel calmness and confidence flow into your body and into the child. Feel quiet and clarity surround you and the child. Whenever you begin to feel upset, for a brief moment picture the most peaceful scene you can think of.

Tell the child:

"You are all right."

"Your body will make itself better."

"The hurt will go out of your body."

"The bleeding will stop itself."

"If you breathe in and out slowly and evenly, you will feel much better."

"Let your body feel as if it's floating."

"Rest quietly and pretend that you are all better and lying in bed quietly, listening to a story."

treatment. Puncture wounds are very small wounds that leave almost no opening on the skin. Most are shallow enough that they don't need to be seen by a doctor. Deep puncture wounds made by large objects—especially in the hand, head, chest, or abdomen—can involve injury to internal tissues even if there is not much damage visible on the surface. If a puncture wound doesn't stop bleeding readily, or is quite deep, it should be seen by a doctor.

The majority of cuts involve only the top layer of skin, require minimal treatment, and rapidly heal by themselves. A cut needs attention by a doctor if (1) it is deep, (2) it doesn't readily stop bleeding, or (3) it contains dirt or foreign bodies that cannot be gotten out completely. A cut is deep if it goes through the skin and is long enough so that the sides of the cut separate and do not stay together. When a cut is this deep, yellow fat globules or shiny connective tissue can often be seen in the wound. *Very deep* cuts or lacerations can involve injury to blood vessels, nerves, or tendons. Such injury may be indicated by loss of movement, loss of sensation, or by blood coming from the wound with great force. Parents should also call the doctor about all but minor cuts on the face and hands. There are many critical structures in the hands that relate to function, and possible problems should be evaluated professionally. Finally, most parents are concerned about the cosmetic effects of facial wounds.

To prevent accidents, children should be instructed in the proper use of sharp objects such as scissors and knives.

Almost all bleeding stops by itself or can be stopped by sustained local pressure. Only very serious bleeding from a major artery requires the use of a tourniquet, and it is best applied by trained people because improper use can actually result in blood vessel and nerve damage.

If foreign particles cannot be removed from a cut, infection can result. Within a day or so there may be swelling, redness, heat, and possibly pus around the wound. Any large cut, scrape, or puncture wound that obviously contains foreign bodies or that shows signs of infection should be seen by a doctor.

Self-help

Minor cuts, scrapes, and *punctures* should be washed thoroughly with soap and water. If possible, the injured area should be submerged in a basin of warm, soapy water. The dirtier the cut, the longer it should be washed. Usually several minutes of soaking, swishing, or stirring will remove most of the dirt or pebbles that have adhered to drying blood or plasma. If dirt still remains, the wound should be held under running water or rubbed with a clean washcloth.

Proper cleansing is important to help the wound heal easily and to prevent infection. If after a day or so the cut becomes tender or begins to swell or redden *mildly,* serious infection can usually be prevented by soaking the injured area in warm water for 15 minutes, 2 or 3 times a day. The warmth of the water increases blood flow which brings antibodies and white blood cells to the area.

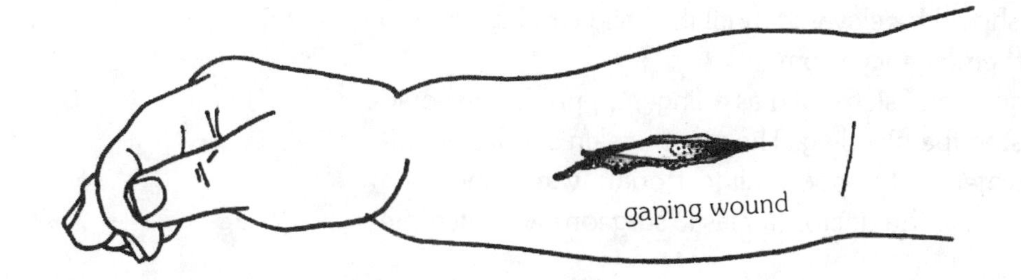

If the sides of a cut do not stay together by themselves, the cut should be seen by a doctor.

Antibacterial creams speed wound healing and lessen chances of infection. Most scrapes, punctures, and small cuts require no bandaging or even a Band-Aid. In fact, they generally heal better if they are exposed to the air and allowed to dry and scab naturally. A scab is nature's own covering and is usually sufficient protection. However, many children like Band-Aids and seem to derive some emotional comfort from them. Band-Aids are also useful for keeping a recent, open cut from getting dirty or bumped.

In treating *deep cuts,* the first step is to *remove any large, obvious foreign bodies.* The next step is to *stop the bleeding.* Several sterile gauze pads, a clean cloth, or a shirt should be placed over the wound. Firm pressure should then be applied on the cloth directly over the wound. After several minutes the pressure can be released. In most cases the bleeding will have stopped, even if it was initially heavy. If bleeding continues, probably pressure was not applied firmly enough for a long enough time, and it should be reapplied.

Almost all cases of bleeding can be stopped or controlled with direct pressure. The body has a remarkable ability to stop bleeding. External pressure simply equalizes that with which the wound is bleeding, allowing blood vessels to constrict and giving time for clotting mechanisms to work. In unusual cases where bleeding persists, pressure should be kept on the

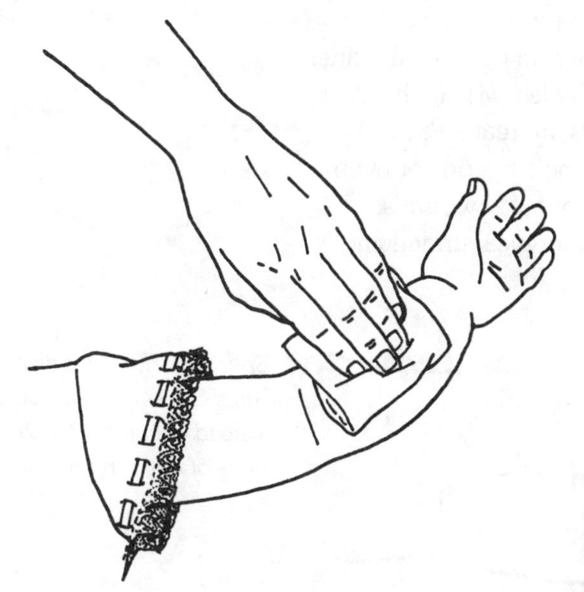

Almost all cases of bleeding can be controlled or stopped by applying direct pressure over the wound.

wound, and the wound should be elevated, until the child can be taken to the doctor or the hospital emergency room.

If a child cuts off a large flap of skin, such as a fingertip, pressure should be applied to the cut to stop the bleeding. The piece of skin should be put in ice-cold water or salt water (½ teaspoon salt to 1 quart water) and taken along to the doctor. Generally, the doctor (a plastic surgeon) will stitch the flap back on.

The doctor

See the Description section for when to call the doctor.

The doctor will clean the wound and check if for any remaining foreign bodies or damage to underlying tissues. Based on the exam, the doctor will decide what treatment, if any, is required.

If the wound is through the skin but is in a place where it will not be opened by movement, the doctor may apply a steristrip bandage. A steristrip is a porous adhesive tape that is applied with a liquid glue. Unlike regular Band-Aids, steristrips are able to withstand pressure and keep the two sides of a wound together. For that reason doctors can sometimes use steristrips in place of sutures (stitches).

Injuries that cannot be closed with steristrips are closed with sutures, which hold skin and subcutaneous tissue together while the body heals itself. A gaping wound that is not sutured must grow new skin over the whole open area, which is much larger and therefore requires more time to heal. A gaping wound also leaves a much larger scar. *Deep wounds should be sutured as soon as possible—definitely within 12 hours—to minimize infection and promote better healing.*

Before suturing, an anesthetic is injected into the sides of the wound to make the process painless. The sutures themselves are simply pieces of fine silk or nylon thread which are tied across the wound at even intervals. The actual number of stitches is relatively unimportant to healing, since the cut heals from side to side, not from one end to the other. In general, the finer the thread and the greater the number of stitches, the less visible the injury will be after it heals. In urban areas where specialists are readily available, some pediatricians refer almost all suturing to pediatric surgeons or even plastic surgeons. This is recommended particularly for facial wounds, wounds of the hand, and for large, deep wounds that reveal underlying structures.

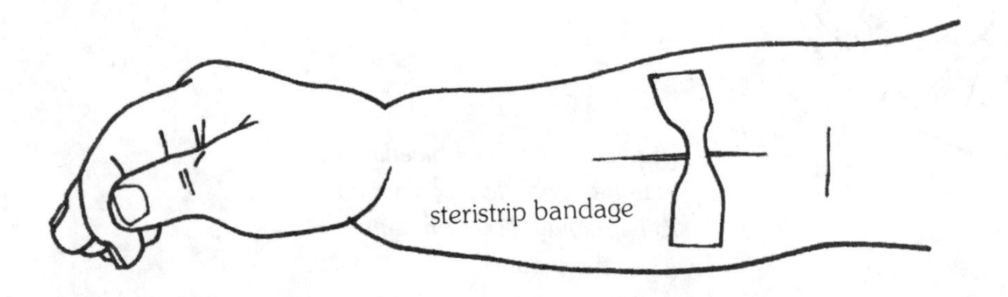

Special bandages called steristrips can sometimes be used instead of sutures to hold the sides of a wound together.

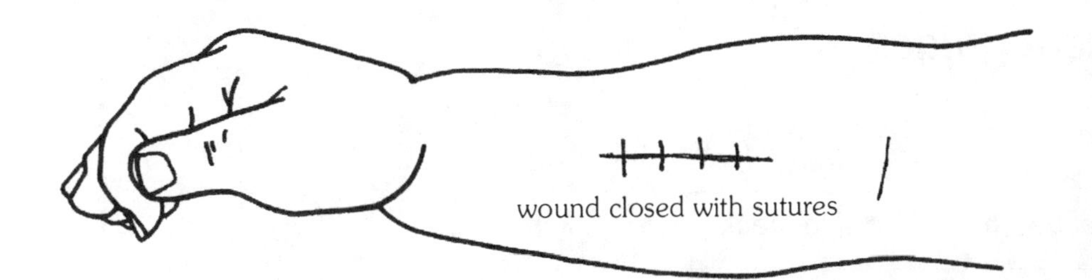

Sutures hold together the sides of a wound and make healing quicker and easier. With a large cut, the resulting scar is much smaller.

Sutured wounds are usually bandaged, and if the injury is a large cut on the arm, the arm is often put in a sling. The sutures are removed between the fourth and tenth day, depending on the location of the cut. Suture removal is not a painful procedure and requires no anesthetic. Children should be told in advance that they will simply feel a slight tugging as the stitches are lifted up, snipped, and pulled out.

In the old days wounds sometimes became infected from tetanus bacteria which live in soil (*see* "Immunizations"). Nowadays this is rarely a danger since almost all children over a year will have had the basic three-shot tetanus series. These children may get no shot or may be given a booster, but they are basically protected against tetanus by the original series. Children who haven't had the series will be given a special immunization that will prevent the possibility of tetanus infection.

If a wound shows signs of infection—increased redness, swelling, heat, pus—the doctor may prescribe antibiotics. Occasionally the doctor will drain pus from the wound if an abscess forms with a white top.

Prevention

Scrapes and minor cuts are not easily prevented. In fact they seem to be firmly associated with early childhood. Large scrapes are generally caused by falls on cement or gravel when children are running or riding bikes. Parents should exercise some caution about where their child engages in certain kinds of play. Most puncture wounds and many lacerations *can* be prevented. Children should be instructed in the dangers and proper use of sharp objects such as scissors, knives, and tools. Puncture wounds are most commonly caused by tacks and nails in boards, so any boards with nails sticking out or sharp scraps of metal should be removed from areas where children play.

Animal bites

Description

Animal bites are treated like puncture wounds and lacerations. They carry a definite added risk of infection from the animal's saliva, and for this reason the wounds should be *cleaned especially carefully and flushed with*

Rabies treatment guide

Bite	Animal health	Treatment: No skin break	Treatment: Skin broken
Dog or cat	Healthy	None	None
	Unknown	None	Vaccine and immune globulin [1]
	Rabid	None	Vaccine and immune globulin [2]
Skunk, raccoon, bat	Possibly ill (bite unprovoked)	None	Vaccine and immune globulin [3]

1. In rabies-free areas, no treatment.
2. Treatment discontinued if tests prove negative.
3. In rabies-free areas, treat only bat bites.

lots of water. Human bites (from other children) carry a significant risk of infection and should be washed carefully and watched for signs of infection.

Animal bites also raise the question of rabies. But a bite from a healthy immunized cat or dog carries no such risk. Rabies is a disease that affects the nervous system and is caused by a virus. It can only be gotten from the saliva of an animal who has active rabies. For the virus to be transmitted, the animal bite must break the skin. An animal who actually has rabies acts very ill and behaves strangely. Currently, the great majority of rabies occurs in wild animals, especially skunks, and to a lesser extent bats and foxes. In the United States, there are only one or two cases of rabies in humans each year. A number of areas in the United States have been declared rabies-free, and no immunization is necessary for most animal bites.

The doctor—Self-help

Any deep bite should be seen by a doctor, and so should any bites from wild animals or sick pets. The doctor will assertively *clean* a deep bite and irrigate it with a syringe full of antiseptic. In general, bites are sutured, except on the hand when they are *left open* and allowed to drain.

If the bite is made by a sick animal or a wild animal, the doctor will decide whether or not to institute rabies immunization based on a complicated set of criteria (see chart). The amount of rabies occurring locally and whether or not the animal can be observed are important considerations. There is a two-part treatment to prevent rabies. The first part is *human rabies immune globulin (HRIG)*, which contains antibodies to protect the person until the vaccine becomes effective. The second part is the vaccine, *human diploid cell vaccine (HDCV)*. This is a relatively new vaccine which is much more effective and less problematic than the old vaccine that was given in the abdomen. A person is given two shots of globulin and five shots of vaccine spread out over a month. The doctor will also give a tetanus booster if needed.

Prevention

Vaccination of pets, including cats and dogs, is an important factor in preventing rabies. Animal vaccination is especially important in rural areas where pets are more likely to come in contact with wild rabid animals.

Immediate, thorough cleaning of a wound with soap and water is actually somewhat effective in preventing rabies infection when the animal is rabid. Children should be taught never to tease or pet sick or strange dogs or touch wild animals that normally would not approach a child. If a child is bitten, the parents should hold or identify the animal if possible and notify the local health department immediately. The health department has facilities for capturing and observing domestic and wild animals. Strangely behaving animals should be reported even when they have not bitten anyone.

Flea bites

Description

Flea bites appear as red, raised areas that often have scabs and show evidence of scratching. If a child scratches the bites a lot, they can become secondarily infected (see *Impetigo.*) Flea bites tend to occur in numbers, though not necessarily in groups. They occur anywhere on the body, but especially on the trunk and scalp. Flea bites are a common cause of an itchy rash, especially in households that have infested pets. Fleas and their bites are most prevalent in late summer and early fall. The fleas themselves may occasionally be seen on the child, the child's bed, or the family pet.

Self-help

Itching can be relieved somewhat with cool baths or calamine lotion. If the bites become infected they should be washed daily with soap and water.

Prevention

Flea bites can be prevented or stopped by controlling fleas in household pets. Unfortunately, flea collars, which are effective, should not be used on pets who are around small children because they give off a strong pesticide.

If collars are resorted to, the pets should be kept outdoors. Flea powder can be used on the pets and their sleeping places, but it should be applied carefully so as to prevent inhaling it or getting it on one's body. If a child's bed is infected, the linens should be laundered, a plastic cover can be put over the mattress, and the pet should be kept off the bed.

Insect bites and stings

Description

When certain insects bite, they introduce small amounts of chemicals under the skin. These chemicals are to some degree toxic, causing a local reaction. Most insect bites are very minor. Some simply cause redness and swelling, some itch, some hurt, but they rarely are cause for real concern. A sting appears as a red, raised area which is generally white in the middle. A central puncture mark, even a stinger, may be visible. The honeybee and some wasps leave their stinger in the wound; the bumblebee does not.

The venom on the stinger is not only toxic, it can cause an allergic reaction. Allergic reactions vary greatly, but in general they cause a greater than normal amount of swelling. Swelling from an insect bite is most visible on the hands and face. If a child gets a number of bites or reacts strongly to a single bite, the whole area around the bite can swell markedly—enough to close an eye or prevent bending a finger.

The only reason there is ever any real cause for concern about an insect sting is that in rare instances a person shows a pronounced allergic reaction to a bite. Such reactions generally follow incidents of increasingly severe local reactions to stings. The child becomes progressively more sensitized to the toxin with each sting. Thus it is uncommon for a very young child to have a true allergic reaction to a sting. A local reaction in a young child often looks more alarming than it really is because of the relatively small size of a child's fingers and cheeks.

Self-help

If the stinger is still in, it should be removed. Ice packs will help to reduce local swelling and may make the child more comfortable. Some people find that *cold-water soaks* or a thick mixture of baking soda and water relieve pain and subsequent itching. Acetaminophen (*e.g.*, Tylenol) can be given in appropriate doses if a child is very uncomfortable.

Young children are often frightened by the sudden, unexpected pain of a sting and this in itself may be the cause of much of their discomfort. Therefore, it is especially important to explain to children what has happened and to reassure them that they will feel better soon. Parents should try to help the child relax.

The doctor

The doctor should be called if the child shows signs of an allergic reaction, has difficulty breathing, faints, develops a rash, or has a severe local swelling that doesn't begin to go down within several hours.

The doctor may prescribe antihistamines which will reduce the swelling and itching. If the child has a true major reaction, which is rare in this age group, the doctor will administer epinephrine, an adrenal hormone.

Prevention

Children should not be made terrified of all insects, but they should be shown how to recognize stinging insects and their common habitats and taught not to tease or try to touch them. If there are large numbers of stinging insects in the area, parents should follow them back to their nests, and the nests should be eliminated by someone who knows how to do it safely.

Burns

Description

Minor burns are painful and often frightening to a child, but they generally heal well and are easy for parents to treat. Most adults are less familiar with burns than with cuts and therefore tend to be more frightened by them. But burns, like cuts, follow a normal course in healing. Burns generally go through a series of rather strange-looking steps as they heal. This is normal and there is no cause for concern unless the burn becomes infected. Increased redness, swelling, heat, and pain after the first day are signs of infection.

Medical personnel divide burns into three categories based on their degree of seriousness. *First-degree burns* are the most minor and only involve damage to the superficial layers of the skin. First-degree burns appear pink or red, will blanch (turn white) if pressed, and feel painful to the child. Sunburn, minor scalds, and brief contact with very hot objects generally result in first-degree burns. *Second-degree burns* involve deeper layers of skin. In a second-degree burn the skin appears blistered or moist and is painful to the touch. It is uncommon for first- and minor second-degree burns to become infected and they tend to heal with little or no scarring. *Third-degree burns* involve all layers of skin. They appear white or charred and initially they are *painless* because the local nerve endings have been destroyed. If more than 10 percent of a child's body has third-degree burns or if there are serious burns on a child's hands, feet, or face, the child will be hospitalized for several reasons: to prevent infection, to administer intravenous fluids to keep up with the child's loss of salt and fluids through the moist surface of the burn, and to give antibiotics.

Self-help

First- and second-degree burns that involve only small areas can be treated at home. The first step is to *apply something cold to the area.* The burn can be put under *cold running water,* or *clean washcloths soaked in cold water or ice can be applied.* The cold relieves pain and reduces tissue damage. It should be continued until the pain improves and may be reapplied if pain

How to prevent burns

Turn pot handles toward center of stove.

Tuck in cords on coffee percolators, fry pans, etc.

Keep children off counters and chairs next to the stove.

Don't pour hot liquids near children.

Set hot cups of liquid (coffee, tea, etc.) well out of children's reach.

Don't ever use boiling water on the stove as a makeshift vaporizer (use the shower instead) and avoid hot water vaporizers if possible.

Never leave toddlers unattended near stoves, heaters, fires, or lit candles.

Instruct toddlers early, emphatically, and often that hot stoves and space heaters will hurt if touched. Demonstrate by holding the child's hand near enough to feel real heat, but not get burned.

Warn visiting children and parents of any special heat dangers in a house.

Be especially careful with infrequently used heat sources like barbecues or hibachis—and always set them up in protected areas.

Don't let children run or play near beach fires, barbecues, or in confined spaces that have electric heaters, wood-burning stoves, etc.

Do not let children dress in or play with very flammable materials or fabrics near any source of heat.

Cover electric sockets with safety caps and keep children away from appliance plugs.

Keep matches out of reach.

Lock caustic materials out of reach of young children.

Do not let young children play with firecrackers.

Warn older children that their hair is especially flammable.

returns. Acetaminophen (e.g., Tylenol) can also be given in appropriate doses to relieve the child's pain. The blisters of a small second-degree burn should not be removed because they provide the ideal protective bandage for healing.

Extensive second- or third-degree burns are a MEDICAL EMERGENCY. They should be briefly washed with cool water. The doctor should be called immediately. Then the child should be wrapped in a clean sheet and taken to a hospital emergency room.

The doctor

The doctor should be called for any third-degree burn and for second-degree burns that are large or involve the face, hands, or feet. If the burn is not too severe, the doctor will usually wash it with plain water and cover it with antibiotic-impregnated gauze pads. These dressings are generally changed every two days for about a week.

The doctor will hospitalize children with large or very serious burns, give them antibiotics, and, if necessary, intravenous feeding.

Prevention

Children commonly get burned or scalded by hot liquids cooking on the stove, by all different kinds of heaters and hot appliances, and by open flames from fires, barbecues, candles, and matches. Electric shock and caustic materials can also cause burns. Much can be done to prevent the possibility of young children getting burned. Parents need to "burn-proof" their house and be attentive to situations in which children are most likely to get burned.

Older children should be educated about the seriousness of burns and about those things that can cause burns. Adults need to be aware of the special problems involving children too young to understand the dangers of extreme heat. A major burn in a young child is a real tragedy that often affects the child's whole life, and it is well worth all the parents' efforts to minimize the possibilities of burns, both in terms of structuring household routines and later in terms of child education.

Bumps, sprains, and broken bones

Description

Young children often fall down, but they rarely hurt themselves seriously. They don't really move that quickly, their bones (some of which are not yet even calcified) tend to be resilient, and they're close to the ground anyway. Moreover, very young children have been shown to have innate fears of edges and falling. From birth, children show anxiety when they are "off balance" or held in a poorly supported position.

Nevertheless, severe accidents (including car crashes and burns) are the major cause of death in children over a year. The most frequent falling accidents (see *Head injuries* also) in the first twelve months involve rolling off of changing tables and falling out of infant seats, high chairs, and cribs. The most common severe accidents among toddlers involve falling down stairs and out of windows. The two- to four-year-old child may also fall while climbing or bike riding or be hit by cars. The results of such accidents can range from minor bumps and scrapes to major injury. In general, the higher and harder the fall, the more severe the injury.

The most common injury in this group is the bump. A bump, or *contusion,* involves breaking many small blood vessels under the skin which then ooze or bleed into surrounding soft tissue. This results in characteristic swollen black and blue areas. As the tissues gradually absorb the dead blood cells, the swelling and discoloration go away.

Strains and sprains result from excess force or twisting of muscles, ligaments, and tendons. Muscles and tendons get strained or pulled; joints and ligaments get sprained or twisted. The joint or muscle may swell and hurt immediately after the accident or not until several hours afterward. Sprains and strains tend to heal more slowly than bumps. They are also more likely to impair function and require rest in order to heal. A severe strain or sprain is often treated like a minor break and can take as long to heal.

Fractures involve breaking, chipping, or splintering the bones underlying the soft tissues. The more severe the injury, the greater the likelihood of a fracture. Sometimes a fracture is obvious, but more often it is difficult to distinguish from a severe strain or sprain. An X ray is the only way actually to verify many fractures. Most doctors have had the experience of having their diagnosis—fractured or not fractured—proved wrong by the X ray. It is most important to X-ray ankles and wrists because they contain many small bones which can be difficult to diagnose. Moreover, improper healing can lead to impaired function and growth.

Certain signs and symptoms point to the likelihood that a fracture has occurred. These are used by doctors as criteria for deciding whether or not to X-ray. Fractures generally involve a combination of (1) obvious deformity or displacement of a bone, (2) pain, (3) specific tenderness to the touch over the fracture point, (4) impaired or abnormal movement, and (5) swelling and black and blue marks.

Bones will naturally heal themselves in a matter of weeks. The important thing is to have them properly aligned and immobilized for a sufficient period of time. A cast simply keeps the ends of the bone in place while they grow together. Bones in young children are growing so fast that breaks generally heal quickly and completely. Children should be reassured that healing is so complete that the bone will be as strong as before the accident and no more likely to break again.

Occasionally young infants get a dislocated elbow. The dislocation is generally the result of the parent's lifting or pulling the child by the hand. The condition is sometimes referred to as nursemaid's elbow because of the standard image of an angry nursemaid dragging an unwilling baby by its arm. If an elbow is actually dislocated, the infant will be unable to bend its arm and there will be tenderness around the elbow. A child with a dislocated elbow should be taken to a doctor who will "pop" the elbow back into the socket.

Self-help

Minor contusions and sprains need little treatment. Swelling and black and blue marks can be kept to a minimum by applying *ice packs* (ice cubes wrapped in plastic bags and a towel). The cold causes constriction of the small blood vessels in the area and thereby reduces swelling and bleeding under the skin. Ice packs can be left on from 5 minutes (minimum) up to several hours. The injured area should also be elevated because this tends to reduce blood flow to the area and helps minimize swelling. In addition to reducing swelling, ice packs tend to reduce pain by numbing the area. The child should rest and not move the injured area until it stops hurting. Large black and blue marks can persist for several weeks.

The doctor should be called if the child is really uncomfortable or if a fracture is suspected. In general, a simple fracture is not an emergency in the sense that it must be treated in a matter of minutes. It is an emergency if the suspected break is accompanied by shock, bleeding, or loss of sensation in the area of the injury.

If a suspected fracture is on a limb, the area should be immobilized, including the joints above and below the injury. For example, if the injury

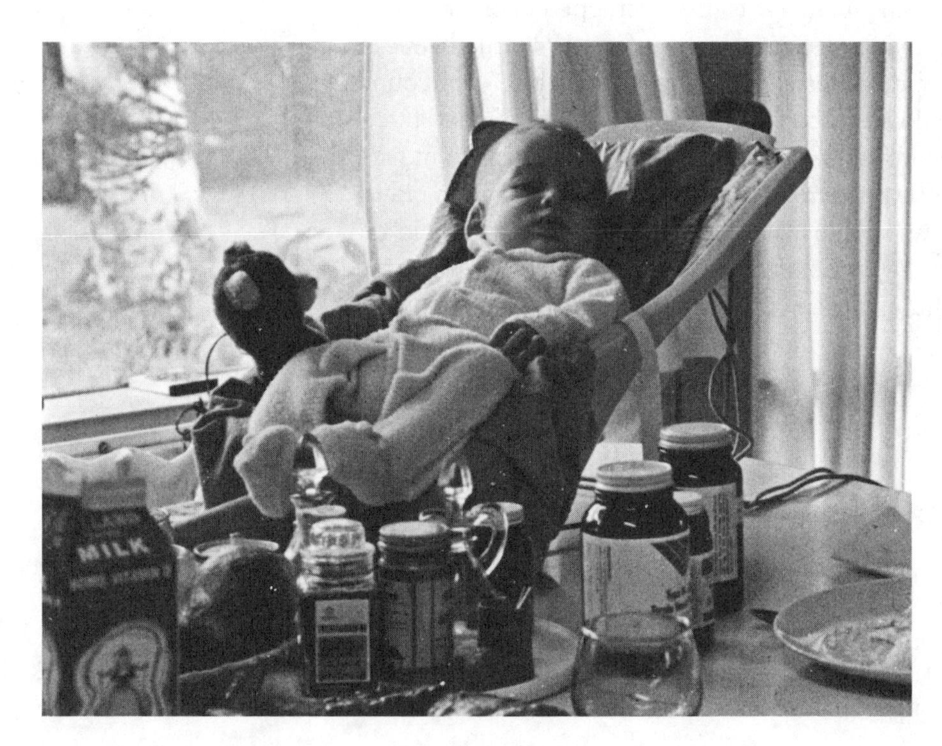

A child in an infant seat should always be buckled in and should never be left alone on a table or counter.

is near the knee, the leg should be immobilized from the ankle to the hip. A simple splint can be made from boards, blankets, and rag ties.

Fences and baby gates can be used to protect young children from high edges and busy streets.

The doctor

If the doctor suspects a fracture, he may arrange to meet the parents at the hospital emergency room rather than have them come to the office. The doctor will examine the injury by touching the area, by moving it, and by asking the child to attempt normal movements. If the doctor suspects a fracture, he will have X rays taken. If the child has a severe sprain or fracture, the doctor will generally call in a specialist, an orthopedic surgeon, who will properly align the ends of the fractures (as shown by follow-up X rays) and immobilize the injured area in a bandage or cast.

Prevention

Many accidents are caused by carelessness and could be prevented. Young children should always be in a car seat and/or seat belt when they are riding in a car. Parents should be familiar with their child's motor capabilities and anticipate developing skills in their safety planning. A baby needs to do something only once to hurt itself. Safety precautions change radically as a child learns to flail, roll over, crawl, walk, and climb. Infants should not be left unattended in positions where they can fall. Parents should keep a hand on a young infant if they have to turn away while changing or bathing the infant. All necessary supplies should be assembled before the bath or change is begun. Infants should be buckled up with safety straps when using infant seats. Even strapped in, an infant in a chair should not be left unattended on a high surface. With one heave, infants under three or four months can flip a seat off a table. Very young infants left on beds should be placed in the center and surrounded by pillows. Crib sides should be raised as soon as the child begins to move about and gates should be put across stairs as older babies start to crawl and climb. Open windows should always be screened. Babies should be watched carefully when they are starting to undertake new skills like standing, walking along furniture, walking unassisted, and climbing up and down stairs.

Tooth accidents

Description

Children occasionally injure their teeth when they fall or are hit. Such accidents almost invariably look worse than they are and are more upsetting to the parents than the child.

Injury can involve chipping or fracturing of the teeth or movement of the teeth in their sockets. There may also be bleeding around the tooth, swelling of the gums, or sensitivity to temperature or touch. Severe trauma—either breaking or loosening of the tooth—may sever the blood and nerve supply, which will cause the tooth to become nonvital. The nonvital tooth may become infected after varying amounts of time. Signs of infection are pain, unusual mobility or looseness of the tooth, or a whitehead on the outside of the gum. After any accident, a tooth may darken or become discolored. This is caused by blood entering the inner pulp of the tooth and does not necessarily indicate the tooth is nonvital.

Self-help

Parents should realize that the accident almost always is not as serious as it looks. First the parent should comfort the child, then assess the situation. If there is active bleeding, parents should press a tissue or washcloth directly on the area until the bleeding slows. Ice can be applied if it makes the child more comfortable. The dentist should be called if the tooth has been knocked out or is cracked, freely movable, or the gums are swollen or bleeding.

The dentist

It is always advisable to call the dentist in the case of a dental accident. It generally needs no treatment, but there are things a dentist *may* do depending on the circumstances. If the tooth is knocked out, the dentist will generally check to see if there are any root fragments still in the socket which will cause infection. Medically, there is no reason to replace a baby tooth with a false tooth. However, occasionally a dentist will make a false tooth (teeth) when the child is two and a half or three and a half and there are particular social, emotional, or speech considerations.

If a tooth is still in the socket, but severely displaced, the dentist may be able to realign it if he is able to see the child soon after the accident. If there is a question as to whether the tooth is vital, the dentist will take an initial set of X rays to compare with a later set. If there are signs of infection the dentist may do root canal work, cap the tooth, or remove the tooth.

Prevention

Most serious tooth accidents are caused by a hard fall in the three-to-four age range. Parents should be conscious of specially hazardous conditions in their house and at the playground, and should not allow play to become too rough. Children should be taught to play carefully with swings, sticks, baseball bats, and similar toys.

Head injuries

Description

The early years of childhood are taken up with learning skills that involve balance, like walking or riding a bike. These skills are acquired by trial and error. Consequently, it is not uncommon for babies and young children to fall and hit their heads. Most of these falls are not serious.

The human skull is made of a number of bony plates which protect the brain. In infants, the bony plates have not yet become completely knit together (see *Fontanels,* page 112). This provides special resilience which cushions the head against blows. For this reason infants sometimes sustain, without any injury, falls that would result in a concussion (loss of consciousness and bruising of the brain) in an adult. Nature seems to have provided babies with extra protection against the common events of childhood.

In a minor head injury a child falls, hits its head, and often is stunned. Within a few seconds the child usually begins to cry. Even quite prolonged or hysterical crying does not necessarily mean that a child is badly injured, because falls are often more frightening than they are serious. In one sense, crying indicates that a child is not badly hurt because it shows the child has not lost consciousness.

In a minor fall the child does not lose consciousness and continues to act normally afterward. There are rarely any problems after this kind of a fall. As with other situations in which children experience a sharp, unexpected pain and are suddenly frightened, they may even cry themselves to sleep shortly afterward. A "goose egg," or actual bump, may develop at the site of the injury. Goose eggs are caused by bleeding into the soft tissues directly under the skin and are not dangerous. Bumps on the head tend to appear big because they can only swell outward due to the hardness of the skull.

In a moderately severe fall a child loses consciousness for a few seconds to a matter of minutes. A child who is unconscious does not respond to touch or speech and appears to be asleep. Loss of consciousness is caused by the shock of the brain shifting inside the skull. The child spontaneously regains consciousness and most likely begins to cry. Later the child may become irritable and drowsy. The child may also vomit and complain of a headache. Any of these symptoms can occur soon after a head injury or, more typically, hours afterward. In general the child recovers and is back to normal in about 12 hours. But the doctor should always be called if there is loss of consciousness or any of the other symptoms.

In a serious fall a child is unconscious for minutes. Upon waking the child usually has significant irritability, drowsiness, headache, and repeated vomiting. The child may show bleeding from the nose, ears, mouth, or eyes, and it may also be confused and unresponsive at times. These are more severe symptoms caused by bleeding and slight swelling of the brain. Bleeding between the skull and the brain is called a subdural or epidural hematoma. Hematomas can occur after a serious fall and, rarely, after a moderate fall. Continued bleeding builds up pressure inside the skull, and if it is significant the pressure must be relieved by surgery or it can be dangerous. The symptoms of a hematoma are personality changes, fluctuating drowsiness and unresponsiveness, vomiting, seizures, abnormal pupil size changes, and loss of movement. The symptoms may not occur for 24 to 48 hours after the fall, and they can begin after the child has apparently recovered from the fall. However, hematomas are uncommon even in more serious falls and occur in only 1 to 3 percent of children who are actually hospitalized for head injuries. In general children with head injuries recover completely by themselves.

Self-help

For a *mild fall* there is no treatment other than reassuring the child. If a goose egg begins to develop at the site of the blow, an *ice pack* can be applied to keep down the swelling. In a mild injury in which there is no loss of consciousness, the parents need not worry about the child napping or going to sleep which often happens due to fright and exhaustion. If the parents are at all concerned, they can wake the child to make sure it is arousable.

If a child loses consciousness after a head injury (concussion), *the doctor may ask the parents to check that the child's pupils are equal in size and that they shut down in response to a bright light. These signs indicate the child is all right.*

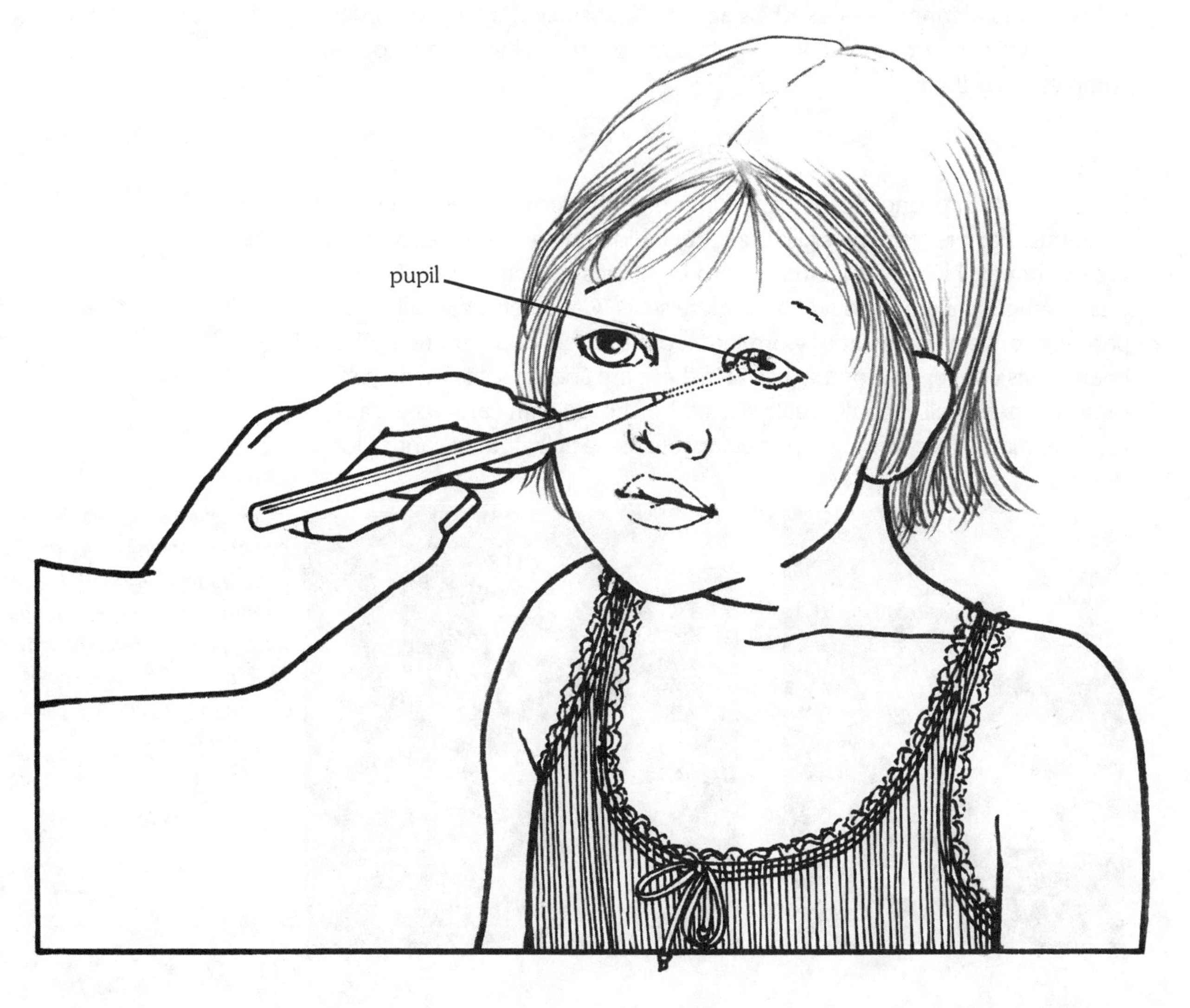

The doctor

If parents are concerned for any reason, they should call the doctor. For all head injuries that are more than minor, the doctor should be seen. The doctor will carefully examine the child, paying special attention to the child's pulse, respiration, and alertness. The doctor will examine the child's head for bleeding and do a neurological exam to make sure the child's movements and reflexes, especially the pupils, are normal. Providing the child appears all right, the doctor will simply have the parents observe the child at home for changes that could possibly indicate bleeding and a developing hematoma. The doctor will advise the parents to be alert to any personality changes, irritability, confusion, vomiting, or unusual drowsiness, and he will generally have the parents wake the child every few hours to make sure it is arousable. The parents may also be asked to make sure the child's pupils are equal in size and close down normally in bright light. There is no cause for concern as long as the child seems well.

In more severe injuries the doctor will do a CT scan and possibly skull X rays and will hospitalize the child for 1 to 2 days for observation. Observation involves periodically checking the child for vital signs, normal pupil reflexes, and alertness, as described above. Almost all of the children who are hospitalized for observation do not develop hematomas and recover completely by themselves.

Prevention

Head injuries in young children are commonly the result of falls or car accidents. For prevention of falls, see prevention in *Bumps, sprains, and broken bones.* Helmets should be worn by babies and children on bicycles; younger children should be in safety seats. Car safety seats allow a parent to drive alone without worrying about sudden stops. Some of the infant seats convert for toddler use and there are special seats made just for toddlers as well. Toddler seats should be chosen with care because toddlers may refuse to sit in a particular seat, especially if they cannot look

Car safety seats are of major importance in preventing serious injuries or death to young children who are passengers in cars. Children who ride on the back of bicycles should be in bike seats and wear helmets.

out the window. An unused or rarely used seat is as dangerous as no seat at all. Larger children should sit with adult seat belts or harnesses.

Swallowed objects

Description

Infants, and even toddlers, may swallow anything they can get their hands on and put into their mouths. Fortunately, *almost anything a child can swallow will pass right through.*

Objects that *are* dangerous are long (1–2 inches, or 3–5 centimeters) sharp things such as needles. Often the parent may not be certain if the child has swallowed a particular object, and as long as the object is not dangerous, it doesn't make any difference. To make sure an object has passed, the parents can strain the baby's stool for several days until the object is recovered.

Swallowed objects

Dangerous objects:
Needles
Straight pins
Open safety pins
Nails and tacks
Batteries

Objects that will usually pass:
Beads
Buttons
Small coins
Fruit pits
Pebbles
Rubber bands
Marbles

The doctor

The doctor should be called (1) if the child swallows any long, sharp object, (2) if the child develops gastrointestinal symptoms such as pain or vomiting, (3) if the child complains the object is stuck in the throat, or (4) if the child swallows a battery. In any of these situations, the doctor may want to X-ray the child. Occasionally, if children have swallowed a dangerous object, they may have to have it removed with a flexible endoscope.

Prevention

The child's house should be "baby-proofed"; that is, small objects should not be left out on tables or on low shelves. Parents should be especially careful with coins, sewing supplies, tool-shop supplies, and older children's toys and games, and should watch their toddlers carefully when visiting other people's houses.

Foreign objects in the ear and nose

Description

In their quest to explore the world and learn about their bodies, children sometimes try to put tiny objects in their nose, ears, or vagina. If they do, the situation is not an emergency and it is not dangerous provided the objects are not sharp. But the objects must be gotten out because they can impair breathing or hearing, and they can become infected. Often the objects are irritating or even painful. The most commonly inserted objects are nuts, cherry pits, peas, beads, and wads of tissues or paper. Frequently a child fails to tell the parents about an object, and parents may discover a foreign body in the nose or vagina only when they notice a smelly, puslike discharge in the area. In particular, a runny nose in only one nostril may indicate a lodged object.

Self-help

Many foreign objects can be gotten out rather readily. The danger in trying to get an object out is that it may be pushed in even farther. This is especially true with smooth, hard objects like peanuts.

To remove an object from a child's ear, the parent should grasp the top of the outer ear and pull up and out. This straightens out the ear canal. Then the child should be told to shake its head or the parent should shake it. If that doesn't work, hard objects can sometimes be flushed out using a Water Pik set at the lowest setting and filled with lukewarm water. This method should *not* be attempted with vegetables or paper because the objects may swell with water.

To remove an object from a child's nose, the parent should have the child blow its nose vigorously ("try to make a loud noise"). The unaffected nostril should be held closed at the same time, to increase the force of the child's blowing. If a child is too young to blow its nose, the parent can try holding closed the unaffected nostril and simultaneously blowing hard into the child's mouth. If the object remains lodged and is near the end of the nostril, the parent can carefully attempt to remove it with tweezers.

The doctor

The doctor should be called if the parents cannot get the object out or if there are signs of infection. The doctor has specialized instruments for removing foreign bodies and can prescribe antibiotics if they are indicated.

Prevention

Small objects should not be left within the young child's reach. In addition, toddlers should be taught not to put things in their ears, nose, or vagina. Parents should simply explain that objects can become stuck and get infected.

Nosebleeds

Description

Nosebleeds are a fairly common occurrence in childhood. They are almost never dangerous, but they often frighten the child and sometimes the parent because compared to minor everyday cuts and scrapes, a nosebleed may involve a lot of blood. However, the actual amount of blood lost usually is insignificant. Generally, the bleeding stops by itself or is easy to stop—and the child should be reassured of this.

Nosebleeds can be caused by dry mucous membranes, trauma, nose colds, scratching the nose, or blowing the nose very hard. They are uncommon in infants. Some children seem to be more susceptible to them than others.

Self-help

Most nosebleeds stop by themselves. The rest stop quickly with the following treatment: The child should sit up and lean slightly forward so as not to swallow the blood. *The parent or child should then squeeze the child's nose firmly between thumb and forefinger. This pressure should be applied continuously for at least several minutes, then released.* Usually the bleeding will have stopped, but if not, pressure should be reapplied for a full 5, and if necessary 10, minutes.

This external pressure stops bleeding by equalizing the pressure within the bleeding vessel and allows the body's clotting mechanisms to go to work. The clot serves as a plug until the body can actually repair the blood vessel. After the bleeding has stopped, the child should sit still for a few minutes and not wipe or blow its nose. This will keep the clot from breaking off and prevent a renewal of the bleeding.

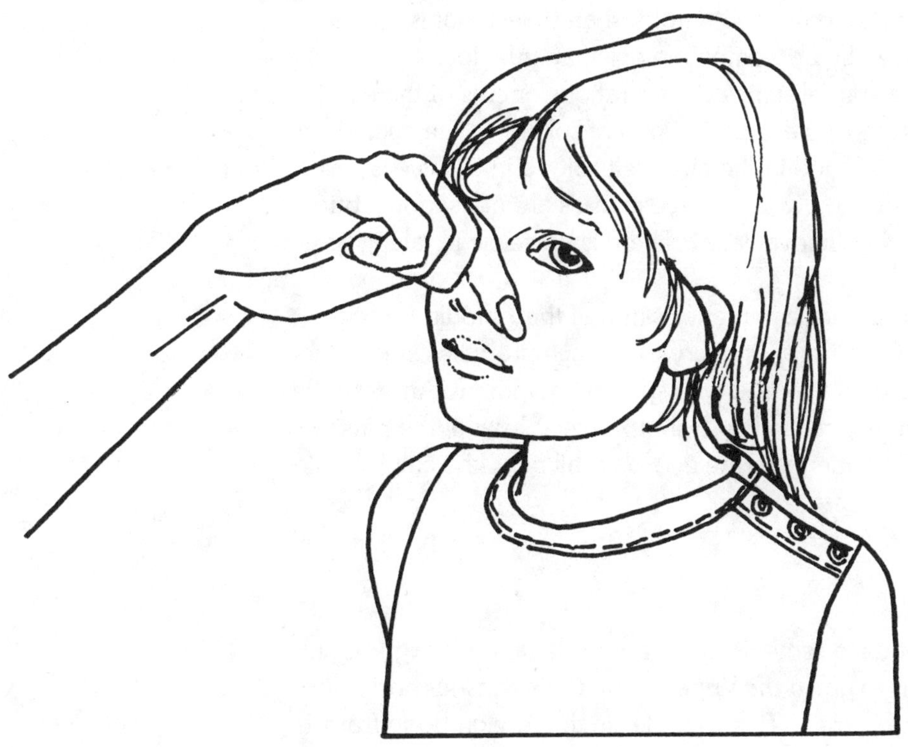

Nosebleeds can be stopped by squeezing the nose firmly between thumb and forefinger for at least several minutes.

The doctor

The doctor should be called if the bleeding does not stop after ten minutes and can only be controlled with pressure. The doctor may pack the nose with gauze. A child with very frequent nosebleeds should have a complete physical exam to make sure there is no underlying problem.

Prevention

Many nosebleeds are caused by falls or fights that cannot be anticipated, but children can be taught not to scratch their nose or blow it too vigorously. Dry mucous membranes can be treated by running a humidifier and/or putting a dab of petroleum jelly on the nasal lining.

Eye injuries

Description

Occasionally accidents occur in which children get something in their eye or scratch it. If a foreign body is caught in the eye, the child will cry or complain of pain and the eye will tear and become bloodshot. Sometimes the foreign body can be seen over the white or colored part of the eye. If a child complains of a foreign body and it can't be seen, it may be caught under the upper eyelid. Most foreign bodies can be removed easily. If not, the child should see a doctor to prevent damage or infection.

Real or suspected injuries to the eye—not just an object that is readily removed—should be seen by an ophthalmologist, an eye doctor. Injuries that should be seen by a specialist include lacerations or cuts of the eye or eyelid, scrapes or abrasions of the eye, any kind of splinter in the eye, burns near the eye, and obvious blood in the eye itself. Blood in the eye is generally caused by a direct blow. Often eye injuries are not serious, but they should all be competently evaluated. There is no sense in taking risks with a child's sight.

All suspected eye injuries are emergencies in that they should be seen within a couple of hours. Sometimes injury to the eye produces little or no symptoms and can only be diagnosed with special equipment. An example of this is a penetrating injury caused by a sharp object. Even if the parent doesn't *see* the accident happen and the eye looks all right, the child should be seen by an ophthalmologist.

Self-help

There are several methods to remove small, nonpenetrating foreign bodies from the eye. The first is to *grasp the upper lid by the eyelashes and pull it out and down over the lower lid.* This can release the foreign body from under the upper lid and allow the tears to wash it out. *Washing the eye with clean water* and an eyecup or small glass is a second method. This is especially effective if the foreign body is a small, nonsticky particle like dirt or sand.

Another method is to remove the foreign body directly. First the object must be located. The child should tilt its head back (and preferably lie down) in very bright light. The parent should spread the child's eyelids with thumb and forefinger. With the eye open thus, the child should be encouraged to look slowly up, down, and to either side. This will allow the parent to see most of the eye and will often show the position of the foreign body. If the foreign body still can't be seen, and the child continues to complain of pain or a scratchy feeling in the upper part of the eye, the parent can attempt to roll back the upper eyelid with a cotton swab to see if the object is caught in the grooves on the underside near the edge (illustration). This procedure does not hurt at all, but it should only be attempted if the parent is reasonably dexterous and the child is calm enough to hold still. Once the foreign body is seen, it can usually be picked up readily with a slightly moistened cotton swab. The cotton is simply touched lightly to the particle. The swab should *never* be rubbed or pushed, but it may help to roll it slightly as it is being pulled away from the eye.

The doctor

If the particle cannot be removed at home or if severe symptoms (pain or continued tearing) persist for more than half an hour, the doctor should be called. And, of course, any obviously serious eye injury should be seen promptly by an eye doctor.

A pediatrician will simply attempt to remove a foreign object as described above, but will be considerably more experienced at it than the parents.

If parents cannot readily see what is caught in a child's eye, they can carefully roll back the child's upper eyelid to make sure the object isn't stuck behind it.

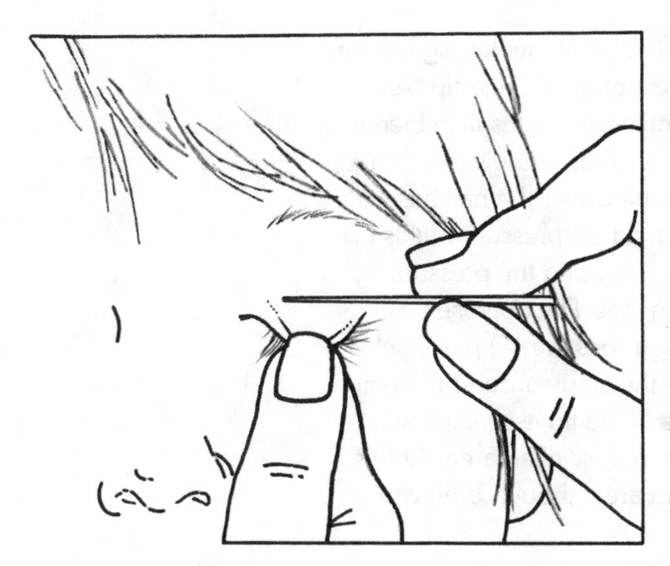

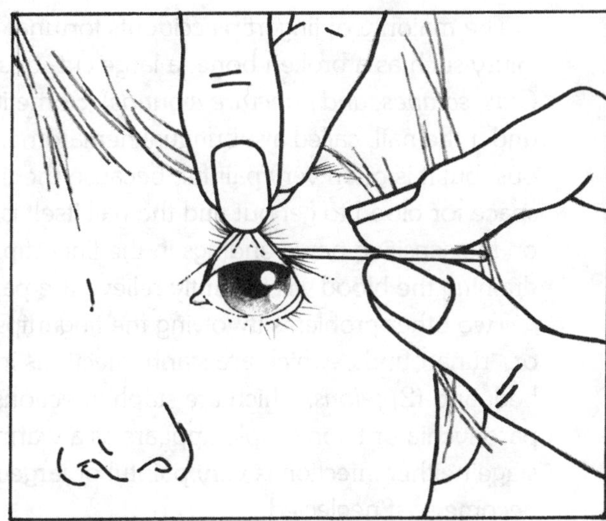

The doctor will insert drops of fluorescein dye, which will show up a particle or an injury under ultraviolet light. An ophthalmologist may also examine the eye with a slit lamp, a powerful magnifier with a very bright light source.

Prevention

Many eye injuries can be prevented simply by not letting young children play with long, pointed objects like branches. Children should be kept away from any machine that throws dust, such as a power saw or sander. Young children are less able to protect their eyes by intentionally squinting, and they should be warned to close their eyes, if possible, when dust or sand is blowing. At the beach or in a sandbox, children should be prohibited from throwing sand, even playfully. Abrasions from something in the eye can be kept to a minimum if children are reminded not to rub their eyes. And of course sharp objects such as knives should be kept well out of reach of very young children and their earliest use by older children should be well supervised.

Injuries and infections of the fingertips and toes

Description

Young children often hurt their fingertips, which seem to be almost the most vulnerable part of their bodies as they play and explore. The most common fingertip injuries involve hitting fingers, catching them in doors, dropping heavy objects on fingers, or having them run over by things like bicycle wheels.

The majority of fingertip accidents fortunately do not involve significant injury such as a broken bone, a large cut, or severing the fingertip (see *Cuts, scrapes, and puncture wounds*). Sometimes injuries result in bleeding under the nail, called a subungual hematoma. Such bleeding is not dangerous, but it is often very painful, because the tissue under the nail has no space for blood to get out and the nail itself is rigid, so pressure builds up on the sensitive nerve endings in the fingertip. Releasing the pressure by draining the blood will instantly relieve the pain (see *The doctor*).

Two other problems involving the fingertips or toes are (1) *paronychia,* or "runarounds," which are staph infections in the tissue around the nail bed, and (2) *felons,* which are staph infections of the tip itself. At first a paronychia or felon simply appears as a warm, red, swollen area. At this stage neither infection is very painful or large in area, though both can become so if neglected.

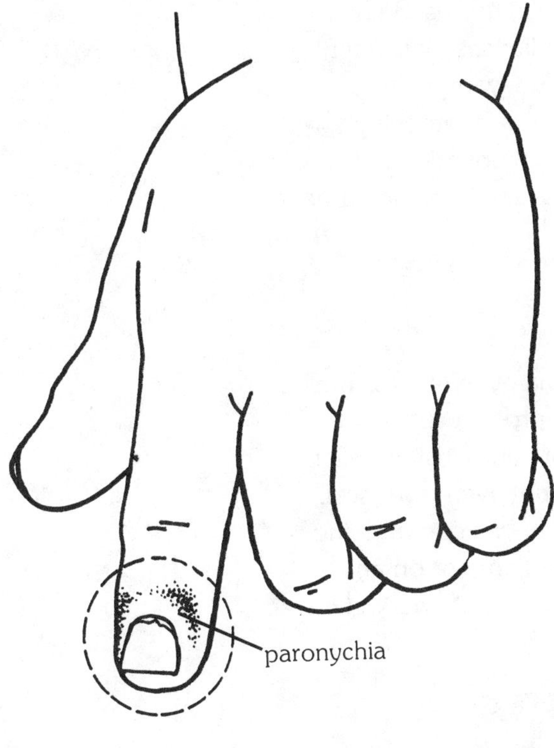

A paronychia *is an infection in the skin around the bed of a nail. It does not heal easily and should be seen by a doctor.*

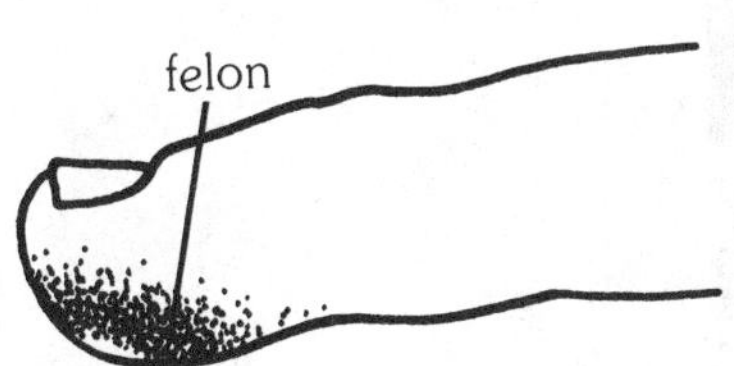

A felon *is an infection of the fingertip. It can be very painful because the nail presses against the infection. A* felon *should be seen by a doctor.*

Both of these infections require treatment because they are near the nail. Paronychia separate the nail from the nail bed, which causes the nail to act as a foreign body and prevents the infection from healing. Felons require treatment because the nail prevents damage and pressure builds up, causing intense, throbbing pain, similar to what happens with subungual bleeding. Also an infection under pressure can spread to the bone, which can be serious.

Self-help

Subungual hematomas that do not cause continued pain will heal by themselves and require no treatment. *Subungual hematomas that cause significant pain are treated by making a tiny hole in the nail.* The hole allows blood and plasma to drain, relieving pain and speeding healing. The nail itself has no nerve endings and the procedure is not painful, so a parent who feels confident can do it at home (see *The doctor*).

Felons and paronychia should be treated assertively in the early stages with warm soaks. The swollen area should be submerged *at least* 3 times a day for 15 minutes at a time. Children may find this tedious, so it is often best to combine the soaks with a bath or water play. The warm water causes the blood vessels to dilate, bringing in antibodies and removing spent cells. This may be sufficient to clear up a paronychia or felon in the incipient stages. If the infection doesn't respond to soaks and becomes large or painful, the doctor should be seen.

The doctor

The doctor will relieve a significant subungual hematoma by making a small hole through the nail of the affected finger or toe. The procedure may sound and look scary, but it is actually painless and it provides instant relief. Because the procedure is not painful, the doctor does not even give local anesthesia. The standard practice is to *straighten a paper clip and heat the end until it is literally red hot.* This can be done in a gas flame or on an electric burner; it cannot be done with matches. *The hot tip is then touched*

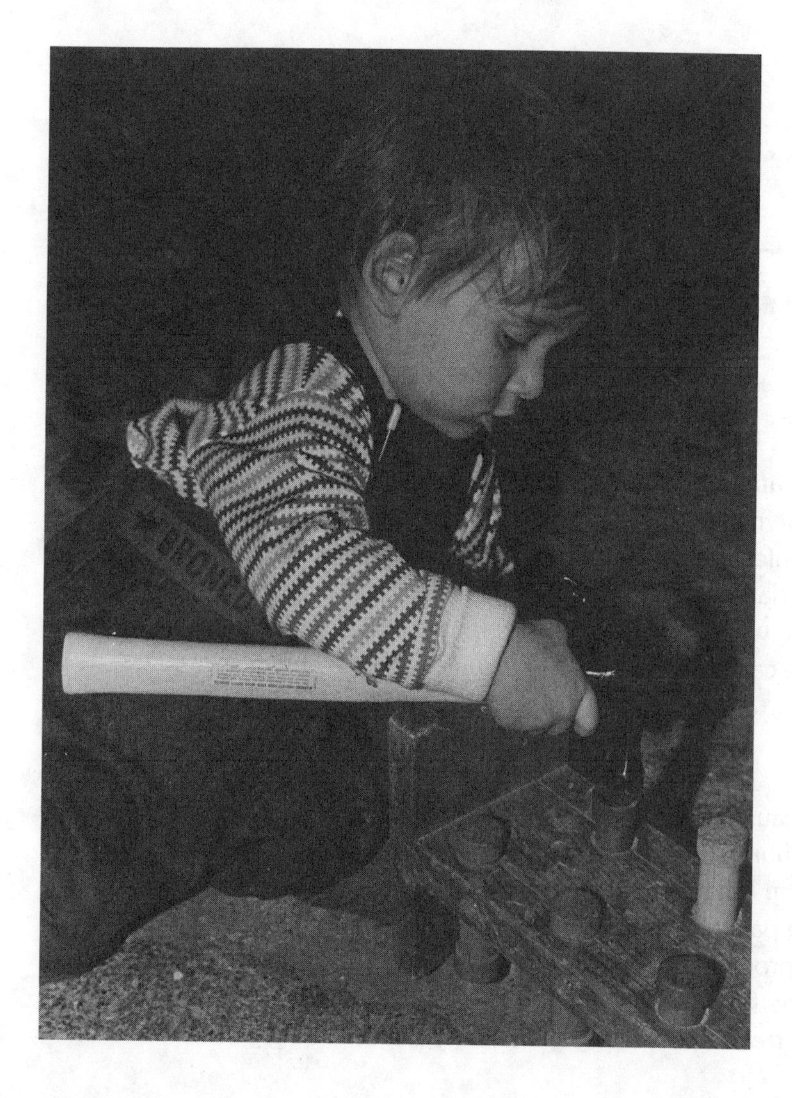

To prevent fingertip injuries, young children should be watched when they play with hammers or heavy objects.

to, not pushed against, the darkest area of the nail. The tip of the paper clip is so hot that it will actually burn a tiny hole in the nail. Because the nail has no nerve endings, the procedure hurts no more than cutting a fingernail with scissors. The pocket of blood under the nail protects the tissues. Some doctors will use a dental drill to make the hole.

Once the opening in the nail has been made, the accumulated blood begins to drain out slowly. Blood and intracellular fluid or plasma will continue to drain out through the hole for a day or so. The affected finger or toe should be soaked 2 or 3 times a day for 5 to 10 minutes at a time. This will help to keep the tiny hole open and allow continued drainage until healing is complete.

The doctor will treat a severe paronychia or felon by draining it. Anesthesia will be injected locally and a small incision will be made to allow the infection to drain externally. The finger or toe should then be soaked frequently.

Prevention

Many subungual hematomas can be prevented by exercising care with young children around car, cabinet, and room doors. Young children should be watched at play with hammers and heavy objects. As early as possible children should be taught that doors can really pinch and dropped objects can hurt.

Paronychia and felons are best prevented by prompt treatment of minor fingertip or toe injuries. Splinters should be removed if they fester much, cuts should be kept clean, hangnails should be trimmed while they are small, and nail biting should be discouraged. Most important, though, actual small infections should be treated immediately and seen by a doctor if they do not clear up promptly.

Febrile convulsions

Description

Febrile convulsions are an unusual response to fever, and are most likely to occur in the early stages of an upper respiratory infection, when a child's fever goes up very quickly (102°F–106°F). The child suddenly loses consciousness and begins to shake or twitch all over with muscle spasms. The eyes roll up in the head; the head may arch backward and the jaws clench. The chest and abdomen may heave irregularly. Breathing is often heavy and may even stop for a few seconds. Occasionally a child may urinate involuntarily during the seizure.

The seizure is always upsetting or frightening to the people who view it, although it is not actually dangerous. *Febrile convulsions stop by themselves within a matter of minutes.* In fact, sometimes there is a question about whether a seizure has really occurred. Often the child does not even know what has happened and has to be told. Generally the seizure does not recur during the illness.

Febrile convulsions do not necessarily ever recur again and rarely mean that a child is epileptic. Febrile convulsions are most common between six months and three years and are more common in boys than girls. Frequently, there is a family history of febrile convulsions. A convulsion can be the first symptom of roseola (see *Roseola infanta*) or an ear infection.

Self-help

Lower the child's fever (see *Prevention*). Watch the child's breathing and wipe away any saliva that might cause coughing. Calm the child.

The doctor

Parents whose child has a febrile convulsion are usually sufficiently frightened to call the doctor. Almost always the doctor will want to see the child to rule out any rare, underlying cause for the convulsion. The doctor will do a normal physical exam, concentrating on neurological signs. The doctor will assess whether the child is very irritable and has difficulty moving its neck. Severe stiffness of the neck is a symptom of meningitis, an inflammation of the lining of the spinal cord and brain which is serious. Meningitis can also cause convulsions, which is why the doctor wants to rule it out (see "Rare diseases"). Sometimes the doctor will do a lumbar puncture to examine a sample of the child's spinal fluid to rule out meningitis. Meningitis is rare. Convulsion is almost always a response to fever. If a child has convulsions on several occasions, the doctor may recommend antiseizure medication, but usually it is not necessary.

Prevention

Febrile convulsions are not only unusual, they are impossible to predict with any certainty.The best way to prevent febrile convulsions is to treat for high fevers (102°F–106°F) in young children. Symptomatic treatment is definitely recommended in the case of children who have had febrile convulsions or who have a family history of them. Acetaminophen (e.g., Tylenol), clothing removal, and tepid sponge baths are all effective in lowering a child's temperature (see *Self-help* under *Upper respiratory infections*).

Breath-holding spells

Description

Children between six months and four years of age can hold their breath until they actually turn blue and pass out. Sometimes the child's arms and legs even shake or jerk. This is a terrifying thing to watch, but is not dangerous at all. The child's powerful, unconscious breathing reflex will take over when the child gets groggy or passes out and the child will *always* begin breathing and regain consciousness by itself. When parents realize this, much of the anxiety of a breath-holding spell is relieved. And parents will be able to handle the situation more easily should it recur. Some children are known to hold their breath when they are tearful and angry or frustrated. This type of behavior disappears as the child grows older.

Self-help

There is no treatment necessary for a true breath-holding episode. If the parents are worried about the child's breathing, a slap on the back will break the spell. If the baby is eating or playing with small toys, the parents should look in the baby's mouth to make sure it is not choking.

The doctor

There is no medical treatment for breath-holding, but parents may want to discuss it with the doctor if it happens repeatedly.

Prevention

The best prevention is to deal with the child's anger and frustration before they get out of control. This is particularly important at certain developmental points and with children who become angered or frustrated easily. If children are able to get help and good, direct communication from their parents, they are less likely to resort to this means of getting attention. Parents should also try to be very calm and firm if the situation does occur, rather than reinforce the behavior by becoming upset.

Choking—foreign bodies in the throat

Description

Young children can inhale or stick objects into their throats which block the passage of air. It is immediately apparent when this happens because the child begins to gag, cough, wheeze, and have difficulty breathing. If the airway is completely blocked, within minutes the child will literally begin to turn blue from lack of oxygen (unusual).

Most often children choke on food, but choking can also be caused by beads, toys, pebbles, gum, or any tiny objects that are put in the mouth. Choking is most common in younger children between six and nine months who are just learning to eat solid, lumpy foods and who love to put things in their mouth. But older children can also choke—generally in excitement.

Household objects babies can choke on

- Coins
- Uninflated balloons
- Marbles
- Pen caps
- Small toy and machine parts
- Solid buttons
- Beads

Self-help

Choking is a frightening experience for both child and parent. The great majority of the time, children are rapidly able to clear their throat by themselves. But occasionally, something remains lodged in the child's throat that makes breathing difficult. In rare cases, the situation can even be life-threatening.

If a child is choking, the parent needs to act quickly. First, the parent must determine whether the child can breathe, cry, or talk, and see if the child can exert a strong cough. If the child can do these things, the blockage is incomplete, and the chances are good that the child can clear out the object without help. For an incomplete blockage, emergency experts currently recommend watching the child closely *without* intervening, because rescue efforts can sometimes make the situation worse. If the child continues to be unable to clear its throat, the parents should have someone call the rescue squad.

The parent should begin FIRST AID if the child cannot breathe, has only a very weak cough, makes a high-pitched noise while inhaling, or begins to turn pale or blue. These are signs of a complete, or almost complete, blockage. This situation is a MEDICAL EMERGENCY and the emergency squad should be called immediately.

If the child is under a year: (1) put the infant facedown along your forearm, holding the baby's jaw in your hand. The baby's head should be lower than its feet. Rest your forearm on your leg for extra support (see illustration).

(2) With your other hand, give the baby four rapid back blows with the heel of your hand, high up between the baby's shoulder blades.

(3) If this does not relieve the blockage, turn the baby over, and firmly press four times on its breastbone with two fingers, just below the level of the baby's nipples.

(4) If the baby still is not breathing, open its mouth with one hand, holding the tongue with your thumb and the jaw with the rest of the fingers. If you can see the foreign body, use the index finger of your other hand to sweep it out of the baby's mouth. If you can't see the object, do not try to sweep it out, because you might push it farther down. *Never* put your finger straight down the baby's throat.

(5) If the baby is still unable to breathe, place your mouth over the

Foods young babies can choke on

- Grapes
- Popcorn
- Chunks of peanut butter
- Raw carrots
- Seeds
- Nuts
- Whole peas
- Meat chunks
- Hot dogs
- Chicken bones
- Gum
- Little hard candies
- Potato chips
- Crackers
- Bread—especially large pieces
- Cookies
- Raisins
- Fruit with pits

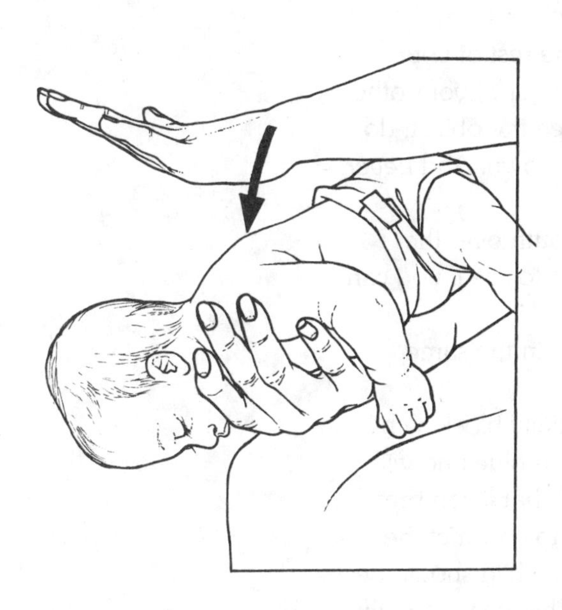

When a baby under a year is choking, the baby should be put facedown along the rescuer's arm, and given four back blows.

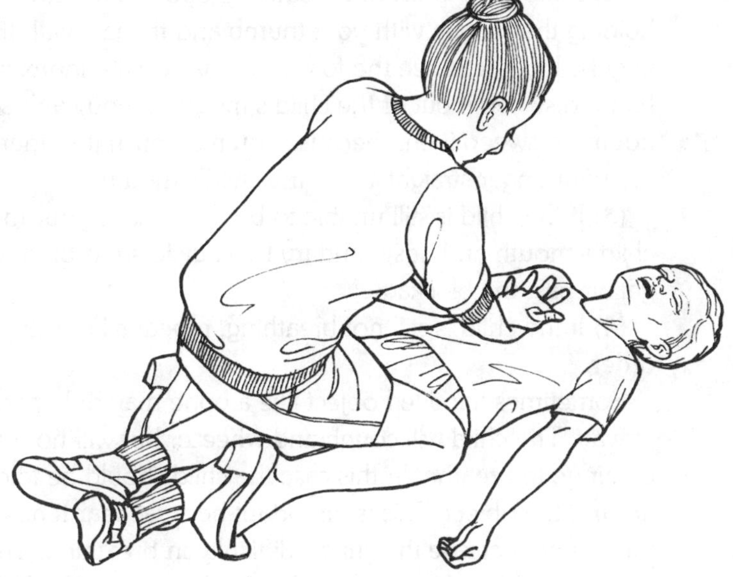

If the child is over a year, put the child on its back and administer abdominal thrusts (see guidelines).

baby's mouth and nose, and try two quick, short breaths to see if you can get air past the blockage.

(6) If the baby is still not breathing, repeat all the steps in the same order.

If the child is over a year: In older children, the *Heimlich maneuver,* or artificial cough, can be used to free the object. The abdominal thrusts of the Heimlich maneuver can be done with the child either sitting, standing, or lying on its back. Generally, a child who is young or unconscious is put on its back. (1) Put the child on its back, and kneel next to the child's feet. Place the heel of one hand on the midline of the abdomen, between the child's belly button and the rib cage. Place the other hand on top of the first, and push firmly but gently, moving your hands inward and upward. With older children you can also do the Heimlich maneuver with the child standing. Stand behind the child and put your arms around its waist. Make one hand into a fist and place it with thumb toward the child, in the midline of the abdomen, slightly *above* the navel, and well *below* the rib cage. Grab your fist with your other hand, and press inward and upward quickly. Several thrusts may be necessary to dislodge the obstruction.

With an older child, abdominal thrusts can be performed from behind.

(2) If the child is still not breathing, open its mouth with one hand, holding the tongue with your thumb and the jaw with the rest of your fingers. If you can see the foreign body, use the index finger of your other hand to sweep it out of the child's mouth. If you can't see the object, do not try to sweep it out, because you may push it farther down. And *never* put your finger straight down the child's mouth.

(3) If the child is still unable to breathe, place your mouth over the child's mouth and nose, and try two quick, short breaths to see if you can get air past the blockage.

(4) If the child is still not breathing, repeat all the steps in the same order.

Sometimes a lodged object like a bone may only partially block a child's airway. The child will cough and wheeze, but will not turn blue and will continue to breathe. In this case the child should be told that it can breathe *around* the object. This is important because fear tends to constrict the throat and increase the child's difficulty in breathing. The child should be encouraged to relax and breathe slowly and evenly. In the meantime, the emergency squad should be called or the child should be taken to the hospital.

The doctor

If the object cannot be dislodged, the parent should call the emergency squad or take the child to the nearest emergency room. The emergency squad is trained in CPR. The doctor can put in an airway, if necessary, and has special equipment to remove the foreign object.

Prevention

Young children should never be given foods that are easily inhaled (for example, peanuts) or that break into large pieces (for example, certain kinds of crackers), and infants should never be allowed to eat while lying on their backs. It's much easier to inhale food in this position.

As children's teeth come in they can gradually be introduced to foods that require chewing, but they should be supervised carefully with new foods and should first be given foods that can be gnawed on or that crumble into small pieces. Toddlers should be watched when they first eat raisins, nuts, seeds, potato chips, hard candies, and gum. Fish should be flaked for bones until a child is old enough to do it, and all children should be discouraged from putting nonfood objects—marbles, pebbles, etc.—in their mouth.

Resuscitation

Description

It is very rare that a layperson has to perform resuscitation. But if a child ever stops breathing for any reason, resuscitation must be begun within 4 minutes and continued until the child begins breathing normally again or until medical help can be obtained. The most common causes for cessation of breathing or heart stoppage in young children are drowning, electric shock, and smoke or gas inhalation. If someone is present who has been trained in first aid, that person should do the resuscitation.

Self-help

When a child stops breathing, it is a MEDICAL EMERGENCY. The treatment for this is CPR (CARDIOPULMONARY RESUSCITATION). This is best learned in a course, but in emergencies it can be done from written directions.

1. Determine if the child is unconscious and actually not breathing. Shake the child gently, and watch to see if the child is breathing.
2. If the child is unresponsive, and does not appear to be breathing, have someone **call for help.** If you are alone, follow the steps below and do CPR for one minute before calling yourself.
3. **Put the child on its back** on a firm, flat surface. If a neck or spine injury seems likely (e.g., a car accident or fall), move the head and neck as a unit, with firm support. In choking, smoke inhalation, sudden infant death symdrome (SIDS), drownings, poisonings, and electric shock, it is unlikely the child will have sustained head or neck injuries.
4. **Open the airway.** Place the hand closest to the child on the child's forehead, and gently tilt the head back. With your other hand, lift up the bony part of the child's chin (see illustration). If there are possible head or neck injuries, kneel behind the child's head and rest your elbows on the ground, place two or three fingers at the angle of the jaw, and lift gently upward to open the airway.
5. **Determine if the child is breathing.** Listen for breath sounds from the mouth, observe if the child's chest is rising and falling, and check for any breaths against your ear. If the child is breathing, wait for help to arrive; if not, begin assisted breathing.
6. If necessary, **breathe for the child.** Continuing to keep the airway open, take a breath and put your mouth over the child's mouth and nose; in an older child, put your mouth over the child's mouth and pinch its nose closed. Blow in a slow breath for one and a half seconds; then take a breath and blow in again. The right volume of air should make the child's chest rise and fall.
7. **Check the pulse.** In a baby under a year, feel for a pulse on the inside of the upper arm, between the elbow and shoulder. In an older child, feel for a pulse on the side of the neck, between the windpipe and muscles.
8. If the child is still not breathing and another person is present, have that person **call for help.**
9. If the baby has no pulse, **chest compressions** must be done to keep blood flowing to the brain. In an infant, put the index finger and middle finger on the breastbone, one finger's width below the baby's nipples, and press down one-half inch to one inch, releasing completely between presses. Do

a hundred presses per minute. In a child, put the heel of one hand on the breastbone, one finger's width from the bottom. Press down one to one and a half inches at a rate of eighty presses per minute.

10. **Do coordinated compressions and rescue breathing.** At the end of every five chest compressions, blow in one rescue breath. After ten cycles (one minute), check to see if the child is breathing unassisted. If not, continue the compressions and breathing, checking every several minutes for breathing. Do not discontinue CPR for more than seven seconds at a time, unless the child begins to breathe or help arrives.

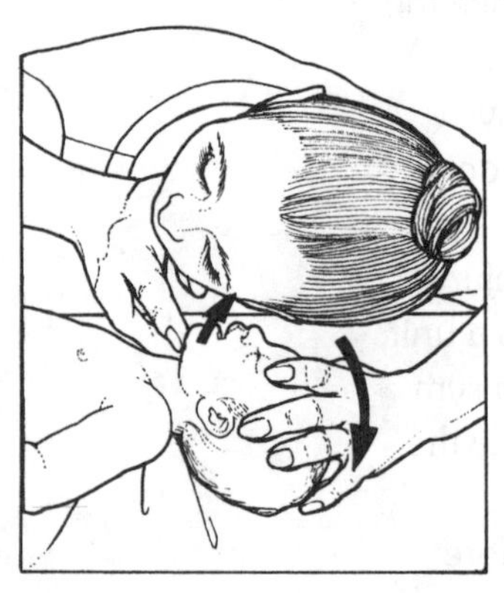

To open the airway, place one hand on the child's forehead and tilt the head back gently. Place the fingers of the other hand under the bony part of the chin and gently lift upward.

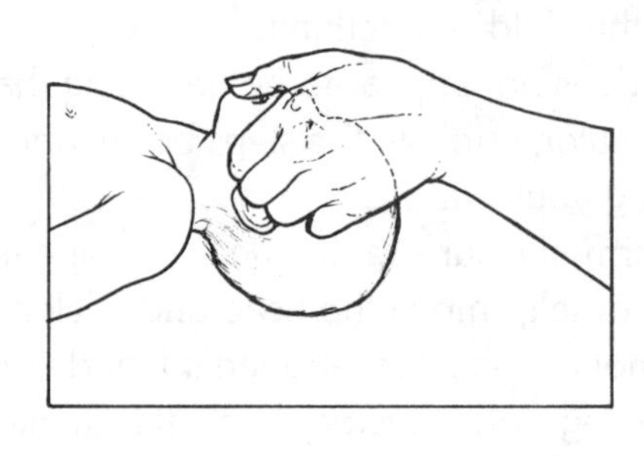

If a neck injury is suspected, open the airway by placing two or three fingers under each side of the child's jaw, and lifting upward.

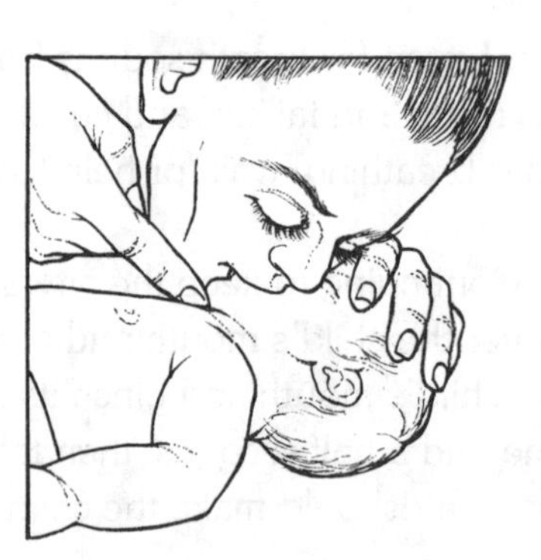

To breathe for a baby, continue to keep the airway open with your hands. Place your mouth over baby's mouth and nose, making a tight seal, then breathe slowly (one to one and a half seconds per breath), causing the baby's chest to rise and fall.

To breathe for an older child, continue to keep the airway open with your hands. Pinch the child's nose closed with the hand you have on the child's forehead and place your mouth over the child's mouth, making a tight seal, then breathe slowly (one to one and a half seconds per breath), causing the child's chest to rise and fall.

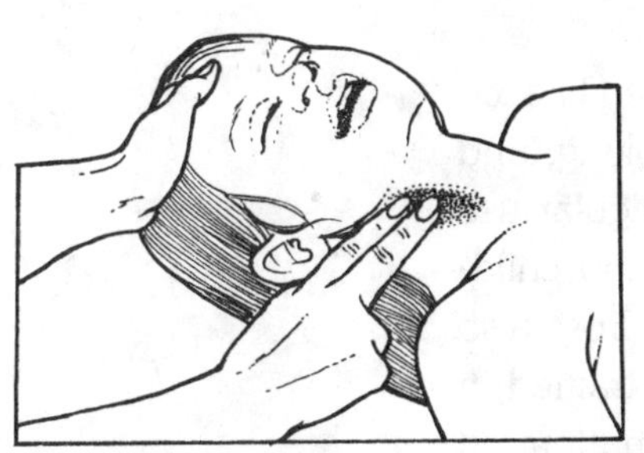

To check for a pulse in a child over a year, gently press index and middle finger in the groove between the windpipe and the muscles on the side of the neck.

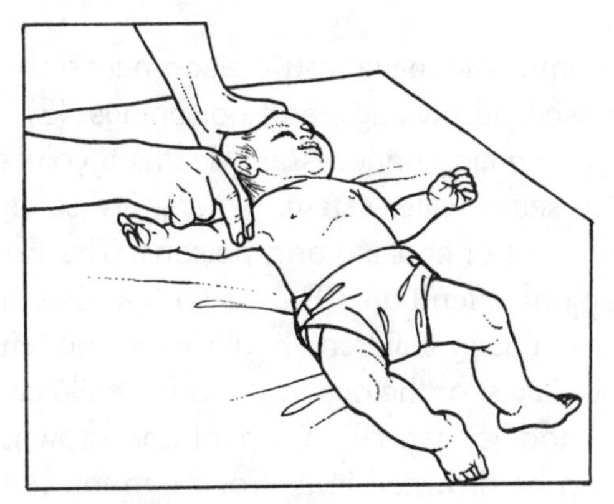

To check for a pulse in a child under a year, gently press the index and middle finger on the inside of the baby's arm, between shoulder and elbow.

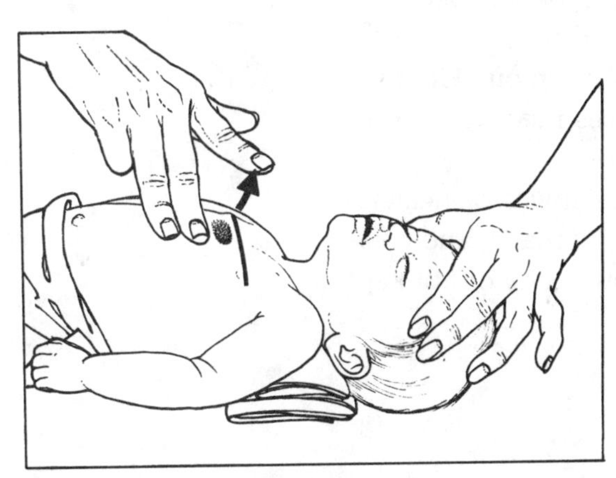

To position fingers for chest compression on a baby under a year, place the index finger on the breastbone at the level of the nipples. The area to be compressed is one finger's width below this, e.g., the location where the middle and ring finger lie. Using two or three fingers, compress the chest one half to one inch, at a rate of a hundred times a minute (approximately one and a half times per second). After every five compressions, pause to breathe for the child.

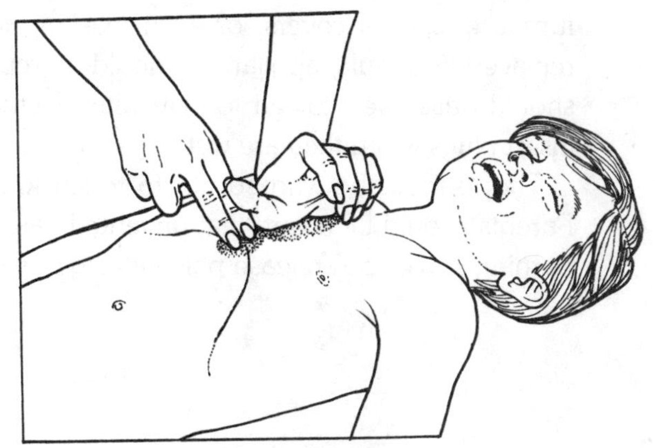

To locate the hand position for chest compression in a child over a year, find the notch where the lowest rib meets the breastbone. Put the middle finger of one hand on the notch, with the index finger on the breastbone. Put the heel of the other hand next to the index finger, and press down one to one and a half inches at a rate of a hundred times per minute (approximately one and a half times a second). Do five compressions in a row, then pause to breathe for the child.

Prevention

The events that most commonly make resuscitation necessary are (1) accidents, including car crashes, drownings, and poisonings, (2) choking, and (3) smoke inhalation. Preventing unnecessary deaths involves regular use of seat belts and safety seats, water safety, general fire safety, and child-proofing the house in terms of choking and poisons. The Red Cross also recommends that everyone attend a CPR class so that they are trained in resuscitation techniques. Young children should never be left unattended around bathtubs, pools, lakes, or the ocean. A young child can drown in a few inches of water. A toddler can fall in a pool and drown, and even a child who can swim can be drowned in a strong current. It is essential to fence pools and streams away from the house. Drowning is a major cause of death in young children who live near water. Children, especially those who live near a lake or a pool, should be taught to swim as early as possible, and should never be allowed in the water without a "buddy." Children who can't swim or who aren't strong swimmers should wear life jackets when they are in boats. All children should be taught to respect the water and to handle themselves properly around it.

Children should be taught not to play with electric plugs or cords, just as they are taught not to touch a hot stove. Plugs should be covered with furniture, special covers, or even masking tape. Eroded wires should be replaced and faulty appliances should be repaired or thrown out. Children should *never* be allowed to play with electric appliances near water or to insert plugs when they are wet.

They should be warned not to touch knobs on gas stoves or heaters. Parents should be aware that unvented gas, kerosene, propane, and coal-burning stoves can release poisonous gases if used improperly or not kept

Swimming areas are extremely dangerous for young children. Parents should watch their children closely and make sure that the children use reliable safety devices until they have learned to swim.

in good repair. Children who live in homes with these kinds of stoves should be taught to recognize the odor of leaking gas.

If most parents think about their houses in terms of safety problems, they will immediately be able to list a few safety hazards that can be corrected or that children should be taught to recognize. A little time now may mean a parent never has to use resuscitation. A child's natural task is to explore the world, and it's a parent's job to protect and educate a child about the dangers of that world.

Accidental poisoning

Description

Poisonings are one of the most common childhood accidents, and they are the fourth most frequent cause of death in the one-to-four age group. Moreover, poisonings are one of the few kinds of accidents that are entirely preventable. Fortunately, over 95 percent of all ingestions are not serious and the doctor will simply instruct the parent to watch the child at home and possibly induce vomiting. Poisonings reach a peak around the age of two when children are at once highly mobile, increasingly dexterous, and very curious, but still young enough to like to put things in their mouth and not really understand that something can be dangerous to swallow. "Not to eat" is the watchword for this age.

All parents know that some substances are dangerous to swallow; fewer parents are familiar with the fact that some substances are dangerous to touch or inhale (see *Poison* lists). Products containing acids or caustic agents in large amounts can burn the skin; many aromatics such as glue, insecticides, or gas fumes can burn the throat or depress breathing. There are a number of substances that are harmless or perhaps even beneficial in small quantities, but are dangerous in large amounts—for example, vitamins, aspirin, acetaminophen (e.g., Tylenol), alcohol, and smoke.

Self-help

A *parent* should *not* induce vomiting without a doctor's instructions because some substances are more dangerous when they come up than when they go down. Strong acids and bases like drain cleaners will cause further burning of the esophagus if vomited up. Aromatics like gasoline and paint thinner can be aspirated into the lungs when vomited, causing possible tissue damage and pneumonia. In the meantime, swallowing milk or water will work to dilute and neutralize any poison that has been ingested.

Poison guidelines

Preventing childhood poisonings

1. Insist on safety closures and learn how to use them properly.
2. Keep household cleaning supplies, medicines, garage products, and insecticides out of the reach and sight of your child. Lock them up whenever possible.
3. Never store food and cleaning products together. Store medicine and chemicals in original containers and never in food or beverage containers.
4. Avoid taking medicine in your child's presence. Children love to imitate. Always call medicine by its proper name. Never suggest that medicine is "candy"—especially acetaminophen (e.g., Tylenol) and children's vitamins.
5. Read the label on all products and heed warnings and cautions. Never use medicine from an unlabeled or unreadable container. Never pour medicine in a darkened area where the label cannot be clearly seen.
6. If you are interrupted while using a product, take it with you. It only takes a few seconds for your child to get into it.
7. Know what your child can do. For example, if you have a crawling infant, keep household products stored above floor level, not beneath the kitchen sink.
8. Keep the phone number of your doctor, Poison Center, hospital, police department, and fire department or paramedic emergency rescue squad near the phone.

First aid for poisoning

Always keep syrup of ipecac and Epsom salt (magnesium sulfate) in your home. The former is used to induce vomiting and the latter may be used as a laxative. These drugs are used sometimes when poisons are swallowed. Only use them as instructed by your Poison Center or doctor, and *follow their directions for use.*

Inhaled poisons

If gas fumes, or smoke have been inhaled, immediately drag or carry the patient to fresh air. Then call the Poison Center or your doctor.

Continued

Poisons on the skin

If the poison has been spilled on the skin or clothing, remove the clothing and flood the involved parts with water. Then wash with soapy water and rinse thoroughly. Then call the Poison Center or your doctor.

Swallowed poisons

If the poison has been swallowed and the patient is awake and can swallow, give the patient only water or milk to drink. Then call the Poison Center or your doctor. ***Caution:*** Antidote labels on products may be incorrect. Do not give salt, vinegar, or lemon juice. Call before doing anything else.

Poisons in the eye

Flush the eye with lukewarm water poured from a pitcher held 6–8 inches from the eye for 15 minutes. Call the Poison Center or your doctor.

Courtesy of Rocky Mountain Poison Center, Denver, Colorado.

The basic principle of poison treatment is to get rid of or dilute the poison safely.

The doctor

The doctor should be called in all cases of ingestion or exposure. It is usually difficult to be certain whether a child has actually eaten something and how much, but it is better to make a phone call than to take an unnecessary risk. Pediatricians inevitably have had a great deal of experience in dealing with possible poisonings and are better equipped to assess whether the child has ingested something, how much, how dangerous it is, and whether or not the child should be brought to the office or hospital. Unless a child has obviously ingested a large amount of a known poison, there's a good chance the doctor will instruct the parent to treat it at home. In any case, the doctor will want to know *exactly* what the child took, so the parent should have the bottle or container in hand. If the doctor does want to see the child, then the parent should take the bottle and its contents.

Prevention

Safe storage and use of cleaning supplies, paints, drugs, insecticides, and automobile products will eliminate much of the possibility of accidental poisoning.

Poisonous plants

Outdoor			*Indoor*	*Wild*
Calla lily	Foxglove	Oleander	Caladium	Jimsonweed
Castor bean	Larkspur	Rhododendron	Diffenbachia (dumb cane)	Mushrooms (a few)
Crocus	Monkshood	Rhubarb leaves		Poison hemlock
Delphinium	Mountain laurel			

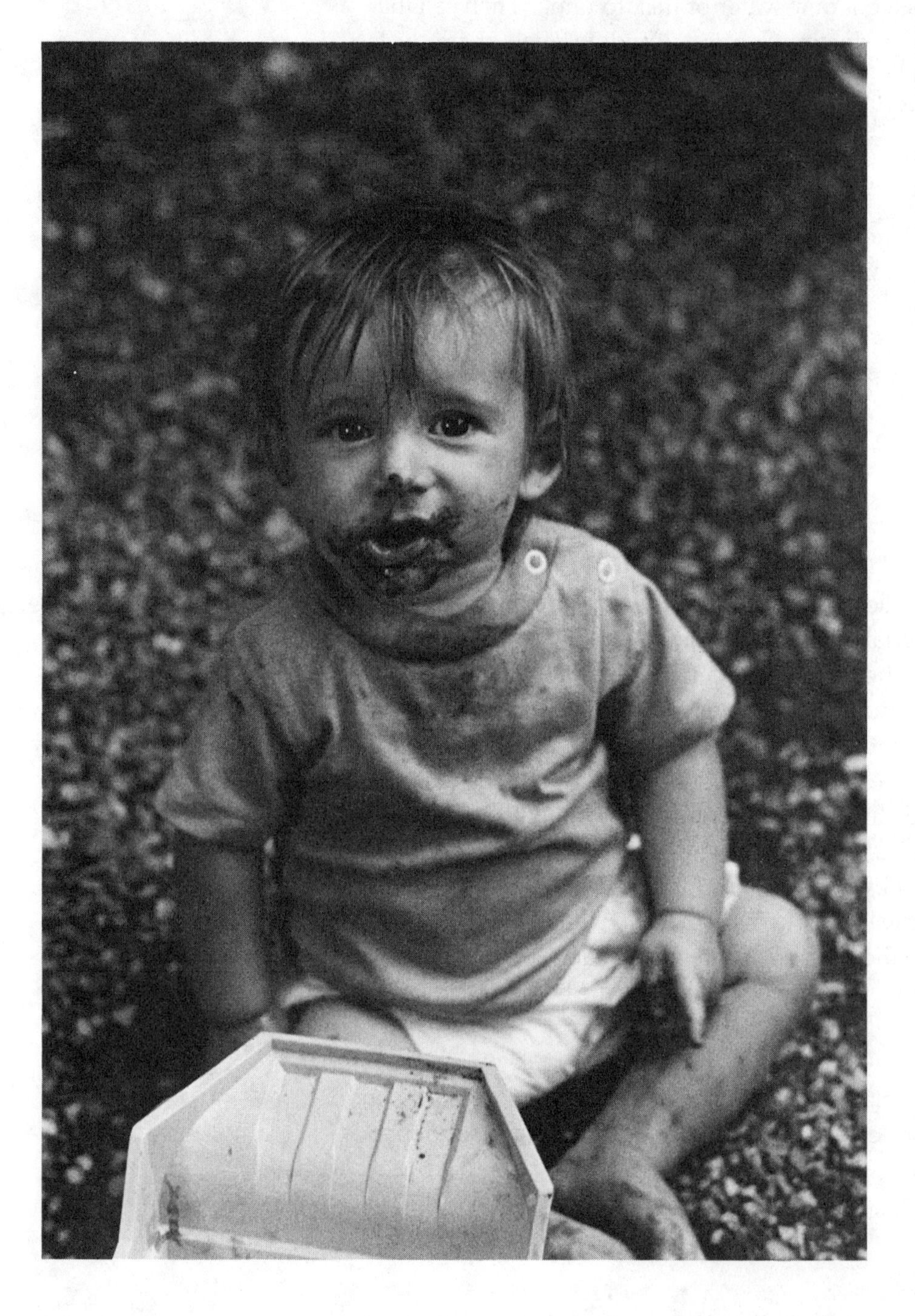

Young babies will put virtually anything in their mouths. They have no understanding of poisons and can't be expected to prevent a poisoning themselves.

Many parents do not actually realize how many common products can be dangerous to swallow, touch, or inhale. Moreover, many parents are caught unprepared when a child begins to crawl, walk, and open things. Before a child even reaches these stages, parents should make a systematic sweep of the house, throwing out products that are not used and raising remaining products well out of reach. Highly toxic products, including drugs of any sort, should be put in locked cabinets. All materials should be labeled if dangerous so they are sure to be kept out of reach.

The most common poisonous substances are household cleaners under the kitchen sink and next to the washer; paints, insecticides, and auto products in the garage, workroom, or basement; and drugs, cosmetics, and cleansers in the bathroom. In addition there are a number of domestic and wild plants as well as some mushrooms that are poisonous (see *Poisonous plants* list).

Common household poisons that may be ingested

After-shave lotion
Alcohol—beverages, cosmetics, rubbing
Ammonia
Amphetamines (diet pills)
Antifreeze
Antihistamines (for allergies)
Ant traps
Aspirin
Automobile polish (liquid wax)
Barbiturates (sleeping pills)
Battery acid
Birth control pills
Bleach (laundry, hair)
Blood pressure medicine
Carbon tetrachloride (cleaning fluid)
Cement
Codeine cough syrups
Cosmetics
DDT
Detergents
Digitalis (heart medicine)
Drain cleaners and openers
Fabric softener
Flea collars or powder
Floor wax
Fly sprays, strips
Furniture polish
Gasoline
Glue
Hair dyes
Hair sprays
Insecticides
Iodine
Iron pills (including fortified vitamins)
Kerosene
Laxatives
Lead (in old wall paint, artists' oil paints, leaded gasoline)
Lighter fluid
Lye
Medications
Metal polishes
Mothballs

Continued

Mouse poison	Rat poison
Mushrooms (some wild)	Roach powder
Nail polish	Rug cleaners
Nail polish remover	Shampoo (some brands)
Nutmeg	Shoe polish
Oven cleaners	Sleeping tablets
Paint—flakes, artists' oil paint	3-in-1 oil
Paint products—removers, thinners, turpentine, synturps	Tobacco
Perfume	Toilet bowl cleaners
Permanent wave products, especially neutralizers	Toilet water
	Tranquilizers
	Tylenol (acetaminophen)

Commonly ingested substances that are only mildly toxic

The doctor should still be called.

Cleansing creams (facial)	Lipstick
Contraceptive pills	Motor oil
Fluoride	Soap
Hand lotion	Vitamins *without* iron

Chapter 11

Using relaxation and imagery in healing

Imagery is one of the oldest healing tools known to man. There are records from Babylonia and ancient Greece on the use of relaxation and imagery in treating illness. Indian yogins have also used imagery techniques for centuries. Recently medical researchers have verified the extraordinary bodily control achieved by yoga masters through imagery, and they have observed that ordinary people can likewise produce healing physiological changes through relaxation and imagery.

Visualizing healing images results in general body changes, including muscle relaxation, changed blood flow, decreased oxygen consumption and output of metabolic waste products, lowered respiration and heart rate, easier breathing, and decreased awareness of pain. Through specific visualizations, even more pronounced physiological changes can be produced. People can radically alter blood flow to a particular area—either increasing blood flow to speed the healing of an infection or decreasing it to stop a wound from bleeding. People can also produce anesthesia in specific parts of the body. Medical doctors are currently using relaxation and imagery to treat a variety of diseases, including asthma, skin diseases, ulcers, infections, and cancer.

Parents can use relaxation and imagery for their children in two basic ways. First, parents can teach older babies to use the techniques them-

The image of a baby surrounded by radiant energy and light is an age-old spiritual visualization. Adoration of the Shepherds, *by Nicolas Dipre, M. H. de Young Memorial Museum, Gift of Samuel H. Kress Foundation.*

selves through pretend games and activities. When children do the exercises, they directly alter their physiology by themselves. In this way children learn the lifelong skill of consciously controlling their bodies. Studies have been done on asthmatic children who have been taught to imagine relaxing situations. When these children imagined such scenes, their breathing became significantly easier. Relaxation caused bronchodilatation, or expansion of the wide tubes of the lungs. This is precisely the same effect caused by asthma drugs, but the children used no medication, only relaxation and imagery. Children can use relaxation and imagery for any illness or injury. These techniques can be used in minor situations not involving the doctor; they can also be used along with medical treatment prescribed by a doctor. Relaxed muscles and increased blood flow will help drugs reach any infection.

The second basic way in which parents can use relaxation and imagery with their child is to use the skills for themselves. This is especially important with very young (even unborn) babies, who cannot do the exercises themselves. When parents do the exercises themselves, they unconsciously communicate their feelings to the baby. As the baby picks up the parents' feelings, its physiology is altered. Some form of telepathy is probably at work here in addition to sensory cues. Research has shown that mother and baby frequently have the same brain-wave patterns and that parents often spontaneously have thoughts that their children talk about later. Reputable scientific accounts about psychic phenomena describe many instances of parents suddenly realizing a child was hurt or needed help when the parent had no way to see or hear the child. This powerful psychic connection between parents and baby probably allows for greater ease in transmission of healing images and their energy.

A healing imagery exercise

Breathe in and out deeply, allowing your abdomen to rise and fall. Deeply relax your whole body. You are now in a state in which your mind is open and receptive. You can visualize vividly and easily. Realize that you are part of the universe. Healing energy can flow into you. You are connected to your baby and your baby is connected to you by strong bonds at a level below conscious thought. Time and space are different at this level—their possibilities are not limited. Imagine how your baby feels, then picture all uncomfortable feelings flowing out of your baby. Picture healing energy, light, and love flowing into you and into your baby. Feel calmness, radiance, and strength flow into you and into your baby. Stay at this level as long as you wish. Keep these images in mind even as you return to your ordinary activities.

By picturing light and energy around the baby, parents can help to speed healing and promote health. Most parents also find that such an image relaxes them.

Receptive imagery for diagnosis and treatment

When a child is hurt or sick, parents can use receptive imagery both to figure out what's wrong and to figure out what will best help the child heal.

Close your eyes. Breathe in and out deeply, allowing your abdomen to rise and fall. As your breathing becomes slow and even, you will feel relaxed. Now deeply relax your whole body in stages. You are now in a state in which your mind is clear and tranquil. You can visualize vividly and easily. Your mind is open and receptive. Imagine your mind is like a screen and you can see images appear and disappear. Now visualize your baby on the screen. Look slowly over the whole baby several times. Look for any areas that appear different from the rest. There may be a murky color, a dark spot, or an area that is red and throbbing. You may even have a sudden, momentary sensation in a particular part of your own body which matches what is happening to the baby. . . . Focus on the area that stands out. If you feel like it, try to make the area right—rub away the murky color, for example, or pinch out the dark spot. . . .

Healing images

Any of these images can be used during a healing visualization. And many of the more graphic, concrete images can be taught to the older baby in the form of an imaginative game.

Picture the child surrounded by light and radiant energy.

Picture the child totally well, happy, and active.

Picture pain flowing out a hole as a murky color or liquid.

Picture the sick or injured area healing:
  A cut filling in with new cells
  A broken bone knitting together with new cells
  White blood cells engulfing bacteria or virus
  An infected ear draining through the eustachian tube
  Bleeding stopping from a wound

Picture the sick area fully healed and healthy:
  Normal skin where there was a rash or cut
  Normal mucous membranes where there was a sore throat

Picture healing energy and love flowing in as warm yellow light.

Now allow images of what will help the baby come to mind—special foods, rest, an exercise, a healing game, a gift, company, or even a magical treatment such as sprinkling imaginary medicine on the hurt area. Finally, allow a healing image to come to mind. Keep this image in mind even as you return to your everyday activities.

Pretend games for healing

These games do not necessarily have to be explained at length or played for a long time. The important thing is to use a metaphor or image that the child is familiar with and can therefore understand. The images below are samples; parents may think of others that are more effective for their child, and children are often marvelous at making up their own images. An image that a child makes up or elaborates on itself is often the most powerful. Once envisioned, the image will work by itself and become a point of reference for

Continued

the child. These images actually change the child's physiology and the child should be told that these pictures will help the body heal itself: "Your body can heal itself. These pretend games will help you get better. Now pretend that . . ." In an emergency situation the parent can simply tell the child calmly and with authority the image *will* happen.

Skin

Rash (eczema, ringworm, prickly heat, dry skin)

Imagine your skin feels smooth like silk.

Imagine that area feels like the smoothest skin of the body.

Imagine the redness disappears as though it's being erased.

Itchiness (poison ivy, poison oak, insect bites, allergies)

Pretend your skin feels cool, just like in a swimming pool.

Pretend your skin feels as if a cool breeze is blowing on it.

Infection (impetigo)

Pretend your skin feels warm as though a warm washcloth were put on it.

Head

Sticky, itchy, or sore eyes (conjuctivitis, sty)

Imagine a black cat or a dark room.

Imagine your eyes being gently bathed with water.

Burning, scratchy eyes (fever, extreme fatigue)

Pretend there is a cool washcloth on your eyes.

Pretend your eyes feel smooth and cool like stones, ice cubes.

Runny nose (cold, allergy)

Imagine someone shuts off the faucet at the top of your nose.

Sore throat (strep throat, tonsillitis)

Imagine sunlight on your throat.

Continued

Earache

Imagine the ache going out of your ear.

Imagine that little men are pounding on the ear and they go away.

Stuffy ears, glue ear (serous otitis media)

Imagine the tube going from the ear to the back of the throat opening up and thin glue flowing out.

Chest

Cough

Picture bad little things jumping out of your throat when you cough.

Imagine your lungs are filled with warm air.

Difficulty breathing (croup, colds, asthma)

Imagine a very happy, relaxing scene—for example, listening to a bedtime story.

Picture tubes in the lungs opening up so that the air can slide in and out easily.

Abdomen

Stomachache

Pretend the hurt falls to your feet and gets lost.

Pretend your stomach feels very warm.

General

Fever

Pretend you are a melting ice cube.

Pretend a cool wind is blowing over your whole body.

Emergency

Cuts

Imagine sticky glue goes across the cut and stops the bleeding.

Continued

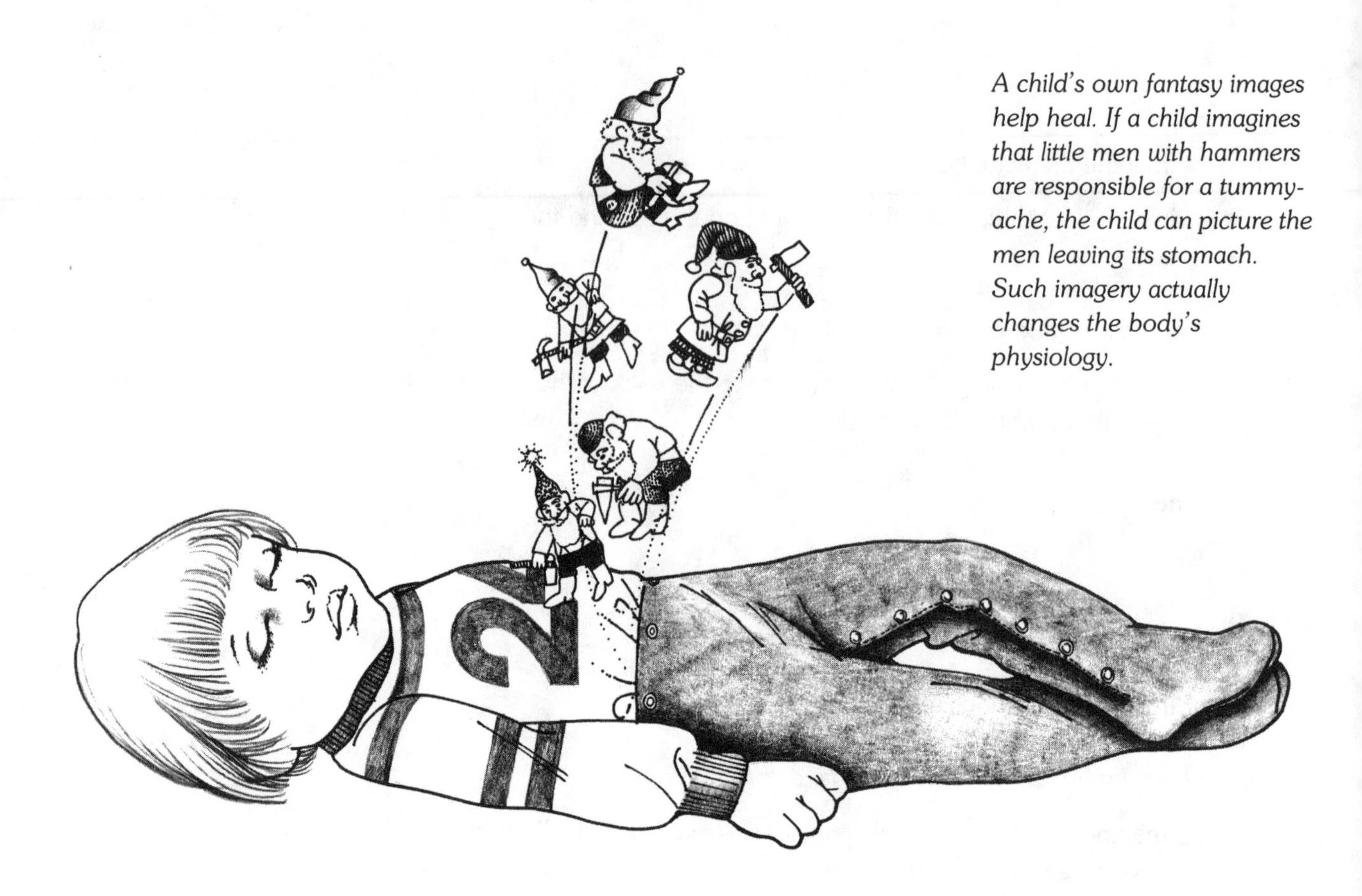

A child's own fantasy images help heal. If a child imagines that little men with hammers are responsible for a tummy-ache, the child can picture the men leaving its stomach. Such imagery actually changes the body's physiology.

Imagine the sides of the cut stick together with glue.

Imagine the line of the cut gets smoother and then disappears.

Nosebleed

Imagine somebody puts a cork in the tiny hole where the blood is coming from.

Bruises

Imagine the hurt floats away like a cloud.

Imagine the black and blue turns into tiny dots and disappears.

Insect bites and stings

Imagine the hurt flies away with the insect.

Imagine the hurt goes out of the sting hole and disappears.

Continued

Imagine the hurt turns into a dot, gets tinier and tinier, and disappears.

Burns

Imagine the burned area feels like ice water.

Imagine the burned area gets smaller and smaller until it's a dot and then disappears completely.

Broken bones

Imagine your body is like a rubber person and it will soon go back straight.

Imagine a person is cementing little white bricks between the bones.

Imagine the bones are being stuck together with white glue and will be stronger than ever.

Fright

Imagine a very happy, relaxing scene—like being at the beach.

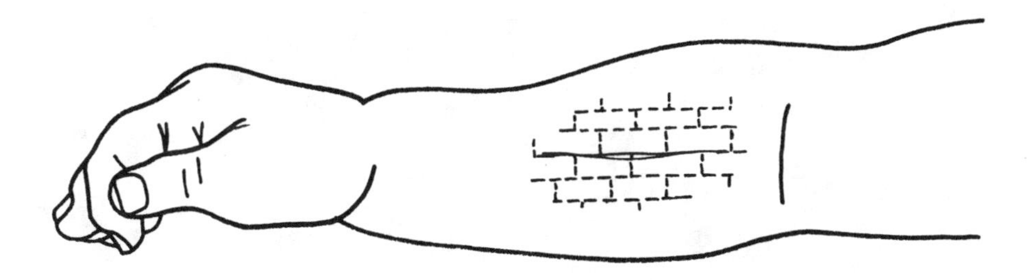

Older babies can speed their bodies' healing processes if they imagine a cut is closing up with tiny bricks.

Chapter 12

Working with the doctor

The role of the pediatrician is a unique one in medicine. More than any other medical specialists, pediatricians are *philosophers,* because they mainly see healthy or mildly ill children, and much of their time is spent answering questions to allay parents' fears. Those questions frequently concern normal incidents in the daily course of development. The answer that the pediatrician gives is generally a combination of scientific research and personal philosophy. The pediatrician's answer involves his or her attitude toward life. Hence the pediatrician-philosopher.

The pediatrician is an authority on children who is readily available to most parents. The doctor has seen thousands of children of all ages and therefore is expected to have knowledge of normal behavior, as well as of health and disease. The pediatrician's knowledge of normal child development is based on observation of children in the office, on discussion with parents, and on scientific training in child development. In the last ten years, a new field of *behavioral pediatrics* has emerged. Recent research has given doctors much greater knowledge of developmental, behavioral, and psychosocial problems in childhood. Most of the questions pediatricians hear have been asked by hundreds of parents before, and the pediatricians' answers are usually in the form of brief talks which contain the same significant points each time. Although these speeches on "normal development" or even on many diseases vary somewhat from one pediatrician to another, they are increasingly based on scientific studies.

The functions of a pediatrician

Prenatal advice on nutrition, drugs, and attitudes toward the baby

Newborn physical exam plus information and advice on (breast) feeding and early infant care

Well baby exams to check on growth and development, administer immunizations, provide advice on feeding, and answer questions on development, behavior, and preschool functioning

Answering questions by phone when a child is ill or hurt

Diagnosis and treatment of minor illness or injury with medical advice and/or drugs

Diagnosis and treatment of emergencies and serious illness with highly technical knowledge, equipment, and medicines

Referral of particular problems to the proper specialists

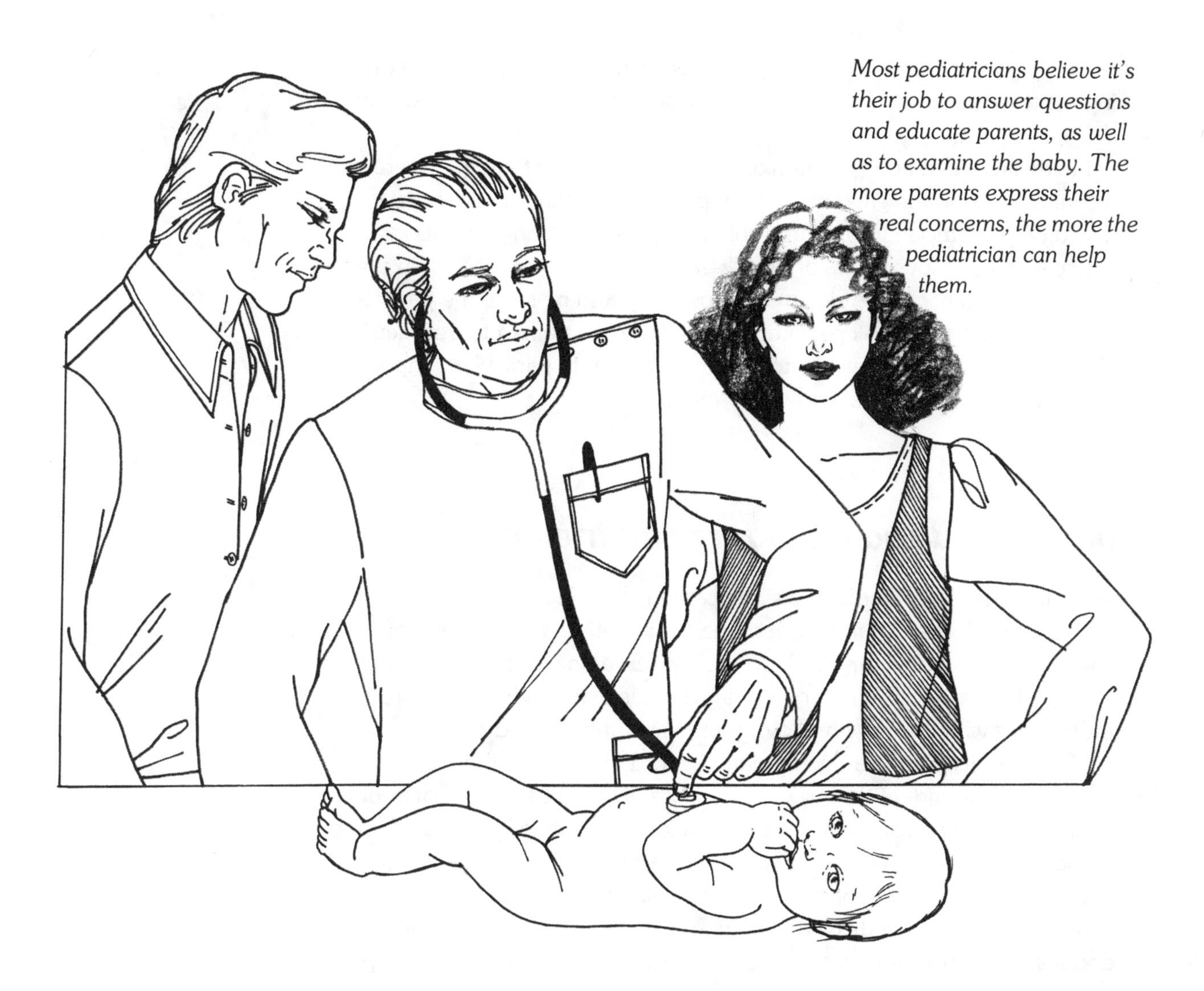

Most pediatricians believe it's their job to answer questions and educate parents, as well as to examine the baby. The more parents express their real concerns, the more the pediatrician can help them.

Doctor visits for well baby checkups

For most parents their major contact with the pediatrician is in well baby checkups. These vary widely depending on the pediatrician. Many doctors focus on the physical exam and on telling parents that development is normal. Some add to this their personal regimen for introduction of foods in the first year. And others encourage lengthy discussions to educate and reassure parents about all aspects of baby care.

Doctor visits for illness and accidents

The second most requent category of doctor-parent contact is treatment of minor illness, either over the phone or in the office. Some doctors encourage phone contact and may even treat things over the phone; others do not. Some doctors are generally conservative in their handling of minor illness, preferring to observe a child and use simple treatment before ordering lab tests and prescribing drugs. Other doctors like to use lab tests and drugs more routinely.

Major illnesses among children are significantly lower than they were half a century ago, so the great majority of parents nowadays never have to consult a pediatrician for major problems. However, many parents carry the specter of serious illness or rare disease in their minds, and often the pediatrician functions to rule out this possibility and reassure the parents that a child is all right. All pediatricians are basically trained to treat serious illness, but some academic doctors concentrate on it, particularly those pediatricians who teach at a medical school.

Choosing and evaluating a pediatrician

It is important that parents take some care in choosing a pediatrician because the doctor can take care of their child for years. A generation ago it was not uncommon for a child to see the same doctor from birth until college. This is less common now, with families being more and more mobile and with the growth of group practices and prepaid clinics.

Most parents choose a pediatrician by word of mouth—the majority on the advice of friends and some on the advice of their obstetrician or another doctor. Basically most parents want a doctor whom they have confidence in medically and whom they can relate to easily.

Parents are usually happier with their choice of a pediatrician if they evaluate their own needs before making a decision. Then when they hear about or see a doctor they are able to ask specific questions which help them decide whether or not they will be happy with that doctor. Both lay people and doctors tend to be happiest with and recommend pediatricians who are most like themselves philosophically. For instance, a parent who attends La Leche International League meetings or an obstetrician who practices natural childbirth will both recommend a pediatrician who encourages breast-feeding. A parent whose child has had serious illnesses or a doctor at a medical school will recommend an academic pediatrician.

Many parents do not realize how widely pediatricians vary, not so much in terms of medical competence, but in style and philosophy. One doctor might spend most time on the physical exam, another on nutritional scheduling, another on psychology. Moreover, doctors' approaches to nutrition can vary widely, from bottle-feeding and introduction of solid foods at two weeks to breast-feeding and delayed introduction of solid foods at around six months. Once parents realize the breadth of differences in pediatric styles, they are in a position to choose a doctor whose style is right for them.

Medical competence in a pediatrician is much more difficult for parents to evaluate. Without medical training it is difficult to know whether a particular way of treating a situation is better than another. Even in accepted medical practice there is a great range in competent treatment of many situations. On the other hand, there is such a thing as bad medical practice. Often parents intuitively pick this up when they feel uncomfortable with the way a doctor is handling a situation. It may be because the treatment varies from similar situations the parents know about, or because the doctor's explanation of the treatment just doesn't make sense to them. Advice or evaluation from a second doctor is one way a layperson can evaluate medical competence, either in initially choosing a pediatrician or in the midst of an uncomfortable situation.

Parents' needs in relation to choosing a pediatrician

Parents should ask themselves how important their need is in each category, and then try to see that the pediatrician they choose meets their major needs. They can ask specific questions of the doctor or of friends who have seen that doctor.

Medical competence

Reassurance of worries

Specific information about nutrition, sleep, etc.

Information about normal growth and development:
- Physical development
- Emotional/psychological development
- Social/behavioral development

Doctor's ability to relate to (young) children

Amount of discussion, answering questions

Specialty knowledge about rare or serious illnesses

Short, efficient visits with little waiting

Telephone availability during day, evening, weekend

Assertive treatment—heavy use of drugs, lab tests

Encourages natural treatment

Economic—cost of care

Encourages breast-feeding

Encourages late introduction of solid foods

Getting satisfaction from the doctor

Choose a doctor that suits your family.

Make lists of questions before an appointment and then make sure the doctor satisfactorily answers each question.

Tell the doctor your own feelings.

Make the doctor aware of you and your child's special needs.

Express disagreement immediately and frankly so it can be resolved.

Make the doctor aware of possible problems in following a prescribed treatment—your own or the child's.

When at home, telephone the doctor if worries persist, something unexpected arises, or treatment doesn't seem to be working.

Make the doctor aware of financial burdens, discuss prices openly, and request generic prescriptions, especially if price is important.

Feel free to explain problems in scheduling or making appointments, such as work or school hours, other children, long waits in the office, long distance to the office.

Helping parents get what they want from a pediatrician

Many parents feel they have little or no influence over what happens to them in the doctor's office. Actually, parents can have a great effect on the kind of care they and their child receive. First, parents must speak up for what they want. This means asking questions about what concerns them and telling the doctor when they don't like or understand something. It means continuing to ask questions and not leaving until they are satisfied. Finally, it means switching to another pediatrician if they are unhappy with their doctor's style, explanations, or competence.

Speaking out certainly works on an individual level. If many people speak out, they can have a profound effect on the style of medicine practiced. In less than a decade, for example, consumer interest has changed much of American obstetrics from caudal anesthesia and delivery by forceps to informed natural childbirth. This change resulted from patients making their wants known and choosing obstetricians who practiced natural delivery.

The more actively parents participate in their child's health care, the more likely they are to get what they want. One of the major goals of this book is to help parents participate more in pediatric care through educating themselves and speaking out.

The physical exam

In the course of a regular visit, pediatricians will do a history and physical exam to make sure a child is healthy and is developing within normal variances. Pediatricians have two basic ways of evaluating a child. First, pediatricians have seen literally thousands of children, and they have a *feeling* for whether or not a child looks healthy. Second, pediatricians know what questions to ask and what physical signs to look for to make sure problems are not arising.

A physical exam consists of experienced general observation and ruling out specific conditions. The office visit is not a mysterious ritual; each step is designed to elicit specific information. In part, the mystery that surrounds medicine comes from the doctor's "backward" approach. That is, the doctor works backward from the signs and symptoms of a number of known diseases to the situation at hand. If a sign or symptom is *not* present, the doctor concludes that the child is all right. In general, doctors don't expect a symptom to be present, but they follow a brief, simple routine which is systematically designed to pick up problems if they are present. Once parents understand the routine, the mystery is gone.

There are two basic types of physical exam that are used, based on the child's age and reason for being seen. The most common is the well baby check or check for minor illness. The second type is the newborn exam, which is done at birth to rule out any serious diseases or birth defects.

The well baby exam

History

The first thing doctors do is take a history; that is, they ask the parents how the baby is. On a first visit doctors will ask questions about the mother's pregnancy and delivery to see if there were any problems. The doctor will ask about rubella, infections, toxemia, RH incompatibility, anesthesia at birth, and whether the baby had any initial difficulty breathing. The doctor will check on the baby's motor landmarks and at what ages they occurred, on the baby's diet and eating habits, and on the baby's history of accidents or illnesses, if any. The doctor will also ask about the family's history (particularly the mother and father's) of allergy, diabetes, or inherited diseases.

If the child has come for a well baby checkup or a normal physical, the doctor will ask what the child has done since the last visit, concentrating on motor landmarks, nutrition, sleep, and social behavior. The doctor will also ask if the parents have any problems or any questions about the child's growth and development. Throughout the history the doctor is able to observe how the child is acting, what the parents are like, and the relationship between the child and the parents. Many doctors consider the history to be one of the most important parts of the checkup. In a well baby check, the history gives the doctor a picture of how things are going and an indication of problem areas and potential illness. For example, a history of feeding problems, poor weight gain, and allergy in the mother may indicate the possibility of low-grade food allergies in the baby. The story of the symptoms and their progression often allows the doctor to make a provisional diagnosis even before examining the child. Each disease has a fairly typical story. During the history the doctor will see if the parents' story matches any typical disease story. Examples of typical disease stories are contained in this book in the *Description* section under each illness in chapter 9, "Diagnosis and Treatment of Common Medical Problems."

After the history the doctor conducts the physical exam. This is usually done with the child's clothes off, in a step-by-step manner, although the sequence may vary. In a well baby check the doctor examines the whole child, but if the visit is due to a specific problem such as an infected finger, the doctor will probably omit parts of the routine exam and concentrate on the problem area.

Weight, height

These measurements give an indication of the child's growth pattern over time, as well as indicating a child's position relative to normal growth curves. A healthy baby will tend to have a fairly smooth rate of growth. Generally the babies are weighed without their clothes, on an infant scale. Their heights are measured with a tape or by laying them on a calibrated board; the head is held against the headboard and one leg is stretched to its full length. Babies often cry at the coldness of the scale and its sense of precariousness, and not infrequently they express indignation at being stretched on the measuring board. By two years of age the child is weighed and measured while standing.

General appearance

The doctor looks to see if the child appears healthy—has good skin color, alertness, energy, and a reasonable weight for its size.

Skin

The doctor looks to see that the skin has a healthy color and is not excessively pale (anemic), blue (cyanotic), or yellow (jaundiced). The doctor will also check to see the skin has good elastic tone, indicating the child is not dehydrated. Finally the doctor will check to see if there are any skin blemishes such as birthmarks or rashes. Many skin lesions are normal in infancy. (See chapter 6, "The Newborn.")

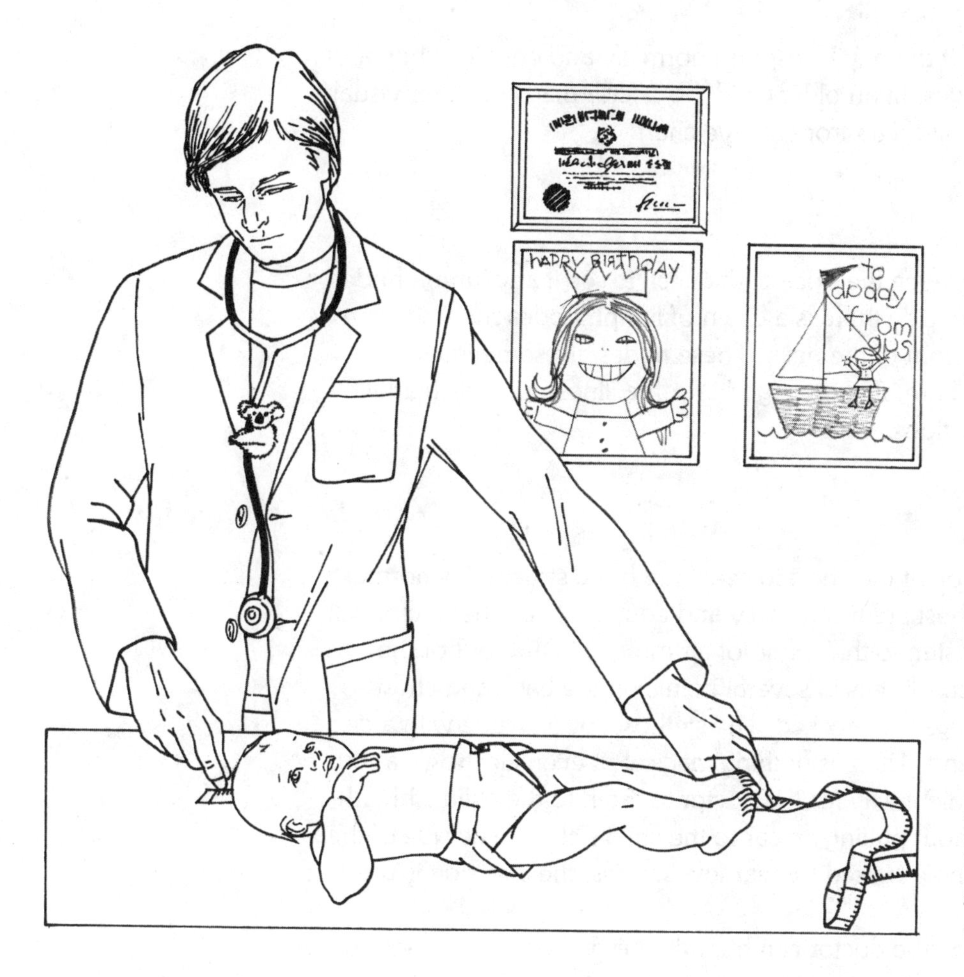

The young baby's height is measured with a tape or by gently stretching the baby out on a measuring board.

Head

In a young baby the pediatrician will check the fontanels (soft spots) and the lines between the skull plates to make sure they are closing at a normal rate. The doctor will also observe the shape of the skull and measure the skull's circumference to make sure it is developing normally. In very rare cases unusual skull shape or size may indicate some kind of neurological condition. While checking the head, the doctor will also glance at the scalp for cradle cap, head lice, etc.

Eyes

The doctor will look at the eyes to see if the baby can follow an object evenly with both eyes. Uneven movement may indicate strabismus. The doctor will examine the membrane of the eyelid for discharge or excessive redness—signs of a possible conjunctivitis. The doctor will look in the child's eyes with an ophthalmoscope, a special optical tool that makes it possible to see the back of the eye (the retina), or its red reflection. The doctor will also notice if the pupils respond normally and equally when a light is shined at the eyes. In an older child the doctor may check for visual acuity by having the child read from an eye chart.

Neck

The doctor will gently touch the sides of the neck to see if any lumph nodes are enlarged. On either side there is a chain of lymph nodes running from behind the ear to the front of the neck. These nodes are sometimes enlarged normally and are often enlarged in some illnesses, particularly in upper respiratory infections.

Chest

First the doctor will look at the chest to see if the bone structure is normal and the walls of the chest are rising easily and equally. Then the doctor will use a stethoscope to listen to the sound of air moving in and out of the child's lungs. The doctor listens at several points on the back and chest so that all areas of the lungs are checked. The stethoscope is a tube with a disc or an opening at the end. There is nothing magical or even electronic about it; it is simply a convenient way for the doctor to listen to the child's breathing (or heartbeat) without putting an ear to the child's chest. The side of the stethoscope with the hole is used to hear low sounds; the disc side is used to hear high sounds.

With the stethoscope the doctor can hear diminished or unusual sounds in the lungs. Normal breathing noises making whooshing sounds, like air going through a pipe. When there is fluid from inflammation in the bronchial tubes, then the doctor hears pops, crackles, squeaks, and wheezes because the fluid impairs the air flow. From the type of sound the doctor can tell much about the nature of an illness. Bronchitis, or infection of the large tubes of the lung, has coarse crackles called *ronchi;* asthma has musical squeaks called *wheezes;* pneumonia, an infection of the tiny air sacs, has fine crackles called *rales.*

Heart

The doctor will also use the stethoscope to listen to the sounds that the heart makes as it pumps. The doctor will be attentive to the rate and the rhythm, as well as the quality of the heart sounds. By listening to the heart of a newborn or very young infant, the doctor can pick up many of the rare congenital heart defects such as improper valve functioning or openings in the walls between the chambers of the heart. These defects produce abnormal heart sounds. The normal heartbeat sounds like lub-DUB (emphasis on the second sound). A defect in a valve or wall produces an extra sound called a murmur. In addition to the normal lub-DUB, a SHHH sound or rumble is heard: Lub-SHHH-DUB. Most murmurs are *not* due to congenital heart defects, but are the result of normal heart function in young children and go away as the child's heart matures (see *Congenital heart defects* in chapter 13, "Rare Diseases"). During a routine physical of a healthy older baby, it is very rare for a doctor suddenly to pick up a murmur caused by congenital heart disease.

Abdomen

The doctor will feel the child's belly to see whether it is tender, hard, or has unusual masses in it. In a well baby checkup this is done to rule out a very rare, surgically correctable kidney tumor. In children with stomach pain this part of the exam is done to rule out appendicitis or any other unusual condition.

The doctor will also check the genitalia and rectum for abnormalities. The doctor may feel along the line where the leg joins the abdomen for possible hernias or enlarged lymph nodes. Enlarged lymph nodes in the junction between leg and torso may be a sign of infection, but they also occur normally.

Extremities

The doctor will check the child's arms and legs for muscle development and coordination. With young babies the doctor checks to see that the creases in the baby's legs are equal and that the legs can rotate outward. This is to check for a rare condition called *congenital dislocation of the hips,* which requires treatment. The doctor will look for bowlegs, knock-knees, toeing-in, and flat feet. The doctor will also watch toddlers walk in order to

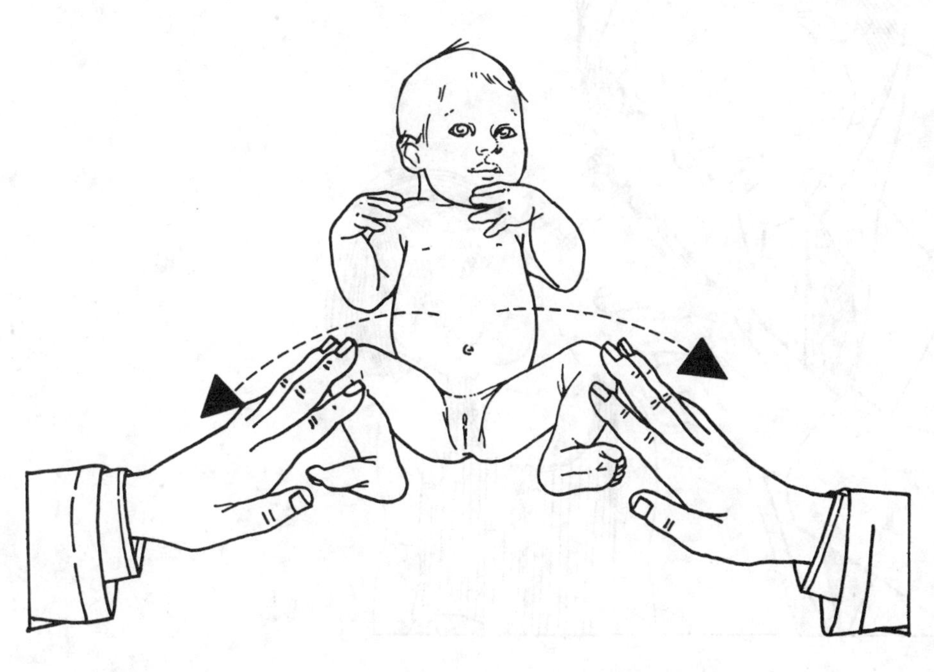

To check for a rare congenital hip condition, the doctor spreads the baby's legs out in a froglike position. There is no "click" if the baby's hip joints are normal. The procedure looks strange but does not hurt the baby.

see that their gait is developing properly. Parents often ask the doctor about bowlegs in the first year or so, and about toeing-in and flat feet during the toddler years. These conditions are common in young children. They generally correct themselves and rarely require treatment. Occasionally pronounced toeing-in is referred to an orthopedist, who may prescribe special shoes.

Mouth, throat, and ears

The examination of the throat and ears is generally saved till the end of the physical exam because it is most likely to be bothersome to a young child. This part of the examination is not painful, but young children often become frightened by it or balk at having to open their mouth, turn their head, or hold still. It is not uncommon for a young child to cry at this point. Sometimes the pediatrician has to hold the child still or have the mother hold the child.

First the doctor will look at the teeth to see the pattern of eruption and to see if there are any obvious cavities. Then the doctor will examine the throat by pressing the tongue down with a depressor and shining in a light.

The doctor looks at the baby's eardrum with an instrument called an otoscope. Healthy eardrums are shiny and cup in slightly.

Many doctors use the light system of the otoscope without its lens system (see below). The doctor looks to see if the back of the throat (the pharynx) or the tonsils are red, inflamed, or mucus-covered. Redness in the back of the throat is the most common and reliable physical sign of a cold. Since colds are by far the most common disease of childhood, a red throat is by far the most frequent "abnormal" finding in a physical exam (see *Common cold* and *Strep throat*).

The doctor will use an otoscope to check the child's ears. The otoscope is nothing more than a light source with a magnifying glass on one end and a funnel-shaped cone on the other end. The light is directed so that it shines through the cone; the cone itself helps to straighten out the ear canal so that the doctor can see the drum. Occasionally the doctor has to clean wax out of the ear with a small, spoon-shaped instrument before the drum can be visualized. A normal eardrum is slightly concave and appears like a metallic reflection. An infected eardrum (otitis media) appears red and swollen; an eardrum with fluid behind it (serous otitis media) appears dull and the fluid level may be visible.

Because ear infection is one of the most common causes of fever and general discomfort in very young children, the ears must be examined in any child with a fever, even though it may make the child cry. In a well baby check, a doctor will occasionally pick up a slightly red drum or fluid behind the ear.

The newborn exam

Most babies are routinely examined several times in the first few days after birth. The first time, the baby is generally examined by the obstetrician right after birth. The second exam, the major one, is done by a pediatrician twelve to twenty-four hours after birth. With minor variations the exam resembles the complete physical just described. The third exam is a brief formality done as part of the baby's discharge from the hospital. If the baby and mother are discharged within a few hours after birth, then only a brief initial exam may be done, usually by a pediatrician. The goal of these exams is to identify and help any newborns who have problems, whether they be due to congenital birth defects, birth trauma, or illness. Parents can be reassured that after the exam the pediatrician will have picked up almost any problem.

The initial exam at birth is generally done after the placenta has been delivered. The doctor looks at the baby to see if there are any obvious birth defects. The doctor then does an Apgar evaluation to assess the baby's whole response to extrauterine life. The doctor checks to see that the baby's heart rate, breathing, muscle tone, and responsiveness are normal. A healthy baby has a heart rate over 100, shows good breathing, good motion, coughs when mucus is suctioned out, and is pink as opposed to

The Apgar score

	0	1	2
Heart rate	Absent	Slow, under 100	Over 100
Breathing	Absent	Slow, irregular	Good, crying
Muscle tone	Limp	Some movement of extremities	Active motion
Response to nasal suctioning	No response	Grimace	Cough or sneeze
Color	Blue or pale	Body pink; limbs blue	Completely pink

blue. Sometime after this, the baby is weighed and measured. A baby is generally considered healthy if its birth weight is within normal range for its gestational age, if it is vigorous and pink, and if it has no obvious birth defects.

In the Apgar evaluation, the baby is given 0, 1, or 2 points in each category depending on its condition at birth. A newborn in the best condition gets an Apgar score of 8–10.

The next exam, which is generally done by a pediatrician, is a full physical. First the doctor observes the baby, noticing its movements, skin tone, and nutritional status. The doctor then goes through the same sequence (skin, head, neck, etc.) as the general physical, but concentrating on whether the structures themselves are fully formed and functional.

Skin

In checking the skin the doctor is especially looking for birthmarks and any signs of cyanosis (blueness) or jaundice (yellowness). Significant yellowness indicates possible blood group incompatibility (Rh or ABO) or infection. Mild jaundice on the second or third day in a healthy baby is usually normal and is the result of immature development of liver enzymes. Significant, persistent blueness can be an indication of heart or lung problems. There are many birthmarks normal to newborns (see *Newborn* description).

Head

In checking the head the doctor is most interested in the fontanels, the natural sutures between the plates of the skull, and the molding due to passage through the birth canal. The doctor checks to see that the sutures do not overlap and that there is no bleeding under the skin of the scalp. The latter condition, called *cephalohematoma,* produces a soft, fluid bulge on the head. It is a not uncommon newborn condition which may be upsetting to see, but which goes away by itself.

Face

The doctor examines the eyes to see that they are structurally complete and normal, with equal movements on both sides. The doctor checks the nose to see that the nostrils are properly open, and the mouth to see that the palate separating the mouth and nose is complete. The doctor checks the ears to see if the external pinna are present and the ear canals are open.

Chest and abdomen

The doctor notes the shape of the chest and abdomen, and makes sure the normal complement of bones and muscles is present. Then the doctor listens to the baby's chest with a stethoscope to make sure that the breath and hearth sounds are normal and the breathing is free and easy (see *The well baby exam* in Chapter 12).

Genitalia, anus, and extremities

The doctor looks at the genitalia and anus, and notes if the urethral opening is normal, the testes are descended (in a boy), the vagina and labia are normal (in a girl), the anus is open, and there is no additional opening in the back (spinal defects or rectal sinuses). On the extremities the doctor checks to see that all the bones are present and normal, and that the child has the correct number of fingers and toes.

Neurological signs and behavior

The newborn physical is completed with a *neurological* exam. This exam is designed to evaluate the functioning of the baby's central and peripheral nervous system. It differs from an adult exam in several ways, as will be apparent. First, the doctor observes the child's movements, posture, and general muscle tone. Then the doctor checks the baby's repertoire of reflexes, including sucking, grasp, and Moro (see chapter 6, "The Newborn," for a complete list and description of the reflexes).

Some doctors complete the neurological with a test of infant behavior derived from an exam developed by Dr. T. Berry Brazelton. The doctor assesses the baby's response to a flashlight, a bell, touch, and animate and inanimate stimuli. The doctor observes how quickly the baby tends to become excited by and quiet after any stimulus. The doctor also evaluates the baby for cuddliness, consolability, self-quieting ability, and other general behavioral characteristics. If the mother is present during the exam, the doctor can also evaluate the mother-infant relationship and bonding (see chapter 6, "The Newborn").

Your child and the doctor

In the first few months of life most babies are relatively unfazed by visits to the doctor. Many enjoy car rides and don't object to strange places like the office or strange people like the pediatrician and the nurse. Also, most young babies don't mind being held or touched, but they may object to the startling coldness of instruments or to being forced to stretch or turn their heads. And most babies seem to have a relatively short memory concerning the brief discomfort of their early injections.

Between six months and three years or so, it is usually quite a different situation. In this period the child has a variety of natural behavior patterns that make doctor visits quite a bit more troublesome—for the baby, the parents, and the doctor. Somewhere around six months most babies begin to be uncomfortable around strangers (especially men) and anxious when away from their parents.

Not surprisingly most babies also begin to show the results of classical conditioning to an unpleasant stimulus—namely the injections. If a doctor were trying to create a situation in which children would have a lifelong fear of doctor visits, there could be no better way than to subject the child to a painful stimulus on most of the visits for the first year. This is a negative side-effect of the present infant immunization schedule. Subsequently, one- to two-year-olds are brought to the doctor only when they are ill. No one likes to travel or be handled when he or she is ill, least of all young children who don't even understand why it is necessary. Moreover, most parents are somewhat anxious when their one- or two-year-old children are sick, which is something the children do pick up.

By three or four most children are into a whole fantasy world, including fears and phobias about injury and illness, as well as their first comprehension of death. Also by three or four many children have had experience with grandparents, parents, or their older friends being seriously ill. In this mixture of fantasy and experience the doctor appears to be a little known but authoritative and perhaps frightening figure. There is no time in a very young child's life, other than a physical exam, when the parents force the child against its will to be handled, and sometimes even hurt, by a relative stranger, while the parents stand by or even hold the child still. This may seem to paint a diabolical picture, but probably for many children this is exactly how a doctor visit is thought of. It is truly sad that the major health figure in most children's lives should be presented to the children in this way. Certainly this picture cannot be a healing one, although most children get better in spite of it. The result of this situation is that many children are afraid to go to the doctor and may even cry about it. In fact, children sometimes magically get better if they think a doctor visit may be in order.

There are several things parents can do that may help to improve this unfortunate situation. First, if parents simply realize that a child may be upset by a doctor visit, they are likely to handle the situation in a more reasonable way, thereby making it easier for the child. Second, it is helpful if parents are frank and open about the doctor and if they educate children about the doctor, his office, and his tools. Third, the parents can provide a "safe base" for children by remaining with them, holding them during the exam, and even by bringing a favorite animal, doll, or blanket along. Finally, if a child becomes very upset, the parents can discuss it with the doctor.

Chapter 13

Rare diseases

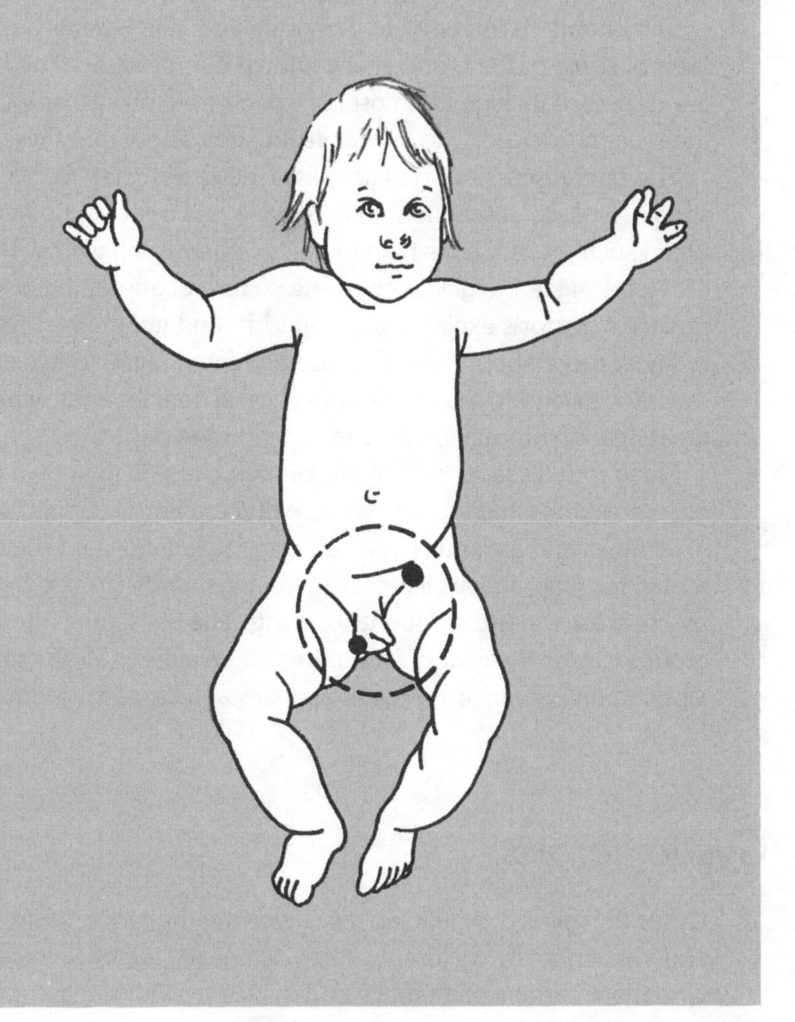

Rare diseases are rare

Due to the remarkable advances brought about by hygiene, immunizations, and antibiotics, many of the serious illnesses that can affect young children are now rare. People's fear of rare diseases is generally far out of proportion to their incidence. Several things contribute to this exaggerated fear: (1) within the last hundred years a significant number of young children did die (of common contagious diseases, not of rare diseases); (2) modern medicine, including pediatrics, focuses its huge resources and teaching on rare diseases; (3) the lay media—particularly television and newspapers—deal almost exclusively with dramatic stories of children and adults who are suddenly struck down by rare diseases.

In actuality the very great majority of young children do not get rare diseases and do not even become seriously ill from common diseases. This is not to say that rare diseases do not exist. Almost all parents have heard of some child in their community who has had one. Inevitably the parents think, "What if it had been my child?" Love and attachment make them afraid, which is a normal fear. What is not healthy—for the parents or the child—is if the parents become frightened of the possibility of a rare disease every time their child becomes ill.

This chapter is intended to demystify and give parents a more realistic view of some of the more widely known rare diseases. The diseases that are discussed include the most common rare diseases, as well as some of the most publicized. The incidence list shows how rare these diseases are.

The brief discussions on each disease are designed to give parents a simple, realistic description of the course and treatment of each illness. Often such explanations help to relieve parents' anxieties. The discussions are not designed to give a complete picture of any of the diseases, nor to replace a doctor's explanation, diagnosis, and treatment. Parents who need to know more about these diseases are encouraged to talk at length with their doctor and to make use of medical school libraries, which contain a great deal of information and are open to the public.

Many rare diseases are genetic or their cause is unknown. Modern science presumes that the diseases are due to chance. Spiritual philosophies in all times and all lands have put forth explanations for their causes. Currently, for most serious illnesses there are support groups that provide practical advice and emotional backing. The assistance offered by these groups can be invaluable for parents and children. Modern medicine is working on prevention of these illnesses and cures for them.

Incidence of rare diseases

Cystic fibrosis
1 in 2000
Sickle-cell anemia
1 in 500 (Blacks)
Congenital heart defects
1 in 100
Pyloric stenosis
1 in 500
Meningitis
1 in 100,000 per year
Cerebral palsy
1 in 1000
Down's syndrome (Mongolism)
1 in 1000
Phenylketonuria
1 in 10,000
Tay-Sachs
1 in 3600 (Ashkenazi Jews)
Sudden-infant-death syndrome (SIDS) (Crib death)
1.6 in 1,000
Childhood cancers
1.3 in 10,000
Kawasaki disease
1.5 in 250,000

Cystic fibrosis

Cystic fibrosis is a genetic disease involving the lungs, gastrointestinal tract, and sweat glands. Children with cystic fibrosis are born to parents *both* of whom are carriers of a particular gene. Any child of these parents has a 25 percent chance of having the disease. There is no cure for cystic fibrosis, but there is great variability in how a given child is affected. Some children with cystic fibrosis die in infancy; many survive into their teens or twenties. These children have frequent lung infections due to thick mucus, and they often have bulky, fatty stools and poor weight gain due to lack of pancreatic enzymes. Children with cystic fibrosis are treated with a special diet, lung exercises, and prompt treatment of lung infections.

Sickle-cell anemia

Sickle-cell anemia is a genetic disease involving the hemoglobin (oxygen-binding molecules) in the red blood cells. The disease is inherited from parents *both* of whom are carriers of a particular gene. *Any* child of these parents has a 25 percent chance of having the disease. The disease almost always occurs among children of black African ancestry. Carriers, people having one normal gene and one sickle gene, do not manifest the disease and are thought to have increased resistance to malaria, which is caused by a parasite that attacks the red blood cells. By natural selection carriers of the trait would tend to be numerous (up to 50 percent) in areas like Africa with a high incidence of malaria.

Children with sickle-cell disease (two affected genes) develop blood clots in the smallest blood vessels. This is due to the strange shape of their red blood cells which is caused by the altered hemoglobin. The sickle blood cells are also fragile and tend to break. This causes anemia—low red blood cell numbers—and results in anemic crises. The most common symptoms are the onset of pains in the legs and belly between nine and twelve months. Presently there is no cure for sickle-cell disease, but crises can be treated for years. A simple blood test shows the presence of altered red blood cells and can diagnose the disease or the trait.

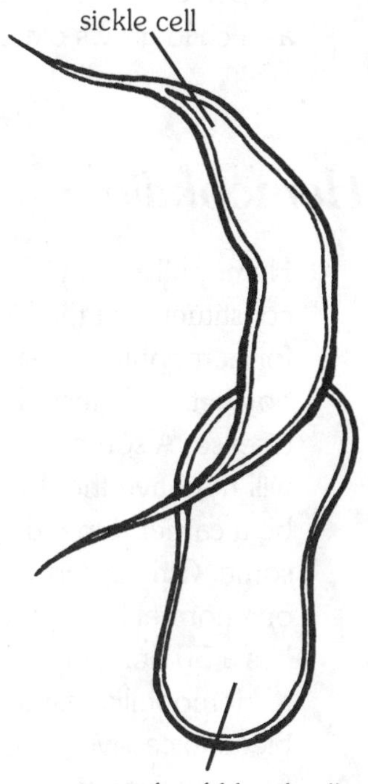

In a child with sickle-cell anemia, the red blood cells take on an unusual shape when they have little oxygen.

Congenital heart defects

In rare cases children are born with structural heart defects. Most heart defects are the result of an inherited predisposition interacting with environmental factors such as drugs or viruses. Generally the siblings of children with congenital heart defects are normal.

The heart is a complex, four-chambered pump and there are a number of different abnormalities involving the valves, the walls between the chambers, and the blood vessels coming to and leaving the heart. Congenital heart disease ranges from mild cases that do not need treatment and cure themselves, to serious cases that require surgery. Over 90 percent of congenital heart defects that don't heal by themselves are now surgically correctable.

Children who have heart defects are unable to circulate oxygen to their body's cells properly. Thus they may appear blue, breathe rapidly, and fail to grow and put on weight in a normal manner. Defects are diagnosed by a combination of physical exam, special X rays, and electrocardiogram. Unusual heart sounds (murmurs) often accompany structural defects, but 99 percent of all murmurs are *not* indicative of any disease and disappear as a child grows older.

Hemophilia

Hemophilia is an inherited bleeding disorder caused by defects in certain constituents of the blood that are responsible for normal clotting. The gene for hemophilia is carried on one of the female's X chromosomes. When a boy gets an affected X chromosome from his mother, he will have the disease. A son of the same mother who gets an unaffected X chromosome will not have the disease, and not be a carrier. A daughter may or may not be a carrier depending on whether or not she gets an affected X chromosome. Girl carriers never actually get the disease because they always have one normal X chromosome. Any son or daughter of a mother with the gene has a 50 percent chance of inheriting the gene.

Hemophilia can range widely in severity. Boys with mild cases may only bleed excessively during severe trauma. Boys with severe cases can have frequent serious episodes of spontaneous bleeding and difficulty in controlling bleeding even from minor wounds. Emergencies are treated by giving the boy blood components that speed clotting. Historically hemophilia has been of great interest because it descended and was expressed for centuries among the royalty of Europe.

Pyloric stenosis

Pyloric stenosis is an abnormality of the opening between the stomach and the small intestine, the pylorus. The circular muscle of the pylorus is greatly enlarged, which prevents normal passage of food from the stomach and causes vomiting. Children absorb little food in the small intestine and therefore show poor weight gain or even weight loss. They may also become dehydrated due to low fluid retention.

The condition shows up very early after birth and by a month of age has progressed from occasional vomiting to frequent and forceful projectile vomiting. (Occasional projectile vomiting is not uncommon among young babies. It is not due to pyloric stenosis and gets better by itself.) After a feeding the baby's upper belly will appear full, and actual churning may be seen as the stomach tries to force food through the narrowed opening. Pyloric stenosis is diagnosed with an X ray of the upper gastrointestinal tract

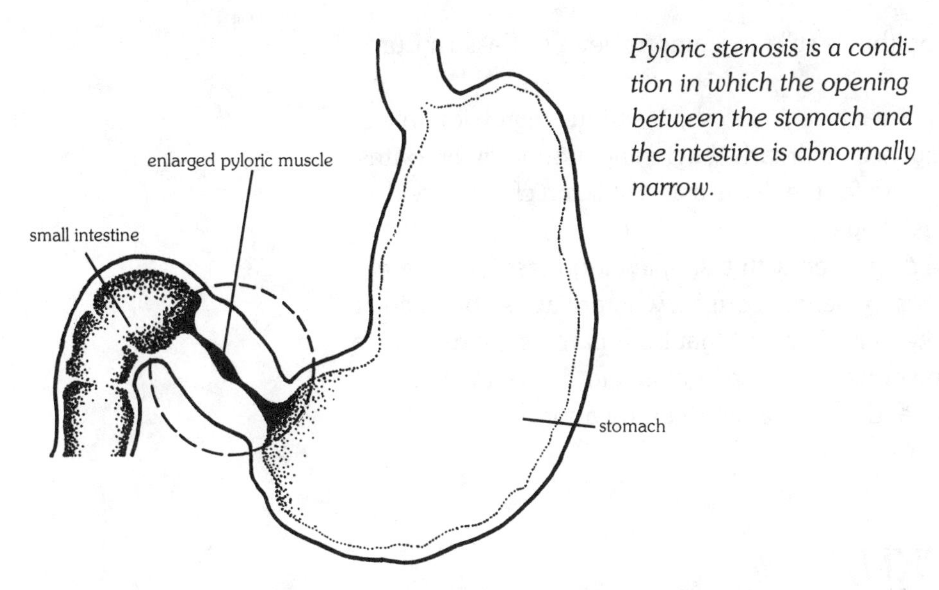

Pyloric stenosis is a condition in which the opening between the stomach and the intestine is abnormally narrow.

and is usually treated surgically. Simple widening of the pyloric opening completely corrects the condition. The cause of pyloric stenosis is unknown. The majority of cases are among boys. Occasionally the child's father has had pyloric stenosis also.

Infant hernias

An inguinal hernia is a small swelling or bulge in the area where the abdomen meets the legs. During normal embryonic development the lining of the abdomen forms the lining of the scrotum (or its female analogue) and separates from the abdomen. A hernia results when this separation is not complete. The mass or bulge consists of abdominal tissue or fluid pushed into this little sac. The condition occurs ten times as frequently among boys as among girls, and simple surgery corrects it. Without treatment the blood supply to the bowel can be squeezed off and the tissue can deteriorate, which can be dangerous.

Another kind of hernia sometimes occurs around the naval. This umbilical hernia does *not* usually need treatment. It corrects itself as the abdominal musculature matures.

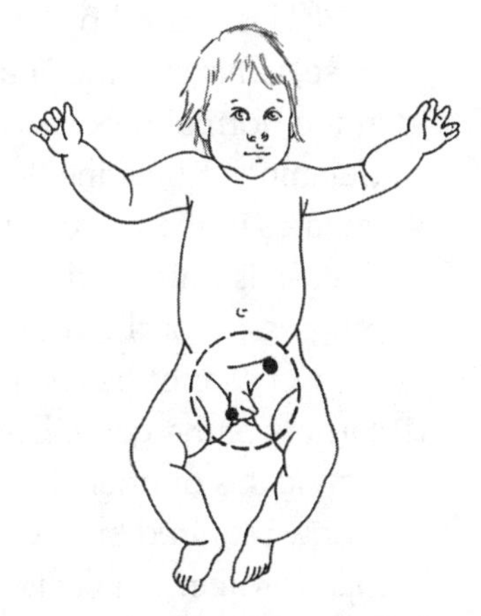

The most common site for infant hernias is in the area where the leg meets the abdomen.

Tay-Sachs disease

Tay-Sachs disease is an inherited disorder of the central nervous system that is extremely rare. Fatty acids accumulate in the brain due to a genetic enzyme deficiency. A child with Tay-Sachs inherits an affected gene from each parent. Both of the parents are normal, but carry the gene. Thus any child of two carrier parents has a one-in-four chance of being affected.

Tay-Sachs is most common (but is still rare) among Jews of Eastern European descent (Ashkenazi).

A baby with Tay-Sachs disease begins to show serious regression in motor, sensory, and intelligence landmarks beginning around five months of age. There is no known cure for the disease and afflicted children seldom survive beyond three years of age.

The carrier state can be diagnosed with a simple blood test. There are programs in most large cities to identify couples who are at risk of having a child with Tay-Sachs. In the unlikely event that both parents are carriers, a test (amniocentesis) can be done early in pregnancy to determine if the fetus will have the disease, and if so, the fetus can be aborted.

Phenylketonuria (PKU)

Phenylketonuria is an extremely rare inherited disorder that causes severe mental retardation. An affected child inherits one gene for PKU from each parent, both of whom are normal but carry the trait. Each child of these parents has a one-in-four chance of being affected.

PKU is caused by low activity of a single enzyme (phenylalanine hydroxylase). This enzyme enables the body to break down one fraction of protein in the normal process of digestion—that is, convert the amino acid phenylalanine to tyrosine. Without normal enzyme activity phenylalanine accumulates in the body in very high levels and is excreted in the urine. If the disease is untreated, brain damage begins in the first weeks after birth and progresses for the next several years.

PKU cannot be disgnosed in the uterus and there is no test to identify carriers of the gene. But PKU can be disgnosed in newborns by testing for high levels of phenylketonuria in the blood or urine. In many states testing is now required by law. The test is not valid until the infant has had sufficient milk (protein) intake to cause accumulation of phenylalanine. Thus an infant who leaves the hospital in less than twenty-four hours should not even have blood drawn for testing. Ideally, a urine test should be done at about two weeks of age.

If the disease is diagnosed by three months of age, the child can be put on a special diet that is low in phenylalanine. Mental retardation is prevented or reduced if the child is kept on the diet for at least four or five years.

Down's syndrome (formerly called Mongolism)

Down's syndrome is a form of mental retardation caused by an extra chromosome. Humans normally have 46 chromosomes—23 from the mother and 23 from the father. Due to a failure of the chromosomes to divide evenly in the formation of the egg (or sperm), a child can be born with an extra chromosome (47 chromosomes). Down's syndrome children have a characteristic appearance in addition to being mentally retarded.

Children with Down's syndrome are much more frequent among mothers over thirty-five years of age. Uneven cell division during egg formation is more common among older women, possibly because all of a woman's egg cells have been present in an incomplete form since birth, and so are older. Generally Down's syndrome is a onetime genetic accident, not a carried disease which is inherited. An older woman who has had a Down's syndrome child has a 1 percent greater chance of having another Down's syndrome child than an older woman who has not had a Down's child.

Risk of Down's syndrome by maternal age

Maternal age	*Frequency of Down's syndrome*
30	1/885
35	1/365
40	1/109
45	1/32

Meningitis

Meningitis is an infection of the lining of the spinal cord caused by various bacteria or viruses. Inflammation of the spinal cord lining can cause stiff neck, vomiting, convulsions, headache, fever, and drowsiness. Each of these symptoms, by itself, is much more commonly caused by other diseases. Spinal meningitis is diagnosed by the presence of cells or bacteria in the spinal fluid. Bacterial meningitis is treated assertively with antibiotics. Although meningitis is a serious disease, most cases are now curable.

Cerebral palsy

Cerebral palsy is a term that refers to nonprogressive disorders of the motor system that are present at birth and appear during the first year. Children with cerebral palsy often have difficulty speaking and controlling muscle movements. Their movements characteristically appear jerky or spastic. A child can be affected variably in the arms, legs, and right or left side. In one-third of the cases the cause is unknown. Other cases are caused by a variety of environmental factors, including prenatal or fetal infection, anoxia (oxygen deprivation), drugs, trauma, and maternal hemorrhage.

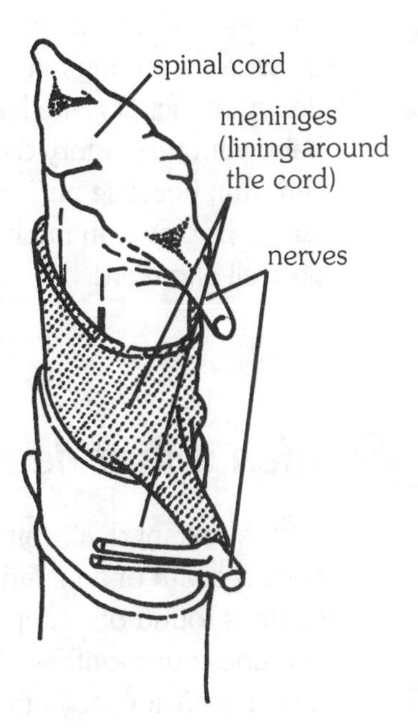

Meningitis is an infection of the lining of the spinal cord.

Muscular dystrophy

Muscular dystrophy refers to a group of genetically linked diseases involving progressive weakness and shrinking of large skeletal muscles. The most common form, which is called Duchennes, is linked to the female chromosome. The gene for Duchennes is transmitted by a mother who carries the gene but doesn't manifest the disease. Each of her sons has a 50 percent chance of getting the gene and the disease; each of her daughters has a 50 percent chance of getting the gene and becoming a carrier of the gene. Women do not manifest the disease because they have one normal X chromosome; men show the disease because they have only one (affected) X chromosome and the genes on it are not overshadowed by another normal X chromosome. A child with Duchennes shows progressive weakness of its legs and arms beginning between the ages of two and six. There is no cure for muscular dystrophy. Treatment involves extensive physical therapy and braces.

Hyaline membrane disease—or respiratory distress syndrome

Hyaline membrane disease refers to a condition in which a newborn's lungs have little air in them and consequently the baby has difficulty breathing. It occurs among premature infants.

A baby with the condition is immediately placed in an incubator to keep it warm and slightly increase the amount of oxygen it is getting. It is given IVs to keep up its fluid levels and to keep its acid-base balance normal. Frequent blood tests are made to keep track of the baby's ability to oxygenate its blood. In severe cases the baby's breathing is aided by a positive pressure breathing machine. It can be a serious disease and can cause death. In fact, it is the leading cause of death among premature babies. A baby with respiratory distress syndrome is moved to a specialized intensive care unit because nursing care and laboratory facilities are of great importance. Babies with mild cases start to improve after three or four days and do well afterward.

Sudden infant death syndrome—crib death

Sudden infant death syndrome (SIDS) refers to the sudden and unexpected death of an infant who is apparently healthy. No medical cause of death is found on autopsy. The peak incidence of SIDS occurs between two and four months; it is rare before two weeks and after six months of age. The incidence in the United States is 1.6 per 1,000 live births. Numerous causes have been suggested, but none have been proved. Some babies may have had a weak respiratory drive, others may have had a laryngeal condition that causes breathing to stop (apnea). It is also suspected that these babies may have brainstem or cardiac abnormalities. There is still little evidence as to whether home-monitoring of babies who have had apnea episodes is valuable. Generally monitoring is reserved for severe cases of diagnosed apnea in which there is a family history of SIDS. Less than 5 percent of all infants who die of SIDS have had apneac episodes. Although still low, the risk that future siblings will die of SIDS rises to 5 in 1,000. Parents always have an extremely difficult time when a child dies so suddenly and inexplicably. Often they feel that they must somehow be to blame, but this is not the case. Psychosocial support is valuable for families who have experienced SIDS, and support groups can offer great comfort. The National Sudden Infant Death Syndrome Foundation can provide information (301-459-3388).

Childhood cancers

Childhood cancers comprise an uncommon group of illnesses whose cause is still basically unknown. Cancer affects only 1 in 10,000 children. Many of these cancers have high cure rates, and children who would have died a few years ago are now surviving due to great advances in medical technology. Currently, treatment includes surgery, radiation, and chemotherapy. Most often, treatment involves a combination of these therapies. Bone marrow transplantation is a relatively new technique that is being used very successfully with a number of childhood cancers.

About 40 percent of all cancer in children under five years of age is *acute lymphoblastic leukemia* (*ALL*), a condition in which immature white blood cells grow at an uncontrolled rate within the bone marrow, crowding out the normal red blood cells, mature white blood cells, and platelets. ALL most commonly develops at about four years of age. Lack of red blood cells can cause the children to be pale and listless (anemic), lack of white blood cells can make the children susceptible to severe infections, and lack of platelets can predispose the children to excessive bleeding. The condition is diagnosed with a blood smear and a bone marrow test. With a combination of chemotherapeutic drugs, more than half of all children with leukemia are now being cured or become long-term survivors.

Neuroblastoma is a malignant tumor that arises from cells in the sympathetic nervous system and adrenal glands. Its incidence is 1 in 100,000. Children with neuroblastoma are most commonly diagnosed at around the age of two. They may have an abdominal mass or they may have bone pain, weight loss, and fever. When children develop this form of cancer under a year the survival rates are very good (80 percent). The rates are gradually improving for older children, in whom the disease is usually more widespread. Inexplicably, in 5–10 percent of all cases neuroblastoma is known to spontaneously regress, most often in children under a year.

Wilms tumor is a malignant tumor of the kidney that is commonly discovered at about the age of three. The incidence is 7 per 1,000,000. The disease presents as an asymptomatic abdominal mass. Treatment consists of surgical removal of the tumor, followed by chemotherapy and radiation. The cure rate is now over 90 percent for a tumor that has not spread outside the kidney, and 80 percent in tumors that have spread.

Retinoblastoma is a rare malignant eye tumor that can affect one or both eyes. The disease is a genetic condition that is either inherited (10 percent) or caused by a mutation. It is most commonly noticed as a yellowish white reflection behind the pupil when a baby is about age two. Treatment involves removal of the affected eye, careful monitoring of the other eye, and if necessary, radiation. In the great majority of cases, the tumor has not spread beyond the eye, and the condition is not life-threatening. Children who have retinoblastoma have a 50 percent chance of transmitting the disease to their own offspring.

Reye's syndrome

Reye's syndrome is a very rare condition affecting the liver and brain that can occasionally be fatal. Its peak incidence occurs at about six years of age, with most cases appearing between the ages of four and twelve. The condition generally develops five to seven days after the onset of a viral illness, such as an upper respiratory tract illness or chicken pox. The symptoms are protracted vomiting, irrational behavior, and stupor. A child who is diagnosed with Reye's syndrome is hospitalized and treated with drugs to lower intracranial pressure. Although very rare, Reye's syndrome has received a great deal of attention because it was found to be more frequent in children who had viral illnesses that were treated with aspirin. Since the FDA required the issuance of a specific warning not to use aspirin in young children with viral illnesses, the rare incidence of Reye's syndrome has declined even further.

Intussusception

Intussusception is a rare condition in which the intestines slide back on themselves, blocking blood flow and causing swelling which eventually obstructs the bowel. It develops most frequently between three months and three years, but the peak incidence is between three months and one year. The symptoms are periodic, severe abdominal pain, followed by vomiting and bloody bowel movements. It is diagnosed with an abdominal X ray or a barium enema. In most cases, the obstruction is cleared by the pressure of the barium enema, and surgery is not required. If left untreated, the condition causes an infection that is fatal. The earlier the condition is treated, the more likely surgery will not be required.

Kawasaki's disease

Kawasaki's disease is a rare inflammatory condition that affects 6 in 1,000,000 children. The symptoms are prolonged high fevers, conjunctivitis, dry lips, red tongue, a general body rash, and peeling of the hands and feet. This condition can be serious if it causes damage to the heart. Generally children recover by themselves, but they are hospitalized to monitor them for heart damage.

AIDS in children

Acquired immunodeficiency syndrome (AIDS) is an illness caused by *human immunodeficiency virus (HIV-1)*. In this condition, the body's immune system becomes damaged and is progressively less able to fight infections. The AIDS epidemic started in 1981, first affecting homosexual men and then striking intravenous drug users of both sexes. It is spread by intimate sexual contact and by contact with contaminated blood products. Currently, 80 percent of children with AIDS are infected *in utero* from mothers who have AIDS, and 20 percent are infected by contaminated blood products used in transfusions. As blood screening becomes even more effective, the percentage of children infected by blood products will decrease, whereas the number of women who pass AIDS to their babies either from intravenous drug use or from sexual contact with infected men is expected to increase. At this time, 22–39 percent of babies born to infected mothers develop AIDS. Why some babies develop AIDS and some do not is unknown. Of the babies who get AIDS from infected mothers, 50 percent will develop the illness in the first year, 80 percent by two years. Children with AIDS are now being treated with the anti-viral drug *AZT*, but up to now, the disease is almost uniformly fatal. As of 1990, children represent 2 percent of AIDS cases in the United States.

Chapter 14

Immunizations

The basic principle of all immunizations involves stimulating the body to produce its own antibodies to the agent that causes the disease. This is done by introducing a small amount of the specific bacteria or virus, or of some related protein. The substance introduced is called the antigen. In response to the antigen, the body produces specific antibodies, which are complex proteins made by the white blood cells. Antibodies hook up to the bacteria or virus and render it harmless. Once some initial antibodies to a disease have been produced, the body has a template or model and can rapidly produce antibodies whenever it is exposed to that particular bacteria or virus. There are several types of vaccines or antigen preparations—vaccines made of live but weakened (attenuated) virus, or of killed virus, or of various bacterial types. Because vaccines contain biological agents, they can cause side effects and do carry a very small risk of adverse reactions. When pediatricians evaluate the need for immunizations, they weigh the balance between the risk of the disease in both the individual child and the population at large, and the potential side effects of the immunization. The American Academy of Pediatrics and the Centers for Disease Control, the federal agency that deals with communicable illnesses, believe strongly that the benefits of the standard vaccines exceed the risks. Currently, pediatricians inform parents about the potential side effects of immuniza-

Immunizations teach the body to recognize a disease and make antibodies against it.

tion, versus the potential risks of not immunizing. In a few instances, pediatricians will not recommend a particular vaccination for a specific reason. In general, only healthy children should receive an immunization. Pediatricians will delay immunization of children who are actively sick, unless it is only a mild cold. Children with immunologic deficiency states or allergies to some component of the vaccine (e.g., eggs or antibiotics) should be given alternative vaccines.

Vaccination is analogous to the natural process that occurs when a person gets a mild case of a disease, recovers, and then is protected from future infections of the disease. The first time people are exposed to a disease they produce antibodies, but not as effectively or rapidly as they will in subsequent exposures. The point of immunizations is to prevent people from getting the symptoms of the disease when they are exposed to it for the first time naturally.

The reason vaccination has been so important in the history of mankind is that the first exposure to certain illnesses is crippling or fatal to a significant percentage of people. A number of dangerous diseases have been virtually eradicated through a combination of hygiene and vaccination. These include smallpox, polio, diphtheria, tetanus, and whooping cough. Smallpox, for example, used to be one of the major killers and it sometimes occurred in epidemics. Now it is essentially eliminated. The incidence of other diseases that occasionally are dangerous has been lowered by vaccination. These include regular measles and German measles.

If the initial illness is generally mild or is dangerous to only one segment of the population, then routine immunization of everyone becomes a matter of debate among doctors and public health officials. An example of this is influenza.

Pediatricians advise that children be immunized against a group of diseases during the first several years. As of 1991, the recommended immunizations are the *DTP series,* which protects the child against *diphtheria, tetanus, and pertussis;* the *MMR,* which protects against *measles, mumps,* and *rubella (German measles); polio* drops; and *HIB,* which protects against *Haemophilus influenzae type b.*

In addition to the advantages that an immunization has for a single child, it has advantages for a whole community or population. The higher the percentage of children inoculated against an illness, the lower the incidence of the disease overall, because the total number of bacteria or virus is lower. This means that even uninoculated children are much less likely to get the disease. In time a situation results in which there are so few cases of the disease, and therefore so few of that disease's bacteria or virus, that the disease is virtually eliminated. At this point people may stop getting immunizations for their children. If the disease then reappears in sufficient numbers, there is a risk of epidemic spread because no one in the community has immunity and everyone is at risk. A 1974 survey showed that only about 60 percent of all preschool children in the United States are vaccinated against diphtheria/pertussis/tetanus, measles, and polio, whereas in

1960, about 85 percent of all children had been vaccinated for these diseases. This has caused some public health officials concern that "half-conquered" diseases could be a risk to large, unimmunized populations. Others believe that the incidence of these diseases is low enough so that there is no serious risk.

When the incidence of a disease drops below the incidence of complications from the vaccine, the vaccine is no longer recommended. For example, up until the early 1970s, smallpox vaccine was routinely administered in infancy and repeated at intervals. Now the World Health Organizaton, the U.S. Public Health Service, and the American Society of Pediatrics all advise against *routine* smallpox immunization.

Infant immunization

Age	*Immunization*
2 months	DTP, polio (drops)
4 months	DTP, polio (drops)
6 months	DTP
12 months	Tuberculosis skin test
15 months	MMR
18 months	HIB
4–6 years	DTP, polio (drops)
5–21 years	MMR

DTP series (diphtheria, tetanus, pertussis)

DTP is a triple vaccine which protects against diphtheria, tetanus, and pertussis. Diphtheria is a bacterial infection which causes a thick membrane to grow across the back of the throat that can block the airway. In the era before antibiotics, diphtheria was often fatal and it still is dangerous. The diphtheria vaccine gives greater than 85 percent protection, has few side effects, and has virtually eliminated diphtheria as a serious illness in childhood.

Tetanus is a bacterial infection of the central nervous system. Tetanus bacteria most commonly live in the soil and enter the body through small wounds. The disease causes stiffness of the neck, excessive irritability to sensory stimuli, convulsions, and spasms in the muscles of the jaw. The jaw symptoms led to the disease being referred to as "lockjaw." Tetanus is a serious disease which is fatal in over a third of all cases. The tetanus vaccine is an excellent immunizing agent, conferring virtually 100 percent immunity. It is one of the safest vaccines available, and reactions to it are very infrequent and limited to local redness and tenderness. Boosters are now recommended at only ten-year intervals.

Pertussis, or whooping cough, is an infection of the lungs caused by the bacteria *Bordetella pertussis.* Whooping cough can be dangerous, even fatal, in the first few years of life. Generally in older children it produces a mild illness. Children under two who get whooping cough initially have a mild cold for about two weeks. The cold is followed by sudden, acute coughing which is violent on expiration and ends with a strange, characteristic whoop as the children try to inhale. The pertussis immunization reduces rates from 90 percent to below 15 percent in exposed children. Unlike other vaccines, the pertussis immunization has a high rate of local side effects, and a very low, but predictable, rate of serious side effects. It is extremely common for children to develop a fever, and local tenderness and swelling 2 to 12 hours after the shot. Local reactions occur in 30–50 percent of immunized children. Acetaminophen (e.g., Tylenol) is effective in treating these side effects. Local reactions are temporary and have no aftereffects. Infrequently, children experience serious, but temporary, side effects, including excessive sleepiness, protracted crying, and limpness and paleness. Although these side effects are not dangerous, the doctor should be called. In rare instances following immunization, children may experience convulsions (1 in 1,750 children), or even more rarely, may develop *encephalopathy* (1 in 310,000), a condition which can cause brain damage. Due to the potential for serious side effects, use of the vaccine was greatly reduced in Great Britain and Japan. Following reduction of the vaccine in Japan, more than 35,000 cases of pertussis occurred, with 118 deaths. Due to these experiences, pediatricians continue to use the vaccine, but follow expanded precautions. The vaccine is not given to any child who has had a severe reaction to a previous dose of DTP, or to a child who has had convulsions or a suspected neurological illness.

The DTP shot is generally given intramuscularly on the outside of the thigh. Most pediatricians alternate the sides they give the shots in to decrease the severity of the local reaction caused by the pertussis vaccine. If fever, irritability, and discomfort do occur 2 to 12 hours after the shot, the infant can be given appropriate doses of acetaminophen (e.g., Tylenol).

Polio

Poliomyelitis is a viral disease which causes muscle paralysis. Initially the child becomes sick with a fever, which is followed by muscle tenderness, then weakness and paralysis 3 to 5 days after the onset. Paralysis is often serious and can even result in death when the respiratory muscles are sufficiently depressed. The thought of polio rightfully frightened parents and children in the days before the vaccine was developed. In 1952 alone, there were fifty-two thousand cases of polio in the United States. In 1975 there were seven. This reduction is due largely to the polio vaccine.

There are two kinds of polio vaccine. Both the attenuated live (OPV or Sabin) and the killed (IPV or Salk) vaccine offer good protection against polio. Currently there is a strong debate among public health officials over the advantages and disadvantages of the two vaccines. The live (OPV) vaccine is the one routinely administered to children in the United States at present. It is recommended and considered safe by the U.S. Public Health Service and the American Academy of Pediatrics. Sabin vaccine is easily administered in drops and it gives proven, long-term immunity. But, in rare instances, children have developed the disease from this vaccine. The live vaccine is now the principal cause of polio in the United States.

(The actual risk of getting even a mild case of polio is 1 in 9 million.) The Salk vaccine (inactivated) cannot cause polio, but must be injected intramuscularly and needs frequent boosters to maintain immunity. Sweden and Finland have totally eradicated polio using the killed vaccine.

MMR (measles, mumps, rubella)

MMR is a triple vaccine which protects against *measles (rubeola), mumps,* and *rubella (German measles).* Measles is a highly contagious viral disease which generally affects preschool children, making them sick, listless, and apathetic. The child has fever, a cough, red eyes, and large red areas of rash that begin at the head and move down to the feet. A child becomes sick 8 to 14 days after exposure and is communicable for 4 days after the rash appears. Measles can have complications including secondary bacterial earaches, pneumonia, and even infection of the brain and nervous system. Even without complications, a child with measles appears and is ill and uncomfortable.

The MMR contains a live attentuated vaccine which affords 95–100 percent protection against measles. Although the vaccine has been in use for over two decades, a large number of people remain susceptible to measles, including unimmunized people; people who received early, ineffective vaccines; and immunization failures. It is recommended that children receive an initial shot at 15 months; if given earlier, maternal antibodies that are still effective will render the vaccine inactive in a large number of cases. Approximately 5–15 percent of children develop a fever, and 5 percent develop a rash within 6 to 11 days after the immunization. Acetaminophen (e.g., Tylenol) can be given for discomfort.

Because the MMR is an attenuated live vaccine, it should not be given to children with immunological defects or an acute illness with fever. It should also not be given to children who are allergic to eggs, because the vaccine is grown on chick embryos. Finally, since the MMR has been associated with febrile convulsions, it should not be given to children who have experienced febrile convulsions before.

Mumps is a childhood infection that is generally asymptomatic, but sometimes causes swelling of the parotid salivary gland at the angle of the jaw. Occasionally, mumps cause severe symptoms, including meningitis, and inflammation of the pancreas, ovaries, or testes. The disease is generally self-limiting and gets better within a week. The mumps component of the immunization is a live attenuated vaccine. It should not be given to individuals with immunologic deficiencies or allergies to eggs. There are no side effects to the mumps component of the vaccine.

Rubella (German measles) is a mild or asymptomatic infection. Signs include a rash and mild respiratory symptoms. Immunization is important because infection during pregnancy, particularly during the first 16 weeks, causes a group of birth defects, including ear, eye, heart, and nervous system abnormalities. Women who have had the vaccine will not get rubella while pregnant. The rubella component of the MMR infrequently produces temporary muscle and joint aches or pains that may persist for several days. Since it is a live attenuated vaccine, the rubella component should not be given to immunologically compromised children.

Haemophilus influenzae (HIB)

Haemophilis influenzae type b is the most significant disease-causing bacterium in childhood. It causes severe infections in more than 80,000 children per year in the United States alone. It causes several serious illnesses, including meningitis, epiglottitis (a rare type of croup), septic arthritis, pneumonia, and infections of the skin and heart. This vaccine is given at 18 months because younger children do not reliably produce antibodies in response to the purified antigen. In respose to the vaccine, a small percentage of children develop swelling, tenderness, and a low-grade fever.

Chapter 15

Common drugs

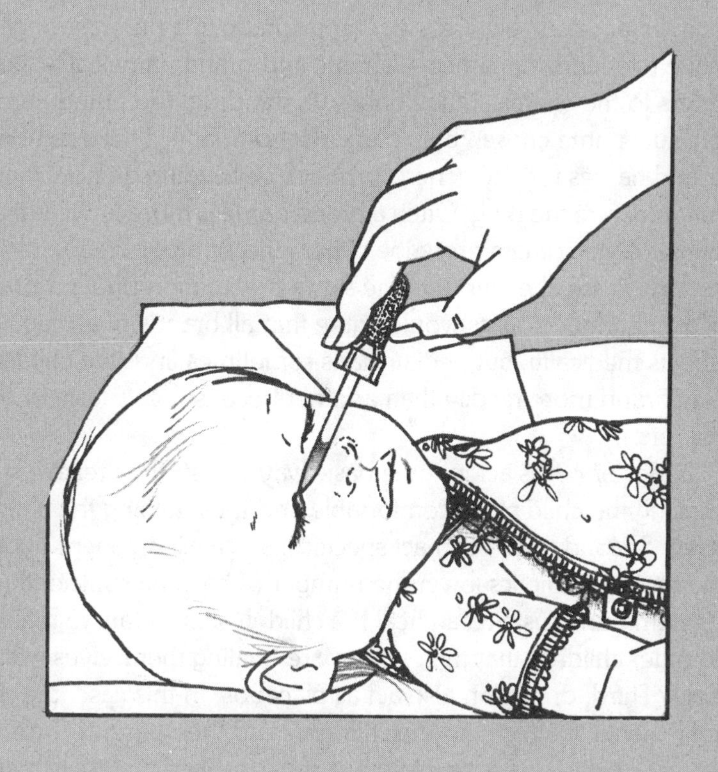

Very few types of drugs are routinely given to children under four years of age. First, young children rarely get serious illnesses, and often the illnesses they do get heal by themselves. Moreover, young children have such small bodies and modern drugs are so potent that doctors tend to be more cautious in prescribing drugs for babies and they are more careful about giving proper dosages. Almost any drug can cause undesirable side effects, can trigger an allergic reaction, and can be overdosed. All these effects are more likely in babies.

Parents should *never* give drugs to babies without a doctor's order. Drugs that are "safe" for adults can be dangerous for children even in small doses. The deleterious effects of many drugs are just beginning to be understood. Thus it is probably a good rule to avoid giving drugs to babies unless a situation demands their use. There are many alternatives to drugs, especially for minor illness.

Some doctors use drugs freely; others are very conservative in their use. Parents can ask their doctors if a drug is absolutely necessary. If not, they can refrain from giving it to the baby. Just knowing that other doctors don't routinely prescribe a drug may be helpful for parents. Adult drugs such as cold tablets, laxatives, and antacids are not necessary for babies and should not be given without strong indication. Even acetaminophen (e.g., Tylenol) does not *need* to be given every time a baby runs a fever.

Most drugs were originally derived from herbs or organic substances. Herbal drug therapy is an ancient form of medicine, perhaps the oldest. Now drugs are generally synthesized in the laboratory because it is more convenient and because they can be made in a purer, stronger form. Drugs have two kinds of names—generic and brand names. The generic name refers to the chemical that makes up the drug; the brand name is simply a product name chosen by a particular company. There can be a number of brand names for any generic product, depending on how many companies manufacture the drug. Often a brand name is more familiar than the generic name. A doctor can prescribe either kind of drug. Frequently generic prescriptions are cheaper than the same preparation under a brand name. Most pharmacologists would agree that all brands of a drug have the same effects medically, but pediatricians sometimes find that children will take one brand more readily than another because of its taste or form (syrup, pill, etc.).

Drugs or herbs act in three basic ways. First, they relieve symptoms, making the child more comfortable and thus helping the child's body heal itself. Second, drugs can act specifically against an agent of disease. For example, antibiotics lower the number of bacteria sufficiently so the child's own immune system can heal the child. It's important to realize and explain to older children that their bodies are healing themselves with the drug's help. Third, drugs can also act as placebos. In this case, the drug has no real chemical effect, but the children (and their parents) believe that they will be healed and the children unconsciously direct their bodies to heal themselves.

Since babies cannot swallow pills, they must be given drops or flavored liquids. Even these liquids must often be given with flavorful foods like jelly, in order to mask the drug's heavy back taste. If parents taste a small amount of the drug, they will have some idea of how the baby feels. An accurate measuring spoon or dropper should be used to administer a prescription because household spoons vary tremendously in the amount they hold.

Aspirin

Doctors advise parents *not* to give aspirin to children during any acute febrile illness, influenza, or chicken pox because the use of aspirin has been associated with a rare neurological condition called *Reye's syndrome.* The exact relationship between aspirin and this syndrome is not clear, but the association has been demonstrated in many epidemiological studies. Reye's syndrome is a very rare condition which typically follows an upper respiratory illness. Its symptoms include vomiting, convulsions, and lethargy or extreme tiredness leading to coma. Although most patients survive, the condition can cause permanent neurological damage.

Acetaminophen (e.g., Tylenol)

Acetaminophen (e.g., Tylenol, Tempera, and Panadol) is the drug most commonly taken by children. It is effective in relieving pain and lowering fever. It is not routinely necessary to treat a fever (see page 295), and acetaminophen does not "cure" a cold. It is most often used for upper respiratory infections, cold, or flu, as well as headaches, muscle aches, and immunization reactions. Acetaminophen lowers a fever by working on the brain's hypothalamic heat-regulating center, and reduces pain by elevating the brain's pain threshold. Acetaminophen is available in chewable tablets, syrup form, and drops. The drug has rarely been found to produce side effects, but should be discontinued if a rash develops, indicating a possible allergic reaction (rare). In high doses, acetaminophen is poisonous, and in the case of an accidental overdose, the poison control center or a doctor should be called immediately.

Antibiotics

Antibiotics are drugs that kill or lower the number of bacteria in a person's body. Antibiotics were discovered by the Chinese twenty-five hundred years ago when it was observed that moldy bean curd cured boils. Antibiotics are chemical substances produced by bacteria and fungi, living things, which in turn kill other bacteria and fungi. In addition to being produced naturally, antibiotics can also be produced synthetically. There are now literally hundreds of different antibiotic compounds synthesized.

Any one antibiotic does not work against all types of disease-causing bacteria; it only works against specific ones. Moreover, through genetic change, a specific bacteria can rapidly become resistant to a particular antibiotic. That is why there are so many different antibiotics. But only three or four of them are commonly used to fight infections. If one antibiotic does not seem to be working—as shown by a follow-up culture or continuing symptoms—the doctor will generally switch to a different one that is likely to be more effective against the bacteria.

To be effective, an antibiotic must kill off or inhibit the growth of bacteria for a long enough time so that they do not reproduce. This in turn enables the body's white blood cells to ingest the bacteria easily and heal the body. An antibiotic can kill only so many bacteria at one time. With continued use, an antibiotic kills more and more bacteria in successive generations, until the bacteria are effectively eliminated. If only half a course of an antibiotic is taken, there is an increased possibility that the bacteria will multiply again.

Antibiotics do not kill virus. So they do *not work* against colds. Antibiotics should only be used with specific indications of bacterial infection, for example, ear infection or strep throat. Antibiotics do kill off normal intestinal bacteria, which aid in digestion. For this reason some doctors suggest eating yogurt during antibiotic therapy. Yogurt contains lactobacilli, a beneficial intestinal bacteria. Unfortunately, adults and even babies can have allergic reactions to antibiotics. The most typical allergic reaction is a skin rash. More serious reactions are unusual in babies. An allergic reaction should be reported to the doctor.

The most common antibiotics are penicillin, sulfa, erythromycin, cephalosporin, and tetracycline. Antibiotics are available (with antifungal agents) in skin creams for topical applications and in drops for eye or ears, as well as in syrup form for internal use.

Penicillin was accidentally discovered by the British bacteriologist Sir Alexander Fleming when he observed that a particular bread mold caused bacteria to die. Penicillin kills bacteria by injuring their cell walls. It works very well against streptococcus and pneumococcus bacteria. A broad-spectrum penicillin that works against a wider number of bacteria is called *amoxicillin.* Amoxicillin has a higher allergic rate and also frequently causes diarrhea. It is most often used to treat strep throat, ear infections, and pneumococcal pneumonia.

Sulfonamides (sulfa drugs) were the first antibiotics to be widely used. All of them contain sulfur. They are broad-spectrum antibiotics which work against a number of bacterial strains. Sulfonamides are most commonly given to babies with ear infections, along with regular penicillin, because babies often have a bacteria, *Hemophilus,* which penicillin does not effectively kill. Sulfonamides are also given in urinary tract infections because they are effective against *E. coli* bacteria.

Erythromycin was originally discovered in the soil. It inhibits the protein synthesis of particular bacteria. Erythromycin is generally given to children who are allergic to penicillin or whose infection has not responded to penicillin.

Tetracycline was discovered when scientists were searching soil samples from all over the world, following the discovery of penicillin. Tetracycline is effective against a wide variety of bacteria, because it inhibits their protein synthesis. Tetracycline can cause brown discoloration of the *baby* teeth if given to pregnant mothers, especially from midpregnancy on, or if given after birth to babies up to six months of age. If given between two months and five years of age, it can cause discoloration of the *permanent* teeth. For this reason tetracycline is rarely used in children below the age of seven.

Cough syrups

A cough is a protective body mechanism which helps clear secretions and dead cells from the throat and bronchial tubes. A child with a cough should be encouraged to cough deeply and raise the mucus, and it *generally does not need cough medicine.* Large amounts of liquids help to keep a cough loose. A teaspoon of honey and warm water will generally relieve a dry cough.

There are two basic types of cough medicine on the market. One kind helps to liquefy phlegm so that it can be coughed up. This kind of cough syrup is called an *expectorant,* and its main ingredient is glyceryl guaiacolate. Robitussin is an example of an expectorant syrup. Expectorant syrups can be soothing, even helpful, in a repetitive, dry cough in an older child, especially if a child is being kept awake by the cough. The second type of cough medicine is called a *suppressant.* It acts on the brain to lower the urge to cough. The main ingredient of this kind of cough medicine is dextromethorphan. This type of preparation is not generally necessary in young children. Cough syrups with codeine, which is a narcotic, should only be given to children under a doctor's direction.

Antihistamines and decongestants

There are two types of drugs that are used to treat symptoms of colds or allergies. *Antihistamines* block the receptors that pick up *histamine,* a chemical released by the body that causes itching, swelling, and a runny nose. Because antihistamines block skin receptors as well as those in the mucous membranes, they are often given for conditions such as chicken pox, bee stings, and poison oak. *Decongestants* are drugs that work on sympathetic nerve endings in smooth muscle, causing a narrowing of blood vessels which reduces swelling and stops a runny nose.

The drugs most commonly prescribed for colds or hay fever in children (e.g., *Dimetapp* and *Rondec*) contain both antihistamines and decongestants. Generally children deal with colds well by themselves, and they do not need cold medicines. Such preparations dry up a runny nose by causing blood vessels to narrow in the nasal membranes; in effect they shut off the body's natural healing impulse to flush out live viruses and remove dead cells.

Both antihistamines and decongestants have side effects. Antihistamines can cause drowsiness, dizziness, gastrointestinal upset, and, occasionally in children, excitability. Decongestants can variably cause a noticeable drowsiness or pronounced restlessness and hyperactivity. Decongestants should never be used for more than a few weeks because they can actually damage the mucous membranes. Moreover, when decongestants are used for a while, they can cause a rebound effect. That is, when the decongestant is stopped, the runny nose returns and is even worse.

Skin creams, ointments, powders, oils, and lotions

There are many skin treatment products for babies, mostly related to problems of diaper care. The principle of most of these products is to make changes in the skin's moisture content. At the optimum, skin feels soft and smooth, neither wet nor dry. The general rule for treating skin conditions like rashes is to return the skin to its optimum moisture content. If the skin is wet and oozy, it should be dried; if the skin is very dry, it should be moistened. Powders tend to dry, while oils, creams, ointments, and lotions

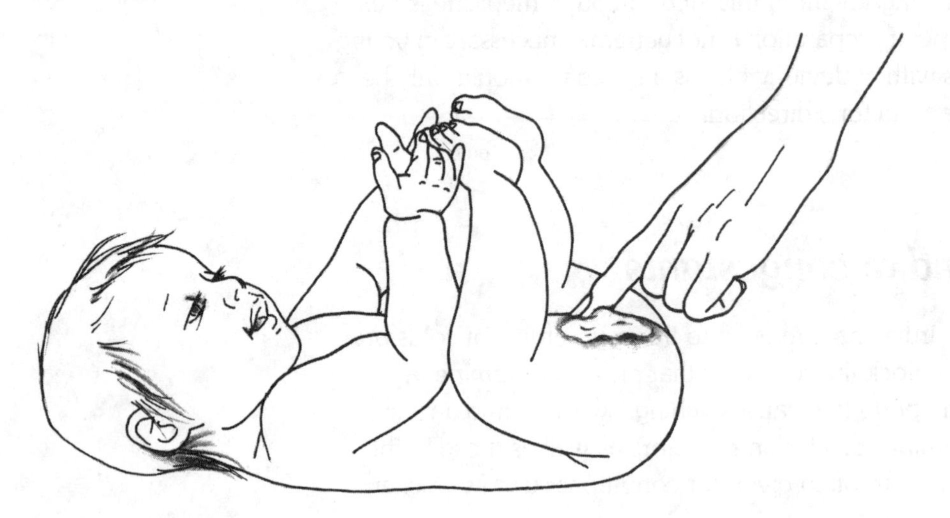

Diaper creams and ointments protect the baby's skin from moisture and irritating chemicals in urine, and thus allow the skin to heal itself.

Problems with skin products and prescriptions

Product	*Problem*
Strong soaps	Remove natural oils and dry skin; can be directly irritative; chemical additives are absorbed into the skin (for example, deodorants in soaps)
Perfumes and other additives in skin products	Irritative, can produce allergic reactions
Talcum powders	Can be harmful to the lungs if inhaled
Cornstarch	Can be a medium for yeast growth in moist areas
Antibacterial creams	Absorbed through the skin; disrupt normal bacteria on the skin
Steroids	Absorbed through the skin; masks symptoms

tend to moisten. Ointments also form a protective barrier which can keep out external moisture like urine.

Chemicals that are put on the skin are absorbed into the body. The skin itself can be adversely affected by substances such as perfumes that are in topical ointments. Parents should thus be careful about what they put on the baby's skin. Strong medicines are to be avoided unless medically necessary, and even nonprescription preparations are to be used sparingly. The more medicine and chemicals in a preparation, the less generally it should be used. Ideally problematic skin conditions should be dealt with before they require strong treatment. In the early stages most skin problems will respond to simple treatments like gentle washing and exposure to sunlight and air.

The strongest skin medicines that are generally prescribed are steroid creams. These preparations may be mixed with antibiotics or antifungal agents. Adrenocorticosteroids are produced in the body naturally by the adrenal glands. Steroids are potent hormones which affect every part of the body. They affect the central nervous system and the metabolism of sugar and protein. Steroids also slow wound healing and decrease cells' response to allergy and inflammation. Steroids are used to treat skin conditions because they decrease inflammation, that is, redness and swelling. This can make the baby more comfortable and may make it easier for the baby to heal itself. But steroids do not remove the cause of or actually cure a rash; the body does that itself. With prolonged use of steroid creams, significant amounts of the drug can be absorbed through the skin, causing side effects and possible harm to the baby. For this reason, most doctors prescribe steroids infrequently and suggest that parents use the creams only for a short time and only for a significant skin problem.

Hints for giving medicines

General suggestions

Don't be upset if a little medicine spills or is spit up, as long as the baby gets most of it.

Give the whole course of the treatment, especially antibiotics. Don't discontinue medication if the baby misses one dose.

Don't double the dose if the baby misses one dose; babies easily overdose on some medicines.

Make medicines palatable if possible; try not to make medicine giving a fight.

Eye drops

Have the child lie down and relax, then close eyes. Put a drop in the corner of each eye, then have the child open its eyes. Drops frighten some children but don't really burn.

Continued

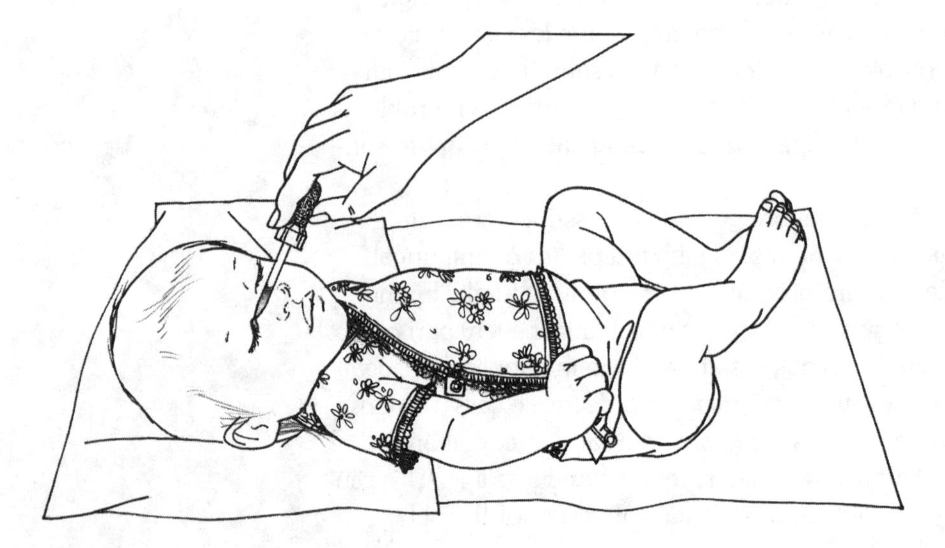

Eye drops can be easily administered by having the child close its eyes and then putting the drops in the inner corner. When the child opens its eyes, the drops will roll in.

Most baby medicines come in liquid form and should be measured with an accurate spoon or dropper.

Nose drops

Have the child tip its head way back. Sometimes nose drops burn the back of the throat a little.

Oral medications

Mix with good-tasting foods such as jams, jellies, fruits, preserves. However, it may not be advisable to mix with baby's favorites or standards.

Measure accurately with measuring spoon or dropper instead of household teaspoon.

Realize that the medicine really may not taste good and the baby's reaction to it is valid.

For young baby, grind tablets such as aspirin between two teaspoons, one on top of another, and put powder into food.

Alternatives to drugs

Drug	*Alternative treatment*
Acetaminophen	Give lukewarm sponge bath; take clothes off if baby is feverish
Cough syrup	Give lots of liquids, honey, and water
Decongestants	Give liquids; rest; and allow body to heal itself
Laxatives	Give fruits, liquids, and bulk in the diet
Antacids	Give milk, soda, bland crackers; rest
Antidiarrhea drugs	Stop solid foods; stop formula, but don't stop nursing; later feed rice and dry toast
Skin drugs	Gently wash area, pat dry; give sunlight and air exposure if irritated area is wet, oil if area is dry
Nose drops or eye drops (nonprescription)	Use dropper or cup to wash eyes with water. Add ½ teaspoon of salt per 1 quart of water to make saline eyewash

Bibliography and recommended reading

Section I

Chapters 1–3

Abt, G. *History of Pediatrics.* Philadelphia: W. B. Saunders Co., 1965.
Ader, R. "Psychoneuroimmunology: Developmental Perspectives" in Krasnegor, N. *Childhealth Behavior.* New York: John Wiley & Sons, 1986.
Aries P. *Centuries of Childhood.* New York: Knopf, 1962.
Moss, G. *Illness, Immunity, and Social Interaction.* New York: John Wiley & Sons, 1973.
Samuels, M., and Samuels, N. *Seeing With the Mind's Eye.* New York: Random House-Bookworks, 1975.
Levine, M. *Developmental Behavioral Pediatrics.* Philadelphia: W. B. Saunders, 1983.
Weil, J. *A Neurophysiological Model of Emotional and Intentional Behavior.* Springfield, Ill.: Charles C. Thomas, 1974.

Section II

Chapter 4

Evans-Wentz, W. Y., ed. *The Tibetan Book of the Dead.* London: Oxford University Press, 1960.
Ferreira, A. *Prenatal Environment.* Springfield, Ill.: Charles C. Thomas, 1969.
Montague, A. *Life Before Birth.* New York: New American Library, 1963.
Nilsson, L. *How Was I Born?* New York: Delacorte Press, 1975.
Samuels, M., and Samuels, N. *The Well Pregnancy Book.* New York: Summit Books, 1986.
Worthington, B., et al. *Nutrition in Pregnancy and Lactation.* St. Louis: C. V. Mosby Co., 1977.

Chapter 5

Arms, S. *Immaculate Deception: A New Look at Women and Childbirth in America.* New York: Houghton Mifflin, 1975.
Barsam, P. "Specific Prophylaxis of Gonorrheal Ophthalmia Neonatorum." *New England Journal of Medicine* 274 (1966): 731–34.
———. "Maternal and Child Interaction." *Ciba Symposium,* 1976.

Klaus, M. "Human Maternal Behavior at the First Contact with Her Young." *Pediatrics* 45 (1970): 187–91.

———, et al. "Maternal Attachment, Importance of the First Postpartum Days." *New England Journal of Medicine* 286 (1972): 460–63.

Klaus, M., and Kennell, J. *Parent-Infant Bonding.* St. Louis: C. V. Mosby, 1982.

Leboyer, F. *Birth Without Violence.* New York: Knopf, 1975.

Winnicott, D. W. *The Child, the Family, and the Outside World.* London: Penguin Books, 1964.

Chapter 6

Addy, D. P. "Infant Feeding: A Current View." *British Medical Journal* 1 (1976): 1268–71.

Ainsworth, M. "Infant Mother Attachment." *American Psychologist* 34 (1979): 932.

Committee on Nutrition. *Pediatric Nutrition Handbook.* American Academy of Pediatrics, 1985.

Condon, W., and Sander, L. "Neonate Movement Is Synchronized with Adult Speech." *Science* 183: (1974).

———. *The Womanly Art of Breastféeding.* La Leche League, 1963.

Jeliffe, D. B. *Human Milk in the Modern World.* Oxford: Oxford University Press, 1979.

Neville, M. *Lactation.* New York: Plenum Press, 1983.

Pipes, P. *Nutrition in Infancy and Childhood.* St. Louis: C. V. Mosby Co., 1977.

Smith, D. S. "Harmful Chemicals and Drugs in Breast Milk." *Pediatrics In Review* 2 (1981): 279.

Thomas A., and Chess, S. *Temperament and Development.* New York: Bruner/Mazel, 1977.

Chapters 7–8

Beadle, M. *A Child's Mind.* New York: Doubleday, Anchor, 1971.

Brazelton, T. B. *Infants and Mothers.* New York: Dell, Delta, 1969.

Gebber, M. "Psychomotor Development of African Children in the First Year and the Influence of Maternal Behavior." *Journal of Social Psychology* 47 (1958): 185–95.

Ilg, F., and Ames, L. *Child Behavior.* New York: Harper & Row, 1955.

Khan, I. *Education from Birth to Maturity.* London: Sufi Publishing Co., 1974.

Koch, J. *Total Baby Development.* New York: Wallaby, 1977.

Leach, P. *Your Baby and Child.* New York: Knopf, 1989.

Leboyer, F. *Loving Hands.* New York: Knopf, 1976.

Lehane, S. *Help Your Baby Learn.* Englewood, N.J.: Prentice-Hall, 1976.

Levine, M. *Developmental Behavioral Pediatrics.* Philadelphia: W. B. Saunders, 1983.
Mussen, P. *Carmichael's Manual of Child Psychology.* New York: John Wiley & Sons, 1970.
———. *Child Development and Personality.* New York: Harper & Row, 1974.
Neuman, E. *The Child.* New York: Harper & Row, Colophon Books, 1976.
Pearce, J. *The Magical Child.* New York: Dutton, 1977.
Pringle, M. *The Need of Children.* New York: Schocken Books, 1975.
Spock, B. *Baby and Child Care.* New York: Pocket Books, 1961.
Stone, L. J., et al. *The Competent Infant.* New York: Basic Books, 1973.
———, and Church, J. *Childhood and Adolescence.* New York: Random House, 1966.

Section III

Chapters 9–15

Kempe, C., et al. *Current Pediatric Diagnosis and Treatment.* Los Altos, Calif.: Lange Medical Publications, 1987.
Nelson, W., ed. *Textbook of Pediatrics.* Philadelphia: W. B. Saunders Co., 1987.
Samuels M., and Bennett, H. *The Well Baby Book.* New York: Random House-Bookworks, 1972.
Samuels, M., and Samuels, N. *The Well Adult.* New York: Summit Books, 1989.

Index

About the authors

Mike and Nancy Samuels are married and the parents of two boys. Mike is a physician and author. He attended Brown University and New York University College of Medicine. He has worked in public health and done years of well baby clinics. In doing the clinics he found he was most interested in talking with young mothers and helping them work out their problems with their babies. He realized that most mothers needed more information to relieve their worries and make their babies healthy. Subsequently, Mike became involved in early efforts in self-help and holistic medicine. His book, *The Well Body Book,* written with Hal Bennett, was a pioneering work in these fields.

Nancy Samuels is an author and a former nursery school teacher. She attended Brown University and Bank Street College of Education. In college she was a pre-med student, and she has always been interested in children and medicine. She became interested in books when she did extensive editing on *The Well Body Book.* The Samuelses' first baby had just been born and Nancy found that book work was very fulfilling and fit in well with the routines of new motherhood.

While Nancy was pregnant with Rudy, their first child, both she and Mike took a course in Jacobson's progressive relaxation in preparation for natural childbirth. This experience showed them the value of holistic tools for health concerning mothers and babies.

Mike became especially interested in the power that relaxation and imagery gave people to create health. He saw in his medical practice how people, including young children, could control their bodies, heal illness, and stay healthy. Together, Mike and Nancy wrote about this and the wider implications of relaxation and imagery in a book called *Seeing With the Mind's Eye.* This was the first book they coauthored, and it was written while Rudy, then two, was in a cooperative play group. The Samuelses found that working together at home was enjoyable and further strengthened the close ties of their family.

When Nancy became pregnant for the second time, their interest in babies, books, and self-help/holistic medicine joined. They felt it was important to write a book that would help new parents understand their babies better, worry less, and learn to create patterns of health. *The Well Baby Book* was written largely while Rudy, then four, was in nursery school, and Lewis, only months old, was napping or sitting in their laps. In subsequent years, the Samuelses coauthored *The Well Child Book, The Well Child Coloring Book, The Well Pregnancy Book,* and *The Well Adult.* This series of health books was written in the same spirit as *The Well Baby Book,* emphasizing self-help and holistic medicine in a reassuring and supportive manner. Mike has recently written *Healing With the Mind's Eye,* a book about using images and visions for personal growth and healing.

The Samuelses live in a small seacoast town in northern California, in a house they built themselves. They have a close family and share many common interests with their sons. Rudy is now in college and Lewis in high school. Music, art, Land Rovers, and Briards have been added to the family's long-standing interests in housebuilding, gardening, photography, and travel.